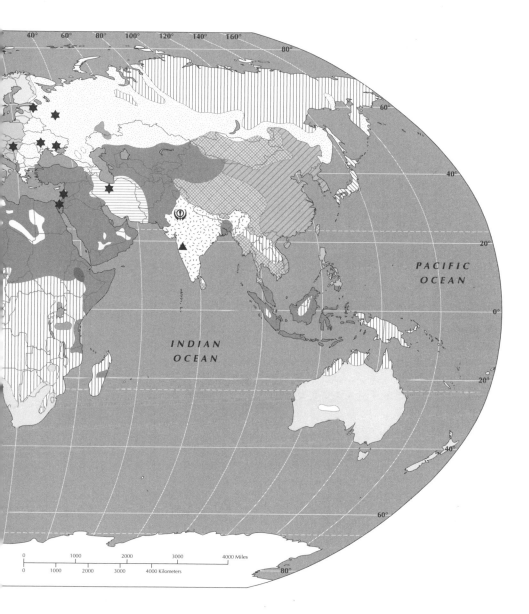

THE WORLD'S RELIGIONS

Worldviews and Contemporary Issues

SECOND EDITION

— ✦ —

William A. Young
Westminster College

PEARSON
Prentice
Hall

Upper Saddle River, New Jersey 07458

Library of Congress Cataloging-in-Publication Data

Young, William A.
    The world's religions : worldviews and contemporary issues /
William A. Young.—2nd ed.
        p.   cm.
    Includes bibliographical references.
    ISBN 0-13-183010-4
    1. Religions.   2. Religion.   3. Sects.   4. Cults.   I. Title.

BL80.2.Y68 2005
200—dc22   2004007542

Editorial Director: Charlyce Jones-Owen
Senior Acquisitions Editor: Ross Miller
Assistant Editor: Wendy B. Yurash
Editorial Assistant: Carla Worner
Marketing Manager: Kara Kindstrom
Production Liaison: Joanne Hakim
Manufacturing Buyer: Christina Helder
Cover Art Director: Jayne Conte
Cover Design: Bruce Kenselaar
Manager, Cover Visual Research & Permissions:
    Karen Sanatar

Cover Photos: *Tibetan Woman*—Keren Su/Getty
    Images; *Hindu Temple Statues*—Jack
    Hollingsworth/Getty Images; *Muslims
    Praying*—M. Freeman/Photolink/Getty Images
Director, Image Resource Center: Melinda Reo
Manager, Rights and Permissions: Zina Arabia
Manager, Visual Research: Beth Brenzel
Photo Coordinator: Joanne Dippel
Composition/Full-Service Project Management:
    Michael Bohrer-Clancy/ICC

Credits and acknowledgments borrowed from other sources and reproduced, with permission, in this
textbook appear on page 406 within text.

Pearson Education LTD., London
Pearson Education Singapore, Pte. Ltd
Pearson Education, Canada, Ltd
Pearson Education–Japan
Pearson Education Australia PTY, Limited

Pearson Education North Asia Ltd
Pearson Educación de Mexico, S.A. de C.V.
Pearson Education Malaysia, Pte. Ltd
Pearson Education, Upper Saddle River, New Jersey

10 9 8 7 6 5 4
ISBN 0-13-183010-4

Contents

EXPLORE WORLD RELIGION!

Prentice Hall is proud to offer new, exciting ways to study the religions of the world. Included with this text is *The Sacred World: Encounters with the World's Religions* CD-ROM, Prentice Hall's new multimedia exploration of the rituals, beliefs, art, and key personalities in nine of the world's major religions.

A multimedia icon 🎥 appears throughout the text, calling out relevant video clips on *The Sacred World* which offer students a better understanding of religion. Below is the integration page, showing the location of icons throughout the text.

Also packaged with this text is TIME *Special Edition: World Religions,* a unique collaboration between Prentice Hall and the editors of TIME magazine, bringing together over 20 important current articles on a variety of religions and religious topics. Relevant articles are highlighted for students at the ends of chapters for further exploration.

INTEGRATION GUIDE
The Sacred World CD Rom
William Young, *The World's Religions,* Second Edition

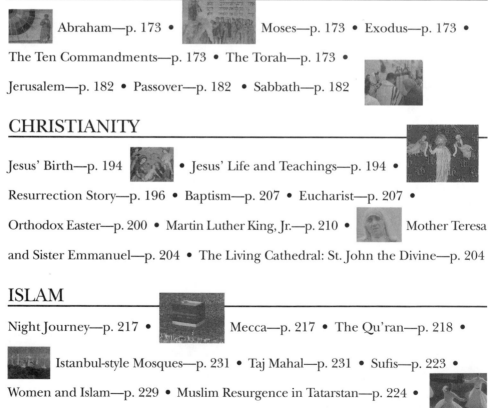

JUDAISM

Abraham—p. 173 • Moses—p. 173 • Exodus—p. 173 •

The Ten Commandments—p. 173 • The Torah—p. 173 •

Jerusalem—p. 182 • Passover—p. 182 • Sabbath—p. 182

CHRISTIANITY

Jesus' Birth—p. 194 • Jesus' Life and Teachings—p. 194 •

Resurrection Story—p. 196 • Baptism—p. 207 • Eucharist—p. 207 •

Orthodox Easter—p. 200 • Martin Luther King, Jr.—p. 210 • Mother Teresa

and Sister Emmanuel—p. 204 • The Living Cathedral: St. John the Divine—p. 204

ISLAM

Night Journey—p. 217 • Mecca—p. 217 • The Qu'ran—p. 218 •

Istanbul-style Mosques—p. 231 • Taj Mahal—p. 231 • Sufis—p. 223 •

Women and Islam—p. 229 • Muslim Resurgence in Tatarstan—p. 224 •

The United States and Islam—p. 236

PREFACE

In nearly three decades of teaching college courses on the world's religions, I have found that students most want to know how religions answer basic human questions such as "Why are we here?" and "What happens after death?" In addition, they wish to learn how religions respond to contemporary ethical issues such as the ecological crisis, economic justice, war, capital punishment, abortion, euthanasia, gender equality, and sexual orientation. They also request an accessible overview of the history and development of religions and their worldviews.

Informed by my students' interests and questions, I have attempted to write a "reader-friendly" introduction to the world's religions, intended for use in classroom surveys, as well as for general readers. It focuses on the basic histories, worldviews, and responses to contemporary ethical issues of the world's religions.

This second edition reorganizes the structure of the book, allowing students to more effectively explore, as well as compare and contrast, religious worldviews and religious responses to some of the most critical issues of the twenty-first century. It also thoroughly updates the surveys of the religions, adding reflections on the status of each religion as the new century begins, and makes current the discussion of ethical issues. Finally, it adds study aids requested by students, including lists of important terms and phrases, and Web sites useful for further study.

Chapter One establishes a framework for understanding religion, with a definition that both distinguishes religion from other human phenomena and structures the analysis of religion. This edition explores more fully the various established methods for studying religion, and clarifies the approach taken in this text. It also discusses general questions, such as "Why are people religious?" and "What is the relationship between religion and science?"

Chapters Two through Thirteen provide an overview of the histories, sacred texts, and worldviews of the major religions of the world. The worldviews are presented using the framework introduced in Chapter One, allowing students to develop their own comparisons. The religions surveyed include indigenous religions (with the religions of the Yoruba of West Africa and Oglala Lakota of the northern great plains of North America as examples); religions of South Asia (Hinduism, Theravada Buddhism, and Jainism); religions of East Asia (Daoism, Confucianism, Mahayana Buddhism, Shinto); and religions of the Middle East and beyond (Judaism, Christianity, Islam, and Sikhism).

Chapter Fourteen focuses on a representative sampling of new religious movements. This edition reorganizes the discussion, in terms of the following distinguishing themes evident in these religions:

- Preparing for the End: Apocalyptic New Religious Movements
- Faith and Spirit: New Religious Movements of Healing and Awareness
- Reviving the Church: Christian New Religious Movements of Renewal
- Nature and Spirit: Earth-based and Ecological New Religious Movements
- Liberation and Enlightenment: New Religious Movements with Asian Roots

- African-American and Afro-Caribbean New Religious Movements
- Native American New Religious Movements
- Focusing on the Human and the Natural: Secular New Religious Movements
- The Quest for Unity: Universalist New Religious Movements

The chapter updates the treatment of new religious movements, and adds descriptions of several that have become prominent since the publication of the first edition in 1995: Aum Shinryko, International Raelian Religion, and Falun Gong.

Chapters Fifteen through Eighteen present in an updated manner the responses of the world's major religions and selected new religious movements to the following critically important twenty-first-century ethical issues:

- The Ecological Crisis: Is the Balance of Life on Planet Earth in Jeopardy?
- The Economic Crisis: Why Hunger and Abject Poverty in a World of Plenty?
- War: When, If Ever, Is War Justified?
- Capital Punishment: When May the State Take a Criminal's Life?
- Abortion: Right to Life or Right to Choose?
- Euthanasia: A "Good Death" or "Playing God"?
- The Changing Roles of Women: Liberation or Confusion?
- Homosexuality: Orientation, Preference, or Perversion?

The final chapter of the book looks to the future, raising questions of how the religions of the world may relate to one another in the twenty-first century, and whether they will find common ground in addressing ethical issues such as the ecological crisis. A new feature of this edition is a reflection on the challenges posed to the world's religions and religious people by the tragic events of September 11, 2001.

Study aids at the end of each chapter include a summary, a list of important terms and phrases, questions for discussion and reflection, and sources and suggestions for further study (including Web sites).

ACKNOWLEDGMENTS

Writing a book of this scope is not a solitary enterprise, even though it is sometimes a lonely one. I am indebted to a host of teachers, colleagues, friends, and family members who have encouraged and challenged me over the years. My parents awakened in me a curiosity about the world, and modeled for me lives of commitment to their own spiritual heritage, but with respect for other religions. My first course in the world's religions, with the late Professor John Gammie at the University of Tulsa, inspired a fascination with the study of religion that has never abated. My understanding of my own religious tradition, other religions, and methods of studying them was refined under the guidance of the faculties of McCormick Theological Seminary and the University of Iowa School of Religion. I would especially like to acknowledge my Ph.D. advisor at the University of Iowa, Professor J. Kenneth Kuntz, and Professor Robert Baird, who shared with me his helpful insights about methodology in the study of religion.

For nearly thirty years I have benefited from my association with faculty and students at Westminster College in Fulton, Missouri. Among the many Westminster colleagues who have affected my own intellectual development I will single out only one: Emeritus Professor Chris Hauer, my colleague in religious studies for more than twenty years, whose breadth of knowledge and insight have been a constant source of stimulation. I have also learned much from my association with other colleagues at a number of institutions too numerous to mention, who have given me an opportunity to try out new ideas and to listen to theirs in a variety of settings, both formal and informal.

The scholars who have reviewed the manuscript of this text at various stages have provided a number of very helpful suggestions. Reviewers for the first edition (and their institutions at the time) included Julius J. Jackson, Jr., San Bernandido Valley College; James Cook, Oakland Community College; James S. Dalton, Siena College; Dale Bengston, Southern Illinois University; Martin S. Jaffee, University of Washington; Adele B. McCollum, Montclair State University; Catherine Wessinger, Loyola University; Roger E. Olson, Bethel College; David L. Barnhill, Guilford College; George E. Saint-Laurent, California State University—Fullerton; David Carrasco, University of Colorado; Daniel A. Brown, California State University—Fullerton; Steven Heine, Penn State University; Diana L. Hayes, Georgetown University; Gary Alexander, University of Wisconsin—Stevens Point; John H. Cartwright, Boston University; Francis Cook, University of California—Riverside; Zev Garber, Los Angeles Valley College; Peter Ochs, Drew University; Robert C. Monk, McMurry University; and Diane Bell, College of the Holy Cross.

Reviewers for the second-edition included Pamela Jean Owens, University of Nebraska at Omaha, and Mark Putnam, University of Northwestern Ohio.

I am grateful for the careful reading of all the reviewers and their proposals, many of which I have adopted. They are not, of course, responsible for any errors of fact or problematic interpretations that remain.

Several opportunities for study and research have had a direct impact on this second edition. Participation in the 1998–99 ASIANetwork South Asia Faculty Development Seminar, directed by Professor Job Thomas of Davidson College, enabled me to study South Asian religions and, through travel in India, experience them directly. I am grateful to the ASIANetwork Board of Directors, and the Ford Foundation, which funded this and other faculty development seminars in Asia. A yearlong sabbatical leave funded by Westminster College allowed me to focus more intensively on the study of Native American spiritual traditions. A three-year appointment as John Ashley Cotton Humanities Scholar at Westminster College, funded by a generous bequest, provided me the time and other resources essential for concentrated work in the critical, final stages of this project.

A number of people at Prentice Hall deserve acknowledgment for their efforts in behalf of this work. For this second edition, Ross Miller, Senior Acquisitions Editor for Philosophy and Religion, Carla Worner, Editorial Assistant, and Joanne Hakim, Production Liaison, have been gracious and supportive. I also appreciate the valuable contributions of Michael Bohrer-Clancy, second edition Production Editor, and the staff of the Interactive Composition Corporation. I am also grateful to Ted Bolen, former Religion editor, and former field representative Wayne Spohr, for their encouragement during the preparation of the first edition. The talented staff at Prentice Hall make writing a textbook not nearly as onerous a task as it could well be.

My family has endured with patience the many hours in which Dad was lost in the world of researching and writing about the world's religions. This book is dedicated to my wife, Sue, who most had to tolerate "the absorbedness of work" (as poet Donald Hall calls it), which tends to create a world of its own. It is also dedicated to the myriad students in scores of college classes who have given me the privilege of introducing them to the world's religions. Without them this book would not exist, and for them I have written it.

William A. Young

SECTION

I

Introduction

efore we begin our study of particular religions, we must first answer some general questions. What is religion? Why are people religious? Why are there so many religions? Why is the study of religion so important today? What is the relationship between science and religion? What are the various ways religion may be studied, and how will religion be studied in this text?

CHAPTER

1

An Introduction to Religion and the Study of Religion

WHAT IS RELIGION?

The Problem of Defining Religion

One person joins the army of her country and enthusiastically kills enemy soldiers. Another refuses to become a soldier and spends time in prison for violating the compulsory service law of his country. One person dances with abandon, holding poisonous snakes, gesticulating wildly. Another sits quietly for hours, seemingly frozen like a statue. One person talks about the earth as her mother and the birds, fish, and land animals as her sisters and brothers. Another speaks majestically of the human sovereignty over nature and implies that other animals are subordinate to humans. One person says that mankind's only hope is through faith in the mercy of the one and only God. Another asserts that many gods exist, but they are powerless to help humans reach the highest goal. Still another denies the existence of God or gods, but seems to have an all-encompassing worldview that takes the place of faith in God or gods.

All of these seemingly contradictory behaviors and beliefs have been identified as "religious" by scholars in the field of religious studies, illustrating the difficulty of identifying the object of their study. If such diverse phenomena are "religious," is there any common denominator that enables us to distinguish religion from other human endeavors?

Scholars are frankly divided on this most basic question. Some argue that it is impossible to define religion in general. Any attempt to define religion as a whole inevitably falls victim, they say, to the bias of a particular religious or nonreligious point of view. Others think that, given the basic diversity among religions, no single definition encompassing all religions is possible. Scholars of this perspective typically leave unaddressed the problem of defining religion.

Other interpreters, including the author of this text, think that a definition of religion in general is not only possible, but essential to the study of religion. A definition may reflect the bias of its author, but readers have a right to know the basic perspective taken in a presentation on a subject, especially one as controversial as religion. If no suitable definition for religion can be found to guide the study, how will students know that what they are studying *is* "religion"? Therefore, we will begin this study of the world's religions with a definition that we will use throughout our discussion.

Adopting a Working Definition of Religion

Many scholars have been sensitive to this problem, and have developed what they call "functional" or "working" definitions of religion. A "functional" definition is one designed for a particular use, in this case the broad study of religion. Such definitions are not intended to capture the *true* essence of religion, but rather intend only a framework for distinguishing and understanding religion. We will not attempt to review the many such definitions of religion proposed over the years. Typically, they have proven appropriate for the particular type of study to which they are related. There is no *one* right working definition of religion. From this perspective, each interpreter should stipulate and explain the definition adopted in his or her study.

The definition of religion developed for this examination of the world's religions is the following:

> Religion is human transformation in response to perceived ultimacy.

My task now is to convince you that this definition is appropriate and helpful for a study of the world's religions in an academic setting. To that end, we will first look at the three key words in the definition (*human, transformation,* and *ultimacy*) then explain the definition as a whole.

Human The first decision one must make is whether to limit "religion" to humanity, or to include other nonhuman life as religious creatures. Are dogs religious? What about plants? Our approach to this question is that if nonhuman beings *are* religious, we have not yet found a sufficiently open form of communication with them to be able to understand and describe their religions in an academic setting. Therefore, for the purposes of this study, we will stipulate that religion is a *human* phenomenon.

It should be noted that the definition leaves open the issue of whether religion is something humans engage in as individuals or groups. In fact, religion involves humans acting both by themselves and as communities, with some religions seeming to stress one over the other. A definition of religion adopted for a general study should not limit itself to either.

The inclusion of the term "human" in the definition also makes clear that religion is being understood as a *human* activity. This is important because some may wish to stipulate that the focus of activity in a definition of religion must be on the nonhuman, as for example in the definition of religion as "*God's* reaching out to humans." For the purposes of this study, religion is human behavior *in response to* some sort of perceived ultimacy such as God. This enables us to deal with what can be directly observed (that which humans say and do) rather than that which is beyond our direct observation (for example, God).

Finally, the word "human" implies that in any religion the observer will find a particular understanding of what it means to be human. We tend to assume that there is one, self-evident view of the nature of humanity (which usually reflects our own particular religious perspective). In fact, we will find a diversity of teachings about the essential elements of "humanity." Do humans have "souls"? If so, are these souls unique? Do humans survive physical death? If so, how? Are humans fundamentally distinct from other living beings? As we study religions we must be sensitive to the diversity of understandings of "humanity" that we encounter.

Transformation   Our definition emphasizes the dynamic quality of religion. Virtually every sort of human thought, feeling, or action *may* be religious. In order for anything human to qualify as religious, according to our definition, it must relate to a process of transformation, meaning *change* from one state of being to another. "Transformation" implies a situation prior to the change, the process of change itself, and the state that follows the change. Therefore, the single word "transformation" points us to three distinct aspects of religion.

First, religion identifies for individuals and/or groups a situation of life from which change is necessary. Such a state might be called the "problem" or "predicament" or, simply, "the human situation." One religion might identify "attachment to the material world" as this basic problem, another "an absence of harmony with the spirit world." We will maintain that a common feature of all religions is the explicit or implicit naming of a state *from* which transformation occurs.

Second, religion implies a state of existence that follows the process of transformation. This end may be expressed as an essentially individual phenomenon, as for example when a Buddhist monk experiences the blissful state called *nirvana*. Or it may be a communal situation, such as the new age that some branches of Judaism associate with their belief in the coming of a messiah. The state may be said to occur for individuals before death, after death, or both. It may come as a result of perceived divine or human initiative. All that can be said in general is that religious transformation involves a "goal," an "ideal state" toward which the transformation is directed.

Third, religion involves a process, a "means" through which the transformation occurs. The "means of transformation" is at the heart of religion. The "means" typically involves identification with myths that tell the fundamental stories of the religion and the acting out of these myths in the form of rituals. In a religious context, language has transformative power. When invoked properly, or dramatically enacted by those entrusted with authority to do so, the "words of religion" enable people to participate in the process of change. As we shall see, in virtually all religions "myth and ritual" are present. We will spend more time later in this chapter discussing these terms since they have specialized meanings, different (especially in the case of myth) from popular usage.

In addition to narratives and ritual acts, the "means" may also include direct experiences of that which inspires the transformation. The practice or belief in such direct experience is called *mysticism*. The transformation often entails the enactment of a right way of relating to others, the world, and one's self (ethics). The means may also involve assent to certain teachings and assertions (belief).

To reiterate a point made earlier, virtually any human activity may become part of the "means of transformation." In a real sense, the study of religion is the study of everything, because nothing can be ruled out *a priori* as nonreligious. And what is religious in one context may be considered nonreligious in another. In one setting, for example, killing an animal may be a matter of obtaining food, with no religious meaning. In other contexts, however, killing an animal may have deeply religious significance, either positive or negative. So, what *are* the criteria for distinguishing a religious phenomenon from other, nonreligious human endeavors?

Ultimacy   There is a fairly broad consensus among scholars today that the critical factor in naming something "religious" is "ultimacy." Religious phenomena are those associated with that which a person or group perceives as ultimate in individual or communal life. "That which is ultimate" means whatever is at the focus of life, that defines what "life" or "true reality" is for a person or community. The ultimate is the center in the circle of life; it conditions and gives meaning to all of existence.

We commonly associate religion with an ultimacy that people experience or believe in as coming from a higher plane of existence than ordinary, earthly reality. We will call this type of perceived extraordinary reality "spiritual" or "supernatural," as opposed to the "material" or "natural" reality of the world directly accessible to the physical senses and interpreted by the rational mind. Indeed, most of the religions to be studied in this text are "spiritual" in their perception of ultimacy.

"Spiritual ultimacy" may be expressed in personal language, the language of "gods" and "goddesses." Those religions whose ultimacy is spiritual and personal speak of the ultimate as one or more gods or spirits. Christianity, for example, is such a religion, for its transformation is in response to an ultimacy perceived as a personal deity. Other religions may have a spiritual sense of ultimacy, but view gods and spirits as either nonexistent or at least not supreme. The Dao of Daoism, for example, although ultimate, is not a god.

The terminology that has developed in Western cultures to describe the various perceptions of spiritual ultimacies reflects a bias in favor of personal description. Belief in the existence of personal gods is called in general *theism*. Belief in the existence of one all-powerful god, to the exclusions of other gods, is called *monotheism*. The belief in the existence of a plurality of personal gods is called *polytheism*. The rejection of belief in personal gods (and by extension spiritual reality in general) is known as *atheism*. Less common examples of theistic belief are *henotheism* (many gods exist, but one is dominant) and *pantheism* (all reality is god).

However, not all perceptions of spiritual ultimacy use personal imagery. We will encounter a number of religions in which ultimacy is understood to be impersonal: a force, energy, or mysterious reality beyond our comprehension. For example, *monism* is the belief in an impersonal ultimacy that is characterized by absolute unity. From a monist perspective, the highest truth is the oneness of all reality.

The term "perceived" is used advisedly in this definition. It is present to clarify that the definition is not claiming to identify the *true* ultimacy, only that which different people have responded to as ultimate. A perceptive (no pun intended) reader might object that "perception" is an exercise of the human mind in relation to this world. How can one perceive that which is, by definition, beyond the realm of ordinary existence? In order to attempt to understand religions with spiritual ultimacies we must be willing to assume for the purpose of the study the *possibility* of the perception of *spiritual* reality.

Secular Religions?

For most of human history, the vast majority of people have responded to what they perceive as spiritual ultimacy, whether personally or impersonally expressed. A characteristic of the modern world is the emergence of perceived ultimacies that are not spiritual, but are of the physical or mental world we experience and express as humans. Since "spiritual" is not a necessary component of our definition, we may include such "secular ultimacies" in the scope of our study and identify them as "secular religions."

One of the most prevalent "secular religions" of the modern world has been Marxism, named after the nineteenth-century economic and social theorist Karl Marx (1818–1883). Marxists typically perceive ultimacy not as a god or some impersonal spiritual reality or force, but as material reality understood in terms of the "laws" Karl Marx described. Marxism identifies transformation of society from a state of "alienation," caused by economic oppression, to the communal utopia of the classless society (which would inevitably arise, Marxists believed, under the stewardship of the Communist Party). We will provide a fuller description of Marxism as a secular religion in Chapter Fourteen.

Marxism is perhaps the most famous "secular religion," but there are others, now more influential than Marxism as the twenty-first century begins. Some would argue that *laissez faire* capitalism is a secular religion that is now more threatening to spiritual religions than Marxism. Under unrestrained capitalism, the pursuit of material wealth can become—for some—a pattern of ultimacy that drives out a meaningful sense of spirituality for individuals and societies. Capitalism is related to a popular, secular perception of ultimacy some consider to be the fastest growing religion in the contemporary world: *consumerism.*

Our contention is that the definition of religion as "human transformation in response to perceived ultimacy" provides a helpful framework for the objective study of the world's religions. It is inclusive enough to encompass the breadth of "spiritual" religions, as well as the "secular" religions we find in the modern world. But it is also narrow enough to provide a series of specific characteristics that enable us to distinguish religious from nonreligious phenomena.

WHY ARE PEOPLE RELIGIOUS?

Many people, probably most people in the world, *are* religious. Given our definition, one could easily argue that *all* people and groups are religious, for everyone seems to engage at some level in transformation in response to some perceived secular or spiritual ultimacy. Readers may wish to reflect on or discuss the question of the universality of religion, now or later in their study. Another, equally interesting question, is "*Why* are people religious?"

One common way to answer this question is in terms of the human needs religions meet. First, religion meets psychological needs. Perhaps the most basic need a person has is to feel a sense of identity and belonging. The perception of ultimacy gives an individual an underlying focus; a fundamental awareness of what is, for that person, the truly real. Religion orders life, and gives life a meaning and purpose that conditions all other experiences. Religion helps people cope with the anxiety of feeling alone and unattached in the world, by linking their own existence with that which is perceived as the foundation of existence. Some critics, most notably Sigmund Freud (1856–1939), have charged that religion causes people to deal with psychological needs in an unhealthy, immature manner. However, religious people themselves typically believe that without their response to perceived ultimacy, their lives would be much less fulfilling.

Second, religion meets social needs. Religion is the foundation not only of individual life, but of communal life, creating bonds within groups who share the same perception of ultimacy. Religions are the most common source of the shared values essential to a functioning society. Religion orders life at all levels of society, from the family to the nation-state. This is most evident in self-consciously religious societies, such as modern Saudi Arabia. However, even in avowedly secular societies, such as contemporary China, it may be argued that a perceived secular ultimacy is the source of the ordering of national life. Critics, such as those influenced by Karl Marx's view of religion as the "opiate of the masses," have charged that religion actually functions as a negative force in societies, causing oppressed people to be unaware of their plight or to feel powerless to change it. Others argue that religion has often been a powerful agent of social change, creating societies that are more just. Regardless, religion is indeed a "sacred canopy" that encompasses all levels of a society.

Another way to answer the question of "why people are religious" is to look not to the psychological or social *functions* of religion, but to ultimacy itself. People seem to be religious because they feel themselves compelled to be. They have no choice; they are by nature religious. They perceive ultimacy and they respond. Asking many religious persons why they are religious is like asking them why they breathe. It is not something about which they feel they have made a voluntary decision. It would seem that if we are to take religious people seriously, we must avoid the temptation to reduce religion to an examination of its various functions. From this perspective, "religion" is a phenomenon in its own right, which has its own reason for being.

WHY SO MANY RELIGIONS?

Although no one keeps an "official" count of the number of religions in the world, those who study religion agree that thousands of different religions exist, and more are springing up each year. We have attempted to account for this incredible variety of religions in the world by including in our definition the word "perceived."

Peoples' perceptions of the world are conditioned by the times and places in which they live, and especially by their languages. Their perceptions of ultimacy, therefore, are inevitably colored by these and other factors. For example, when expressing the idea of a "paradise," it is not surprising that religions that developed in a desert environment pictured paradise as an oasis, with lush trees and plenty of life-giving water. The language of religion is often metaphorical, with words drawn from everyday or extraordinary experience pointing us toward that which is perceived as ultimate. For example, in a culture in which the form of government is monarchical, it is not surprising that the ultimate may be expressed using royal language. God is a king, who rules. Many today believe that recognizing the metaphorical quality of the language of religions is a key step in understanding (and not being threatened by) the diversity of religions in the world.

Is it possible to penetrate to a deeper level than the metaphorical to find a common *essence* to all religions? Or are the metaphors of each religion so essential to the religion's identity that, at the most basic level, religions are fundamentally different? As you study the religions described in this text, you are invited to develop your own theories about the basic unity or diversity of religions in the world.

WHY IS THE STUDY OF RELIGION SO IMPORTANT IN THE TWENTY-FIRST CENTURY?

When asked why the study of religion is important, most of us engaged professionally in the field are tempted to give the "Why climb Mount Everest?" answer: because it's there. That is only a partially flippant response. Religion is pervasive, and, from what we are able to gather about the earliest evidence of human life, it always has been. Anyone seeking to understand the world in which he or she lives must confront religion seriously.

More specifically, the study of religion is critical today because of its role in a variety of the arenas of human life: political, artistic, and economic, to mention but a few. One need only look at a daily newspaper to see the influence of religion in politics. The events of September 11, 2001 brought home the role of religion in horrendous acts calculated to have profound political effect. However, religion has also been at the center of political movements that have improved the lives of people, such as the nineteenth-century campaign to end slavery in the United States. Today, whether involving Islam and Judaism in the Middle East, Hinduism and Sikhism in India, or branches of Christianity in Europe and the Americas, the political conflicts of the world have a distinctly religious tone. In more tranquil settings, transformation in response to perceived ultimacy often determines the agenda for political discussion and the parameters of political action. For example, in the important political question of population control, differing attitudes on the permissibility of abortion and forms of birth control, rooted in varying religious perspectives, are a prime ingredient in the debate.

Religion is also a driving force in the arts. The clearest examples are in traditionally religious cultures. One need only stroll through a museum featuring paintings from the European Middle Ages to witness how pervasive was the influence of religion on the art of that time. Today, the artistic influence of religion may be less obvious, but should not be ignored. Listen to any type of contemporary music, and ask yourself how varying perceptions of ultimacy are being expressed in the songs you hear!

Economic decisions are also rooted in peoples' perceptions of ultimacy. How resources are viewed and used in a society depends on a people's religion. For example, an indigenous society relates to nonhuman animals in a much different way than a materialistic society. Indigenous people perceive ultimacy as present in all of nature, so the maintenance of harmony with all living beings is critical to how they draw upon the resources of the world to meet their daily needs. In a society where material ultimacy dominates, nature is typically viewed as "stuff" to be used however humans wish. As the early twentieth century students of the relationship between religion and economic life, Max Weber and R. H. Tawney, demonstrated, the rise of capitalism in Europe was linked to the emergence of Protestant Christianity. One can hardly understand economic issues without attention to their religious underpinnings!

As we study the religions of the world, we will focus particular attention on how religions respond to some of the major political, social, ethical, and economic issues of the twenty-first century.

In addition to these objective reasons for studying religion, there are subjective factors to consider. Why is it important for *you* to study religion? You may or may not consider yourself a religious person, probably making that determination on the basis of your participation in structured religious activities. Even if you think of yourself as "nonreligious," it is nearly impossible for you to avoid religious questions. Who does not contemplate his or her place in the universe? Who does not wonder what "life" is, and whether "life" extends beyond physical death? This study will enable you to confront how people throughout history have answered these and other fundamental issues. If you are a self-consciously religious person, you will have the opportunity to compare your answers to the basic questions of life with those of other religious people. The process may not be comfortable, but it will be educational in more than a detached way.

Finally, we should consider what might be called the "moral imperative" for studying religion. We live on an increasingly small planet, shrinking because of the growing numbers of humans inhabiting the earth, and the amazing communications technologies that link even the most remote regions. If the human species is to survive, we must learn to live together and cooperate in solving the environmental and political problems we face. The key to cooperation is understanding the "other." How can we hope to understand other peoples unless we are willing to study their religions, their responses to perceived ultimacy? It may sound melodramatic, but it is arguably true that our future depends on peoples' willingness to understand sympathetically other peoples' religions.

WHAT IS THE RELATIONSHIP BETWEEN SCIENCE AND RELIGION?

A commonly held perspective today (especially in academic circles) is that science has replaced religion as the accepted mode of understanding reality. Surely, it is argued, what people once explained through their religions, educated people now understand by applying scientific reasoning. For example, people once thought that illness was caused by evil spirits; through science we have cast aside that view and embraced an understanding that illness has natural origins, even though we may not fully grasp what they are. Does not religion hold people back in the critically important quest to understand the world and ourselves?

While one may want to make the case that science *should* supplant religion, the pervasiveness of religion today shows that this has not yet happened for the vast majority of humans. In the modern world, then, both science and religion are present. Here we will only summarize a few of the different perspectives on how science and religion relate, using the fundamental question of origins to illustrate them.

Many people believe that religion and science are two competing, incompatible ways of approaching the world—that they are enemies. Some religious people stubbornly reject scientific explanations that, they believe, conflict with the religious viewpoint. Some Jews and Christians, for example, reject the biological theory of evolution; they believe it contradicts the Biblical teaching of creation by God in six, days which they accept as the true and accurate account of origins. On the other side, some scientists refuse to acknowledge the legitimacy of religion because of their perception that religion always depends on supernatural explanations that conflict with the naturalistic theories of science. They contend that those who seek to be scientific in their outlook must reject religion. For example, some scientists argue that since the Bible represents a prescientific view of the world, the Bible is at best antiquated and at worst dangerous, because it thwarts the scientific work necessary to cope with the complex problems of contemporary life. Attempts by religious people to thwart the teaching of the theory of evolution in public schools, they contend, endanger public support for and understanding of science at a time when science is more essential than ever to the well being of humanity.

Others stake out different territories for science and religion. "Good fences make good neighbors," and so it is with these two different ways of looking at the world, some would say. Religion begins where science ends, it might be argued. From this perspective religion and science are more like strangers than enemies. Science helps us understand the world naturally; religion examines the underlying causes and purposes of existence. For example, the Biblical story of creation deals with such questions as "Why does the universe exist? What is the purpose of life?"

Scientists studying origins are silent on these fundamental questions, focusing instead on such issues as "How did the universe come into existence?"

A third position is that science and religion are neither opposed nor separate, but are rather interrelated and complementary ways to approach life. From this point of view, both science and religion are trying to respond to the mysteries of existence. At some points the responses may diverge, but, increasingly, advocates of this position would argue, science and religion are coming to the same basic insights from their different directions. According to this perspective, religion and science are neither enemies nor strangers, but partners in the quest for truth. For example, some modern physicists think that their discoveries about the basic state of indeterminacy or flux in nature accords with the teachings of religions such as Buddhism and Daoism about the fundamentally fluid nature of reality. On the other hand, some religious thinkers (especially in Judaism and Christianity) are drawing on scientific theories such as evolution to explore new ways of perceiving ultimacy.

Have you thought about the relationship between science and religion? If so, do you consider religion and science to be enemies, strangers, or partners? (To pursue this topic further, see Barbour 2000.)

HOW MIGHT RELIGION BE STUDIED?

There is no single accepted method in the academic study of religion. That should not be surprising given the fact, as we have acknowledged, that there is no consensus on just what "religion" is, yet there is wide agreement that virtually any human activity or belief may fall at one time or another within the domain of religion. In fact, religious studies is by nature an interdisciplinary activity, drawing on the methods of a wide variety of academic disciplines. We will outline some of the approaches to the study of religion by dividing them in terms of the fundamental purpose of the study. Then we will clarify the way in which religion will be examined in this work.

Evaluative Methods of Studying Religion

One way to distinguish methods in the study of religion is in terms of the purpose of the study: religion may be studied for the sake of *evaluation* or *description*. Sometimes the two are combined, but for the purposes of an introductory study it is important to distinguish them. Those whose goal is evaluation are seeking to judge the truth of religion or religions. They want to know whether the claims of individual religions (or religion in general) have merit, and seek to establish criteria for assessing them. Two common evaluative methods are the *religious* and the *philosophical.*

Religious   As we have already acknowledged, any observer inevitably looks at other religions from the perspective of his or her own perception of ultimacy. In the "religious" method, however, the student has as a fundamental goal an assessment of the truth of other religions from one religion's point of view. For example, if I am a Zoroastrian, I might examine other religions to look for the degree to which they accord with truth as understood from a Zoroastrian perspective. The same approach may be taken with any religion as a starting point. Or I might start my study from the perspective that there is no truth to the claim that spiritual reality exists. I would then study religions with spiritual ultimacies in order to refute their teachings. Since I would hold as ultimate the assertion that there is no spiritual reality, this perspective would still fall under the heading of a "religious approach to religion" (using our definition of religion).

Philosophical   Another method of studying religion with an evaluative goal is the *philosophy of religion*. Here, however, the truth claims of religions are assessed not from the perspective of a particular religion, but from the standpoint of their susceptibility to being proven or disproven on the basis of rational argument. Does God (or any spiritual ultimacy) exist? Is there life after death? Are there miracles? A philosopher of religion will carefully analyze each of the terms of these assertions to determine the degree to which they may be said to have any rational meaning, and to have a basis in observable reality.

Descriptive Methods of Studying Religion

By contrast, a descriptive study of religion is designed not so much to make judgements about the truth of religion or religions, but rather to understand religion and the roles religions play in human life. Those committed to describing religion typically suspend judgment on the question of the truth or falsity of that which they are studying, at least while they are engaged in descriptive study. Descriptive methods include the *phenomenological, historical, functional,* and *comparative.*

Phenomenological   Simply stated, the phenomenological approach to the study of religion attempts to understand religion from the perspective of religious persons themselves. Perhaps you have heard the popular saying, derived from a Native American proverb, that you should not judge a person until you have walked a mile in his or her moccasins. The phenomenological method, in the sense used here, holds that "understanding" should precede "evaluation" when it comes to studying religion, and that a primary goal of the initial phase of study should be to understand the religion as much as possible "from the inside." In other words, when studying Islam the goal should be to understand Islam as Muslims do. That is an idealistic, perhaps utopian objective. How can we possibly perceive ultimacy as others do? In addition, Islam means different things to different Muslims. The fact that we cannot fully attain the phenomenological goal does not mean that we should not try, advocates of this method argue. What is required is a willingness to consciously "bracket off" one's own assumptions about religion in general—and other religions in particular—long enough to see the world from another religious point of view. We must attempt to let religions "speak for themselves," and listen sensitively to what we hear.

Historical   The historical approach seeks to understand the religions as they have come into existence and developed through time. An historical study will typically examine the origins of a particular religion, its earliest expressions, its spread and often times divisions, and its progress up to the present.

Functional   A functional study seeks to understand the function or role religion plays in a particular human context. Psychologists of religion typically study the function of religion in the makeup and development of individuals. Sociologists of religion examine the role religion plays in human groups, from the family to the entire society. Anthropologists of religion engage in a method of study functional in intent, but often phenomenological in spirit. They typically focus on the place of religion in the cultures of indigenous and other peoples, through a process of participation in and observation of the people of that culture. The common denominator in the functional approach is that the primary interest is in understanding the role of religion in the life of an individual, society, or culture. The functional approach overlaps with the evaluative when the question of whether religion is "functional" or "dysfunctional" in the various contexts is raised.

Comparative   The comparative method seeks to understand religion by looking for that which is common among religions. Its basic question is whether there is an "essence" that all religions share. The method also focuses on fundamental patterns of religious expression. For example, a comparativist might find common meanings in the use of water in the rituals of various religions.

HOW WILL WE STUDY THE WORLD'S RELIGIONS?

Our method of studying religions in this work will be fundamentally descriptive. Readers are urged, to the maximum degree possible, to put aside their own assumptions about the truth of religion or religions, and seek to understand the variety of religions studied in this book on their own terms. In other words, if you begin this study fervently believing in the truth claims of a particular religion, try hard not to assess other religions from your own religious perspective. Instead, resolve to try your best to understand what each religion means to its own adherents. Or, if you come to this study antagonistic toward religion (perhaps because of a negative experience with a particular religion) you are also encouraged to set aside your prior perspective. Simply coming to a basic understanding of the world's religions is hard enough; carrying one's own baggage along on the journey of discovery can make it much more difficult. Once you have achieved an understanding of the various religions of the world, you will be in a better and fairer position to make informed judgments about them, and your discussion of religions with others will be freer of the biases we so often carry into such dialogues.

Our descriptive study of the world's religions will be *historical, comparative,* and—above all—*phenomenological.* We will examine the origins and stages of development of each religion, and (after the indigenous religions) its written, sacred texts. From the perspective of phenomenological study, at the most basic level, religions order reality. In other words, each group of religions and each individual religion has a "worldview" rooted in its distinctive "perceptions of ultimacy." To appreciate this critically important dimension of religion, we have created a "framework for understanding" religious worldviews. At the outset of the discussion of each group of religions, and at the heart of our examination of each particular religion, we will typically apply this framework as a tool of analysis. In addition, the framework will provide a basis for descriptive (rather than evaluative) comparison of religions.

A Framework for Understanding and Comparing Religious Worldviews

The framework for understanding religious worldviews that we will employ is based on the definition of religion developed for this study: human transformation in response to perceived ultimacy. We have already begun to analyze the elements of this definition; it can be further expressed in terms of seven questions that may be asked of each religion in order to develop an understanding of its worldview. This framework will be useful in both understanding and comparing the religions we are studying.

What Does It Mean to Be Human? Each religion has its own view of what constitutes human nature and the relationship between humans and other beings. If the religion is spiritual (rather than secular), humans are understood to have not only material, but also spiritual natures. For example, some spiritual religions claim that humans have individual souls, while others reject the notion of separate human souls. Religions also place humans in the world. For example, some religions are anthropocentric (human-centered), claiming a unique spiritual identity for humans and a relationship of dominance over the rest of the world; others are biocentric (centered on all living beings together), rejecting the view that humans have special spiritual status or are superior to other forms of life. Still others might be called ecocentric (centered on all reality together), embracing the spiritual interconnectedness and ultimate identity of all life.

What Is the Basic Human Problem? Each religion identifies a situation common to humanity, which results in the need for transformation. For example, some religions identify the fundamental human dilemma as entrapment in a cycle of birth, death, and rebirth. Others see the human problem as a lack of harmony with the rest of life. Still others see the problem as human separation or alienation from a personal god.

What Is the Cause of the Problem? Religions also include understandings of what is at the root of the basic human dilemma. Religions that see the problem as separation from a personal god often see the cause as human disobedience of the deity's will. By contrast, religions identifying the problem as being stuck in the cycle of rebirth tend to view human desire and ignorance of the spiritual as the causes. And religions stressing disharmony put the emphasis on human forgetfulness of the way of harmony.

What Is the End or Goal of Transformation? If religions identify a basic human problem and the cause of the dilemma, they also envision an ideal state for humans. We may call this state the end or goal of transformation. For example, religions in which the problem is entrapment in the cycle of rebirth claim that the ideal state is liberation from the cycle; typically, they are rich in imagery of the nature of the liberated existence. However, religions focusing on human disobedience of a personal god portray a state of existence in which humans are reconciled with the deity, typically enjoying a life beyond earthly existence.

What Are the Means of Transformation? At the heart of each religion are means that will enable the transformation to occur. For religions in which liberation from the cycle of rebirth is the end or goal, the means of transformation focus on the overcoming of material attachment and spiritual ignorance. However, if the end or goal is repairing the breach with a personal god caused by human disobedience, the means will involve reorientation to the way of life ordained by the deity. For religions in which the end or goal is harmony with all living beings, the means typically are all-encompassing, involving every aspect of life.

What Is the Nature of Reality? If religions do indeed order reality, then it is important to understand how each religion constructs time and space. For example, for religions in which the issue is the cycle of birth, death, and rebirth, the understanding of time is obviously cyclical, with beginnings and endings of each cycle. By contrast, other religions understand time as moving from a beginning to a definitive end. Space is also understood from the perspective of the perceived ultimacy. For example, as we shall see in Chapter Two, indigenous religions are typically rooted in particular places and construct ordered space around a specific center.

What Is the Sacred and How May the Sacred Be Known?   In this study we use the term "sacred" as a synonym for the perceived ultimacy that distinguishes each religion. While it is common to think of the sacred as synonymous with the spiritual, that is not the case in our approach. Rather, that which is perceived as ultimate may be either spiritual or secular. The sacred may be the personal god or gods of a theistic religion or an impersonal energy or force. An important and related question is how the sacred may be made known. For example, for religions in which the problem is spiritual ignorance, the sacred is often made known through a disciplined pursuit of spiritual knowledge. However, monotheistic religions often claim that the only way the sacred may be known is through some act of self-revelation on the part of the god at the center of the religion, typically through the agency of a person or persons.

It may be useful for you at this point to consider your own responses to these seven questions. Do you find them difficult to answer, or do responses spring easily to mind? Regardless of your answer, as you study other religious worldviews, you will have the opportunity to reflect on your own. But remember, please place the priority on *understanding* other religions, before you evaluate them!

Symbols, Myths, and Rituals

Because of their central importance to the academic study of religion, we must clarify three important, interrelated terms: *symbol, myth,* and *ritual.*

Symbols   In general, a *symbol* is something that stands for something else. Drivers know that a red, octagonal sign at an intersection means "Stop!" The sign "symbolizes" the concept of "stopping" within the rules established for driving. Symbols may be objects, like the sign, or they may be gestures or sounds. When a baseball umpire raises his or her right hand, a strike is being called. When a movie director says "Cut!" the actors know that they should stop the scene. Religion is full of symbols in this general sense: objects, gestures, and sounds that reveal some aspect of whatever is ultimate in the religion. In Hinduism, for example, pictures of deities often show the god as having a number of arms as a visual way of expressing the power of the god. When a Jew says "*Shema' yisrael . . .* " ("Hear, O Israel . . . "), he or she is articulating a belief in the unity of the personal diety at the heart of Judaism.
      However, many students of religion suggest a somewhat more specialized meaning for the term "symbol" when applying it to religion. More than simply representing something else, a religious "symbol" enables people to participate in that to which the symbol points. For example, when Hindus walk around (circumambulate) the object that symbolizes a particular deity, they are actually experiencing the sacred reality of that god. When a Roman Catholic priest lifts the "host" and says the prescribed words, the wafer is not a mere *representation* of the "body of Christ." When worshippers take the bread, they believe they are actually receiving Christ.

Although religious people often disagree on the precise meaning of symbolic "participation," the belief that symbols (whether simple or elaborate) are essential to their contact with that which they deem ultimate is held in common. In studying a religion, awareness of the rich symbols that are present, and their particular usage, is critical to understanding.

Myths   The dominant contemporary usage of the term "myth" is much different than its specialized meaning in the study of religion. In current general usage, myths are "false stories" because they conflict with what we know empirically to be true. For example, we might say that the belief that casual contact spreads the AIDS virus is a myth, because scientific research has shown that to be untrue. To say in response to someone's story, "That's a myth!" is to denigrate the account, relegating it to the realm of the unbelievable.

In the academic study of religion, the term "myth" has a specialized meaning. In our study we will use "myth" for stories about whatever people perceive to be ultimate, and which they therefore accept as *true* reality. Myths are often called "foundational stories" because they typically serve to create the basic patterns of order (cosmos) for those who believe them. They are paradigmatic, meaning that they reveal the way life is to be understood and lived by those who are grasped by the particular ultimacy with which the myth is concerned.

In the popular understanding, only "primitive" (and now discredited) religions had myths. They may be interesting to study (like the myths surrounding the Olympian gods), but they are now "dead." Contemporary students of religion typically take the position that *every* religion (whether spiritual or secular) has myths, for every religion has narratives about that which is ultimate—foundational stories that are at the heart of the religion.

One of the most common types of myths is the "myth of origins" (*cosmogonic myth*), which recounts the story of how that which is ultimate gave rise to all experienced reality. For Judaism and Christianity, for example, the first chapters of the Book of Genesis constitute a myth of origins, a story about the beginnings of space and time that reveals the nature of the cosmos created by God. Virtually every religion has a myth of origins that fulfills a similar function. One of the fruitful ways to compare religions is to examine the cosmogonic myths popular in the religions.

Other myths relate to that toward which ordinary time is moving, rather than that from which it comes. They are called *eschatological myths,* and they are particularly common in the religions that hold a linear view of time. For example, the Christian Bible ends with a book that tells the myth of the "end time." As in the Book of Revelation, most end-time myths tell of how the order present in the time of origins will be completely restored at the end of time. Religions that take a cyclical view of time, like Hinduism, still have mythic accounts of the end of the current age, which will be destroyed before the next cosmic cycle begins.

Because they "stand outside ordinary time," myths speak of a time that is eternally present and repeatable (see Eliade 1959: 68–113). That is, if the story of the myth is not limited to a particular time, then it is equally true and real at the particular moment at which it is told. The telling of a myth relates not so much to something that happened within time (although myths may relate to historical events), but draws the eternal into the present reality. For example, for Jewish people the story of the deliverance of the people of ancient Israel from slavery in Egypt (told in the Book of Exodus in the Hebrew Bible) is a "foundational story" or myth. Although the story of the deliverance presumably occurred in some form within time, the story about these events is a "myth," which speaks of how God interacts with his people at all times. When the story is recounted, those who accept it as "myth" experience it not only as an account of what "happened," but what continually "happens."

One of the critical steps in the study of any religion, spiritual or secular, is to ask, "What are its myths?" Myths are not confined to religions with spiritual ultimacies. So-called secular religions have "foundational stories" that order the cosmos they inhabit, and eschatological stories that reveal that toward which time is moving. For example, Marxism constructs a narrative of historical events to show how the phenomenon of class struggle keeps repeating itself. It also envisions the "classless society" that will represent the culmination of ordinary, class-conscious history. The vibrancy of a religion can be measured in part by the power of the religion's myths to continue to lay the foundations for ordered reality for the people who tell them. Living myths are not only stories told but realities lived. They provide the models for living, for groups as a whole as well as for individuals.

Rituals A term equally important in the study of religion in general is *ritual*. If myths are stories outside time and space, which order reality for those who accept them as true, then "rituals" are those actions within time and space that bring the power of myth into the lives of the people who practice them. Ritual is symbolic action that enables persons to participate in transformation in response to ultimacy. The source of ritual is myth. Rituals are often, one might say, "myths enacted." Myths express their order in word and image; rituals dramatize the ordering of the cosmos in terms of performance. For example, if the story of the deliverance of Egypt is a basic Jewish myth, then the Passover celebration is the ritual through which the myth is enacted, and through which the people may participate in the transformation in response to the ultimacy perceived in the myth. Through participation in the ritual, the individual or community steps outside ordinary time and space and enters, during the ritual, into sacred, "ordered" time and space.

Rituals create "sacred space," areas set apart or distinguished (temporarily or permanently) from ordinary usage to become arenas for the experience of the ultimate. Whether the context is a magnificent cathedral or a small home shrine, it is the conducting of rituals that transforms these spaces into "true space," where encounters with ultimacy order and give meaning to life.

Rituals order time, creating "moments" amidst ordinary time into which the sacred enters to create cosmos. Some ritual observances are recurrent, creating a calendar for those who share the same perception of ultimacy. For example, in traditional Christian cultures the year is ordered according to the series of festivals that enact the Christian myth (such as Easter and Christmas). "The periodicity of ritual time . . . ensures the perpetual grounding of world in its myth. Through daily, weekly, monthly, or annual ritual time, myth is recoverable." (Paden 1988: 101). In most religions there are "great" festivals that order the entire year at the time of transition from one year to another. Typically, there is a time of purification involving restriction and denial, followed by a time of celebration and rebirth. For example, the Christian "new year" is created by the sequence of the purificatory period called Lent, climaxing in death on Good Friday, followed by the time of rebirth at Easter.

In addition, there are other festivals of renewal on a monthly, weekly, or daily basis. In many indigenous religions, and in traditional practice in other religions, all of time is sacralized through the daily repetition of rituals.

Periodic rituals are for groups, but also for individuals. In most religions, individuals celebrate their birthday, marriage day, or the death of a family member as recurrent times of renewal. For the times of transition in the life of the individual

A bride and groom after having their marriage blessed at a Hindu temple in South India. Rites of passage at times of life transitions such as marriage are universal.

(birth, adulthood, marriage, death), there are "rites of passage," to mark as well as order these moments.

Today rituals are often dismissed as a "waste of time" by those for whom the associated myths have no power. However, look at your own life or the lives of others and ask yourself if you and they do not have certain "rituals" that order life? For some people in modern, materialistic society the "weekend" is ritual time, with the Friday or Saturday night "party" serving as a focus and frame for the experience of "true reality." At the party they "step outside ordinary time" and enter into a transformed reality that creates a sense (at least temporarily) of meaningfulness for an otherwise rather meaningless existence.

LOOKING AHEAD: AN OVERVIEW
OF THE REST OF THE TEXT

In the present study our basic approach is *phenomenological*. Our goal is to let each religion speak for itself, presenting it in a way that could be affirmed by the people who themselves perceive ultimacy in this manner. However, we will draw on other methods, especially the historical and comparative, as we describe the religions.

In each chapter we will use an historical approach to relate the basic story of each religion, following (for the most part) its chronological development. We will also use the framework for understanding presented earlier in this chapter as we seek to understand the worldview of each religion.

We have organized our presentation of the religions of the world in the following manner. First, we will examine the "indigenous religions" that find expression throughout the world as the earliest form of religion. Fortunately, indigenous religions survive, and so we study them not only as the original and most basic type of religion, but in their contemporary expression. Next, we will turn to the major geographic areas of the world to study the religions that originated in and/or dominated these regions in the historical period: the religions of South and Southeast Asia (Hinduism, Theravada Buddhism, and Jainism); the religions of East Asia (Daoism, Confucianism, Mahayana Buddhism, and Shinto); and the religions of the Middle East, Europe, and the Americas (Zoroastrianism, Judaism, Christianity, and Islam; we will also discuss Sikhism in this section). We will then examine some of the "new religions" of the world, religious movements that have developed in the last two centuries in the context of the major religious traditions, or that have emerged afresh.

Once we have surveyed the world's religions historically, phenomenologically, and comparatively, we will turn to responses of the world's religions to some of the major issues of the twenty-first century: ecological crisis, economic justice, war, capital punishment, abortion, euthanasia, gender equality, and sexual orientation.

We will conclude our survey with various views of what the future holds for the world's religions, and efforts to find common ground so that religions may address the most critical issues the world faces. We will also raise the question of relations among religions after the events of September 11, 2001.

At the end of each chapter we will provide a summary and a list of key terms and phrases in the chapter (many of which are defined in the Glossary at the end of the book). Then we will raise a series of questions for group discussion and/or individual reflection. These are not so much "review" or "study" questions; rather, they are questions with no clear "right" or "wrong" answers, intended to provoke thought and conversation. If they do their job, this book will become a dialogue between the reader and the religions being studied, or a "town meeting" of readers, rather than just a monologue by the author.

There is nothing more fascinating and rewarding than a serious, open conversation about religion! There is also nothing more fraught with the potential for misunderstanding and animosity. Please be respectful and gentle with one another if you are using this book as the basis for a discussion about religion in a group of persons with diverse attitudes about the subject.

Finally, each chapter will include a list of references and sources for further study (both books and internet sites).

Two concluding comments about this study of religion are necessary before we actually embark on it. First, to reiterate an important point: none of us is able to entirely shed the cultural, social, and psychological influences that have been a part of the formation of our experience of the world. This holds true for the author as well as for readers. I am aware that my decision to approach religion phenomenologically, with support from the historical and comparative methods, has been shaped by my own particular journey.

Your response to what you have read so far and what is to come will be guided by your own set of experiences with religion. The only real antidotes for the inadvertent blindness sometimes caused by preconditioning are self-awareness, self-criticism, and humility. If we allow ourselves to be aware of how our own presuppositions are affecting our understanding, if we constantly ask ourselves whether we are being fair in our statements about what we are studying, and if we acknowledge that we ourselves do not yet have a complete grasp of the truth, the study will be an effective and rewarding one.

Second, establishing "understanding" as the primary goal does not mean that "evaluation" is not important. The perspective of the author is that he should not do the work of evaluation for the reader. If this book is being used in a classroom setting, I hope that evaluative discussions will be allowed by the teacher. The class will be much more interesting if you not only seek to understand religion, but engage in an open and frank (but respectful) discussion about the truth of religion and religions. However, I encourage you not to short-circuit the process. Before you move to the stage of evaluation, make sure you have first tried hard to understand the religion you are judging!

CHAPTER SUMMARY

The legendary founder of Daoism (see Chapter Six), Lao Zi, is reputed to have said, "The journey of a thousand miles must begin with a single step." If you complete a study of the world's religions, even an introductory one such as this book intends, you will feel as though you have journeyed at least a thousand miles by foot! There is much ground to cover! The purpose of this first chapter has been to help you get started in your journey.

In this chapter we first discussed the problems associated with defining religion and whether developing a definition of religion is a necessary starting point for a study of religion. We adopted as our working definition of religion for this study, "*human transformation in response to perceived ultimacy,*" briefly explaining each of its elements.

We then asked "Why are people religious?" "Why so many religions in the world?" "Why is the study of religion so important today?" and "What is the relationship between religion and science today?" In each case we reflected on various possible answers.

We then introduced the two types of academic study of religion. We distinguished between studies of religion for the purposes of evaluation and understanding. "Evaluative" methods include what we called the "religious (or theological) approach to studying religion" and the philosophical. "Descriptive" approaches that focus on "understanding" include the phenomenological, historical, functional (psychological, sociological, or anthropological), and comparative methods. We explained that we will draw particularly on the historical and comparative methods to complement the fundamentally phenomenological approach in this book.

Phenomenological study entails trying to let the religions speak for themselves as much as possible. Using our definition of religion as a basis, we developed a "framework for understanding" religion that addresses each religion with the following questions in order to understand its unique worldview:

- What does it mean to be human?
- What is the basic human problem?
- What is the cause of the problem?
- What is the end or goal of transformation?
- What are the means of transformation?
- What is the nature of reality?
- What is the sacred and how may the sacred be known?

We then focused special attention on three terms central to the study of religion: symbol, myth, and ritual.

The chapter concluded with an overview of the rest of the book. In addition to a study of the worldviews of religions, the second distinctive feature of this text is a consideration of the responses of the world's religions to some of the most important ethical issues of the twenty-first century.

You are ready now to embark on what will be, if you undertake it with curiosity and an open mind, a fascinating journey!

IMPORTANT TERMS AND PHRASES

The study of any subject requires the development of a distinctive vocabulary. Here is a list of the important terms and phrases from this chapter to add to your "religious studies vocabulary." You will find them explained in the chapter, and, in many cases, defined in the glossary at the end of the book. Similar lists will be included in other chapters.

> atheism, capitalism, comparative method, consumerism, cosmogonic myth, eschatological myth, evaluative versus descriptive, functional definition of religion, functional methods (e.g., psychology, sociology, anthropology), human transformation in response to perceived ultimacy, Marxism, monotheism, myth, periodic rituals, phenomenological method, philosophy of religion, polytheism, religious (theological) approaches to studying religion, rites of passage, ritual, secular religion, symbol, theism

QUESTIONS FOR DISCUSSION AND REFLECTION

1. As you begin a study of the religions of the world, what is your basic attitude toward religion? Do you consider yourself a religious person? Why or why not? Write down a brief sketch of your experiences with religion (including both positive and negative experiences). How have these experiences shaped your current attitude toward religion?

2. How many different religions have you *directly* encountered? What was the nature of your encounter(s)? What do you feel you learned from them?

3. What do you hope or expect to derive from a serious study of religion? Jot down the general and specific questions you have right now about religion in general or particular religions.

4. Look up the word "religion" in a dictionary. Do any of the definitions listed seem more (or less) appropriate for a thorough, objective study of the world's religions than the definition proposed in this chapter?

5. Do you think that a study of religion should include "secular religions" as we have proposed in this chapter? Why or why not?

6. Are science and religion in opposition to one another, concerned with different ways of knowing, or complementary? Take a provisional position on this question as it relates to the issue of understanding the origins of the cosmos.

7. Pick up a major newspaper or a weekly news magazine (or access one on the web). Also, watch coverage of the news on broadcast and cable television. Make a quick list of the stories that reflect the influence of religion. From this sample, how well do you think the contemporary news media covers religion?

8. Consult the "framework for understanding religion" in this chapter, and give your own provisional responses to each of the questions. What, for example, do *you* think is the basic human problem, and the cause of that problem? If you

find that you do not have clear responses to these questions, why do you suppose that is the case?

9. What assumptions do you bring to the study of religion? Do you see the value of "bracketing off" these assumptions and trying to understand what each religion means to its own adherents? Why or why not?

Sources and Suggestions for Further Study

Barbour, Ian, 2000. *When Science Meets Religion: Enemies, Strangers, or Partners.* San Francisco: HarperCollins.

Campbell, Joseph (with Bill Moyers), 1988. *The Power of Myth.* New York: Doubleday. (See also other works by Campbell, a popular interpreter of the world's religions, including *The Hero with a Thousand Faces* and *The Masks of God.*)

Cunningham, Lawrence and John Kelsey, 2001. *The Sacred Quest: An Invitation to the Study of Religion,* 3rd ed. Upper Saddle River, NJ: Prentice Hall.

Eliade, Mircea, 1959. *The Sacred and the Profane: The Nature of Religion.* Trans. Willard Trask. New York: Harper and Row. (See also other works by this important figure in the development of the phenomenological method of the study of religion, including *Cosmos and History* (1954), *Myth and Reality* (1963), *Patterns in Comparative Religion* (1963), and *Rites and Symbols of Initiation* (1965).)

Eliade, Mircea, ed. 1987. *The Encyclopedia of Religion.* New York: Macmillan.

Hick, John, 1992. *An Interpretation of Religion.* New Haven: Yale University.

Paden, William, 1988. *Religious Worlds: The Comparative Study of Religion.* Boston: Beacon.

Paden, William, 2003. *Interpreting the Sacred: Ways of Viewing Religion.* Boston: Beacon.

Pals, Daniel L. 1996. *Seven Theories of Religion.* New York: Oxford University.

Runzo, Joseph and Nancy M. Martin, 2000. *The Meaning of Life in the World Religions.*

Smith, Jonathan Z., ed. 1995. *The Harper-Collins Dictionary of Religion.* San Francisco: HarperCollins.

Smith, Wilfrid Cantwell, 1991. *The Meaning and End of Religion.* Minneapolis: Fortress.

Streng, Frederick J. 1998. *Understanding Religious Life.* 3rd ed. Belmont, CA: Wadsworth.

Web Sites

Note: All internet sites begin with http://

www.wabashcenter.wabash.edu/Internet/front.htm
(a guide to internet resources for the study of religion, provided by the Wabash Center for Teaching and Learning in Theology and Religion)

religion.rutgers.edu/vri/index.html
(a virtual index for the study of religion, maintained by the Department of Religion at Rutgers University)

www.acs.ucalgary.ca/%7Elipton/
(a religious studies web guide, maintained by the University of Calgary Library)

interfaithcenter.org
(the web site of the New York City Interfaith Center, with links for study of the world's religions)

www.sacred-texts.com
>   (an internet archive of sacred texts from the world's religions)

d1.dir.dcn.yahoo.com/society_and_culture/religion_and_spirituality
>   (the Yahoo directory for sites on numerous religions)

beliefnet.com
>   (a commercial site with information and links regarding the world's religions)

TIME   Refer to Pearson/Prentice Hall's **TIME Special Edition: World Religions** magazine for these and other current articles on topics related to many of the world's religions:

•❖ *The Religious Experience: Birth and Childhood; The Legacy of Abraham; Mohandas Gandhi*

•❖ *The Impact of Religion: Cult Shock; Relaxing in a Labyrinth; Will Politicians Matter?; Essay—God Is Not On My Side. Or Yours.*

Prentice Hall's **Research Navigator** helps students in their further study of the world's religions. Visit ***http://www.researchnavigator.com*** for help on the research process and access to databases full of relevant material, including the New York *Times.*

SECTION

II

The World's Religions— Histories and Worldviews

※

In this section (Chapters Two through Fourteen) we will study the histories and worldviews of the world's oldest major religions and of a representative sampling of the world's smaller and newer religious movements. We will utilize the phenomenological, historical, and comparative methods of studying religion described in Chapter One. The religions will be grouped in the following "families": indigenous religions (focusing on case studies drawn from African and Native American religions), South and Southeast Asian religions (Hinduism, Theravada Buddhism, and Jainism), East Asian religions (Daoism, Confucianism, and Mahayana Buddhism), religions originating in the Middle East and beyond (Judaism, Christianity, Islam, and Sikhism), and new religious movements. After using the "framework for understanding" developed in Chapter One to introduce the worldview or general characteristics of each family of religions, we will survey the stages of development and sacred texts of the particular religions. We will then typically apply the framework for understanding again, to survey the worldviews of the individual religions.

CHAPTER

Indigenous Religions— Quest for Harmony

AN ORIENTATION TO INDIGENOUS PEOPLES AND THEIR RELIGIONS

"Indigenous" means "pertaining to a particular area." Indigenous religions are those religions native to a specific geographic area, such as North America, Africa, or Australia. In each region of the world we find religions that were present when modern people first entered the area and/or reflect an earlier stage of cultural development than the state-level societies dominating the world today. This does not mean that indigenous religions have not changed over time. *All* religions change, as do all human activities and institutions. However, many of the religions of contemporary indigenous peoples in their traditional manifestations are, to a significant degree, in continuity with the beliefs and practices of the religions of their ancestors. Such religions are fascinating in their own right. They can also help us become aware of basic patterns found in the religions we will study in subsequent chapters.

In this chapter we will discuss problems associated with studying indigenous religions, introduce the traditional worldview of indigenous religions, and treat as case studies the religions of the Yoruba people of West Africa and the Oglala Lakota (Sioux) of North America.

Problems in Studying Indigenous Religions

We must acknowledge the serious problems faced by any outsider who tries to describe indigenous religions today. The first is the word "religion" itself. "Religion" is a Western term, which usually implies an organized set of beliefs and practices to be distinguished from a "nonreligious" sphere of life. As we shall see, indigenous peoples make no such distinction. An Oglala Lakota leader once told the author, "We have no word 'religion' in our language. It is not a word appropriate to our traditional way of life." Many scholars have begun to use the term "spirituality" instead or "religion" when speaking of the sacred ways of indigenous peoples. We have chosen to use the word "religion" in this chapter because we are committed to using a broader definition of religion ("human transformation in response to perceived ultimacy"). Although indigenous peoples typically have no word for "religion," they do have patterns of ultimacy central to their cultures.

The second problem reflects an even more blatant bias. Until quite recently scholars seeking to describe these religions often called them "primitive" religions, adopting the stereotype that religions which developed after them are "advanced." However, the intricate and sophisticated teachings and practices of these religions show them to be as fully "developed" as any other religions.

Other appellations are more descriptive, but still reflect a modern, Western bias, and suggest a third problem—"naming" this group of religions. These religions have been called "preliterate" or "nonliterate" religions, indicating that they do not have written scriptures—instead, their myths and legends are transmitted orally. These designations imply a lack of a literature, but that is not true: sacred traditions are revered and preserved orally in virtually every indigenous culture. Other interpreters have called these religions "prehistoric," but this is misleading because they have continued into and, in many cases, show the influences of, the historical era.

The search for a more descriptive "name" has led some scholars to call the indigenous religions "basic" or "primal" religions, reflecting their status as the original religions (and in some ways the foundation for later religions). These designations are not themselves prejudicial, but they risk misunderstanding by those who assume that "basic" or "primal" means simple or not complex. Others have adopted the term used for the level of social organization most common in these religions, calling them "tribal" or "small-scale traditional" religions. They have also been called "native" religions. However, both "tribal" and "native" have taken on misleading, stereotypical meanings in modern societies, and "small-scale traditional" is misleading because many of these religions were associated with very large groups of people.

In our discussion in this chapter and the next we will use the designations "indigenous" or "traditional" religions, because these terms seem the most descriptive and the most neutral of the titles so far suggested.

Of course, *any* "naming" of these religions as a group has serious limitations, for each indigenous religion is unique. Even initiates into these religions typically receive only a portion of the full panoply of sacred knowledge associated with the religion. Outsiders, even those who spend a great deal of time with the people, have access to isolated bits of information that they must try to put together into a meaningful whole. Moreover, these religions depend on oral rather than written traditions, which must be passed from generation to generation.

Despite these difficulties, much progress has been made toward an understanding that can be communicated at least partially to outsiders such as the author and readers of this book. Anthropologists and ethnographers have documented literally hundreds of indigenous cultures, recording the rich oral traditions and variegated beliefs and practices they exhibit. Some indigenous people have themselves published their own accounts of their traditional religions.

The Traditional Worldview of Indigenous Peoples

The framework we have established for understanding religions (see Chapter One) serves as well as a pattern for introducing the traditional worldview of families of religions. Here we will examine the shared worldview of indigenous religions. In subsequent chapters we will encounter the shared worldviews of the religions of South and Southeast Asia, the religions of East Asia, and the religions of the Middle East and beyond. Comparing and contrasting these basic worldviews is a helpful way of establishing contexts for understanding the complexity of the world's religions. As with all generalizations they are intended as learning tools rather than as final, definitive descriptions.

Humanity: Members of a Larger Spiritual Family   It is common to hear members of indigenous communities call nonhuman living beings "people." For example, birds are said to be "winged people," trees "standing people," and fish "people who swim in the waters." This is not the result of a limited vocabulary in indigenous languages, but because all beings, in the shared indigenous worldview, are typically understood to be members of one spiritual family. From this perspective, we humans live in a biocentric, as opposed to anthropocentric, world. Humans are not thought to be at the center of the world or superior to the rest of creation. As the Lakota people say in their songs and prayers in reference to all living beings: *mitakuye oyasin* (all my relations, or we are all related). Humans are typically thought to have souls, the "sacred wind" as some indigenous cultures say. However, other beings also have souls or spirits. It is the human responsibility to respect and live in harmony with all other living beings.

Problem: Life out of Balance   For indigenous people *all* life is spiritual. The spiritual world is not separate from us; we live in a spiritual world at all times, whether we are aware of it not. Indeed, as must be stressed, there is but one world from the perspective of the indigenous worldview. We humans live amidst spiritual beings and forces, seen and unseen. The basic human problem is failure to respect the intended spiritual equilibrium of all life, human and nonhuman, and to live within it.

The Hopi people of the American Southwest have a word in their language that expresses well the problem the indigenous worldview identifies. It is *koyaanisqatsi,* meaning "life out of balance." Often, indigenous people will speak of a path of harmony which they are intended to walk, and the problem as departing from that path on to a road of disharmony or error.

The problem is usually expressed collectively. At issue is the spiritual balance of the community as a whole (family, clan, tribe, or nation) in the context of the balance of all life. An individual's spiritual imbalance is problematic because it undermines the harmony of the group, not merely because of the consequences for the person alone or his or her immediate family. Social chaos and individual disease or dislocation are assumed to be fundamentally spiritual problems.

Cause: Forgetfulness and Individualism   For indigenous peoples balance need not be *created;* it is already and everywhere present for those who learn to be attentive. Imbalance is caused by forgetting the way of life patterned after the spiritual, and turning to a false, error-filled path resulting in "life out of balance." Forgetfulness may be brought on when people allow themselves to fall under the influence of spirits who seek to lead them astray, or when they become too enamored with inappropriate activities—such as the pursuit of one's own or one's family's material well-being at the expense of the group as a whole (often extending to the community of all living beings).

In particular, those who live merely to gratify their own needs and desires, forgetting that they are members of and have obligations to an all-encompassing spiritual family, are said to have forgotten who they are.

End: Maintenance and Restoration of Harmony   The fundamental transformation that indigenous people realize is necessary is to maintain equilibrium with the spiritual, and to restore that balance when it is lost. Although indigenous religions usually speak of an existence after the present life, it is not often thought of as the principal goal to be sought.

Since the spiritual is everywhere potentially present, balance must be sought with everyone and everything, at all times. When spiritual equilibrium is present, that which the group needs for its material well-being will follow. The Diné (Navajo) of the American Southwest speak of this state as *hozho,* usually translated as "beauty," but meaning the state of harmony and wholeness. Walking in *hozho* means living in a state of balance with all living beings.

Means: Patterning All Life   Indigenous religions typically have no written "scriptures," but rather oral myths and legends that reveal the spiritual paradigms the group is to follow. They are passed from generation to generation. As we will see, spiritual patterns involve individual rituals (rites of passage, for example). There are also many prescribed group rituals that must be carried out in order to preserve or restore harmony.

Some indigenous religions may have priests who carry out the rituals. Another typical religious leader is the *shaman.* The term comes from Siberian indigenous religion, but is now widely used for a "sacred person" who has entered fully into the spirit world, and who thereafter is gifted with the ability to make journeys there for the sake of the well-being of his/her people. Through these ecstatic journeys, the shaman acquires a knowledge used to heal sicknesses, instruct a person or group on proper courses of action, and even cause good things to happen. A shaman, typically, not only has had a spontaneous, powerful spiritual experience that has empowered the specialist, but also has studied sacred lore with another shaman. Someone who has been called to be a shaman, and has accepted the status by passing through the process of apprenticeship, is particularly venerated and retains the position throughout his/her life.

A shaman often uses and sometimes gives to others special sacred objects, which indigenous people believe can assist them in their pursuit of harmony. An example would be the feathers sometimes worn by indigenous religious leaders, or the special rattles or drums often used in ceremonies. These have been called by Western scholars of earlier generations "fetishes," but the corruption of the term *fetish* in modern psychological usage makes it of dubious value in phenomenological study. The "sacred pipe" we will encounter in our study of the Oglala Lakota is an example of a sacred object.

The term *magic* is usually associated with indigenous religions, and is popularly thought of as a manipulation of objects or persons by someone who knows the proper formula or ritual. Indigenous people often use what interpreters call *imitative magic,* when they behave ritually like that which they are seeking to influence. For example, to ensure fertility in the growing of crops, intercourse is sometimes feigned in ritual. To the outside observer such practices may *seem* to be designed to try to force an outcome. Indigenous people themselves view these practices rather as following a pattern that the spirits have prescribed, so that they may live in balance and restore lost harmony.

Another widely misunderstood practice common among indigenous religions has been given the name *taboo* by outside observers. If something or someone is "taboo," it is thought to be so spiritually potent that touching the object or person, or engaging in the prohibited behavior, will have disastrous consequences. In most indigenous cultures menstruating women are taboo, as are warriors before and after a battle (until they have been ritually purified). It is often considered a taboo to speak the names of the dead or for initiates to eat certain foods.

Since violating a taboo is not the only source of ritual impurity, indigenous religions typically have a standard rite of purification. Water and smoke are frequently used in these rituals to create cleansing and to restore harmony.

Some, but not all, indigenous religions prescribe sacrifices, in which something animate or inanimate is offered to the spirits or the Creator. Offerings may be made to placate spirits which the groups believe have been offended, or to propitiate spirits for some particular blessing.

Because of the attitude toward nature in indigenous religions (see Chapter Fifteen), it is not surprising that groups develop spiritual relationships with particular animals, plants, or even "inanimate" objects. Spiritual bonds between groups (typically subgroups within a larger group) and animals are most common. The animal (sometimes called a *totem* by some Western scholars) is thought to be the special protector of the group, and the group shows reverence for the animal. Totemic groupings are a common way of distinguishing members for particular ritualistic functions. Each group has its own specialized rituals and mysteries that are not revealed to those outside the group, although knowledge may be shared within the group. To become a part of a totemic group requires a ritual of initiation, in which the member's ordinary identity is stripped away, and a new identity is ritually assumed.

Many interpreters have pointed out that totemism and other practices and beliefs of indigenous peoples persist in modern cultures, often in camouflaged form. We have already noted the continuation of rites of passage in religious and nonreligious settings. A school mascot could be considered a vestige of totemic practice. A rabbit's foot or even an item of clothing believed to bring luck is an example of a sacred object thought to have special powers.

Reality: Sense of Place within the Rhythms of Life   Language today is typically thought of as a "symbolic activity." We recognize that when we speak a word, the word is different from the thing about which we have spoken. However, for indigenous people, "words have a special potency or force that is integral to their specific sounds: What is named is therefore understood to be really present in the name in unitary manner, not as a 'symbol' with dualistic implication, as is generally the case with modern languages. . . . Recitation of a myth of creation, for example, is understood to be an actual, not a symbolic recapitulation of that primordial creative process or event, which is not bound by time" (Brown 1988: 3; see also 88–89). Therefore, when an indigenous person skilled in sacred matters speaks of the sacred, the sacred is experienced as present. In general, the desire to experience sacred reality in order to be a part of that which is perceived as true reality is a pattern found in all religions.

Indigenous people also view time differently than is typical in the modern world. Under the influence of the western religions and with the nineteenth-century rise of historicism, most persons have come to view time as a linear process. What has happened in the past will not be repeated in the future in any literal sense. By contrast, for indigenous people time unfolds in a rhythmic and cyclical manner rather than as a straight line. Traditional indigenous people do not seek progress in life. They seek to experience the true reality of the spiritual amidst the cyclical patterns of life. They typically look to a sacred time of origins, which stands outside the circle of profane time.

Through a panoply of rituals, indigenous peoples order the circle of life in a sacred manner. For example, in the cycle of an individual's life there are special moments, times of passage from one stage to another—birth, infancy and early childhood, entrance to adulthood, marriage, and death. By ordering these times in a sacred manner through rituals (called by interpreters *rites of passage*), the individual's life cycle becomes a manifestation of the sacred. These rites of passage involve typical stages (see Van Gennep), here illustrated with actions typical of the funeral rituals associated with death: First comes separation from the preceding status, as when a corpse is removed from its place of living to be prepared for passage to the next stage. Next comes the stage of "liminality," the passage itself, as when the body is placed in a carrier (e.g., a casket) and taken in a procession on a symbolic journey to its next stage of existence. At this stage the change in status is accomplished, as when the deceased person becomes an ancestor. Finally comes reincorporation, as when the corpse, now having passed into a new status, reenters the social world in its new identity through being burned, buried, or exposed to the elements.

Many observers have pointed out that modern cultures maintain rites of passage for the fundamental transitions of life, whether in spiritual or secularized fashion. For example, groups ranging from college fraternities and sororities to urban gangs often reflect in their rituals of initiation the pattern of separation, transition, and reincorporation associated with rites of passage.

Similarly, the yearly cycle of the seasons may be approached in a sacred manner. The Christian adaptation of the seasonal rituals of indigenous European peoples to the special historical moments in the life of Christ (as with the celebration of Christmas and Easter) is an indication of the continuing influence of indigenous religions.

Just as sacred time may be "made present," sacred space may also be created. This is apparent in the structures built for ritual purposes. However, it is true in "ordinary" life as well. For example, the building of a village or a dwelling is, for indigenous people, a sacred act, which must be done according to the pattern revealed in myth. When indigenous people enter sacred space, whether during a special ritual time or during daily existence, they perceive themselves in a reality ordered by the spiritual, and thus "truly real."

Sacred: Everything Is Spiritual   In the major religions of the world today, participants typically draw a clear distinction between the spiritual realm and the material or profane world. Most Jews, Christians, and Muslims, for example, speak of God as separate from the world, viewing the deity as the transcendent creator, sustainer, and judge. Most Hindus call material reality *maya* (illusion), and differentiate between the eternal, spiritual reality and the temporal, material reality of this changing world.

There is no such strict distinction between the spiritual and material in the worldview common among indigenous peoples, for whom "everything is alive" and therefore everything is potentially spiritual. Indigenous peoples believe that all reality is saturated with spirituality. As previously discussed, indigenous people understand that while humans are spiritual beings, so are birds, deer, trees, lakes and streams, the sky, and the earth as a whole. Modern Western interpreters, with their penchant for labeling things, call this attitude that all reality is infused with spirits, and therefore alive, *animism* (from the Latin word *anima*, "spirit" or "soul").

If the spiritual is everywhere and at all times potentially present, then what we might call ordinary activities are, for indigenous peoples, by nature spiritual. For example, the life-sustaining act of hunting or farming is seen as a spiritual activity by many indigenous peoples, and is undertaken with the same care and reverence as any other ritual. The same could be said of making a basket from plants or a blanket from an animal skin.

If *everything* is potentially spiritual, then *all* life must be lived as a ritual. Everyday activities are patterned after myths that tell the story of how the world and its inhabitants came into existence. By recapitulating the myth in a ritualized action, the people participate in the creation of the cosmos in which they find harmonious life. As one native person remarked, "We do not believe our religion, we dance it!" (cited by Brown 1988: 123).

The attitude toward spiritual beings is quite complex, because if all life is spiritual then spiritual beings are everywhere potentially present. Western missionaries have often attacked indigenous peoples as "heathens" or "idolaters" because they seem to worship material objects and a plethora of spirits rather than "the one true god." From a phenomenological perspective this reflects judgment before understanding. In fact, examination of a variety of indigenous religions suggests that many recognize a high god, who is perceived as a transcendent creator, just as in Western religions.

However, in indigenous religions the *high god* is but one dimension of the spiritual, and, on a day-to-day basis, not necessarily the most important. Veneration is due not only the creator but the other divine beings who are also active in creating and maintaining the world, as well as the spirits with whom one comes into contact daily or periodically. Spirits are present and deserve awe and respect amidst the daily routine. However, at times, particular spirits may appear (in some groups in the form of masked members of the tribe) and a special ritual occur. Modern observers sometimes say that indigenous peoples seem to live in fear of the spirits they perceive all around them. It would be more accurate to say that they live with reverence for these spirits, recognizing that harmony in life depends on maintaining good relations with other spiritual beings, seen and unseen.

Let us turn now to specific indigenous religions in their own contexts. We will introduce the religion of the Yoruba people of West Africa and the religion of the Oglala people of the Great Plains of North America.

THE YORUBA OF WEST AFRICA

Introduction

One of the first Portuguese explorers to land on the southern coast of Africa reported that, "The people . . . have no religion" (Booth 1977: 1). Unfortunately, most of the rest of the world still has little awareness of traditional African religions. Those who do are most likely to have distorted impressions, with images of wicked "witch doctors" casting evil spells, and cannibals preparing dinners of boiled missionaries. Our goal here is to counter this lack of understanding and misrepresentation of indigenous African religions, focusing on the religion of the Yoruba people of West Africa.

With population estimates running as high as one hundred million, the Yoruba are a people who have spread throughout the world, descending from one of the most influential cultures of West Africa. Most of the approximately fifteen million Yoruba in Africa in the early twenty-first century live in the southwestern region of the modern nation of Nigeria, with others residing in surrounding countries such as Benin, Ghana, and Togo. About twenty subgroups within Yoruba culture have been identified, each with its own distinctive linguistic, political, and religious patterns. In fact, the use of the single term Yoruba to collectively designate these related peoples may very well be a nineteenth-century development. Many Yoruba were forcefully taken to the Americas as slaves, where they have become a significant presence in Brazil (where they are known as "Nago"), Cuba ("Lucumi"), Jamaica, and North America. A significant (but difficult to estimate) number of contemporary African-Americans are descended from Yoruba slaves.

Archaeological and religious evidence suggests that the Yoruba have lived in their West African homeland since the fifth century B.C.E. Before the end of the first millennium, the Yoruba had developed a complex urban society, with the important city of *Ile-Ife* dating from the ninth century.

There is a vast oral collection of Yoruba poetry and prose, organized into collections called the *odu*, through which knowledge of the Yoruba way of harmony is passed orally from generation to generation.

Yoruba Religion: Harmony with the Orisa

Gods and Spirits   The complexity and intricacy of the Yoruba spirit world challenges the notion that the religions of indigenous people are "primitive." Our understanding as outsiders must be acknowledged to be superficial.

According to the Yoruba worldview, the cosmos has two levels, *Orun* and *Aiye*. Orun is heaven or sky, and is the abode of the Supreme God and the other gods (*orisa* [pronounced "oh-rish′-a"]) and ancestors. Aiye is the place of habitation for humans and other animals, as well as the home of the *omoraiye*, ("the children of the world"), the beings responsible for witchcraft and sorcery.

The Yoruba name for the Supreme God is *Olorun Olodumare*. Olorun ("owner of the sky") is the Lord above all, who dwells in the heavens and is the source of all life. Although people may pray to Olorun, there are no shrines in Olorun's honor, and no rituals or sacrifices to influence Olorun.

The *orisa* in general are projections of the power of Olorun, found in elements of nature and among the distinguished ancestors. According to some Yoruba legends, there are 401 *orisa*, all of whom were once humans who lived especially notable lives. This is a way of symbolizing the variety of *orisa* and of ways of responding to them ritually.

Orisa-nla (also called *Obatala*) is but one of the *orisa*, although as the one who forms babies in their wombs, he is often said to be the most important. He is worshipped throughout the Yoruba homeland. To mock infants, including those who are misformed, is to insult Orisa-nla their creator. He is worshipped with offerings of pure water, and his color is white. His followers often wear white clothes. The two main taboos associated with Orisa-nla are drinking palm wine and having contact with dogs.

In Yoruba mythology the deity to whom diviners turn most for guidance is *Orunmila*, for he was present at creation and knows the destinies of human beings. With the belief that humans have a destiny given by Olorun which they have forgotten, the practice of *ifa* or divination is particularly important.

The trickster figure in the Yoruba pantheon is *Esu*, who traverses the earth, reporting on people to the heavenly *orisa*, and deceiving people into wrong actions. Sacrifices to the *orisa* must include a portion for Esu, to ensure that the offering reaches the intended divine recipient. Esu mediates the conflicting qualities of reverence and irreverence, good and evil, allowing him to serve as a mediator between heaven and earth. The association of Esu with the Devil by Christian missionaries is an example of the imposition of a foreign understanding that distorts the culture's own understanding.

Different orisa are popular in different areas. *Sango,* King and Thunderer, once the demonic king of Oyo, is worshipped in towns that once were part of the Oyo empire. He guarantees the moral order, punishing those who violate social norms. He is also one of the deities who most frequently "mounts" (takes possession of) worshippers. Another popular *orisa* is *Ayelala,* once a slave girl who was sacrificed in place of a man who had done a wicked deed. She is now the deity who punishes immorality.

Ogun, the most widely worshipped of the *orisa,* is the Yoruba god of war and iron, with associated powers both of formation and destruction. He lives at the fringes of society and is feared, because he can turn his power to kill or destroy on his own people without warning. He also watches over the hunter and forester. Like other *orisa* he specializes in particular areas of life, in his case violence and, through his patronage of iron, culture. He is also viewed as the guarantor of justice; in court traditional Yoruba swear to speak the truth by kissing a piece of iron in the name of Ogun. Drivers often carry a representation of Ogun as an amulet to ward off accidents. Here is an example of a song, sung to seek Ogun's protection of the iron objects owned by the petitioner (Ray 1976: 80):

> Ogun, here are Ehun's kola nuts;
> He rides a bicycle,
> He cultivates with a machete,
> He fells trees with the axe.
> Do not let Ehun meet your anger this year,
> Take care of him.
> He comes this year,
> Enable him to come next season.

Another Yoruba deity, who possesses both male and female qualities is *Orisa-oko,* patron of farmers. *Ile,* the earth, is the dry land of the creation myth. When a Yoruba child is born, the baby is laid on the earth, and at death the deceased is returned to the womb of the earth. According to a legend, when *Ile* became angry she caused crops to fail and living beings to become sterile.

Yoruba do not exclusively worship one *orisa.* Instead, a particular family or village is under the sway of an assemblage of *orisa,* evident in the variety of *orisa* images in their shrines. Each person has his/her own personal orisa (or *ori inun,* "inner head"), symbolic of a personal destiny, an array of possibilities and limitations, which cannot be altered.

Humans consist of *ara* (matter) formed by Orisa-nla, into which Olorun breathes *emi,* spirit. When a Yoruba dies, the body returns to the earth and the spirit is reincarnated as a new child.

As with other indigenous religions, ancestors play an important role in Yoruba religion. Certain ancestral spirits may return, through masked dancers who appear at popular yearly festivals, with special messages for those left behind. Within families the head of the family is charged with seeing that the ancestors are properly venerated. In addition to the family ancestors, there are also "deified ancestors," leaders who because of their particular contributions are now venerated. They are worshipped within a particular locality rather than within a family.

It is also important to understand the Yoruba conception of *ase,* the divine energy that causes things to come into existence and to pass away. Orisa manifest *ase,* yet it is present in all things. In all situations it is the force that opposes chaos.

Myth of Origins: Orisa-nla Brings Life to the Marsh   According to one version of the Yoruba myth of origins, at the beginning Olorun lived in the heavens with other deities. The heavens and the earth were close together, and the earth was a desolate marsh. The heavenly beings at times came to earth to hunt. When Olorun decided to make the land firm, he commanded *Orisa-nla* ("Great Divinity") to carry out the plan. When Orisa-nla came to earth, he threw down soil and released a five-toed hen and a pigeon. When the hen spread the soil, the marshy waters were forced back and dry land appeared. Then trees were planted, and Olorun breathed life into sixteen humans and sent them to earth. In other versions of the myth, Orisa-nla became drunk on palm wine and *Oduduwa*, his rival in the myth, is the creator. In this version Ile-Ife is the place of creation. Yoruba oral history remembers Oduduwa (or *Odua*) as the original king and creator of the Yoruba people, ruling from Ile-Ife.

Religious Leaders   At the family level, the responsibility for maintaining the proper rituals and ensuring that all members are following the basic guidelines of balanced life falls on the *olori ebi,* the head of the family. In towns or cities the *oba* (chief, leader) is in charge of the proper conducting of rituals. In the Yoruba worldview, all leaders originally came from Ile-Ife, where the gods established the earthly kingdom.

In addition, there are priests associated with the shrines of Ife and those throughout the Yoruba homeland. Each of the many deities has its own priesthood. For example, the *aworo* (or *babalawo,* "father of secret things") priesthood is associated with Orunmila. They are most often consulted for advice through an elaborate process of divining. Such advice is sought both for individual concerns and to determine the course of events affecting the family or larger group. Becoming a priest requires a long period of training and apprenticeship.

In addition to the priests who conduct the sacrifices and other aspects of ordered religious practice, there are *elegun,* shamans who are spontaneously possessed by and become intermediaries for spirits. However, any Yoruba, most often in the context of one of the festivals, may be possessed or "mounted" and enter into an ecstatic state.

The *oloogun* is the Yoruba religious functionary who specializes in healing, often working in cooperation with a priest. Because healing comes from the gods and spirits, the *oloogun* are viewed merely as channels for the rejuvenating power.

Rituals   The most important annual Yoruba festival is *Odun Egungun,* which focuses on the ancestors of the father's family. The *egungun* are masks created from layers of cloth, made of dark colors with white edges, and also the Yoruba males who wear them. The masked dancers enter with dignified pace, then engage in whirling motions that cause the cloth layers to fly out in various patterns. The dancers manifest the presence and power of the ancestors. Their masks are handed down from generation to generation.

The *Gelede* festival at the time of the spring rains is given in honor of the female "mothers" (*awon iya wa*). All women are recognized as possessing awesome creative and destructive power, but this festival particularly honors women elders and ancestors. It is a joyous, though reverential, celebration. It takes place in the market, where transitions occur, and where women dominate. (The men who dance are seen as agents of the women.) At night masked dancers enter the market, with the white and bearded Spirit of the Ancestresses as Great Mother and the Spirit Bird, with a long and pointed red beak, prominent in the masquerade. They represent the foremothers. During the night ceremony the various gods are called upon, Ogun as the virile one and Esu as the deceiver and messenger. The particular concerns of the people are voiced, and prayers are made for long life and many children.

Sacrifices are very important in Yoruba ritual, with offerings of prayers, nuts, or animals. Sacrifices reflect the character of the *orisa;* so, for example, the war god Ogun receives the carnivorous dog as his sacrificial food. In return, the power of the *orisa* passes to the worshipper.

Yoruba rites of passage have their own distinctive characteristics. Before birth a mother visits a *babalawo* so that the priest may divine the newborn's destiny and ascertain (with a healer's assistance) which medicines to take to ensure a good birth and what taboos to practice. After the birth the parents then make an offering at the shrine of the orisa most important to the family.

Yoruba children receive instruction throughout their early years about the rituals and customs of the family and larger community. Males are typically circumcised early in life in preparation for marriage. After intricate negotiations between the two families, carried out by a mediator and including divination, the wedding takes place. After elaborate preparations in the homes of both the bride and bridegroom, the bride is led in procession to the bridegroom's home for the marriage ceremony.

Upon death, particularly when the deceased is the head of a family or other important person, an elaborate funerary rite occurs. The person is buried in the family compound, with appropriate sacrifices so that the person will be received into *orun rere* ("good heaven"). Masked dancers then emerge from the dead person's home, beginning a time of feasting and dancing. If the person is worthy of the status of an ancestor, a shrine marks the place of burial and becomes a place of worship for the family, who consider the ancestor to be present with them.

As with other indigenous religious traditions, the Yoruba have distinct religious societies. One of the principal Yoruba secret societies is the *Osugbo* or *Ogboni* society. Initiates are taught to understand their special house as a microcosm of the universe. Thus, the mystery seems to be, as it often is in such groups, the original unity of all reality, which goes beyond all the opposites of ordinary human experience.

Amulets and other sacred objects are used for protection against hostile powers. Small objects, made potent by incantations, may also be used to negatively influence enemies.

Islam was introduced to the Yoruba centuries ago, but was not widely embraced until the Yoruba began to be victimized by slave traders and came under the control of the British in the nineteenth century. Then many Yoruba converted to Islam, perhaps in part as a form of protest against the efforts of Christian missionaries endorsed by the British (beginning about 1840).

New Religious Movements   As we shall see in Chapter Fourteen, new religious movements often emerge from larger religious traditions. This has been the case with the Yoruba. Particularly influential among the Yoruba has been the *Aladura* ("People of Prayer") Movement, which began in response to the missionary activity of the Church of England (the Anglican Church). It originated not as a separate movement, but as a supplement to the rituals and organization of the Anglican Church.

Groups within the Aladura movement began to create their own distinct identities. One such group is the *Egbe Serafu* ("Seraphim Society"), inspired by the vision of angels received by a young woman named Abiodun Akinsowon during a Christian ritual in 1925. The appeal of the groups which make up the Aladura movement is their emphasis on charismatic leadership, visionary interpretation of the Christian Bible, inspired prayer, and healing.

Other new religious movement developed among Yourba who had been taken as slaves to the Americas, and have a background in traditional Yoruba religion. One is *Santeria,* a synthesis of Yoruba religion and Spanish Catholicism, originating among slaves in Cuba but eventually spreading throughout the Americas and beyond. Santeria uses Catholic saints as "fronts" for various *orisa.* For example, Ogun is worshipped in association with St. Peter. Orunmila is represented by St. Francis of Assisi. The sacrificing of animals by Santeria groups in the United States has sparked controversy and led to law-suits by Santeria priests seeking to defend their freedom of religious expression.

The religion popularly known as *Voodoo* or *Vodou* (also known as *Vodun*) has its roots in Yoruba religion. It developed among Yoruba slaves in Haiti and, like Santeria, spread to other countries, including the United States. Most of the adults of Haiti still practice forms of Vodun, and it is estimated that as many as sixty million people worldwide are associated with the religion. Unfortunately, the popularization of distorted images of Vodun is still widespread. In fact, like Santeria, Vodun combines the worship of various groups of spirits (called *loa*) with Catholic saints. A particular feature of Vodun ritual is dancing leading to possession of the dancer by one of the *loa.* Most commonly, the possession releases the healing power of the *loa.*

THE OGLALA LAKOTA (SIOUX) OF THE GREAT PLAINS OF NORTH AMERICA

Introduction

When Europeans first encountered the native inhabitants of what we now call North America, they, like the Europeans who first visited Africa, thought they had discovered a people with no religion. Christopher Columbus wrote of the people he found on the first islands that he "discovered" in the new world in 1492: "They have no religion and I think that they would be very quickly Christianized; for they have a very ready understanding." Several years later, the explorer Amerigo Vespucii (from whom we take the name "America") wrote, "While among these people we did not learn that they had any religion" (cited by Gill 1982: 3, 5).

Prejudice closes the eyes of the observer to the reality and value of what is different. Both Columbus and Vespucii thought the peoples of the lands to which they had come had no religion, because what they observed had no parallel with their own experience of religion. They assumed that to be "religious" a people must follow the same patterns they had known.

Regrettably, the attitude represented by Columbus and Vespucii dominated the European response to the indigenous peoples of the "new world" for centuries. In some quarters it continues today. A television commercial for cough drops broadcast in the 1990s shows three Eskimo (Inuit) men, each with a different remedy. The younger man contrasts the effectiveness of the drops he uses with the "traditional remedies" of his father and uncle. The seemingly inoffensive commercial is, at one level, a parody of the perceived "silliness" of the rituals of the indigenous peoples of the Arctic.

The purpose of this section is to identify and understand the family of religions Columbus could not recognize, focusing on the sacred ways of the Oglala Lakota of the Great Plains.

Outsiders know the people whose religion we will now study as one group within the "Sioux" nation, one of the 530 Native American tribes in the United

States (450 of which have federal recognition). However, "Sioux" is a French corruption of the Algonquian *nadowesiih* ("little adders"), which was applied to the Lakota by another native nation, and adopted by the French missionaries and traders. Over time, "Sioux" was adopted as a self-designation, particularly when speaking to outsiders, despite its originally pejorative connotation. However, many "Sioux" wish to be known by the term for their nation in their own language.

The Lakota have been the subject of many Hollywood movies, mostly quite stereotypical treatments ranging from the vicious savages of the Westerns of the 1940s and '50s to the "noble savages" of the 1990 Oscar-winning *Dances with Wolves*. While the latter film gives a very sympathetic portrayal of this group of native Americans, they deserve more in-depth and realistic attention than the Hollywood movie genre allows.

We will focus particular attention in this chapter on one of the seven divisions of the Lakota nation, the Oglala, whose principal home is now the Pine Ridge Indian Reservation of South Dakota, near the Black Hills. We will first trace the history of the Oglala Lakota. We will then describe their traditional religion and what has happened to the Oglala Lakota and their religion in recent decades.

A Brief History of the Oglala Lakota

According to the Lakota worldview, the ancestors emerged from beneath the Black Hills (see the section on myth of origins, following). In the version of Lakota history reconstructed by modern historians, by the 1700s the Lakota (who may have migrated originally from the east coast and settled in Minnesota), after being forced westward, lived in groups of extended family bands called *tiyospaye* on the plains of what is now South Dakota. During most of the year the autonomous bands lived alongside rivers and streams in encampments of lodges, which could be moved to follow the buffalo herds. The buffalo provided the basis for a subsistence (but adequate) lifestyle. In the winter the Oglala established camps in more sheltered areas.

By the mid-1700s the Oglala had obtained their first horses, increasing their mobility. A hunter/warrior could show his valor and earn "coup points" by riding into a buffalo herd and striking the lead animal a blow on the nose, or into an enemy camp and hitting a foe with a glancing blow.

Throughout most of the nineteenth century the Oglala and other branches of the Lakota had an uneasy, sometimes violent, interaction with European settlers and the soldiers sent to protect them. War broke out in 1854, and the Lakota distinguished themselves as brave warriors in conflicts, especially the Red Cloud Wars of the 1860s. Some of the most renowned leaders of the "Indian Wars" were the Oglala warriors Red Cloud and Crazy Horse. Their power was sufficient to force the Fort Laramie Treaty of 1868, in which the U.S. Government promised that the Black Hills were "for the absolute and undisputed occupation of the Sioux." However, when gold was discovered in the Black Hills in 1874, the treaty was broken and whites flooded onto Lakota land. Oglalas were a part of the coalition that attacked and destroyed General George ("Long Hair") Custer's forces at the Battle of the Little Big Horn (Custer's "Last Stand") on June 25, 1876.

Their victory was shortlived. By 1880 the Oglalas and other Lakota had been subjugated and forced onto reservations, "the natural and best home of all red men," one white leader of the time said. The Pine Ridge Reservation was established in 1878. Although it had only one small area of farmable land, the Oglala were told to become self-sufficient farmers, following the European model.

The great Lakota leaders were systematically humiliated or murdered. As one U.S. Senator said in 1881, "these Indians must either change their modes of life or they will be exterminated" (Hughes 1983: 117). According to tradition, Crazy Horse, before he was killed in 1877, had this to say to the victors (cited by Matthiesen 1992: ix):

> We did not ask you white men to come here. The Great Spirit [*Wakan Tanka*] gave us this country as a home. You had yours. We did not interfere with you. . . . We do not want your civilization! We would live as our fathers did, and their fathers before them.

By the 1880s a concerted effort to annihilate traditional Lakota culture and religion was well underway. Children were taken to boarding schools where they were forbidden to speak Lakota or wear traditional clothes, in order to "kill the Indian, and save the person." The Lakota ceremonies described in the following sections were outlawed. This prohibition continued as official government policy until 1934—and unofficially well beyond, despite a congressional act in 1978 guaranteeing all American Indians the right to practice freely their traditional religions.

On December 29, 1890, about three hundred Lakota men, women, and children were slaughtered by soldiers from Custer's 7th Calvary regiment at a settlement called Wounded Knee on the Pine Ridge Reservation. The soldiers had been sent to crush the Ghost Dance among the Lakota, a movement that had been started by a Paiute prophet named Wovoka in the 1880s (see Young 2002: 273–99). Wovoka taught Indians a circle dance that he said was the prelude for the restoration of traditional Native American cultures and the destruction of their white oppressors. Although the movement was peaceful, government agents and missionaries feared the Ghost Dance movement would lead to violence.

After the Wounded Knee massacre most Oglala lived in poverty on the Pine Ridge Reservation, dependent on the few jobs and welfare allotments provided by government agencies. Isolated holy men kept alive the traditional Oglala ceremonies and values but, under intense pressure from government agents and missionaries, many Oglala gave up their distinctive ways, taking European names and lifestyles and joining Christian churches.

The 1934 Indian Reorganization Act forced the Oglala to elect a central tribal council, in violation of their traditional political organization into autonomous *tiyospaye*. In 1973 Wounded Knee became the site of a seventy-one-day occupation led by the intertribal American Indian Movement (see Matthiessen 1992: 58–82).

Some Oglala Lakota have been leaders in the legal movement to force the U.S. Government to honor treaties made with the Lakota and other native Americans. In 1980 a Supreme Court decision offered the Lakota $105 million in compensation for the theft of the Black Hills in violation of the Fort Laramie Treaty, in return for Lakota abandonment of their legal claim. Those who filed the suit refused, however, to accept the financial settlement. One Lakota leader said, "How can we put a price on our Mother?" The dispute over the Black Hills remains unsettled.

In recent years, many Oglala have attempted to find a balance between adapting to modern society and preserving their Oglala identity and traditional rituals. For example, Oglala Lakota College in Kyle, South Dakota is committed to educating Lakota students with skills appropriate for modern life, but with the foundation of traditional Lakota values. A resurgence of commitment to traditional spirituality among the Lakota is very much in evidence today.

Oglala Lakota Religion: The Way of the Sacred Pipe

Until recently most nonnative Americans grew up with a few quite stereotypical ideas about Native American religion: the Great Spirit, the peace pipe, and the

Happy Hunting Ground. All are distortions of aspects of the religions of the people who, like the Oglala, inhabited the Great Plains in the nineteenth century. Our task here is to describe—as best we can, given our status as outside observers—the actual religion of the Oglala Lakota.

Myth of Origins: Emergence from the Black Hills   As recorded by a white physician, Dr. James Walker, who worked on the Pine Ridge Reservation in the 1890s, the Lakota myth of origins begins with these words (Dooling 1992: 3):

> In the beginning was Inyan [stone], who had no beginning, for he was there when there was no other, only Hanhepi, the Darkness. Inyan was soft and shapeless, but he was everywhere and he had all the powers. These powers were in his blood, and his blood was blue. His spirit was Wakan Tanka.

As the myth continues, Inyan takes part of himself and spreads out a great disk, *Maka,* the Earth. Over *Maka* is a blue dome, from the blood of Inyan, the Sky, called *Skan.* The fourth of the Sacred Beings is *Wi,* the Sun. Though four, they are one, *Wakan Tanka.* A companion is created for each of the four Sacred Beings.

Eventually, under the Black Hills the *Pte Oyate* (Buffalo People) and *Ikce Oyate* (Real People, a Lakota self-designation) live together. Some of the *Ikce Oyate* emerge from the Black Hills, accompanied by *Pte Oyate* who pledge to support their life on the earth's surface. On the plains east of the Black Hills the Lakota live harmoniously with the buffalo. However, when the Lakota begin to forget that they must live in balance with all living beings, they begin to suffer. The buffalo withdraw and life becomes harsh. At this point, a mythic figure known as White Buffalo Calf Woman comes to the people with a gift intended to help them to live in harmony once again. We shall return to her story.

Holiness: *Wakan Tanka* and *wakana*   The Lakota conception of the sacred (*wakan*) or holiness (*wakana*) defies easy classification. On the one hand, there seems to be a central deity, *Wakan Tanka,* to whom the Oglala pray. When addressed as "Grandfather" (*Tunkashila*), *Wakan Tanka* is not manifest; when invoked as "Father," *Wakan Tanka* is manifest, as for example through the Sun. The feathers of the highest flying bird, the eagle, symbolize *Wakan Tanka.*

However, *Wakan Tanka* also represents "sixteen important supernatural beings and powers, half of which existed prior to the creation of the earth, half as a result of it." (Powers 1987: 436). As one expert has said, "Rather than a single being, *Wakan Tanka* embodied the totality of existence . . . " (DeMaillie 1987: 28). In the sacred language of *wakan* persons, *Wakan Tanka* is called *Tobtob* ("four times four"), symbolic of the fact that all sacred things come in fours.

As with many other indigenous peoples the earth is understood as Mother (*maka ina;* or when unmanifest, as Grandmother). Marla Powers (1986: 35) records a typical Oglala prayer to Mother/Grandmother Earth:

> O you, Grandmother, from whom all earthly things come, and O You, Mother Earth, who bear and nourish all fruits, behold us and listen: Upon You there is a sacred path which we walk, thinking of the sacredness of all things.

Wakan is not confined to "deities." Everything has a *wakan* or spirit. Birds and animals have spirits, just as humans, so they are called the "winged people" and the "four-legged people." Every being, even the smallest ant, has a *wochangi* or sacred influence, so humans must learn to be attentive, so that they can receive the *wochangi* of other beings.

Sometimes holiness is spoken of as an impersonal force (*wakana*), which is everywhere potentially present. The Oglala also speak of *wakan* beings, spirits of ancestors and other "ghosts," who can appear to "sacred persons" or others during visions.

The Sacred Hoop: Circle Symbolism   A principal Oglala symbol for holiness is the circle. Like *Wakan-tanka,* the circle has no end (Black Elk 1932: 164–65):

> Everything the Power of the World does is done in a circle. The sky is round, and I have heard the earth is round like a ball, and so are the stars. The wind [. . .] whirls. Birds make their nests in circles, for theirs is the same religion as ours. The sun [moves in a circle as does the moon]. Even the seasons form a great circle (and so does the life of each human being).

Each year, in the Summer, Lakota have traditionally gathered for a "camp circle," reflecting the symbolism of the nation as a *sacred hoop*. In the middle is an area for dances, with a tree at the center. The circle creates Oglala cosmos, a sacred space that gives the Oglala an experience of true reality. The entrance to the circle is always at the east, nearest the rising sun. During the camp circle the Sun Dance (see below) is performed. The loss of tribal unity was expressed by Black Elk in the imagery of the "sacred hoop" being broken, and the flowering tree at its center dying.

From the highest of the Black Hills, known to Lakota as "the heart of everything that is," it is easy to understand the Lakota conception of the earth as a "sacred hoop." The Oglala's traditional home, the tipi, also manifests the circle symbolism. Viewed from above, a tipi forms a circle. The crossed poles of the tipi formed a center, with the four cardinal directions.

Cardinal Directions   For the traditional Oglala, the four cardinal directions (north, south, east, and west) and the two central directions are very important. According to Fools Crow, "in these six directions is found everything needed for renewal, physical and intellectual growth, and harmony." The sacred powers given by the directions include, he says, "joy, good health, growth, endurance, wisdom, inner peace, warmth, and happiness." In the important pipe ceremony, the pipe is smoked and pointed with its stem pointing out in a clockwise circle, to the west, north, east, and south; then down to Grandmother Earth, up to Grandfather, and "in an almost imperceptible higher movement to *Wakan-Tanka*" (Mails 1979: 58).

Leaders   The spiritual leaders of the Oglala are known as *wicasa wakan* (sacred man) or *winyan wakan* (sacred woman). They are intermediaries for the people to the spirit beings and their powers. They can speak with animals and call on the power of *wakana* for the healing of individuals as well as for the well-being of the people as a whole.

The process of becoming a sacred person usually involves overcoming some misfortune, receiving instruction from another *wakan* person, crying for a vision (see below), serving an apprenticeship, and finally "ordination" (Powers 1977: 59–63).

Ritual Clowns   Oglala religion included an important role for "ritual clowns," called by the Oglala *heyok'a* (Lewis 1990: 140–52; Walker 1980: 14, 155–57; DeMaillie

1984: 232–35). They are also known as the "contraries." A *heyok'a* is designated by a vision of the thunder beings who come from the west. Thereafter, the contrary is obligated to do everything in reverse, to ward off the dangers of lightning and storm. On dance days they may engage in disorderly, even deviant behavior. The effect is a comic relief, especially appreciated at times of stress and despair, balancing the solemnity of the occasion. Their outrageous behavior is thought to be a source of curative power, and they are considered potent healers.

The Giveaway Ceremony To avert a misfortune, or to seek renewal after one and to offer thanksgiving, or to prepare for a special occasion, an Oglala family may give away some, even all, of its most valued possessions to others. Economically, giveaways have allowed for a ritualized avoidance of the concentration of wealth in one family. They stress the positive values of sharing and concern for the well-being of the group as a whole. The holy man Fools Crow describes a giveaway ceremony he and his wife held in 1928, after the death of his daughter Grace (Mails 1979: 117):

> We . . . invited the poorest people in our district. Of our 183 horses, we gave away nearly half. We had 42 cows, and we gave half of them away. We gave away all of our poultry. We gave away our clothing [. . . .] All we kept of our furniture was the kitchen stove and the cooking utensils.

White Buffalo Calf Woman and the Gift of the Sacred Pipe The most important sacred implement for Oglala religion, as it is for many other native American groups, is the *sacred pipe* (in Lakota, *cannunpa wakan*). The sacred pipe is used in all Oglala rituals. It symbolizes the cosmos as a whole.

The myth of the gift of the sacred pipe is one of the most commonly recorded Oglala narratives. According to this story, the pipe was brought to the people by *Ptehincalasan Win* ("White Buffalo Calf Woman"). At a time when the Lakota people were suffering because they had forgotten the importance of living in harmony, a beautiful maiden appeared to two hunters. She instructed them to prepare a special lodge in their village. They did, and the next day the maiden came to the village carrying a gift for the people, the sacred pipe. She told them that the red stone bowl of the pipe was the earth. Carved in the stone was a buffalo calf, representing all the four-leggeds. The wooden stem symbolized all that grows on the earth. The twelve feathers stood for the Spotted Eagle and all the winged creatures. She told them that when they prayed with the pipe, they would be praying with and for everything and everyone. The seven circles on the round stone, she said, were the seven rites in which the pipe would be used. When she left, the woman said that she would look back at the people in each of the four ages to come, and at the end she would return. As she walked away she turned into a buffalo calf, then into a white buffalo, and next a black buffalo, which bowed to each of the four directions and disappeared.

Today the pipe brought by White Buffalo Calf Woman is kept at Green Grass on the Cheyenne River Reservation in northern South Dakota. The pipes used in Lakota rituals today are understood to be extensions of the power of this original pipe.

When a sacred pipe is to be used in a ceremony it is taken from its special pouch by the sacred person to whom it has been entrusted. The *wakan* person typically raises the pipe in both hands, above his or her head, and then points the stem of the pipe in each of the four directions, to invoke the power of the West, North, East, and South. Tobacco, sealed in the bowl of the pipe during its consecration, is then lit. Those smoking the pipe repeat the pointing of the pipe in the four directions, puffing on it four times. Smoking or even touching a sacred pipe in any but the prescribed manner or by anyone but those of the highest integrity is taboo. However, nonspecialists may use their own individual sacred pipes, praying with them in the four directions.

On August 20, 1994, a female white buffalo calf was born on the Heider farm in southern Wisconsin. Word of the birth of the calf, whom the Heiders named Miracle, quickly reached the Lakota reservations, and many Lakota elders related it to the promise of the White Buffalo Calf Woman to return at a time of great need, a prophecy noted by earlier generations of Lakota holy men like Nicholas Black Elk (e.g., Brown 1953: xix–xx; see Pickering 1997).

Has the prophecy of the return of White Buffalo Woman been fulfilled? Has the power of the Buffalo to renew life returned? That is, of course, not a question for a descriptive study to answer, but it is clear that many Lakota people and others believe it to be the case. They are convinced that White Buffalo Calf Woman has returned to offer not only the Lakota but all humanity an opportunity (perhaps the last) to learn the way of harmony she first came to teach.

The Seven Rituals   According to some traditions, with the sacred pipe White Buffalo Calf Woman gave the Oglala seven rituals (the sweat lodge, vision quest, sun dance, preparation for womanhood, making of relatives, keeping of the soul, and throwing the ball). The following descriptions of the first three of the rituals are based principally on the accounts of Powers (1977: 89–103) and the holy man Black Elk, as told to a white scholar (Brown 1953: 10–138).

A Lakota sweat lodge on a South Dakota reservation. The sweat lodge ritual of purification and renewal is central to Lakota (Sioux) spirituality and is also practiced in other Native American cultures.

THE SWEAT LODGE—TO RENEW LIFE   This ritual of purification or renewal is often conducted in preparation for participation in other rites, such as the vision quest or sun dance, or for a great endeavor. It may also be done as a ceremony in itself, as a means of petitioning for a need or offering thanksgiving for a blessing. (For descriptions of contemporary Lakota sweat lodge rituals, see Bucko 1998.)

The "sweat lodge" itself is a domed structure of bent willow branches covered traditionally with buffalo robes and other skins (although tarps and blankets are now typically used), with hot stones in a pit in the center. The lodge is the cosmos, and the rocks Grandmother Earth. The fire is the life-giving power of *Wakan-Tanka.* The water symbolizes the *wakinyan* (thunder beings), who come from the West inspiring awe but bringing goodness. The round pit in the center of the lodge is the center of the universe, where *Wakan-Tanka* comes to the worshippers.

From the entrance of the lodge, a path of eight paces is made, running east and west. At the eastern end is a mound of earth dug from the pit inside the lodge. The mound is an altar, called "grandmother." Two paces further is the "fire without end," in which the stones are heated. Both men and women may participate in the sweat lodge ritual, but typically not together.

As the fireplace is being prepared, the participants offer a prayer such as the following (Brown 1953: 33–34):

> O Grandfather and Father Wakan-Tanka, maker of all that is, who always has been, behold me! And You, Grandmother and Mother Earth, You are wakan and have holy ears; hear me! We have come from You, we are a part of You, and we know that our bodies will return to You [. . . .] By purifying myself in this way, I wish to make myself worthy of You, O Wakan-Tanka, that my people may live!

The ritual itself begins with participants following the leader into the lodge on all fours, symbolic of their return to the womb of Mother Earth. As each participant enters, he or she says *mitakuye oyasin*. A sweat lodge ritual typically has four "doors" or rounds. As each begins, the flap over the opening of the lodge is closed, and the heat gradually emanating from the rocks becomes intense. The sweat lodge leaders calls the spirits to the lodge with songs, and give thanks to *Tunkashila*. A sacred pipe may be passed and prayers offered by the leader and participants. It is understood that whatever is said in the lodge remains there. Participants often speak of feeling completely cleansed and renewed when they leave the lodge, again saying *mitakuye oyasin*.

As one Lakota shaman has put it, in describing the sweat lodge ritual (Halifax 1990: 26):

> We go into that sacred lodge to purify ourselves. We go in there to see just who we really are, and in the darkness to see how we go on this Earth. We make ourselves really humble, like the littlest creature, and we pray to the Spirit that we may be healed, that all may be healed. We see that we are not separate from anything. We are all in this together. And we always say *mitakuye oyasin*, all my relations.

THE VISION QUEST—CRYING FOR A VISION   Under the guidance of a *wakan* person, any person may seek to enter the spirit world. A young person might undertake a vision quest in order to receive guidance for his or her life. A soldier might go before leaving for war. Preparation for the sun dance may also involve seeking a vision in this manner. A family member might go to request healing for a sick or dying relative. A person might also "cry for a vision" as a way of giving thanks to *Wakan Tanka* for some special blessing.

After purification through fasting, typically lasting four days, and participation in the sweat lodge ritual, the person seeking a vision is led by his guide to a sacred hill. The only thing taken is a blanket. No food or water are allowed. The seeker is given a sacred pipe to have throughout the ritual. A pit is dug in the ground at the center. At times the worshipper will climb into this pit, covered with brush. The cardinal directions are marked. The person walks to each of the points, returning to the center, crying for a vision, all day long. The rituals may last from two to four days, though shorter durations are typical today. The seeker may neither eat nor drink while lamenting. When the person finally lays down exhausted, a vision may come. The seeker may be spoken to by animals or visited by the *wakinyan* (thunder beings). Often the vision reinforces a sense of "nothingness" in comparison to the *wakan* power.

Sometimes visions come to persons spontaneously, often during a time of illness, as was the case with the "Great Vision" of Black Elk (Black Elk 1932: 17–39). These are "visions without crying" or "power visions" and they are commissions to a special leadership role among the people.

THE SUN DANCE—FOR THE PEOPLE   The Sun Dance is always held in the Summer. When the Oglala still lived freely on the prairie, sun dances occurred over a four day period when the bands gathered for a "camp circle" and a common buffalo hunt. In the 1870s, so many Lakota gathered for the ceremony that the diameter of the encampment was up to four miles, with forty groups of from six to twelve dancers, each with a holy man (Steinmetz 1990: 27; for descriptions of Sun Dances in the modern period, see Mails 1979: 118–38 and Hollar 1995: 139–78).

The role of the Sun must be clarified. According to Fools Crow, the Sun, like the sacred pipe and the cardinal directions, is an instrument of *Wakan Tanka*. "We respect it and pray to it," he says, "because it watches over the world and sees everything that is going on. It also serves God by bestowing special gifts that it has upon the world. But the sun is not God." During the ritual, dancers are able to see the sun with their eyes open (although they do not stare constantly at the sun, as sometimes is reported). Fools Crow says that "in it we see visions" (Mails 1979: 119).

On the first day of the ceremony a hole is dug in the center of the camp circle, and a large lodge is built around it. On the second day a cottonwood pole is ritually selected and brought by procession into the camp. On the third day the pole is raised at the center of the lodge.

During these three days, those who have taken a vow to participate in the dance prepare themselves under the guidance of a *wakan* person. They decide whether to dance gazing at the sun, pierced, suspended, or dragging buffalo skulls. In the latter three forms, the dancer is pierced by the sacred person and rawhide thongs are attached to the dancer's flesh.

On the fourth day the dancers who have chosen to gaze at the sun do so throughout the day. The pierced dancers continue until the pressure causes the thongs to break free. The dance ends when the last dancer has succeeded in breaking the hold of the thongs. The lodge and pole are left in place, until they deteriorate and return to Mother Earth.

According to Black Elk, the Sun Dance was introduced as a rite of penance, when the people had begun to forget *Wakan Tanka*. At the conclusion of the dance, the dancers are told, "By your actions you have strengthened the sacred hoop of the nation. You have made a good center which will always be with you, and you have created a closer relationship with all things of the universe" (Brown 1953: 99–100).

The Renewal of Oglala Lakota Religion   The approximately 35,000 Oglala Lakota on the Pine Ridge Reservation today *are* faced with tremendous problems of poverty, inadequate housing and health care, unemployment, and alcoholism. The reservation includes the poorest two counties in the nation, with an average unemployment rate of 86 percent in recent years.

However, the sacred hoop of the Lakota is alive. Traditional Oglala religion is being preserved and renewed in several ways. The first method is revitalization of the distinctive myths and rituals of the Oglala. Many Oglala agree with Frank Fools Crow who, after a vision quest on Bear Butte, said he recognized that "our only hope was to fall back upon our traditional way of life. It was the only foundation we had that would give meaning and purpose to us" (cited in Beasley 1992: 39).

Four of the traditional rites are being practiced once again, including the Memorial Feast (inspired by the "keeping of the soul" ritual), the sweat lodge, the vision quest, and especially the annual Sun Dance.

The Sun Dance embodies the challenges facing the Oglala today (see Hollar 1995). In 1960, with the permission of the Bureau of Indian Affairs, the Oglala Tribal Council allowed the practice of piercing to be reinstituted (although Fools Crow had been doing it since the early 1950s). Fearful that the sacred nature of the Sun Dance was being compromised in the official dances, some traditional holy men have closed their dances to non-Lakota or non-Indians. However, for most Oglala the Sun Dance continues to help create a sense of tribal identity and unity. It also contributes to intertribal understanding, since many Native Americans from other groups participate. The numbers of men and women dancers have been approximately equal in recent years, with a tendency toward more people being pierced. The Dance has proliferated in recent years, with fifteen or more held each summer on the Pine Ridge Reservation.

The second way Oglala religion is being preserved is through the renewal of rituals rooted in the tradition, though not part of the traditional "seven rituals." For example, the *Yuwipi* ritual of curing sickness is popular (Powers 1982). It is an ancient ritual, but it only became a major ceremony during the reservation period. In this ceremony a "*yuwipi* man" is wrapped in a blanket. He calls in the spirits he has previously encountered in visions to untie him. The *yuwipi* man can heal the sick, find lost objects, prepare persons for a vision quest, and receive answers to prayers.

The third method of preservation is through Christianity, serving as a vehicle for the expression of traditional Lakota beliefs and rituals. Many Oglala have converted to Christianity in the last century; most, like Nicholas Black Elk and Red Cloud, to Roman Catholicism (the "black robes"), or like Frank Fools Crow to Episcopalianism (the "white robes), whose missionaries first reached the reservation. There is also a small Presbyterian presence on the reservation. Evangelical Christianity has come to the reservation in the form of churches like the independent, pentecostal Body of Christ Church (Steinmetz 1990: 153–62, 174–76; Lewis 1990: 119–23).

Some Christian priests and ministers have tried hard to incorporate native practices such as the sacred pipe into Christian rituals. For example, since 1961 the Lakota Catholic Church at Pine Ridge has been decorated with a mural that represents the Christian Trinity with Lakota mythological symbols; the Holy Spirit is represented by an eagle with twelve tongues of fire. Beginning in 1965, a Catholic priest, Father Paul Steinmetz, prayed at funerals and other services with the pipe, claiming that the Pipe is Christ. Father Steinmetz contends that the Pipe is Christ in the sense of the Pipe symbolizing the source of all life and functioning as a mediator among the Lakota (Steinmetz 1990: 35–39).

The Christian aspects of the Sun Dance have also been emphasized. For a number of Oglala, no contradiction is seen in practicing Christianity *and* traditional rituals. Typically, these Oglala see Christianity as a matter of institutional membership and the native ways as a powerful spiritual source to be turned to in times of need (Powers 1977: 129).

Finally, some Oglala have joined the Native American Church, a religion combining traditional Indian spirituality with Christian symbolism, focusing on the sacramental use of the peyote cactus (see Chapter Fourteen).

THE CONTINUING IMPACT OF INDIGENOUS RELIGIONS IN THE TWENTY-FIRST CENTURY

With the subjugation of indigenous peoples in the nineteenth century, some government officials and missionaries triumphantly announced the end of "paganism." However, as the twenty-first century begins, indigenous religions are not only *not* dead, they are, as we have just illustrated, undergoing renewal.

Indigenous religions have a continuing impact in the inspiration they give to the modern environmental movement. The indigenous attitude of seeking to live in harmony with nature has influenced many environmentalists to seek a spiritual basis for their political and educational efforts (see Chapter Fifteen).

Surviving indigenous religions have also had a tremendous impact on those attempting to recover the pre-Christian beliefs and rituals of Europe. This "movement," known in general as "neo-paganism," has taken a variety of forms. We will examine one of them, Wicca, in Chapter Fourteen.

Finally, many people in the "historical" religions we will survey in subsequent chapters have begun to take a new attitude toward indigenous religions. Rather than viewing them as forms of idolatry that should be exterminated, many people are affirming them as legitimate and powerful manifestations of holiness that have much to teach people living in the modern world. Many people of various religions are recognizing that the basic patterns of indigenous spirituality are the foundation for the development of their own traditions. For them, the study of indigenous religion is, at least in part, a journey in search of their own roots.

CHAPTER SUMMARY

The purpose of this chapter was to introduce readers to the religions of the indigenous peoples of the world. We discussed some of the problems associated with the study of indigenous religions, especially the issue of whether outsiders may hope to understand the complexities of these religions without badly distorting them. In the past, scholars have labelled these religions using "primitive," "preliterate," "basic," and other terms. We chose "indigenous" because it is more descriptive, and because it is increasingly being used by representatives of these religions as a self-designation.

Using the "framework for understanding" developed in Chapter One, we then examined what might be called the general indigenous worldview:

HUMANITY: Members of a Larger Spiritual Family
PROBLEM: Life Out of Balance

CAUSE: Forgetfulness and Individualism
END: Maintenance and Restoration of Harmony
MEANS: Patterning All Life
REALITY: Sense of Place within the Rhythms of Life
SACRED: Everything is Spiritual

As examples of indigenous religions we examined the religions of the Yoruba people of West Africa and the Oglala Lakota of the Great Plains of North America.

We then turned to a discussion of the continuing impact of the indigenous religions in general in the twenty-first century.

IMPORTANT TERMS AND PHRASES

animism, fetish, high god, indigenous, magic, *Olorun, orisa, Orunmila, Esu, Ogun, Orisa-nla, Odun Egungun, Gelede, Aladura, Santeria,* rites of passage, shaman, taboo, totem, *mitakuye oyasin,* ghost dance, sacred hoop, sacred pipe, sweat lodge, sun dance, vision quest, *wakan, Wakan Tanka, Tunkashila, wicasa wakan, winyan wakan, heyok'a,* giveaway ceremony, White Buffalo Calf Woman, Wounded Knee, *Yuwipi*

QUESTIONS FOR DISCUSSION AND REFLECTION

1. What would be lost if indigenous religions ceased to exist? How important is it that they be preserved? What, if anything, can be done to keep them from disappearing?

2. The accumulation of individual wealth over an extended period is frowned on in many indigenous cultures. Why is that the case? Why has the attitude toward wealth changed in many modern societies?

3. People participating in indigenous religions may spend considerable time attending to the practices that they believe are necessary to maintain balance. Discuss the criticism that they are "wasting time," which could be more productively spent on activities that will help improve their material condition.

4. Many outsiders are now seeking to participate in Lakota rituals, especially the sweat lodge and the sun dance. Do you think this is an appropriate practice? Would you participate in one or both of these rituals if given the opportunity? Why or why not?

5. Put yourself in the place of a group of Native American leaders presented with opportunities to develop coal and natural gas resources on sacred tribal land, which would involve allowing toxic wastes to be dumped. If you agree to these deals, your people will get much-needed financial resources to develop schools, hospitals, and industries to provide jobs. If you do not agree, the sacred land will be preserved as the symbolic "center of the universe." What would you do? In a group setting, simulate a meeting of leaders to discuss the issue. Can you reach consensus? (Note: You may wish to consult the indigenous environmental teachings in Chapter Fifteen as you consider this question.)

6. Should the Black Hills be returned to the Lakota people? Why or why not?

SOURCES AND SUGGESTIONS FOR FURTHER STUDY

INDIGENOUS RELIGIONS IN GENERAL

ELIADE, MIRCEA, 1964. *Shamanism: Archaic Techniques of Ecstasy.* Trans. Willard Trask. Princeton: Princeton University.

GILL, SAM, 1982. *Beyond "The Primitive": The Religions of Nonliterate People.* Englewood Cliffs, NJ: Prentice Hall.

HARVEY, GRAHAM, ED. 2002. *Readings in Indigenous Religions.* New York: Continuum.

LEWIS, I. M. 1989. *Ecstatic Religion: A Study of Shamanism and Spirit Possession.* 2nd ed. New York: Routledge.

VAN GENNEP, ARNOLD, 1960. *Rites of Passage.* Trans. Monika B. Vizedom and Gabrielle L. Caffe. London: Routledge.

AFRICAN INDIGENOUS RELIGIONS (GENERAL)

BOOTH, NEWELL S., JR. 1977. *African Religions: A Symposium.* New York: NOK Publishers.

KING, NOEL Q. 1986. *African Cosmos: An Introduction to Religion in Africa.* Belmont, CA: Wadsworth.

MBITI, JOHN S. 1990. *African Religions and Philosophy,* 2nd ed. New York: Praeger.

OLUPONA, JACOB K. 1991. *African Traditional Religions in Contemporary Society.* New York: Paragon House.

RAY, BENJAMIN C. 1976. *African Religions: Symbol, Ritual, and Community.* Englewood Cliffs, NJ: Prentice Hall.

RAY, BENJAMIN C. 1987. "African Religions: An Overview," *Encyclopedia of Religion,* ed. Mircea Eliade (New York: Macmillan), vol. 1, 62–69.

THE RELIGION OF THE YORUBA

DESMANGLES, LESLIE G., 1992. *The Faces of the Gods: Vodou and Roman Catholicism in Haiti.* Chapel Hill, NC: University of North Carolina.

DREWAL, MARGARET, 1983. *Gelede: A Study of Art and Feminine Power among the Yoruba.* Bloomington, IN: University of Indiana.

GBADEGESIN, SEGUN, 1991. *African Philosophy: Traditional Yoruba Philosophy and Contemporary African Realities.* New York: Peter Lang.

GLEASON, JUDITH, 1987. *Oya: In Praise of the Goddess.* Boston: Shambhala.

KARADE, BABA IFA, 1994. *The Handbook of Yoruba Religious Concepts.* Red Wheel/Weiser.

MURPHY, JOSEPH M., 1993. *Santeria.* Boston: Beacon.

NEIMARK, PHILIP, 1993. *The Way of the Orisa.* SanFrancisco: Harper SanFrancisco.

PEEL, J. D. Y., 1968 *Aladura: A Religious Movement Among the Yoruba.* Oxford: Oxford University.

PEMBERTON, JOHN III, 1987. "Yoruba Religion," *Encyclopedia of Religion,* ed. Mircea Eliade (New York: Macmillan), vol. 15, 535–38.

NATIVE AMERICAN RELIGIONS (GENERAL)

BECK, PEGGY, ANNA LEE WALTERS, AND NIA FRANCISCO, 1995. *The Sacred: Ways of Knowledge, Sources of Life.* Redesigned edition. Tsaile, AZ: Navajo Community College.

BROWN, JOSEPH EPES, 1988. *The Spiritual Legacy of the American Indian.* New York: Crossroad.

BROWN, JOSEPH EPES, WITH EMILY COUSINS, 2000. *Teaching Spirits: Understanding Native American Religious Traditions.* New York: Oxford University.

DELORIA, VINE, JR., 1994. *God is Red: A Native View of Religion.* Revised edition. Golden, CO: Fulcrum.

DELORIA, VINE, JR., 1999. *For This Land: Writings on Religion in America,* ed. James Treat. New York: Routledge.

GILL, SAM, 1983. *Native American Traditions: Sources and Interpretations.* Belmont, CA: Wadsworth.

HUGHES, J. DONALD, 1983. *American Indian Ecology.* El Paso: Texas Western.

YOUNG, WILLIAM A., 2002. *Quest for Harmony: Native American Spiritual Traditions.* New York: Seven Bridges.

OGLALA LAKOTA RELIGION

BEASLEY, CONGER, JR., 1992. "The Return of the Lakota," *E Magazine* (September/October), 37–42, 65.

BLACK ELK, (NICHOLAS) AND JOHN G. NEIHARDT (FLAMING RAINBOW), 1932. *Black Elk Speaks. Being the Life Story of a Holy Man of the Oglala Sioux.* New York: William Morrow. (Pocket Books Edition, 1972.)

BROWN, JOSEPH EPES, ED., 1953. *The Sacred Pipe. Black Elk's Account of the Seven Rites of the Oglala Sioux.* Norman: University of Oklahoma. (Penguin Edition, 1971.)

BUCKO, RAYMOND A., 1998. *The Lakota Ritual of the Sweat Lodge: History and Contemporary Practice.* Lincoln: University of Nebraska.

CATCHES, PETE, 1997. *Oceti Wakan (Sacred Fireplace).* Pine Ridge, SD: Oceti Wakan.

DEMAILLIE, RAYMOND J., ED., 1984. *The Sixth Grandfather: Black Elk's Teachings Given to John G. Neihardt.* Lincoln: University of Nebraska.

DEMAILLIE, RAYMOND J., 1987. *Sioux Indian Religion: Tradition and Innovation.* ed. with Douglas R. Parks. Norman: University of Oklahoma.

DOOLING, D. M., ED., 1992. *The Sons of the Wind: The Sacred Stories of the Lakota.* San Francisco: HarperCollins.

HALIFAX, JOAN, 1990. "The Third Body: Buddhism, Shamanism, and Deep Ecology," in *Dharma Gaia,* ed. Allan Hunt Badiner. Berkeley, CA: Parallax, 20–38.

HOLLAR, CLYDE, 1995. *Black Elk's Religion: The Sun Dance and Lakota Catholicism.* Syracuse: Syracuse University.

LAZARUS, EDWARD, 1991. *Black Hills, White Justice: The Sioux Nation versus the United States, 1775 to the Present.* San Francisco: HarperCollins.

LEWIS, THOMAS, 1990. *The Medicine Men: Oglala Sioux Ceremony and Healing.* Lincoln: University of Nebraska.

MAILS, THOMAS, 1979. *Fools Crow.* New York: Doubleday.

MATTHIESSEN, PETER, 1992. *In the Spirit of Crazy Horse.* New York: Penguin.

PICKERING, ROBERT B., 1997. *Seeing the White Buffalo.* Denver: Denver Museum of Natural History.

POWERS, MARLA, 1986. *Oglala Women: Myth, Ritual, and Reality.* Chicago: University of Chicago.

POWERS, WILLIAM K., 1977. *Oglala Religion.* Lincoln: University of Nebraska.

POWERS, WILLIAM K., 1982. *Yuwipi: Vision and Experience in Oglala Ritual.* Lincoln: University of Nebraska.

POWERS, WILLIAM K., 1986. *Sacred Language: The Nature of Supernatural Discourse in Lakota.* Norman: University of Oklahoma.

POWERS, WILLIAM K., 1987. "Lakota Religion," *The Encyclopedia of Religion,* ed. Mircea Eliade (New York: Macmillan), vol. 8, 434–36.

STEINMETZ, PAUL B., S. J., 1990. *Pipe, Bible and Peyote Among the Oglala Lakota.* Knoxville: The University of Tennessee.

WALKER, JAMES R., 1980. *Lakota Belief and Ritual.* ed. Raymond J. DeMaillie and Elaine A. Jahner. Lincoln: University of Nebraska.

WALKER, JAMES R., 1982. *Lakota Society.* ed. Raymond J. DeMallie. Lincoln: University of Nebraska.

WALKER, JAMES R., 1983. *Lakota Myth.* ed. Elaine A. Jahner. Lincoln: University of Nebraska.

Web Sites

cs.org
    (Cultural Survival, an organization committed to assisting indigenous peoples)

afrikaworld.net/afrel/
    (links on various aspects of traditional African religions)

scholars.nus.edu.sg/landow/post/nigeria/yorubaov.html
    (an overview of Yoruba culture and religion)

www.public.iastate.edu/~savega/amer_ind.htm
www.hanksville.org/NAresources/
    (sites with links for the study of Native American cultures)

religioustolerance.org/nataspir.htm
religiousmovements.lib.virginia.edu/nrms/naspirit.html
    (sites with introductions to Native American spirituality and links for further research)

puffin.creighton.edu/lakota
    (links for the study of Lakota culture and religion)

TIME

Refer to Pearson/Prentice Hall's **TIME Special Edition: World Religions** magazine for these and other current articles on topics related to many of the world's religions:

➥ *The Religious Experience: Birth and Childhood*

Prentice Hall's **Research Navigator** helps students in their further study of the world's religions. Visit *http://www.researchnavigator.com* for help on the research process and access to databases full of relevant material, including the New York *Times*.

CHAPTER

3

Hinduism—Many Paths to the Summit

INTRODUCTION

The family of religions studied in the next three chapters (and Chapter Thirteen) is united by a shared geographical origin, an interrelated history, and a common underlying traditional worldview. The religions known to the world as Hinduism, Buddhism, Jainism, and Sikhism all originated in South Asia, in what are now the countries of India, Pakistan, Bangladesh, Sri Lanka, Bhutan, and Nepal. Hinduism is still the dominant religion of India, encompassing a broad range of beliefs and practices. The roots of Hinduism can be traced to the second millennium B.C.E. It is a minority religion in the other countries of South and Southeast Asia.

Jainism began in sixth-century B.C.E. India when the teachings of one austere holy man became the basis of a new religious movement. It continues as one of the smallest religions in India, but with influence far beyond the relatively few Jains.

Buddhism also began in sixth-century B.C.E. India, but survived by spreading beyond India to become the major religion of Southeast and East Asia. As a separate religion, Buddhism faded in India, its teachings absorbed into Hinduism. Theravada Buddhism, the form of Buddhism described in the next chapter, is dominant in Sri Lanka and Southeast Asia.

Sikhism, to be discussed in Chapter Thirteen, traces its roots to fifteenth-century India.

After orienting ourselves to South and Southeast Asia and the worldview common to the aforementioned religions, we will examine in this chapter the history and worldview of Hinduism. We will conclude with reflections on Hinduism at the outset of the twenty-first century.

AN ORIENTATION TO SOUTH AND SOUTHEAST ASIA

Lands and Peoples

The countries of South Asia are India (by far the largest in size and population), Pakistan (bordering India on the west), Bangladesh (on India's eastern border), and four small countries (Bhutan and Nepal in the mountains along India's northern border; and Sri Lanka and the Maldives, small island nations south of India).

At the beginning of the twenty-first century the population of India was over one billion and growing fast enough to overtake China as the world's largest country by mid-century. Over two-thirds of the people in India live in villages. The two major ethnic groups in India are Indo-Aryans (called simply Aryans), most of whom live in northern India, and Dravidians, who dominate in southern India. Pakistan, with a population of over 150 million, includes Aryans, Dravidians, and people of Arabic descent. The Sinhalese of Sri Lanka and the Maldives came from northern India; the Tamils of Sri Lanka originated in southern India. In Nepal and Bhutan are both Aryans and people of Tibetan and Mongolian heritage. These nations have much smaller populations.

There are nine countries in the geographic region known as Southeast Asia: Myanmar (Burma), Kampuchea (Cambodia), Laos, Thailand, and Vietnam on the peninsula; Malaysia; Indonesia; the Philippines; and Singapore.

The early twenty-first century population of Southeast Asia is over 550 million. Indonesia, with a population of about 235 million in 2003, is by far the largest. The ancestors of most of the people of Southeast Asia migrated from China long ago. They drove the indigenous peoples of the region into mountainous areas where some still reside. Many people have also migrated from India into the region.

The branch of Buddhism widely known as Theravada dominates the Southeast Asian countries of the peninsula, except for Malaysia and Vietnam. Islam is the chief religion of Malaysia and Indonesia, and Christianity (brought by the Spanish) is the major faith in the Philippines. There are also many Hindus in the region, especially in Malaysia and Indonesia.

A Brief History of India

Since all the religions examined in the next several chapters originated in India, a brief overview of the history of India will provide a context for an understanding of their stages of development.

The historical period in India began about 4,500 years ago when a flourishing civilization arose in the Indus River Valley, in an area now located in Pakistan. Archaeologists have learned much about the sophisticated *Indus Valley Civilization* (ca. 2500–1500 B.C.E.) from the excavation of two of its major cities, Harappa and Mohenjo-daro. This civilization disappeared mysteriously over a period of time.

Most historians agree that about 1500 B.C.E. bands of *Aryans* (from the Sanskrit word for "nobles") migrated from central Asia, through the mountains into northern India, although some scholars today think they were indigenous to India. The Aryans were a nomadic people, who measured their well-being in terms of the size of their herds and the number of their progeny. Their language (Sanskrit), religion, and social organization are documented in the earliest texts of the *Vedic* scriptures. "Hinduism" traces its roots to these *Vedas,* the sacred writings of the Aryans (see below). The Aryans forced the Dravidians into southern India. Although the Aryan class system (the basis of the later caste system) came to dominate all of India, the Aryans never fully conquered the south.

Late Aryan religion, dominated by a priestly class known as *Brahmins* who sought an esoteric knowledge, provided the foundation for the basic worldview which all of the religions studied in this chapter reflect. However, the religious system controlled by the Brahmins, and the rigid class distinctions of Aryan culture, met resistance. Both Buddhism and Jainism developed from the sixth-century B.C.E. reaction of two great religious teachers against the excesses of *Brahminical* religion.

In 326 B.C.E. Alexander the Great's army swept into northwest India, initiating contact between the great cultural heritages of Greece and India. The invading army was eventually driven out, and significant interaction between India and the West was not to resume for over a thousand years.

From about 322 B.C.E. until 185 B.C.E. the Maurya Empire (named after its founder, Chandragupta Maurya) united almost all of India for the first time. The most famous Maurya ruler was *Ashoka,* who died in 232 B.C.E. A successful conqueror, Ashoka renounced violence, became a Buddhist, and inspired the spread of Buddhism throughout India and beyond. He sought to rule by *dharma* (see below) rather than force. During this period the most famous text of "Hinduism," the *Bhagavad-Gita,* was probably written, as part of a large epic, the *Mahabharata,* which envisioned a united India.

What has become known as the "Golden Age" came to India with the ascendancy of the Gupta dynasty in northern India in the fourth Century C.E. During the Gupta Empire (ca. 320–500 C.E.) there was a rebirth of Aryan culture, and significant developments in art, science, and medicine.

For almost the next thousand years India was invaded again and again, first by the Huns from central Asia, later by Muslims from Arabia and Afghanistan, and finally by Europeans. The Muslims began to enter India in the seventh century, not long after the Prophet Muhammad's death, beginning a long, slow period of conquest.

The greatest Muslim dynasty in India, the Moghul Empire, was established in North India in 1526 C.E. and continued until the early 1700s. Its glory is seen in architectural wonders like the famous Taj Mahal ("crown palace"), built between 1632 and 1647 in the city of Agra. One of the first Moghul rulers, Akbar (1542–1605), is remembered by Hindus with fondness, because of his commitment to religious tolerance. Sikhism, which sought to combine the best from the two traditions, emerged and became a significant religion; it continues to play an important role in India. Other Moghul rulers were less tolerant of religious diversity, exacerbating tension between Hindus and Muslims, which is still an important dynamic in South Asian life.

Europeans had begun to arrive in India in the 1500s. Portuguese traders seized ports on the western coast, following the voyage of Vasco de Gama in 1498. They vied with Dutch, French, and British traders for control of commerce.

Great Britain soon became the dominant European power in India. The British East India Company established trading centers in Bombay, Calcutta, and Madras. The Company took advantage of the decline of the Moghul Empire and became the principal political power in 1757. A century later, after a rebellion against the East India Company, the British government took direct control and established British India. The British negotiated with leaders (often known as *maharajas* ["great rulers"]) who were given control over some areas called the Indian States in exchange for a pledge of loyalty to the British. A British viceroy was appointed to govern. The British brought organization to political and economic life, establishing transportation and communications systems. During British rule many Indians were educated in British schools and assimilated to Western culture and values. However, resistance to British control and a renewal of traditional Indian culture soon began.

The political movement for Indian independence continued under the leadership of the largely Hindu Indian National Congress (founded in 1885) and the rival Muslim League (1906). Discontent grew after the Amritsar Massacre of 1919, when a British general ordered his troops to fire on an unarmed crowd. A year later Mohandas K. Gandhi (known as *Mahatma* or "great-souled one") became leader of the Indian National Congress. In addition to challenging British rule through a campaign of passive, nonviolent resistance, he challenged the iron-grip of the traditional caste system on Indian society and was a mediator between Muslims and Hindus. Gandhi skillfully orchestrated the movement of civil disobedience that ultimately convinced the British to allow India to become independent in 1947.

However, because of Hindu-Muslim strife, historic India was partitioned by the British into the Hindu nation of India and the Muslim nation of Pakistan (divided into two parts, West and East Pakistan). The partition divided the region dominated by Sikhs, causing some Sikhs to begin an as yet unsuccessful movement to create an independent Sikh state in the Punjab area. In 1971 India assisted East Pakistan in rebelling and a new independent nation, Bangladesh, was formed.

Unfortunately, violence between Muslims and Hindus as well as Sikhs and Hindus continues to threaten the fragile unity of India. Nevertheless, since independence the people of India and Pakistan have made great strides in addressing the poverty, disease, hunger, and illiteracy which have plagued the area for so long. India remains the largest democratic nation in the world.

The Traditional South Asian Worldview

Tour *The Sacred World* CD!

As we will see, the religions of South and Southeast Asia have significant differences, but they share the following general perspective about the fundamental problems humans face and the transformation needed to resolve them. This worldview is a helpful framework for comparing and contrasting the distinctive teachings of Hinduism, Jainism, Buddhism, and Sikhism.

Humanity: Our "*Karmic*" Selves   Although these religions have differing views on the spiritual nature of humans, they agree that human action unfolds according to the principles of the law of *karma*. As a result, we humans have "*karmic*" selves separate from our spiritual natures. Our karmic selves act and are acted upon.

Karma (from the Sanskrit for "action") is the law explaining the cause-and-effect relationship operative in human behavior. It is a key link in the basic South Asian world view. It is especially important in Hinduism, Buddhism (where the concept is known in early Buddhism by the Pali name *kamma*), and Jainism. Each religion expresses a different understanding of the nature of karma, but they all agree that it is central to our understanding of humanity.

The difference between karma and the Western idea of moral accountability expressed in sayings like "you reap what you sow" is that *karma* is not just a *part* of what we are as humans; karma fully explains us as physical, emotional, and intellectual beings. We sometimes say in modern America, rather flippantly, "you are what you eat" or "you are what you wear." From the Indian perspective, this is not just an off-hand comment—it is true. The "self" who eats breakfast, gets dressed, goes to class, watches TV, reads a book, and goes to bed *is* determined according to the law of karma. Hence, it may be called the *"karmic" self*. We are determined by the law of karma as is the trajectory and speed of a ball by the angle and force of the bat with which it is hit!

Although the religions of South and Southeast Asia share the view of a karmic nature separate from the spiritual, they have significant differences, as we shall see, on the question of just what the spiritual nature of humans is.

Problem: Attachment   According to the traditional South Asian worldview, the reason human beings engage in deliberate behavior is that we have desires. For example, it is nearly lunchtime as I write these words, and I am sensing a strong desire for food. Some desires are sensual, such as my longing for lunch. Some desires are for nonmaterial things such as recognition or sympathy. For the traditional worldview underlying the religions originating in India, desire is at the root of the fundamental human problem. Because we desire, we act, and because we act we develop a sense of our own separate identity as willful beings. It is this attachment to the karmic self, rooted in desire, which entraps us. Although each of the religions of South and Southeast Asia, describes attachment in somewhat different ways, they share the perception that the attachment caused by desire must be overcome if ultimate transformation is to occur.

Cause: Desire and Ignorance   As we have seen, according to the South Asian view, desire is the culprit. It is the link that holds the karmic chain together. Unless it is broken, we are trapped.

In addition, an underlying problem, commonly identified in South Asian religions, is that we do not know who we truly are spiritually. Because we are attached by desire to our karmic selves, we are blinded to the truth that there is a spiritual dimension to our existence. In other words, an important cause of our dilemma is that we are spiritually ignorant, and need to be enlightened to our true nature.

End: Liberation and Enlightenment   The state of existence *toward* which the religions which originated in South Asia seek ultimate transformation is expressed as "liberation from the cycle of rebirth." As we will see, the religions have quite different teachings about the nature of liberation. However, the religions share the view that since our basic human problem is karmic entrapment in the cycle of rebirth, our ultimate goal is to break the attachment and escape from the cycle. In addition, we need to become enlightened, to "wake up" to who we truly are spiritually.

Means: The Way of Dharma (Duty)   The religions that originated in India have diverse teachings about the paths to follow that lead to escape from the cycle of rebirth. However, they share a general understanding that there is a universal human "duty" to pursue liberation and to pattern human life accordingly. This concept is expressed by the Sanskrit word *dharma* (and the Pali word *dhamma*).

In its broadest sense, the concept of dharma describes the proper order of things and the principles of conduct implied by that order. It is the "duty" implicit in the very structure of existence. Thus, as noted, we all share the dharma of seeking liberation. Moreover, in individual and communal life there is also a "social" dharma to be followed. Where dharma is not observed, chaos results. Each of the religions of the region affirms dharma, but they disagree significantly on the way dharma should be manifest in individual and social life.

Reality: The Cycle of Rebirth   The beer commercial that told viewers: "You only go around once!" was not (or should not have been) shown in countries dominated by the religions that originated in South Asia. The reason is that the religions we are studying in this chapter agree that the effects of karma are not limited by physical death. We humans can and do "go around" more than once!

According to the religions with which most readers of this book are probably familiar, life is lived as a one-way trip. You live, you die, and then your enter into a life after death, Western religions teach. A cynic in the cultures shaped by this "linear" understanding of life usually drops the notion of "life after death" and agrees with the bumper sticker that reads, "Life's a bummer and then you die."

In the religions that originated in South Asia, time is not thought of as a linear process. A cynic in India might say, "Life's a bummer and then you die, and then you are reborn, and then you die, and then you are reborn. . . ." Unless a person has found a way to break free from the law of karma, that person will be reborn into another (not necessarily human) life. This "cycle of rebirth" (or *samsara* as it is known in Sanskrit) is an accepted premise of the traditional South Asian worldview.

As popularized by some writers in the West, "reincarnation" is an exciting journey, and people should be eager to explore their "past lives." It has no such allure in Hinduism, Jainism, Buddhism, and Sikhism. To use the terminology that we have developed to speak about religion, in the religions that originated in India the cycle of rebirth is the state of being *from which* persons seek ultimate transformation.

We should also note that the cycle of rebirth is also a description of reality as a whole. In the worldview that developed in South Asia, not only do individual humans pass through cycles of birth, death, and rebirth, the universe as a whole undergoes this process, passing through ages called *kalpas*. Therefore, "creation" is thought of differently in the religions discussed in this chapter than it is in the religions of the West. "Creation" is not a one-time event that happened when the cosmos originated. "Creation" occurs at the beginning of each cosmic cycle, and will occur again after reality as a whole goes through a process of dissolution.

Sacred: A Diversity of Views   The religions that originated in India all affirm the reality of the spiritual. However, beyond that point these religions range from the monotheism of Sikhism to the spiritual atheism of Jainism and Theravada Buddhism. Within Hinduism we will encounter a diversity of language regarding the sacred, with imagery both personal and impersonal, sometimes in the same text.

With an overview of the history of India and at least a preliminary explanation of the traditional South Asian worldview as a framework, let us now turn to the first of the major religions that originated in India, with the goal of understanding its unique history and distinctive teachings.

STAGES OF DEVELOPMENT AND SACRED TEXTS

The Problem with the Name "Hinduism"

The first thing to understand about "Hinduism" is the difficulty in naming this religion. Its roots can be traced to the Vedas, the sacred writings associated with the Aryans. For nearly 3,000 years there was no one "name" for the complex of beliefs and practices that were evolving in this "Vedic" tradition. The closest the tradition came to a self-designation is the Sanskrit *sanatana dharma,* which means "eternal duty" and refers to the inherent human orientation toward liberation from the cycle of rebirth.

When Muslims began to arrive in India, they were frustrated by the lack of a single label for the religion of the people in the land they were entering. In this context, the name "Hinduism" emerged to distinguish clearly the existing practices from the Islamic faith of the new arrivals. "Hindu" refers simply to the people who lived in the region of the Indus River. Our English term "Hinduism" technically means, then, the religion of the Hindus. When the British arrived in India, they adopted the "Hindu" designation.

Therefore, the name "Hinduism" is an arbitrary appellation imposed by outsiders for an array of religious beliefs and practices within India. Only gradually did Hindus accept the name Hinduism to describe a distinct religion, but by the nineteenth century it was widely accepted as such by religious leaders in the Vedic tradition. For this reason, it is appropriate to use the term "Hindu" as the name for a distinct religion in a phenomenological study. It is best, however, to consider Hinduism as a family of religions, with a shared heritage and some basic teachings in common, but with considerable diversity as well. As we shall see, the same can be said for all the world's major religions!

In this section we will follow the basic phases in the evolution of Hinduism from its origins in the Vedic culture and the Vedic scriptures; the emergence of the rules and customs still evident in Hindu society; the two great epics of Hinduism (the *Mahabharata* and *Ramayana*); the development of the two great branches of Hinduism, which continue into the present ("devotional" and "philosophical" Hinduism); and finally the reform movements that arose in Hinduism in the nineteenth and twentieth centuries in response to European influences.

Religion of the Indus Valley (Harappan) Civilization

The preliminary stage in the development of Hinduism is the religion of the Indus Valley (or Harappan) Civilization (ca. 2500–1500 B.C.E.). We know of the religion of this urban culture only through artifacts discovered principally in the ruins of the two main cities of Harappa and Mohenjo-daro. No written texts have been discovered. Although some of the small stone seals are inscribed, the language of the culture has not yet been deciphered. We are left then to speculate on the meaning of such finds as "fertility" figurines and the seals, many of which have seemingly religious scenes on them. Some suggest the strong possibility of a link between the religion of this period and later developments. For example, one seal shows an apparent deity in a pose suggestive of the posture and symbols of the later Hindu deity *Shiva*.

The Religion of the Vedas: The Rig-Veda and the Upanishads

 Tour *The Sacred World* CD!

The Vedas (from the Sanskrit term for "knowledge") are the most venerated writings in Hinduism, although they are not the only sacred texts. Although the Vedas are written texts, they are still transmitted orally by priests who recite verses from them on special occasions. It is most likely that the Vedas were written down over a nearly two-thousand year period, from about 1500 B.C.E. until about 400 C.E.

Of the four basic books in the Vedas, we will focus on the earliest and most important, the *Rig-Veda* (literally, "the Veda of verses of praise"). It is primarily a collection of more than one thousand hymns to the gods of the Aryan pantheon. These gods have faded from popular worship for the most part, or have been incorporated into the worship of more popular deities, but the hymns to them are important in their own right.

The most prevalent deity in the Rig-Veda is *Indra,* the god of thunder and rain, the ruler of the space between the heavens and the earth. He is a warrior deity, celebrated in over 250 hymns, described anthropomorphically as huge, bearded, and hard-drinking, with a thunderbolt as his weapon. In Vedic mythology Indra is particularly renowned as the victor over the demon *Vitra,* who withholds the waters which bring fertility to the earth. The hymns sometimes address Indra as king of the gods. Indra appears in later Hinduism (and Jainism), but in a subordinate role.

Another important god of the Aryan pantheon is *Agni,* the god of fire and sacrifice, who appears in over two hundred hymns. *Agni* is also used as a term for the sacrificial fire itself. As the god of fire, *Agni* receives the burnt sacrifices offered to other deities and brings the offerings to the gods.

Varuna is the Vedic deity who maintains cosmic order (personified as *rita*). He is all-seeing and all-knowing. Varuna punishes those who violate the cosmic order and forgives those who acknowledge their shortcomings. In a sense he is a rival to Indra.

The most intriguing Vedic god is *Soma,* the lord of plants. The name *soma* means "pressed" and refers to the pressing of a particular plant to produce an intoxicating drink. In Vedic times worshippers thought *soma* produced insight and immortality. The ritual drinking of *soma* apparently played an important role in Aryan life, and is an example of the practice of using hallucinogenic drugs for religious purposes.

Typically, the hymns of the *Rig-Veda* seek not a spiritual immortality, but a long life on earth, with much wealth and good health. It is almost as though a barter system applies: Worshippers make their offerings, and the deities respond with blessings. Spiritual reality is affirmed, in the form of a pantheon of personified deities (and other spiritual beings). However, they are treated almost as a means to a this-worldly end.

Other deities in the *Rig-Veda*'s mythology include *Yama,* god of the dead; *Vishnu,* later a principal Hindu deity, but at this stage a fairly minor god; and *Rudra,* god of destruction (precursor of the later deity Shiva).

We find in one famous creation poem from the Rig-Veda (x.129) early signs of a quest for a mystical knowledge of the unity (or nonduality) that lies beyond all that we can perceive with our senses. The gods are clearly secondary to the primal reality, although the hymn seems to leave open the question of whether there might be one supreme god related to the Oneness at the root of everything. The poem ends (v. 7) with this cryptic stanza (Mahony 1998: 57):

No one knows whence this creation has come into being.
Perhaps it formed itself. Perhaps not.
Only he who looks down from the highest heaven truly knows.
Or maybe he does not know.

Another creation poem of the Rig-Veda (x.90) uses sacrifice as a metaphor to speak of the ordering of human life. This suggests a movement away from concern for the actual practice of sacrifice to an exploration of the symbolic meaning of the sacrificial actions of the priests and the words associated with them. The focus is on a Supreme Person (*Purusha*) whom the gods offered as a cosmic sacrifice. When Purusha was dismembered in the sacrifice, his mouth became the priests, his arms the warriors, his thighs the producers, and his feet the workers. This is one of the earliest allusions to the four-fold class (*varna*) system that would later develop (see below) and evolve over time into the complex caste system in India. In the Purusha Hymn the hierarchical pattern of priests, warriors, producers, and workers is presented as the result of a paradigmatic act in mythic time, validating its replication in the social order of Aryan India.

We also find in the hymns of the Rig-Veda early references to the reverence for cows that would become and remains an important aspect of Hindu culture. For example, one hymn (vi.28) associates cows with Indra and their milk with Soma.

The Rig-Veda constitutes but one of the four basic collections of texts or books of the Vedas. The others are the *Yajur-Veda* (a collection of ritual materials and directions for the sacrifices and invocations for the gods); the *Sama-Veda* (a collection of verses from the Rig-Veda arranged musically); and the *Atharva-Veda* (over seven hundred hymns together with spells, incantations, remedies, and charms for use in the home). Each of the four basic collections was broken into four parts: hymns (*mantras*), ritual material (*brahamas*), symbolic and allegorical interpretations intended for those who had taken a vow to be "forest dwellers" (*aranyakas*), and philosophical utterances (*upanishads*).

Because of their importance for the development of Hinduism let us now turn to a discussion of the *Upanishads*. The term means "to sit near by" and refers to the practice of a student sitting at the feet of a spiritual teacher to receive instruction. The Upanishads are the basis for later philosophical reflection. It is often said that virtually all of Hindu religious philosophy is in one form or another commentary on the Upanishads. In them we find developed the quest for a mystical, intuitive knowledge of that which is the one source of all reality.

Although the Upanishads are diverse, they do develop much of the perspective that became the basis for classical Hinduism. They speak over and over of the one supreme reality from which all other reality comes, and name this oneness Brahman. For example, the Mundaka Upanishad uses the image of a spider spinning a web as a metaphor for Brahman. Just as a spider emits and reabsorbs its thread, so does all reality arise from and return to what this Upanishad calls the Imperishable. Simply put, Brahman is the sole principle of unity in the cosmos. Brahman is eternal, infinite, unknowable to the rational mind. Brahman is often described, and is usually pictured as, an *impersonal* reality, for to assign personal qualities to Brahman would be limiting. However, some passages use personal imagery, causing some interpreters to conceive of the ultimate oneness as a personal, all-powerful, all-knowing deity. We will revisit this tension over the impersonal versus personal character of the ultimate.

If Brahman is beyond the ordinary knowing we associate with this world, how then can Brahman be known at all? The resolution of this dilemma in the Upanishads is to assert that the true nature of every living being is an eternal soul (called the *Atman*), which, in truth, is one with Brahman. The basic human problem is ignorance (*avidya*) of who we truly are. Indeed, everything else in the universe besides the Brahman/Atman unity is nothing more than an illusion (*maya*) created by our ignorance. According to the Upanishads, each of us is Atman, but we are attached, by desire, to the illusion of a distinct karmic self (*jiva*). One helpful way to understand this concept is to think of the Atman as the the Self (with a large "S") and the physical, distinct, karmic self as the self (with a small "s").

The Upanishads introduce into Indian thought the concept of the law of karma, which we have already described. It is the "self" which acts and which is shaped by the consequences of karma. The Self (Atman) does *not* act, for it is eternal and unchanging. Because of our ignorance, we do not know the true, spiritual reality of Atman/Brahman, and we are left with the illusion that our true nature is the self that *does* act. Until this ignorance is overcome, the Atman remains trapped in the cycle of rebirth (*samsara*), another concept introduced by the Upanishads. Once true knowledge is obtained, then the Atman reaches liberation (*moksha*) from the cycle of rebirth. "True knowledge" is not "knowledge" in the ordinary sense; if it were, by reading about these concepts you might experience liberation. "True knowledge" is mystical and intuitive; it involves an indescribable experience of oneness that is obtained through total self-discipline and meditation. We will have more to say about meditation, and we will encounter this sort of "knowing beyond ordinary knowledge" in other religious traditions.

Hindu Society: The Laws of Manu

Tour *The Sacred World* CD!

The Laws (or Code) of Manu (from the Sanskrit for "a thinking being" or "mankind") constitute a collection of ethical and religious guidelines for individuals and society as a whole, written between approximately 200 B.C.E. and 200 C.E. In the Vedas, Manu is the primal human being, and this basic collection is traditionally attributed to him. The Laws of Manu claim, therefore, to provide the pattern for right conduct laid down at the time of origins. Its teachings concerning the dharma (duty) of the four principal classes (already introduced in the Rig-Veda) and the four stages of life for Indian men of the upper classes (*asramas*) are at the heart of the still-influential Hindu caste system.

This is the appropriate point to clarify the crucial Hindu social reality that became known as "caste." The term "caste" actually comes from the Portuguese word *casta,* which means "race." It first appeared in reference to Indian society when Portuguese traders encountered the social divisions within India in the sixteenth century. The Sanskrit term used to refer to these divisions is *varna* (color). We will use an English translation of *varna* (class) to designate the social system at its early stage, and reserve "caste" for what later developed as the system evolved. We have already observed the four basic "classes" in the Rig-Veda. These are *brahmins* (priests and sages); *kshatriyas* (warriors); *vaishyas* (producers [merchants, bankers, and farmers]); *shudras* (workers or servants).

Like the Rig-Veda, the Laws of Manu assert that the four classes are rooted in the ordering of the cosmos. In Vedic times there was apparently some mobility among classes. In the Laws of Manu, the system seems to have rigidified, with clear statements about the dharma of each class.

The compensation for the lack of mobility among the classes is reincarnation, also described in the Laws of Manu. According to karma, whoever fulfills his or her dharma in one life will experience a higher birth in the next. Whoever performs evil actions (those in conflict with dharma) will be born at a lower level, including the possibility of being born as a plant or nonhuman animal. For example, a later text (*Garuda Purana* 5) says that, in accord with the law of karma, someone who murders a cow in this life becomes himself humpbacked (like a cow) in the next. Someone who commits illicit sexual acts becomes a eunuch. Those who steal grain become locusts.

Although not specified in the Laws of Manu, by 300 B.C.E. numerous *jati* or birth groups had begun to develop within the four-fold *varna* system. The *jati* formed the basis for the later multileveled caste and subcaste system still observable in Indian today, especially in rural areas. In this elaborate system, for a higher caste member to touch a member of a lower caste causes ritual impurity. By tradition, marriage and social contact were extremely limited among *jati*. However, because of narrowly defined occupational specializations for each caste, *jati* were interdependent. Despite their origin in association with particular occupations, the social mobility of the modern era, especially in urban areas, has eroded such ties for *jati* and made the caste system less significant. However, in rural areas *jati* often maintain an occupational relationship. Especially in village settings, the *jati* provide a social network in which people are employed and provided for. Its important social function, especially in villages, has made attempts to reform the caste system very challenging.

In addition to the *varna* system there arose the tradition that some *jati* are so polluting that they must be considered to be outside the four classes, and constitute a fifth social grouping, known as the untouchables or "scheduled castes," or today as *dalits* ("oppressed"). For example, cremation workers are polluted by their contact with dead bodies and are thus "untouchable." Other *jati* are polluted by their contact with human waste or leather. According to the traditional Hindu social system, for those in the four classes (especially the higher classes) to touch such persons causes pollution requiring significant ritual cleansing. Hence, when members of untouchable *jati* violated the taboos of separation, they were often severely punished, even killed, by members of higher castes. While the anonymity of urban life has undermined such traditions, in rural areas discrimination and violence against members of untouchable *jati* who have been accused of violating social taboos is still practiced. It continues to be a serious problem in modern India, and we will return to it.

The highest three classes in the *varna* system became known as the "twice born," because boys in these classes traditionally engage in an initiatory rite of passage (*upanayana*) in which they symbolically experience a "second birth."

The Laws of Manu prescribe four stages of life for young men of the three higher *varna*. The first stage is student (*brahmacarin*), in which a young man, after *upanayana,* is to study the Vedas under the guidance of a teacher. After the next rite of passage, marriage, the young man becomes a householder (*grihastha*). During this stage he performs the daily sacrifices, produces sons, and provides for his family's welfare. The third stage is forest-dweller (*vanaprastha*), entered after one's children are grown. During this state a man devotes himself to a simple life, studying the Vedas, withdrawing from the desires of earthly life. If his wife accompanies him, they remain chaste. After reaching an attitude of nonattachment, the man is ready to enter the final stage, that of a renunciant (*sannyasin*). Here he lives alone, without possessions, seeking a state of being without desires. These stages remain the ideal for upper-class Hindu men in modern India. However, not many Hindu men today undertake the rigors of the final two phases.

The dharma of a woman, according to the Laws of Manu, includes service to her father, then marriage to her husband, and performance of the household duties. Hindu women do not pass through the four stages, but they too are born into a class and, in some circumstances, they can take the vow of *sannayasin*. We will have much more to say about the role of women in Hinduism in Chapter Eighteen.

The evolution of the practice of venerating cows is also seen in the Laws of Manu, in the directive to the *vaisyas* to "protect cattle" and in the listing of "the killing of cows" as an act to be avoided. The eating of a vegetarian diet is also set forth in the Laws, as the "eating of flesh should be avoided."

In addition, the Laws of Manu contain rules on marriage, daily rituals, funeral rites, forms of hospitality, duties of kings, debt, inheritance, and civil and criminal law. Also found are warnings about the possibility of rebirth in a "hell" for those whose deeds are particularly evil.

The Epics: Ramayana and Mahabharata

Besides the *Vedas* and the Laws of Manu, the other most important literature in the development of Hinduism, during what is sometimes called the "classical" period, were two major epics. One was the Ramayana ("the story of Rama"), the tale of the exploits on earth of the god-king Rama and his wife Sita. As we shall see, the Ramayana plays an important role in one of the most serious issues in modern India. The other epic is the Mahabharata ("great epic of the descendants of Bharata"). Both are long stories, transmitted orally for generations, with textual traditions beginning as early as 400 B.C.E. The *Mahabharata* is one of the longest epics ever written; its hundred thousand verses make it seven times the length of the Greek epics, the Iliad and the Odyssey, combined. Stories from both epics are performed in elaborate annual dramas throughout India. In recent years they have inspired wildly popular series on Indian television. We will focus here on the *Mahabharata.*

The *Bhagavad-Gita*   In the sixth book of the mammoth Mahabharata, there is a relatively short section (seven hundred verses), which stands on its own as perhaps the most important single sacred text in Hinduism. The Bhagavad-Gita ("Song of the Lord"), as this section is known, has inspired generations of Indian religious and political leaders. Mahatma Gandhi called it a "dictionary for life," and Jawaharlal Nehru, the first Prime Minister of the independent India, kept a copy by his bedside throughout his life. It has also served for the last several centuries to introduce people beyond India to the Hindu religion. For example, the American transcendentalists Ralph Waldo Emerson and Henry David Thoreau incorporated some of the Bhagavad-Gita's teachings into their writings. The explosion of the first atomic bomb in the New Mexico desert in 1945 caused one of the scientists associated with its development, Robert Oppenheimer, to quote a line from the Bhagavad-Gita that speaks of the destruction of all reality. This poem still plays a critical role in Indian life. In the early 1990s dramatic adaptations of the Bhagavad-Gita generated the largest television audiences in India.

On the eve of a great battle, the Pandava warrior, Arjuna, expresses despair over the prospect of civil war and the chaos it will bring. *Krishna,* serving as Arjuna's charioteer, responds to Arjuna's dilemma, and the body of the Gita (as it is often known) is a dialogue between the two. As the conversation progresses, Krishna reveals himself to be an *avatar* (incarnation, earthly manifestation) of the God Vishnu, who appears on earth to bring comfort and instruction at times of trouble. In the climax of the Gita, Krishna allows Arjuna to have a mystical encounter with the deity in his spiritual form.

Amidst the poetic narrative of the Gita, the reader finds a synthesis of the major concepts already enunciated in the Upanishads, as well as the introduction of new ideas. The Gita reflects the major theme of the Mahabharata as a whole in stressing the importance of dharma. Krishna teaches Arjuna that as a warrior he must fulfill his dharma and go into battle against his kin. To explain his advice, Krishna tells his friend that human beings cannot avoid acting. Therefore, their acts must be guided by class dharma. The key is to act in such a way that you are not attached to the results of your actions. Krishna reaffirms the Upanishadic teaching about human nature. We have a material, karmic nature, the "self" that acts; but we also have an eternal, spiritual nature, the "Self" (*atman*) that does not act. If we are attached to our actions, we are identifying with the temporal self, the karmic self, and we are bound by karma within the cycle of rebirth. If we can overcome attachment to the results of our actions, we are identifying with our eternal, unchanging Self. If Arjuna fulfills his dharma as a warrior, but without attachment to the effects of his deeds, he will be acting in a spiritually proper manner. This teaching about human action, which expresses one of the three basic approaches to spiritual fulfillment in Hinduism, can be applied to any situation, and therefore has had wide appeal.

Beyond the emphasis on acting in accord with dharma (but without being affected by those actions), the Gita offers other spiritual advice. It teaches that one seeking spiritual liberation may follow a path of mental and spiritual exercises through which the *atman* is experienced. This is the path of meditation (or the way of knowledge), the second of the major spiritual paths that attained popularity in Hinduism.

Depending on the tendencies associated with the attributes of their material natures, others may take a third path, offering all their actions as sacrifices to a personal god. This path of devotional service (*bhakti*) became the most widely practiced type of Hinduism. The Gita makes clear that anyone, regardless of class, gender, or age, can practice devotional service to the Supreme Lord. Whatever one's particular abilities, they can be offered to God as a sacrifice. According to the Gita, God loves humans and is concerned about them, taking various forms (avatars) to express this compassion. To respond to God's compassion with a life of devotion to God is to take the path to ultimate communion with God. We will discuss all of these paths more fully when we consider the Hindu worldview.

The Gita also teaches readers about the nature of the ultimate. As with humans, the ultimate has two natures, a lower, material nature (*prakriti*) and a higher, spiritual nature (*purusha*). One of the enticements of the Gita is its ambiguity. Is the ultimate described in the Gita impersonal, the Brahman of the Upanishads? Or is the ultimate the supreme Lord, a personal god? Which is the superior spiritual path, selfless action guided by dharma, meditation on the impersonal absolute, or devotion to a personal god? If the ultimate *is* personal, is Vishnu or Krishna the supreme Lord? Is the Gita's last word about the nature of the ultimate monistic or monotheistic—or perhaps pantheistic? This ambiguity has inspired commentators to write volumes on the Gita, without generating definitive answers to any of these questions. Perhaps the ambiguity is intentional, to make us aware that as humans we cannot pin down clearly the nature of the Ultimate, or the best means of ultimate transformation. If this be the case, then the Gita offers support for tolerance and respect among differing religious traditions.

For those who would like to read the Gita as a whole, a variety of inexpensive translations into English are readily available (e.g., Prabhupada 1983, Miller 1986, and Mitchell 2000).

Devotional Literature and Movements: The *Puranas*

Tour *The Sacred World* CD!

Although their precise time of origin is unknown, the set of writings called the *puranas* came into prominence in the period after the Bhagavad-Gita, (about 400 through 900 C.E.), called by some scholars the postclassical phase in the development of Hinduism. The *puranas* are stories and teachings primarily concerned with the personalities and exploits of three gods (called, as a group, the *trimurti*) and their accompanying goddesses. The gods are *Brahma* (the creator), *Vishnu* (the preserver), and *Shiva* (the destroyer). Brahma's principal consort is *Sarasvati* (goddess of wisdom and learning); Vishnu's is *Lakshmi* (goddess of fortune); and Shiva's traditional consort is *Parvati* (daughter of the mountain Himalaya).

Although the creator-god figures in many stories in the *puranas,* Brahma is the least important of the three major deities. Unlike Shiva and Vishnu, no devotional movements focusing on Brahma developed. Like other deities, however, Brahma has a special animal (*vahana*) on which the deity rides. In Brahma's case it is the swan. Brahma is depicted as red, with four bearded faces (symbolizing his all-knowing nature) and four arms (many arms symbolize the power of the deity).

Vishnu, whom we have already encountered in the Bhagavad-Gita, is the god of love, compassion, and forgiveness. As revealed in the Bhagavad-Gita, Vishnu comes to earth in many forms (avatars) to help humanity at times of trouble. The *Bhagavata Purana* speaks of nine current incarnations of Vishnu. Besides Krishna in the Bhagavad-Gita, and the god-king Rama, they include several animals, such as a boar who raised the earth at the time of the primordial waters, and creatures such as a man-lion. Notably, *Siddartha Gautama* (the founder of Buddhism) is one of the classic avatars of Vishnu, reflecting the Hindu absorption of Buddhism into its own teachings. The literature also looks toward a tenth avatar, *Kalkin,* who will appear at the end of the present age on a white horse to punish the wicked and reward the righteous.

In addition to his earthly incarnations, Vishnu is the preserver of the entire cosmos. For his devotees, Vishnu is the Supreme Person who transcends, yet is the source of all reality. The coming into existence of the material world is but his *lila* (sport or play), which has no effect on his ultimate nature. As Arjuna learns in the Bhagavad-Gita, everything (including the rest of the gods) will be absorbed into Vishnu at the end of the present age.

The religious movement focusing on devotion to Vishnu is known as *Vaishnavism,* and devotees are called *Vaishnavites.* They express their love for Vishnu and deities associated with Vishnu (most notably Rama and Krishna) in poems and songs, and seek liberation by responding to Vishnu's love for humanity with a life of devotion to their Lord, the one Supreme God.

Shiva is the arguably the most popular of the three major deities of devotional Hinduism. Known principally as "the destroyer," Shiva is the god of death, disease, and destruction. However, he is also the god of regeneration. Given the Indian view of cyclical life, these two functions are not contradictory. Before renewal can take place, there must first be destruction. Therefore, like Vishnu, Shiva takes the role of the Supreme Lord, who rules over the cosmic process.

Shiva's association with reproduction leads to his portrayal in some pictures with a constantly erect penis. Two of the principal symbols associated with Shiva are the *lingam* and *yoni,* stylized representations of the male and female sexual organs, respectively. These symbols are usually found in shrines associated with Shiva.

Among the popular epithets of Shiva are "Lord of Creatures" and "Lord of the Dance." Portrayed as *Nataraja* (Lord of the Dance), Shiva is shown in a dancing pose, maintaining the rhythm of the universe through his exuberance. Yet his face is in calm repose, because he is not affected by or attached to his cosmic dance.

The devotional movement which identifies Shiva as the Supreme Lord is called *Shaivism* and the devotees *Shaivites.*

Under the general term *Devi* (Goddess) worship, movements have sprung up around various goddesses. One of them, *Kali,* is one of the most well-known deities in Hinduism. In the popular pictures of Kali—used, like the portrayals of other deities, as objects of devotion—she is often depicted wearing human skulls around her neck, ripping the flesh of her victims, and drinking blood. Her bloodthirsty habits are legend. One groups of followers of Kali, the *thagi* (from which the English word "thug" is derived), were once a secret society in north and central India. Until the practice was outlawed in British India, they robbed and strangled victims as a way of showing devotion to Kali. As with Shiva, the more horrific side of Kali must be understood in the context of her role in regenerating the cosmos. Without destruction there can be no regeneration.

Sometimes called simply the Great Goddess, Devi is worshiped as a mother who always desires the well-being of her children. Throughout India, Devi temples attract worshippers, who often come to the Goddess with a specific request: that a disease be healed, an examination passed, or a job secured, for example. Women often ask the Goddess for assistance in bearing a male child. Her main forms as a wish-bestower, especially Lakshmi, goddess of wealth, and Sarasvati, goddess of learning, have been particularly important. While some forms of Devi worship are common throughout India, others are regional. For example, Kali, Lakshmi, and Sarasvati are worshipped throughout India. By contrast, temples and festivals for *Draupadi,* heroine of the Mahabharata, are more common in south India, while *Radha,* the beloved of Krishna, is more typically worshipped in the north.

One of the most popular legends from the *puranas* is the story of *Ganesha,* the elephant-headed son of Shiva and Parvati, one of the most beloved deities in the Hindu pantheon. According to many versions of the tale, Ganesha received his elephant head in an unusual way. Not recognizing Ganesha as his son, Shiva beheads him. The enraged Parvati threatens to destroy the universe and all the gods unless her son's head is restored. Shiva sends his attendants to bring the first suitable head they can find. They return with the head of an elephant, and Shiva restores his son with the new head. Ganesha is worshipped in his own right as a god who overcomes obstacles and upholds dharma. Shrines with images of the elephant-headed god can be found throughout India, and are often found in the entryways of Hindu homes. His popularity is increasing in modern India, as persons turn to him to help them adapt to changing times.

For most Hindus today the means of ultimate transformation is devotion (*bhakti*) to a personal god (often called *bhakti-yoga* or *bhakti-marga*), which will be discussed more fully below. The fact that each movement considers its deity supreme is accepted within Hinduism, and has not led to the internecine strife common in other contexts when claims of supremacy are made for different deities.

Within *bhakti* Hinduism we find two complementary orientations. For most Indians, the concerns of family and home take precedence over more refined spiritual concerns, as they do for most of the world's peoples. In India full commitment to spiritual matters is popularly reserved for *sadhus* (holy persons) and those who have taken the vow of *sannyasin* (renunciation of all worldly attachments). The issues of acquiring sufficient food for the family, carrying out daily responsibilities, and dealing with sicknesses and other family problems are the primary concerns of others. Thus, they look to a deity for help in facing mundane matters, and tend to approach *bhakti* from this perspective. Their acts of devotion (*puja*) to a god are for the purpose of seeking divine assistance and comfort in meeting the challenges of daily living and confronting the tragedies of life. Through their devotional service, they may hope to attain a higher birth in a subsequent life.

However, the ultimate goal of devotion to a personal god is liberation (*moksha*) from the cycle of rebirth after one's current life. In this approach, devotees will typically divorce themselves as much as possible from the attachments of daily living, and treat all their activities as an expression of love for the deity. Some will take the vow of a *sannyasin* (either at the fourth stage of life, or earlier), in order to practice the total devotion associated with this expression of *bhakti.*

For many devotional Hindus, as for persons in the devotional traditions of other religions, both motivations are present in their worship of a personal god.

A particular kind of practice found in devotional Hinduism is called *shaktism* (*shakti* means "power, might"). Shakti is the active energy of a god, usually depicted as the feminine aspect (balanced with the passive side, depicted as masculine). In Hindu mythology and iconography, *shakti* is often depicted as a goddess (as in the expression by Shaivities of *shakti* in the person of Kali), and these goddesses are called *shaktis*. Shaktism is the practice of seeking to identify with this active power and draw upon it for material or spiritual pursuits. "Right-handed" shaktism is the more philosophical expression of this belief in the union of the two powers, while "left-handed" shaktism is the more magical and esoteric.

Related to left-handed shaktism is the religious phenomenon known as *tantrism*. It is an unorthodox practice found in Tibetan Buddhism, Jainism, and Sikhism, as well as Hinduism. *Tantra* is the Sanskrit word for "that which extends, spreads." In a broad sense, tantrism is religious practice outside the Vedic tradition, including rituals open to persons not of the Brahmin class. Tantras themselves are manuals of magical words and spells used in this unorthodox practice. Hindu tantrism refers more specifically to the worship of deities for worldly purposes, but also to a mysterious, radical method (involving occult practices) for seeking *moksha*. Tantrics are known for cultivating the more sensual aspects of human nature as a way of seeking spiritual advancement.

Like Jainism and Buddhism, Hindu tantrism began in reaction against the control of religion by Brahmins. Hindu tantrics emphasize the union between the masculine and feminine in divinity. The universe comes into existence through the union of the male god's potency and the *shakti* of the goddess. Rather than the ascetic renunciation of the sensual, as in mainstream Hinduism, tantrism attempts to harness sensual energy for spiritual (or mundane) purposes. The practitioner learns to draw upon the "dormant power" (*kundalini*) within himself or herself, and is then initiated into a "circle" (*cakra*) of other tantrics, equally divided among males and females. The males symbolize Shiva and the females Shakti. In a highly stylized ritual, the worshippers engage in sensual behavior, consuming intoxicants and finally engaging in sexual union. Key to the final step is the retention of semen by the male, demonstrating control over mind, breath, and ejaculation. This symbolizes the experience of cosmic withdrawal into oneness, rather than the creative extension of power, and is is seen as an abbreviated (but risky) path to *moksha*. Needless to say, Hindu tantrism as a spiritual path is a practice reserved for a very few, highly committed (and unorthodox) seekers. Its practice has been in decline in modern Hinduism, though it is still evident. Tantrism is visible to the general population in the erotic art often seen in the form of sculptures on Hindu temples, such as those in the famous complex of temples at Khajuraho in northern India. Tantric literature was compiled between 500 and 1500 C.E.

In addition to the *puranas*, other texts, called *agamas*, arose in the devotional tradition. Their development coincides with growth of temples housing images of the gods, between about 400 and 900 C.E. They are principally ritual texts that regulate the *puja* and other devotional practices associated with the deities in temples and home shrines. The "seeing" (*darshana*) of the god or goddess, as manifest in the image, is often the goal for those who go on pilgrimage to one of the temples.

Philosophical Literature and Movements: The Yoga School and Advaita Vedanta

The other major branch of Hinduism that inspired a number of movements, alongside the devotional, is often called "philosophical," because the ultimate focus is on knowledge of the spiritual, seen to be a state beyond devotion to a personal god. We should note here that in South and East Asian traditions we do not find the distinction between "philosophy" and "religion" found (especially since the Enlightenment) in the West. The knowledge sought in Hindu philosophy is not "objective" knowledge about the world, but a direct, experiential knowledge of the sacred. In this branch, the term *darshana* ("seeing") refers to the various philosophical schools. Although the most popular tradition identifies six philosophical systems within Hinduism, there are in fact a myriad of positions. The divergent schools arose from distinct commentaries on Vedic texts, especially the Upanishads. We will restrict our attention to two of the more prominent systems of thought: the *Yoga* school and *Advaita Vedanta.*

The Yoga School   *Yoga* is probably the one Hindu term known to most persons outside India. However, it is often misunderstood. It is usually thought of only as a form of physical exercise involving difficult postures. In fact, physical (*hatha*) yoga, in which various physical exercises involving various positions are practiced, is but one aspect of the broader phenomenon. In its widest sense in Hinduism, yoga (from the Sanskrit term for "to yoke or join") refers to a variety of methods that seek to join the individual soul to the Ultimate, and thus achieve liberation from rebirth. Thus, *bhakti* yoga is the spiritual path that emphasizes devotion to gods or goddesses, or both. More narrowly, yoga refers to a particular philosophical school developed by the fourth-century C.E. sage Patanjali, who wrote a philosophical treatise on meditation in the form of a commentary on the *Yoga Sutra* (*sutras* are collections of aphorisms). The meditative discipline based on his work became known as *raja yoga* (meaning the "king" or supreme yoga). Its practice involves working through a series of defined stages, including the following:

- *Yamas*—Vows of restraint pledging not to hurt living creatures and chastity
- *Niyama*—Internal control, calmness
- *Asanas*—Bodily postures, including the popular lotus position, to assist concentration and control
- *Pranayama*—Breath control
- *Pratyahara*—Control of senses
- *Dharana*—Extreme concentration on a single object
- *Dhyana*—Withdrawal from all attachments through meditation
- *Samadhi*—Entering into a trance in which oneness with Brahman, and therefore liberation, is experienced

Those engaged in raja yoga sometimes perform remarkable physical feats, such as reclining calmly on a bed of nails or walking on hot coals, demonstrating control over their bodies. Philosophically, the school is "dualistic," emphasizing that the universe has two basic principles—the material (*prakriti*) and the spiritual (*purusha*). Attachment to the material must be overcome through the above steps, so that the *atman* may experience union with *purusha*.

Advaita Vedanta   Another important Hindu philosophical system is *Advaita Vedanta,* one of the three *vedanta* schools (all of which are based on commentaries on the Upanishads). Advaita Vedanta literally means the "nondual or monistic system based on the Upanishads." The other Vedanta schools are *Dvaita* (meaning "dualistic," and therefore recognizing the distinction between material and spiritual reality) and *Vishishtadvaita* (a "qualified nondualism" in which the both the distinction of the material and spiritual and their ultimate unity is expressed).

Advaita Vedanta developed in the ninth century C.E. when a philosopher named Shankara (788–820) wrote a commentary on an earlier work known as the

Vedanta Sutra. The Advaita Vedanta school emphasizes the absolute oneness of *brahman.* All else is illusion (*maya*). To illustrate this point, Shankara used the example of a person seeing a coiled object on the ground and jumping back, thinking it to be a snake. On closer examination he found it to be only a piece of rope. According to Shankara, our minds, overcome with desire, interact with the energy of the truly real to create the illusion that the material world is real, as a person in the desert driven by thirst sees an oasis that is not there. Until we penetrate the veil of illusion, we will assume that the world of diversity we see and experience is the true reality. Shankara spoke of the path to liberation as having two phases. In the first phase, we worship a personal god (for Shankara it was Shiva) in order to bring spiritual reality into focus and to begin our spiritual quest. In the second phase, we move beyond a personal god to the higher experience of Oneness. For Shankara personal gods are nothing more than the supreme oneness (*brahman*) *with* attributes, not to be confused with the impersonal reality or *brahman without* attributes.

This monistic interpretation of Hinduism, in which a personal god is understood as the provisional manifestation of impersonal *brahman,* rather than as the highest spiritual reality (as is the case in the *bhakti* movements), has been popularized in the West by modern Indian intellectuals who hold the *advaitan* position. It is sometimes mistakenly presented *as* Hinduism, rather than as one major branch within the Hindu family.

Hindu Reform Movements and Reformers in the Nineteenth and Twentieth Centuries

Tour *The Sacred World* CD!

Beginning in the eighth century C.E., "Hinduism" had to respond to the religions brought by those who entered South Asia. First it was Islam, a religion with teachings in some cases diametrically opposed to Hindu views. As a result, for over a thousand years Hindus and Muslims have maintained a sometimes violent, usually peaceful, coexistence. The most striking religious effect of the introduction of Islam into India was the development in the fifteenth century C.E. of the new religion of Sikhism, which sought to synthesize the best of the two traditions.

The coming of Christianity to India had a more profound effect on the development of Hinduism in the modern world. This was especially true after the British allowed Christian missionaries to enter India in the nineteenth century. They brought not only the Christian gospel, but also schools and other institutions that introduced Indians to Western values and customs. As a result, movements and teachers arose who sought to blend what they considered the best of Christian and Western views with their own Hindu traditions, or defend Hinduism against the perceived invasion of alien values and customs.

The Brahmo Samaj   The first such Hindu school of reform was the *Brahmo Samaj* (Society of God), founded in Calcutta in 1828 by Ram Mohan Roy (1774–1833), a brahmin who had studied a variety of religions. He became convinced that the truth behind all religions was that there is one personal God. He accepted the ethical teaching and congregational worship of Christianity (but not the divinity of Jesus), and sought to purge all polytheistic and, in his view, superstitious practices and references from Hinduism. His goal was a universal religion and a reform of society based on belief in the one God and the highest ethical principles. He joined with the British in opposing practices such as *sati*, the custom of a widow placing herself on the funeral pyre of her husband to be consumed with him.

The Arya Samaj   In response to reform movements that leaned heavily on Western teachings and sought to move beyond "Hinduism" to a "universal religion," others sought to reform Indian society by returning to Vedic values. One such movement was the *Arya* (from Aryan) *Samaj*, created in 1875 in Bombay by Swami Dayanand Saraswati (1824–1883). In this movement, the word *Arya* means a noble human being—one who is thoughtful and charitable, who thinks good thoughts and does good actions. According to Arya Samaj, the way to become an Arya is to commit oneself to the values and rituals of the Vedic tradition rather than embracing traditions external to India, such as Christianity or Islam.

Ramakrishna   An influential nineteenth century reformer was Sri Ramakrishna (1836–1886). Ramakrishna was a *brahmin* and a priest of the goddess *Kali*. He longed for a mystical experience, and attained union with the divine (*samadhi*) through concentration on an image of Kali, whom he called Mother. He then undertook a twelve-year spiritual journey, during which he had religious experiences following the disciplines of Jainism, Buddhism, Islam, and Christianity. He became convinced that all religions were simply different paths to the same summit.

Ramakrishna's disciple, Vivekananda (1862–1902), became one of the first Hindu missionaries to the West, carrying the philosophy of Advaita Vedanta to the first Parliament of Religions at Chicago in 1893. He spoke of the oneness of all religions, and the experience of the oneness of all reality. In India, the Ramakrishna Order was established among his disciples. They were often highly educated Indians who began schools, hospitals, and other institutions for the betterment of the poor.

Aurobindo Ghose   Sri Aurobindo Ghose (1872–1950) was the son of an Indian physician who had become convinced of the inferiority of Indian culture. Aurobindo's father sent him to European schools, including Cambridge University in England, where he received many academic awards. Ghose had no exposure to the classical texts of India until he returned home to begin an academic career. He taught himself Sanskrit and became enthralled with the spiritual depth of the Hindu classics and the value of Indian culture.

After a period of political activity in support of Indian nationalism, Ghose withdrew to form an *ashram* (spiritual center) in southern India, which continues to attract students from all over the world. He spent the rest of his life practicing and teaching a form of yoga called Integral Yoga. He wrote a number of highly acclaimed works, including a rendition of the epic poem *Savitri*, reflecting his own spiritual odyssey, and the philosophical work *The Divine Mind*, in which he related the spiritual progress of the individual to a cosmic evolution.

Synthesizing his education in Western science with his own spiritual heritage, Ghose spoke of the phases of evolution as life out of matter, mind out of life, and ultimately spirit out of mind. Our purpose as humans, he wrote, is to facilitate this final stage, bringing union to matter, life, mind, and spirit.

Mohandas Gandhi   The last Hindu reformer we will discuss is the best known and historically the most important—Mohandas K. (Mahatma) Gandhi (1869–1948). Educated to be a lawyer in England, the young Gandhi, when he began a legal practice in South Africa, found that he could not shed his Indian heritage. He experienced discrimination against people considered to be inferior, and he committed his life to the liberation of people from such injustices.

Gandhi drew on his own Hindu background, especially the teaching on dharma and nonattached action in the Bhagavad-Gita; the ideals of the Sermon on the Mount of Jesus in the Christian New Testament; and the teaching of *ahimsa* (non-injury to life) from Jainism.

Gandhi returned from Africa to his homeland to lead a nonviolent struggle for independence. He challenged the traditional caste system, especially the degrading treatment of persons known to the British as the "scheduled castes," the "untouchables" who were thought to be so low they were not even a part of the traditional fourfold class division. Gandhi called the "untouchables" *harijan* (children of God), and was influential in the adoption of a constitution that prohibited discrimination on the basis of caste.

Some orthodox Hindus viewed Gandhi as a heretic because of his reform of caste and his willingness to cooperate with Muslims. Gandhi was assassinated by an orthodox Hindu, but his influence continued. The American civil rights leader of the 1960s, Dr. Martin Luther King, Jr., cited Gandhi's nonviolent teachings as an inspiration in his campaign to win justice for Black Americans.

Independent India

The modern state of India is a secular nation, the largest democracy in the world. In its 1948 constitution, India adopted the Western ideals of freedom of religion and equal protection under the law. Special efforts were instituted to redress past injustices by reserving jobs and scholarships for lower caste persons, especially members of the "scheduled castes" and "scheduled tribes" (the indigenous people of India, often called *adivasis* ["first dwellers"]). As the twentieth century ended, these efforts were bringing cries of "reverse discrimination" from persons in the higher castes, who claimed that they were losing losing opportunities they had earned, because of efforts to help the lower castes.

Despite a political commitment to human rights, the traditional Hindu teaching of karma makes it very difficult to overcome the inherent inequalities and injustices of the caste system. This has caused some Indian intellectuals to renounce Hinduism altogether, claiming that it is incompatible with the development of a modern, secular society. On the other end of the spectrum, Hindu extremists have decried the excesses and social instability brought on by the adoption of Western ideals. They call for a return to a society strictly based on the values of the Vedic tradition, such as those expressed in the Laws of Manu. In the middle are those who seek to maintain the best of Hindu spirituality, integrating these values with the respect for individual freedoms introduced by Westerners. (We will return to these issues when we discuss Hinduism in the twenty-first century.)

In the last century, numerous Hindu teachers have come to the United States. Some have begun movements that continue today as expressions of the Hindu tradition in North America. The well-known International Society for Krishna Consciousness (better known as the "Hare Krishnas") will be discussed in Chapter Fourteen: New Religions.

THE HINDU WORLDVIEW

Why are there so many gods in Hinduism? Is one god better than the others? Why do Hindus worship cows? Why do Hindus believe that after they die they will be reborn in another life? What controls the kind of birth they will experience? Why is

Hindu society divided into "castes"? Is the caste system as restrictive now as it once was? These are the questions often raised about Hinduism. We have touched on some of them already. In this section we will confront the others as we summarize the worldview of Hinduism as it is practiced today.

Humanity: An Eternal Soul (*Atman*)

According to Hindu teaching first expressed in the Upanishads, our true nature is the eternal, unchanging soul (*atman*). The *Chandogaya Upanishad* (3.14) describes the *atman* as smaller than a grain of rice yet larger than all the worlds. In other words, it is not defined by space (or by time). It is separate from the material, changing karmic self, or *jiva,* and is eternal.

Problem: Trapped by *Karma*

The *atman* is trapped in a cycle of rebirth (*samsara*) because of the law of karma. The law of karma stipulates that we are inevitably determined in our future actions by the effects of our past actions. Until the inexorable enchainment of karma is broken, the *atman*'s journey through unending rounds of rebirth will continue. The level of existence of the *atman* is controlled by the actions of prior lives. Each action tends toward a particular effect, and that effect will be realized, whether in the current life or another. For example, a person whose actions are slovenly may cause the *atman* to experience rebirth as a sloth.

Cause: Desire and Ignorance

The entrapment of the *atman* by karma is a result of desire causing us to act with attachment and *avidya* (ignorance) of our true nature. The Hindu understanding of "ignorance" is different from the ordinary meaning of the concept in the West. *Avidya* is not a lack of knowledge; it is spiritual confusion about our true human nature and the true nature of all reality. It is delusion, believing that the changing world in which we live day to day is the only reality.

Hinduism teaches that, because of our ignorance, we inevitably assume that the material world is the only reality, and we become attached to that world. We seek ultimate fulfillment in the activities of the material world—such as relations with other persons, work, leisure activities, eating—unaware that attachment to these is entrapping us. We assume that the "self" that acts is the only self, and we fail to realize that beneath this changing, acting "self" is the eternal *atman.* Therefore, for Hinduism as for other religions that share the common South Asian worldview, at the heart of the issue is desire that causes us to act and that leaves us deluded about that which should be our principal concern—spiritual liberation.

End: Liberation (*Moksha*) from the Cycle of Rebirth

According to classical Hinduism, life has four aims. They are *dharma* (right conduct); *artha* (material gain); *kama* (pleasure, mainly thought of in sexual terms); and finally *moksha* (liberation from the cycle of rebirth). This clearly shows that Hinduism is not the world-denying religion some have accused it of being. With these four aims, Hinduism recognizes that there is a time and a place for pursuing material gain and enjoying sexual pleasure, in so far as both are within the context of right conduct. There is even a well-known handbook, the *Kama Sutra,* to guide couples in the pursuit of sexual pleasure. Within classical formulation, the proper context to pursue material wealth and sexual pleasure is at the "householder" stage, when a person is married and fulfilling familial responsibilities. However, there is a higher goal in life, the fourth aim, *moksha,* the culmination of life. It may be realized within this life; it is *not* merely a state of existence after death.

The branches of Hinduism share *moksha* as the ultimate goal. However, they differ on the nature of the liberated state. The *bhakti* movements speak of the communion of the *atman* with a personal deity in an eternal state of "enjoyment or bliss." The philosophical schools tend toward a more impersonal view. They typically emphasize that *moksha* is beyond description. All that we can say is that once the *atman* experiences liberation, there is no more rebirth, only a state of complete and total release. The monistic school (Advaita Vedanta) speaks of *moksha* as a coming to awareness of the identity of the *atman* with the cosmic oneness (*brahman*), a state of absorption often called *samadhi.*

Means: The Paths of Action, Devotion, and Knowledge

 Tour *The Sacred World* CD!

The most common way of designating the different paths to liberation within Hinduism is to speak of *karma yoga* (the way of action), *bhakti yoga* (the way of devotion), and *jnana yoga* (the way of knowledge). Sometimes the term *marga* (which literally means "path") is used instead of *yoga.* Although a variety of other yoga (referring to the process of joining or yoking the *atman* with the spiritual source) are found in Hinduism, these three are the most widely recognized.

Karma Yoga: The Path of Action   Karma yoga is the path followed by most Hindus, although it is often combined with others. It simply means living in accord with dharma (duty, determined principally in Hinduism by gender, caste, and stage of life). For traditionalists, the Laws of Manu set forth the basic guidelines for living. They include the rituals one must perform, the occupations one may enter, and the ways one should interact with others. The Bhagavad-Gita added the notion of carrying out one's caste dharma with an attitude of detachment, and treating all of one's actions as sacrifices to the Supreme Lord. Karma yoga has the virtue of simplicity and accessibility. Traditionalists believe that by karma yoga, lower-caste individuals can only improve their rank in the next life, while others believe karma yoga opens the door to *moksha* for any, regardless of caste and gender.

Bhakti Yoga: The Path of Devotion   *Bhakti* yoga is the path of devotion to a personal deity. Rooted in the Vedic practice of sacrifice to various gods, it came into prominence with the Bhagavad-Gita, and increased in popularity with the emergence of Shiva and Vishnu as the principal deities in the Hindu pantheon. Hindus are remarkably tolerant of peoples' right to choose different deities as the object of their devotion. One common way of explaining the diversity of gods is to recognize them as manifestations of the one Supreme Lord, who gladly accepts being worshipped by a variety of names and forms. This tolerance is extended beyond the Hindu names for gods to the ways of knowing the divine in other religions. Nevertheless, different *bhakti* movements recognize their particular God (Shiva, Vishnu, Kali, or Krishna, for example) as ultimate. For philosophical schools, which speak of an ultimacy which goes beyond personal identity, this path is often considered a preliminary to the highest form of spiritual attainment, knowledge.

RITUALS AND FESTIVALS   Hinduism does not set aside one day of the week for worshipping the gods. Expressions of devotion (*puja*) are to be a part of one's daily routine. However, each deity has temples, to which the faithful make pilgrimage as a way of showing devotion, and special days during the year set aside for festivals. One of the most famous is the Jagannatha Temple at Puri, which houses an image of Vishnu. Once a year the image is taken from the temple and moved by a special vehicle (called a "juggernaut"). However, literally thousands of other temples and shrines dot the Indian landscape. The highlight of a visit is the experience of *darshan,* when the worshipper spiritually sees and is seen by the deity, through the image of the god or goddess.

The annual Hindu ritual calendar includes the following festivals in which the deities are worshipped in special ways:

- *Holi*—This spring festival commemorates a myth in which the son of a demon king is spared from a fire because, to the dismay of his father, the son has taken refuge in Lord Vishnu. During the festival, people throw colorful paints on one another and men sing raucously after consuming a special beverage, breaking down social distinctions. Bonfires enact the consuming fire of the story. Holi marks the burning away of self-conceit, selfishness, greed, lust, and hatred—in fact, of all undesirable tendencies, propensities, thoughts, and behaviors.

- *Mahasivaratri*—During this solemn ritual, worshippers follow the example of Lord Shiva and engage in fasting and other austerities.

- *Rama Navami*—This spring festival marks the birth of Lord Rama, one of the incarnations of Vishnu. The day has become particularly important in the Hindu nationalist movement, for whom the time of Rama's rule is heralded as the ideal Hindu society, and for whom his birthplace (at the northern city of Ayodhya) is Hindu India's sacred center.

- *Ganesh Chaturthi*—Lord Ganesh, the remover of obstacles, is honored in this summer festival. It includes the carrying of large images of Ganesha into the sea or other body of water.

- *Navarathri*—This autumn festival focuses on Durga, the Goddess who defeats evil and regenerates life.

- *Deepavali (Diwali)*—This autumn festival of lights, in which fireworks are common, honors Lakshmi, the goddess of wealth.

SACRED RIVERS   The most popular pilgrimage spots for all Hindus are found along the banks of the River Ganges, and other holy rivers such as the Narmada. Known as Mother Ganges, the river (first among the seven holy rivers of India) is thought to be a goddess herself, related mythologically to both Shiva and Vishnu. To bathe in the life-giving and purifying waters of Mother Ganges is a source of inestimable joy for virtually all Hindus. To be cremated along her banks and have one's ashes deposited in her waters is the hope of pious Hindus. Of the many sacred cities along the Ganges, the most prominent is Benares (today known as Varanasi or simply Kasi) in north-central India.

COW VENERATION   One of the more controversial forms of worship in Hinduism is veneration of the cow. With so much hunger in India, why does the government not encourage the eating of the cows that wander through villages, towns, even cities? At certain times of the year in some locations, cows are venerated as deities, with garlands of flowers placed on their necks.

A cow and autorickshaw on a street in Bangalore, center of India's computer industry. The cow, revered by Hindus as the sustainer of life, is typically given the right-of-way even in urban areas in India.

According to even as enlightened a leader as Mahatma Gandhi, "cow protection" is at the core of Hinduism. Why? The reasons are both symbolic and practical. For Gandhi, the cow represented all nonhuman life. Respect for her instills awareness that we humans are dependent on the nonhuman world for our very existence. Veneration of the cow also fosters, Gandhi believed, an attitude of giving freely to others. She is indeed a Mother of all humanity, to be honored, not slaughtered and eaten. Her protection is deeply rooted in the spiritual tradition of India, where she is associated with the mother goddess.

More practically, the cow *is* critical to survival for many Indians. For example, her dung is an essential fuel, a disinfectant, and an ingredient in mortar for building. Supporters of cow protection point out that to kill a cow would provide a few meals; to allow her to roam, with her products of milk, butter, and dung accessible to even the poorest, has enabled countless Indians to avoid starvation and homelessness.

Jnana Yoga: The Path of Knowledge   *Jnana* yoga (the way of knowledge) is the path of meditation that leads ultimately to an intuitive experience of the ultimate, usually spoken of as *brahman*. Through a process of moral, physical, mental, and spiritual discipline, the seeker slowly and patiently reaches a point of final preparation. Then, in a single moment of blinding enlightenment, the goal is reached, and the door beyond rebirth opens into an indescribable state of union with the ultimate. After the experience, one continues living in a blissful state in this world, until the effects of past actions are worked through. Then, upon death, the *atman* is liberated, and there is no more rebirth.

Serious students of *bhakti* and *jnana* yoga believe that meaningful advancement requires placing oneself under the guidance of a spiritual teacher, usually called a *guru*. To be a guru, one must demonstrate exceptional spiritual awareness and an ability to lead others toward the same end. The devotion shown to gurus, through prostration in the presence of the guru or offerings of gifts, is part of the process of gaining spiritual merit. Unfortunately, some unscrupulous religious leaders have played upon the practice of having a guru to manipulate and extort naive followers. Since there is no central authority to exercise discipline in Hinduism, it is very difficult to control such excesses.

Reality: Penetrating the Veil of Maya

The most common term associated with the Hindu understanding of the material world is *maya* (illusion). The various branches of Hinduism share the belief that the material world obscures the spiritual. Because of our ignorance, we fail to see that we must penetrate through this "veil" to the unchanging spiritual reality. Where they differ is whether the world of *maya* is real in some sense, or actually "unreal." Some schools says that *maya* results from the creative energy of the Supreme Lord (a personal god) through which God brings the material world into existence. *Maya* is real, but should not be confused with God's higher, eternal nature. Other schools believe that *maya* results from human ignorance; when we "wake up" we will discover that there is but one true Reality, and that all else has only a temporary, provisional existence. A variety of other views can be found among other schools.

Despite these rather technical philosophical differences, Hinduism in general teaches that the material world comes into existence and is dissolved in a cosmic process of rebirth.

Sacred: Many Gods and Beyond the Gods

Tour *The Sacred World* CD!

Readers who have studied the whole section on Hinduism are now well aware that the Hindu conception of the sacred is complex. Within Hinduism we find all types of theism as well as monism, dualism, and more. The clearest division in the Hindu understanding of the spiritual is between those who speak of the highest reality as beyond all distinctions and therefore impersonal (*brahman*), and those who steadfastly hold to an understanding of the supreme as personal. Unfortunately, some of the most popular interpreters of Hinduism misrepresent the breadth of Hindu teaching by presenting the impersonalist view as "Hinduism." In describing Hinduism phenomenologically we must simply acknowledge and respect the fundamental divergence between "personalists" and "impersonalists."

HINDUISM IN THE TWENTY-FIRST CENTURY

Hinduism as a Global Religion

Although the vast majority of Hindus reside in India, Hinduism in the twenty-first century is truly a global religion. The spread of Hinduism beyond South Asia began long ago, as Hindu traders and farmers established themselves in Africa and Southeast Asia. Today there are large and growing Hindu communities in Europe, Canada, and the United States; indeed, throughout the world. New Hindu temples are springing up in communities large and small.

Increasingly, the global Hindu community is interconnected. Here is but one example, known to Hindus as the "Ganesha Milk Miracle." On September 21, 1995, a New Delhi man dreamed that Lord Ganesha, the elephant-headed God of Wisdom, was thirsty for milk. The next morning the man rushed to a nearby temple where he offered a spoonful of milk to a stone image of Lord Ganesha. The milk disappeared, consumed (according to the worshipper) by the deity. Within hours, word that Ganesha was accepting milk offerings spread throughout India, and millions of people flocked to the nation's temples. Soon, with Hindus in India contacting family members in other countries through phone calls and e-mail messages, images of Ganesha in Hindu temples around the world were accepting milk offerings. According to many observers, the "Ganesha Milk Miracle" sparked a global resurgence of Hindu devotion.

Hindu Nationalism in India

Another turning point for Hinduism and India, which will continue to have influence in the twenty-first century, occurred on December 6, 1992, when a mob of 300,000 Hindus tore down a sixteenth-century Muslim mosque, called the Babri Masjid, located in Ayodhya. The incident at Ayodhya was the culmination of a well-orchestrated plan by Hindu nationalist leaders, who were exploiting a growing rejection of the secularism that had dominated India since Independence in 1948, and an anger at perceived special treatment for minorities, especially Muslims. The Babri Masjid was the symbolic center for Hindu hostility, since it was thought to have been built on the site of a destroyed Hindu temple that marked the birthplace of Lord Ram, the god-king Rama. In a wave of violence across India after the destruction of the Ayodhya mosque, several thousand Muslims and Hindus were killed.

A coalition of traditionalist Hindu organizations, united by their commitment to the *Hindutva* ("Hindu-ness") of India, came together in support of the destruction of the Muslim mosque and rebuilding of a Temple dedicated to Lord Ram at Ayodhya. They included the *Visha Hindu Parishad* (VHP), a cultural movement; the *Rashtriya Swayamsevak Sangh* (RSS), a paramilitary group; and the *Bharatiya Janata Party* (BJP), a political party. By 1998 the BJP had ridden the fervor over Ayodhya, and the growing commitment to Hindu nationalism among Hindus, to national victory. As the twenty-first century began, the BJP dominated a coalition government, led by Prime Minister Atal Bihari Vajpayee.

The opponents of the BJP have warned that its program of Hindu nationalism is a veiled form of intolerant "fundamentalism," which will destroy the fragile Indian democracy, and the religious pluralism that the founders of modern India (e.g., Gandhi and Nehru) championed. In response, the BJP leaders claim that its program for India includes respect for all faiths. At the same time, it calls for recognition that India is united by a three-thousand-year-old Hindu culture. Pride in that culture (claims the BJP, and the other groups within the Hindu nationalist movement) is not incompatible with an Indian democracy with a "civilized, humane, and just civil order," in which there is no discrimination based on caste, religion, class, color, race, or sex. Despite its support for a rebuilt Hindu temple at Ayodhya, the BJP has so far restrained its supporters, and full reconstruction of the Ayodhya temple has not occurred.

Sporadic violence between Muslims and Hindus continues. On February 27, 2002, Hindu zealots on their way home from a mission to rebuild the Ram temple in Ayodhya taunted Muslim vendors on a rail platform. The train was set ablaze, killing fifty-eight Hindus. In subsequent days, more than six hundred Muslims were killed. It is important to emphasize that despite the violence, the vast majority of Hindus and Muslims in India continue to live side by side in peace, as they have for centuries.

Other important movements, which will continue to be very important in the twenty-first century, are those committed to the liberation of untouchables (called today *dalits*, "the oppressed") from their social and political oppression, those focused on improving the status of women in India, and others with an environmental orientation.

Chapter Summary

In this chapter we first oriented ourselves to the land, people, and history of South and Southeast Asia, an area in which more than 30 percent of the people of the world live. We then briefly surveyed the long and rich history of India, as background for our study of the religions that originated in South Asia and spread to Southeast Asia and beyond (Hinduism, Theravada Buddhism, Jainism, and Sikhism).

Before turning to the religions of South and Southeast Asia, we established a framework for understanding, by outlining the traditional worldview shared by these religions: the law of action (*karma*), the problem of attachment caused by desire and ignorance, the cycle of rebirth (*samsara*), the quest for liberation from the cycle of rebirth (*moksha*), and the fulfillment of "duty" (*dharma*).

Hinduism is more a family of religions than a single religion. Our survey of the stages of development and sacred texts of Hinduism included discussion of the religion of the Indus Valley Civilization (which preceded the emergence of "Hinduism"); the classical Hindu texts—the Vedas (focusing on the Rig-Veda and the Upanishads); the formation of traditional Hindu society as reflected in the Laws of Manu; the great epics of India, the Ramayana and Mahabharata, focusing on the section of the latter known as the Bhagavad-Gita, arguably the most important text in Hinduism; devotional movements and the deities associated with them (especially Vishnu, Shiva, *and* Devi [the Goddess]), and philosophical movements, emphasizing the Yoga School and Advaita Vedanta. We then examined the role of nineteenth and twentieth century Hindu reformers.

In our discussion of the distinctive Hindu worldview we utilized our framework to describe the view of human nature as the eternal *atman* (eternal soul) separate from the karmic nature (*jiva*), the basic problem as the eternal soul (*atman*) trapped in the cycle of rebirth (*samsara*), the cause of this problem as desire and ignorance (*avidya*) resulting in attachment, the view of material reality (*maya*), the goal of liberation (*moksha*) from the cycle of rebirth, the means to this goal (the various types of yoga), and the sacred (encompassing various forms of theism and monism). In discussing the Hindu worldview, we responded to frequently asked questions about Hinduism, such as, What is the caste system and is it still present in modern India? and Why are cows worshiped in Hinduism?

We concluded the chapter by examining Hinduism in the twenty-first century. We focused on Hinduism as a global religion and the growing Hindu nationalist movement in India.

Important Terms and Phrases

Advaita Vedanta, *ahimsa*, Aryans, *atman*, avatar, *avidya*, Bhagavad-Gita, *bhakti*, *bhakti-yoga*, Brahma, *brahman*, Brahmin, caste, dharma, *devi*, guru, Indus Valley Civilization, *jiva*, karma, *karma-yoga*, *jnana-yoga*, Kali, Krishna, *maya*, *moksha*, *samsara*, *shakti*, Shiva, tantrism, Untouchables, Upanishad, Veda, Vishnu, yoga

QUESTIONS FOR DISCUSSION AND REFLECTION

1. Based on your experiences, do you agree that there is a "law of karma" that explains the course your life takes?

2. Do you feel that you (or others you know) are trapped by attachment to the material world caused by desire (craving)? Do you agree that attachment to "things" causes ignorance of the spiritual dimension of life?

3. Can you think of any beneficial aspects of the traditional Hindu class/caste system? Why has reforming the system proven so difficult in India, especially in rural areas?

4. When Robert Oppenheimer, one of the creators of the atomic bomb, saw his creation explode in the New Mexico desert, he uttered a verse from the Bhagavad-Gita: "Time I am, the great destroyer of the worlds, and I have come here to destroy all people. . . ." What might he have intended by quoting this verse?

5. Do you agree with Krishna in the Bhagavad-Gita that performing actions without attachment to the results is necessary in order to attain true self knowledge?

6. What did you think of "cow worship" before reading this chapter? Has your perspective changed after reading the discussion of cow veneration?

7. The American writer Mark Twain said that although we in the West may consider the people of India poor and ourselves rich because of our material prosperity, in matters of the spirit we are the paupers and they are the millionaires. What are your reactions to Mark Twain's observation?

SOURCES AND SUGGESTIONS FOR FURTHER STUDY

BORMAN, WILLIAM, 1986. *Gandhi and Non-violence.* Albany: State University of New York.

ECK, DIANA L., 1996. *Darshan: Seeing the Divine Image in India.* 2nd rev. ed. New York: Columbia University.

HAWLEY, JOHN S. AND DONNA MARIE WULFF, EDS., 1986. *The Divine Consort: Radha and the Goddesses of India.* Boston: Beacon.

JAFFERELOT, CHRISTOPHER, 1996. *The Hindu Nationalist Movement in India.* New York: Columbia University.

KINSLEY, DAVID, 1993. *Hinduism: A Cultural Perspective.* 2nd ed. Englewood Cliffs, NJ: Prentice-Hall.

LARSON, GERALD JAMES, 1997. *India's Agony Over Religion.* Delhi: Oxford University.

MAHONY, WILLIAM, 1998. *The Artful Universe: An Introduction to the Vedic Religious Imagination.* Albany: State University of New York.

MILLER, BARBARA STOLER, TRANS. 1986. *The Bhagavad Gita: Krishna's Counsel in Time of War.* New York: Bantam.

MITCHELL, STEPHEN, TRANS., 2000. *Bhagavad Gita: A New Translation.* New York: Three Rivers.

O'FLAHERTY, WENDY, 1973. *Shiva: The Erotic Ascetic.* New York: Oxford University.

O'FLAHERTY, WENDY, 1980. *Karma and Rebirth in Classical Indian Traditions.* Berkeley: University of California.

O'FLAHERTY, WENDY, 1981. *The Rig Veda: An Anthology.* London: Penguin.

PRABHUPADA, A. C. BHAKTIVEDANTA SWAMI, TRANS., 1983. *Bhagavad-Gita As It Is*. Los Angeles: The Bhaktivedanta Book Trust.

Web Sites

hinduismtoday.com
> (a newsmagazine featuring articles on Indian spirituality)

www.hindunet.org
> (links to various Hindu sites; reflects a Hindu traditionalist perspective)

hinduwebsite.com
> (featuring links to other sites dealing with Hinduism)

www.asia.si.edu/devi/
> (on the Goddesss [Devi], from an exhibit at the U.S. National Museum of Asian Art at the Smithsonian Institution)

 Refer to Pearson/Prentice Hall's **TIME Special Edition: World Religions** magazine for these and other current articles on topics related to many of the world's religions:

➥ *The Religious Experience: Mohandas Gandhi*
➥ *The Impact of Religion: In the Heart of Hate*

 Prentice Hall's **Research Navigator** helps students in their further study of the world's religions. Visit *http://www.researchnavigator.com* for help on the research process and access to databases full of relevant material, including the New York *Times*.

CHAPTER

4

Theravada Buddhism—
The Middle Way

INTRODUCTION

As with Hinduism, the name "Buddhism" is a somewhat misleading attempt to organize an array of diverse religious traditions. Like "Hindus," "Buddhists" call themselves followers of the *dharma* (or *dhamma* in the Pali language). However, the Buddhist understanding is quite different from Hindu teaching, and disagreements among followers of the Buddha about the meaning of *dhamma* are found.

Buddhism began in India in the sixth century B.C.E., and its early development occurred in South Asia. However, as we shall see, it faded as a separate religion in India (although it has been revived in India in recent decades), and survived principally because it spread from India and took root in other cultures of Southeast and East Asia. Today, Buddhism is a global religion.

As it evolved, Buddhism divided into two branches, often called the two "vehicles." In this chapter we will study the first phase of Buddhism, tracing its origin and early development and discussing the texts and teachings of *Theravada*—a representative school of the earliest of the two major branches of Buddhism, which flourishes today in the island nation of Sri Lanka and several countries of Southeast Asia. This branch of Buddhism is also called *Hinayana* ("the small vehicle"). In Chapter Eight we will study the other segment of Buddhism, called *Mahayana* ("the large vehicle"), which thrives in a variety of separate movements in East Asia.

STAGES OF DEVELOPMENT AND SACRED TEXTS

Founder: Siddartha Gautama

Tour *The Sacred World* CD!

"Buddhism" had a single founder, a remarkable teacher who discovered and shared with others a path to liberation from the cycle of rebirth that is appropriately called "the middle way." Whatever their differences, all "Buddhists" join in honoring this man. Buddhists may differ dramatically on their understanding of the nature of the founder's teachings and the significance of his life, but a principal factor that distinguishes them from other religions is their focus on this man.

Gautama was his family name; his parents called him Siddartha. He was born in about 563 B.C.E., a member of the warrior caste (*kshatriya*), not far from the holy city of Varanasi (Benares) in northern India. We have little information about his life that historians would accept as certain beyond a doubt; legends fill the void. What follows is the religious biography his followers wrote.

Siddartha's wealthy father, a chieftain of the Sakya clan, desperately wanted him to become the emperor of India. According to one tradition, a soothsayer told his father that Siddartha was fated to become either a great political leader or a homeless monk. To ensure the former, his father raised Siddartha in luxury, protecting him from the unpleasantness of life that might raise religious questions in his mind. Siddartha married a lovely princess and she gave birth to a son. At the instructions of Siddartha's father, servants carefully screened the poor, sick, and dying from his sight.

Despite all the affluence, Gautama began to feel an inner longing, an emptiness he could not fill with wine and song or even the pleasures of family life. He began to venture out alone, without his "advance party." As his chariot journeyed through an "unsanitized" area, Siddartha experienced what Buddhist tradition calls "the four passing sights." The first was a sorrowful old man. The second was a man racked by illness. The third was a dead man being carried on a funeral pyre. For the first time in his life Siddartha had seen that life is not all pleasure and joy, but includes misery, suffering, and death. And he realized that he too was destined to grow old, become ill, and die. His despair continued to deepen until one day he saw the "fourth sight," a monk, calmly walking alone in a yellow robe.

One night Siddartha crept out of his palace, leaving behind his wife and son. This turning point in the Buddha's life is called "the great renunciation." He shaved his head, clothed himself in the robes of a monk and set off to discover the way to escape the inevitable suffering of material existence. Thus began a six year quest. He started out with an open mind about the teaching of the Hindu *brahmins*. First, he tried and mastered a meditative approach such as that implied in the Upanishads, but to no avail. Then he tried rigid asceticism, similar to the teaching of the Jains (see Chapter Five). For five years he denied himself, to the point that his diet consisted of a single grain of rice a day. Five other ascetics joined him, only to watch as he fainted dead away beside a stream. When he revived, Siddartha determined that self-denial would not lead to spiritual fulfillment. He accepted a meal and vowed not to deny himself to such an extreme. This left him in a quandary; neither of the commonly accepted paths to spiritual awareness had succeeded.

Not far from a place in northeastern India now known as Bodh Gaya, Siddartha sat down under a fig tree (known to Buddhist tradition as the *bodhi* or enlightenment tree). He told himself he would not arise until he reached a state of spiritual enlightenment. According to Buddhist legend, as he sat, *Mara*, the god of desire and death, appeared to him and tempted him to turn back to his old life of pleasure. However, Siddartha remained firm in his quest. He pointed to the earth with his right hand, as if to call upon the earth to be his witness. At that moment, now aware that it was desire that had kept him entrapped, he suddenly "awakened" to a new life beyond its grip. He was now a *Buddha*, one who had "woken up." He was enlightened. The state of desirelessness he now entered was *nirvana*.

Siddartha Gautama, Buddha, now faced another momentous decision. Should he tell others the new way of ordering life (*dhamma*) he had discovered, or should he keep it to himself, allow his existing *karma* (*kamma* in Pali) to dissipate, so that he could enter into the state beyond rebirth (*parinirvana*)? His fateful choice was to communicate his teaching to others, so that they too could follow the path to awakening. His first students were the five ascetics, who had left him disgustedly when they saw him accept refreshment after he had fainted. In a place called the Deer Park, he proclaimed to them his teaching. That first public proclamation of *dhamma* is now known as the "Deer Park Sermon." The Buddha spoke to his former colleagues of a "middle way" between the two extremes of his own life—self-denial and self-indulgence. This path, he said, had led him to the truth, and if they followed it, they too would be enlightened. What he told his fellow seekers has become known as the "Four Noble Truths." They form the core of Buddhist teaching.

- The first of the four noble truths is that life is suffering, a state of existence none of us can avoid experiencing no matter how hard we try.
- The second truth is that the cause of this suffering is desire, a desire that leads us to attachment to the illusion that there is something permanent and unchanging in life.
- The third truth is that we are not trapped; there is release from the suffering of life.
- The fourth of the noble truths is that the way to find release is to follow the Eightfold Path.

We will have more to say about each of the Four Noble Truths, and the Middle Way that the Buddha taught, when we summarize the distinctive worldview of early Buddhism.

The five ascetics were convinced by the Buddha's sermon. They resolved to follow his example, and thus became the first members of the *sangha,* the Buddhist order of monks. According to Buddhist tradition, this exchange set in motion the "Wheel of the Law" (the *dhamma/dharma chakra*), which continues wherever the teaching of the Buddha is put into practice.

For forty-five more years the Buddha preached the truth of the Middle Way. At the age of eighty he died quietly near Varanasi. According to Buddhist tradition, when he lay down he entered the state beyond the cycle of *samsara* called *parinirvana.* He would not be reborn again. His last words to his disciples were, "Work out your own salvation with diligence."

Formation of the Order of Buddhist Monks and Nuns (Sangha)

Tour *The Sacred World* CD!

Those who joined the early *sangha* (literally, "community" or "assembly") came from all the social classes of India. Two of the early leaders were a *brahmin,* Sariputta, and a *kshatriya,* Buddha's cousin Ananda. As the *sangha* grew, there was a need for rules of behavior. The "Three Refuges or Jewels" developed as the basic vows of an initiate into the *sangha:* I take refuge in the Buddha; I take refuge in the *dhamma;* I take refuge in the *sangha.* The new monk was pledging to follow the example set by the Buddha, to live a life guided by the teaching of the "middle way," and to accept the discipline of the order. The monks who took these vows followed the Buddha's example of wandering and preaching during the dry season, and remaining together during the rainy monsoon season, July through October.

At first, after the Buddha's death, the form of government in the *sangha* was democratic, with the assembly coming to consensus on matters of common concern.

A diorama of Siddartha Gautama teaching the Four Noble Truths of Buddhism to his first four disciples at the Deer Park in Sarnath, India, near Varanasi (Benares) on the Ganges River.

However, as the movement grew, a hierarchical ranking developed, perhaps inevitably. Permanent monasteries sprang up, and the once-unified *sangha* divided into separate orders with different leaders. These monasteries became important centers of secular as well as religious power in India.

Although only men joined the *sangha* at first, a number of women requested initiation. After much thought, the Buddha approved allowing women to become nuns, with the same ability to pursue the path leading to liberation as monks.

For both monks and nuns, the basic rules of monastic life came to be known as the "Ten Precepts." Simply stated, they are:

- Refrain from taking life (*ahimsa*).
- Do not take what is not given.
- Practice chastity.
- Do not lie or deceive.
- Do not take intoxicants.
- Consume food in moderation, and never after noon.
- Do not gaze upon spectacles such as dancing and singing.
- Do not ornament your body.
- Do not recline on high or wide beds.
- Do not accept gold or silver.

The first five rules also applied to the followers of Buddha who could not leave their ordinary lives to become monks or nuns. These lay devotees could also gain merit by showing kindness to the monks, offering them food when they came along with their begging bowls and listening attentively to their teaching.

The Spread of Buddhism Beyond India

A decisive turning point in the history of Buddhism occurred when the powerful King *Ashoka* of the Mauryan Empire renounced the violence that had made him a successful conqueror, and accepted the truth of the Buddha's teachings. Ashoka became the monarch of much of northern India in about 270 B.C.E. and ruled for thirty-five years. During his reign he instructed his subjects to observe the Buddha's teachings and sent missionaries abroad to carry the Buddha's message as far as Egypt and Greece. Ashoka's life, and his conversion from violence to the nonviolent message of Buddhism, was the subject of a popular movie produced in India in 2001.

The process of expansion of Buddhist teaching beyond India actually began when Ashoka's emissaries to Sri Lanka, the island nation south of India, succeeded in establishing shrines and monasteries. Sri Lanka remains today one of the centers of preservation of the earliest forms of Buddhism.

Later, Buddhist missionaries spread throughout the countries of Southeast Asia—Myanmar (Burma), Thailand, Kampuchea (Cambodia), Laos, Malaysia, and Vietnam—beginning in the third century C.E. It took centuries for Buddhism to become the dominant religion in all these countries, but for the past six or seven hundred years all of them except Vietnam and Malaysia have been largely under the spell of the more conservative branch of Buddhism.

The Pali Canon

The major sacred texts in the early phase of Buddhist history are known collectively as the *Pali Canon.* The term Pali comes from the language of the texts, which Theravada Buddhists claim was the spoken language of the Buddha. Composition of the texts in Pali is a symbol of the rejection of the authority of the Sanskrit Vedic literature.

The Canon is also called the *Tripitaka* ("three baskets"): *Vinaya Pitaka* ("the basket of disciplinary regulations"), *Sutta Pitaka* ("the basket of discourses"), and *Abidhamma Pitaka* ("the basket of higher philosophy"). The thirty-one separate texts in the Pali canon originated during the first five hundred years after the death of Buddha, first as oral traditions before they were written down. The first basket included guidelines for all aspects of the life of a Buddhist monk. The second basket contained the basic teachings of Buddha; whether they accurately represent the actual words of Buddha is a matter of dispute. One of the most important texts in the Theravada tradition comes from this basket. It is known as the *Dhammapada,* sayings on morality. The third basket focuses on an analysis of the nature of existence as it is understood in Theravada teaching.

As is customary with sacred texts, commentaries arose on the Pali Canon, and some of them became important Theravada documents. According to tradition, a Buddhist teacher named Buddhaghosa from Sri Lanka complied the commentaries into a collection known as the "Way of Purification." He also turned the isolated incidents about Buddha found in the *Tripitaka* into the story of Buddha's life we have told above.

The Two Major Branches of Buddhism

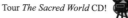

Tour *The Sacred World* CD!

The Conservative Branch: The Theravada School The form of Buddhism that King Ashoka adopted, and which began to spread to Sri Lanka and beyond, has become known as Theravada (literally, "the way of the elders"), although that is somewhat anachronistic. To be precise, Theravada was actually one of a number of schools that emerged out of a complex series of debates and splits involving disputes over which were the true teachings of the Buddha. Among the conservative schools in this debate, Theravada alone survived as a representative. Therefore, it is common to generalize and call the traditionalist, conservative branch of Buddhism by the name Theravada. From the beginning, Theravada and the other conservative schools claimed to preserve in the purest form the authentic and true message of the Buddha. Attempts to reconstruct the life of the Buddha and his teachings depend on these accounts, since they provide the earliest evidence. However, we must acknowledge that these accounts reflect the biases of that tradition.

The Liberal Branch: The Mahayana Schools   After the death of King Ashoka, the center of Buddhism in India shifted to the northwest of the country. By the first century B.C.E., out of the disputes and divisions among Buddhist teachers, a new movement had coalesced. It became, in effect, the second major branch of Buddhism, known to its adherents as *Mahayana* (meaning "large method, vehicle, or raft").

In the basic Indian worldview, "river" often alludes to the cycle of rebirth, with the far bank of the river symbolizing liberation from the cycle. *Yana* literally translates as "means," but in the context of the "river" analogy it can be understood as the "raft" or "vehicle" used to carry persons across the raging river of rebirth to the safe shore of liberation. From a Mahayana perspective, the conservative branch of Buddhism, which we have called Theravada, is more accurately Hinayana (the "small vehicle or raft"). The contrast is that in the teachings of Mahayana a large vessel, with a pilot, carries many persons to liberation. (As we shall see, however, this analogy does not hold for all of the schools within the Mahayana movement!) In Hinayana, each person must row himself to the opposite shore in a small raft which holds only that person, having the example of the Buddha and others but with no external assistance.

The Mahayana movement came into existence in India, but it flourished in the nations of East Asia when Mahayana missionaries carried their interpretation of Buddhism from northwest India into China in the first century C.E. We will discuss the various Mahayana sects and their teachings and texts in Chapter Eight.

THE THERAVADA BUDDHIST WORLDVIEW

Tour *The Sacred World* CD!

Whether what follows is the actual teaching of the historical Siddartha is open to question. However, we are certain that these are the views of the Theravada community about what the Buddha taught.

Humanity: Soullessness (*Anatta*) and Dependent Origination

The fundamental Theravadan teaching about human nature is that, at the depth of who we are, there is no permanence. This is the opposite of the Hindu claim that beneath the changing surface of life exists the *atman,* the eternal self that does not change. For Theravadans the truth of our human nature is *anatman* (*anatta* in Pali), which literally means "no eternal self." We may wish there to be an eternal self, a part of a personal god or a oneness with the world spirit, but it is just that, wishful thinking, according to Theravada Buddhism.

We have already stipulated that all of the religions that originated in India, including Buddhism, accept the idea of the cycle of rebirth. How can Theravada Buddhists hold *both* the teaching that there is "no self" *and* the idea of rebirth? Who is reborn, if there is no permanent substance to our nature, no *atman?* One of the things the Buddha refused to do, according to Theravada teaching, was to engage in speculation about questions such as this. Instead of arguing such points philosophically, the Buddha spoke in images. When speaking about rebirth he used the example of a flame being passed from candle to candle. Nothing substantial moves between the tapers. The energy of the lighted candle causes the wick of the other candle to ignite. It is the heat that causes a new flame. So it is with human existence. As long as a life is "on fire" with desire, its influence will be passed into a new existence, "igniting" a new life. When the candle flame is extinguished, it no longer causes a new flame. When the flame of desire in a human life is blown out, there is no more "rebirth."

If we have "no souls," then who are we as distinct human beings? What accounts for separate identities? The Theravadan answer to this question is the teaching of what are called "aggregates" or *skandhas* (*kandhas* in Pali). In this view, who we are at any given moment is actually a coming together of the five *skandhas:* form (physical factors), feelings, perceptions, volitions, and awareness or consciousness. As long as these "forces" are held together, a distinct and separate being "exists." They are not "elements" that themselves have permanence. They are nothing more than bundles of various types of energy, which result in a personality in constant flux, from moment to moment.

What holds these forces together? This is the place for *karma* (*kamma* in Pali). It is the "law of action" that accounts for the seeming permanence of the *skandhas.* When the hold of the law of karma is broken, the forces will dissipate. And what allows the law of karma to be effective? Desire. Without desire, karma would have no power.

The formal expression of the view that human existence is nothing more than an always changing, interlocking circle of causes and effects is a teaching called "dependent origination" or "the chain of causation." Observation of the flow of human existence, from the Theravadan perspective, identified twelve "links" in this chain. Two of the links (ignorance and karma) arise from prior existence; eight account for present existence (consciousness, name and form, the six sense organs, contact, sensation, desire, attachment, existence); the last two lead to another existence (birth, suffering).

The fourth-century-C.E. Theravada philosopher Vasubandhu explained the teaching of soullessness in this way (Conze 1959: 196–97):

> When a flame burns a piece of wood, one says that it wanders along it; nevertheless, there is nothing but a series of flame-moments. Likewise there is a continuous series of processes which incessantly renews itself, and which is falsely called a living being.

Problem: The First Noble Truth—Life Is Suffering (*Dukkha*)

The basic human problem that the Buddha identified is expressed in the first of the Four Noble Truths (Rhy Davids 1881: 148):

> Birth is suffering; decay is suffering; illness is suffering; death is suffering. Presence of objects we hate is suffering; separation from objects we love is suffering; not to obtain what we desire is suffering.

The place to begin one's spiritual journey, according to the Buddha's teaching, is with admission that the suffering of life is unavoidable. So it was with Siddartha himself. Until he removed the blinders his life of luxury had given him and faced the reality of human suffering, he could not start on his spiritual quest. He came to realize that although he was leading of life of material abundance, he was indeed suffering. Until he awoke to that reality, he was lost!

This teaching is illustrated in a famous story of the Buddha, often called the "Parable of the Mustard Seed" (see Rogers 1870: 271–72). It is the tale of Kisa Gotami, a widow whose only son dies. In traditional Indian society a woman's status depends on her ability to give birth to a son. If she becomes a widow, she relies on her son for security. So it is easy to understand why Kisa Gotami was overwhelmed with despair when her only son died. In her grief she carried the dead child to her neighbors, asking them for a medicine to cure him. Seeing that the boy was dead, the neighbors recoiled, thinking her to be insane.

Finally, someone directed the grieving widow to the Buddha, telling her that he was a physician. When Kisa Gotami begged him for medicine that would cure her son, the Buddha answered her calmly and with compassion, saying "Bring me a handful of mustard seed." As she left to secure some mustard seed, the Buddha added, "The seed must come from a house where no one has lost a child, husband, parent, or friend." Kisa Gotami went from house to house in the village, asking for mustard seed. Each time, the people started to give her the seed, but when she asked if they had lost a loved one or friend, they said, "Alas! The living are few, but the dead are many. Do not remind us of our deepest grief!" She went to every house in the village, but there was none that had not known the sorrow of death.

An exhausted Kisa Gotami sat down that night. Suddenly it came to her that this is the way of human life. She realized how selfish she had been, to think that she alone was in grief. Suffering, she realized, was the fate of all. Kisa Gotami arose and carried her son's body to the cremation grounds. Returning to the Buddha, she took refuge in him and found comfort in his teachings. Her spiritual journey had begun.

According to Theravadan teaching, the contention that all life is suffering (*dukkha* in Pali) is simply a realistic statement about the way things are, not the result of a pessimistic outlook. Admittedly, this is a difficult concept to grasp. Most of us try to condition ourselves to "look on the bright side" and believe that "things are not as bad as they seem." For the Theravadan these sentiments are wishful thinking and inhibit our spiritual quests. Many of us would contend that a close relationship with a family member or friend brings joy into our lives. However, the one unavoidable fact about a relationship is that it will end. Friends leave physically or figuratively, or we leave them. The breaking apart of a relationship, however satisfying that relationship may have seemed, is painful. Its ultimate effect is suffering. From this perspective, any aspect of life, no matter how seemingly pleasant, already has the seeds of the suffering that is the common denominator of all human experience.

In order to focus their meditation on the reality of suffering, some Theravadan monks engage in what is known as "corpse meditation," gazing on bodies in various stages of decay. It is common in Theravadan monasteries to have piles of bones or skeletons displayed to drive home this fundamental point.

Cause: The Second Noble Truth—Suffering Is Caused by Craving (*Tanha*)

If the basic reality of life is suffering (*dukkha*), what causes this condition? The second Noble Truth gives the answer (Rhys Davids 1881: 148):

> It is that craving that leads back to birth, along with the lure and the lust that lingers longingly now here, now there: namely, the craving for sensual pleasure, the craving to be born again, the craving for existence to end.

To an extent, this is the same analysis of the cause of the human dilemma as found in Hinduism (see Chapter Three) and which we will encounter in Jainism (see Chapter Five): desire that leads to attachment. We suffer because our desire leads us to become attached to things or people and deluded as to the real nature of our situation in life. For example, we desire the pleasures of friendship, so we become attached to other persons, only to suffer when disputes arise and when friendship ends. We would not suffer if we were not attached, and we would not be attached if we did not desire.

Theravada Buddhism goes beyond Hinduism, however. Hinduism teaches us to direct our desire away from our physical natures toward the spiritual, to seek union with God or oneness with Brahman. Theravadans believe that even desire for spiritual ends leads to attachment. So it was with Siddartha. It was not until he gave up his desperate quest for enlightenment that he became enlightened. As long as he desired liberation, it was denied him. His attachment to the idea of liberation was as entrapping as his earlier attachment to the material world. If, as the Second Noble Truth states, "we desire existence to end (i.e., escape from the cycle of rebirth)," it will never come.

Such an insight is difficult to understand in a culture that counsels us to "go for it." "You've got to want it," we are told. On the other hand, most of us can recall a time when desiring something actually stood in the way of attaining it. For example, trying too hard to learn to ride a bicycle can actually make it more difficult to keep your balance. When you stop trying too hard, it sometimes "just happens." The Theravadan teaching is to extend this idea to *all* of existence. To let go of *all* desires, no matter how good they may seem, is seen as essential to authentic spiritual life.

End: The Third Noble Truth—The Extinction of Craving (*Nirvana*)

The difference between Theravada Buddhism and some modern thinkers who deny that there is any eternal "self" is that Theravadans do not think that this is the last word about our destiny. Our entrapment in an existence characterized by suffering need not be the final chapter in our stories. The Buddha found escape, and so can those who follow his example. His Third Noble Truth is that there is a way out of the suffering caused by desire.

Like other religions that originated in India, the "goal" for Theravada Buddhism is liberation from the cycle of rebirth (*samsara*). However, the problem for Theravadans is obvious: With "no permanent self," how can there be a "goal," for who reaches it? Theravadans answer that speculation on such questions is fruitless and unproductive.

A famous story of the Buddha, often called the "Parable of the Arrow" (see Warren 1896: 120–21), illustrates this point. One day the Buddha told a follower that a man who had been shot with an arrow refused to allow the arrow to be removed until he was told the name of the warrior who shot him. When his companions told him, he said, "Before you take out the arrow, tell me the warrior's caste!" The questions continued until the man died, the arrow unremoved. Why speculate on matters not directly related to our suffering, the Buddha was teaching his followers.

All we can know from the experience of the Buddha and others who have followed his teachings, Theravadans say, is that when craving is extinguished suffering ends, as does rebirth. In the words of the Third Noble Truth, there is a cessation to suffering.

What follows suffering? In a word, *nirvana* (Pali *nibbana*) arises when craving ends. Nirvana literally means "blowing out." Existence is ablaze with craving; that is the cause of suffering. When the flame of passion is "blown out," suffering ends.

It is far easier to say what nirvana is *not* in Buddhism, than to say what nirvana *is*. Nirvana is not a state of existence after death. Nirvana is a phenomenon experienced whenever a person "wakes up," as did the Buddha. A common image in South Asian religions for liberation and enlightenment is the lotus flower. The lotus typically grows in marshy areas. Its lovely, pure flower emerges, untainted by the muddy waters. This symbolism of the lotus flower is invoked in a Theravadan text known as *The Questions of King Milinda,* to point toward the truth of nirvana (Conze 1959: 157):

> As the lotus is unstained by water, so is Nirvana unstained by all the defilements.

For Theravada Buddhism, the person who follows the example of the Buddha and is enlightened is called an *arhant* (Pali for "worthy one"; also written *arhat* or *arahant*). Like Buddha, an *arhant* has overcome attachment and desire and, once earthly life is ended, will no longer be reborn. Nirvana is *not* heaven, for that would imply a place where souls dwell. But, paradoxically, nirvana is also not merely negative. Descriptions of nirvana in Theravadan literature speak in such terms as calm, peace, joy, bliss. Does this mean that an arhant continues to exist after death? A distinction *is* drawn between nirvana and *parinirvana* (the state the *arhant* enters after death), but it should not be overemphasized. Some Theravadans have suggested that nirvana is a state beyond both being and nonbeing. In the final analysis, the question of the nature of survival beyond death is one most Theravadans stubbornly reject as too speculative, and not helpful in dealing with our basic problem.

Means: The Fourth Noble Truth— The Eightfold Path of the Middle Way

Tour *The Sacred World* CD!

The Fourth Noble Truth expresses the Theravadan teaching on the means to liberation. It states that the way that leads to the cessation of suffering is the "holy eightfold path." The steps in the path are:

- Right Belief
- Right Aspiration
- Right Speech
- Right Conduct
- Right Means of Livelihood
- Right Endeavor
- Right Mindfulness
- Right Meditation

This is the "middle way" between self-denial and self-indulgence, a moderate and focused way of living. Notably absent are rituals or expressions of devotion to a personal god. In Theravada Buddhism adoration of deities has no place as a part of the means to reach liberation.

"Work out your own salvation," the Buddha had said on his deathbed. The eightfold path provides the guidelines, but each individual must traverse it by himself or herself. No outside assistance from gods or other humans is possible. You are on your own!

Some explanation of each of the steps may help clarify the eightfold path as a whole. These steps are not so much a set of directions to be followed sequentially as eight principles that need to be applied to the particular situation of each person.

The first step, right belief (also called right understanding or right views), means holding a correct view of the nature of reality. It includes accepting as true the Four Noble Truths and the attitude toward life associated with the Buddha. That implies recognizing what had become known as the "three marks of existence": *anatta* (no soul), *anicca* (impermanence), and *dukkha* (suffering). It also entails believing in the Theravadan notion of dharma. In Hinduism dharma referred to right conduct in the context of the caste system, as well as one's "duty" to seek liberation. Early Buddhism redefined dharma (Pali *dhamma*) to mean (1) the truth as taught by Buddha and contained in the Pali canon, (2) proper conduct, which applies to all regardless of caste, and (3) reality itself and the laws (such as karma and dependent origination) that explain how reality functions.

The second step, right aspiration, purpose, or thought, means freeing one's mind from sensual desires, greed, and malice. It also means taking on thoughts of nonviolence, renunciation, and compassion. At this stage one seeks to replace cruelty and unconcern with gentleness, benevolence, and good will. The point is not to attach oneself to particular persons with a caring attitude, but to practice a "universal goodwill" that extends equally to all.

The third step, right speech, includes not speaking falsely, not gossiping, abstaining from harsh words, avoiding vulgar or prejudicial talk, and not falling into the habit of useless chatter.

The fourth step, right conduct or action, means not killing other living creatures, not stealing, and avoiding illicit sexual behavior, intoxicants, and gambling.

The fifth step, right means of livelihood, forbids four types of occupations: those that involve killing, those engaged in commerce or services for hire, anything that involves trickery or deception, and any work that entails astrology. In general, it means earning a living in ways consistent with Buddhist ideals.

The sixth step, right endeavor or effort, refers to avoiding any sort of unwholesome action that will have a negative karmic influence, and pursuing beneficial deeds. It requires constant alertness as to what one is doing.

The seventh step, right mindfulness or alertness, means devoting oneself assiduously to focused observation of oneself and others. Contemplation begins by focusing on one's breathing to become aware of the body and its impermanence. It also includes awareness of the ebb and flow of one's feelings, then one's mental activities, and finally the objects of one's mind.

It is at this level that monks might engage in gazing on decaying bodies and bones, the idea being to let the reality of impermanence completely occupy the mind. The Dhammapada includes these instructions for monks engaging in "corpse meditation" (146–51; Radhakrishnan 1950: 108–09):

> Behold this [. . .] body full of wounds, put together, diseased, and full of many thoughts in which there is neither permanence nor stability.
> This body is worn out, a nest of diseases and very frail. This heap of corruption breaks to pieces, life indeed ends in death[. . . .]
> The splendid chariots of kings wear away; the body also comes to old age but the virtue of the good never ages, thus the good teach to each other.

The final step, right meditation or concentration, arises as one's mind is brought sharply into focus as a result of the prior step. At this stage a calmness and peace comes as one enters the state of *samadhi*. For Hindus *samadhi* meant absorption into the spiritual; in Theravada Buddhism it is not absorption into something outside oneself, but rather a "one-pointedness" in which all attachments have been broken. Once at this stage, nirvana is at hand and, in a flash of intuition, that state of final bliss dawns.

The steps of the eightfold path correspond to the three instructions of Theravada tradition: morality, concentration, wisdom. Morality (*sila*) includes right speech, action, and livelihood. Concentration (*samadhi*) encompasses right effort, mindfulness, and meditation. Wisdom (*prajna*) envelops right belief and aspiration. Since wisdom built on concentration, and both built on morality, the "path" is not so much linear as interconnected.

Everyone should attempt to live by the eightfold path, and (theoretically) enlightenment is open to anyone regardless of caste, gender, or whether lay or ordained. In practice, in Theravada Buddhism, becoming an *arhant* and reaching nirvana have been limited to monks who have the freedom to devote themselves fully to the path. In Southeast Asia, where Theravada Buddhism is centered, monks and nuns group together in monasteries and convents. The monks wear yellow robes, shave their heads, and own only a very few possessions, including a begging bowl. Each Theravada monk and nun pledges to live by the ten precepts outlined in the section as monastic life.

In Theravadan countries the religious life of lay people involves following the first five precepts, spending a limited time in a monastery (for young men especially), showing kindness to monks and nuns, receiving instruction from them, and showing reverence for the Buddha by visiting shrines containing images and/or relics of the Buddha. The images are highly idealized, symbolic representations; for example, the Buddha is portrayed with long ears (a symbol of enlightenment) and a beatific gaze to indicate that he has experienced nirvana. A relic might be a reputed tooth of the Buddha, or one of his bones. Lay people also commit themselves to a modified version of the last five precepts.

The most important monuments in Theravada Buddhism are *stupas,* distinctive dome- or bell-shaped structures that house relics associated with the Buddha or other early leaders. Atop the dome (thought to symbolize the cosmos) one always finds three disks (to denote the umbrellas used to shield royalty). The disks represent the Buddha, who has gone beyond the attachments of this world. In India, where numerous ancient *stupas* remain, the dome shape predominates. In Southeast Asia the bell-shape became more popular, rising to a single point at the top. *Stupas* are important pilgrimage sites. Perhaps influenced by Hindu practice, worshippers come to give homage to the Buddha, circumambulating the structure and reciting verses from sacred texts. Flowers and other offerings may be left. Gold foil may be pressed into the walls of the stupas by wealthy lay people. Virtually all of the *stupas* have elaborate carvings of various mythic beings adapted from the popular beliefs of the region.

The question naturally arises: Is this not worship of the Buddha as a deity? Setting up images that are venerated seems suspiciously like the *puja* of devotional Hinduism. Indeed, these practices have been called Buddha-*puja*. The Theravada answer has always been to say that the Buddha is *not* being worshipped as a deity; rather, followers are simply showing reverence to one who has attained enlightenment and symbolically committing themselves to follow his example.

Reality: Impermanence (Anicca)

If there's one basic truth, we sometimes tell ourselves, it is that nothing remains the same. Look at a photograph of yourself taken five, ten, or more years ago! According to Theravada Buddhism, this commonsense realization is the truth about *all* reality.

All reality is impermanent (*anicca*). This applies both to human nature, as we have already seen, and to the cosmos as a whole. Hinduism sees a permanent, unchanging personal God or impersonal Oneness (*brahman*) beyond the impermanence of this world; Theravada Buddhism sees no such cosmic permanence. Like the waves in the ocean, all reality is in flux, constantly in motion.

Theravadans today point out that their theory about reality is better supported by contemporary science than the idea of permanence. Physics, for example, continues to penetrate into the nature of matter and finds not permanence but flux, no discrete entities but an interwoven field of energy. Perhaps, Theravadans would say, it is only our desire which creates the illusion of permanence!

As in Hinduism, Theravada Buddhism teaches that the cosmos itself passes through cycles of birth, death, and rebirth. After the age of destruction in the current cosmic cycle, according to Theravada teaching, a new Buddha, known as *Maitreya*, will usher in a new age of cosmic harmony. When he comes, Maitreya will attract by his preaching hundreds of thousands, so that *arhats* fill the earth. He will continue preaching the true dharma for sixty thousand years, and reach literally hundreds and hundreds of millions of living beings. He will then enter nirvana, but his dharma will continue another ten thousand years.

Sacred: Spiritual Atheism

Theravada Buddhism is an atheistic religion, denying a central role for a personal god or gods. It is not just that Theravada Buddhism is "agnostic" about the gods, without claimed knowledge concerning the existence or role of deities in human existence. Theravada Buddhism claims that gods have no role to play in human liberation, any more than any other spirits or human agencies do. Each person by himself or herself must "work out his or her own liberation."

To be precise, Theravada Buddhism, like Jainism, is atheistic in a functional rather than a theoretical sense. Theoretical atheism denies that gods exist. Functional atheism is not concerned about the question of the existence of gods; it only knows that whether they exist or not, they are irrelevant to human destiny. Theravada Buddhists simply avoid speculation on the issue of whether gods or spirits exist, because such idle thought is not productive for what is truly important— overcoming suffering.

That which is spiritual in early Buddhism is nirvana, the state entered when craving is extinguished. It is not a deity like Vishnu, nor a cosmic spirit like *brahman*, but for Buddhism nirvana is spiritual.

THERAVADA BUDDHISM IN THE TWENTY-FIRST CENTURY

After centuries of slow decline and a recent history of suffering from active political oppression in some countries, Theravada Buddhism is in resurgence in much of South and Southeast Asia.

In India, where Buddhism nearly vanished into Hinduism, the religion is experiencing a remarkable resurgence. The revival began during the 1950s when members of scheduled castes (the "untouchables") began to convert to Buddhism in large numbers, in order to escape the oppression of the Hindu caste system. In 1956, Dr. Bhimrao Ambedkar, the architect of the Indian Constitution, and himself an "untouchable," converted to Buddhism with hundreds of thousands of his followers.

Early in the twenty-first century there were over ten million Buddhists in India, many associating with Theravada teaching. Sarnath, the site of the Buddha's first sermon near Varanasi (Benares), long a Buddhist pilgrimage site with a major *stupa*, has been revitalized, with centers for various schools of Buddhism. An All-India Action Committee has led a campaign to restore Bodh Gaya, where the Buddha experienced enlightenment, as a Buddhist site.

When Sri Lanka became independent from British rule in 1947, Theravada Buddhism became the official national religion. However, there has been great instability and considerable violence because of conflict between the Hindu Tamils of northern Sri Lanka and the Sinhalese Buddhists of the South. The Tamils want an independent Hindu state, and the Sinhalese are committed to preserving Sri Lankan unity as a Buddhist nation. In the early twenty-first century about two-thirds of the nearly twenty million residents of Sri Lanka were Theravada Buddhist. An active Buddhist reform movement continues to exert considerable influence in Sri Lanka.

Myanmar (Burma) continues to be an overwhelmingly Theravada Buddhist country, with 85 percent of the population of over forty-two million associated with Theravada schools. This may contribute to the intensely self-reliant, reclusive attitude that dominates the nation. An attempt to develop a social and economic order based on Buddhist principles has been stalled by various factors, most recently a repressive military regime.

Thailand also is a Theravada country, with almost 95 percent of the population of nearly sixty-three million associated with Theravada Buddhism. The greatest threat to Buddhist influence in Thailand is the lure of materialism that has increased as exposure to modern, secular ways has grown. One influential Thai Buddhist reform movement, the *Dhammakaya*, emphasizes that economic modernization is not incompatible with Buddhist teaching, and focuses on the pursuit of individual peace. It has won the support of the Thai royal family and is popular among those who have benefitted from the globalized economy. However, other Thai monks have led efforts to reform corrupt governmental structures and develop more environmentally responsible policies and programs.

Kampuchea (Cambodia), with a population in 2000 of thirteen million, is the home of one of the most impressive Theravada complexes in the world, the twelfth-century temple called *Angkor Wat*. After the Communist revolution of 1976, Buddhism suffered greatly in Kampuchea, with thousands of monks driven from monasteries or killed. Recent attempts to restore Kampuchea after the withdrawal of the Vietnamese in 1989 include hints, if not clear indications, of a Buddhist resurgence.

A communist regime in the small nation of Laos (six million) has also greatly damaged the status of Theravada Buddhism in that country, although there are recent signs of Buddhist restoration in Laos also.

In all these countries, and in Mahanyana countries as well, a movement known as "engaged Buddhism" is growing. In brief, it is a movement seeking to relate Buddhist teaching to the actual suffering of the world today. For example, proponents of engaged Buddhism have taken the lead in applying Buddhism to the ecological crisis and the search for economic justice (see Chapter Fifteen).

CHAPTER SUMMARY

Buddhism began in the sixth century B.C.E. in reaction to the perceived excesses of Hinduism at that time. Its founder, Siddartha Gautama, is known as the "Buddha." He charted a "middle way" between self-indulgence and self-denial. After his own enlightenment, he initiated an order (*sangha*) of monks and nuns. Buddhism faded in India, but flourished in the countries of Southeast Asia. It divided into two main branches:

Theravada ("Way of the Elders") and Mahayana ("The Large Raft"). The most important Theravada sacred texts are found in a collection known as the Pali Canon.

We surveyed the worldview of the Theravada branch of Buddhism, identifying the view that humans have no eternal souls, the problem as the suffering characteristic of all existence, the cause as craving, the view of reality as impermanence, the goal as nirvana, the means as the "eightfold path," and the view of the sacred as a type of "spiritual atheism."

We concluded the chapter by considering the role of Buddhism in South and Southeast Asia in the early twenty-first century.

IMPORTANT TERMS AND PHRASES

anatman, anicca, arhant, Ashoka, *bodhi,* dependent origination, *dhamma, dukkha,* Four Noble Truths, four Passing Sights, functional atheism, Great Renunciation, *kamma,* Mahayana Buddhism, Maitreya, *nirvana,* Pali Canon, *parinirvana, sangha,* Siddartha Gautama, *skandhas, stupas, sutras,* theoretical atheism, Theravada Buddhism

QUESTIONS FOR DISCUSSION AND REFLECTION

1. Siddartha Gautama was spiritually blind until he saw with his own eyes the suffering of the world. Are people today who are isolated (or who isolate themselves) from the pain and anguish of existence necessarily spiritually blind?

2. Theravada Buddhism stresses self-reliance in spiritual matters. How important is it to engage in your own pursuit of truth?

3. The Buddha said that we should not waste precious energy speculating on spiritual questions. We should instead devote ourselves to the pursuit of enlightenment. What are the pros and cons of this position?

4. What evidence do you see for and against the Buddhist teaching that everything is impermanent?

5. Was the Buddha correct in saying that "all life is suffering"? Try to think of something enjoyable that does not pass away and lead to suffering in some form.

6. What is "bliss" to you? Compare your understanding with the "bliss" of the Buddhist nirvana.

SOURCES AND SUGGESTIONS FOR FURTHER STUDY

ARMSTRONG, KAREN, 2001. *Buddha.* New York: Viking.

CONZE, EDWARD, 1959. *Buddhist Scriptures.* London: Penguin.

HARVEY, PETER, 1990. *An Introduction to Buddhism: Teachings, History, and Practices.* Cambridge: Cambridge University.

HESSE, HERMANN, 1982. *Siddarhta.* Trans. Hilda Rosner. New York: Bantam Classics.

LESTER, ROBERT C., 1973. *Theravada Buddhism in Southeast Asia.* Ann Arbor: University of Michigan.

RADHAKRISHNAN, SARVEPALLI, TRANS., 1950. *The Dhammapada.* London: Oxford University.

RAHULA, WALPOLA, 1974. *What the Buddha Taught.* Rev. ed. New York: Grove.

RHYS DAVIDS, T. W., TRANS., 1881. *Buddhist Sutras.* In *Sacred Books of the East,* ed. Max Müller. Vol. 11. Oxford: Clarendon.

ROGERS, T. E., TRANS., 1870. *Buddhaghosa: Buddhist Parables.* London: Trubner & Co.

STRONG, JOHN S., 1995. *The Experience of Buddhism: Sources and Interpretations.* Belmont, CA: Wadsworth.

WARREN, HENRY CLARKE, ED., 1896. *Buddhism in Translations.* Harvard Oriental Series No. 3. Cambridge, MA: Harvard University.

Web Sites

buddhanet.net/
  (Buddhist Information and Education Network)

ciolek.com/WWWVL-Buddhism.html
  (a virtual library for Buddhist studies)

members.tripod.com/~Arumugam/buddhiststudies
  (a guide to the study of Buddhism on the internet)

nibbana.com
  (links to Theravada Buddhist sites and texts)

accesstoinsight.org
  (dedicated to providing accurate, reliable, and useful information concerning the practice and study of Theravada Buddhism)

Refer to Pearson/Prentice Hall's **TIME Special Edition: World Religions** magazine for these and other current articles on topics related to many of the world's religions:

➥ *Buddhism: Buddhism in America; The Dalai Lama—"It's Time to Prepare New Leaders;" Essay— Lost Without a Faith*

Prentice Hall's **Research Navigator** helps students in their further study of the world's religions. Visit *http://www.researchnavigator.com* for help on the research process and access to databases full of relevant material, including the New York *Times*.

CHAPTER

5

Jainism—The Way of Noninjury

INTRODUCTION

In the history of religions, we find numerous examples of religious movements that began as attempts to reform an existing tradition. In India, in the sixth century B.C.E., reactions surfaced against the Vedic sacrificial system and the control of religion by the Brahmins. Two reformers became founders of major religions. The first was Siddartha Gautama, the founder of Buddhism, whose life and influence we explored in the preceding chapter. The other was Nataputta Vardhamana, better known as *Mahavira,* the founder of Jainism.

Jainism is a relatively small religion. Today, approximately four million persons are Jains, and they are concentrated around Mumbai (Bombay), India. However, the impact of Jainism on other religions, and its uncompromising commitment to its own ascetic ideals, make Jainism an important world religion.

The name Jainism comes from the Sanskrit term *jina,* which means "conqueror." Within the religion, a *jina* is a honorary title given to great teachers. Jains are those who seek to follow the example of these figures and win the battle over that which keeps them trapped within the cycle of rebirth.

STAGES OF DEVELOPMENT AND SACRED TEXTS

Founder: Mahavira and the Tirthankaras
Tour *The Sacred World* CD!

According to Jain tradition, within the current cosmic cycle, twenty-four exemplary teachers have become *tirthankaras* (literally "crossing finders or makers"). The image is that of a person who finds the place where a river can be forged. As we have already noted, in the religions that originated in India, a river often symbolizes the cycle of rebirth. So a *tirthankara* is someone who has found the successful means for finding a way to cross over and go beyond the cycle of rebirth. The way can serve as an example for others to follow.

Jains date the origins of their religion to the first of the twenty-four *tirthankaras*. Academic historians recognize certain evidence for only the last in this series (and perhaps the next to the last, a man named Parshva). The last *tirthankara* was born about 597 B.C.E. in northeastern India near the modern city of Patna. Like Siddartha Gautama, Nataputta Vardhamana was born in the warrior class (the *kshatriyas*) and raised in luxury. Legends abound about this man, making it difficult for historians to determine what is true and what is imaginary. Since we are attempting a phenomenological perspective, we will recount his story as faithful Jains tell it.

Like Siddartha, Nataputta became disillusioned in his comfortable life. At the age of thirty he left his wife and young daughter. He spent more than twelve years wandering naked through central India, seeking to abandon the worldly fetters that he felt kept his spirit bound to endless rebirth. At first he joined with others who shared his commitment to self-denial, but ultimately he determined to avoid attachment to any other being. He rarely stayed more than one night in any place, lest he develop attachments to anyone or any location. Although he was not the first to try to live by the principle of *ahimsa* (noninjury), he took it to the extreme in his own life. He carried a broom to sweep his path clean of all forms of insect life, and he strained the water he drank through a cloth so as not to consume even the smallest life form. He was not the first to try to deny his physical body, for renunciation was a common strategy of Hindu holy men. However, he took asceticism to an extreme. He meditated uncovered in the intense heat of summer sun, and in the winter rain he shunned shelter and gladly endured the hardship for the sake of its positive spiritual effect. One tradition states that people in one village tried to light a fire under him while he meditated, in order to get him to move, but he sat still. They stuck pins in his ears; he remained oblivious.

In the thirteenth year of his quest he reached his goal. He became a *jina;* he won the victory over desire and attachment. For the remaining years of his life, he spent his time teaching his message of extreme asceticism and *ahimsa*. People began to follow him and practice the lifestyle he exemplified. In about 527 B.C.E. he died by voluntarily starving himself, the ultimate act of self-denial. His soul now dwells, with those of other *jinas,* in a state of eternal bliss at the top of the universe.

His followers, who transformed the example of his life into a world religion, call him with reverence Mahavira (which means "Great Man" or "Hero"). They proclaim him the twenty-fourth and last *tirthankara* for the present cosmic cycle.

The Jain Community

Tour *The Sacred World* CD!

By the time Mahavira died, a movement had developed around him. At his death, leadership passed to the survivors among his first disciples. The movement began to spread from central India to the south and to the northwest. During the Maurya dynasty of the third century B.C.E., the Jain movement benefited from royal support for the ascetic lifestyle.

As the movement spread, divisions inevitably occurred. The earliest split was on the issue of whether monks should be allowed to wear clothes or go naked. One group thought that the ascetic ideal and Mahavira's own example supported nudity. Another group argued that allowing monks one white garment would not compromise the principle. By the first century C.E., Jains either supported monastic nudity (the *Digambaras*, meaning "sky-clad") or identified with those monks who accepted the white garment (the *Shvetambaras*, meaning "white-clad"). The latter group accepted women into their order, while the Digambaras did not. Over the centuries the Shvetambaras became prominent in the West and Northwest while the Digambaras enjoyed success in Central and Southern India. Gradually, Jainism faded in the latter areas and now survives principally in northwest India, around Bombay (now known as Mumbai).

The "Jain community" is more than these religious orders, however. Throughout Jain history there has been a close association between monastics and the laity. Lay persons revere the monks and nuns and provide for their basic necessities and, in turn, receive instruction in the principles of Jain living.

Jain Texts: The *Agamas*

The Sanskrit term *agamas* means "tradition," and refers to any body of teachings handed down by an unbroken succession of sages. As we have seen, in Hinduism the term covers a set of writings related to the personal deities. In Jainism, *agamas* is the most general designation for the writings considered sacred.

The sacred writings of the Jains are religious and philosophical in character. Each of the two major sects maintains its own canon. Included in the Shvetambara scripture are the remembered sermons and discourses of Mahavira. The Digambaras hold that the original teachings of Mahavira are lost, but maintain that in their texts the essence is preserved.

The *agamas* are seen as helpful in guiding a person to the right path, but they do not possess the complete "truth." As we shall see below, in Jain teaching nothing in the material world, including scripture, is capable of expressing pure knowledge.

THE JAIN WORLDVIEW

Humanity: Eternal, Infinite Souls (*jivas*)

In the Jain worldview, every living being has a spiritual soul (called *jiva;* note that, in Hinduism, *jiva*, which means "life principle" in Sanskrit, refers to a person's material nature). These souls are by nature perfect, blissful, all-knowing, eternal, and infinite in number.

Problem: Souls "Weighed Down" by Actions (karma)

Like Hinduism, the fundamental problem Jainism recognizes is that spiritual souls are confined by karma to the cycle of rebirth. However, for Jains karma is not just a law; karma is a form of very subtle matter (*ajiva*). The human dilemma is that when we act, karmic matter attaches to and "weighs down" the *jiva*. The more karma a soul accumulates in a given existence, the lower down the ladder of existence that soul is born. Being born as a human indicates that the *jiva* has worked its way a long way up the scale, and has a unique opportunity to rid itself of existing karma and stop the accumulation of more.

According to Jainism innumerable souls may be born in human or nonhuman bodies, depending on the karma they have accumulated. In a passage from a Jain text, the possible fates are described (*Uttaradhyayana* III.2–7. Jacobi 1895: 15–16):

> The universe is peopled by manifold creatures who are, in this Samsara, born in different families and castes for having done various actions.
> Sometimes they go to the world of the gods, sometimes to the hells, sometimes they become Asuras (demons) in accordance with their actions.
> Sometimes they become Kshatriyas (nobles) or Kandalas and Bukkasas (outcastes and untouchables), or worms and moths, or [. . .] ants[. . . .]
> But by the cessation of Karman (karma), perchance living beings will reach in due time a pure state and be born as men.

One of the more interesting implications of the Jain view of our human problem is its view of knowledge (*anekantavada*). Although our souls are in their pure nature "all knowing," when attached to karma they are limited in knowledge by their particular situations. Therefore, no one point of view can claim to be comprehensive. Each is limited to its own set of assumptions and perspectives. A contemporary Jain scholar calls this view of knowledge "multiplism" (Ram-Prasad 2001), emphasizing its recognition of multiple perspectives. The famous parable of the blind men and the elephant illustrates this teaching. In this story three blind men encounter an elephant. Each touches a different part of the elephant. When asked to describe what they have experienced, each answers in a different way. The man who touched the side speaks of confronting a stone wall. However, to the man who felt the tail of the elephant, it is a rope. The last man, who reached out and held the ear of the elephant, was just as certain that it was a fan. Each man spoke truthfully, because his experience was limited to his own situation. The point is that as long as we are "blinded" by our particular karmic context, we will see things only in part, and our knowledge will be limited.

Cause: Activity

For Jainism the cause of karmic bondage is not just desire, although the more attached one is to the material world and its pleasures, the more karma will be accumulated. Jains believe that *all* actions, no matter now well-intentioned, produce karma and burden the *jiva*. Therefore, only a commitment to inactivity or to activity that focuses on liberating the *jiva* will be effective in stopping the further accumulation of karmic matter.

End: Becoming a Conqueror (*jina*) and All-Knowing One (*kevalin*)

The goal in Jainism is for the soul to be liberated from its bondage to karma so that its true nature can be realized. In Jain cosmology liberated souls rise to the top of the universe (a place called *loka*) where they dwell eternally in full consciousness, knowledge, and bliss. The liberated soul is a *kevalin*, an "all-knowing one."

Through liberation one's soul joins Mahavira and others who have escaped the bondage of karma to become themselves *jinas* (conquerors). In effect, they attain a state higher than the gods, who remain bound by an invisible form of karma. However, unlike Hindu monism, there is no state of unity realized upon liberation; the individual souls remain separate. And there is no ultimate communion with a personal god as there is in the *bhakti* traditions in Hinduism. Yet, unlike Theravada Buddhism, souls do exist.

A Jain text describes the liberated soul as follows (*Kundakunda Niyamasara* 176–77. Bhaskar 1991: 153):

> The Supreme Soul (Paramatman) is free from birth, old age, and death; he is supreme, pure, and devoid of the eight karmas; he possesses infinite knowledge, intuition, bliss, and potency; he is indivisible, indestructible, and inexhaustible. Besides, he is supersensuous and unparalleled, is free from obstructions, merit, demerit, and rebirth, and is eternal, steady, and independent.

Means: Self-Denial and Noninjury (*ahimsa*)

Like Theravada Buddhism, Jainism is a religion of self-reliance. Jains believe that in the quest to become *jinas,* they are on their own. The gods cannot help, for they too are working out their own liberation. Priests cannot invoke any special powers. The Vedas (and all scriptures, even the Jain writings) are limited by the point of view of their writers, so they have no ultimate authority.

The key word in the Jain teaching about the path to liberation from the cycle of rebirth is *asceticism.* Only through a lifestyle of active self-denial can one hope to work off existing karma and avoid accumulating more karma, and only through ridding the soul of karma can liberation be attained. Asceticism can be considered a form of vigorous spiritual exercise, which "burns off" karma and controls one's appetite for more, just as intense physical exercise reduces calories and curbs one's desire for food.

For the Jain the ideal way of living is to follow Mahavira's example and avoid all attachments. Although, according to Jain teaching, the path to liberation is open to all regardless of caste, gender, or membership in a religious organization, in practice only monks and nuns can maintain the extreme discipline required. For the laity some attachments in family life and in the community are inevitable.

Jain monks and nuns commit themselves to the "Five Great Vows." Jain lay people follow them in modified form. They are listed in a Jain text (*Acaranga Sutra* 24. Jacobi 1884: 208–13) as follows:

> The first great vow, sir, runs thus: I renounce all killing of living things[. . . .]
> The second great vow, sir runs thus: I renounce all vices of lying speech arising from anger or greed or fear or mirth[. . . .]
> The third great vow, sir, runs thus: I shall renounce all taking of anything not given[. . . .]
> The fourth great vow, sir, runs thus: I renounce all sexual pleasures, either with gods or men or animals[. . . .]
> The fifth great vow, sir, runs thus: I renounce all attachments, whether little or much, small or great, living or lifeless[. . . .]

Of these vows, the first (*ahimsa*) is the hallmark of Jainism. Monastics are obligated to go to extremes to avoid taking life, consciously or unconsciously. All Jains are vegetarians, in order to minimize the taking of life in the production of their food. However, when walking, a Jain monk even sweeps the path before him so as to avoid inadvertently stepping on living creatures. Like Mahavira, he strains the water he drinks and wipes out his begging bowl (if he has one; Digambara monks use only their hands for begging). The great gift Jainism has shared with the rest of the world is this unqualified commitment to noninjury.

Others may judge *ahimsa* impractical, but it is an ideal that calls forth the nobility in others. It had a great impact on Mahatma Gandhi, who was influenced by the Jain community in Bombay where he spent his early years. He transformed this ideal into a highly successful political strategy of nonviolent resistance, which was then adopted by Dr. Martin Luther King and other leaders of the American civil rights movement.

For the Jain laity a modified set of principles evolved. They are to avoid taking life knowingly. Hence, they may not work at occupations such as farming in which life is taken as a matter of course. They are to remain faithful to their spouses in marriage. They are to place limits on their material holdings. This ideal has inspired many Jains (who have become quite wealthy in business, law, and banking) to give away considerable sums of money for charitable causes. They are to live simply, avoiding unnecessary travel. They must observe periods of meditation and self-denial, spending days living as monks or nuns. They must support the ascetics. Their strong commitment to a moral lifestyle has often earned Jains the admiration of others in the communities where they live.

A casual observer of Jain practice is bound to be confused when visiting a Jain temple. One will see there statues that look to the outsider like images of deities, with Jain laity presenting what appear to be offerings and walking around (circumambulating) the images in an apparent display of devotion. Is this not *puja,* the worship of deities we observed in Hindu devotionalism? Although Jain practice was probably influenced by Hindu *puja,* appearances can be deceiving. When Jains bow before a statue of Mahavira or one of the other *tirthankaras,* they are not worshipping a "god." Rather, they are focusing on the example given by these "crossing finders." They are pledging themselves to follow the spiritual path blazed by Mahavira and the others. However, this is not to deny that there is a popular piety in Jainism, in which worshippers may seek material gains through the "merit making" of revering the images or showing kindness to monastics.

The worshipper enters the temple, saying, *Namo Jinanam* (I bow to the Jina). Jain temple *puja* might include ritual bathing of the image, symbolic of the bathing of the newborn *tirthankara* by the gods. The worshipper may touch his or her forehead with the liquid used to bath the image in a sign of reverence.

Fasting also plays an important role in Jain ritual, for monks and nuns, but also for lay people, with the most pious lay people devoting as many as ten days each month to refraining from or limiting the intake of food. In November/December, during *Maunagiyaras,* a day of total silence and fasting is observed. The day is viewed as the anniversary of the birth of many of the *tirthankaras.*

One of the highlights of the Jain ritual calendar is *Mahavira Jayanti,* the celebration of the birth of Mahavira. It falls during March or April of the solar calendar.

Paryusana Parva, an eight-day ritual during August/September, is the most important festival in Jainism. It commemorates the time when Jain monks and nuns suspend their wandering during the rainy season to stay in one place. There they instruct lay people in the principles of Jainism. Today, communities invite Jain scholars to give lectures on the teachings of the faith. Paryusana Parva is a time of repentance for any acts of violence committed during the previous year, with ascetic activities performed to remove the accumulated karmic matter. One day is entirely devoted to fasting. The period often ends with a festive meal.

Like Hindus, Jains observe the festival of Diwali, during the months of October/November. For Jains it marks the anniversary of the liberation of Mahavira. The traditional lighting of Diwali lamps signifies for Jains the keeping alive of Mahavira's teachings about enlightenment.

A worshipper, wearing a veil to avoid injuring even the smallest living beings, makes an offering at a shrine in a Jain temple in Mumbai (Bombay), India. Although Jains do not worship gods, many Jain lay people (but not monks or nuns) do engage in acts of devotion to show reverence to heroes of the faith such as the founder, Mahavira.

At some Jain temples there are hospitals for sick or injured animals. Perhaps the most famous is a hospital for rats. The point of such institutions is that the Jain commitment to *ahimsa* is uncompromising. Birds and dogs have souls, and deserve the same respect as humans or other living beings.

Like Hindus, devout Jains also have shrines in their homes and perform daily *puja* at them. Many Jains begin their day by lighting a lamp in front of the images. Spreading grain for birds in the morning and filtering water to remove any small animals are ritual acts of charity and nonviolence. *Samayika* is a forty-eight-minute meditative practice, often performed twice a day by the most faithful. *Pratikramana* is performed in the morning, with a prayer of repentance for any acts of harm committed during the night, and in the evening for the harm done during the day. The prayer may be:

> I forgive all living beings,
> Let all living beings forgive me;
> All in this world are my friends,
> I have no enemies.

Reality: A Dualism of Matter (*ajiva*) and Spirit (*jiva*)

According to Jain teaching, reality is divided into only two categories: matter (*ajiva*) and spirit (*jiva*). In each of these categories an infinite number of individual particles exists. In the spiritual realm, as noted, an infinite number of discrete souls are present. According to Jain teaching, these souls were not created by a personal god, nor do they emanate from some World Spirit. They have eternally existed as individual units, all of the same nature—pure knowledge and goodness.

Souls are further classified in terms of the number of senses they possess. Humans, gods, animals, and other spiritual beings have five senses, while at the other extreme plants have but one sense (touch).

Matter is by nature evil and, when attached to souls, obscures their purity and goodness. It is composed of gross matter but also space, time, motion, and rest. As noted, karma is a particularly subtle form of matter. Jain philosophers have noted that this "atomistic" approach to describing reality accords well with what modern science is discovering about the composition of matter.

Sacred: Spiritual Atheism

Just as Theravada Buddhism, Jainism is a religion that is at the same time atheistic, yet spiritual. Jainism is atheistic not in the sense of denying the existence of gods. In the Jain cosmology gods exist, but they play no role in ultimate transformation. It is fruitless to pray to them or to "put one's trust in them," because they too are seeking liberation. They exist simply as other types of *jivas*, with their own particular form of matter (which renders them invisible).

JAINISM IN THE TWENTY-FIRST CENTURY

According to the Jain view of time, we are currently in a period of decline that will last 21,000 years. During this phase Jainism and other religions will fade away as will all human virtue. Another 21,000-year period will follow, bringing an end to human civilization. This will complete the downward spiral of the cosmic cycle, and a period of ascendancy will then begin.

This helps explain why Jains have never been concerned about spreading their religion. In addition, each person must decide alone to begin the arduous trek to liberation. Whether or not that person calls himself or herself a "Jain" (or proclaims membership in another religious movement) is irrelevant to spiritual success. Only one's own commitment to rigid self-denial and noninjury matters.

Nevertheless, in recent decades Jainism has become somewhat more open to other religions, and has spread to other countries. In the 1970s a Jain monk for the first time left India to travel to world conferences on religion. And in recent years Jain temples and centers have been established in the United States, Canada, Africa, and elsewhere. There are over two dozen Jain temples in the United States. Many Jains are highly educated and have joined the migration of Indian professionals to the West, carrying their religion with them. The economic success of the Jain community continues to create tension for many Jains between the Jain tradition of self-denial and the lures of the materialistic world available to the affluent.

In 1991, in an effort to pass Jain values and traditions to a new generation, American Jains established the Young Jains of America (YJA). It holds periodic conventions, such as one in 2002 with the theme "Walking the Path of Jainism: Today's Youth, Tomorrow's Future." The organization claimed 3,500 members in 2003.

CHAPTER SUMMARY

Jainism began in the sixth century B.C.E. as a reaction to priestly control of Hinduism. It is an ascetic religion through which members seek to liberate their souls from attachment to matter. To study the stages of development and sacred texts of Jainism we first studied the life of the principal founder, Mahavira. We then discussed the basic branches within Jainism and Jain scriptures (the *agamas*).

Our survey of the Jain worldview identified the view of humanity as having eternal souls (*jivas*); the basic problem as these spiritual souls "weighed down" by karma; the cause as all forms of activity; reality as a duality of spirit and matter, and a pluralism of either spiritual or material particles; the goal as becoming a "conqueror" (*jina*), an "all-knowing one" (*kevalin*) whose soul rises to the top of the universe; the means as asceticism; and the view of the sacred as a type of "spiritual atheism."

We concluded the chapter with a brief examination of Jainism in the twenty-first century.

IMPORTANT TERMS AND PHRASES

agamas, ahimsa, ajiva, asceticism, Digambaras, Jain view of knowledge, *jina, jiva,* karma, *kevalin, loka,* Mahavira, Shvetambaras, *tirthankaras*

QUESTIONS FOR DISCUSSION AND REFLECTION

1. Many Jain lay people are quite successful business leaders. What in their religion accounts for this tendency to prosper? What problems might material success raise for Jains?

2. Why do Jains establish hospitals for animals, even rats? When there is so much human suffering, is this a justifiable use of resources?

3. Is Jain *puja,* making offerings to images at home or in a temple, inconsistent with Jain teaching? Why or why not?

4. In the Jain view, all worldly knowledge, even that found in scriptures, is relative. Would the world be better off if this teaching were more widely adopted? Why or why not?

SOURCES AND SUGGESTIONS FOR FURTHER STUDY

BHASKAR, BHAGCHANDRA JAIN, TRANS., 1991. "Jain Texts." In *World Scripture: A Comparative Anthology of Sacred Texts,* ed. Andrew Wilson. New York: Paragon House.

BHATTACHARYYA, NARENDRA NATH, 1999. *Jain Philosophy.* New Delhi: Munshiram Manoharlal.

CHAPPLE, CHRISTOPHER KEY, 1993. *Nonviolence to Animals, Earth and Self in Asian Traditions.* Albany: State University of New York.

CORT, JOHN E., ED., 1998. *Jain Communities and Culture in Indian History.* Albany: State University of New York.

JACOBI, HERMANN, TRANS., 1884. *Gania Sutras, Part I.* In *Sacred Books of the East,* ed. Max Mueller. Vol. 22. Oxford: Clarendon.

JACOBI, HERMANN, TRANS., 1895. *Gaina Sutras, Part II.* In *Sacred Books of the East,* ed. Max Mueller. Vol. 45. Oxford: Clarendon.

JAINI, PADMANABH S., 1979. *The Jaina Path of Purification.* Berkeley: University of California.

RAM-PRASAD, C., 2001. "Multiplism: A Jaina Ethics of Toleration for a Complex World." In *Ethics in the World Religions,* ed. Joseph Runzo and Nancy M. Martin. New York: Oneworld Publications, 347–69.

TOBIAS, MICHAEL, 1991. *Life Force: The World of Jainism.* Berkeley, CA: Asian Humanities.

Web Sites

www.jainism.org
   (a definitive source for the study of Jainism, with many links)

jainworld.com
   (intended to make the core values of Jainism accessible to all)

www.cs.colostate.edu/~malaiya/jainhlinks.html
   (a Colorado State University site with numerous links)

 Prentice Hall's **Research Navigator** helps students in their further study of the world's religions. Visit *http://www.researchnavigator.com* for help on the research process and access to databases full of relevant material, including the New York *Times.*

CHAPTER

6

Daoism—The Way of Nature

INTRODUCTION

Commentators have labelled the next hundred years the "Pacific Century." The fasting growing economic powers in the world are on the "Pacific rim," among the nations of East Asia—Japan, China, Taiwan, and Korea. Study of East Asian languages and cultures has rapidly expanded in Western colleges and universities, as students prepare themselves for international careers oriented toward East Asia.

Anyone seeking to understand East Asia ignores at his or her peril the religions that have developed in these cultures. The values and customs of East Asian nations are rooted in the religions we will study in the next four chapters—Daoism, Confucianism, Shinto, and Mahayana Buddhism. We will begin our study in this chapter with a general orientation to East Asia, and a brief survey of the history of China and the traditional Chinese worldview. We will then examine the stages of development, sacred writings, basic teachings, and responses to contemporary ethical issues of Daoism. In the next chapter we will consider Confucianism, in Chapter Eight examine the Mahayana Buddhist schools of East Asia, and in Chapter Nine discuss the native religion of Japan, known as Shinto.

AN ORIENTATION TO EAST ASIA

Lands and Peoples

The five independent nations in modern East Asia are China, Japan, the two Koreas (North and South), and Taiwan. China covers 90 percent of the land; its 1.3 billion people make it the most populous country in the world. Japan is a series of islands to the east of China; in the early twenty-first century its population was about 127 million. Korea is on a peninsula located between China and Japan. The population of South Korea stands at nearly 49 million; North Korea's is about 22.5 million. Taiwan is a small island nation south of Japan, just off the Chinese mainland, yet it has a population of nearly 23 million. East Asia is the most crowded region in the world, with a population density almost five times the world average.

In addition to its geographic and population dominance, China has exercised great cultural influence over the entire area. For example, the Confucian ethics developed in China play an exceedingly important role in the everyday life of people throughout East Asia. The Confucian emphasis on proper decorum and obedience to authority are hallmarks of East Asian society.

Politically, China and North Korea are the among the handful of countries still dominated by Marxist Communism. Since the end of World War II, Japan has been a parliamentary democracy. Taiwan is largely ruled by Chinese who left the mainland when the Communists took control in 1949. China claims that Taiwan is one of its provinces and should return to Chinese control. South Korea has a constitutional form of government with democratically elected leaders, but opponents have claimed abuse of human rights by some regimes. Efforts to unify Korea after World War II failed, leading to an armed conflict in the early 1950s that drew in the United States (under the flag of the United Nations) and many other countries.

Economically, North Korea still has the central planning characteristic of a Communist state; China, on the other hand, has allowed a great deal of free enterprise in recent years and is in the midst of surging growth. Japan's industrial and trade success has made it a world economic superpower and brought its people one of the highest standards of living in the world. South Korea and Taiwan have also adopted the capitalist system, which has brought significant economic growth, although many workers complain of low wages and poor working conditions.

A Brief History of China

To provide a framework for the study of the religions of East Asia, let us survey in this chapter, at least superficially, the history of China. In Chapter Eight we will give a brief overview of the histories of Japan and Korea.

The Shang Dynasty emerged in central China about 1750 B.C.E. During the Shang Dynasty, a highly organized society developed the Chinese form of writing still in use.

The next dynasty was the Chou (ca. 1122–222 B.C.E.), begun when the Chou people of western China gained control. Their power centered in the north and west, with semi-independent states in the east. In the late Chou period (a time often called the Warring States Period), these states fought one another continuously, creating a great deal of political and social chaos. This was the context for the emergence of some of the great schools of Chinese thought, including Confucianism and Daoism.

The short lived Ch'in dynasty (221–206 B.C.E.) brought the first strong, central government to China. Before it collapsed, the rulers of this dynasty had begun work on the four-thousand-mile Great Wall of China.

During the Han dynasty (202 B.C.E.–220 C.E.), Confucianism became the foundation for the government and educational system. Chinese influence began to spread into other countries, and the first trade with Europe occurred. Late in the Han dynasty, Indian missionaries brought Buddhism to China.

With the breakup of the Han dynasty, China split into three competing kingdoms, and a series of short dynasties took power in the north and south. Buddhism spread, with monasteries established throughout the land. This is the period during which the various Chinese schools of philosophical Buddhism originated.

The next major dynasty, the Tang (618–907), brought prosperity to China. The capital, Ch'ang-an (now Sian), was a great cultural center. Chinese schools of

Buddhism such as the Ch'an (the Meditation School) and Ching-t'u (the Pure Land School) developed and gained influence. However, Confucianism enjoyed a revival during the ninth century.

During the Sung Dynasty (907–1279) Confucian-educated civil servants dominated the government. The Neo-Confucian school, combining Confucian ethics with Buddhist and Daoist philosophy, received state endorsement.

During the thirteenth century Mongol invaders swept into China from the north. The Mongol leader Kublai Khan established the Yuan dynasty (1279–1368), the period during which the Italian trader and explorer Marco Polo (ca. 1254–1324) reached China.

The Ming dynasty (1368–1644) brought stability and prosperity, with Chinese influence spreading throughout East Asia. Viewing themselves as culturally superior, Ming leaders rebuffed European trade efforts and Christian missionaries.

The Ch'ing dynasty (1644–1911) brought China under the rule of Manchuria. The island of Taiwan came under Chinese control in 1683. A period of order and wealth extended until rapid population growth caused decline in the late eighteenth and nineteenth centuries. In the 1800s China began to export massive amounts of tea and silk to Europe, but still sought to limit European influence. The Opium War (1839–1842) between China and Great Britain, caused by Chinese resistance to the smuggling of opium into China, ended in a British victory. The treaty of Nan-ching gave Hong Kong to Great Britain, and opened some Chinese ports to the British. Special privileges were soon secured by other European powers and the United States. Hong Kong was restored to Chinese rule in 1997, but is allowed a degree of political and economic autonomy.

China was weakened by the Taiping Rebellion (1851–1864) and a war with Japan (1894–1895). In the face of growing Western political, economic, and religious influence, a Chinese secret society (known as the "Boxers" by Westerners) led a rebellion in 1900.

A nationalist movement led by a Western-educated physician, Sun Yat-sen, mounted a successful revolution which established a republic. The last emperor of China, a six-year-old boy, surrendered the throne in 1912. A period of struggle ensued. Chiang Kai-shek succeeded Sun Yat-sen as head of the Nationalist Party in 1925 and united China in 1928.

The Japanese conquest of China began in 1931 when Manchuria was seized. By 1938 the Japanese controlled most of China. When World War II ended in 1945, a civil war broke out between the Nationalists and the Communists (led by Mao Zedong).

The victorious Communists established the People's Republic of China in 1949, and the Nationalists fled to Taiwan. Religions were repressed by the Communists, especially after the Cultural Revolution of 1966. Since the death of Mao in 1976 religious groups have been allowed greater freedom, but government control continues. Pressure for more political freedom has increased as China has opened its markets and increased contact with the West. However, a student-led democracy movement was suppressed in 1989 and its leaders executed or jailed. Since that time, further political reform seems to have been thwarted, while economic modernization continues.

The East Asian Worldview and Indigenous Religions

The traditional worldview of China forms the basis for popular, indigenous Chinese religion. In addition, elements of this worldview had an important influence on the classical Chinese and Japanese religions, as we shall see. We will blend at this point a discussion of the traditional Chinese worldview with a discussion of the major characteristics of indigenous (or popular, as it is sometimes called) Chinese religion.

Humanity: An Underlying Harmony   If there is a key word in the traditional Chinese worldview, which influenced the rest of East Asia, it must surely be *harmony*. The perception of an underlying harmony that humans must seek to discover within themselves and manifest in their individual and social lives runs deep, expressed in a variety of ways in the religions we will study. To some degree this harmony is similar to the "balance" that we identified as a feature of the indigenous worldview in general (see Chapter Two).

In humans, as in all reality, the harmony is reflected in a balance of the complementary forces, *yin* and *yang* (see below). In the traditional Chinese worldview, these forces in humans are identified as souls or spirits. Each person has both *yang* (*shen*) and *yin* (*kwei*) spirits. At death the *shen* soul (*hun*) becomes an ancestral spirit, while the *kwei* soul (*p'o*) merges with the ground when the body dissolves.

Problem: Disharmony   If harmony is the key word, then the condition that gives rise to the need for transformation, according to this view of the world, is, of course, *disharmony*. Humans are susceptible to losing the pattern of harmony that is so observable in nature, and therein lies the basic human problem. As we shall see, Confucianism and Daoism (and other religions of East Asia) may describe the situation of disharmony quite differently, but the word applies to the diagnosis of the basic human problem they all affirm.

Cause: Turning from Harmony   Whether humans lose sight of a preexistent harmony that runs through all life, or fail to create and maintain harmony by not performing the proper rituals and committing themselves to the right ordering of their lives, is, as we shall see, an important point of contention among the religions of East Asia. They identify different specific reasons for disharmony.

According to popular Chinese religions, restless spirits are often the culprits in causing disharmony (although it is the human failure to properly acknowledge and tend to them that causes disharmony to persist). However, all agree that humans choose the path that leads to disharmony, and it is up to them to initiate the action (or recognize the "inaction"!) that will realize harmony.

End: Harmony in This Life   Harmony is, in the Chinese worldview, primarily a this-worldly phenomenon. The ideal of families living in harmony, and a society ruled and inhabited by virtuous persons living harmoniously, is an important part of the "goal" in popular Chinese religions (and the others as well). Although life beyond death is a facet of this worldview, the emphasis is placed on the desired transformation occurring within life on earth.

In popular Chinese religion, as in popular religions of other cultures, the specific goals are health, a full life span, prosperity, harmony within the family, continuity of the family lineage, and protection from natural and human disasters.

Means: Discerning and Living in Harmony   Indigenous Chinese religious practices are not the domain of one social class or geographic setting. They may be found in both villages and cities, observed by educated and uneducated alike. The means of realizing harmony (at the level of popular religion) that we will survey here are ancestor veneration; the maintenance of worship of gods at temples, shrines, and family altars; and divination. In addition, the important concepts of *de* (virtue) and *xiao* (or *hsiao,* filial piety), are fundamental.

De (pronounced "day" and also transliterated as *te*) means inherent power or virtue. In a sense, it is the principle which allows or creates harmonious human life. Where virtue is valued, there is harmony; where it is absent, there is chaos. Although Confucianism and Daoism developed quite different teachings about virtue (as we shall see), they both focus on the question of how to lead virtuous lives, and that concern is deeply imbued in the Chinese way of life.

Although filial piety (*xiao*) rose to prominence later as one of the principal Confucian virtues, it is a principle deeply rooted in China, as well as in other East Asian cultures. Specifically, filial piety refers to the loyalty shown by a son to his father. More generally, it is the respect and reverence anyone in an inferior social position shows for superiors. It is at the root of the Asian respect for authority that even the most casual observer in China, Japan, Korea, or Taiwan immediately notices. It is principally seen at the family level, but has at times been transferred or extended to the emperor, the nation, a political party, or, in modern Japan especially, to the corporation. It should be noted that even as juniors are to show loyalty to elders, elders are to treat their juniors with courtesy and concern.

Reverence for elders extends to ancestors, who play an exceedingly important role in the worldview of the cultures of East Asia. Traditionally, the ancestors have been considered spirits who continue to play an important role in family life. If proper respect is shown to them they will assist the family. If veneration is not shown to the ancestors, their displeasure can bring hardship.

Many of the popular deities of indigenous Chinese religion are particularly important ancestors who have been accorded the status of gods. For example, the deity *Ma-tsu,* goddess of fishermen, was at first the soul of a young girl who died before her marriage. Other deities are gods and goddesses associated with natural elements such as the soil. Proper worship of these deities determines whether there will be good crops and fertility in general. In each location a mound of earth represents the spirit of the soil. In addition, each region, city, village, and family has its own particular gods.

Divination is the "deciphering" of reality in order to determine the significance of present or future events. In China, divination was practiced from earliest times. At first diviners read cracks on heated bones and tortoise shells. Over time the cracks were identified with the *yin* and *yang* forces, an unbroken line (—) with the *yang,* and a broken line (– –) with the *yin.* These two types of lines may be arranged in triads eight different ways, to form the Eight Trigrams. The trigrams may be paired to yield sixty-four possible hexagrams. These patterns were interpreted in the classic manual of interpretation for Chinese divination, the *I Ching* (Book of Changes). Diviners dropped sticks on the ground to form the trigrams (or hexagrams), and then, using the *I Ching,* interpreted their significance in relation to the particular concern being addressed. Use of the *I Ching* has become popular in the West, and the manual and instructions for its use are available in many bookstores. Other forms of divination have developed in China, including geomancy (reading the signs found in the earth) and palmistry.

Reality: The Harmony of *Yin* and *Yang*   Long before Daoist and Confucian philosophies had crystallized in China, the view had become popular that two interacting, interdependent, complementary forces—*yin* and *yang*—are present in all reality.

The yin/yang symbol reflects the traditional East Asian view of the nature of reality. It manifests the opposite, but complementary forces in the cosmos. The yin (the dark side) is passive, soft, and feminine, while the yang (the light side) is active, hard, and masculine. The wavy line between the two indicates the forces are in constant motion, and the two dots show that the forces are interdependent.

The *yang* force is described with the following adjectives: active, hard, warm, dry, bright, positive, expansive, procreative, and masculine. Its symbol is the tiger. The *yin* force has the opposite characteristics: passive, soft, cold, wet, dark, negative, contracting, and feminine. Its symbol is the dragon. These forces are not considered from a moral perspective. One is not good and the other evil.

Everything in nature and society consists of these two energies interacting. In some things the *yang* force dominates, or is in ascendancy; in other things the *yin* force; but in all things (including humans), both are necessarily present. During one period the *yin* force may be prominent, while the *yang* recedes, or vice versa. For example, a person may ordinarily have a dominant *yin*, and thus be a quiet, reserved person, but at times of arousal the *yang* takes precedence.

In the indigenous Chinese religion that predates the great philosophies, the spirits present everywhere are either the heavenly *yang* (*shen*) spirits or earthly *yin* (*kwei*) spirits.

In nature the five basic elements are either *yang* or *yin*. Wood and fire are *yang*, while metal and water are *yin*. Earth belongs to both. The interaction of *yin* and *yang* (and the five elements) can be seen in the changing seasons. *Yin* is dominant in winter, gradually to be replaced, as spring and summer come, by *yang*. As the ripened fruit falls to the ground, so the *yang* gives way to *yin*, and as new life emerges from the cold ground, *yang* comes to prominence again.

The symbol for *yin* and *yang* together is a circle, cut in half by a curving line. One side of the circle is dark, with a white spot, while the other is white, with a dark spot. The curving line symbolizes the dynamic interaction between the two forces within all reality (represented by the circle). The two dots indicate that the *yin* is present in the *yang*, and vice versa.

Traditionally, wisdom in China is associated with understanding and conforming to the *yin* and *yang* forces in their interaction. There is a strong sense that there is a right (auspicious) time for actions and a right place to build structures, which are in proper harmony with the interacting forces. The alternation between growth and decline, waxing and waning of the moon, and success and failure all reflect the cosmic interaction.

Sacred: A Fundamental Harmony   According to the Chinese worldview, and throughout East Asia, there is a strong perception of an underlying order in the cosmos as a whole, in nature, and in human societies. What accounts for that order? Different religions in East Asia speak of this fundamental harmony in distinct ways at different times. However, no East Asian religion is immune from the influence of this perception of a harmony that is the underlying reality all must recognize.

Early in Chinese history, two concepts emerged concerning the spiritual world, which have had a strong influence on the understanding of government in China. During the Shang Dynasty, a deity who went by the name of *Shang Ti* ("Ruler on High") became the object of worship. He was thought to determine when and if crops would grow and whether human projects would be successful. The Emperor's diviners consulted him, for example, to find out when to go to war or sue for peace. Like the Indian Vedic deity *Varuna* (see Chapter Three), *Shang Ti* was the guarantor of the moral order. He ruled over a celestial hierarchy, modelled after the government bureaucracy, with deities in charge of the "ministries" of Thunder, Epidemics, Fire, and so on. *Shang Ti* evolved into the Jade Emperor, the central deity in popular Chinese religion to this day.

During the Chou dynasty, a more impersonal designation for the concept of a heavenly power developed—*T'ien* (Heaven). Until the last emperor left the Chinese throne in 1906, the Emperor was known as the Son of Heaven. He conducted special ceremonies intended to maintain the harmony between Earth and Heaven.

According to the traditional Chinese worldview, rulers maintain power only as long as they retain the mandate of heaven. First expressed in the twelfth century B.C.E., this concept has influenced the attitude toward government in China ever since, especially during periods of imperial rule. It holds that when rulers fail to exercise their responsibility to maintain harmony in society through the promotion of virtue, they lose their right to govern, and a revolution is not only in order, it is inevitable. This concept places a heavy burden on any government to create a strong sense of moral order in the society, which the people can recognize and endorse. It also lends support to the view that revolutions are a necessary ingredient in the cosmic order. This concept was invoked by the most recent Chinese revolutionaries, the Communists under Mao Zedong.

DAOISM: THE WAY OF NATURE

The name "Daoism" (also written as Taoism) is ambiguous. It may refer to the philosophical tradition traced to the legendary sage *Lao Tzi* (also written as *Lao Tzu*) and first expressed in the collection of poems called the *Daodejing* ("The Classic of the Way and its Power," also written as *Tao-Te-Ching*). Since the Han dynasty this tradition has been called *Dao jia* ("the philosophy of the Dao"). This is the "Daoism" most widely known in the West today, mostly because of widespread exposure to translations of the Daodejing. Philosophical Daoism has faded as a distinct movement in East Asia, but it did have an influence on the Meditation School of Buddhism (Zen) that continues to exercise considerable influence in Japan. It also had a profound influence on the arts and literature in both China and Japan.

However, the Daoism currently practiced in Taiwan and other Chinese communities (but still largely dormant in the People's Republic) is more closely associated with a tradition known as *Dao jiao* ("the teaching of the Dao"). Specifically, *Dao jiao* involves the worship of deities and the propitiation of spirits through rituals carried out by hereditary Daoist priests. It is one facet of a popular religious movement that, as we shall now see, evolved from philosophical Daoism, transforming some of its basic teachings.

In our presentation of Daoism we will trace its development from a mystical philosophy of life that did not focus on gods and had no use for rituals, to a popular religious system with a pantheon of deities and a plethora of rituals.

Stages of Development and Sacred Texts

Tour *The Sacred World* CD!

The Legendary *Lao Zi* The legendary founder of philosophical Daoism is known to tradition as Lao Zi ("the old Master"). Some interpreters question if a man called Lao Zi ever existed as an historical person; others see a real person behind the legends. According to a second-century B.C.E. biography, Lao Zi was born in 604 B.C.E. As an adult, he took a government post. However, he left his position as an archivist because he came to the realization that governments with their laws and bureaucracies distort the simplicity by which humans should live. He withdrew from society and resolved to live a solitary life. He was besieged by visitors (including Confucius, according to the legend) and decided to leave society all together. According to tradition, as he traveled by, the gatekeeper at the pass into the western regions persuaded Lao Zi to write down his philosophy of life. In short, enigmatic poems he wrote a treatise on how to live, calling it the *Daodejing*. The earliest name for the

Daodejing was *Lao Zi,* so it is entirely possible that the legend of the "old Master" arose to provide a specific author for this ancient book.

The *Daodejing*   Regardless of who wrote this work, the Daodejing stands alongside works such as the Bhagavad Gita of India as one of the great classics of religious literature. Many contemporary interpreters think that it was actually written sometime between 350 and 275 B.C.E., during the latter days of the Warring States Period. However, like other literary classics, it is timeless in its basic meaning.

The Daodejing is a short work, with eighty-one brief chapters, including only about 5,500 words. The short, enigmatic poems that constitute its chapters have been the subject of hundreds of commentaries and translations. The Daodejing has become the most widely known Chinese classic. It may have been written originally as a political work, a manual to instruct those who would aspire to rule in the art of governing, but like all great literary works it has various levels of meaning.

Politically, the Daodejing must be considered a failure. No Chinese government, or probably any other in history, has made a serious attempt to implement on a large scale its philosophy of passive government. Its lasting impact has been at other levels. The Daodejing's teaching of natural, simple living has inspired millions of readers to examine their own lifestyles and to let go of that which has been forcing them into uncomfortable, even destructive patterns. It has also served to spiritually inspire many with its teaching of a mystical, harmonious process that is true reality.

Since the Daodejing is the basis for Daoist philosophy we will discuss its teachings more fully in the next section.

Zhuang Zi   Another important Daoist philosopher was a fourth-century B.C.E. teacher named *Zhuang Zi* ("Master Chuang," also written as *Chuang Tzu*), legendary author of a work that goes by the same name.

The *Zhuang Zi,* second in importance in Daoism only to the Daodejing, argues against other philosophical schools popular at the time to show that the Dao cannot be understood rationally, and that one must let go of dependence on knowledge and words in order to live harmoniously. It distinguishes between the Dao and the words used to describe the Dao, saying that the two belong to different orders of understanding, as footprints differ from the shoes that make them. We must, the Zhuang Zi says, give up all thoughts about the Dao in order to experience oneness with the Dao.

The Zhuang Zi also argues that there is an original, natural equality of all things, which humans lose sight of as they accumulate knowledge and build civilizations. The Zhuang Zi is much less political than the Daodejing, emphasizing instead a natural, spiritual freedom to which we must seek to return.

Most scholars today think that the principal sections of the Zhuang Zi were written about the same time as the Daodejing. The philosophical traditions represented by these two works were combined in the third century C.E. into the movement that became known as Philosophical Daoism.

The Development of Daoist Rituals and Magical Practices   In speaking of the eternal Dao, sections of both the Daodejing and Zhuang Zi seem to suggest that whoever is in harmony with the Dao lives forever. This intimation of immortality in the classic texts, combined with the popular concern for health, happiness, and long life, became the basis for a new branch of Daoism, often called in the West "Religious," "Ritual," "Applied," or sometimes "Magical" Daoism. By the second century C.E. there was an organized Daoist "religious" movement, focusing on the pursuit of immortality and well-being, which continues today. The facet of this movement dealing with rituals of cosmic renewal, carried out to renew the community's relationship with deities and spirits, is called *Dao jiao*.

The cosmological background for "religious" Daoism is the teaching (common to many religions) that humans are a microcosm, reflecting in their natures the structure of the cosmos as a whole. According to philosophical Daoism, the unmanifest Dao is the source of all reality, and the manifest reality of this world, including humanity, is the result of the interaction between the *yin* and *yang* forces. "Religious" Daoism emphasizes the teaching that the "breath" (called the *qi* and also written as *ch'i*) of the Dao creates the *yin/yang* dynamic. However, when *qi* divides into *yin* and *yang*, death and dissolution enter into reality, because these forces tend to become imbalanced. In humans this results in the deterioration of the body and, eventually, death. If the creative balance can be restored, then *qi* will not dissipate and humans can avoid death and decay. Whoever attains the perfect balance becomes a *hsien* (immortal being). The quest for immortality can be documented in China by the third century B.C.E.

A variety of paths to "immortality" developed. One was alchemy, the search for some elixir that could be taken to preserve the vital force. Another was a hygienic and dietary regime, in which foods with energies thought to correspond to the five basic elements were eaten, and foods that caused the vital essence to dissipate were avoided. Breath control techniques and physical exercises also developed as a means to preserve the *qi*. Sexual practices (similar to Indian tantrism; see Chapter Three) involving the suppression of orgasm were also thought to contribute to maintenance of the original creative balance. Finally, living a life of virtue was thought to be essential to becoming an "immortal."

In addition to becoming a *hsien*, this branch of Daoism also responded to the popular desire for assistance in confronting the dilemmas of everyday living. A hereditary priesthood arose, which could be called upon to conduct rituals to aid people in all sorts of circumstances.

The second-century Daoist movements, which developed to assist individuals in the pursuit of immortality, had a political dimension. They envisioned the coming of a new age of the Dao, and some of the Daoist communities resorted to military means to achieve it. Various Daoist schools, with numerous individual communities, organized, and competed with one another for influence.

Associated with this branch of Daoism is an elaborate array of hierarchically arranged spiritual beings, organized on the bureaucratic model of the Han dynasty. Highest is the unmanifest Dao, next the primordial chaos or breath (*qi*), followed by the Three Officials (or Three Heavenly Worthies). These were the Jade Emperor, Lao Zi, and the Marshal of supernatural beings. Temples and shrines, in which Daoist priests conducted rituals to honor these deities and seek their blessing, sprang up all over China. Further down are the various divine ministries, inhabiting nine heavens; still lower are the spirits of demons, humans, ancestors, and animals. The popular practice of Daoism approached a type of animism in which everything was thought to be inhabited by spirits who must be properly respected. Some of the more popular spirits were not exclusively Daoist. One was the "God of the Stove," the *shen* thought to sit in the kitchen corner in every home and watch over the family.

As early as the fifth century C.E. a canon of Daoist scriptures had been collected. The canon in use today dates from the fifteenth century and includes charms, descriptions of gods, alchemical texts, histories of Daoist movements and biographies of leaders, as well as the Daodejing and other philosophical texts. Only a small portion is actually used in Daoist rituals.

The Worldview of Daoist Philosophy

Any discussion of Daoist philosophy should be prefaced by the caution found in the Daodejing (Legge 1891: 100):

> He who knows does not speak; he who is (ever ready to) speak about it does not know it.

Daoist philosophy defies the neat summarization and classification that is the style of textbooks such as this! Daoist truths must be experienced for oneself. Therefore, what follows should be considered only an invitation to a personal investigation of Daoist philosophy. The place to start a search is with one of the many available translations of the Daodejing (e.g., Mitchell 1988). In this section we will merely call attention to some of the basic teachings of that work. The numbers in parentheses indicate the number of the poem that readers may wish to consult in relation to the particular observation. In a sense, the one-word answer of Daoist philosophy to all the questions of our framework for understanding is "Dao," but that is the place to end, not begin the discussion!

Humanity: The *Dao* Within   According to Daoism, humans, like all reality, are a part of the cosmic process known as the Dao (25). The Dao naturally comes to expression through us, manifest in the *yin* and *yang* forces. The Daodejing teaches that when humans yield to the workings of the Dao, they are soft and supple and their lives are harmonious (76). They are truly alive. They are one with the Dao (23).

Problem: Resisting the Flow of the *Dao*   In a sense, as with the teachings we encountered in the religions that originated in India, the basic problem humans face, according to the Daodejing, is that we do not know who we truly are. Our fundamental choice is either to acknowledge that reality and let ourselves go with the flow of the Dao (23), or to resist who we are and try to establish our own, separate identities (13).

Cause: Striving for Permanence and Virtue   As Buddhism teaches, the Daodejing suggests that when we allow ourselves to succumb to the illusion of a unique, permanent self we fall victim to desire and craving (1, 9). We strive to "become," to "make something of ourselves." For philosophical Daoism this human striving for permanence is the cause of the dilemma to be overcome.

The *Daodejing* also makes the intriguing claim that if we strive to be virtuous, the result will not be harmony but chaos. Poem 38 expresses this teaching in these words (Legge 1891: 80–81):

> when the Tao was lost, its attributes appeared; when its attributes were lost, benevolence appeared; when benevolence was lost, righteousness appeared; and when righteousness was lost, the proprieties appeared. Now propriety is the attenuated form of lealheartedness and good faith, and is also the commencement of disorder.

End: The Harmony of the *Dao*   The goal of human life is the same as the goal of all life: harmony with the Dao (15, 55). For humans this means a natural and simple life (8), seeing both life and death as a part of the eternal Dao (16, 33). As the Zhuang Zi puts it, "birth is not a beginning; death is not an end. There is existence without limitation; there is continuity without a starting point" (*Zhuang Zi* 23. Giles 1926: 304).

The ideal life is that of the Sage (22, 33, 47). The goal of Daoism is at both an individual and communal level, for if those who are leaders practice the life of natural goodness, then society will be in harmony with the Dao.

The notion of a "goal" is ironic in Daoism, for the "goal" is to realize the natural, cosmic process that is already present. "Goal" implies striving, and that is the problem we must overcome. Therefore, in a sense the real goal in Daoist philosophy is to stop having a goal!

Means: Action without Assertion (*wu wei*)   What is the simple life through which one experiences harmony with the Dao? The term *wu wei* ("inaction" or "nonpurposiveness") expresses it most clearly. To practice *wu wei* is to act without asserting oneself (2, 47). On the one hand, *wu wei* means to have no ambitions, no desire for fame or power, no need to influence or dominate others. It is to be not what others think you should be, but to simply "be yourself" in the most basic and natural sense.

Such a person may seem weak-willed, passive, even stupid to those who live by desire and striving. However, such a person "achieves without achieving." How can that be? By living spontaneously, the person is allowing the Dao to come to its true expression, and "virtue" (*de*) will be natural rather than contrived (18, 38). Rather than seeking to "do good" for others, goodness will naturally emanate from the person in nonmanipulative acts of kindness. Others will be positively influenced not by an *effort* to influence them, but by the power of the Dao being actualized. As we will see, this attitude toward the "virtuous life" is much different than that taught by Confucian ethicists.

In governments the best course is noninterference (60). In education it is best not to seek knowledge actively, but to be passively open and receptive (47). You cannot learn what is truly important from those who would presume to have the knowledge to teach you (19). Far better than knowing the world outside is knowing who you truly are (72, 33). (Do you agree? If so, why are you reading this book? Are you learning anything?)

Poem 54 puts it this way (Legge 1891: 97–98):

> Tao when nursed within one's self,
> His vigour will make true;
> And where the family it rules
> What riches will accrue!
> The neighborhood where it prevails
> In thriving will abound;
> And when 'tis seen throughout the state,
> Good fortune will be found.
> Employ it the kingdom o'er,
> And men will thrive all around.

To sum up, "in letting go, it all gets done" (48).

Reality: The Power of the *Dao*   As we have already mentioned, in Daoism the world we directly experience is the manifestation of the unmanifest Dao. In other words, it is the actualization of the Dao (42). The pattern of the Dao is one of return, a process of coming into being, maturing, and then decaying and returning to the

Dao (16, 32, 40). Everything is a part of this cyclical process. Everything has its own *de*, its destiny or "power" (21, 51), which, when not opposed, will naturally manifest itself in the process of living. You might find it interesting to compare this teaching to the dharma, which we encountered in South Asian religions.

Sacred: The Nameless and Eternal *Dao* We have spoken frequently already of the Dao ("Way"), but we have avoided trying to explain what the Dao means. That is because the Dao which can be named or explained is *not* the Dao. The enigmatic first poem of the Daodejing creates the sense of the mystery of the Dao, which saturates the text (Legge 1891: 47–48):

> The Tao that can be trodden is not the enduring and unchanging Tao.
> The name that can be named is not the enduring and unchanging name.
> Having no name, it is the Originator of heaven and earth; having a name, it is
>   the Mother of all things.
> Always without desire we must be found,
> If its deep mystery within us be,
> Its outer fringe is all that we shall see.
> Under these two aspects, it is really the same;
> but as development takes place, it receives the different names.
> Together we call them the Mystery.
> Where Mystery is the deepest is the gate of all that is subtle and wonderful.

We should first clarify what the Dao is not. The Dao is not God, at least in any personal sense (4, 60). The Dao is not a *being* of any sort, yet all beings are manifestations of the Dao.

The best we can do is mention the metaphors the Daodejing uses to try to point us toward the Dao. One of the most frequent images is the flow of water (78). Like a stream the Dao is in constant motion, and over time wears down all that opposes it. Reality itself is the flow of the Dao, and those who are "truly real" are those who are going with that flow.

Feminine images point us toward the Dao. The Dao is the Mother, the source of life (1, 25). The Dao is the womb of all reality. The Dao is also like a valley (6), for it is the emptiness of the valley that gives it reality. Stated more philosophically, the Dao is the "nonbeing" from which all "being" comes (40, 25), yet the Dao is also everything that is! The Dao is also like a block of wood, from which the carved image emerges, the course of creativity (15, 32), the Void (11), or a deep pool (4).

Where can you find the Dao? Look within yourself (21).

Daoism in the Twenty-First Century

Religious Daoism today is found principally in Taiwan and Hong Kong, as well as Chinese communities in Malaysia, Thailand, Singapore, and wherever sizeable Chinese groups have settled (for example, San Francisco). In these communities Daoist priests are visible and very active. They perform rituals of healing for individuals and lead communal worship.

Daoist monasteries were closed in the People's Republic of China, and have not been as readily reopened in recent years as other religious institutions. According to the official policy of the Communist government, Daoism is a superstition rather than a religion and therefore does not have the same protections as Christianity,

Buddhism, and Islam. However, the government has moderated its position, and allowed (and in some cases supported) the rebuilding of Daoist temples. Daoism is also being reintroduced into other public places. For example, restaurants are being allowed to display small altars to Daoist deities of wealth and protection. Individuals in China are also less reserved about their observance of Daoist traditions. For example, paper "hell bank notes" are openly burned by relatives of those who have died, in order to improve the ancestors' status in the afterlife.

The growing popularity of *tai-ch'i*, the exercise regimen and approach to the martial arts based on the Daoist teachings, is evidence of the vitality of Daoism in the twenty-first century. The principles of yielding, softness, centeredness, slowness, balance, suppleness, and rootedness found in *tai-ch'i* are all drawn from Daoism. The influence of Daoist philosophy is seen in the names of movements in the *tai-ch'i* form, such as Push the Boat with the Current, and Wind Sweeps the Plum Blossoms. The influence of "religious" Daoism, especially its astrological elements, is seen in other *tai-ch'i* movements, such as Step Up to Seven Stars, and Embrace the Moon.

The influence of Daoism is also seen in the growing popularity of the practice of *feng shui* (the art of reading the *yin* and *yang* forces present in particular settings, in order to insure the harmony of buildings and activities), and acupuncture.

The rapidly growing new religious movement known as *Falun Gong* (see Chapter Fourteen) also draws on Daoism in its teachings.

In East Asia the teachings of philosophical Daoism were largely absorbed into the meditation school of Buddhism. The tradition is still preserved, however, by individuals (including many in the West) who find in the Daodejing and other classical texts an appealing philosophy of life. Its teachings of the return to a natural way of life are particularly attractive amidst the conflicts and turmoil of an increasingly frenetic world.

CHAPTER SUMMARY

After orienting ourselves to the lands and people of East Asia, we surveyed the history of China. The traditional worldview of East Asia includes a view of reality as the interaction of balancing forces (*yin* and *yang*), the use of divination, social relationships based on loyalty and deference to those in a superior role and respect and courtesy for those in an inferior position, a sense of an underlying harmony, the importance of virtue, and the political consequences of this harmony.

We then encountered Daoism, tracing its development from a mystical philosophy that taught a life of harmony with the mysterious Dao, to a religion aimed at attaining physical immortality and material well-being through propitiation of gods and spirits. We summarized the worldview of philosophical Daoism, drawing on the Daodejing as our principal source.

The chapter concluded with comments on the resurgence of Daoism in the twenty-first century.

IMPORTANT TERMS AND PHRASES

qi (*ch'i*), Dao, Daodejing (Tao-te-ching), *de* (*te*), filial piety (*xiao*), *hsien*, I Ching, Lao Zi (Lao Tzu), mandate of heaven, *Shang Ti*, *tai-ch'i*, *T'ien*, *wu wei*, *yin* and *yang*, Zhuang Zi (Chuang Tzu)

QUESTIONS FOR DISCUSSION AND REFLECTION

1. As you experience the natural world and the behavior and personalities of people, do you observe *yin* ("passive") and *yang* ("assertive") forces at work, balancing each other?

2. What evidence might be cited to support (or challenge) the Daoist perspective that everything is the manifestation of the Dao?

3. What do you think accounts for the appeal of philosophical Daoism to many people in Europe and the United States?

4. What is meant by the Daoist principle of "going with the flow"? Is this Daoist principle different from what people in Western societies usually mean when they use the same expression?

5. Do you agree with the Daodejing that when people try to make themselves good and virtuous, the result is chaos?

6. What is meant by the Daoist principle of "simple living"? Is it possible in the fast-paced modern world?

7. Do you agree with the Daodejing that death should be accepted as part of the process of life? Why or why not?

8. If the Dao that can be named is not the true Dao, how can we say anything at all about the meaning of the Dao? Is the Dao meaningless?

SOURCES AND SUGGESTIONS FOR FURTHER STUDY

CHAN, WING-TSIT, COMP. AND TRANS., 1963. *A Sourcebook in Chinese Philosophy.* Princeton: Princeton University.

THOMPSON, LAURENCE G., 1995. *Chinese Religion: An Introduction.* 5th ed. Belmont, CA: Wadsworth.

CREEL, H. G., 1982. *What Is Taoism?* Chicago: University of Chicago.

GILES, HERBERT A., TRANS., 1926. *Chuang Tzu: Mystic, Moralist, and Social Reformer.* 2d ed. Shanghai: Kelly and Walsh.

HOFF, BENJAMIN, 1983. *The Tao of Pooh.* New York: Penguin.

KOHN, LIVIA, 1993. *The Taoist Experience.* Albany: State University of New York.

KOHN, LIVIA, ED., 2002. *Daoist Identity: History, Lineage and Ritual.* Honolulu: University of Hawaii.

KOHN, LIVIA, ED., 2001. *Daoism and Chinese Culture.* Cambridge, MA: Three Pines.

LEGGE, JAMES, TRANS., 1891. *The Sacred Books of China: The Texts of Taoism, Part I.* In *The Sacred Books of the East,* ed. Max Müller. Vol. 39. Oxford: Clarendon.

LEGGE, JAMES, TRANS., 1892. *The Sacred Books of China: The Texts of Taoism, Part II.* In *The Sacred Books of the East,* ed. Max Müller. Vol. 40. Oxford: Clarendon.

MITCHELL, STEPHEN, 1988. *The Tao te Ching: A New English Version.* New York: HarperPerennial.

ROBINET, ISABELLE, 1997. *Taoism: Growth of a Religion,* trans. Phyllis Brooks. Stanford, CA: Stanford University.

ROTH, H. D., 1999. *Original Tao: Inward Training (Nei-yeh) and the Foundations of Taoist Mysticism.* New York: Columbia University.

WELCH, HOLMES, 1965. *Taoism: The Parting of the Way.* Boston: Beacon.

Web Sites

newton.uor.edu/Departments&Programs/AsianStudiesDept/china-phil.html
www.clas.ufl.edu/users/gthursby/taoism/
helios.unive.it/~pregadio/taoism.html
    (academic sites with links for the study of Daoism and other religions in East Asia)

taopage.org
    (a resource for the study of Daoism)

taorestore.org
    (the site of the Taoist Restoration Society)

 Prentice Hall's **Research Navigator** helps students in their further study of the world's religions. Visit *__http://www.researchnavigator.com__* for help on the research process and access to databases full of relevant material, including the New York *Times.*

CHAPTER

7

Confucianism—The Way of Virtue

INTRODUCTION

Some interpreters suggest, somewhat whimsically (but with a grain of truth), that if philosophical Daoism is the *yin* of East Asia, then Confucianism is the *yang*. After your study of both, consider whether this is an apt description.

Confucianism is originally a Western term, applied by early Christian missionaries to China in order to understand the scholarly tradition they found dominant (Jensen 1997). In China, the tradition called Confucianism in the West was known as the *ru* tradition (*rujia*), a literati (intellectual) movement rooted in the self-cultivation of moral virtue. Like the designation "Hinduism," "Confucianism" is now accepted as an appropriate label for this tradition by those within it. For two thousand years, until the early twentieth century, Confucianism dominated the philosophy of education and the approach to government, first in China, then in Korea and Japan. It is undergoing a contemporary resurgence.

Indeed, the influence of Confucianism on East Asian culture is difficult to overemphasize. Many would attribute the miraculous postwar recovery of Japan, Korea, and Taiwan (not to mention the resurgence of China) to an innate commitment to Confucian ideals.

In this chapter we will follow the development of Confucianism from the time of Master *K'ung* (Confucius) to the twentieth century suppression of Confucianism in China under the Communist government. Then we will describe the Confucian worldview, contrasting it with Daoist teachings. Finally, we will discuss the status of religion in the People's Republic of China, and the renewal of Confucianism in China in the twenty-first century.

STAGES OF DEVELOPMENT AND SACRED TEXTS

Founder: Master *K'ung* (Confucius)

As was the case in other great movements, the followers of the man known in the West as Confucius created biographies that blended actual history with legend. Nevertheless, we can reconstruct the basic aspects of his life with some confidence.

Confucius was born in the ancient, feudal state of Lu, now the area known as Shantung, in about 551 B.C.E. The name Confucius is a Latinized version of *K'ung fu-tzu*, which means "Great Master *K'ung*." *K'ung* was his family name; his given name was *Ch'iu*. Shortly after his birth, his father died and his mother had to sacrifice to provide him with an education, helping to instill in him the value of learning. At about the age of fifty, Confucius was appointed to a high office in the administration of the Duke of Lu. However, his policies were not adopted and he resigned or was forced out of office. He was about fifty-five when he began a thirteen-year period of wandering from state to state, teaching a program of political and social reform. At age sixty-seven he returned to Lu and spent the rest of his life teaching, and (according to tradition) editing the Confucian classics. When he died, in about 479 B.C.E., he was discouraged by his failure to have more influence on government. However, he left a band of followers committed to his teaching.

The Analects and Other Texts

The *Analects* (*Lun Yu*) are the reputed sayings and conversations of Confucius. They were compiled after his death, over a long period of time, in various layers. However, the major Confucian teachings are present in the Analects, making them an important source for the ideas of Confucius himself and his early disciples. The Analects became the principal cornerstone of both the Chinese educational system and the examination system for government officials. It has also continued to serve as an inspiration for personal reflection, much as the Bhagavad Gita has done in India.

The Analects are one of the *Four Books,* which serve as a basis for our understanding of Confucian teaching. The *Great Learning* (*Ta Hsueh*) was a chapter from the *Book of Rites* (39), which served as an introductory text for students beginning their study of Confucian ethics. The *Doctrine of the Mean* (*Chung Yung*) was also excerpted from the Book of Rites (Chapter 28). It deals with the relationship between humanity and the moral order. The *Book of Mencius* is the third-century B.C.E. collection of the sayings of one of Confucius's principal disciples. It is the first attempt at a systematic philosophical statement of the teachings of Confucius.

The tradition that Confucius himself wrote the Five Classics is not considered historically accurate by contemporary scholars, but they are nonetheless important in the study of Confucianism. They include the *Shu Ching* (Book of History), the *Shih Ching* (Book of Poetry), the *Li Chi* (Book of Rites), the *I Ching* (Book of Changes), and the *Ch'un Ch'iu* (Annals of Spring and Autumn). It is quite possible that these anthologies existed by the time of Confucius, and that he made use of them in his own teaching, perhaps even editing them.

Formation of the Confucian School, and Confucianism as State Teaching

According to tradition, the principal disciples of Confucius became teachers themselves. In addition to the Four Books, the disciples produced the popular *Book of*

Filial Piety (*Hsiao Ching*). Although not rigidly organized in this early period, they formed what we may call a Confucian School.

These were turbulent times. The feudal order was breaking up, and many rival schools emerged. In addition to Confucianism and Daoism, other schools included the Mohists (who sought to unite all people in a loving community) and the Legalists (who argued for a strict law administered by force as the basis for society).

Two of the leaders of the Confucian School deserve special mention. Master *Meng* (known as *Mencius* in the West, ca. 371–289 B.C.E.) emphasized the Confucian virtue of humaneness (*ren* or *jen*), but rejected the Mohist notion of a universal goodwill with no regard for kinship or social standing. He taught that humaneness must interact with righteousness (*i* or *yi*), so that how one expresses concern for others is related to their relative position in society. He said that rulers must place the needs of others before their own, and if they do not they lose the mandate of heaven. His most famous teaching is that humans are by nature good, and this became one of the principal themes of Confucian teaching. Master Meng observed that anyone who sees a child fall into a well will save the child without considering the personal consequences, and concluded that each of us must have a natural tendency toward goodness. However, this natural humaneness must be cultivated.

Xun Zi (also transliterated as *Hsun Tzu*, ca. 297–238 B.C.E.) was the most important Confucian teacher in the Han dynasty. He taught that the most important virtue is *li*, propriety. He also rejected Mencius's view of human nature, saying that humans are basically evil. Xun Zi claimed that goodness requires strict education, and an important element in training is participation in the rituals of the society.

The turning point for the official acceptance of Confucianism came in 136 B.C.E., when Confucians were given the responsibility for educating youth for positions in government. For the next two thousand years, until 1905, Confucianism remained the basis for the educational system of China. It also heavily influenced the subject matter taught in other East Asian countries.

Confucius also became the object of state piety. As early as 195 B.C.E., a Han dynasty emperor had performed a sacrifice at the grave of Confucius. This practice continued, and Confucius was posthumously awarded titles of nobility and veneration. Temples dedicated to Confucius were built, and the sacrifices offered to Confucius became ever more involved. The temples included images of Confucius, and he became, in effect, a deity. About the same time as the Protestant Reformation in Europe (see Chapter Eleven), the state cult of Confucius was simplified and he became known as "Master K'ung, the Perfectly Holy Teacher of Antiquity."

Neo-Confucianism

During the Sung Dynasty (960–1279 C.E.) the movement known in the West as Neo-Confucianism called for a return to the basic principles of Confucianism in response to the growing influence of Buddhism and Daoism in China. It also incorporated some of their philosophical ideas into Confucian teaching. The two principal branches of Neo-Confucianism were the School of Principle and the School of Mind. *Zhu Xi* (also written as *Chu Hsi*) (1130–1200) was the main figure associated with the former, and *Wang Yangming* (1472–1529) was the chief proponent of the second.

Zhu Xi was successful in winning acceptance for Master Meng's view that humans are essentially good. He also made popular the concept of the Great Ultimate, the rational principle that is at the essence of all reality and that is evident to any who objectively study nature. He thus transformed the principle of *li* into a cosmic force. Each human being also has such a principle at the core, he taught, working itself out as goodness. The influence of philosophical Daoism, modified by traditional Confucian values, is evident. Zhu Xi advocated, and modelled in his own life, a method of introspection (somewhat similar to Buddhist meditation) as a means of bringing oneself into a way of acting that is in harmony with the Great Ultimate.

Wang Yangming emphasized that the underlying rational principle is discovered less from an investigation of nature than from an examination of one's own mind. He came to the conclusion that it is the mind that shapes the objects we perceive. The rational principle we discover within, he said, is a guiding light, an innate bearing toward goodness. He taught that our minds are like mirrors. When polished by proper instruction, the natural ability of the mind to reflect virtue is manifest. Like Zhu Xi, Wang Yangming taught that quietly sitting is the effective method of awakening to this inner principle.

Is Confucianism a Religion?

As we shall see, Confucian teaching is ambiguous on the question of religion. Confucius himself seems to have taught that it was important to conduct rituals to ancestors and other spirits, but for the value of these rituals in ordering society rather than as a means of *spiritual* transformation. Assuming the definition of religion introduced in Chapter One, we can consider early Confucianism a *secular* religion. The ultimate transformation that Confucius and the early disciples envisioned related to secular society rather than to any kind of spiritual reality.

Confucianism, however, according to our use of terminology, *became* a spiritual religion, rooting ultimacy in a force that undergirds the world of self and society. Neo-Confucianism revived Confucian teaching about the importance of human virtue as a means to create social harmony, but also incorporated Buddhist and Daoist philosophy to give Confucianism a stronger spiritual basis.

In addition, as we have already noted, the worship of Confucius transformed the teacher into a spirit to be venerated. This is not to say Confucius was thought to be a god, any more than any venerated ancestor is a god. It does show that there was more of a spiritual dimension to Confucianism as it developed.

Is Confucianism a religion? The answer, like the question, is ambiguous. From our perspective, the most appropriate answer is that the Confucian ethical system may function as a secular religion, and Neo-Confucianism may be considered a religion with spiritual ultimacy.

The Decline of Confucianism

With China's turn to the West in the early twentieth century, Confucianism as state orthodoxy faded (see de Bary 1991). Confucianism no longer served as the foundation for the educational system, and the worship of Confucius declined. By the 1920s the dominance of Confucianism in "family life, education, and government service were eroded beyond recognition" (Berthrong and Berthrong 2000: 236). After taking power in 1949, the Communist government in China outlawed sacrifices to Confucius and banned the study of Confucian classics. Confucius was considered an advocate of the feudal system that Communism was rebelling against. We will turn to the revival of Confucianism in recent decades, after considering the Confucian worldview.

THE CONFUCIAN WORLDVIEW

The emphasis here will be on the basic Confucian teachings as attributed to Confucius, developed by Master Meng, and reaffirmed in Neo-Confucianism.

Humanity: Social Relationships and Microcosm

In the West we are accustomed to viewing humans as autonomous individuals. In the Confucian worldview, humans are seen in terms of the web of relationships in which each individual is embedded, in the family and in the state. The formal expression of this understanding is known as the Five Basic Relationships: parent and child, husband and wife, elder and younger brother, friend and friend, and ruler and subject. When the mutual obligations of these hierarchical relationships are understood and enacted, harmony results.

Like other religions that originated in China, Confucianism views humanity, like other aspects of reality, as characterized by the interaction of *yin* and *yang* forces. The earthly *kwei* and heavenly *shen* souls of mankind reflect this interaction. Humans are also composed of the five basic elements, like all reality. In others words, humans are a microcosm of the cosmos as a whole.

Problem: Social Chaos

Like Siddartha Gautama, Confucian teachers based their analysis of the fundamental human problem on observation of human experience. For Siddartha, suffering caused by craving was the dilemma humans must confront. For Confucius and Master Meng, the predicament was manifest in the social chaos of the Warring States period, brought on by the collapse of the feudal system.

Cause: A Breakdown of Virtue

What caused the social chaos? Confucian teaching observed that when rulers and the educated elite did not live virtuous lives, a social breakdown occurred. In particular, this breakdown occurred because people failed to follow their social roles. For example, princes failed to behave as princes should, and fathers no longer performed the roles they should play. At the same time, as Mencius observed, people were not corrupt by nature, and virtue seemed to depend on how people were educated. Confucian teaching pointed to an earlier age when rulers naturally displayed virtue (*de*), and sought to recover that kind of society.

End: Leaders of Character (*jun-zi*) and the Harmonious Society

The goal Confucius sought was the restoration of the harmony of the feudal order, and the right pattern of human relationships. Like Lao Zi, Confucius felt that the harmonious society would be created by sages, "ideal persons" who lived virtuous lives, and that they would do so by the force of their moral character. The "gentleman" (*jun-zi* or *chun tzu*) that Confucius envisioned would remain committed to virtue through all of life's hardships. *Jun-zi* had meant an aristocrat, a person of noble birth; Confucius taught that anyone could become an "ideal person" through a process of moral formation leading to harmony (*ho*). For Confucius the ideal was not to withdraw from the world, but to realize one's inherent human potential for goodness, immersing oneself in human life—first in the family, but also in society through public service. *This* is the Confucian way to achieve identification with the cosmic order.

According to the Master, the gentleman was the son always filial, the father ever just and kind, the official unfailingly loyal and faithful, the husband completely righteous and judicious, and the friend always sincere and tactful. Confucius directed his efforts to the education of young men, so his pronouns were male. Many interpreters have observed that there is nothing gender-specific about the basic ideal.

Means: The Virtuous Life

Tour *The Sacred World* CD!

For Confucius the path to the harmonious society—and the "ideal persons" who would create it by the force of their moral character—lay in education in specific virtues. The gentleman would maintain a balance between what we might call "inner" (*nei*) virtues (relating to one's basic attitude and orientation) and "outer" (*wai*) virtues (having to do with how one behaves toward others).

The primary inner virtue is *ren* (humaneness; also written as *jen*). The humane person is not concerned about self-gain or recognition, but desires to seek the good of others as an end in itself. The Chinese character for *ren* is composed of the character for "person" and the character for "two." This suggests that in all one's considerations, the other person is included naturally. The humane person instinctively recognizes the inherent worth and value of every person, from the highest in society to the lowest. For rulers this meant a concern for the needs of every person.

Related to *ren* is *shu* (reciprocity), the Confucian equivalent to the "golden rule." *Shu* means not doing to others what you would not have them do to you.

Another inner virtue is *hsueh*, translated as "self-correcting wisdom." A person with *hsueh* is constantly evaluating his or her behavior against the standard of moral excellence of the "ideal person." In the process, one realizes that the goal has not yet been reached; *none* of us ever reaches the ideal. We all have room to grow. This leads to an attitude of humility, rather than pride, about one's character.

These "inner" virtues must be balanced by "outer" virtues. It is not enough to be a person of good character; one must put goodness into action.

The most basic external virtue is *li* ("propriety, good form"). *Li* has a variety of meanings in different contexts. It can refer to the rites and rituals of a society; it can mean courtesy in human interaction, or treating others with reverence and respect. In general, *li* is a right and proper order to be followed in any circumstance. According to Confucian teaching, without *li* a society loses sight of how to conduct proper worship. The right relationship between the genders is confused; children and parents do not know how to treat one another. In short, human relationships lose their compass. As one scholar has put it, *li* is "the traditional, primarily social mechanism for constituting community and generating its social political order[. . . .] *Li* is not passive deference to external patterns. It is a making of society that requires the investment of oneself and one's own sense of importance" (Ames 2002: 101, 102).

In the area of human interaction, *li* manifests itself in the five basic relationships already described, but expressed with male imagery: father and son, husband and wife, the eldest son and younger brothers, ruler and subjects, elder and junior male friends. Where there is *li*, people recognize this ordering of society, and know how to treat one another with courtesy and respect within the relationships.

Li includes religious rituals, which in China meant ancestor veneration and worship of the deities and other spirits. For Confucius the real value of these rites and the other ceremonies of society was that they maintained social harmony when properly conducted. He also taught that to find the proper way to conduct the rituals we must look to the past, to that time when society was in harmony.

Confucian temples are known as *wen miao* ("temples of culture"). In the main hall of a Confucian temple are found the tablets identifying Master K'ung as "Most Holy Former Master." For much of Chinese history, the birthday of Confucius was a state holiday, a time for special pilgrimages to the Confucian temples. According to Confucian teaching, the Master was an honored ancestor, not a deity. For ordinary people, however, Confucius was a god, who could be invoked for blessings and who performed miracles.

Two other outer virtues deserve mention. One is *xiao* (or *hsiao*, "filial piety"), which we have already identified as a characteristic of the underlying East Asian worldview. Confucianism is the principal carrier of this virtue, however. "Filial piety" means respect for one's elders, especially within the context of the family. In modern, secular societies, reaching maturity usually means "leaving home," and no longer accepting the authority of one's parents. In traditional, Confucian societies, a child never "leaves home." Respect and reverence for elders continues throughout life, and, with the veneration of ancestors, beyond. You will not find many nursing homes in societies rooted in Confucian values, because keeping one's elders within the context of the family is seen as a basic social obligation. Not only are they kept physically, but they are valued and honored. Confucius emphasized respect for elders and others in authority, but it is important to emphasize that "filial piety" also includes parents treating their children (and those in authority treating people in their charge) with respect and courtesy.

Confucian tradition also speaks of a virtue known as the "rectification of names" (*cheng-ming*). In general, this is to say that words are important. When they are degraded and lose their meaning, society suffers. In particular, titles must be respected. If one carries the title "prince," then behavior must be in conformity with the best that title implies. In the contemporary idiom we might speak of "roles." Each of us has a number of social roles. You might define yourself as student, daughter, sister, friend, and worker, for example. Each name implies a code of moral behavior. If you fail to act in conformity with what is expected of you as a "sister," then the social setting in which "sisterhood" is important will became confused and chaotic. The same applies to all roles.

Whoever lives a "balanced" life in a Confucian sense displays a force of character, a moral charisma (*de*) that has a positive, constructive influence on others. If the ruling class manifests *de*, then citizens will follow their example, and the "good society" will exist without resort to force. In an important sense, all of Confucian teaching is oriented toward *de*, for when we learn to manifest the virtue that is natural to our human character and shaped by the social roles in which we find ourselves, the result will be inner harmony for each of us and harmony for society.

Reality: Life-Giving, Relational, Harmonious

According to Confucian teaching, the universe is "fundamentally oriented toward the production and promotion of life." All reality is relational, beginning with the hierarchical relationship between heaven and earth. It matters not which in any relational pair is superior, but that they function effectively and promote life in the relationship. There is a given pattern to which things should conform, both in our human nature and in society. When we accept our role and seek to live in conformity with it, then reality is harmonious. You might say, from a Confucian perspective, "we *are* our relationships."

Moreover, the harmony of the cosmos depends on an ordered, virtuous society. In an age when we are seeing what the lack of virtue can do to the environment and to human relationships, the Confucian view of reality has a particular appeal.

Sacred: Making the *Dao* Great

Like Siddartha, Confucius sidestepped questions such as, "What is the nature of the spiritual?" He is reputed to have said that you cannot treat spirits and divinities properly before you learn to treat your fellow human beings properly (*Analects* 11:12; Ware 1955). He advised his followers to treat the spirits "as though they were real" (3:12). Some have called his teaching a "spiritual agnosticism." He professed no knowledge of the spiritual, but still felt that maintaining religious rituals was critical to his central concern: social harmony.

Confucius spoke of the Dao, but not like a philosophical Daoist. According to the Analects, it is humans that make the Dao great, not the Dao that makes humans great (15:29). In other words, if there is to be a "way" for things to go, an underlying harmony, it will be because humans manifest it in their commitment to virtue. For philosophical Daoists, the way to virtue is to let the Dao happen. Striving to be virtuous results in a lack of virtue, they argued. For Confucians, the way to the Dao *is* to seek virtue actively. From this perspective, perhaps Confucianism *is* the *yang* and philosophical Daoism the *yin* of East Asian culture!

As Confucianism developed, more refined and abstract images of that which is ultimate developed. In the Doctrine of the Mean (*Chung Yung*), a work attributed to *Tsesze,* grandson of Confucius and teacher of Master Meng, the author reflects on the nature of absolute truth and its unseen manifestation (*Doctrine of the Mean* 24–25. Yutang 1938: 86):

> Thus absolute truth is indestructible. Being indestructible, it is eternal. Being eternal, it is self-existent. Being self-existent, it is infinite. Being infinite, it is vast and deep. Being vast and deep it is transcendental and intelligent.

CONFUCIANISM AND OTHER RELIGIONS IN THE PEOPLE'S REPUBLIC OF CHINA

In 1937 the Chinese Nationalist leader Chiang Kai-shek erected a shrine with a tablet of Confucius surrounded by busts of Western scientists such as Galileo and Newton. It was intended to symbolize a new China, synthesizing the best of Chinese tradition with the best of Western science and technology. As the twenty-first century begins, events in China seem to suggest a similar attempt, but now the "best of Chinese tradition" includes more than a half-century of Communist rule.

When Mao Zedong led the successful Communist Revolution that created the People's Republic of China in 1949, he established as a goal the weeding out of all religion and philosophical idealism from Chinese life. Until 1966 the official policy of the communist government was that religion would die a natural death. The new socialist democracy would choke religion's social roots—as a tool of exploitation by the ruling classes. Education and improved living standards of the masses would choke its intellectual root—ignorance of the real forces causing their misery.

The Communist government recognized as religions Buddhism, Christianity, and Islam. The Chinese constitution of 1951 allowed freedom of individual religion, but placed all religious institutions and leaders under strict government control.

Separate associations were created to oversee the activities of each religion and to make certain that they were supportive of the communist goals. For example, the "Chinese National Patriotic Movement" was the government agency that administered Catholicism.

Confucianism was considered an idealistic philosophy, and Confucius a sponsor of the feudal order that oppressed the people. Religious Daoism was dismissed as a superstition that should be actively repressed.

In 1966 the Great Proletarian Cultural Revolution initiated a period of severe repression of all religions. Religions had not died a natural death, so government policy changed, to pull up and destroy all its poisonous roots. All churches, mosques and monasteries were ordered closed, and the buildings given over to more "socially useful" purposes, turning them into museums, schools, and warehouses. Religious leaders and all vestiges of religion became the target of the fanatical "Red Guard" who sought to eliminate from Chinese life the "four olds": old ideas, old customs, old habits, old culture. The constitutional right to private free expression of religion was ignored, and even home altars became the target of Red Guard attack.

Mao died in 1975, and the new leadership discredited the Cultural Revolution. In 1978 the constitutional guarantee of free, private religious expression was reintroduced. In recent years religious institutions have been allowed to reopen, including schools to train a new generation of religious leaders. The numbers of Christians, Muslims, and Buddhists are steadily growing, and there are even signs of a resurgence of Daoism and folk religion (see Chapter Six).

Much has changed since the birthplace of Confucius was ransacked during the Cultural Revolution. After being condemned as a "class enemy," Confucius has been rehabilitated in the People's Republic of China. His ancestral home has been rebuilt, and Confucian moral teaching is not vilified as it once was. Indeed, schools dedicated to teaching Confucian values are springing up all over China, some with government funding. In Beijing, children as young as five are sent to special classes in which they memorize passages from the Confucian classics. Their parents hope that they will internalize the values the texts embody. Statues of Confucius, once pulled down, are now being re-erected, even in government institutions. On the 2,550th anniversary of the Sage's birth in 1999, scholars known as the New Confucians gathered in Beijing to discuss the future of Confucianism in a "post-Confucian" East Asia (Berthrong and Berthrong 2000: 244).

The current leadership of the People's Republic of China seems to be trying to draw on the Confucian heritage of respect for authority and commitment to moral virtue to balance the rising tide of consumerist individualism and distrust of those in authority, especially among the youth. As many have observed, from the outset Mao Zedong and other communist leaders adapted Confucian virtues to their teaching (of loyalty to "the people" and to the Communist Party) even while they vilified Confucius and Confucianism.

The revival of Buddhism in China today is illustrated with the return of images of the popular *bodhisattva Kuan Yin* (*Guanyin;* see Chapter Eight). During the Cultural Revolution, the Red Guard searched homes for statues of Kuan Yin as evidence that the residents must be enemies of the state. Now government factories produce images of Kuan Yin to sell to the public, and pilgrims flock to reopened shrines to Kuan Yin.

Whether or not this new receptivity to religion is part of an effort to improve the image of China in the West or a sincere change of heart is open to question. As long as Communism is the "state religion of China," openness to other religions will be limited. While individual freedom of religion is recognized, attempts to spread religion are still controlled, and only the right to propagate atheism is constitutionally guaranteed. The democratic reforms essential to the creation of a society that respects religious pluralism have been repressed.

CHAPTER SUMMARY

While philosophical Daoism teaches a way of cosmic harmony, Confucianism is preoccupied with social harmony. The founder, Master K'ung, taught aspiring leaders a way of virtue that he believed would create harmony in society.

We first summarized the stages of development and sacred texts of Confucianism, which was founded on the basis of the teachings of a sixth-century B.C.E. government official, Master K'ung (Confucius). A set of Confucian classic texts embodied his teachings. Confucianism gained prominence as the official state philosophy in China, and was taught for more than two millenia in schools. Later Confucians developed a religion that revered Confucius as a saint, if not a god. Early Confucianism seemed to have been a secular religion, but later Confucianism adopted a spiritual understanding of ultimacy.

During most of the twentieth century, Confucianism suffered in China—first when China looked to the West, and then as a result of a campaign against Confucianism in the early decades of the People's Republic.

We reviewed the Confucian worldview, with its emphasis on social relationships and social harmony as the highest goal. We contrasted Confucianism with Philosophical Daoism. Confucian ethics seeks the cultivation of virtues such as *ren* (humaneness) and *li* (propriety and righteousness), with the "ideal person" manifesting a balance between "inner" and "outer" virtues.

We concluded the chapter with a discussion of the revival of Confucianism in twenty-first-century China, and a discussion of religion in the People's Republic of China.

IMPORTANT TERMS AND PHRASES

Analects, *cheng-ming,* Confucius (Master K'ung), *jun-zi,* filial piety, Five Classics, *hsueh, jen (ren), li,* Master Meng (Mencius), Neo-Confucianism, *shu,* Xun Zi (Hsun Tzu)

QUESTIONS FOR DISCUSSION AND REFLECTION

1. Do you agree that Daoism is the *yin* and Confucianism the *yang* in the Chinese religions?

2. Would you like to live in a society guided by the Confucian worldview? Why or why not?

3. Do you have moral virtues that you try to live by? If so, compare them to the Confucian virtues. If not, is your approach to morality more like the Daoist?

4. Do you agree that good societies depend on leaders living moral lives? Does the morality of a society depend on the virtue of its leaders?

5. Why do you think that religions did not fade away in Communist China, as the leaders thought they would? Why is the influence of Confucianism likely to continue to grow in twenty-first-century China?

6. Should Confucianism be considered a religion?

SOURCES AND SUGGESTIONS FOR FURTHER STUDY

AMES, ROGER T., 2002. "Rites as Rights: The Confucian Alternative." In *Applied Ethics: A Multicultural Approach.* 3rd ed., ed. Larry May et al. Upper Saddle River, NJ: Prentice Hall, 101–11.

BERTHRONG, JOHN H., 1998. *Transformations of the Confucian Way.* Boulder, CO: Westview.

BERTHRONG, JOHN H. AND EVELYN NAGAI BERTHRONG, 2000. *Confucianism: A Short Introduction.* New York: Oneworld.

BUSH, RICHARD C., 1970. *Religion in Communist China.* Nashville, TN: Abingdon.

DE BARY, W. T., 1991. *The Trouble with Confucianism.* Cambridge, MA: Harvard University.

HALL, DAVID AND ROGER AMES, 1987. *Thinking through Confucius.* Albany: State University of New York.

JENSEN, LIONEL M., 1997. *Manufacturing Confucianism: Chinese Traditions and Universal Civilizations.* Durham, NC: University of North Carolina.

LEGGE, JAMES, TRANS., 1885. *The Sacred Books of China: The Texts of Confucianism, part 4. The Li Ki: A Collection of Treatises on the Rules of Propriety or Ceremonial Usages.* In *The Sacred Books of the East,* ed. Max Mueller. Vol 27. Oxford: Clarendon.

OLDSTONE-MOORE, JENNIFER, 2002. *Confucianism: Origins, Beliefs, Practices, Holy Texts, Sacred Places.* New York: Oxford University.

WARE, JAMES R., 1955. *The Sayings of Confucius.* New York: New American Library.

YAO, XINZHONG, 1997. *Confucianism and Christianity: A Comparative Study of Jen and Agape.* Brighton, UK: Sussex Academic.

YUTANG, LIN, ED. AND TRANS., 1938. *The Wisdom of Confucius.* New York: Random House.

Web Sites

main.chinesephilosophy.net
    (general site on Chinese philosophy, with links to Confucian sites)

www2.kenyon.edu/depts/religion/fac/Adler/reln471/links471.htm
    (links for the study of Confucianism, maintained at the Religious Studies Department, Kenyon College)

Prentice Hall's **Research Navigator** helps students in their further study of the world's religions. Visit *http://www.researchnavigator.com* for help on the research process and access to databases full of relevant material, including the New York *Times.*

CHAPTER

8

Mahayana Buddhism— The Great Vehicle

INTRODUCTION

In this chapter we continue our discussion of the religions of East Asia. In Chapter Six we provided an orientation to the lands and people of East Asia and a brief history of China. The schools associated with the Mahayana Branch of Buddhism that took root in China migrated to Korea and then Japan, where they became influential. In this chapter we will first briefly survey the histories of Japan and Korea. We will then compare in general the two major branches of Buddhism: Theravada and Mahayana. Next, we will examine two of the Chinese Buddhist movements (the Pure Land and the Meditation Schools) as they developed in Japan; one distinctively Japanese school of Buddhism (Nichiren); and the form of Buddhism that flourished in the mountain nation of Tibet (the Tantric School). We will conclude with a brief examination of Mahayana Buddhism in the twenty-first century.

A BRIEF HISTORY OF KOREA AND JAPAN

Korea

Three of the four provinces established in Korea by the Chinese, who occupied the Korean peninsula in 108 B.C.E., were liberated by 75 B.C.E., but much of northwestern Korea remained under Chinese control for centuries. This contact resulted in heavy Chinese influence on the development of Korean civilization.

The classical Three Kingdoms of Korea (Paekche, Koguryo, and Silla) were formed by 300 C.E. During the fourth and fifth centuries C.E., Buddhism entered Korea from China and became the major religion. In the late seventh century C.E., Silla gained control of the entire peninsula. From this time on, the Confucian educational system and values had a profound impact on Korea.

The name Korea (from *Koryo*) is the product of tenth-century developments. After a century of Mongol occupation, Koryo regained its independence in the late fourteenth century. The Yi dynasty, which took control in 1392 and renamed the country *Choson*, lasted until the early 1900s. Buddhism's dominance gradually lessened during this time.

After successfully resisting Japanese and Chinese attacks, the country was closed to foreigners in the seventeenth and eighteenth centuries. Christian missionaries were largely rebuffed when they began to enter Korea in the nineteenth century, but their success after World War II has resulted in a large Christian minority in Korea today. Japan forced Korea to reopen some of its ports by 1876, and took total control of the peninsula in 1910.

In 1945, after the defeat of Japan in World War II, Japanese domination of Korea finally ended, and the United States occupied the southern half of the country, with Russian troops in the north. After failed attempts to unite the two halves of the country, and the withdrawal of American and Soviet forces, troops from North Korea invaded the South in 1950, and a war began—with U.S. and other forces in defense of the South under the United Nations flag. The war ended without a peace treaty in 1953, and thousands of U.S. troops remain in South Korea. Under often strict constraints on civil liberties, South Korea has become a regional economic power. North Korea is one of the last nations under strict Communist control.

By the early twenty-first century, North Korea had become a nuclear power, and a tense standoff between North Korea and the United States and other nations threatened the stability of the region.

Japan

The early history of Japan is shrouded in mystery. The mythological version of Japanese origins is recounted in the *Shinto Myth* (see Chapter Nine). As we shall see, traditional Japanese religion (Shinto) traces its roots to the divine creation of the Japanese islands.

Historians speculate that the ancestors of the modern Japanese came to the islands originally from Korea, Mongolia, and Malay, possibly as early as 6000 B.C.E. Until the fourth century C.E., the land was divided into independent tribes and clans, who practiced indigenous religions that had many of the attributes described in Chapter Two. Then the Yamato clans took a central role, claiming that their leader was a descendant of the sun goddess.

Historians, however, know remarkably little about Japan until the Chinese introduced writing, Confucianism, and other new ideas, beginning in the late fifth century C.E. Fifty years later, Buddhism came to the Japanese islands from China and Korea and soon became the dominant religion in Japan. However, the introduction of writing enabled Japanese scholars to write down the Shinto myths and legends circulating among the clans.

The Taika Reform (beginning in 646) established a strong central government under the control of an emperor, on the Chinese model. In 858 the Fujiwara family gained control and ruled Japan in name for three hundred years. Real power, however, was increasingly in the hands of the lords of independent estates, who hired warriors (*samurai*) to protect them.

In 1192 a military government, with the central leader called a *shogun,* began. Shogun rule lasted until 1867. During this time Emperors continued, but they surrendered effective power to rule to the Shoguns. In 1281 a Mongol fleet, sent by Kublai Khan, threatened Japan, but was destroyed by a typhoon (called by the

Japanese the *kamikaze,* "divine wind"). During this period several movements that combined Shinto and Buddhist teachings developed. (Shinto and Buddhism had, in fact, been combined functionally for centuries.)

Portuguese sailors first reached Japan in 1543. The Spanish priest Francis Xavier brought Christianity a few years later. By the early 1600s the Netherlands and England had opened trade with Japan. In 1603 the Tokugawa family took control of the shogunate. During the Tokugawa Period (1603–1867) ties were cut with the outside world. Christianity was virtually eliminated, and a Shinto revival movement gained momentum.

In 1853 the American navy forced Japan to open trade. A series of treaties gave an unfair advantage to the Western powers. During the Meiji ("enlightened rule") period (1868–1912), Japan became a modern industrial and military power. China was defeated in 1895, and the Japanese fought Russia to a standstill (1904–1905). A new educational system, which made Shinto the official ideology, developed. A distinction was drawn between "nonreligious" State Shinto and the Shinto practiced by religious sects. Confucianism also played an important role in the development of this state ideology.

During the 1920s and '30s Japan came under increasing military control, and the creation of a Greater East Asia Co-Prosperity Sphere under Japanese control became a goal. When the United States responded by cutting off the export of crucial raw materials, Japan attacked the United States forces at Pearl Harbor, Hawaii, on December 7, 1941.

After the defeat of Japan in World War II, a new constitution creating a parliamentary democracy was drawn up. With the imposition of freedom of religion in this constitution, the door opened for the development of a host of new religions (such as *Soka Gakkai,* a lay movement associated with Nichiren Buddhism—see Chapter Fourteen). Since 1945 Japan has made a miraculous economic recovery, becoming one of the handful of economic superpowers in the world. However, as the twenty-first century began, Japan was suffering from economic stagnation.

MAHAYANA BUDDHISM IN EAST ASIA

Of the two major branches of Buddhism, the oldest, *Theravada* ("Way of the Elders"), dominated the nations of Southeast Asia, while the other, *Mahayana* ("The Large Vehicle"), spread into East Asia and became the principal form of Buddhism in China, Japan, and Korea. We have already discussed the origins of Buddhism in India and the teachings of the Theravada School (see Chapter Four). In this section we will focus on the history, texts, and teachings of a few of the more prominent Mahayana schools of East Asia: Pure Land, Zen, Nichiren, and Tibetan.

The Spread of Mahayana Buddhism into East Asia

Through the support of King Ashoka, Buddhism flourished in northern India by the first and second centuries C.E. Buddhist missionaries carried the teachings of Buddha into Central Asia. At some point in the first century C.E., Buddhist monks crossed the deserts to China, probably with merchants. From then on, steady traffic between India and China carried more Buddhist teachers into China, and Chinese pilgrims to India to study Buddhism in its homeland.

Monasteries sprang up throughout China, and new Buddhist schools such as *Ch'an* (Zen) and Pure Land emerged and gained popularity. By the seventh century C.E., Buddhism had gained prominence throughout China.

As noted above, Buddhism spread to Korea from China, beginning by the fourth century C.E. It gained its strongest foothold in the southeastern province of Silla. When Silla gained control over the whole country in the seventh century, Buddhism flourished. Its dominance lasted until the fourteenth century, but then it entered a period of slow decline.

When Buddhism reached Japan from Korea in the sixth century, the imperial court was more receptive than the military rulers. During the Heian and Kamakura periods Buddhism was the dominant religion in Japan, but a Shinto revival in the Tokugawa Period moderated Buddhist influence somewhat. The pressure of the emergence of State Shinto (see Chapter Nine) in the late nineteenth century also put pressure on Buddhism. However, Buddhism reemerged in the twentieth century, particularly after World War II, to play a very significant role in Japanese life.

Buddhism came to Tibet by way of Nepal in the seventh century C.E. It met strong opposition from supporters of the indigenous, animistic religion of Tibet, called *Bon*. Several centuries later, however, Buddhist monks from India had succeeded in establishing a number of large monasteries in Tibet. The abbots of the monasteries held political as well as spiritual power. Disputes among the monasteries led to the creation of several sects of Tibetan Buddhism. The Yellow Sect, led by the Dalai Lama, won out in the struggle and became the dominant form of Buddhism in Tibet.

Mahayana Buddhist Texts of India

Theravada Buddhism has an authoritative set of sacred texts, the Pali Canon (see Chapter Four). Mahayana Buddhism has no such collected canon, but rather a diverse set of writings, with each Mahayana school emphasizing its favorites. Most of the classical Mahayana texts were written in India in Sanskrit during the first five centuries C.E., and later freely translated into Chinese and Tibetan. However, some of the texts were composed by monks in China and Japan. We will mention only a few of the major Mahayana texts in this chapter.

The Lotus Sutra   Probably the most popular Mahayana text is the Lotus Sutra, also called the "Lotus of the Good Law" (*Saddharma Pundarika Sutra*). It contains the supposed sayings of the Buddha delivered on Vulture Peak (near Bodh Gaya) in India. In the Lotus Sutra Buddha explains that he taught his first disciples the spiritual self-reliance of Theravada doctrine because they were not ready for the ultimate truth. That truth is the revelation that the historical Buddha is but a manifestation of the real Buddha. The true Buddha is the cosmic Buddha who wants to show compassion for all beings.

The Lotus Sutra also teaches that there are three ages of the dharma: the age of authentic dharma, the age of false or counterfeit dharma, and the age of the final dharma, when a *bodhisattva* (see below) would come to reveal the true cosmic Buddha vehicle in a direct and simple way so all could understand it. There are frequent references to the merit that comes to those who revere the Lotus Sutra. Although beloved by most Mahayana schools, the Lotus Sutra assumed the role of ultimacy in several movements, including the Nichiren school to be discussed below.

The Diamond Cutter Sutra and the Heart Sutra   The Diamond Cutter Sutra (*vajracchedika prajnaparamita*), usually called simply the Diamond Sutra, contains teachings on transcendent, nondual wisdom (*prajna*). *Prajna* is found in the emptiness of all distinctions, which gives form to all reality. In its purest form, it is *prajnaparamita,* the wisdom that goes beyond ordinary perception.

The Diamond Cutter is one of the so-called Wisdom Sutras. Another is the Heart Sutra, which speaks of *prajna,* but also identifies the source of the wisdom-that-goes-beyond as the Bodhisattva *Avalokitesvara* ("The Lord Who Looks Down with Compassion").

The Garland Sutra   The Garland Sutra, another Mahayana text, reveals that the distinct forms of the world as we experience it are the result of the delusion of our material minds. The only true reality is the Original Mind, the unitary Buddha nature. Stanzas from a poem from the Garland Sutra reflect this perspective (*Garland Sutra* 20. Cleary 1984: 451–52):

> It's like a painter
> Spreading the various colors:
> Delusion grasps different forms
> But the elements have no distinctions.
> [. . .]
> If people know the actions of mind
> Create all the worlds,
> They will see the Buddha
> And understand Buddha's true nature.

MAHAYANA AND THERAVADA BUDDHISM CONTRASTED

According to Mahayana schools, Siddartha taught much more than is contained in the Pali Canon and manifest in the Hinayana schools (the Mahayana name for the Theravada tradition). They claim that the Buddha taught much in secret to disciples who could understand this higher truth. He threw down many leaves, so to speak, and only a few picked them *all* up.

The "Three Bodies" of the Buddha

According to Theravada teaching, there is only one Buddha in each age, enlightened beings who have traversed the path to *nirvana* on their own. By contrast, according to a Mahayana concept known as the "three body doctrine," there are three separate bodies or natures of the Buddha. One is the earthly body or manifestation of the Buddha (*nirmana-kaya*)—in our age, Siddartha. Another is the heavenly body of the Buddha (*sambhoga-kaya*), in the form of Buddhas (such as *Maitreya, Vairocana* and, the most popular, *Amitabha* of Pure Land Buddhism) and *bodhisattvas* who inhabit fully spiritual realms. The heavenly Buddhas are also called *Dhyani* ("contemplative") Buddhas. The last is the cosmic body or nature of the Buddha (*dharma-kaya*), who is present in all reality. From this perspective, *each* human and every other being has the nature of the Buddha.

Bodhisattvas

In Theravada Buddhism, the *bodhisattva* is a "Buddha in the making," Maitreya in the current era. Mahayana teachers adopted and reinterpreted the doctrine of the *bodhisattva.* For Mahayana Buddhists, the *bodhisattva* (literally "a being [intended] for enlightenment") has postponed final enlightenment and nirvana for himself or

herself in order to help other beings in their spiritual quests. To become a
bodhisattva, a person must manifest the innate qualities necessary, and then take the
Great Vow of compassion for all living beings. Any person is potentially a *bodhisattva,*
because anyone may take the vow. However, it takes many lives to fulfill the vow. An
elaborate literature developed to explain the stages in the career of a *bodhisattva*
and how to begin the process. As they progress on the path, *bodhisattvas* accumulate
a store of merit that they can share with others who turn to them for help.

The "*bodhisattva* vow" is described in this passage from a Mahayana text
(*Sikshasamuccaya* 280–81 [*Vajradhvaja Sutra*]. Conze 1964: 131–32):

> A bodhisattva resolves, "I take upon myself the burden of all suffering; I am
> resolved to do so; I will endure it. I do not turn or run away, do not tremble, am
> not terrified, nor afraid, do not turn back or despond[. . . .] All beings I must set
> free[. . . .] I must rescue all these beings from the stream of Samsara, which is so dif-
> ficult to cross, I must pull them back from the great precipice, I must free them
> from all calamities, I must ferry them across the stream of Samsara. I myself must
> grapple with the whole mass of suffering of all beings.

Some *bodhisattvas* have reached the point in their journeys at which they exist in
heavenly realms and from there provide divine aid to those who show devotion to
them. One of the most prominent celestial *bodhisattvas* is known in Sanskrit as
Avalokitesvara (probably "the Lord Who Looks Down from Above"), already
mentioned. In the Indian texts he is portrayed as a prince; in China, Japan, and
Korea this *bodhisattva* takes on feminine qualities, and is known as the Goddess of
Mercy (*Kuan Yin* in China [also transliterated as *Guanyin*], *Kannon* in Japan, and
Koan-Eum in Korea). Her maternal compassion is a great source of consolation for
millions of people throughout these countries. They turn to her for divine aid in
virtually any circumstance. She is frequently shown standing or seated on a lotus,
holding a child, wearing a crown with an image of Amitabha Buddha. Her devotees
believe that she will lead the faithful to the Western Paradise of Amitabha.

Sunyata ("Emptiness")

Finally, in contrasting Mahayana with Theravada Buddhism, we should stress again
the important teaching of *sunyata* ("emptiness"). The concept appears in
Theravada texts, where it seems to mean the absence of value in the changing flux
of existence. In Theravada Buddhism it had a pragmatic function, helping a monk
or nun overcome attachment to worldly life. In Mahayana, *sunyata* became an
important concept for those schools more philosophical in their orientation.

The Sanskrit works of the prominent Indian Buddhist philosopher of the
second-third centuries C.E., *Nagarjuna,* founder of the *Madhyamika* ("Middle Way")
school, are particularly important for an understanding of the concept of *sunyata.*
Nagarjuna argued that our ideas and language subtly bind us to the constructions of
reality that we create, and therefore render us attached to that which is not truly
real. We must come to a realization of the "emptiness" or "openness" (*sunyata*) of all
things and of all our perceptions of things. Only through coming to a realization of
sunyata can we truly wake up and realize the freedom that the Buddha taught.

Nagarjuna made the provocative assertion that *samsara* and *nirvana* cannot effectively be distinguished from one another. By this he meant that both rebirth and
escape from rebirth are products of our human mental construction. Beyond them
both is the ultimate truth of *sunyata.* Although *sunyata* is a difficult concept to grasp

(for in "grasping" it, all concepts dissolve!), there is none other more important for an understanding of Mahayana Buddhist philosophy.

A later Mahayana school of philosophy in India called *Yogacara* expressed the concept of *sunyata* in a more positive vein. This school stressed that if one experiences the "emptiness" of all distinctions in the perceived world, this leads to an awareness of Pure Mind, or Mind-in-itself, which is freed from the entanglements of our ordinary minds. The only way to discover this Pure Consciousness is to explore one's own mind and probe to its depths, ultimately beyond all ordinary "knowing." This teaching had a profound influence on the development of the school of Mahayana Buddhism most widely known by its Japanese name, Zen.

MAJOR MAHAYANA SCHOOLS IN EAST ASIA

The doctrine of "emptiness" became the basis for more than one of the schools that emerged in China and Japan. Besides Zen, the school known in China as *T'ien-Tai,* and in Japan as *Tendai,* taught that there is no distinction between *sunyata* and this experienced world.

According to this school, founded in China in the sixth century C.E. and brought to Japan about two hundred years later, all the Buddhas are present in one grain of sand, and Buddhahood can be manifest in the ordinary life of lay people as much as in the heavenly Buddhas or monks.

T'ien-Tai/Tendai is but one of a number of separate Mahayana movements that emerged in China, and then took root in Japan and Korea. We will focus here on two of the most significant Chinese schools, which have had a profound influence not only in Japan but in America—the Pure Land and Meditation Schools. We will also discuss a movement that began in Japan and has spread to America—Nichiren Buddhism. All three were influenced in different ways by T'ien-Tai/Tendai. Finally, we will examine what happened to Mahayana Buddhism when it was introduced in Tibet.

Pure Land: The Devotional School

The Pure Land School is based on a Sanskrit text that tells the story of the heavenly Buddha, Amitabha ("infinite light"), who resides in a celestial region known as the Western Paradise or Pure Land. The text describes the Pure Land as a rich, fertile, heavenly place, with jeweled palaces, inhabited only by gods and men, not by ghosts or demons (*Sukhavativyuha Sutra,* ch. 15–18. Conze 1959: 232–36):

> This world Sukhavati, Ananda, which is the world system of the Lord Amitabha, is rich and prosperous, comfortable, fertile, delightful and crowded with many Gods and men. And in this world system, Ananda, there are no hells, no animals, no ghosts, no Asuras [demons] and none of the inauspicious places of rebirth[. . . .]
>
> And this world system Sukhavati, Ananda, emits many fragrant odours, it is rich in a great variety of flowers and fruits, adorned with jewel trees, which are frequented by flocks of various birds with sweet voices, which the Tathagata's miraculous power has conjured up[. . . .]
>
> And all the wishes those beings may think of, they all will be fulfilled, as long as they are rightful[. . . .]
>
> And all the beings who have been born, who are born, who will be born in this Buddha-field, they all are fixed on the right method of salvation, until they have won Nirvana[. . . .]

The Pure Land school teaches that any human can attain Buddhahood through faith in Amitabha. The first stage in this process is rebirth in the Western Paradise, where one receives preparation for nirvana and Buddhahood.

When this teaching reached China by the fourth or fifth century C.E., it was adapted to the view that we live in the last of the three declining periods of Buddhist teaching. In this perverse age, people must rely on the grace of Amitabha rather than their own ability to discover the truth. This "easy path" of reliance on a "god" for help in attaining liberation met with wide acceptance among lay people. The Chinese Pure Land school taught that merely by calling on the name of Amitabha in faith at death, one could experience rebirth in the Western Paradise.

The real success of the school, however, came in Japan, where it was introduced first as an element within the Tendai tradition. Amitabha is known as *Amida* in the Japanese Pure Land tradition. By the twelfth century the Pure Land teaching became the basis of a separate Japanese Mahayana School, known as *Jodo shu* ("Pure Land School"). *Jodo-shu* taught the expression of faith in Amida by chanting his name over and over again. The chant *Namu Amida Butsu* ("I place my faith in Amida Buddha"), called simply the *nembutsu,* became the basis for a devotional tradition that is still extremely influential.

The most popular Pure Land school is an offshoot of *Jodo-shu* known as *Jodo-Shinshu* ("True Pure Land School"). Its innovation was to say that if a person has a true attitude of humility and faith in Amida, then repetition of the chant is not a necessary prerequisite for rebirth in the Pure Land. Instead, one should chant in response to having received Amida's grace, rather than as a means of attaining his compassion. Faith comes as a freely bestowed gift of Amida, not as a state generated by the believer.

Pure Land Buddhism came to America with Chinese and Japanese immigrants. The first official *Jodo Shinshu* missionaries arrived in 1899 and formed the North American Buddhist Mission. After the imprisonment of Japanese Americans during World War II, the name was changed to the Buddhist Churches of America to symbolize a commitment to adapt to American culture.

The teaching of the Pure Land Schools is straightforward and simple, making it especially attractive to those impatient with the more esoteric teachings of other Buddhist movements, such as the one we will now discuss—Zen.

Zen: The Meditation School

Tour *The Sacred World* CD!

The school of Buddhism most widely known in the West is the Meditation School, known in China as *ch'an* (based on a Chinese rendering of the Sanskrit term for meditation—*dhyana*) and in Japan as *Zen.* As we shall see, Zen teaches skepticism about ordinary language and mocks attempts to explain truth rationally. Therefore, we preface this discussion of Zen with the same sort of warning given before the section on Philosophical Daoism: those who talk do not know! Although the same might be said of other religious traditions, it is especially true for Zen.

Stages of Development   The roots of Zen can be traced to the meditation practiced by Siddartha Gautama and his followers, and the Indian philosophical schools that stressed the doctrine of *sunyata* or "emptiness" (see above). According to Zen tradition, the Buddha once held a lotus before his disciples, smiled, and said nothing. Only one of his followers experienced the truth of this silent sermon, while the rest remained confused. This disciple smiled in return, showing the Buddha he had awakened to the truth beyond words. Hence began the tradition of "mind-to-mind" teaching from a master to his disciple.

Zen tradition has focused on an Indian monk called *Bodhidharma* (ca. 470–543) as the one who brought this insight to China. According to legend, when Bodhidharma was brought before the Chinese Emperor, the monk chastised the emperor, telling him that all his temples to the Buddha and copying of Buddhist texts were worthless. He is reputed to have sat in rapt meditation before a wall for nine years. Bodhidharma is often portrayed as having no eyelids, having cut them off so that he could avoid falling asleep and thus spend more time meditating. He is regarded as the First Patriarch of Zen in China.

Regardless of the precise method of introduction, when Buddhist meditative practice and the idea of *sunyata* reached China, they found a receptive audience among philosophical Daoists (see Chapter Six).

Bodhidharma was followed by subsequent Patriarchs, the most famous among them the sixth, *Hui-neng* (ca. 638–713). He was an illiterate kitchen laborer, who nevertheless experienced enlightenment. He is the traditional author of the Platform Sutra, which helped the Meditation School in China establish its own basis apart from the Indian texts. It popularized an approach to meditation known as "sudden enlightenment," in which radical techniques such as shouts, slaps, and even cutting off a student's finger were used to try to shock students out of their dependence on ordinary thought. This led to the creation in China of a school that emphasized "sudden enlightenment," as opposed to the more scholarly approach, where quiet meditation and study of philosophical texts was thought to lead to a "gradual awakening." Some extreme advocates of "sudden enlightenment" apparently burned Buddhist scriptures and destroyed images of the Buddha. One teacher is reputed to have said, "If you meet the Buddha, kill him!"

The Chinese meditation school took root as distinct movements in Japan in the late twelfth and early thirteenth centuries c.e. These two movements, *Rinzai* and *Soto*, continue today, with the latter being the larger, and the former better known for its teaching techniques. Rinzai emphasizes seated meditation on the word puzzles known as *koans* (see below) to lead to the experience of enlightenment. Soto puts more emphasis on the practice of seated meditation itself as the means of enlightenment.

The influence of Zen in Japanese culture has been very significant. As will be discussed in the next chapter, Zen played a crucial role in the formation of the *Bushido*, the code of behavior of the samurai warrior. According to Zen teaching, the ultimate truth is found in the tiniest detail of nature and amidst ordinary activities. Therefore, seemingly mundane activities such as the serving of tea become rituals that manifest the underlying harmony behind the seeming distinctions of this world. Under the influence of Zen, a Japanese approach to beauty developed in which the spontaneous and natural are appreciated over the ordered and conventional. Ink painting in which the artist quickly draws the brush over the paper, leaving flowing marks that cannot be changed, is one example. Another is *haiku* poetry, in which, in a single breath, the poet expresses an immediate experience of a single moment. One famous haiku by Basho (1644–1694) illustrates the technique (Miyamori 1970, 132):

An ancient pond!
A frog leaps in;
The sound of water!

Ironically, in the arts influenced by Zen there *is* convention (such as the haiku pattern, or the elements of the tea ceremony), but within the seeming limitation there is spontaneity and immediacy. The forms represent the presence of the absolute truth in a single moment. Japanese painting and gardens, in which elements seem to come to their own natural expression in a fluid beauty (with much space left empty), also reflect the Zen understanding.

Zen, alongside Philosophical Daoism, also influenced the development of the martial arts of China and Japan. The various schools share the insight that you should not try to overwhelm your opponent with aggressive, self-exerted force. Rather, when one moves with the existing flow of energy, the advantage comes naturally.

Zen has become very popular in the United States. Zen Centers can be found in most cities and in some rural areas, offering the opportunity to practice Zen techniques of meditation for a short time or for extended periods. They are typically led by Westerners who have studied under Japanese Masters and reached enlightenment. The regimen is very similar to that in Japanese monasteries. In addition, Zen has been popularized by a number of books that offer a critique of Western, American culture from a Zen perspective.

The Zen Worldview   According to Zen teaching, every individual has the nature of the Buddha. The problem is that we deceive ourselves into thinking we are not the Buddha. It is as though the Buddha is the sun and our nature is a calm pool that perfectly reflects the Buddha, but the surface of the water is disturbed and the perfect light breaks up into a myriad of seemingly separate particles.

For Zen teachers, one of the fundamental problems (if not *the* problem) to be overcome is rational thinking, which causes us to view ourselves as separate from that which we are observing. We must awaken to the Pure Mind (the Buddha Nature) obscured by the ordinary mind. This passage from the ninth-century C.E. Zen master, *Hsi Yun,* is an example of such teaching (Blofeld 1958: 36):

> The Pure Mind, the source of everything, shines forever and on all with the brilliance of its own perfection. But the people of the world do not awake to it, regarding only that which sees, hears, feels, and knows as mind. Blinded by their own sight, hearing, feeling, and knowledge, they do not perceive the spiritual brilliance of the source-substance. If they could only eliminate all conceptual thought in a flash, that source-substance would manifest itself like the sun ascending through the void and illuminating the whole universe without hindrance or bounds.

We deceive ourselves through becoming attached to the pleasures of this world and the diversity of objects that we think we see. But we also deceive ourselves through becoming attached to the desire to escape attachment to the world. We are trapped both by our normal consciousness of the world and our desire to be liberated from it!

How can we find our way out of this dilemma? Like early Buddhist teaching, and in contrast to the Pure Land school, Zen emphasizes that one cannot rely on forces outside oneself to discover the truth. The truth lies within, for only in looking inward can we awaken to the reality that there is no distinction between ourselves and the rest of reality. The journey is one of self-discovery, as one turns inward to penetrate to the depths of one's own existence in order to experience the "emptiness" or "voidness" that is at the heart of everything. This theme is evident in a poem by the seventh-century C.E. Chinese patriarch of the Meditation School, *Seng*

Ts'an (Conze 1964: 296):

> Stop talking, stop thinking and there is nothing you will not understand.
> Return to the Root and you will find the Meaning;
> Pursue the Light, and you will lose its source;
> Look inward, and in a flash you will conquer the Apparent and the Void.
> For the whirligigs of Apparent and Void all come from mistaken views;
> There is no need to seek Truth; only stop having views.

Zen texts echo Daoist philosophy in heralding the natural way of living, without trying to "make things happen." Through meditation one can overcome the illusion of "duality," that there is an "I" who stands over against the "world." The goal of Zen is the sudden experience of the same kind of "awakening" that Siddartha had under the *bodhi* tree. The experience of *satori*, as it its known in Japanese Zen, is of oneness with everything; one wakes up to the Buddha-nature present in all reality, and therefore to one's true nature. The Zen experience can be approximated thus: "There is no 'goal.' I am already enlightened. I have always been in nirvana. I am already the Buddha! There is no path to follow. I am already at the destination! I was simply confused about what already exists!" Until you break free from this "dualistic" prison, you will never discover the truth, Zen teaches.

The techniques in Zen focus on breaking the grip of the rational mind. We must eliminate analytical thinking. A Zen master (*roshi*) may give his students word puzzles called *koans*, designed to confound rational thought. Famous examples of such puzzles are "What is the sound of one hand clapping?" and "What did your face look like before your parents were born?" The student meditates on the question, and then has an interview with the master. The master will know if the student's answer to the question indicates enlightenment. For example, a master gave the *koan* "Does a dog have a Buddha nature?" to a student. When that student *barked* "*Mu!*" (No!) to the master, the master knew he had experienced illumination.

Students of Zen often practice seated meditation (*zazen*). Some masters have been known to slap or yell at their meditating students to try to shock their thinking. Zen masters respect the fact that no two individuals will experience *satori* in the same way. Each person must follow the way best suited to his or her personality.

It is sometimes said that Zen rejects *all* scriptures and all philosophical reasoning. This is not true, for there are Zen writings and Zen philosophical teachings. What Zen rejects is attachment to scriptures, to philosophies, even to the Buddha himself. Sometimes this point is made in a rather shocking way, as in the Zen picture of two monks warming their backsides on the fire from a chopped-up, burning statue of the Buddha.

Here is how a day in a Zen monastery in Japan might go: Arise early (as early as 3:00 A.M.), wash, recite sutras, have a private session with the Master. After breakfast, *zazen*, then clean house, listen to a lecture, go begging for food. After the midday meal, two or three hours of *zazen*. Then engage in manual labor for several hours. After eating and more recitation of sutras, another several hours of *zazen*, perhaps a visit with the *roshi*, then to bed about 8:00 or 9:00 P.M. The bed is a straw mat; it is also the place to sit during meditation, and the dinner table.

Zen does not teach that a person, once enlightened, should withdraw from the world, but rather continue to go about daily routines. As one Zen teacher put it, "My supernatural power—drawing water and carrying firewood." Enlightenment leads one to see that the Truth is present in the ordinary activities of life, and that each moment is both void of meaning in any ordinary sense, yet full of transcendent meaning. The Buddha *is* everywhere present.

One of the most popular sets of Zen drawings is the "Search for the Bull." In this collection of ten drawings, a boy sets out to search for a missing bull. The bull is trailed, found, and (at the fourth panel) caught. He is tamed and led home in the next panels. Then there is an empty panel, symbolizing that both the self and the bull are transcended in the experience of emptiness. However, the drawings continue with a picture of the boy using the bull in ordinary activity.

Have you begun to understand Zen? And then again, if you think you understand Zen, then you clearly do not! What *did* your face look like before your parents were born?

Nichiren: The Political School

Nichiren Buddhism is actually a group of schools that trace their origin to a thirteenth century Buddhist priest named *Zennichimaro* (1222–1282), who was given the honorific name *Nichiren* ("Sun Lotus"). Nichiren studied all the forms of Buddhism popular in Japan—Tendai, Zen, Pure Land, and an esoteric and mystical sect called Shingon. He finally accepted the assertion of the founder of Tendai that the Lotus Sutra is the supreme Buddhist teaching, particularly in its emphasis on placing one's trust in the truth of this scripture for the current age of the destruction of dharma.

The Lotus Sutra portrays Buddha as the Compassionate One who pours out his mercy on all, as the Buddha himself makes clear in this passage, portraying himself as a massive rain cloud bringing peace in this world and the joy of nirvana (*Lotus Sutra* five. Soothill 1987: 127–28):

> I am the Tathagata ["the one thus come," one of the titles of Buddha],
> The Most Honoured among men;
> I appear in the world
> Like unto this great cloud,
> To pour enrichment on all
> Parched living beings,
> To free them from their misery
> To attain the joy of peace,
> Joy of the present world,
> And joy of Nirvana.

Nichiren called on people of all backgrounds to show their faith in the Buddha by reciting the formula: *Namu myo-ho-renge-kyo* ("Hail to the wonderful truth of the Lotus Sutra!"). He denounced the government of his time and the other forms of Buddhism, especially Pure Land, as corruptions of the truth. As a result of his radicalism he was imprisoned.

Nichiren interpreted a series of natural disasters as a sign that the final age of dharma (*mappo*) predicted in the Lotus Sutra had begun. His prophecy that Japan would be attacked by a foreign power seemed to come true with the threatened invasion of the Mongols (halted only by the *kamikaze*), and he won wide public acclaim. However, government officials sought his death; though he was spared execution, he was exiled.

When he returned, he selected Mount Fuji as the earthly manifestation of the mythical mountain where the Buddha is said to have spoken the Lotus Sutra. He established a temple on nearby Mount Minobu as the center for the movement he had initiated.

Nichiren was adamant in his condemnation of other forms of Buddhism. He called Pure Land "a hell" and Zen "a devil." He also argued that Buddhism must have a national as well as an individual impact. Only if Japan adopted the true religion that he had revealed would the nation be at peace. And only if the Japanese carried this truth to the world, would the world find peace. He claimed that in the 2,200 years since the death of *Sakyamuni* ("the enlightened sage of the Sakya clan"—another name for Siddartha) only he, Nichiren, had fulfilled his prophecy.

His followers believed that Nichiren was the earthly manifestation of *Jogyo*, one of the *bodhisattvas* who was in the heavenly audience when the Buddha delivered the Lotus Sutra, and who is committed to proclaiming its truth. They formed a movement that eventually split into two separate branches. The branch that continued Nichiren's radical tendencies was *Nichiren Sho-shu* ("the true school of Nichiren"). Nichiren Sho-shu taught that the teachings of Nichiren were superior not only to other forms of Buddhism but to all other religions. In addition, the Lotus Sutra is not only the best of Buddhist scriptures, it is the *only* scripture needed in the *mappo* age. The heart of the Lotus Sutra is the chant described above.

The hidden truth of the Lotus Sutra is that the Buddha existed from eternity and will always exist. When this age of the destruction of the dharma ends, it will be replaced with an era of cosmic harmony for those who take refuge in the teachings of the Lotus Sutra.

Today, roughly 30 percent of Japanese Buddhists are in the Nichiren tradition. One of the principal forms of Nichiren Buddhism in Japan—and its most influential manifestation in the United States and around the world—is a lay organization known as *Soka Gakkai* ("Value Creation Society"), one of the "new religions" of Japan. We will discuss Soka Gakkai in Chapter Fourteen.

Tibetan Buddhism: The Tantric School

Tour *The Sacred World* CD!

Tantrism is a term used to refer to "unorthodox" movements in Hinduism, Jainism, and Buddhism. The Buddhist Tantric School originated in India but took root in Tibet, becoming the dominant expression of Buddhism in that secluded, mountainous land.

The history of Tantrism in Tibet can be traced to an eighth-century holy man named *Padma-Sambhava* who came from India. He brought the Buddhist teaching called *Vajrayana* ("Diamond" or "Thunderbolt Vehicle"), in which the union of male and female deities was thought to overcome the duality of life in *samsara*. It also taught that certain magic formulae were effective in channeling physical and psychic energies into the experience of sudden enlightenment. The indigenous religion of Tibet, a form of animism known as Bon, was synthesized with Tantrism, creating an elaborate complex of beliefs and practices. For example, the belief in demons was incorporated from Bon, with the notion that the Buddhas have the power to drive them off.

The omnipresent prayer wheel is also a reflection of this synthesis. The wheel is actually a drum into which are placed written prayers and pages from Buddhist sutras. To turn the crank of the drum energizes the words and is considered an act of devotion to the Buddhas as well as an effective way to ward off evil. Ingenious monks design water wheels that will perpetually turn their prayers.

One of the most widely used magical formulae in Tibetan Buddhism is the Sanskrit *mantra: Om mani padme hum* ("Om! the jewel is in the lotus, hum!"). Its meaning remains a mystery to the uninitiated, but its use is widespread.

Like Hindu Tantrism, at the center of Tibetan Tantrism are cosmic pairs of deities, but in Tibet they are Buddhas rather than Hindu gods and goddesses. In Indian tantrism the active energy in the pair is the female, while the male is passive. In Tibet the male Buddhas are portrayed as the possessors of dynamic power, and their female consorts are the quiescent possessors of wisdom. The pantheon includes five celestial Buddhas, with one at each of the cardinal directions and one in the center. They all emerge from the *Adi-Buddha,* the Buddha essence that is the source of all other Buddhas and all reality. Human devotees can identify with the Buddhas and their consorts by fasting and meditation, and the repetition of magical utterances. As a result, one's identity is merged with the Buddha. This leads to the Vajrayana experience, in which enlightenment comes like a thunderbolt, cutting like a diamond through all that stands in the way of illumination.

Just as in its Indian counterpart, Tibetan tantrism teaches that humans are the cosmos in miniature. The cosmic energies are present in the human body and can be channeled through the proper meditative techniques.

At the center of Tibetan Buddhism are the *lamas* ("superior ones"). Although the term is sometimes used to refer to all Tibetan monks, lamas are more specifically monks (or lay people) who possess special magical powers, revealing that they are incarnations of Buddhas and *bodhisattvas*. In each monastery there is a hierarchy of lamas.

Selfless *bodhisattvas* committed to the unity of all living beings also play a central role in Tibetan Buddhism, as this passage from a Tibetan text reveals (*Acharya Shantideva* 8.112–17. Batchelor 1979: 117–18):

Why should I be unable
To regard the bodies of others as "I"?
It is not difficult to see
That my body is also that of others[. . . .]

Only through acquaintance has the thought of "I" arisen
Towards this impersonal body;
So in a similar way, why should it not arise
Towards other living beings?

In the fourteenth century a reform movement in Tibetan Buddhism led to the creation of a new school. It became known as the Yellow Hat School, because the monks (called Yellow Hats) wore the color yellow to symbolize a return to the pure teachings of Buddha, and to distinguish themselves from those who resisted reform, who wore red (called Red Hats). The reform imposed a stricter discipline on monks (reintroducing celibacy, for example), but did not abolish all signs of Tantrism.

Because of the celibacy rule in the Yellow Hat order, the succession of leadership could not be hereditary. To meet this need the theory of the reincarnation of the abbots (heads) of monasteries developed. According to this concept, the grand lamas of each monastery were the incarnations of Buddhas. After their deaths, they were reborn in another human form. After the death of an abbot an elaborate search for his successor began. It might take years. The goal was to find a young child, born forty-nine days after the abbot's death, who demonstrated clear familiarity with some of the abbot's belongings and who had the magical marks of the abbot on his body. Other magical signs were sought through divination. The child was then taken from his family, raised in the monastery, and installed as abbot.

In the sixteenth century the Grand Lama of the monastery at the main city of Tibet, Lhasa, took the name the *Dalai Lama.* The head lama of Lhasa had been

Tibetan Buddhist monks prepare to dismantle the colored sand mandala they have just spent several days creating. A mandala is a sacred picture, often in the form of a circle. A Tibetan sand mandala represents the celestial palace inhabited at the center by Buddha, surrounded by other spiritual beings. Each element is highly symbolic. The sand mandala is used to facilitate meditation, and is always destroyed after its construction because of the Buddhist belief in non-attachment and impermanence.

considered an incarnation of the *bodhisattva Avalokita* (Avalokitesvara). According to one tradition, as a result of his work in revitalizing Buddhism in Mongolia, he was given the title of honor Dalai ("ocean") to symbolize the infinite wisdom of the *bodhisattva* he incarnated. The Dalai Lama is understood by Tibetan Buddhists to be the "ocean of wisdom." The Yellow Hat school gained more power and influence, and not only became the dominant Buddhist movement in Tibet but spread into Mongolia, Russia, and Siberia.

Beginning in the seventeenth century, the Dalai Lama became the symbol of the nation of Tibet, considered both its temporal and religious leader. By this time, one-fifth of the people of Tibet lived in monasteries, which were great fortresses in addition to being religious centers.

The fourteenth and present Dalai Lama, Tenzin Gyatso, was identified when he was five years old, in 1940. When the Chinese took control of Tibet in 1951, he tried to work within the framework of the Communist regime. After the destruction of monasteries in Tibet and Mongolia by the Chinese government in 1959, and a subsequent invasion of Tibet by the Chinese, the Dalai Lama fled to India. There he established a center for the preservation of Tibetan culture. He has traveled extensively to make known the plight of the Tibetan people, and to call for understanding among world religions and peace among the nations of the world. For his work he was awarded the Nobel Peace Prize in 1989. He has made a number of lecture tours of the United States. A citation of a Tibetan text on the Dalai Lama's official web site (www.dalailama.com) reflects his commitment to his traditional role:

> For as long as space endures, and as long as living beings remain, until then may I, too, abide, to dispel the misery of the world.

The most famous text in Tibetan Buddhism is the *Bardo Thodol* ("the between state in which there is liberation through hearing"). It is popularly known in the West as the *Tibetan Book of the Dead*. The work focuses on the liberation of a person during the forty-nine-day period between the moment of death and the next incarnation. This period is the *bardo*, the "time between." The book gives elaborate instructions to those who are attending a dying person. Typically, a lama sits at the head of the person and chants magical formulae that are intended to help the person to be reborn in the Western Paradise of Amitabha rather than on earth. As death approaches, the dying person is given instructions on how to attain liberation.

Then, after the funeral, during the entire *bardo*, a picture or effigy of the deceased may become the focus of further instruction. The Bardo Thodol has become popular in the West, and has been the subject of extensive psychological and philosophical interpretation.

MAHAYANA BUDDHISM IN THE TWENTY-FIRST CENTURY

In South Korea, Buddhism is in the midst of a period of revival. Economic prosperity has created lay patrons for Buddhist monasteries, and schools that are committed to spreading Buddhist values throughout the culture. There is even an "All-Buddhist Network" on South Korean television.

In Japan, Buddhism began to recover after World War II from a century of government attacks. Today, most Japanese families are registered with a Buddhist monastery (in addition to a Shinto shrine), so that Buddhist death rituals may be performed for family members. As in China, devotion to the *bodhisattva* Kuan Yin

(Kannon in Japan) is on the rise, particularly at pilgrimage sites. Several movements related to Nichiren Buddhism, including Soka Gakkai (see Chapter Fourteen) and *Reikukai Kyodan* ("Spiritual Friends Association"), have millions of members in Japan and exercise considerable influence. The schools of Zen Buddhism have nearly ten million lay members. The impact of Zen in shaping Japanese culture continues. The Pure Land Buddhist schools are also still popular.

Perhaps the most remarkable Mahayana Buddhist development in the twenty-first century is the rapid growth of Tibetan Buddhism throughout the world, especially in the West. The Dalai Lama has carried the teachings and rituals of this once reclusive religion around the globe, as he has travelled to promote understanding of the plight of the Tibetan people and world peace. Other lamas are also active in spreading the religion, and groups of Tibetan monks publicly creating and then destroying their elaborate sand mandalas have served to make many Westerners aware of the Tibetan Buddhist worldview.

The Free Tibet Movement, with the involvement of celebrities like Richard Gere and Stephen Seagal, has also attracted attention not only to the political situation in Tibet, but to the religion of the Tibetan people. By the early twenty-first century, centers of Tibetan Buddhism had sprung up in the United States and other Western countries, attracting converts seeking greater spiritual meaning for their lives. While these new Tibetan Buddhists remain loyal to the authority of the Dalai Lama and the traditional practices, they are also adapting their observance of Buddhist teachings to their own nonmonastic, more individualistic lifestyles.

After the fall of the Soviet Union in 1989, with the support of the Dalai Lama, Tibetan Buddhism has been restored to portions of Mongolia and is enjoying a resurgence.

CHAPTER SUMMARY

We first surveyed the histories of Japan and Korea, as background for further discussion of the religions of East Asia.

Although the Mahayana branch of Buddhism is based on *sutras* mostly written in India, it grew to maturity in East Asia. We outlined the spread of Buddhism from India into East Asia, identified the major Mahayana texts, contrasted Mahayana with Theravada Buddhism, and briefly surveyed the major Mahayana movements: the Pure Land School, the Meditation School (better known as Zen), the Political School (Nichiren), and the Tantric School (in its Tibetan form).

IMPORTANT TERMS AND PHRASES

Amitabha (Amida), Avalokitesvara (Avalokita), Bardo Thodol, Bodhidharma, *bodhisattva,* Bon, Buddha-nature, Dalai Lama, Diamond Cutter Sutra, *koan,* Kuan Yin (Kannon, Koan-Eum), lama, Lotus Sutra, Mahayana, Maitreya, Nichiren, *mappo* age, Nagarjuna, *prajna, Prajna-paramita,* Pure Land (Western Paradise), Pure (Original) Mind, *satori, sunyata,* Vajrayana, Zen

QUESTIONS FOR DISCUSSION AND REFLECTION

1. If you could associate with one, and only one, of the branches of Buddhism (Theravada or Mahayana), which would you choose? Explain your choice.

2. If you could associate with one, and only one, of the schools of Mahayana Buddhism (Pure Land, Zen, Nichiren, or Tantric), which would you choose? Explain your choice.

3. Contemplate the Zen Buddhist teaching that "rational thinking" is the fundamental problem we must overcome. What is the "mind beyond mind"? What *did* your face look like before your parents were born?

4. According to one Zen teacher, the highest truth is found in chopping wood and carrying water. Does that make sense to you?

5. Which do you prefer: the Zen Buddhist view that "heaven" is a creation of our minds, which has no substance; or the Pure Land teaching that heaven is a spiritual place of supreme enjoyment?

6. Do you know anyone (personally or by reputation) who seems to have the qualities of a *bodhisattva*? What are those characteristics?

7. Why has the current Dalai Lama had such a significant impact on people around the world?

SOURCES AND SUGGESTIONS FOR FURTHER STUDY

ANESAKE, MASAHARU, 1966. *Nichiren, the Buddhist Prophet.* Gloucester, MA: Peter Smith.

BATCHELOR, STEPHEN, TRANS., 1979. *A Guide to the Bodhisattva's Way of Life: the Bodhissatva-acharyavatara.* Dharamsala, India: Library of Tibetan Works and Archives.

BLOFELD, JOHN [CHU CH'AN], TRANS., 1958. *Zen Teachings of Huang Po: On the Transmission of Mind.* New York: Grove.

CLEARY, THOMAS F., TRANS., 1984. *The Flower Ornament: A Translation of the Avatamsaka Sutra.* Vol 1. Boulder: Shambhala.

CONZE, EDWARD, ED. AND TRANS., 1959. *Buddhist Scriptures.* London: Penguin.

CONZE, EDWARD, ED. AND TRANS., 1964. *Buddhist Texts through the Ages.* New York: Harper Torchbooks.

GYATSO, TENZIN, THE FOURTEENTH DALAI LAMA, 1995. *The World of Tibetan Buddhism: An Overview of Its Philosophy and Practice,* trans. Geshe Thupten Jinpa. Boston: Wisdom Publications.

HANH, THICH NHAT, 1996. *Culminating the Mind of Love: The Practice of Looking Deeply in the Mahayana Buddhist Tradition.* Berkeley: Parallax.

KAPLEAU, PHILIP, ED. 1967. *The Three Pillars of Zen.* Boston: Beacon.

MIYAMORI, ASATAR-O, 1970. *An Anthology of Haiku, Ancient and Modern.* Westport, CT: Greenwood.

RAY, REGINALD A., 2000. *Indestructible Truth: The Living Spirituality of Tibetan Buddhism.* Boston: Shambhala.

SEAGER, RICHARD H., 1999. *Buddhism in America.* New York: Columbia University.

SOOTHILL, WILLIAM E., TRANS., 1987. *The Lotus of the Wonderful Law.* Atlantic Highlands, NJ: Humanities.

SUZUKI, SHUNRYU, 2002. *Not Always So: Practicing the True Spirit of Zen,* ed. Edward Espe Brown. New York: HarperCollins.

UNNO, TAITETSU, 1998. *River of Fire, River of Water: An Introduction to the Pure Land Tradition of Shin Buddhism.* New York: Doubleday.

WILLIAMS, PAUL, 1989. *Mahayana Buddhism: The Doctrinal Foundations.* New York: Routledge.

WRIGHT, DALE, 2001. "Practices of Perfection: The Ethical Aim of Mahayana Buddhism." In *Ethics in the World Religions.* ed. Joseph Runzo and Nancy M. Martin. New York: Oneworld, 219–33.

Web Sites

(see also sites on Buddhism listed in Chapter Four)

www.ne.jp/asahi/pureland-buddhism/amida-net/
(information on the Pure Land School)

ciolek.com/WWWVL-Zen.html
(a virtual library for the study of Zen Buddhism)

dalailama.com
(official site of the Dalai Lama, head of Tibetan Buddhism)

ciolek.com/WWWVL-TibetanStudies.html
(a virtual library for the study of Tibetan Buddhism)

www.nichirenshoshu.or.jp
www.nst.org
(sites of schools of Nichiren Buddhism)

TIME Refer to Pearson/Prentice Hall's **TIME Special Edition: World Religions** magazine for these and other current articles on topics related to many of the world's religions:

•➔ *Buddhism: Buddhism in America; The Dalai Lama—"It's Time to Prepare New Leaders;" Essay— Lost Without a Faith*

 Prentice Hall's **Research Navigator** helps students in their further study of the world's religions. Visit ***http://www.researchnavigator.com*** for help on the research process and access to databases full of relevant material, including the New York *Times.*

CHAPTER

9

Shinto—The Way of the *Kami*

INTRODUCTION

Shinto (or "Shintoism," as it is also known), the traditional religion of Japan, has played a critical role in the formation of Japanese culture and the Japanese national identity. Despite reports of its demise in recent decades, Shinto continues to be a significant force in Japanese life in the contemporary world.

In this chapter we will summarize the origin and development of Shinto, present the basic Shinto worldview, and comment on religion in Japan as well as Korea in the twenty-first century.

STAGES OF DEVELOPMENT AND SACRED TEXTS

The Origin and Meaning of "Shinto"

Like Hinduism and other native religious traditions, "Shinto" defies easy classification. Its very name reflects the problem. Shinto comes from two Chinese words that we have already encountered (*shen* and *dao*), and means the "way of the spirits." Shinto was in fact the name developed to try to understand the native traditions of Japan when Buddhism was introduced, just as the name Hinduism came out of a need to distinguish indigenous Indian beliefs and practices from Islam, when the Muslims entered India. Indeed, in the early stages of the development of religion in Japan, there was no "Shinto," only a variety of indigenous religious traditions.

The same Japanese characters pronounced *shen dao* can also be pronounced (when the two characters are separated) *kami-no-michi*, "the way of the *kami*." We will discuss the meaning of *kami* more fully below, but in general *kami* refers to anything or anyone inspiring awe, respect, and devotion. It is the Japanese word for "the sacred." The goal of life, according to Shinto teaching, is to live in harmony with the *kami*.

The Shinto Myth: Japan as the Land of the *Kami*

The roots of Shinto are found in the myth of the origins of the Japanese islands. The Shinto Myth probably had a long oral history, but it was first compiled in written form in 712 C.E., in a work known as the *Kojiki* ("Chronicle of Ancient Events"). The Kojiki was a complete history of the world from the creation down to the middle of the seventh century; together with the *Nihongi* ("Chronicles of Japan"), written down by 720 C.E., it forms the core of the traditional Japanese understanding of national identity and history.

According to the Kojiki, the Japanese islands were created at the beginning of time by two *kami,* the original male, *Izanagi* ("male-who-invites"), and female, *Izanami* ("female-who-invites"). A story of the pollution and cleansing of Izanagi foreshadows the central role of ritual purification in Shinto. From the left eye of Izanagi came the deity most revered in Japan, the sun-goddess, *Amaterasu.* A long list of other deities also came into being in Japan. For example, the storm-god, *Susa-no-wo,* emerged from the nostrils of Izanagi, and subsequently engaged in a series of struggles with Amaterasu. Later, concerned about the disorder on the islands, Amaterasu sent her grandson to rule. According to legend, his great-grandson, *Jimmu Tenno,* was the first human emperor of Japan, and the ancestor of all subsequent imperial houses. The traditional date for his ascendancy is 660 B.C.E.

Therefore, according to the Shinto Myth, the emperor of Japan is a descendant of the sun-goddess herself, and is known as the "manifest *kami.*" The Japanese islands were the center of creation, and the Japanese people are all descended from the *kami.* Indeed, Japan is "the land of the *kami.*"

The following excerpt from the Shinto Myth describes the creation of the Japanese islands by Izanagi and Izanami (*Kojiki,* Bk. One, Ch. 1, 3–4. Philippi 1968: 47–51) from a floating mass "resembling floating oil and drifting like a jellyfish":

> The heavenly deities, all with one command, said to the two deities Izanagi-no-mikoto and Izanami-no-mikoto: "Complete and solidify this drifting land!" Giving them the Heavenly Jeweled Spear, they entrusted the mission to them.
>
> Thereupon, the two deities stood on the Heavenly Floating Bridge and, lowering the jeweled spear, stirred with it. They stirred the brine with a churning-churning sound, and when they lifted up [the spear] again, the brine dripping down from the tip of the spear piled up and became an island. This was the island Onogoro. Descending from the heavens to this island, they erected a heavenly pillar and a spacious palace.
>
> At this time [Izanagi] asked his spouse Izanami, saying: "How is your body formed?"
>
> She replied, saying: "My body, formed though it be formed, has one place which is formed insufficiently."
>
> Then Izanagi-no-mikoto said: "My body, formed though it be formed, has one place which is formed to excess. Therefore, I would like to take that place in my body which is formed to excess and insert it into that place in your body which is formed insufficiently, and [thus] give birth to the land. How would this be?"
>
> Izanami-no-mikoto said: "Then let us, you and me, walk in a circle around this heavenly pillar and have conjugal intercourse."

Popular Japanese Religion

Tour *The Sacred World* CD!

Long before there was "Shinto," there were religious practices in Japan. Many were incorporated into the myths and rituals of Shinto, but there remains a level of popular Japanese religiosity which should be considered on its own terms. As in China, popular or folk religion in Japan—which reaches back into prehistoric times—has always included divination, inspired healings, ancestor veneration, spirit possession, and the worship of other deities and spirits. Through popular religion, people express a desire to live in harmony with the cycles of nature and to respect the spiritual power manifest in natural phenomena. Their primary concern is well-being in their daily lives. Some scholars have called this popular Japanese religion "folk Shinto."

One specific feature of Japanese popular religion deserving of special mention is the role of women. The *miko*, a woman shaman (on the nature of shamanism, see Chapter Two), was an important religious leader in early Japan, and remains so in remote Japanese villages today. Young girls are still apprenticed to shamanesses in some rural areas. While possessed by a spirit, a *miko* may utter poems or sing ballads extolling the beauty of nature or lamenting the death of a loved one. They also transmit traditional folklore through their singing, recitation of poetry, and religious paintings. Her empowerment enables the *miko* to be an effective healer and communicator with the spirit world.

The role of women in Japanese religion was diminished with the introduction of Confucian ethics (and was not fully recovered in Shinto). However, in some of the new religions that have emerged in modern Japan and gained in popularity since World War II (see Chapter Fourteen), the role of charismatic women leaders has been reestablished. Korea also has a long tradition of shamanesses, who are called *mudang*.

Medieval Shinto: Theoretical Amalgamation with Buddhism

As Buddhism, which had been introduced to Japan from Korea in the mid sixth century C.E., began to spread outside the Japanese court into the villages, Shinto priests adapted by erecting Buddhist temples within the Shinto shrines. As a result, theoretical teachings developed about the relationship between Buddhist deities and the Shinto *kami*. The most common was the idea of "original substance, manifest traces." Shinto scholars argued that the original substance was found in *kami*, and the manifest traces were the Buddhist deities, while Buddhist teachers argued the opposite.

Several different schools of "mixed Shinto" emerged, each trying to resolve the question of the relationship between the *kami* and Buddhist deities in a different way. The most popular was *Ryobu* ("two-sided") Shinto, which treated the two as manifestations of the same reality. For example, Amaterasu was said to be the same as the very popular Sun Buddha, *Vairocana*. During the Kamakura period, Buddhism nearly supplanted Shinto through a process of absorption and redefinition.

Another feature of medieval Shinto, and its amalgamation not only with Buddhism but also Confucianism, deserves special attention: the *bushido* ("military-warrior-way") of the *samurai* warrior. It was developed in the Kamakura Period, and systematized in the Tokugawa Period. Although it has been compared to the medieval European knight's code of chivalry, it has a decidedly East Asian character. The unwritten code bound the samurai to their feudal lords with loyalty and to nature with reverence. Some of the virtues associated with *bushido*, in addition to loyalty and reverence, are courage, truthfulness, respect, and justice.

The most famous *bushido* virtue is honor, to the extent that death is preferable to disgrace for the true samurai. The warrior always carries two swords: one to do battle with the enemy, and another, shorter sword to commit ritual suicide (*seppuku*) if honor requires. Bushido reflects the influences of Confucianism in its emphasis on filial piety, loyalty, and the five basic relationships; Zen Buddhism in its focus on self-discipline and spontaneity of action; and Shinto in its aesthetic appreciation of nature and pride in one's ruler.

The legendary courage of Japanese *kamikaze* pilots and other Japanese combatants during World War II is a modern version of *bushido,* with loyalty to the feudal lord transferred to the Emperor and nation. Today, some have called the Japanese businessman the modern samurai, with absolute obedience to his corporation, whose well-being is more important than his own. Occasionally, even today, there are examples of ritual suicide carried out by a man (*harakiri*) and his wife (*jigai*). The spiritual aura of the martial arts, still evident in modern Japan, can be traced, in part, to the *bushido.*

The Revival of Shinto

Efforts to restore Shinto as the central religion of Japan began as early as the fourteenth century, but it was during the Tokugawa period, beginning in the seventeenth century, that the revival became an important force. This was the time when Japan's military leaders tried to close Japan to foreign influence. They joined with Shinto scholars in promoting a return to the "Ancient Way." The leading scholar was Motoori Norinaga, who taught that Japan was superior to other countries, which are bound to give allegiance to the Mikado, the Japanese emperor. This ideology was to play an important role in the promotion of Japanese expansionism in the mid twentieth century, just as nineteenth-century German scholarship helped support the Nazi racial ideology of "Aryan" superiority.

Shinto as a State Religion (1868–1945)   The introduction of Western values that followed the forced reopening of Japan by American naval forces under Commodore Perry in 1853 led to a reaction that sought to secure Shinto as the national ideology. This effort continued during the Meiji Period (1868–1912) and until the end of World War II in 1945. For example, the Constitution of 1881 stated in Article III that "the Emperor is sacred and inviolable." This was an abstract endorsement of the Shinto Myth's contention that the emperor was the Manifest *Kami,* a descendant of the Sun Goddess.

An attempt was made to force Buddhism and Christianity out of Japan. Failing in the effort to purge foreign religious influences from Japan entirely, the strategy shifted to the creation of a State Shinto ostensibly separate from religious practice. State Shinto (*Jinja-Shinto*) included most of the rituals and shrines, placing them under the control of a government Bureau of Shrines. All Japanese were required to register at a shrine.

The Shinto Myth's teachings concerning the sacredness and centrality of Japan were ordered to be taught in schools. The Imperial Rescript on Education (1890), the basis for the educational system, called the Imperial Throne "coeval with heaven and earth" and the Way of the Ancestors "infallible for all ages and true in all places." Until 1945, this is what every Japanese schoolchild was taught to accept without question. Students bowed daily before a picture of the Emperor. A 1911 order required teachers to take their students to Shinto shrines for festivals, in order to teach them the reverence that is the foundation of national morality. (Whether there is a substantial difference between these practices and the civic rituals conducted and observed in the schools of other nations is an interesting topic of discussion.)

The government listed more than one hundred thousand shrines during this period. Some were run by the government, but most were local shrines. Sixteen thousand priests served the major state shrines. They were instructed not to carry out overtly religious ceremonies, but the national rituals conducted by these priests were hard to distinguish from religious rites.

State Shinto was officially nonreligious. The spiritual side of the Shinto Myth was deemphasized; the *kami* of the Myth were said to be human beings who had attained legendary status. However, from the perspective of the definition of religion adopted for this study (see Chapter One), State Shinto *was* a religion, albeit a secular one. Loyalty to the nation and to the Emperor as its symbol became the goal. Transformation was through giving oneself fully to the nation and to the Emperor, making "His august will" one's own.

The *Kokutai-ni-hongi* (1937) told citizens that when they go to the shrines to perform rituals they will be " 'dying to self' to become one with the State." The following excerpt from the *Kokutai-ni-hongi* illustrates the perspective of State Shinto that the basic dilemma facing the Japanese during this period was the influence of Western (Occidental) individualism (Gauntlett and Hall 1974: 82):

Of late years, through the influence of the Occidental (Western) individualistic ideology, a way of thinking which has for its basis the individual has become lively. Consequently, this and the true aim of our Way of loyalty which is "essentially" different from it are not necessarily [mutually] consistent. That is, those in our country who at the present time expound loyalty and patriotism are apt to lose [sight] of its true significance, being influenced by Occidental individualism and rationalism. We must sweep aside the corruption of the spirit and the clouding of knowledge that arises from setting up one's "self" and from being taken up with one's "self" and return to a pure and clear state of mind that belongs intrinsically to us as subjects, and thereby fathom the great principle of loyalty.

With the creation of State Shinto, an officially religious branch of Shinto was also recognized. Sectarian Shinto (*Kyoha-Shinto*) included thirteen separate Shinto sects that had developed by the late nineteenth century. Some focused on *kami* in nature, making prominent features of nature objects of worship; others tended toward the individual desire for health and well-being. The most prominent among this group was *Tenri-kyo,* which emphasizes faith-healing and is still a popular movement in postwar Japan. Still other Shinto sects tried to maintain the spiritual side of the Shinto Myth and the traditional rituals of purification.

State Shinto played an important role in the fostering of Japanese support for the expansionist policies that led the country into war with the United States, Britain, and other Western powers. The most dramatic example of its influence is the phenomenon of the *kami-kaze,* the Japanese pilots who crashed their planes into the enemy ships approaching Japan toward the end of the war. They were named after the "divine wind" that had turned back another foreign invasion in 1281, and they manifested the idea that if the people were loyal Japan would remain inviolable.

Shinto after World War II   In December 1945, four months after the dropping of the atomic bombs on Hiroshima and Nagasaki by the United States and the unconditional surrender of Japan to the allied powers, the occupation government arranged for the publication of a "Shinto Directive." It required the abolition of government support, sponsorship, perpetuation, dissemination, and control of State Shinto. It also included the mandate that the Shinto Myth be withdrawn as the basis of Japanese education.

A month later the Emperor's Rescript stated that the Emperor was not divine, Japan was not the center of the universe, and the Japanese people were not superior to any other people. Emperor Hirohito called on the Japanese people to work toward the improvement of all humanity, not just their own country. A new constitution guaranteed religious freedom and forbade state involvement in religious activities.

In this changed environment a host of "new religions," including some influenced by Shinto teachings, gained popularity. A few, such as *Soka Gakkai* (see Chapter Fourteen), have become quite influential in modern Japan and have spread to other parts of the world.

After the war, Shrine Shinto replaced the now outlawed State Shinto. The number of shrines dropped to about eighty-five thousand, with control held at the local level. Due to land reform, shrines lost their holdings and were forced to either close or provide other services, such as preschools or kindergartens, for support. Many priests, accustomed to receiving government support, had to take at least part-time jobs. Still, the custom continued of a hereditary priesthood associated with specific shrines. A private Shrine Association was formed to provide coordination and support for the formerly government-controlled shrines.

THE SHINTO WORLDVIEW

As in other Asian religions, there is no central authority establishing an orthodoxy in Shinto. Shinto has different meanings for different people. It is also important to note that allegiance to Shinto is not viewed as exclusive. Typically, Japanese register with both Shinto Shrines and Buddhist institutions, so that about 75–80 percent of the Japanese people can be considered both Shinto and Buddhist in their general religious affiliation.

Humanity: The People of the *Kami*

The Shinto Myth makes clear that since the Japanese islands are the land of the *kami* (see below), the Japanese are the people of the *kami*. This perspective creates a strong sense of rootedness in the land, similar to the sense found in other indigenous religions (see Chapter Two). It also helps us understand the strong sense of solidarity and interconnectedness associated with Japanese culture. Both were weakened by the defeat of Japan in World War II and the introduction of Western values; today they are threatened by the consumerism that characterizes contemporary Japanese life.

Problem: Impurity and Disharmony

For the traditional Shinto associated with the shrines, the basic dilemma to be overcome is impurity brought on by disharmony with the *kami*. Failure to maintain harmony with the *kami* leads to chaos for individuals, families, and the nation as a whole. According to Shinto teachers, one manifestation of this state is individualism, when people promote themselves over their families, their clans, their companies, or their nation.

Cause: Lack of Reverence for the *Kami*

People will naturally follow the path of harmony with the *kami*, unless they lose their reverence for them. When nature is viewed as lifeless material to be used however people please, rather than as alive, beautiful, and inspiring, people lose reverence for the kami. When the ancestors and ancient heroes are forgotten, and people pursue individual pleasure rather than the good of family and society, they lose reverence for the *kami*. If they lose their pride in being Japanese and living in the land of the *kami*, they lose reverence. Lack of reverence results in a state of pollution, from which people must be transformed through rituals of purification and forgiveness.

End: Purity and Harmony

As with Daoism, Shinto's ultimate goal is cosmic harmony, with all elements in balance. However, like Confucianism, the focus of Shinto harmony is this-worldly and social. The ideal for Shinto is a Japanese people living harmoniously: with one another, with the land, and, at the root of it all, with the *kami*. Such is the life of purity toward which all Japanese should strive, according to traditional Shinto teaching.

A practical accommodation has been worked out between Shinto and Buddhism in Japan. Shinto is concerned with life before death, maintaining harmony and purity in the here and now. Buddhism enables people to deal with the impermanence of life and the reality of death, offering a path to deliverance from the suffering of life in the world.

Means: Shrines, Rituals, and Self-Cultivation

The principal path to harmony and purity in traditional Shinto is through participation in temple rituals. Some rituals are national, others local, and some for clans and families. At each level Shinto priests perform the ceremonies of purification.

The most popular national Shrine is now, as it has been for centuries, the Grand Imperial Shrine of the Sun Goddess Amaterasu located at *Ise*. To some extent it is like Mecca for Muslims; every Japanese who takes seriously the Shinto traditions tries to visit Ise at least once. Like most Shinto shrines, the Imperial Shrine at Ise is a simple structure, made of unpainted cedar. The symbols of Amaterasu are not pictures or statues, but objects associated with the myth of the goddess—a mirror, sword, and string of stone jewels. As part of the concern for purification and renewal, the Shrine is torn down and rebuilt every twenty years.

Virtually every Japanese village has a Shinto shrine, at which the rituals passed down from ancient times are still carried out. Typically the rectangular compound is surrounded by a fence, to demarcate the "sacred space." A sacred threshold, a gateway called the *torii*, marks the entrance to the shrine. A path leads from the *torii* to the outer shrine, called the *haiden*. As the worshipper approaches the *haiden*, the person washes his or her hands and mouth with water for purification. In other contexts, salt is used as a purifying agent in Shinto rituals. Then the worshipper bows, claps hands to get the attention of the *kami*, rings the bell, drops an offering in a box, leaves a prayer on a piece of paper, and then departs while bowing low. Beyond the outer shrine one finds the inner holy place, called the *honden*. This shrine is not entered by worshippers, for it contains the sacred object associated with the *kami* of the shrine. The object is never seen, except once a year at an annual festival when it is taken and carried through the village.

In addition to the local festival associated with the *kami* of each shrine, there are a series of national rites that are still widely observed. Twice each year the Great Purification is held, on June 30th and December 31st. Before World War II the Emperor, as the Manifest *Kami,* would pronounce forgiveness for the sins of the nation. The type of cleansing wand used in this ceremony to symbolize the "wiping away" of impurities is used by Shinto priests in other, less formal settings. Someone who has bought a new car, for example, might bring it to a priest to be purified with the cleansing wand and thereby made safe.

Other important national Shinto festivals include the New Year, which begins at midnight on December 31 (after the purification ceremony) and continues for three days. This is a time when ordinary life in Japan comes to a standstill, and millions of people travel to their ancestral homes to visit local Shinto shrines and Buddhist temples. Gifts are exchanged, and children typically receive envelopes full of money from relatives. About a month before the New Year, at the beginning of December, people traditionally put up an "entrance pine" (*kadomatsu*) in their homes and businesses to welcome the *kami* whose blessings are sought.

A number of festivals relate to individuals and their stages of life. On January 15th "coming of age day" is celebrated. Twenty-year-olds come to Shinto shrines to seek the blessing of the *kami* on their new status. The Girl's (Doll's) Festival is observed on March 3rd and the Boy's Festival (now called Children's Day) on May 5th. The famous Chrysanthemum Festival is held on September 9th. The respect for older people in Japan is reflected in the the Festival of the Elderly celebrated on September 15th.

The agricultural year is also observed in rural areas in a series of festivals linked to the phases of the cultivation of rice, beginning at the end of March. Shinto's ability to adapt to change and absorb new traditions is seen in the rising popularity of

Shinto priests commonly use a haraigushi, a wand made of linen or paper streamers attached to wooden sticks, in formal purification ceremonies and also to cleanse new buildings or vehicles.

Christmas as a national festival, replete with Santa Claus impersonators at festively decorated shopping malls.

People visit Shinto shrines not only at prescribed occasions, but at times of family importance. The rites of passage of birth, puberty, and marriage are conducted by Shinto priests. In the case of birth, the rite is at the shrine, when the family presents the child to be received as part of the "family of the *kami*." Traditional marriages are elaborate, expensive affairs in which priest and bride wear traditional dress, while the groom wears a Western style morning coat. People also visit shrines to seek the *kami*'s blessing and intercession at special times of family concern. The exception is at death, when the funeral rites are conducted by Buddhist rather than Shinto functionaries.

In addition to Shrine Shinto, the practice of Shinto continues in other contexts. One is the home, where many families still maintain a *kami-dana* ("god shelf"). The ancestors of the family and other *kami* special to the family are memorialized on wood or paper tablets with their names inscribed. Miniatures of the special symbols of the sun goddess Amaterasu or other major *kami*, and objects or pictures of ancestors, are also found. Devout families practice daily rituals, involving offerings of food and a prayer. Many others turn to the home shrine at times of special concern or crisis in the family.

Families often have both a shelf for Shinto *kami* and another shelf for Buddhist deities and the names of ancestors (*butsu-dan*).

In addition to shrines and rituals, moral self-cultivation plays an important role in Shinto teaching. Moral behavior, and particularly sincerity (*makoto*) and acting with "a truthful heart," are emphasized. In this context, Shinto reflects the influence of Confucian virtues introduced from China and Korea.

Reality: The Land of the *Kami*

Under the influence of Buddhism, Shinto scholars developed an interest in the nature of reality, and searched for the "original essence" that is the foundation of all that is. In addition, we find a distinct understanding of reality in the Shinto Myth. The Myth teaches the Japanese that their islands are the center of the universe, that Japan is the land of the *kami*, and that all nations are destined to bow before the Manifest *Kami*, the Emperor. This is what might be called an organic conception of reality, in which humanity, nature, and the spiritual all interact in one balanced whole. In a word, the linchpin of this organism is "Japan."

In addition, the *kami* manifest themselves in particular places, creating sacred space. Virtually any place may become such a manifestation, as is evident by the number of shrines. Within homes, the *kami* are present on the *kami* shelf, sanctifying and purifying the home. They are present in the village, the region, and in national shrines. Therefore, in daily life, communal life, and national life, those who seek purification and live in harmony with the *kami* will live out their lives in sacred space.

At the same time, the Japanese have a remarkable ability to absorb the ways of others and incorporate them into their own culture. From the introduction of Confucianism and Buddhism centuries ago to the fascination with American popular culture today, the Shinto heritage supports openness to new ideas. Two Shinto principles reflect this attitude. One is *musubi* ("creativity and production"), which reflects a pragmatic attitude always ready to draw upon new ideas that have promise, whatever their source. The other is *chuto-hanpa* ("a little of this, a little of that"), which implies a willingness to combine ideas from different sources.

Sacred: The *Kami*

We have spoken frequently of the *kami,* for they are at the heart of Shinto, but the reader is probably still wondering just what the kami are. Interpreters of Shinto have long struggled with a simple way to describe the *kami.* As we have already indicated, the *kami* are not just deities, although some *kami* are gods. According to Shinto tradition, eight million (or eight hundred thousand) *kami* exist. This is a symbolic way of saying that the number of *kami* is infinite. *Kami* may be family ancestors, national or local heroes, persons with extraordinary spiritual powers, celestial bodies such as the sun or moon, topographical features such as mountains or rivers, natural forces like the wind and thunder, particularly inspiring natural objects such as rocks and trees, animals (foxes and horses are particularly honored), Buddhas and *bodhisattvas,* and, of course, the Manifest *Kami,* the Emperor. Natural features considered *kami* are often designated by being surrounded or connected with a straw rope.

In sum, anything or anyone is potentially a *kami. Kami* symbolize the sacred quality of human existence, nature, and the cosmos as a whole. All reality is infused with *kami,* but some *kami* are transcendent, making Shinto in its traditional form similar to the understanding of the spiritual in indigenous religions of other cultures.

RELIGION IN TWENTY-FIRST CENTURY JAPAN AND KOREA

Japan

The irony of religion in modern Japan is that while the vast majority of Japanese consider themselves nonreligious, religions (especially Shinto, Buddhism, Confucianism, and the "new religions" like Soka Gakkai to be discussed in Chapter Fourteen) have a continuing and significant impact on Japanese life. Many people still participate in Shinto and Buddhist rituals at least periodically, and although the number of home altars has declined, they are still present (if not regularly attended) in many homes. Confucian virtues still have a strong impact on the way Japanese view themselves and treat others. And millions of Japanese have been attracted to a host of new religious movements.

Has Japan become a strictly secular, materialistic society, with spiritual traditions preserved only in vestigial form? If so, the argument could be made that the effective religion for most Japanese (as is the case in other affluent societies today) is consumerism. The perceived ultimacy may be simply wealth and the comfortable lifestyle wealth brings, and the transformation the frantic commitment to the accumulation of material things so evident in Japan today.

At the same time, as in other societies that have gone through a period of rapid modernization, there are growing numbers of Japanese traditionalists calling for a recommitment to the heritage of Shinto, with its strong sense of nationalism. And the new religions, with their varied approaches to individual spirituality, have attracted growing numbers of persons for whom materialism has left a void in their lives, or who see one of the religions as a vehicle to improving their position in society.

Whatever happens, it will be interesting indeed to observe the future of religion in the "land of the *kami.*"

Korea

More than in other East Asian societies, Christianity has taken root and grown significantly in South Korea, to the extent that it is a significant force in modern Korea.

Like Japan, South Korea has become quite a secular society. Only 25 percent of the population acknowledge a religious affiliation; of this number, about 70 percent claim Buddhism, and 30 percent Christianity. However, this gives the Christian churches a much stronger voice than in other East Asian societies. Some Christians have been leaders in the efforts to bring greater respect for human rights and protection for the rights of Korean workers. As in Japan and China, Confucian virtues continue to have a very strong impact.

North Korea is still an officially Communist state, with few observable signs of the change in attitude being observed in China. A secular religion focusing on the communist leader Kim Il Sung still flourishes in North Korea (while "Maoism" has faded in China). It is known as *Juche* and focuses on the "Great Leader," who died in 1994 but is still considered the leader of the nation; it claims twenty-three million adherents. Thousands of mourners daily come to his memorial in Pyongyan to express their devotion. North Korean children are taught that the Great Leader is a father figure who protects them against the external evils that threaten them. His son Kim Jong Il ("Dear Leader") now shares in his father's deification. However, in North as in South Korea, Confucianism continues to be a dominating force in social relations.

CHAPTER SUMMARY

Shinto, the native religion of Japan, is rooted in a mythic account of the creation of Japan as the center of the cosmos and the land of the *kami*. *Kami* are gods, persons, places, or things that inspire reverence and awe. *Kami-no-michi*, the Japanese self-designation for Shinto, teaches a way of harmony. In this chapter we traced the development of Shinto: the emergence of the Shinto myth, the role of popular religion, the introduction of the name "Shinto," the period of amalgamation of Shinto with Buddhism, the Shinto revival, and the modern era in which an attempt was made to distinguish Shinto as a national ideology from "religious Shinto." We highlighted the role of State Shinto in Japan before and during World War II, and discussed the fate of Shinto after the war.

We then described the Shinto worldview. Like other East Asian religions Shinto seeks harmony. In the case of Shinto the harmony is with the *kami*. An elaborate system of shrines and rituals provides the means for the maintenance of harmony. The maintenance and restoration of purity also plays an important role in Shinto.

Finally, we reflected on the state of religion in twenty-first century Japan and Korea.

IMPORTANT TERMS AND PHRASES

Amaterasu, *bushido, haiden, hondon,* Izanagi, Izanami, Jimmu Tenno, Juche, *kami, kami-dana, kami-no-michi, kokutai-ni-hongi,* manifest *kami, miko, Ryobu,* samurai, Shinto Directive, Shinto Myth, State Shinto, *Tenri-kyo*

QUESTIONS FOR DISCUSSION AND REFLECTION

1. Do you think that Shinto will survive in the twenty-first century? Will it become simply a set of customs rather than a living religion, as some scholars predict?

2. Compare and contrast State Shinto with patriotic loyalty to the United States or another country.

3. Did the United States and its allies do the right thing in allowing the Japanese emperor to stay on his throne, but forcing him to renounce the teaching that he was a descendant of Amaterasu, the sun goddess?

4. Why do many people in Japan consider themselves participants in both Shinto and Buddhism? Do you understand and agree with the idea of identifying with more than one religion at the same time?

5. Is Shinto's ability to absorb features from other cultures and religions (e.g., Santa Claus and Christmas) a strength or a weakness?

SOURCES AND SUGGESTIONS FOR FURTHER STUDY

BREEN, JOHN AND MARK TEEUWEN, ED., 2000. *Shinto in History: Ways of the Kami.* Honolulu: University of Hawaii.

ELLWOOD, ROBERT S., JR. AND ROBERT PILGRIM, 1985. *Japanese Religion: A Cultural Perspective.* Englewood Cliffs, NJ: Prentice Hall.

GAUNTLETT, JOHN OWEN, TRANS. AND ROBERT KING HALL, ED., 1974. *Kokutai no Hongi: Cardinal Principles of the National Entity of Japan.* Newton, Massachusetts: Crofton.

LITTLETON, C. SCOTT, 2002. *Shinto: Origins, Rituals, Festivals, Spirits, Sacred Places.* New York: Oxford University.

PHILIPPI, DONALD L., TRANS., 1968. *Kojiki.* Tokyo: University of Tokyo.

PICKEN, STUART D. B., 1994. *Essentials of Shinto: An Analytical Guide to Principal Teachings.* Westport, CT: Greenwood.

WOODWARD, W., 1972. *The Allied Occupation of Japan and Japanese Religions.* Leiden, Netherlands: E. J. Brill.

YAMAMOTO, YUKITAKA, 1987. *Way of the Kami.* Stockton, CA: Tsubaki America.

Web Sites

www.csupomona.edu/~plin/ews430/shinto1.html
 (a site with links on Shinto beliefs, culture, and practices)

jinja.or.jp/english/
 (the site of the Shinto Online Network Association)

ecai.org/shinto/charter.html
 (site of the Center for Shinto Studies and Japanese Culture)

www.shinto.org/
 (site of the International Shinto Foundation)

 Prentice Hall's **Research Navigator** helps students in their further study of the world's religions. Visit *http://www.researchnavigator.com* for help on the research process and access to databases full of relevant material, including the New York *Times*.

CHAPTER

10

Judaism—The Way of Torah

INTRODUCTION

Three of the world's major religious traditions (Judaism, Christianity, and Islam) originated in the geographic area known as the Middle East—a region covering parts of northeastern Africa, southwestern Asia, and southeastern Europe. Another smaller religion, Zoroastrianism, which influenced the development of the other three, also began in the Middle East. These religions will be the subject of the next three chapters.

Because of the shared belief in a single all-powerful personal deity, these religions are known as the monotheistic religions. They also have in common a strong concern with distinguishing between good and evil and identifying the ways of living that are good or "right." Therefore, some interpreters group this family of religions under the heading "ethical monotheism."

Judaism, Christianity, and Islam are also grouped together as the Abrahamic religions, for in their sacred texts they each claim descent from a common ancestor, Abraham, who was called by God to renounce the worship of other gods and live by faith in the one true God (see Feiler 2002).

Because Judaism and Christianity spread beyond the Middle East and now dominate the Western world (Europe and the Americas), they are sometimes called "Western religions," to distinguish them from the Eastern religions that dominate in Asia. Judaism, Christianity, and Islam are today global religions in their scope and impact.

Dispersed from their homeland by persecution, Jews have established communities throughout the world. The creation of the modern state of Israel in 1948 has allowed many Jews to return to the land of their ancestors. Christian and Muslim missionaries carried their religions into all areas of the world. Christianity is presently the dominant religion in Europe, the Americas, Australia, the Philippines, and New Zealand. Outside Israel, Islam now is the major religion in the Middle East, with a majority as well in some areas beyond the Middle East—in Central Asia especially. In Africa, Islam and Christianity have both been introduced as missionary religions, with varying degrees of success in displacing indigenous religions. In most of the developing countries of Africa, Islam is the fasting growing religion.

Before we turn to the histories and distinctive teachings of these religions in the next several chapters, we will survey the geography, demography, and history of the region in which they originated. As we have done with the other families of religions, we will also provide an orientation to the traditional worldview that is an important part of the background necessary for understanding these religions. We will illustrate the worldview with examples from Zoroastrianism.

AN ORIENTATION TO THE MIDDLE EAST

Lands and Peoples

The present-day countries now included in the swath of land called the Middle East, which includes parts of three continents, are Egypt and Sudan in Africa; Saudi Arabia, the two Yemens (Aden to the north and Sana to the South), Oman, the United Arab Emirates, Qatar, Bahrain, and Kuwait in the Arabian peninsula; Iraq and Iran in southwest Asia; and Israel, Lebanon, Jordan, Syria, Cyprus, and Turkey in the eastern Mediterranean. There is considerable ethnic and cultural diversity in the region, the source of much conflict over the centuries. Most of the Middle East is desert, with people concentrating along the seacoasts and river valleys. The discovery and exploitation of huge deposits of oil in the region has brought much development in the last century, creating pockets of great wealth amidst widespread poverty.

A Brief History

About 4000 B.C.E. two of the world's earliest civilizations emerged in the Middle East—the Egyptian along the Nile River in northeastern Africa, and the Sumerian in the area known as Mesopotamia (the land between and along the Tigris and Euphrates rivers). Beginning in 800 B.C.E. the great civilizations (and other societies in the region) were occupied and destroyed by invaders. Alexander the Great conquered most of the Middle East by 331 B.C.E., bringing Hellenistic (Greek) culture, which spread throughout most of the region. The Romans took control of most of the Middle East three hundred years later; it was during Roman rule that Christianity emerged.

In the seventh century C.E. followers of the Prophet Muhammad—according to Islam, the final prophet of God—swept out of the Arabian peninsula and conquered much of the region. As a result, Muslim culture and the Arab language, which still dominate the area, were introduced. In the eleventh century the Seljuk Turks came from Turkestan in Central Asia and seized control of Asia Minor (modern Turkey) and Arab Syria, including (in 1071) Jerusalem and the rest of the Holy Land.

In the twelfth and thirteenth centuries, successive Christian armies from Western Europe mounted invasions that succeeded in temporarily recapturing Jerusalem and other portions of the Holy Land. But eventually the Europeans were driven from the area by Muslim armies.

The Ottoman Empire began about 1300, and took control of much of the Middle East as a portion of its vast holdings. The Ottoman Empire was at its pinnacle during the sixteenth and seventeenth centuries. When it faded in the nineteenth century, European powers began to exert increasing influence on the region. After World War I much of the area was placed under British or French control. By the end of World War II most countries had attained independence.

Growing immigration by Jews seeking to return to their ancestral homeland created tension with the Arabs occupying the land, which the Jews called Israel, but the Arabs knew as Palestine. In 1947 an attempt sponsored by the United Nations to divide Palestine into a Jewish state (Israel) and an Arab state (Palestine) was rejected by the Arabs. The Palestinians were supported by other Arab states in the region, while the Israelis received the backing of European nations and the United States. A series of wars (in 1948, 1967, 1973), two Palestinian *intifadas* (uprisings) beginning in 1988 and 2000, and a series of diplomatic efforts have thus far failed to resolve the dispute.

An Islamic revolution in Iran in 1979 was an indication of a growing movement to purge Muslim nations of Western influences. A war between Iraq and Iran began in 1980 and continued throughout most of the decade. In 1990 Iraq invaded Kuwait, as a result of a disagreement over oil rights and other issues. Because of the threat posed to the large oil reserves in the area, a coalition of nations led by the United States drove the Iraqis from Kuwait in 1991. After the terrorist attacks of September 11, 2001, conducted by the *al-Qaeda* network led by a Saudi, Osama bin Laden, the United States and other nations mounted a sustained campaign to destroy terrorist organizations and confront governments in the region believed to support them. In 2003 a coalition led by the United States invaded Iraq and deposed Saddam Hussein, ending his autocratic regime. However, terrorist attacks continued.

The Middle East continues to be one of the world's hottest trouble spots as the twenty-first century begins. Religion has unfortunately played an inflammatory role in the hostilities that have spawned so much violence, but it also has the potential to play a crucial peacemaking role in resolving the tensions underlying them.

The Traditional Worldview

The religions that originated in the Middle East share a worldview that distinguishes them as a group from the religions of Asia and indigenous religions. In describing this traditional perspective we will draw examples from Zoroastrianism, the monotheistic religion founded in ancient Persia (modern Iran) after the one God (known as *Ahura Mazda*) spoke to the prophet Zarathustra (known in the West as Zoroaster) in a vision and commissioned Zoroaster as his messenger. The center of Zoroastrianism today is the *Parsi* ("Persian") community in Mumbai (Bombay), India, descended from Persians who migrated to India over a thousand years ago. It is estimated that there are about a quarter of a million Zoroastrians today, including many in immigrant communities in Great Britain, Canada, and the United States. Many scholars believe that the worldview of Zoroastrians had a significant influence on the development of the teachings of the other religions in this family.

We should note that what follows represents the *traditional* worldview of these religions. Especially in Judaism and Christianity we find movements that have adapted some elements of the traditional perspective in response to the development of the modern, scientific outlook.

Humanity: At the Center of Creation   These religions emphasize the special place of humans as spiritual beings in the created order: humans are superior to other living beings, existing in a special relationship with God not shared by other creatures. Thus, these religions are sometimes called *anthropocentric* in their understanding of the relationship between humanity and the rest of creation. However, because of their special spiritual status, humans also have a special responsibility in caring for God's creation.

Part of the special human status is the ability to reason, and with it the freedom to choose how to lead one's life. Enlivened by God, humans have tremendous capacity for goodness, but this freedom also gives them the ability to cause great evil.

Problem: Tension with the Creator　For the religions that originated in the Middle East, the critical human dilemma is relational. The problem is the breaking of the relationship between humans and their divine creator. This is perhaps best expressed as tension with the Creator. These religions share a belief in a single, all-powerful, personal deity who has revealed a path for humans to follow in life. When humans fail to follow that path, they alienate themselves from their Creator. Within these religions the traditional emphasis is on the ultimate fate of those who turn from God. Those who do not experience transformation will continue to be alienated from God after death, in a state of eternal separation.

Zoroastrianism teaches that humans are free to choose between the competing forces of good and evil in the world. These forces are personified as two eternal spirits: a good spirit (*Spenta Mainyu*) and an evil spirit (*Angra Mainyu*). Both emanate from the one God, Ahura Mazda, and exist in a balance, with both being necessary for life. According to Zoroastrianism, the principal problem that humans face is to avoid the lure of the forces of evil, which seek to thwart the following of the path of goodness established by Ahura Mazda.

Cause: Turning the Wrong Way　What causes humans to be alienated from the Creator? The human problem, according to these religions, is brought on by turning the wrong way. An important aspect of the special relationship that humans have with God is the availability of knowledge concerning the way God desires humans to live. In their desire for independence and power, humans often (or always) choose a path in conflict with the divine will.

Why are humans disobedient? The emphasis on human freedom to choose is in tension with the common belief in these religions that a force of evil in the cosmos seeks to draw humans away from the path established by God. This personified force is not equal in power to God, but can tempt people to disobey God. In Zoroastrian teaching, Angra Mainyu is known as *Satan* ("accuser"). He has an entourage of demons who tempt human beings, under his direction.

In these religions humans have only one life in which to choose the path of righteousness. Zoroastrianism emphasizes human accountability. Humans will suffer or enjoy the consequences of their decision to follow the good or evil force. In the ethical dualism of life, truth (*asha*) stands against falsehood (*druj*). It is up to the individual to recognize the distinction, and to choose and honor the truth.

End: Restoration and Life after Death　The goal in these religions is the restoration of the relationship with God broken by humans turning the wrong way. Restoration relates both to individuals and to society. Within these religions, some emphasize the restoration of individuals while others stress the healing of societies. For individuals the experience of restoration may occur before death, but it is the state of existence after death that attracts the most attention. Typically, these religions include the idea that those who experience salvation will enter into a state of eternal well-being after death, whereas those who do not will remain alienated from God beyond this life (whether eternally so or not is a matter of dispute).

A formulation of the idea of life after death found in these religions is the image of a time of judgment by God at the end of history. At this endpoint, those who have been reconciled with God enter into their final reward and those who have not been saved are condemned. Accompanying this concept is the belief that the dead will be raised from their graves at this end time, and participate with those still living in the final judgment.

The state of wholeness and well-being at the end of time is a restoration of the harmony with God that existed at the beginning. At the beginning there was a paradise in which humanity, God, and nature were in an ideal relationship. The imagery of the original paradise is used to picture the state of existence that is the destination for those who respond to the will of God.

Restoration occurs not just for individuals, but for communities and the entire cosmos. The idea that God acts within history to restore groups of people is common. One way to look at the coming "end" is to stress a state of restoration for people together. Sometimes this restoration of society, in which everyone together is living in obedience to God, is pictured within history. You can also find imagery within these religions that paints a picture of a restoration of the entire cosmos to a state of well-being.

The goal for Zoroastrians is a life after death in paradise, a place of beauty where all who have followed the path of righteousness will spend eternity. According to the teaching concerning the destiny of individuals, after death the individual soul remains with its body for three days. On the fourth day the soul goes to the place of judgment. The image of a scale is used. If deeds of evil outweigh good deeds, then the person is sentenced to punishment. If good deeds predominate, even slightly, then the person's soul is destined for paradise.

According to Zoroastrianism, the souls continue their existence in paradise or hell until the end of time. When the world comes to an end, Ahura Mazda wipes away all evil. All souls are raised for a final judgment. Both the good and evil are subjected to an ordeal of fire and molten metal. The souls of the righteous are not burned by the fire. The souls in hell are purified in the terrible ordeal, and those that survive this process will join with the souls of the righteous, and a new age—in which there is no evil, death, or disease—will begin. Angra Mainyu and his minions will be destroyed. Thus, the ultimate outcome seems to be a qualified universal salvation, although those who choose evil will pay a terrible price before they are healed from their wickedness. Some, it seems, are so wicked that there is no goodness in them to be purified.

Means: The Way   What brings about the restoration of individuals and communities? Each religion, of course, has its own distinct prescription. What they share is the image of a "way" revealed by God. The "way" is revealed through a person, and includes the concept of living in obedience to God. Typically, the way of obedience is contrasted with a way of disobedience. The image of a need to "turn away" from the path of disobedience and embrace the path of obedience is common. The way includes guidelines for individual and social morality. In each of these religions, sacred writings play a central role in making known God's way to salvation.

In Zoroastrian teaching, the general ethical principles Ahura Mazda has revealed for humans to follow are good thought, good word, and good deed. Zoroastrians are to practice the virtues that follow from these principles: truthfulness, charity, justice, and compassion.

In keeping with the sacredness of the elements of nature, Zoroastrians are to avoid their pollution. Traditionally, Zoroastrians were expected to practice what today might be called an ecological approach—to farm wisely without unnecessary damage to the earth, and to care for animals (especially the cow).

The rituals in Zoroastrianism reflect these basic principles. At the center of worship is the offering of prayers to Ahura Mazda for help in leading a life of goodness, free from impurities and pollution. Instead of offering sacrifices of animals or even vegetables, Zoroastrian priests (dressed in white to symbolize purity) preside over the offering of sandalwood to the sacred flames that burn unceasingly in the Fire Temples, the Zoroastrian houses of worship. The fire symbolizes the divine presence, power, and purity. The priests wear masks to avoid polluting the sacred fire. Many Zoroastrians maintain a sacred flame in their homes.

The most famous Zoroastrian rite of passage is at death. To avoid the contamination of the elements, the corpse of a deceased person is neither buried nor burned. Instead, it was traditionally exposed in a special enclosure called a *dakhma* ("tower of silence"), a round structure open to the sky. Vultures that stayed near the tower quickly stripped the body. Since this practice is increasingly frowned upon, especially in urban areas, alternatives have developed, such as placing the body in a special sealed casket so that it will not contaminate the elements, or cremating it with an electrical heat that does not involve a flame.

Reality: A Beginning and an End   These religions understand time from a perspective that seems to be diametrically opposed to the cylical view of time in indigenous religions and the religions of South and Southeast Asia. In the worldview of the religions that originated in the Middle East, time *does* have a beginning and an end. The cosmos began at a specific moment and it will end with the creation of a final, timeless state of being. This "linear" conception of time has a number of implications that affect these religions and the cultures for which they provide the myths. For example, this conception places a great deal of importance on both the beginning and the end of time. There is a strong sense of destiny, of things being oriented toward a final culmination. Reflection on the "end time" is known as *eschatology*. These religions share an eschatological orientation. There is also a great deal of interest in what happened at the beginning of time, and how what happened at the beginning affected what followed.

A linear view of time, combined with an emphasis on the special place of humans in creation, results in more concern with human history than we find in other religions. In Judaism and Christianity, and Islam especially, historical events take on an importance equal to the events of the mythic period at the beginning or end of time. In fact, in these religions historical occurrences take on a mythic meaning. For example, each religion has a calendar determined by a particular event of foundational significance, such as the birth of Jesus or the migration of the prophet Muhammad from Mecca to Medina.

This linear trajectory also applies to individuals. According to these religions, you "only go around once." You are born, you live, and you die. This increases the urgency to participate in ultimate transformation in this life, and may help explain why at least two of these religions (Christianity and Islam) are so intent on spreading their messages and converting others to their religion. These religions share a special concern with what happens to humans after they finish their linear journeys. Life after death is an important concern, especially in Christianity and Islam.

How did reality come into existence? All these religions consider the ultimate source to be the God who is the only reality beyond time and space. At a specific moment God created the cosmos; God will also bring the cosmos to an end. What will happen at the *eschaton* (the end time) has been or will be determined by God.

Zoroastrianism was the first religion to introduce the linear understanding of time, with existence moving from its creation by Ahura Mazda to a final culmination. The world is real; it is not an illusion. It is the proving ground for humans. Their response to that which happens within time will determine their destiny when the time of fulfillment comes.

Zoroastrianism considers the basic elements of earth, fire, water and air to be sacred. To pollute them is a wicked act for which perpetrators will be held accountable.

Sacred: Monotheism   Among these religions there is consensus that the ultimate is a personal God, who is the sole source of all life and who has no equals. In the traditional teachings, God is all-powerful and all-knowing. Nothing can occur unless it is caused or allowed to happen by God. Emphasis is placed on the "will of God" being absolute. From this perspective, God is separate from the creation—that is, transcendent. God cannot be portrayed in a picture or a statue, because God is beyond all forms. God is personal in the sense that God relates to the creation and to humans, with characteristics such as love and anger. These religions share the view that God loves the world and the creatures of the world.

God is beyond gender, but it is most common to encounter male metaphors for God in the sacred writings of these religions. God is pictured as a heavenly father, a divine king, or a warrior. The traditional model for God's relationship to creation is hierarchical. God stands above creation and gives orders that are carried out. These religions typically envision spiritual intermediaries (e.g., angels) between the one God and creation.

Given the strict monotheism in these religions, two issues require special attention. If God is fundamentally separate from the creation, how can God be experienced, and how is God known? In general, these religions all place importance on God's revelation to humans. God chooses to make known to humans the divine existence and the way humans may enter into a relationship with God.

Another issue these religions must confront is sometimes called the "problem of evil." If God is all-powerful and loves the creation, why does God allow evil to occur? Two answers to this question are common. One is that there are divine forces that cause evil. The myth of a spirit who rebelled against God and who is the direct force behind much evil in the world is found in these religions. In addition, humans are seen as having freedom to decide between good and evil, with much of the evil in the world caused by human decision. However, these religions share the view that while evil is present in the creation, God will ultimately triumph over it.

At the time of Zoroaster, Iranian religion was apparently polytheistic. His contention that Ahura Mazda ("Wise LORD") was the *only* God worthy of praise, the creator and judge of all, was revolutionary. Ahura Mazda is the invisible, eternal ruler of the universe.

Zoroaster also taught that Ahura Mazda manifests his will through Spenta Mainyu ("Good Spirit") and six "Immortal Holy Ones": Good Thought or Mind, Best Order or Right, Absolute Power, High Devotion or Piety, Perfection, and Immutability. These six are sometimes called angels, sometimes modes of divine or ethical action. They are attributes by which the invisible, unapproachable LORD is known.

JUDAISM: THE WAY OF TORAH

What Is Judaism?

Judaism, of course, is the name of a religion, and our focus in this chapter will be on Judaism as a religion. However, Judaism also designates the culture, civilization, way of life, and shared story of the Jewish people. Within Judaism, in this more expansive sense, are found not only people who affirm the spiritual teachings of the religion of Judaism, but also others who are steadfastly secular in their orientation yet still associate themselves with Jewish culture.

It is critical to make clear that although it is appropriate to speak of the "Jewish people" as those who identify with the religion, culture, or story of Judaism, "Jew" is *not* a racial designation. There is no factual basis for the pseudoscientific theory of a "Jewish race," which was developed in the nineteenth century, exploited by the Nazi Party of Germany in its program of extermination of the Jewish people of Europe during World War II, and resurrected by various neo-Nazi groups and others today.

Jews are those who by birth or by conscious decision and action identify themselves with the heritage and continuing experience of the Jewish people. And Judaism is the shared story of the Jewish people. Therefore, to understand Judaism both in its narrower sense as a religion and in its broader sense, we must begin with the story of the Jewish people.

Stages of Development and Sacred Texts

Tour *The Sacred World* CD!

The story of Judaism begins with a people remembering their past. These memories are recorded in an anthology of sacred writings that became known as the *Tanak* (an acronym formed from the first letters of the three sections of the text in Hebrew— *torah* ["Law, instruction"], *nevi'im* ["Prophets"], *kethuvi'im* ["Writings"]). The collection is also known as the Hebrew Bible.

Origins and Ancestors   The Tanak begins by recounting the creation of the universe by the one God (Genesis 1–2). The emphasis is on God as the sole creator, the goodness and order of creation, and the special place of humanity (created in the "image of God"). Next comes the primal history of mankind: the first man (Adam) and woman (Eve) in the Garden of Eden, their expulsion from paradise because of their disobedience, the great flood that destroyed the earth because of the wickedness of humanity, the ark in which Noah and his family and pairs of all the animals were saved, the covenant God made with Noah and all flesh in which God promised not to destroy the world again with a flood, and (after further disobedience) the scattering of the nations throughout the earth with different languages (Genesis 3–11).

Then the story focuses on the relationship between God and the one nation God chose to play a special role in history. First, the story of the ancestors of Israel, and the special covenant God entered into with Abraham and his descendants, is recounted (Genesis 12–50). The term "covenant" is often used in the Tanak to refer to various pacts initiated by God and entered into with Israel. Sometimes the covenant is a promise made by God; on other occasions the covenant includes specific stipulations for the people of Israel to follow.

After an encounter with God, in which he is told that his descendants will become a great nation in a land of their own as well as a source of blessing to other nations, Abraham and his wife Sarah journey from Mesopotamia to the land that was to become Israel. The promissory covenant to Abraham and Sarah is renewed with the son of Abraham, Isaac, and his wife Rebecca, and Isaac's son, Jacob, and his wives Rachel and Leah. Jacob is also called Israel ("he who wrestles with God"; see Genesis 32:28). The twelve sons of Jacob/Israel are remembered as the ancestors of the twelve tribes that would make up the nation of Israel. In the name of the nation is the notion of a people who wrestle with God, an apt description for the relationship described in the Tanak. The Book of Genesis ends with the sons of Jacob having gone into Egypt where one of them, Joseph, who had been sold into slavery by his brothers, has become a chief officer of the Pharaoh.

Moses and the *Torah*   In the Book of Exodus, the Tanak's narrative next focuses on a man named Moses who led the descendants of Abraham out of bondage in Egypt. The descendants of Abraham have become slaves, and they cry out to God to deliver them. To Moses God reveals a special name (written in most English translations of the Hebrew Bible as "LORD"). The LORD instructs Moses to confront the Egyptian Pharaoh and demand that he set the people (called at this point the Hebrews) free. The people miraculously escape from Egypt (in a series of events that are commemorated in the festival of Passover) and begin a journey toward the land that the LORD had promised to give to the descendants of Abraham. At the mountain called Sinai, where the LORD had first appeared to Moses in a burning bush, the LORD gives to Moses the Ten Commandments and other laws, as the basis of a new covenant relationship with the people of Israel. The LORD promises to be the God of this nation and protect them, if the people will agree to follow the laws he has revealed through Moses.

The revelation of the LORD to Moses on Mount Sinai is the root of the concept of *Torah,* the instruction given by God on how the people of Israel are to keep their part of the covenant agreement. Torah is also the name given to the first five books of the Tanak (Genesis, Exodus, Leviticus, Numbers, Deuteronomy), because these books recount the giving of the Torah. This section of the Tanak is also called the Books of Moses (because of the traditional belief that Moses is their author) and the Pentateuch ("five books," after the Greek translation). However, the term Torah may also be used when speaking of the Tanak as a whole. More broadly, Torah refers to the total revelation from God as understood by classical Judaism: the Tanak (the written Torah) and the related authoritative commentary (called the oral Torah). We will discuss the oral Torah more fully later in this chapter.

After the encounter with the LORD at Mount Sinai as recounted in the Book of Exodus, the rest of the Pentateuch tells the story of the people's wandering in the wilderness and the instructions that the LORD wanted them to follow. The guidelines cover both their relations with one another and their relationship with God. The people were to carry with them the Ark of the Covenant, in which the tablets of the Ten Commandments were kept. The Ark was the symbolic throne of the LORD; it was to be kept in a tent that is meticulously described in the Torah. Despite the grumbling and lack of trust of the people, the LORD continues to provide for the people's needs. The tribes they encounter are defeated with the help of the LORD. The people are told that if they follow the covenant they have made with the LORD, then they will have a good life in the land the LORD is going to give them, a "land flowing with milk and honey." However, if they fail to obey the laws, they will die.

The Rise and Fall of Ancient Israel: The Roles of Kings and Prophets   In the next section of the Tanak, the prophetic books, the story of the history of the people of Israel continues. The "Former Prophets" (Joshua, Judges, First and Second Samuel, First and Second Kings) narrate the story of the people of Israel from their occupation of the land of Canaan through the creation of a united nation of Israel by the tenth century B.C.E., ruled first by the charismatic King David and then by his son, Solomon, who builds the first Temple in Jerusalem and creates a mini-empire. The successors of Solomon are unable to maintain the unity of Israel, and the nation splits into a northern kingdom (Israel) and a southern kingdom (Judah). Israel falls to the Assyrians in the eighth century B.C.E. and Judah is overrun by the Babylonians in the sixth century. The Babylonian conquest of Jerusalem and destruction of the Temple (597–587 B.C.E.) is a watershed event in the history of ancient Israel. It marks the beginning of the Babylonian exile (which lasted until 538 B.C.E.).

The narrative in the Former Prophets is not a mere recounting of events, but a theological history told from the perspective that when people were obedient to the LORD the nation flourished, but when they were not loyal, catastrophe struck.

Interspersed with the story of political leaders in the historical narrative are accounts of prophets, men and women who confront the people and their leaders with God's warnings about violations of the covenant, including the worship of other deities. The prophets are not so much predicters of the future (as the term in modern usage implies), but emissaries commissioned by the LORD to challenge the people to obey the covenant, and to warn them of the dire consequences if they do not.

The other section of the prophetic books is called the "Latter Prophets." These books are largely the collected utterances and writings of the prophets of ancient Israel. They are not arranged in chronological order, but rather in terms of length. There are three "major prophets" (Isaiah, Jeremiah, Ezekiel) and twelve "minor prophets" (combined in the Tanak as the Book of the Twelve).

Although each prophetic book has its own unique themes, in general all the works stress the covenant between the LORD and Israel and interpret the various calamities in the life of the nation as a result of covenant disobedience. But they also stress that the LORD, the creator of the ends of the earth, chose the nation Israel and will not give up easily on the people. Some of the prophets look ahead to a new, eschatological age, after judgment, when the fortunes of the nation (or a remnant of the people) will be restored and all nations will live together in peace. In some cases, this time of renewal is associated with the hope of the restoration of the Davidic kingship.

Return from Exile and the Birth of Judaism   Before we turn to the third section of the Tanak, the *kethuvi'im* ("Writings"), we will briefly recount what is known of the remainder of the biblical period in the history of Judaism. The Babylonian exile ended when the Persians defeated the Babylonians beginning about 538 B.C.E. Many Jews remained in Babylon (located in the present-day Iraq), which became an important center of Jewish life and scholarship for the next thousand years. Those leaders who returned to Israel rebuilt the Temple and the walls of Jerusalem. This new Temple, constructed on the site of the original Temple built by Solomon, is known as the Second Temple.

During the Second Temple period, the Torah (or some portion thereof) was embraced as the national constitution of the Jewish people. It is likely that during the Babylonian exile, when there was no access to the Temple, places of gathering (*synagogues*) had already emerged for the hearing and study of the teaching (Torah) believed to be revealed by God to Moses on Mount Sinai. Scribes and Torah teachers, who copied and interpreted the Torah, were important religious leaders. With the restoration of the Temple, priests also played an important role in Jewish life once again.

The period of Persian control of Israel continued until Alexander the Great conquered the region in 333 B.C.E., beginning the Hellenistic period. Hellenistic (Greek) culture was to exert significant influence on the Jewish community, both in the homeland and throughout the *Diaspora*, referring to the dispersion of the Jewish people from their homeland in Israel throughout the world.

By the second century B.C.E. a Seleucid dynasty based in Syria controlled the Jewish homeland. The emperor Antiochus Epiphanes enacted a particularly ruthless policy of Hellenization. In reaction, some Jews mounted a revolt, led by the Hasmonean family. It became known as the Maccabean revolt (from the epithet

Maccabeus, meaning "hammerer," assigned to the first of the Hasmonean military rulers, Judas). In 164 B.C.E., in December, Judas's forces liberated the Temple. After their victory over the Seleucids, the Hasmoneans created a dynasty that gave Israel a century of political and religious independence, until the entry of the Roman general Pompey into Jerusalem in 63 B.C.E. For the rest of the biblical period Israel was under Roman control. A watershed event was the destruction of the Second Temple by the Romans after a Jewish revolt in 70 C.E.

We return now to our overview of the final section of the Tanak, the Writings. The Writings contain a variety of types of literature. Included are narrative books that parallel and extend the story told in the Former Prophets (First and Second Chronicles, Ezra, Nehemiah). Also found in the Writings are two short stories that focus on two heroic women (Ruth, Esther). A unique work is the Book of Daniel. It is an apocalyptic writing, meaning that it purports to reveal the mysteries of the end of history and the beginning of a new age. The other books of the Writings are largely poetic. They include a collection of hymns associated with worship in the Jerusalem temple and other poems (Psalms), wisdom books that are of both a practical and speculative nature (Proverbs, Job, Ecclesiastes), an anthology of love poetry (Song of Songs), and a collection of poems of sorrow occasioned by the destruction of Jerusalem by the Babylonians (Lamentations). Within the Writings are some of the most profound and artful literary works in the Tanak.

The background of the religion of Judaism is found in the Tanak's story of the ancient nation of Israel, the people who "wrestled with God." The Tanak, however, is only the beginning of the Jewish story. Even as the writings comprised by the Tanak were being collected as a canon of sacred writings, new developments were underway that helped to shape the religion of Judaism.

The name "Judaism" actually came into existence after the nation Israel was conquered and the people had lost their national identity as "Israel." Judaism referred originally to the religion of the people of the Persian province of Judea. The term Jew also was first used after the Babylonian Exile to refer to the people of Judea and other descendants of the people of Israel who lived in communities dispersed around the Mediterranean world.

Classical Judaism and the Oral Torah   Even before the end of the Biblical period, institutions that were to become especially important in the next phase of Jewish history were emerging.

SYNAGOGUE   The Jews of the Diaspora were cut off from the Temple, the center of worship in biblical Judaism. To fill the void, the synagogue (from the Greek word for "assembly") developed. Synagogues were local centers of study and prayer. Since Jews in the Diaspora could not perform the sacrificial ritual prescribed in the Torah, they instead focused on services of prayer and intense study of the written Torah. When the Second Temple was destroyed by the Romans in 70 C.E., the synagogue became even more important. It continues today for many Jews as the central religious institution beyond the family.

In the post-Biblical period, rabbis replaced priests as the central office in the practice of Judaism. The term *rabbi* ("my master") probably emerged in the first century C.E. as a title for a person of learning who could interpret Jewish teaching to others. Rabbis were also instrumental in the development of the body of tradition known as the oral Torah. Their precursors were the scribes or Torah teachers of the early Second Temple period.

MISHNAH AND *MIDRASH*   The origins of what is known as the *oral Torah* are found in the Jewish communities' need to apply the commandments of the written Torah to changing times. For example, the written Torah stipulates that to obey the covenant with the LORD people must keep the Sabbath holy (Exodus 20: 8–11). However, what specifically does that mean? A series of guidelines, which emerged out of deliberations among Jewish teachers of the Torah, developed over time to make clear what Jews could and could not do on the Sabbath in order to keep the basic commandment. By the second century C.E. a large body of these legal guidelines had come into existence in oral form. About this time one collection was written down by Rabbi Judah, a teacher who lived in a Jewish academy near the Sea of Galilee in Palestine (the Romans had given this name to the land of Israel). Rabbi Judah's collection of about four thousand legal instructions was called the *Mishnah* ("repetition"). It was one of several *mishnahs,* but became the one deemed authoritative.

The Mishnah gave not only the legal decision that resulted from the deliberations, but the conflicting opinions as well. Some of the legal scholars involved in the exchanges recorded in the Mishnah were quite conservative in their interpretations, others more liberal in adapting the legal principles of the Tanak to changing times. The tradition was accepted that the laws of the Mishnah carried the same authority as the Tanak. It was therefore the first stage in the development of what became known as the oral Torah (in contrast to the written Torah).

The *Midrash* ("search, interpret") consists of interpretation of the Tanak by rabbis during the first five centuries C.E. Some of the commentary was legal in nature; some was not. The legal interpretation was called *halakah* ("path"), a term to which we will return; the rest was nonlegal commentary or *haggadah* ("telling"), which was intended to inspire readers with stories and sayings.

TALMUD   These writings did not end the process of reflection and deliberation over the meaning of God's instruction and the development of the oral Torah. The continued discussions among leading rabbis were compiled by the fifth century in two written versions, one in Palestine and the other in Babylon. These extensive collections of both *halakah* and *haggadah* were called *Gemara* ("tradition, completion"). The Palestinian Gemara was combined with Rabbi Judah's Mishnah to create the Palestinian *Talmud* ("learning, teaching") by about 425–450 C.E. The Babylonian Gemara added to the Mishnah formed the Babylonian Talmud by 500–525 C.E. Both Talmuds are indeed libraries of volumes so immense that the phrase "sea of Talmud" was coined to describe their extent and depth.

The Babylonian Talmud attained acceptance by the Jewish community. Therefore, the Jewish sacred texts include not only the Tanak (the written Torah) but also the Talmud. In a sense, with ongoing interpretation of the application of the tradition to new circumstances by contemporary rabbis, oral Torah continues to be created.

Sadducees, Pharisees, and Other Movements   If we could enter a time capsule and visit the Jewish world at the beginning of the Common Era we would encounter a number of different "schools." To understand the development of Judaism we need to consider these groups.

During the period of the Second Temple, the High Priest of the Jerusalem Temple became the civil as well as religious head of the Jewish community. The High Priest and priestly families allied with him formed a party known as the *Sadducees* (from the name for the leading family of priests, *Zadokites*). This wealthy, aristocratic movement distanced itself from some of the popular religious ideas of the time (such as the apocalyptic expectation of a new age in which the dead would be raised from their graves). They rejected the emerging oral Torah and maintained that only the five books of Moses (the Pentateuch) had authority over the life of the community. The Sadducees tended to favor cooperation with the Roman authorities, who by this time had taken control of Palestine, as the best way to maintain stability. They were also more willing to adopt the Hellenistic cultural values the Romans embraced. After the destruction of the Temple in 70 C.E., their influence faded.

Another party, opposed to the Sadducees, took the name *Pharisees* (possibly "separatists"). The Pharisees emphasized living in joyful obedience to the gift of the Torah. They also stressed the need to adapt the guidelines of the written Torah to changing circumstances in order maintain righteousness. This placed them in opposition to the Sadducees. They also were more open to new teachings, such as the resurrection from the dead, and the hope of the coming of a messiah to restore the nation of Israel. After the destruction of the Temple they became virtually the ruling party within the Jewish community, replacing the sacrifice at the Temple with a worship of "the lips and the heart." The Talmud is a product of the Pharisaic movement.

The Sadducees and Pharisees were not the only parties in Judaism at this turbulent time. Another was the *Zealot* party, which favored a violent revolution to overthrow the Romans. The Zealots believed that by taking up arms they could hasten the coming of the messiah. It was a Zealot revolt, which broke out in 66 C.E., that led to the Roman destruction of the Temple in 70.

The Jewish historian Josephus and other authorities also identify a party known as the *Essenes.* They lived in monastic communities preparing for the coming of the new age. The Essenes considered the other schools of Judaism corrupt.

It has been widely assumed that it was an Essene community along the shores of the Dead Sea that produced the Dead Sea Scrolls. The Dead Sea Scrolls, which began to be discovered in 1947, included both Biblical texts in Hebrew (one thousand years older than the next oldest Hebrew manuscript) and sectarian documents that described the lifestyle and beliefs of the community that produced them. The latter writings portray a community that considered itself the elect of God, who would emerge triumphant in a final battle between the Children of Light and the Children of Darkness.

We should also mention, at least in passing, Jewish communities that were heavily influenced by Hellenistic (Greek) culture, in which Greek philosophy was used to interpret Jewish teachings.

Out of this crucible two Jewish movements ultimately survived. One was the Pharisaic, which defined the form of Judaism that forms the basis of Judaism as it was passed through the centuries. The other was called by contemporary Jewish interpreters the *Nazarean,* for it was composed of the followers of a rabbi from Galilee named *Yeshua* (Joshua, in Hebrew; or, in Greek, Jesus) of Nazareth. To this latter group we shall return later in the next chapter. Now we will pursue the development of classical or Pharisaic Judaism.

Judaism during the Middle Ages and Enlightenment   During the Middle Ages the Jews of the Diaspora were largely at the mercy of the two religions that had come to dominance in the Middle East and Europe, Christianity and Islam.

When Christianity became the official religion of the Roman Empire in the fourth century C.E., the antagonism that had characterized the attitude of most Christian leaders toward Jews rigidified (because of Jews' unwillingness to recognize Jesus as the messiah sent by God to restore Israel).

In the tenth and eleventh centuries many Jews fled from the Middle East to Spain, where there was a thriving Jewish community. Thus began an era of great achievement in all areas of Jewish life. For example, the twelfth-century physician and scholar Moses Maimonides wrote works that reconciled the best in contemporary science and philosophy with Jewish themes.

One of the most fascinating medieval developments in Judaism was a mystical movement that goes under the name *Kabbala* ("tradition"). Exponents of Kabbala drew on numerology to probe the hidden meanings of the text of the Hebrew Bible. A mystical work written in the late thirteenth century, called the *Zohar* ("Splendor"), became as popular and influential as the Tanak and Talmud among many Jews. The Zohar portrays God as a boundless energy (*ein sof*) from which emanates ten spheres, such as wisdom, beauty, and strength. These forces are variously male and female, in interaction with one another. One aspect of the Kabbalistic enthusiasm was a heightened messianic expectation.

When the Christian Crusades began, one consequence was wholesale Christian attacks on Jews throughout Europe. Jews who refused to convert to Christianity were expelled from England in 1290, from France in 1394, and from Spain in the year that Columbus left for his voyage of discovery, 1492. The Jews who remained in Italy, Germany, and Austria were forced to live in segregated areas called ghettos. The term "ghetto" is of Italian origin, arising from the practice decreed by Pope Paul IV in 1555 that Jews living in the papally controlled areas of Rome had to live in separate quarters. Catholic authorities forced Jews to wear "Star of David" badges, a precursor to the practice adopted by the Nazis during World War II.

The Jews who fled Spain into the Middle East have become known as the *Sephardim* ("Spanish"), while those who fled to Poland and surrounding areas became the *Ashkenazim* ("Germans"). The Ashkenazim developed a dialect combining German and Hebrew, which is called *Yiddish*. They were able to flourish by becoming successful in trade and moneylending.

In addition to these developments in the history of Judaism in Europe, throughout these centuries Jewish communities continued to exist and often flourish in the Muslim world (in North Africa and the Middle East) and in areas as far away as Asia.

When the Protestant Reformation swept across Europe, it appeared that Christian intolerance toward Jews might change. Martin Luther spoke warmly of the Jews in his early writings, defending them against the popular "blood libel" charge that Jews murdered Christian children and used their blood in the Passover ritual. However, when Jews refused to convert to a reformed Christianity, as they had also declined to convert to the Catholic Church, Luther in one of his later writings (*Concerning the Jews and Their Lies,* 1543) called the Jews "poisonous bitter worms" and suggested that the German princes of the day rid the land "of this insufferable devilish burden—the Jews."

In Eastern Europe a series of *pogroms* (spontaneous attacks) in the seventeenth century resulted in the death of half a million Jews. The blood libel accusation was widely accepted in both the Christian and Muslim worlds. The persecution inspired a new round of messianic excitement. One messianic claimant, Sabbatai Zevi, was widely acclaimed, but enthusiasm was crushed when he was arrested in Turkey while on his way to Jerusalem in 1665. He converted to Islam when faced with a choice of conversion or death.

An eighteenth century movement called *Hasidism* has had a lasting impact on Judaism. Hasidic communities can still be found throughout the Jewish world. The founder of Hasidism was a delightful storytelling faith healer who became known as the *Baal Shem Tov* ("Master of the Good Name"). He became convinced that God should be enjoyed as well as studied. He rejected overemphasis on study of the Talmud and taught people to dance in joy in addition to their study. He said God is everywhere present. Hasidic communities formed around charismatic leaders called *tzadikim* ("righteous ones").

The European Enlightenment of the eighteenth century also had a profound effect on Jewish life. Jewish leaders like the German intellectual Moses Mendelssohn urged Jews to leave the ghetto and assimilate to the newly forming societies based on reason and respect for human rights. The American and French revolutions promised freedom and justice for Jews as for other citizens. Jews were admitted to universities and to the professions. Many Jews, like their Christian neighbors, gave up their distinctive religious traditions to live a new, secular life.

Branches within Modern Judaism

REFORM JUDAISM   The attitude that Judaism should adapt to a changing world was strongest in nineteenth-century Germany. In German synagogues rabbis began reading the sabbath liturgy in German rather than Hebrew. The idea of the coming of a messiah who would lead Jews back to a restored Israel was dropped. Emphasis was placed instead on Jews being loyal citizens of the countries in which they lived. A famous phrase in the early Reform movement was, "We know no homelands but the land of our birth." Some rabbis contended that strict adherence to the dietary laws of the written and oral Torahs was no longer as necessary as commitment to the ethical teachings of the Torah. All of this led to the creation of the *Reform* Movement, dedicated to the preservation of the basic principles of Judaism by adapting them to changing circumstances. The Reform Movement spread from Germany throughout Europe and to the United States, where today it is particularly popular.

ORTHODOX JUDAISM   In response to the liberalism of the Reform movement other rabbis formed what became known as *Orthodox* Judaism. Orthodox Jews reacted particularly strongly to the Reform contentions that the written and oral Torahs were not the direct word of God and that their guidelines were not all of equal importance. The Orthodox were and are concerned about strict observance of the commandments of the Torah. Judaism could survive different ideas, they believe, but not abandonment of the keeping of the instructions that reflect obedience to God and that distinguish Jews as a people. For the Orthodox community, strict adherence to the traditionally stated commandments of the Torah is a matter of Jewish survival.

CONSERVATIVE JUDAISM   Some Jews looked for a middle ground between the Reform and Orthodox approaches, and found it in the *Conservative* Movement, which was also founded in the nineteenth century. Conservative Jews are willing to use the vernacular language in worship and apply historical study to traditional teachings. Therefore, Conservative Jews combine a commitment to observe the commandments of the Torah with a recognition that the legal tradition continues to evolve. Like Reform Jews, Conservative communities ordain women as rabbis (a practice not adopted by Orthodox Jews).

RECONSTRUCTIONISM   A fourth branch of Judaism is *Reconstructionism,* which developed out of the Conservative Movement in the 1920s and '30s. It stresses that Judaism is a civilization, and that the maintenance of Jewish culture is the key to

Jewish well-being in the modern world. Its founder, Mordecai Kaplan, called Judaism "an evolving religious civilization." This movement has created "Jewish Community Centers" as places where Jewish culture can be celebrated and continued by Jews of differing religious orientations. The particular position of Reconstructionism on religion is that Judaism must be interpreted in a modern scientific framework. For example, the idea of "God" must be seen in the light of evolving human experience.

We should also note the *Havurah* ("fellowship") movement in the United States, which holds its meetings in individual homes instead of synagogues or temples. Another potent force, particularly in Judaism in the West, is a feminist movement (see Chapter Eighteen).

Judaism in the Modern World

THE ZIONIST MOVEMENT   The new toleration and acceptance of Jews in nineteenth-century Europe turned out to be short-lived and superficial. In 1894 a young Austrian journalist named Theodore Herzl was covering the trial of Alfred Dreyfus, a French officer and a Jew who had been charged with being a spy. The conviction of Dreyfus on the basis of very weak evidence convinced Herzl that Jews were not as safe in Europe as they thought. He joined the emergent movement called *Zionism* ("Zion" is a symbolic name for Jerusalem) and became its chief negotiator. The Zionist goal was to find a homeland for Jews where they would be safe from persecution. The preference was Palestine, and the Zionists began buying land and starting Jewish settlements there in the early 1900s. By 1909 a new Jewish city (Tel Aviv) had been established, and by 1920 there were fifty thousand Jews in Palestine. The Jewish immigration caused the Arabs of Palestine, who had lived in the land for centuries (but without independence), to fear that they would lose their homeland. The British (who, after World War I, exercised authority over Palestine) at first encouraged, then—under Arab pressure—limited Jewish settlement. In 1939 the British established a quota of fifteen thousand Jews per year to be allowed into Palestine.

THE HOLOCAUST   The final reversal of the acceptance of Jews into modern European society was the coming to power of the Nazi regime in Germany under Adolf Hitler. Drawing upon pseudoscientific racial theories developed by German academics, and the history of Christian persecution of Jews, Hitler announced a goal of making Germany and all of Europe *Judenrein* ("free of Jews").

When Hitler took power in 1933, the first stage of his plan began. Jews were forced out of their positions of responsibility in German society and Jewish property was expropriated. In 1935 laws were passed that identified categories of "Jewishness," ranging from full Jew to mixed Jew, and the discriminatory policies were institutionalized. Many Jews fled to other countries, after paying an exorbitant exit fee and leaving all their property, but strictly enforced quotas in most countries (including the United States) closed the door to many Jews trying to escape.

With the onset of World War II in 1939, Germany quickly began a policy of killing Jews. At first special squads followed the advancing German army and shot many of the Jews in the "liberated" areas. As the war progressed, more "efficient" killing centers were built in Poland. In areas under German control, Jews had been forced into ghettos, from which they were rounded up and transported to extermination camps like Auschwitz. Most were taken directly to large chambers (ostensibly for a disinfecting shower) and gassed with a pesticide, Zyklon B.

By the time the war ended, about six million Jewish men, women, and children had been exterminated by the carefully orchestrated plan of genocide. Two-thirds of the Jews of Europe had been killed. In Poland the Jewish population before the war was more than three million. In 1945 there were fifty thousand Jews left in Poland. The name *Holocaust* (*Shoah* in Hebrew, the term for a "total sacrifice") was used to describe what the Nazis had done in effectively wiping out the Jews of most of Europe.

The Holocaust has caused many Jews (and others) to reconsider the traditional belief in a God who acts in history. If God has the power to intervene, they ask, why would God allow innocent children to die in Nazi gas chambers? Some Jews have given up belief in such an active God, and consider their Judaism simply a matter of cultural identity. Other Jews have developed new understandings of God and God's relationship with humans, dropping the notion that God has the power to intervene at will in history. Still other Jews view the Holocaust as a terrible punishment on Jewish infidelity and have committed themselves even more strongly to the traditional Jewish ways and the belief in a providential God. Regardless, the Holocaust is considered by most Jews the single most important event in the history of Judaism, especially in the modern world. Its impact is still unfolding.

JUDAISM AND THE STATE OF ISRAEL   The Zionist dream of a homeland for Jews was finally realized with the birth of the modern state of Israel in 1948. For most Jews today, to say that Israel is merely the product of the political movement known as Zionism is misleading. "Israel" is more than a political state; it is a place where Jews are free to live as Jews—a Jewish homeland. It is a refuge against the revitalization of anti-Semitism, a place where Jews will protect other Jews from those who seek to destroy the Jewish people. Israel is a critical expression and symbol of Jewish identity as a people.

The State of Israel recognizes a "right of return" to the Jewish homeland for all the Jews of the world. Recent decades have seen a flood of Jewish immigrants to Israel from the former Soviet Union and other places where anti-Semitism is on the rise. Many Reform Jews, who before World War II opposed the creation of the state of Israel and the Zionist movement, have become strong political and financial supporters of Israel.

The state of Israel is officially nonreligious. In fact, for many Israelis it may be argued that Zionism functions as a secular religion, in which the nation fulfills the role of ultimacy. However, within Israel, Orthodox groups exercise considerable influence.

The Jewish Worldview

Tour *The Sacred World* CD!

Judaism as a religion has not traditionally emphasized conformity to a set of beliefs. At the heart of traditional Judaism is not so much belief but practice, following the commandments.

Until the emergence of the Reform movement in the nineteenth century, there was not much disagreement with the notion that the common denominator uniting the diverse movements in Judaism was observance of all the commandments (although what exactly observance means in particular circumstances has always been a subject of discussion and debate in even the most orthodox circles). Today, however, the challenge of the Reform and Reconstructionist movements to this pattern, and reinterpretations offered within the Conservative movement, must be taken into account in any discussion of the Jewish worldview. For example, Reform Judaism has typically encouraged considerable *individual* deliberation in deciding the degree to which the keeping of the commandments (especially those involving diet and ritual) is important to one's Jewish identity.

Humanity: In God's Image   The first chapter of the first book in the written Torah (Genesis), describes the creation of humanity in God's image (Genesis 1:27 [NRSV]):

> So God created humankind in his image,
> in the image of God he created them;
> male and female he created them.

While interpreters debate just what "in God's image" means, the phrase suggests a close relationship between humanity and the Creator, and an equality between male and female.

A biblical psalm (Psalms 8:4-5 [NRSV]) reflects on the divine/human relationship and the status of humans in creation with these words:

> What are human beings that you are mindful of them,
>   mortals that you care for them?
> Yet you have made them a little lower than God,
>   and crowned them with glory and honor.

These passages support the view that traditional Judaism is fundamentally anthropocentric. However, with the honor of being in God's image, humans are also given by God the responsibility of caring for creation.

According to Jewish teaching, humans have souls, the "breath of God" breathed into them at creation. A passage from the Talmud compares the relationship between God and the world with that between the soul and the body (Simon 1959: 54):

> Just as the Holy One, blessed be He, fills the whole world, so the soul fills the body. Just as the Holy One, blessed be He, sees, but is not seen, so the soul sees, but is not itself seen. Just as the Holy One, blessed be He, feeds the whole world, so the soul feeds the whole body. Just as the Holy One, blessed be He, is pure, so the soul is pure. Just as the Holy One, blessed be He, abides in the innermost precincts [of the Temple in Jerusalem], so also the soul dwells in the innermost part of the body. Let that which has these five qualities, come and praise Him who has these five qualities.

Problem: Missing the Mark   All branches of Judaism agree that humans have the freedom to decide whether to follow the will of God or to rebel against it. In contrast to traditional Christian teaching, Judaism does not teach that humans are inherently sinful. Classical Judaism speaks of two contrasting tendencies (*yezers*) that are at war in each human's nature: a good impulse and an evil impulse. These impulses are not external forces, but internal tendencies that are present in every human being. Those who choose to follow the "evil impulse" inevitably engage in deeds that "miss the mark."

Traditional Judaism has emphasized both the intention behind acts that violate the will of God and the acts themselves. The rabbis distinguished between acts that were particularly heinous and those which were not as severe, but all violations of the commandments were considered a break with God.

Reform Judaism has tended to focus on the ethical commandments, to the extent that many Reform Jews believe ignoring the dietary and ritual laws is not a violation of the will of God. They argue, for example, that the dietary law was appropriate when it was formulated (for health reasons, and to maintain a distinctive Jewish identity), but that in the modern world the restrictions have become irrelevant. They believe that Jewishness should not be seen as a matter of the food you eat or the type of prayers you say, but rather in terms of one's fundamental orientation toward the ethical lifestyle found in the Jewish tradition.

Cause: Disobedience   Like other monotheistic religions, traditional Judaism teaches that God has revealed the way people are to live. Our choice is whether to obey God and follow the path (in Judaism the *halakah*), or disobey God. The dimension added by Reform Judaism is a certain flexibility to reflect the different circumstances people face.

End: Next Year in Jerusalem   In the formative period of classical Judaism we find a variety of beliefs about the future fulfillment for those who keep the Torah. In particular, there was no consensus on the role of a messiah in the future, or the fate of people after death. With the emergence of the Pharisaic view as normative, the following developed as one widely held understanding. According to this viewpoint, at some time in the future—at a time known only to God—a human descendant of King David anointed by god (the messiah) will appear and enter into Jerusalem. The messiah will restore the nation of Israel, with Jerusalem at the center. This belief is expressed in the toast that is part of the Passover liturgy, as the participants look with anticipation and hope to the coming of the messiah: "Next year in Jerusalem!"

When the messiah comes, a new age, the "age to come," will begin, bringing universal peace, harmony, and justice for all nations. Those who have died before the coming of this age will be raised from their graves to be judged. Those Jews who have been obedient to the Torah, and those Gentiles (non-Jews) who have followed the minimal commandments given by God to all humanity after the Flood, will enter into this new Kingdom of God. The ideal place of burial for many traditional Jews is the cemetery on the Mount of Olives near Jerusalem, where they will be ready to meet the messiah when he returns to Zion.

On the basis of this teaching many Orthodox Jews opposed the creation of the state of Israel in 1948, because the messiah had not come and it was not yet time for the nation to be restored. The belief is widespread that the messiah will not come until all Israel is living obediently, as is the accompanying belief that Jews can "force" the coming of the Messiah by their faithfulness. This has been a motivating force in the work of some Orthodox groups to try to encourage Jews who have never kept the Torah (or who have stopped keeping it) to live observant lives.

Reform Judaism has tended to interpret the teaching about the messiah symbolically rather than literally. Rather than expecting an actual messianic figure, the Reform movement has emphasized that a "messianic age" of universal peace and justice will only come if humans learn to cooperate with God in bringing it about. The role of the Jewish community, according to this view, is to model the commitment to ethics that will bring humanity into the new age. There is no one teaching in the Reform movement on whether individual humans survive death (or, if they do, what form that life takes).

There is surprisingly little reference in the Tanak to life after death. For the most part, texts speak of *sheol*, the place for all the dead, where they exist as "shadows" cut off from the worship of God. Some texts may acknowledge a belief in life after death with God (e.g., Psalm 16:10–11, 49:15, 73:24). However, it is in the Book of Daniel in the Writings that we find the clearest statement of a belief in an individual resurrection of the dead at the end of history (see Daniel 12:1–3).

In the Mishnah we find a fuller expression of the teaching about the judgment by God at the end of time (Abot 4.29, Herford 1930: 122–23):

> Those that are born are for death; and the dead are for life again, and they that live [again] are to be judged; to know, to make known, and to be made aware that He is God, He is the Maker, He the Creator, He the Discerner, He the Judge, He the witness, He the adversary and he will judge, blessed be He, in whose presence there is neither obliquity nor forgetfulness, nor respect of persons, nor taking of bribes. And know that all is according to reckoning.

Means: The Way of Torah   At the heart of all branches of Judaism is the Torah, the instruction from God on how to live obediently, which includes both the written and the oral Torah. Disagreement comes on what it means to follow the way of Torah in the modern world. You will find heated debate within any of the branches of Judaism on the way in which specific situations are affected or addressed by the teachings of the Torah. However Torah is interpreted, there is consensus that following the way of Torah is not a burden, but a joy. Torah is God's gift to the Jewish people, and being obedient to Torah is a way of showing gratitude. As one Rabbi said, "The reward for keeping one *mitzvah* (commandment), is another!"

Orthodox Jews believe that the authority of the Torah resides in its origin. They hold that the whole Torah, written and oral, was revealed by God to Moses on Mount Sinai. The commandments of the written and oral Torah are therefore the actual word of God to the Jewish people. The only exception to keeping particular commandments is when a person's life is at stake. For example, if a Jew is threatened with death, then it is acceptable to break the commandments in order to avoid being killed. This was the traditional basis for defending the public conversion of Jews to other religions at times of persecution.

From an Orthodox perspective, a Jew should keep a *kosher* ("ritually correct") diet, not simply for practical considerations, but because God has clearly instructed Jews to do so. The kosher laws govern which foods may be eaten, how the allowed foods are to be prepared, and the acceptable manner of consumption. The Talmud contains a large collection of such instructions, based on verses in the Tanak. All forms of vegetation are permissible, but only animals that have both cloven hooves and dual digestive tracts. Fish must have both fins and scales. Birds of prey and those that lack a crop, gizzard, and talon are also forbidden. Allowed fish may be eaten when caught, but fowl and the other allowed animals must be ritually slaughtered. The rules of slaughter are so complex that specially trained butchers perform this function in traditional Jewish communities. Once slaughtered, every effort must be made to remove all blood from the meat. In serving the food, meat and dairy products must not be mixed. Separate dishes are maintained for the two.

Reform Judaism makes the keeping of a kosher diet a matter of individual conscience. Those Jews who believe that it is a valuable practice in enabling them to lead a Jewish lifestyle should maintain a kosher diet, but those who do not recognize its value should not maintain the tradition for its own sake.

A calendar of festivals is also critical to the way of Torah. At the center of the Jewish calendar is the weekly *sabbath,* the twenty-five hour period beginning Friday at sundown. As with the other holidays, the basis of the sabbath is a scriptural tradition about the key moments in the history of God's involvement with the nation of Israel. The sabbath is a reenactment of the creation myth, the seventh day when God rested (Exodus 20: 8–11), as well as a remembrance of God's mercy in delivering the people from bondage in Egypt (Deuteronomy 5: 12–15). In the observance of the sabbath at home, the day of rest is greeted as a guest, with a blessing for the day (*kiddush*) said over bread and wine at the sabbath meals and over the lighting of the sabbath candles. Two loaves of sabbath bread are served as symbols of the double portion of *manna* that fell from heaven in the Sinai wilderness. Special prayers are said, and at the conclusion of the sabbath a *havdalah* ("separation") ceremony is held to bid farewell to the sabbath and to distinguish this holy day from the rest of the week.

Orthodox and Conservative Jews attend sabbath services in the synagogue on Saturday mornings, where selections from the Torah are publically read as part of a yearly cycle. Reform Jews typically hold sabbath services on Friday evening, after sundown, in houses of worship called temples. Calling the local place of worship a temple is a symbol of the Reform belief that the temple is in whatever place the Jewish community gathers, not just in Jerusalem. For the Orthodox the *only* temple is the one in Jerusalem, which will be rebuilt when the messiah comes.

Orthodox observance of the sabbath requires abstention from all forms of labor (except where health is at stake), including riding in automobiles, lighting or extinguishing lights, or even carrying money. Conservative Jews attempt to keep the commandments, but with some adaptation (such as allowing the driving of automobiles to the synagogue on the sabbath). In Reform communities individuals decide for themselves which of the sabbath restrictions or observances have spiritual meaning.

Although the sabbath is set aside as a day of rest, according to traditional Judaism individuals should participate in services of prayer and praise three times daily, including the sabbath. The sabbath morning service is made special because of the reading from the Torah in the synagogue at this service.

Throughout the year a series of other festivals remember and reenact other central historical events in the life of the Jewish people. The Spring celebration of *Passover* or *Pesach* ("lamb") is an eight- (or seven-) day commemoration of the deliverance of the Israelites from Egypt. It occurs in March or April. The name of Passover refers to the angel of death "passing over" the homes of the Hebrew families, when the first-born of the Egyptians were killed. On the first one or two nights of the celebration families gather for *seder* ("order") meals. The Passover *haggadah* is read at the seder, recalling the Egyptian bondage and deliverance. The participants remember the time when "we" were slaves in Egypt, making present the experience of deliverance and expressing the solidarity of the Jewish community. The foods eaten at the seder recall the exodus experience: *matzoh* ("unleavened bread"), bitter herbs, roasted meat, and greens.

In ancient times Passover was one of the three annual pilgrimage festivals, during which Jewish males were required to come to Jerusalem for special Temple rituals. Fifty days after Pesach is the celebration of *Shavuot* ("weeks"). It is also known as the festival of first fruit, harvest, or Pentecost. It remembers both the bringing of the first fruits of the harvest to the temple, and the receiving of the Torah from God.

The third pilgrimage festival was *Sukkot* ("booths"). A celebration of the autumn harvest, it also recalls the time when the Israelites wandered in the wilderness and lived in portable dwellings called *sukkot*. It takes place in September or October and extends for seven days.

The "high holy days" of the Jewish calendar are *Rosh Hashanah* ("New Year") and *Yom Kippur* ("Day of Atonement"). Rosh Hashanah is celebrated in September or October each year. It begins with the sounding of the ram's horn (*shofar*) as a call to repentance that initiates a ten-day period of penitence, during which Jews review their lives over the past year and prepare for a new year of Torah obedience. During Rosh Hashanah, sweets are eaten as a symbol of the hope for a pleasing year. This

The Jewish Festival of Passover celebrates God's deliverance of the Hebrew slaves from bondage in Egypt. At the Passover meal (seder) a special plate holds the various symbols of the ritual, such as bitter herbs that represent the suffering of the people before their liberation.

holiday ends with Yom Kippur, traditionally a day of abstinence from work, with prayers for forgiveness and reconciliation. Many Jews spend the entire day in the Synagogue. An elaborate Temple ritual for Yom Kippur is described in the Bible and Talmud, in which the High Priest entered the Holy of Holies in the Temple for the only time in the year. A goat was sent into the wilderness carrying the sins of the people (hence the term "scapegoat").

Other festival days on the Jewish yearly calendar include the Feast of Dedication (*Hannukah*), remembering the rededication of the Temple after it had been profaned during the Maccabean revolution. It takes place in November or December and involves the lighting of a candle each day, for eight days. Thus it is called the Festival of Lights. The Feast of Lots (*Purim*), celebrated in February or March, recalls the Jewish victory celebrated in the Book of Esther.

The Jewish rite of passage is the *Bar* (or *Bat*) *Mitzvah* ("son or daughter of the commandment"). Traditionally, when a boy reaches the age of thirteen he becomes an adult member of the community, and can be counted among the minimum of ten adult males (*minyan*) required for a synagogue. He prepares for this passage by studying Torah and learning to read Hebrew. In Reform and Conservative communities the rite of passage has been extended to girls, while in Orthodox communities the *Bat Mitzvah* includes public presentation, but not the Torah reading common to Bar Mitzvahs. In all branches the Bat Mitzvah typically occurs when the girl is twelve.

Another rite of passage is the ritual of circumcision (removal of the foreskin of the penis) of a male infant on the eighth day after birth (or an adult male Jewish convert). This ritual is known by the Hebrew name *berit* ("covenant"), because the ritual is the symbol of the covenant made by God with Abraham and his descendants (see Genesis 17:10–12).

Other rites of passage occur, as they do in other religious traditions, at marriage and death. In Jewish tradition the wedding ceremony takes place under a *chuppah* or wedding canopy, made with a prayer shawl (*tallis*). The *chuppah* is symbolic of the home that the bride and groom will make; being open on all sides, it implies that the couple's home will always be welcoming to all who enter. A blessing (*kiddush*) is said and the bride and groom share a cup of wine, blessing the marriage. At the heart of the traditional Jewish wedding ceremony are the seven blessings (*sheva b'rochot*). Traditionally, the groom signs a marriage contract (*ketubah*) outlining his responsibilities to his wife. In modern ceremonies both the bride and groom often sign the *ketubah*. The most famous Jewish marriage custom is the breaking of a glass by the groom at the end of the ceremony, after which those in attendance shout "*mazel tov!*" ("good fortune"!).

At death, the body of the deceased is ritually cleansed and buried (never cremated), because of the belief in resurrection of the body. During a seven-day period following the death (called *shiva*), those closest to the deceased refrain from normal activities.

Traditionally, Jews have believed that in their relations with others they are to imitate the characteristics of God. Just as God cared for the poor and needy, so are God's people to show compassion. In the Biblical legislation, care for the stranger and the widow is especially enjoined. In general, the Torah requires not only love of God but also love of neighbor. In a famous incident described in the Talmud, the great Rabbi Hillel was asked by a non-Jew if he could recite the whole Torah while standing on one foot, to which Hillel responded, "What is hateful to you, do not do to your neighbor: that is the whole Torah, while the rest of it is commentary thereof; go and learn it." The Torah also requires personal piety. The ideal is to sanctify all of life. (As noted, Reform Judaism has placed greater emphasis on the ethical over the ritual and the dietary laws.)

According to rabbinic teaching all people may manifest the love and justice of God, each in their own way. The particular Jewish obligation is to manifest the love and justice of God by following the Torah. This passage from the Talmud suggests that the meaning of life for Jews is to be found in bringing joy to others and making peace between opposing parties (Petuchowski 1982: 112):

> Rabbi Baruqa of Huza often went to the marketplace at Lapet. One day, the prophet
> Elijah appeared to him there; and Rabbi Baruqa asked him, "Is there anyone among

all these people who will have a share in the World to Come?" Elijah answered, "There is none[. . . .]" Later, two men came to the marketplace; and Elijah said to Rabbi Baruqa, "Those two will have a share in the World to Come!" Rabbi Baruqa asked the newcomers, "What is your occupation?" They replied, "We are clowns. When we see someone who is sad, we cheer him up. When we see two people quarreling, we try to make peace between them."

All branches of Judaism agree that to live a life of obedience to Torah through study is critical. As noted, synagogues are places not only of prayer but of study. In Talmudic times the centers of Jewish leadership were academies where scholars gathered to study and interpret Torah. In Orthodox communities today, *yeshivas* (schools) offer instruction in the Talmud.

Reality: It Is Good!   The first chapter of the Book of Genesis is the basis for the Jewish understanding that the created order is good, not evil. God has created the world as a place of abundance to be enjoyed, and charged humanity to respect and maintain the harmony of the creation. Judaism has steadfastly avoided that dualism that says that matter (including the human body) is evil and spirit (including the human soul) is good. It is not our bodies that are evil, but the acts that we commit when we follow the evil impulse within us. Not only has God created the world, God sustains the world day by day, and therefore is present in the world.

Traditional Judaism teaches that not only God is present in the natural order, but God acts within human history, and history is moving toward a time of fulfillment.

Sacred: The Great "I Am"   When God appeared to Moses on Mount Sinai, in the fire of a bush that burned but was not consumed (Exodus 3:2), the sacred name for the deity (called the *tetragrammaton,* because it has four Hebrew consonants: YHWH) was revealed. As we have noted, in most modern English translations, "LORD" is used when *YHWH* appears in the Hebrew. For Jews the tetragrammaton symbolizes the holiness and transcendence of God. Traditionally, the tetragrammaton is not pronounced. Instead, the more common Hebrew name for lord (*adonai*) is said when *YHWH* appears in the biblical text. The transcendence of God is also emphasized in Judaism by the commandment against any images of God and the circumlocutions used in prayers, such as "The Holy One of Israel, Blessed be He," and "Master of the Universe."

The clear distinction between the creation and the Creator implies that God is far above us. However, Jewish tradition also makes room for the immanence of God. For example, the *shechinah* ("presence") is God's indwelling nature, said to reside in Israel and the Torah. In this passage from the Talmud, the first-century-C.E. Rabbi Gamaliel explains the *shechinah* to the Roman emperor (Schachter 1959: 251):

The Emperor said to Rabbi Gamaliel, "Ye maintain that upon every gathering of ten [Jews], the Shechinah (Divine Presence) rests. How many Shechinahs are there then?" Rabbi Gamaliel called Caesar's servant, and tapped him on the neck, saying, "Why does the sun enter into Caesar's house?" "But," he [the ruler] exclaimed, "The sun shines upon the whole world." [Rabbi Gamaliel said,] "Then the sun, which is but one of the countless myriads of the servants of the Holy One, blessed be He, shines over on the whole world, how much more the Shechinah of the Holy One, blessed be He, Himself?"

For Judaism the transcendent and immanent God is one and indivisible. At the heart of Judaism is the oft-repeated *shema,* which begins: "Hear, O Israel! the LORD is our God, the LORD alone!"

This traditional portrait of God has been subject to much reinterpretation by modern Jewish scholars, who seek to reconcile the idea of God with the contemporary scientific worldview of natural causes and effects, and with the horrible reality of the Holocaust, which seemed to challenge the idea of a compassionate God who acts in history to deliver Israel. Some Jews today are willing to give up entirely the concept of a supernatural, personal deity in favor of an understanding of God as a personification of natural or human qualities.

Judaism in the Twenty-First Century

In the early twenty-first century estimates of the total number of Jews in the world range as high as eighteen million. Of these, five to six million live in the United States, four to five million in Israel, and about three million in the former Soviet Union. In the world as a whole, most religious Jews follow the Orthodox path of full obedience to all the commandments of the Torah. However, in Europe and North America, Reform Judaism is the largest movement. In the United States approximately 40 percent of religious Jews are members of Reform communities and 40 percent are associated with Conservative congregations, while about 20 percent are Orthodox Jews. In Israel it is estimated that 80 percent are "secular" Jews, while among the religious Jews the vast majority are Orthodox.

The Palestinian-Israeli Conflict   The continuing conflict between the Israelis and the Palestinians inside Israel and in the "occupied territories," as well as those in refugee or exile status outside Israel, has created a great deal of tension in the Jewish world. In Israel and among Jews worldwide there is a wide spectrum of opinion on how best to deal with the issues raised by the demands of the Palestinians for independence in a nation of their own.

Some Jews want to restore the land of Israel as "Judea and Samaria," the Israel envisioned in the Biblical period. They reject the alleged right of Palestinians to a homeland of their own within the traditional boundaries of Israel. They point out that, unlike the Jews, the Palestinians never had a separate homeland in the past, and assert that Palestinians outside Israel should be absorbed into surrounding Arab countries. They are strong advocates of the movement to place permanent Jewish settlements in the "occupied territories."

On the other side are Jews who say that Israel should close all settlements in the occupied territories, withdraw at once from all the land taken in the wars with Arab states, and cooperate fully in the creation of a Palestinian state within these borders. In between are a variety of opinions.

A peace process begun in 1993 broke down in 2000, and a cycle of violence, in which thousands of Palestinians and hundreds of Israelis have died, continued into the early twenty-first century. As this chapter is written, a "road map" for peace, sponsored by a group known as the "Quartet" (the United States, Russia, the European Union, and the United Nations) is being promoted. However, suicide bombings by Hamas and other Palestinian groups committed to the destruction of the State of Israel (so that an Islamic, Palestinian state can be created), and a strict policy of reprisals by the Israeli government, including targeted assassinations of Palestinian leaders and the destruction of homes of suspected militants, make peaceful resolution of the conflict any time soon seem unlikely.

Resurgence of Anti-Semitism   The problem of hatred of Jews, which has led to violence against Jews for millenia, has not disappeared in the twenty-first century. More than 300 serious incidents of anti-Semitism were reported worldwide in 2002; this compared to 228 serious incidents in 2001. The Anti-Defamation League, a Jewish organization that monitors evidence of anti-Semitism in the United States, identified 1,559 reports of anti-Semitic incidents in 2002, up from 1,432 in 2001.

The contemporary resurgence of anti-Semitism has a number of causes. Neo-Nazi movements have long made claims of a worldwide Jewish conspiracy a central feature of their ideologies. The economic dislocation and a deepening sense of powerlessness following the breakup of the former Soviet Union have fostered the reappearance of scapegoating of Jews and anti-Semitic outbreaks in Eastern Europe. Racist Christian groups in the United States also blame Jews for a host of problems. Perhaps most threatening is the rise of anti-Semitism in the Muslim world. Before the September 11, 2001, terrorist attacks, Osama Bin Laden identified the "Crusader-Jewish" alliance as the principal enemy of Islam, inspiring *al-Qaeda* cells and supporters to mount attacks on Jews. Unfortunately, the *Protocols of the Elders of Zion,* a forged document that purports to be evidence for a worldwide Jewish conspiracy, has been promoted in the Muslim world as part of the campaign against the Jewish State of Israel. In addition to virulent and violent anti-Semitism, subtle forms of hatred against Jews are still evident in communities where Jews are ostensibly fully accepted.

Assimilation   Assimilation occurs when Jews turn away from their religion or traditions and attempt to blend into the larger culture in which they live. In the United States today about half of Jews marry outside their religion, and many no longer raise their children in the faith. Many Jewish families have simply faded away from the Jewish community and lost contact with Jewish tradition. Jewish authorities point out that if this trend continues the survival of a distinct Jewish community in countries like the United States is threatened. However, programs to rekindle a sense of cultural and religious identity among Jews have had success, and a sizeable core group of committed Jews remains strong.

CHAPTER SUMMARY

 In this chapter we began our study of the major religions that originated in the Middle East—Zoroastrianism, Judaism, Christianity, and Islam. Except for Zoroastrianism, all these religions have spread throughout the world and can today be found in virtually all countries.

After surveying the lands, peoples, and history of the Middle East, we summarized the traditional worldview shared by these religions, using Zoroastrianism to illustrate our "framework for understanding." The distinctive characteristics of this worldview are a shared belief in a single, personal, supreme God, creator and judge of all that is; a belief that humans have a special, spiritual status and are at the center of God's creation; a view of time as linear, with a beginning and an end; a belief in reward or punishment after death; and an emphasis on God's revelation of a "way" of ethical living.

We then surveyed the stages of development and sacred writings of Judaism and the Jewish worldview, noting where there has been reinterpretation of traditional teachings by some Jews today.

We concluded the chapter with a look at issues facing Judaism in the twenty-first century, focusing on the Palestinian-Israeli conflict, a resurgence of anti-Semitism, and assimilation.

IMPORTANT TERMS AND PHRASES

Ahura Mazda, Angra Mainyu, anthropocentric, anti-Semitism, Ashkenazim, assimilation, Avesta, Bar (Bat) Mitzvah, Conservative Judaism, Diaspora, eschatology, *haggadah, halakah,* Hasidism, Holocaust, Kabbala, messiah, Midrash, Mishnah, *mitzvah* (plural, *mitzvoth*), Orthodox Judaism, Oral Torah, Parsis, Passover, Pharisees, problem of evil, rabbi, Reconstructionism, Reform Judaism, revelation, Rosh Hashanah, Sabbath, Sadducees, Satan, Sephardim, Septuagint, Spenta Mainyu, synagogue, Talmud, Tanak, Torah, the LORD, Yiddish, Yom Kippur, Zionism

QUESTIONS FOR DISCUSSION AND REFLECTION

1. Explain why you agree or disagree with the following assertions.
   a. Only those Jews who keep the commandments are true Jews.
   b. The Torah is no longer relevant because the world today is totally different from the world in which the Torah was written.
   c. The diversity within modern Judaism is healthy for the religion.
   d. A Jew concerned about the survival of the Jewish people should not marry a non-Jew.

2. Have you ever felt as though others were responding to you on the basis of a stereotype? Have you ever experienced or witnessed the stereotyping of Jews (or members of other religions)? What did you do? How serious is the problem?

3. Should the death of six million Jews in the Holocaust cause reconsideration of the traditional belief in a God who acts in history to deliver people at their time of need?

4. Respond to the assertion that the State of Israel should not surrender any land to the Palestinians for a Palestine state because God promised all the land to the Jewish people.

5. How seriously does assimilation threaten Judaism (and other religions)? Has your own understanding and practice of religion changed as a result of assimilation to dominant cultural pressures?

SOURCES AND SUGGESTIONS FOR FURTHER STUDY

BERGER, ALAN L., ED., 1994. *Judaism in the Modern World.* New York: New York University.

BOYCE, MARY, 1982. *A History of Zoroastrianism.* 2 vols. Leiden: E. J. Brill.

FEILER, BRUCE, 2002. *Abraham: A Journey to the Heart of Three Faiths.* New York: William Morrow.

FISHBANE, MICHAEL, 1987. *Judaism.* Hagerstown, MD: Torch.

GILBERT, MARTIN, 1985. *The Holocaust: A History of the Jews of Europe during the Second World War.* New York: Henry Holt.

GILLMAN, NEIL, 1992. *Sacred Fragments: Recovering Theology for the Modern Jew.* New York: Jewish Publication Society.

GREENBERG, IRVING, 1988. *The Jewish Way: Living the Holidays.* New York: Summit.

HAUER, CHRIS E. AND WILLIAM A. Young, 2001. *An Introduction to the Bible: A Journey into Three Worlds.* 5th ed. Upper Saddle River, NJ: Prentice Hall.

HERFORD, R. TRAVERS, ED. AND TRANS. 1930. *Pirke Aboth: The Tractate 'Fathers' from The Mishnah.* New York: Jewish Institute of Religion.

HESCHEL, ABRAHAM, 1987. *God in Search of Man: A Philosophy of Judaism.* Northvale, NJ: Jacob Aronson. (1955)

MEEKS, WAYNE, ED., 1993. *The HarperCollins Study Bible: New Revised Standard Version.* New York: HarperCollins.

MONTEFIORE, C. G. AND H. LOEWE, EDS., 1963. *A Rabbinic Anthology.* New York: Meridian.

PETUCHOWSKI, JAKOB J., TRANS. AND ED., 1982. *Our Masters Taught: Rabbinic Stories and Sayings.* New York: Crossroad.

ROTH, CECIL AND GOEFFREY WIGODER, EDS., 1972– *Encyclopedia Judaica.* 16 vols. Jerusalem: Keter.

SCHACHTER, JACOB, TRANS. 1959. *The Babylonian Talmud,* ed. I. Epstein. Vol. 24. New York: Rebecca Bennet.

SIMON, MAURICE, TRANS. 1959. *The Babylonian Talmud,* ed. I. Epstein. Vol. 1. New York: Rebecca Bennet.

WIESEL, ELIE, 1960. *Night.* New York: Bantam.

WIESEL, ELIE, 1972. *Souls on Fire: Portraits and Legends of Hasidic Leaders,* trans. Marian Wiesel. New York: Random House.

Web Sites

www.avesta.org
> (site includes complete text of the Zoroastrian scripture, and links to other Zoroastrian sites)

maven.co.il
> (a Jewish web dictionary with links for sites related to the branches of Judaism)

judaism.about.com/
> (a basic site on topics in Judaism, with links)

uahc.org
> (the site of the Union of American Hebrew Congregations, the association for Reform Jewish congregations)

ou.org
> (the site for the Orthodox Union, linking Orthodox Jewish congregations)

uscj.org
> (the site of the United Synagogue of Conservative Judaism, linking Conservative Jewish congregations)

TIME   Refer to Pearson/Prentice Hall's **TIME Special Edition: World Religions** magazine for these and other current articles on topics related to many of the world's religions:

➡ *The Religious Experience: The Legacy of Abraham*

➡ *Judaism: Pop Goes the Kabbalah; A Ritual for All Ages; Jerusalem at the time of Jesus*

 Prentice Hall's **Research Navigator** helps students in their further study of the world's religions. Visit ***http://www.researchnavigator.com*** for help on the research process and access to databases full of relevant material, including the New York *Times.*

CHAPTER

11

Christianity—The Way of Jesus Christ

INTRODUCTION

Christianity has more followers than any religion of the world—more than two billion, or roughly one out of every three persons on earth. The admonition of Jesus to his disciples at the end of the Gospel of Matthew (28:19–20) to go into all the world and make disciples of all nations has been largely fulfilled.

Like other religions with a "founder," the various Christian movements are linked by their profession of faith in Jesus of Nazareth, whom they proclaim to be the Christ, the messiah. Christians all share the belief in a transformation wrought by the life, death, and resurrection from the dead of Jesus. However, they differ in their understanding of the meaning of these events. Many also share the rituals of baptism for the forgiveness of sins and a meal that reenacts the last meal Jesus ate with his disciples. Christians have a linear view of time, in which they look forward to a life beyond this life for individuals and a new age of peace and harmony for humanity.

In this chapter we will study the development of Christianity from the time of its founder, Jesus of Nazareth, to the present; the Christian worldview as expressed traditionally and reinterpreted by some contemporary Christians; and the status of Christianity in the twenty-first century.

STAGES OF DEVELOPMENT AND SACRED TEXTS

Founder: Jesus of Nazareth

Tour *The Sacred World* CD!

Jesus of Nazareth was a Jewish rabbi from the region of Galilee in the first century C.E., who attracted a small band of followers through his ministry of healing and teaching. After a short ministry he was executed by Roman authorities. Historians would have paid him little notice, but his followers made the astounding claim that Jesus had been raised by God from the dead. They kept alive his teachings and the stories of his life, and eventually wrote them down in different versions. They proclaimed the message that through the death and resurrection of Jesus, God had made a new covenant with humanity, and that, through Jesus, God offered redemption to all.

As with other "founders," the stories of the life of Jesus told in the New Testament reflect both historical events and beliefs about the significance of these events. The four New Testament gospels (Matthew, Mark, Luke, and John) were not written as biographies in the modern sense, but rather affirmations of faith in who Jesus was and what his coming meant. The "gospel" (from the Old English word for "good news") stories are, however, almost our only source of information about the life of Jesus. The following is a reasonable reconstruction of the basic events in the life of Jesus, based on what the gospels tell us.

Legends about the birth of Jesus (preserved only in the Gospels of Matthew and Luke) agree that Jesus was the son of a young virgin named Mary in Bethlehem, a small town several miles from Jerusalem in Judea. Her husband was a carpenter from Nazareth in Galilee named Joseph.

All of the gospels agree that Jesus lived in Nazareth in Galilee when he began his ministry, but they tell us almost nothing about his childhood. Jesus was about thirty when he left Nazareth and ventured to the Jordan River, where he encountered a prophet named John the Baptizer who was proclaiming a message of repentance. Jesus was baptized by John in the Jordan, apparently culminating a period of spiritual awakening for Jesus.

Following his baptism Jesus spent time in the wilderness of Judea fasting. Three of the four gospels portray this as a forty-day period of testing, during which Jesus was tempted by Satan. He then returned to Galilee where he began to challenge people to repent, telling them that the Kingdom of God was at hand. The "Kingdom of God" was a symbol in Jewish apocalyptic teaching of a radically new age, in which people would live in harmony with God and with one another. Jesus called together a group of close disciples; the gospels say that there were twelve. This number is symbolic of the twelve tribes of Israel, and reflects the view of his followers that the disciples of Jesus were a "new Israel" with whom God was entering into a new covenant. In addition to these twelve men, there were also women in the close band of followers of Jesus, according to the gospels.

The length of the ministry of Jesus is disputed. Only the Gospel of John implies a three-year period; the other gospels portray events that could have taken place in one year. Nor is it clear how many trips Jesus made to Jerusalem during his ministry.

Jesus taught people that compassion for others was more important than meticulous observance of the commandments. He warned people of the perils of wealth, and the importance of being ready for the coming Kingdom of God. The Gospel of John, in particular, says that Jesus taught that he himself was the Son of God who was "one" with the Father. It is in the Gospel of John that Jesus says, "No one can come to the father except through me." Scholars disagree on whether these reflect the actual sayings of Jesus or the developed interpretation of the significance of Jesus among his followers. Jesus often taught using the rabbinic device of parables—sayings and stories that drew on events and characters with which people could easily identify.

Jesus also worked miracles, according to the New Testament gospels. He healed the sick, the blind and the lame. He fed the hungry and cast out demons. He walked on water and calmed stormy seas. He even raised the dead. These claims may seem amazing to modern ears, but such miracles were often associated with other prophets and charismatic teachers in first-century Judaism.

More amazing at the time, to a Jewish community particularly concerned with righteous living, was the tendency of Jesus to associate with known sinners and social outcasts. He maintained that his message was especially intended for those who were not considered righteous.

Opposition to Jesus among some religious leaders and political authorities began to grow and, according to the gospels, he withdrew from his public ministry to spend time with his closest followers. He then went to Jerusalem for the Festival of Passover. The gospels say that he was enthusiastically greeted when he entered Jerusalem and was proclaimed to be the messiah. He also taught at the Temple and challenged the religious authorities. After a last meal with his disciples, he was arrested and condemned to death by Pontius Pilate, the Roman procurator of Judea.

Jesus died on the eve of the sabbath; his body was placed in a rock tomb. On the morning after the sabbath ended, several of the women among his disciples came to the tomb to anoint his body, as the Torah required, and found it empty. According to the gospels, Jesus had been raised from the dead. In several different legends, recorded in the gospels, Jesus appeared to his disciples at various times during the next forty days before he ascended into heaven.

The New Testament and the Birth of Christianity

Tour *The Sacred World* CD!

The New Testament not only preserves virtually the only evidence about the life of Jesus, it is also the primary source for the birth of Christianity.

The New Testament is actually a library of twenty-seven separate sacred writings that came into existence over an extended period of time. Most scholars think that the earliest writings in the New Testament (the first letters of the Apostle Paul) were written fifteen to twenty years after the death of Jesus. The latest books were probably composed in the mid-to-late second century C.E. In addition to the New Testament canon, there are a number of other Christian writings that were written throughout the period, including various gospels. The name "testament" is another word for "covenant."

The Christian compilers of the New Testament believed that these writings bore witness to a new covenant that God had made, extending the "old" covenant with the nation of Israel to include all people. Some of the prophets of Israel had envisioned a "new covenant" between God and Israel (e.g., Jeremiah 31:31–34). The writers of the New Testament thought that through Jesus, whom they proclaimed as the messiah, God had initiated this new covenant. They believed that the people who responded to Jesus's call to discipleship, and to the message about him, were a "new Israel" that God had assembled for a new age. There are a number of works available that will introduce readers to the critical interpretation of the New Testament (e.g., Hauer and Young 2001). Detailed examination of the individual books of the New Testament is beyond the scope of our study.

Historians have sifted through the historical references in the New Testament, and drawn also on other Christian and non-Christian literary works (as well as archaeological evidence), to reconstruct the origins of Christianity. What follows is a very general overview that emphasizes the broad consensus of the majority of historians.

Spiritual encounters with the risen Christ gave the immediate followers of Jesus both a message and the courage to proclaim it. The earliest church in Jerusalem centered around the Galileans who had come to Jerusalem with Jesus and remained there after his death. The community organized itself like other sectarian Jewish groups (including the group that produced the Dead Sea Scrolls). There was apparently an inner circle of leadership—Simon Peter and the two sons of Zebedee, James and John. After the execution of this James, another James (a brother or cousin of Jesus) apparently took his place as a leader of the Jerusalem community. Peter became a missionary, taking the message of the crucified yet risen Christ to Jewish communities in Palestine and the surrounding area. According to the New Testament book called the Acts of the Apostles, the Jerusalem followers held their material goods in common. They met in homes to commemorate the resurrection of Jesus, but they also continued to observe the Jewish calendar and worshipped at the Temple. As the Christian message spread, the Jerusalem community was looked upon with respect and reverence.

The early Jewish followers of Jesus understood the message that they were proclaiming mostly as a fulfillment of Jewish expectations. As the message began to spread into non-Jewish circles, the focus inevitably shifted. The Apostle Paul (a Pharisee who had had a transforming encounter with the risen Christ on the road to Damascus, Syria), and other missionaries committed to winning Gentiles to faith in Christ, naturally drew on imagery from the wider Hellenistic culture to interpret to those not familiar with Jewish tradition the meaning of God's sending the Christ, his Son, into the world. The message became more one of a personal salvation from a decaying world, from death, and the evil powers of the world. Even more importantly, Paul and other Gentile missionaries taught that Gentiles did not have to live under the commandments of Torah in order to experience the redemption that God offered through Jesus. According to Acts, the movement first called itself simply the Way, and acquired the name "Christians" for the first time in Antioch, Syria—probably (as with the names of other religions) from outsiders seeking to understand this new group.

Through the efforts of missionaries such as Paul, Christian communities began to spring up around the Mediterranean world, in both Jewish and Gentile settings, by the middle of the first century C.E. Although it was probably overdramatized in the sources, the first Christians suffered persecution at the hands of both the Sadducean leaders in Jerusalem and Roman authorities. The proclamation of Jesus as Lord was seen as a challenge to imperial prerogative. By the time of Paul's death in Rome (ca. 62 C.E.), however, Christianity had a relatively secure, if tenuous, foothold in the Roman empire.

Worship within the earliest Christian communities apparently revolved around gatherings in homes, in which the last meal of Jesus with his disciples was reenacted as a way of experiencing his presence. The practice of baptizing converts to the faith (borrowed from Judaism, and based upon the remembrance of the baptism of Jesus) continued. Paul speaks of a number of "gifts of the Spirit" present among the followers of Christ, including both "ecstatic" gifts (like speaking in tongues and prophesying) and more ordinary gifts (such as teaching and administration). He said, and others undoubtedly agreed, that it was most important for the followers to share the unconditional love for one another that God had shown in sending his Son into the world. Emphasis was placed on giving up the "old life" dominated by sinful desire and behavior, and taking on a "new life, a new nature" in Christ in which the fruits of the Spirit would be manifest.

The year 70 C.E. was a watershed in both the Jewish and Christian traditions. It marked the Roman destruction of Jerusalem and the Second Temple after a Jewish revolt. After 70 C.E. association with Judaism was less beneficial for Christians, because of the Roman response to the Jewish revolt.

The period before 70 C.E. is called the apostolic age in Christian history. After 70, the post-apostolic period (70–ca. 125 C.E.) began. It was inevitably characterized by growing institutionalization, as the Christians organized their movement. This process accelerated as the initial expectation of an imminent end to history and the return of Christ began to fade. Bishops oversaw the churches of a region, while elders and deacons (who were already functioning during the apostolic period) exercised leadership in individual churches. The term "church" translates the Greek *ekklesia* ("gathering, those called together"), and refers at this stage to the people in the Christian community, either locally or all together, never to a physical structure or a "denomination."

We should not leave the impression of a uniformity of belief and practice in the early stages of the Christian movement. The New Testament itself reflects differing points of view and ways of expressing the faith. It took several centuries for Christian "orthodoxy" to emerge, and not long thereafter for differing interpretations of it to begin to lead to the divisions still evident in Christianity. Some of the early disagreements were over the "natures" of Jesus. Was he a human being, called by God to special work? Was he divine, and in his appearances on earth only apparently human? Or was he both human and divine, and if so, how were these natures related? A variety of groups, linked together by historians under the name "Gnostics," claimed that Jesus was a divine savior who only appeared to be human. Marcionism, named after the second century theologian Marcion, held that there are two gods, one of justice, who created the world, and another of goodness, the father of Jesus Christ, who redeemed the world.

In response to such movements, other Christian leaders sought to develop standards of belief among Christians. One of the earliest expressions of this tendency is the Apostles' Creed, recited by converts to Christianity upon baptism, and still used by many Christian communities as a statement of faith.

The Institutionalization and Spread of Christianity

As the Christian church grew, each of the major cities of the Roman Empire had a Christian community headed by a bishop. Over time the Bishop of Rome became the principal bishop. According to tradition, the Apostle Peter was the first Bishop of Rome, and Peter's centrality among the apostles and in the Jerusalem church supported his leadership. The Roman church and its supporters claimed that among the successors to the apostles the first was the Bishop of Rome, the successor to Peter. By the end of the fourth century the title *pope* was in use to describe the Bishop of Rome. The term "apostolic succession" refers to the principle that the authority of church leaders derived from their historical connection with the apostles of Jesus. That authority passed to those ordained by the apostles and their successors.

Among the Christian churches of the eastern Mediterranean region (e.g., Syria) there was no one central bishop comparable to the Bishop of Rome. For there churches, ultimate authority resided in the gathering of bishops in ecumenical ("general") councils.

In 313 C.E. the Emperor Constantine, after the latest in a series of persecutions of Christians, ordered in the Edict of Milan that Christianity be protected alongside other religions. Twelve years later he convened the Council of Nicaea to reconcile disputes among Christian leaders over the vexing question of the natures of Christ. The Council produced the still-popular Nicene Creed, which affirmed that Christ was "begotten, not made, of the same substance with the Father. . . ." On his death bed Constantine accepted baptism and became a Christian himself.

Under the reign of Theodosius (379–395) Christianity completed its amazing rise from outlawed sect to the official religion of the Roman empire. In 451 another ecumenical Council at Chalcedon in Asia Minor attempted to resolve the dispute over the two natures of Christ by affirming that Christ is "truly God and truly man."

Among the early theologians of Christianity, the one with the greatest influence on the subsequent shape of Christianity was Augustine, Bishop of Hippo in North Africa (354–430). Augustine's conceptualizations of the transcendence of God, the trinity, original sin, divine grace, faith, the sacraments, and the role of the church in history all helped shape orthodox Christian teaching as it is still expressed today. His *City of God* is an inspired defense of the Christian understanding of history against the charge that Christianity had caused the defeat of Rome by the Goths.

Beginning in the third century C.E., a monastic movement institutionalized the Apostle Paul's emphasis on celibacy and the New Testament warning against dependence on material wealth. Monasticism, with its emphasis on self-denial, prayer, and a secluded life, spread from Egypt throughout the Christian world.

The Bishop of Rome evolved into a political as well as spiritual power, but the patriarchs of the East refused to recognize his primacy in either area. In addition, a variety of theological and liturgical differences divided East and West. For example, the churches in the East tended to emphasize more strongly the divinity of Christ, and allowed clergy to be married. The date usually given for the split between Eastern and Western Christianity is 1054, when the Pope Leo IX excommunicated the Patriarch of Constantinople, and Patriarch Michael Cerularius returned the favor, resulting in the "Great Schism" between the two churches. An atmosphere of mistrust continued until 1965, when Patriarch Athenagoras and Pope Paul VI officially overturned the excommunications of 1054.

By the Middle Ages Christianity had become by far the major religion in Western Europe. Except for Muslim dominance in Spain (under the Moors), Europe has remained largely Christian until the present. Accommodations were made to indigenous religions (as, for example, in the dating of Christmas and the naming of Easter), but Christianity succeeded in supplanting native religions, and withstanding the Muslim attempts at invasion. The papacy was the firm anchor during a period that saw the decline and fall of the Roman Empire. Like any power without competition, the Western Church became corrupt. Papal power was often used for material gain, and ordinary people were viewed as a source of wealth to be exploited.

Despite official corruption, Christian theology continued to develop and thrive in the Middle Ages. The writings of Thomas Aquinas (ca. 1225–1274), in particular, had a lasting influence. His major contribution was to draw upon the philosophy of Aristotle to defend rationally such basic Christian conceptions as the claim that God is the creator of the universe, so that they could be accepted on the basis of reason, not just revelation. Thomas set out to show that Christian revelation fulfills rather than contradicts the rational pursuit of truth. The depth and profundity of works such as the *Summa Theologica* make them still fertile ground for those seeking to reflect rationally on Christian teachings.

Reform Movements in Christianity

Beginning in the late Middle Ages, a variety of efforts were undertaken to reform Christianity and restore its original vitality and teachings. These efforts continue to the present.

One of the first major Protestant reformers was the German Martin Luther (1483–1546). Luther became convinced through his study of Scripture that every

Christian was a priest and that salvation was not for the Church to dispense through the sacraments; rather, it was God's free gift received by each individual in faith. He challenged the corruption of the Roman Catholic church, most famously through the posting of his "95 Theses" on the door of the castle church in Wittenberg in 1517.

Other reformers quickly emerged. Perhaps the most influential was John Calvin (1509–1564), who reemphasized the Augustinian doctrines of the sovereignty of God and depravity of humanity. In his role as minister of the church in Geneva, Switzerland, Calvin exercised a great deal of influence in both secular and religious affairs. He discouraged frivolity and stressed hard work and industry. He encouraged the development of businesses through the use of money loaned at interest. The role of Calvinism in the development of capitalism in Europe has been widely acknowledged.

Besides the Lutheran and Reformed (Calvinist) wings of the Protestant Reformation, another group of reformers sparked the Anabaptist movement. Among them were Jacob Hutter (d. 1536), and Menno Simons (ca. 1494–1561), the founder of the Mennonites. The name Anabaptist ("baptism for a second time") comes from the practice of baptizing people as adults rather than as infants (as was the case not only in the Roman Catholic church but also the other branches of the Protestant Reformation). Anabaptists are perhaps best known for their advocacy of pacifism and the strict separation of church and state. Many Anabaptist groups have been persecuted for their beliefs.

In England a formal break with Rome came in 1533, when King Henry VIII refused to accept the Pope's denial of his request for an annulment of his marriage. Henry then founded the Church of England, with himself as its head. In Scotland a follower of John Calvin, John Knox, led a movement that ultimately resulted in the creation of the Church of Scotland, which in turn inspired Presbyterian movements in England and later the United States. "Presbyterian" comes from the New Testament word for "elders," and refers to the belief that the government of the church should be vested in "elders" chosen by the people rather than bishops.

The Roman Catholic Church responded to the various Protestant reforms by instituting a reformation of its own, called the Counter-Reformation. The Council of Trent (1545–1563) set forth positions in opposition to those taken by the Protestant reformers. While Protestants emphasized that Scripture alone was the standard by which teachings of the church should be judged, the Council of Trent stated that the tradition of the Catholic church had equal authority with Scripture. The Council reaffirmed that several books of the Old Testament were indeed Scripture (calling them the *Deuterocanon,* or "second canon"). Most of the reformers had rejected this idea because the books were not part of the Hebrew canon. Most Protestant churches call these works—which include Tobit, Judith, First and Second Maccabees, the Wisdom of Solomon, the Wisdom of Jesus ben Sirach (Ecclesiasticus), Baruch, and supplements to Esther and Daniel—the Apocrypha ("hidden writings"). The Council of Trent also reaffirmed the seven sacraments of the Catholic church, since most reformers claimed that only two (the Lord's Supper and Baptism) were Scriptural.

Major Christian Movements

Tour *The Sacred World* CD!

In this section we will summarize briefly the modern histories and some of the major emphases of the three major branches of Christianity: Roman Catholic, Eastern Orthodox, and Protestant.

Roman Catholicism   From the Council of Trent until the nineteenth century the teachings and structure of the Roman Catholic church remained fairly stable. Papal authority had been challenged in the wake of the French Revolution of the late eighteenth century and the rationalist spirit that swept across Europe after the Enlightenment. However, a nineteenth century movement called Ultramontanism ("across the mountains") strengthened the power of the papacy. In the nineteenth century several major papal proclamations affected church teaching. For example, in 1869 the First Vatican Council promulgated the doctrine of papal infallibility, which said that under certain conditions the utterances of a pope are without error. The conditions were that the pope must be speaking *ex cathedra*—that is, while discharging the office of pastor and doctor of Christians—and speaking to the universal church on matters of faith and morals in his full capacity as successor of St. Peter.

At the end of the nineteenth century a movement called Catholic Modernism tried to examine Church teaching in the light of the modern study of the Bible and the accepted theories of contemporary science, such as evolution. The movement was condemned by Pope Pius X in 1907, but its influence continued among many Catholic scholars. The movement called Neo-Thomism had more success in winning official acceptance for its interpretation of the teachings of Thomas Aquinas using modern developments in philosophy and science.

The most transforming event in the history of Roman Catholicism since the Council of Trent began in 1962 when Pope John XXIII opened the Second Vatican Council. The Council sought to modernize the Church in response to positive developments in the world at large. Among the many changes brought about by the Council were increased use of the vernacular languages in worship, the sharing of papal authority among all the bishops, an increased role for laity in the government of local parishes, acceptance that members of other churches share in God's work of salvation and are legitimate Christians, recognition of the validity of non-Christian religions, and the declaration that all Jews were not to be held responsible for the death of Jesus. Pope John XXIII's successor, Paul VI, presided over the last three sessions of the Second Council.

John Paul II, who was elected as pontiff in 1978, was the first non-Italian pope in modern history. He particularly identified with the plight of the poor and oppressed of the world, and has also been a strong supporter of traditional teaching on birth control and other matters of personal morality. He also opposed the ordination of women and any modification of the teaching that priests who seek ordination before marriage must remain celibate. By the twenty-fifth anniversary of his papacy, John Paul II was slowed by failing health but still traveled around the world to promote the Catholic faith and foster good relations with other Christians and people of other religions. He had become one of the longest-serving pontiffs, and without doubt the most widely traveled pope in history, completing his hundredth trip in 2003.

Eastern Orthodoxy   The Eastern Orthodox branch of Christianity (sometimes called simply the Orthodox Churches) consists of a number of independent national churches, such as the Russian Orthodox Church and the Greek Orthodox Church. Each church is led by a Patriarch, Metropolitan, or Archbishop. There are patriarchates today in Istanbul (formerly Constantinople, in Turkey), Alexandria (Egypt), Antioch (Syria), Jerusalem (Palestine), Russia, Romania, Bulgaria, Serbia, and Georgia. Other Orthodox churches are in Greece, Cyprus, Poland, the Czech Republic Slovakia, the Ukraine, Albania, and Finland. Immigrants have brought the Orthodox Church to Europe, the Americas, Japan, and Australia. The ideal of unity among the Orthodox churches has persevered, despite their essential independence as a result of different political histories.

A great deal of unity in doctrine and liturgy among the Orthodox churches has also been maintained, in part because they all accept as infallible the creeds and dogmas of the seven ecumenical councils. The Orthodox emphasis is on the incarnation of the invisible God in the liturgy and devotional practices of the church—the point is the *experience* of God's holy presence in the sacraments, icons, prayers, and pageantry of the Church. The energies of God (such as glory, light, grace, and love) fill the world and can be personally experienced. Doctrine is not so much expressed in words but sung and lived in the richness of the liturgy. Orthodox worship services are virtual works of art.

Through a life of devotion individuals can become "partakers of the divine nature." The famous *icons* (from the Greek for "image" or "likeness") found in Orthodox churches and homes are stylized paintings on wood or canvas of Christ, Mary, angels, saints, and Biblical scenes. The icons often represent those who have experienced "deification," and now serve to inspire others on that same path. Like the Bible (a verbal icon) the painted icons manifest God's presence, but they are to be venerated rather than worshipped. In Orthodox teaching the honor given to the icon is "passed over" to that which it manifests.

At the close of World War II, every national Orthodox church except the Greek found itself in a hostile political environment. The Russian Orthodox Church, for example, was forced to cooperate with an officially atheist Communist government. After a long struggle, the Russian and other Eastern European Orthodox churches were permitted to send delegates to the World Council of Churches in 1961. As already noted, in 1965 the Patriarch of Constantinople met with Pope Paul VI and officially renounced the Great Schism of 1054. Ecumenical dialogue with both Protestants and Roman Catholics has continued since then.

With the demise of Communism in the former Soviet Union and Eastern Europe a new day of openness and opportunity dawned. In the United States, Eastern Orthodox jurisdictions continue to reflect the ethnic diversity of these immigrant churches. However, there are signs of increased cooperation that may someday lead to greater unity.

Protestantism   All but one of the five major branches of Protestantism active today began during or shortly after the Protestant Reformation. Today they are typically known as "denominations," reflecting the influence of a particularly American phenomenon. "Denomination" refers to a church as a voluntary association that people join. This is in contrast to the practice of national churches with which people are automatically associated, unless they choose to remove themselves. With a wide variety of national churches and dissenting groups in the United States, the principle of separation of church and state was rooted in practical necessity as well as the ideology of individual freedom. The pattern of "denominations" competing in an open religious marketplace for members has spread from the United States to be the characteristic pattern for Protestant churches in the world today (even where national churches are still technically present).

The Lutheran branch of Protestantism was established in Germany and the Scandinavian countries (Denmark, Norway, and Sweden), and has been carried into other areas by immigrants from those countries. The largest among the Reformed churches is the Presbyterian; others include various national Reformed churches (such as the Dutch Reformed). Splitting from the Presbyterians in the United States was the Disciples of Christ denomination and various others.

Another branch is the Baptist, united by the common acceptance of believer baptism. One expression is the Anabaptist wing, including the Mennonites and a famous offshoot of the Mennonites, the various Amish churches. Another expression includes the Baptist churches that trace their roots to the Puritan movement in England during the sixteenth and seventeenth centuries. Among the Puritans who settled in the American colonies were Baptists, including Roger Williams. Today the Southern Baptist Convention is both the largest association of Baptist churches and the largest Protestant denomination in the United States. One of the other major Baptist groups is the American Baptist Churches in the United States of America.

The Anglican Communion, including the Church of England and the Episcopal Church in America, is often called a branch of the Protestant movement because, as we have seen, its origins trace to a break from the authority of the pope in the sixteenth century. However, Anglicanism technically remains Catholic in its own self-understanding and in many of its doctrines, so it is misleading to call it a wing of Protestantism.

The Methodist movement split from the Church of England under the leadership of John and Charles Wesley in the eighteenth century, and spread into other countries. The Congregationalist movement, which emphasizes that the true church is a gathering of people together in a particular place, not an association of local churches or a hierarchy, also emerged out of the Anglican Church in England, as did the Quaker movement (the Society of Friends). Like the Baptist movement, they both arose in the religious turmoil of seventeenth-century England, when the Puritan movement was at its strongest.

The final branch of modern Protestantism is the Pentecostal, including such denominations as the Assemblies of God. This movement began in the late nineteenth- and early twentieth-century in the United States, and emphasizes the literal interpretation of Scripture, a "baptism of the Spirit," and the manifestation of the ecstatic gifts of the Spirit (such as speaking in tongues).

In the nineteenth century, Protestant and Catholic missionaries spread into virtually every country and culture to proclaim the Christian gospel. This involved ministering to the full range of physical, social, and spiritual needs of people. Christian missionaries established schools, hospitals, and other institutions of social welfare. As we noted in Chapter Two, Christian missionaries have often attacked the religions of indigenous peoples, and sought to replace the culture of the native peoples as well as their religion. However, many Protestant churches and the Roman Catholic Church have changed their understanding of mission work in recent decades, to emphasize the development of local leadership and respect for the cultures of other peoples. The movement has come full circle, with missionaries from mission churches begun in the nineteenth century being invited to bring their understanding of the Christian message back to the countries of the original missionaries!

In the twentieth century, Protestantism has been particularly affected by the emergence of a movement known as Fundamentalism. In response to growing openness among many Christian leaders to developments in modern science (such as evolutionary theory in biology) and the application of critical methods to the study of the Bible, some Christians reacted by reasserting teachings that they thought were threatened. These included belief in the inerrancy and verbal inspiration of the Bible, creation in six days, and the virgin birth, bodily resurrection, and second coming of Christ. Each of these doctrines had been reinterpreted by Christians who sought to adapt Christian teaching to the new scientific worldview. Some Fundamentalists have remained within traditional denominations and tried

An image of the Virgin Mary and the baby Jesus at a Catholic shrine in Chennai (Madras), India. The pieces of yarn tied to the shrine's screen are common offering by Indian women seeking divine help in giving birth.

to influence the leadership and doctrine of the church, while others have rejected "denominationalism" and started independent churches. The term "fundamentalist" is now being widely applied to traditionalist movements in other religions.

Other Developments

Tour *The Sacred World* CD!

The Charismatic Movement   Another important twentieth-century development in Christianity is the charismatic movement. The term "charismatic" comes from the New Testament term for "gift of the Spirit." It has a more specialized meaning than the general understanding of "charisma" as the ability to inspire people. This movement emphasizes the "baptism of the Holy Spirit," in which persons experience what they believe to be the power of the Spirit in their lives. The presence of the Spirit is particularly manifested in the ecstatic gifts. Charismatics believe that they can call upon the power of God in faith, and God will respond with physical healing and other forms of divine assistance. Within virtually all Protestant denominations (and Roman Catholicism) charismatic fellowships have formed. The Charismatic Movement is sometimes called neo-Pentecostalism, and the older Pentecostal churches such as the Assemblies of God are considered exponents of "Classical Pentecostalism."

The Ecumenical Movement   The ecumenical movement is another important twentieth-century development that has principally involved Protestants, but affected Roman Catholicism and the Eastern Orthodox Churches as well. The term *ecumenical* derives from a Greek word used to refer to "the whole inhabited world." The ecumenical movement seeks to increase cooperation among Christian churches, particularly in their mission to the world. In addition, the movement seeks to heal the historical divisions among churches. It also tries to mobilize Christians to confront social problems of poverty and injustice.

The World Council of Churches, which now has nearly three hundred member churches, is a principal expression of the ecumenical movement. Member churches come from the Protestant and Eastern Orthodox branches of Christianity, but do not include the more conservative Protestant churches or the Roman Catholic Church. National movements such as the National Council of Churches of Christ in America also try to increase cooperation. At the local level, there has been increased cooperation, particularly in mission work, among congregations. Since the Second Vatican Council the Roman Catholic Church has been very open to forms of ecumenical cooperation but not actual membership in some ecumenical bodies.

Finally, related to the ecumenical movement is the trend toward union among Protestant denominations. Negotiations among Protestant churches have led to more than fifty such unions since World War II. Some have been the reunion of denominations that had split over doctrinal or political disputes, while others have brought together separate churches for the first time.

THE CHRISTIAN WORLDVIEW

In summarizing the Christian worldview we will emphasize the traditional teachings, but also acknowledge the reinterpretation of these doctrines supported by many Christians today. We will distinguish here between "conservatives" or "traditionalists" who defend traditional teachings, and "liberals" or "modernists" committed to reinterpreting them in light of modern science and critical reflection.

Humanity: One in Christ

Christianity joins Judaism in affirming that humans, male and female, have been created in the image of God and charged by God to care for the earth. From the Christian perspective, humans are more than their material bodies; they have souls. Under the influence of Greek philosophy, Christianity has traditionally emphasized a distinction between soul and body.

According to the Apostle Paul, in Christ all humans are one in Christ, regardless of their ethnicity, social status, or gender (Galatians 3:28, [NRSV]):

> There is no longer Jew or Greek, there is no longer slave or free, there is no longer male and female; for all of you are one in Christ Jesus.

Problem: Separation from God

Like other religions that originated in the Middle East, Christianity teaches that the fundamental human problem is alienation from God. Among the religions in this family, Christianity has tended to emphasize most strongly the underlying state of existence that separates humanity from God. This state of existence is called "sin" and refers to an inherent orientation that humans have to turn away from God. Acts of disobedience ("sins") follow from this state, but the real dilemma that needs to be addressed is the underlying quality of being ("sinfulness").

Traditionally, Christianity has largely emphasized the problem as an individual matter. Individuals are "sinners," and the resolution is personal transformation. However, sin is also seen as a "corporate" concern. Nations can be sinful, as can other human communities. Liberal interpretation has focused on this dimension of sin, to argue that persons need to be liberated not only from their own "sin," but from their entrapment in and by sinful social structures. Moreover, environmental theologians point out that life beyond humanity is endangered by the effects of human sin, and any doctrine of sin must include its ecological dimensions.

Cause: Original Sin

The doctrine of *original sin* developed in Christianity to explain the pervasiveness of sin. This doctrine holds that humans are by nature sinful creatures. Although never directly stated in the Bible (and not accepted by Jewish or Muslim interpreters, or even all Christians), Christians have tended to see in the story of Adam and Eve the basis of a doctrine of "original sin." Moreover, there are passages in the New Testament (e.g., Romans 5:12–19) that may be considered as support for the teaching. The early Christian theologian, Augustine (see above), was the first to express clearly the view that humans inherit the sin of Adam. It should be noted that Augustine developed the theory of "original sin" to counter another Christian theologian's view that all humans are born free from sin, and may choose between good and evil.

This traditional view that all humans inherit the sin of Adam is widely held in Christianity, especially among those on the more conservative side. Other Christians do not view Adam and Eve as actual historical persons whose sin is passed on naturally through human generations. They assert that humans are fully free to choose whether to sin or not. Still others accept original sin as a symbolic way of expressing the reality that all humans share an inclination toward sinfulness in placing "self" over God and others.

In addition, traditional Christianity accepts the existence of Satan and his demonic forces and teaches that Satan seeks to draw persons into sinful behavior. Liberal interpretation tends to view Satan as a symbol for the reality of evil in the world, rather than as a literal being.

End: The Kingdom of God in Heaven and on Earth

Many Christians believe that "life after death in heaven" is the chief goal toward which Christian life is oriented. "Heaven" is seen as a spiritual realm in which God dwells and to which those who experience salvation will go after death to live in eternal blessedness. This is the Kingdom of God, in their view. "Hell" is a place of torment where the damned are destined to spend eternity separated from God. Traditional Catholic teaching adds "purgatory," a place of purification for those who die while still in a state of sin. It is believed that prayers for the souls of the dead can help them attain purification and pass from purgatory into heaven.

According to traditionalist understanding of Biblical teaching, entrance into heaven or hell will occur at the end of time, after the resurrection of the dead and a final judgment. This emphasis on the fate of individuals after death has been challenged by interpreters on the Christian left (as well as some conservative Christians who view it as a distorted reading of the Bible).

Liberal Christians tend to agree with non-Christian critics, who point out that Christian teaching about life after death has often been used to convince oppressed people that they should accept passively their horrible condition on earth because they are going to a "better place." The goal of Christianity, they say, is not so much to prepare individuals for life after death, but to transform life in this world, so that people can experience, here and now, the fullness of life that God intends. They point out that Jesus instructed his disciples to pray for the coming of the Kingdom of God to earth as it is in heaven. In their view, the teachings of Jesus have a this-worldly, rather than an other-worldly emphasis, which contemporary Christians need to reaffirm. "Heaven" and "hell" are symbols of life in harmony with God's intentions or life apart from them, rather than actual places or even states of existence after death, some liberal Christians have contended.

Means: Grace, Faith, and the Sacraments

Tour *The Sacred World* CD!

A basic Christian teaching is that humans are powerless to save themselves from sinfulness. Humans have hope for salvation only because of God's *grace.* God sent his only son, Jesus, into the world to deliver the world from sinfulness. According to traditional Christian teaching, Christ's death on the cross has atoned for human sinfulness, and his resurrection opens the way for humans to enter into eternal life. Anyone who responds to God's free gift of divine grace enters into a new, spiritual life in Christ characterized by love, joy, peace, and hope. The process of growing in this new spiritual life is called *sanctification.*

How is grace made available to humans? In traditional Catholic and Orthodox teaching, Christ established the Church and through the Church humans have access to grace. In particular, the *sacraments* of the Church are the instruments of divine grace. In 1439 the Council of Florence declared that there are seven sacraments: baptism, confirmation into the Church, penance (the rite of forgiveness), eucharist (holy communion, the Lord's Supper), marriage, holy orders (ordination), and anointing of the sick (unction). These were reaffirmed by the Council of Trent.

The Protestant reformers challenged both the number of sacraments and the interpretation of their significance. They said that the only two sacraments instituted by Christ are baptism and the Lord's Supper. The Reformers also said that the sacraments are signs, not instruments of grace. God's grace is received by individuals when they respond in faith to what God has done in Christ, not through the mediation of the Church, they argued. They reemphasized the Apostle Paul's teaching of *justification by faith* to describe what enables humans to overcome sinfulness. The "radical reformers" of the Anabaptist movement rejected the notion of sacraments as related to divine grace altogether, preferring to call baptism and the Lord's Supper "ordinances" instead. Division over the nature and meaning of the sacraments is one of the most significant obstacles to the overcoming of divisions among the Christian churches.

Christianity is still divided over the meaning of the sacrament of Holy Communion (also called the Eucharist or the Lord's Supper). The teaching of the Catholic and Orthodox Churches is called *transubstantiation,* meaning (in its traditional formulation) that the elements of bread and wine are converted into the substance of the body and blood of Christ. The Lutheran position is called *consubstantiation,* meaning that the substance of the body and blood are spiritually present *with* the elements. Other Protestants either follow the Reformed view that Christ is symbolically present when the Church gathers for Communion, or that the meal is merely a memorial of the Last Supper. Some Catholic and Protestant theologians have begun to find common ground in the seemingly opposed traditional teachings.

As we have already noted, the issue of whether to baptize Christians at infancy or when they become themselves believers is a source of division. In addition, the meaning of baptism is also disputed. In Catholic tradition it is necessary for salvation.

Liberal interpreters have tried to move the discussion of the "means of salvation" away from both the subjective individualism of Protestantism and the instrumentality of the Church in traditional Catholicism. Participation in the work necessary to bring about the world of peace and justice that God intends is seen as the way Christians manifest that they have accepted God's grace. This work is the compassionate alleviation of suffering, and action to transform sinful social structures and institutions.

The New Testament, of course, is full of instruction on the way to be obedient to God as disciples of Jesus. According to the New Testament, the right way to live is to "imitate Christ." On the one hand, that means emulating the teachings and actions attributed to Jesus in the Gospels. On the other hand, "imitating Christ" means incorporating into one's life the sacrificial lifestyle symbolized ultimately by the crucifixion, and the spiritual "new life" symbolized by the perceived resurrection of Jesus from the dead.

For most Christians the day in the week set aside for worship is Sunday, called the Lord's Day. It commemorates, they believe, the day when Jesus rose from the dead, and thus the new beginning for all humanity. In the Catholic, Orthodox, and some Protestant traditions the worship on Sunday is called the *mass* (from the Latin *missa,* derived from *dimissio,* meaning "dismissal"). It is a celebration of the Eucharist, with a prescribed order that ends with the words "Go, the mass is ended." Until the Second Vatican Council the Catholic mass was said by a priest in Latin. Since that Council, the mass has been said in the language of the people for whom it is being celebrated. A movement generally known as "traditional Catholicism" has sought to restore pre–Vatican II worship and theology. Protestant worship put less emphasis on the drama of the mass and more on the reading and interpretation of Scripture. In the Pentecostal tradition worship is more spontaneous, with the outpouring of the Spirit manifest in speaking in tongues, healings, and prophesying. Some Protestant groups (notably the Seventh-Day Adventists; see Chapter Fourteen) observe the Jewish Sabbath as their day of worship, claiming that Jesus and the early Christians followed this practice.

Roman Catholics, Eastern Orthodox, and many Protestant churches observe a liturgical calendar, celebrating the various festivals of the Christian year with prescribed readings from Scripture and ritual observances. The two central cycles in this calendar revolve around the celebration of the resurrection and birth of Jesus. The New Testament sets the date of the resurrection in relation to the Jewish Passover. Various reforms of the calendar have led to different calculations of the dates in Western (Catholic and Protestant) and Eastern (Orthodox) traditions, so the Orthodox Easter frequently falls from one to four weeks after the Western Easter. Over time, the tradition developed of a forty-day preparation for the celebration of Easter, called Lent (from the "lengthening" of the days during spring). On the fortieth day after Easter, the Ascension of Christ into heaven is celebrated, and on the fiftieth day Pentecost (commemorating the descent of the Holy Spirit on the Apostles in Jerusalem), the traditional date of the founding of the Christian Church.

A second cycle of festivals developed around the indigenous celebrations of the winter solstice. The earliest to appear was the feast now called Epiphany ("appearance") on January 6th (an Egyptian date for the solstice), commemorating both the birth and baptism of Jesus. In Rome the celebration of the birth of the Invincible Sun (December 25th) became the date for the celebration of the birth of Jesus. The Roman Church adapted January 6th as a day of commemoration of the arrival of the wise men in Bethlehem. The four weeks of preparation before Christmas became known as Advent ("coming"), and celebrated not only a time of getting ready for the celebration of the birth but the anticipation of the Second Coming of Christ.

In addition to these cycles the Christian liturgical calendar includes festivals commemorating saints, typically on the dates of their deaths. The process of "canonizing" saints developed to regulate the calendar. Many Protestant churches deemphasized this aspect of the calendar. Finally, theological concepts (such as the Trinity) have become the basis for special days of observance.

More conservative Protestant churches have rejected some or all of the liturgical calendar of observances because, in their view, it lacks clear Scriptural authority.

The reaction in Christianity in general, but particularly within Protestant circles, to a perceived overemphasis on rituals and doctrines is called *pietism*. Personal prayer and study of the Bible is, in the pietistic tradition, more important than participation in public worship or assent to doctrines. Pietism spread to England and the United States through the English Puritan movement.

Reality: Creation and the Cosmic Christ

Like the other religions that originated in the Middle East, Christianity views reality as the creation of the one God, who transcends the created order. The creation is "good," as created by God. Humanity has been charged with the care of the creation, and the responsibility for maintaining the divinely wrought harmony. However, human sinfulness leads to the abuse and corruption of creation.

Christianity introduces the notion that Christ, as fully divine (as well as fully human), participates in the creation. The New Testament portrays Christ not only as the agent of divine creation but as present in creation, bringing harmony and unity to all reality. The hymn at the beginning of the Gospel of John portrays Christ as the Word, through whom all things came into being (John 1:1–2).

Like the other religions in this family, Christianity is *eschatological* in its view of time. Christian teaching is that time began with God's creation. Since Christians believe Christ is God's agent in the ordering of reality and is present in all reality, the Christian measurement of time naturally is calculated on the basis of the historical manifestation of Christ. Christians traditionally have looked ahead to a time of fulfillment, when God will again send Christ into the world to restore the original harmony (the Second Coming). Christians sometimes speak of already living in the end time, because with the first coming of Christ they believe the new age has broken into time. This helps explain the Christian sense of living in tension with the "world," by which is meant reality corrupted by sinfulness and evil. Christians believe that through faith in Christ they have already experienced a foretaste of the new age, and therefore they feel alienated from the "world" even while they still live in it.

Many liberal Christians, like many Reform Jews, have reinterpreted the traditional eschatological teaching. Rather than looking forward to the literal return of Christ, they see the teaching of Christ's "Second Coming" as a symbolic way of saying that God's intention is for the terrible mess humans have created on earth to be cleaned up. Modernist Christians tend to believe that if this is to happen, however, humans must cooperate with this divine intention and create through their efforts the new age of harmony.

Sacred: One God, Three "Persons"

The traditional Christian understanding of the sacred is expressed in the doctrine of the *trinity:* one God, three "persons." The New Testament does not directly express a trinitarian view of the nature of God, but it does sow the seeds for the doctrine by portraying Christ with the qualities of divinity and emphasizing the role of the Holy Spirit. In particular, the commandment of Jesus to baptize "in the name of the Father, Son, and Holy Spirit" (Matthew 28:19) and Paul's use of the threefold formula in a doxology (Second Corinthians 13:14) form the Scriptural basis for the doctrine.

It took until the fourth century, however, for the theory to be formulated in a final, orthodox version. The Council of Nicaea in 325 C.E. stated that the Son is "of the same substance" as the Father. Debate raged at the Council over one Greek letter. The Greek word for "of the same substance" is *homoousios*. If one letter (an *iota*) had been added, as some at the Council argued, the creed would have said that Jesus is "of a similar substance" (*homoiousios*) as the Father.

The First Council of Constantinople in 381 C.E. upheld the divinity of Father, Son, and Holy Spirit, but said that within the Godhead the Father is "unbegotten," the Son is "begotten," and the Spirit proceeds from the Father. In a move that contributed to the growing hostility between the Eastern and Western churches, the Western church added the word *filioque* ("and the Son"), expressing as dogma the teaching that the Holy Spirit proceeded from the Father *and* the Son.

This formulation hardly resolved the arguments, however. Christian theologians have wrestled with ways to explain how Christians can maintain the unity of God (and avoid tritheism, the worship of "three gods"), yet preserve the humanity of Jesus (and avoid docetism, the teaching that Jesus only appears to be human), and the relationship of the Spirit to the Father and Son (and avoid pantheism, the view that God is present in all reality). Christians consider the Trinity a mystery that defies logical explanation or proof, but that, when accepted in faith, can be understood as revealing the truth about God's nature.

Many contemporary theologians have rethought the doctrine of God in light of the modern worldview and challenges to the traditional view posed by events like the Holocaust. A movement known as "process theology" has, for example, sought to reinterpret the traditional notion that God is a power external to the world who causes events to happen in strict accordance with a preexistent divine plan.

CHRISTIANITY IN THE TWENTY-FIRST CENTURY

Tour *The Sacred World* CD!

The issues facing Christianity in the twenty-first century have evoked responses that cross the traditional demarcations of Roman Catholic, Eastern Orthodox, and Protestant. As we have seen already, phenomena such as the charismatic and ecumenical movements involve members of not only the Protestant churches where they originated but the other branches as well. In general, as the twenty-first century begins, Christians are divided among three broad perspectives, in addition to the historical divisions outlined earlier:

- those who think that emphasis should be placed on adapting traditional Christian teaching and practice to the new insights, methods, and situations emerging in our rapidly changing and increasingly secular world;
- those who argue that traditional teachings (whether derived from the Bible, the church, or an inspired leader) should be even more strongly affirmed in the face of the challenges posed by the modern, secular world; and
- those who seek a middle ground, affirming the core of traditional teachings but also some aspects of the modern perspectives and approaches.

Although they are not clearly expressed institutionally, the patterns in Christianity reflect the Reform, Orthodox, and Conservative movements in Judaism. Other labels that might apply are "liberal, conservative, and moderate," "left-wing, right-wing, and centrist" or "modernist, traditionalist, and accommodationist."

On the "liberal" side are those who think that with too much emphasis on traditional teachings, Christianity risks becoming increasingly irrelevant in the rapidly changing modern world. Christians toward the left on our hypothetical spectrum also think that Christianity has traditionally placed too much emphasis on private, individual morality and not enough on transforming society in response to the fundamental principles of justice and love taught in the Bible. Like those in the Reform movement in Judaism, liberal Christians believe that their position is actually a reaffirmation of the basic principles of the faith.

During the American Civil Rights movement of the 1950s and '60s, liberal Christians took an active role in bringing Christian teaching to bear on the struggle to overcome discrimination against Blacks and other minorities. More recently, liberal Christians have been active in the movements for gender and sexual-orientation equality, justice for oppressed peoples, and environmental responsibility.

On the more radical side of the liberal wing of Christianity, movements have developed that provide a theological basis for militant political action to redress injustices. They continue to be influential in the twenty-first century.

Black theology arose during the Civil Rights movement to challenge the perceived racial bias of traditional Christian theology. Some black theologians call for a totally new black Christianity, which recognizes that "God is black." Others work within existing church structures to overturn teachings and practices rooted in racism.

Similarly, feminist theologians have sought to overcome the masculine orientation present in Christianity, including the limiting of talk of God to masculine language and the refusal in some churches to allow for the ordination of women as priests or ministers. Some feminist theologians argue that a complete break with traditional Christianity is necessary in order to affirm feminine imagery for God and the role of women in religion. Others have sought to reinterpret traditional Christian teaching from a feminist perspective (see Chapter Fighteen).

Black theology and feminist theology are sometimes considered branches within a larger theological movement called liberation theology. In general, liberation theology stresses that the fundamental activity of God is the liberation of humans from whatever keeps them in bondage. Drawing heavily on biblical stories such as the exodus from Egypt, the prophets of ancient Israel who spoke of God's demand for social justice, and the sayings and work of Jesus, liberation theologians say that God is to be found today on the side of the poor and oppressed of the world (see Chapter Fifteen).

Environmental theologians emphasize that God's redemptive work is not limited to, or necessarily focused on, humanity, but rather includes the entire cosmos. Some see in the Biblical tradition, and in the teachings of selected Christian leaders throughout history, the basis for an "ecological Christianity" sensitive to the well-being of the whole environment. We will have more to say about this development in Chapter Fifteen.

More conservative Christians have emphasized the message of personal salvation. The fundamental role of the Church and of individual Christians, they believe, is the worship and praise of God and working to spread the gospel of Jesus Christ to individuals, offering them salvation from their sinfulness so that they may have eternal life. Many Protestants on the right side of the spectrum believe in a literal interpretation of Scripture. Conservative Christians point out that Jesus did not try to change society; rather, he challenged individuals to repent and prepare themselves for the Kingdom of God (which is typically understood in the conservative camp as heaven). Many conservative Christians also point out that the Apostle Paul taught Christians to respect political authorities not undermine them. Some conservatives emphasize the imminent return of Christ to transform this sinful world, making attempts by Christians to alter society not only unnecessary but a sign of a lack of faith in God's promises.

In recent decades, many conservatives have become politically active, because, they assert, society is too dominated by secularists and religious liberals who have too little respect for "traditional values." For example, with the legalization of abortion in the United States, conservative Christians have joined together to work to overturn what they view as a direct violation of the teaching of Christianity about the "sanctity of life" (see Chapter Seventeen). Some conservative Christian leaders have allied themselves with conservative politicians, or entered politics directly, in order to fight for their understanding of Christian principles. On the more radical side of the conservative wing, there is talk of creating a "theocracy" (a government in which religious leaders assume political leadership) to protect Christian values.

In the current highly charged atmosphere, there does not seem to be much room for the "moderate" camp in Christianity. Moderate Christians are those who see merit in both the liberal concern for Christian involvement in righting social wrongs and the conservative emphasis on personal salvation and traditional moral values. They may be involved in some of the activities of both wings, but they reject the more radical stances that so often seem to gain attention. For example, moderate Christians might support a woman's right to choose to have an abortion, as do liberals, but agree with traditionalists that abortion has inappropriately become a method of birth control that devalues life.

In a recent, controversial study (*The Next Christendom*), Philip Jenkins has argued that the center of Christianity is shifting from the Northern hemisphere, with its more liberal orientation, to the more traditionalist South (what has been called "the third world"), where the Christian population is exploding (e.g., 480 million in Latin America, in contrast to 260 million in North America). According to Jenkins, it is more accurately labelled the "two thirds" world. Jenkins contends that "[b]y 2025, 50 percent of the Christian population will be in Africa and Latin America, and another 17 percent will be in Asia." As the center shifts, the trend will be in the traditionalist direction. "Christianity is actually moving toward supernaturalism and neo-orthodoxy," Jenkins contends, "and in many ways toward the ancient world view expressed in the New Testament: a vision of Jesus as the embodiment of divine power, who overcomes the evil forces that inflict calamity and sickness upon the human race." The impact, he says, will be as great as the social and political upheaval caused by the Protestant Reformation. Whether Jenkins is right in his prediction, clearly he is correct in saying that "in its variety and vitality, in its global reach, in its association with the world's fastest-growing societies, in its shifting centers of gravity, in the way its values and practices vary from place to place—in these and other ways it is Christianity that will leave the deepest mark on the twenty-first century" (2002).

CHAPTER SUMMARY

In this chapter we introduced readers to the largest religion in the world today—Christianity. Given its size (two billion adherents), we should not be surprised that Christianity is a complex religion.

To introduce Christianity we told the story of its development from the life of its founder, Jesus of Nazareth, until modern times. We surveyed the life of Jesus on the basis of the evidence found in the New Testament, the early history of the movement that proclaimed Jesus to be the Christ (*messiah*) and the crucified and risen Lord, the institutionalization and spread of Christianity through the Middle Ages, the various reform movements that began with the Protestant Reformation, and the branches of modern Christianity (Roman Catholic, Eastern Orthodox, and Protestant). We concluded our survey with a discussion of various other movements such as the ecumenical and charismatic.

In our discussion of the Christian worldview we highlighted both the traditional understanding of doctrines such as sin and salvation and efforts to reinterpret these doctrines in response to modern developments.

The chapter concluded with a discussion of the spectrum found within Christianity as the twenty-first century begins, and a trend that will shift the center of Christianity from the northern to the southern hemispheres as the century unfolds.

IMPORTANT TERMS AND PHRASES

Anabaptist, Anglican, apocalyptic, apostolic succession, Augustine, Baptist, John Calvin, charismatic movement, Constantine, consubstantiation, cosmic Christ, Council of Trent, Counter-Reformation, covenant, denomination, ecumenical, ecumenical councils, eucharist, *ex cathedra,* fundamentalist, Gnostic, gospel, grace, Great Schism, icons, John Paul II, Kingdom of God, liberation theology, *logos,* Martin Luther, Lutheran, Mary (mother of Jesus), mass, Methodist, natures of Christ, original sin, Orthodoxy (Eastern), Paul, Pentecostal, Peter, pietism, pope, Protestant Reformation, Reformed, sacraments, sanctification, Second Coming, Second Vatican Council, Thomas Aquinas, transubstantiation, trinity, 70 C.E.

QUESTIONS FOR DISCUSSION AND REFLECTION

1. Compare and contrast the Christian story of the life of Jesus with the Buddhist narrative of the life of Siddartha Gautama (see Chapter Four) and the Jain account of the life of Mahavira (see Chapter Five).

2. Compare and contrast Christian beliefs about Jesus Christ with Buddhist beliefs about the Buddha (see Chapters Four and Eight) and Jain beliefs about Mahavira (see Chapter Five).

3. Should someone who seeks to follow Jesus as an ethical teacher or inspired prophet, but does not believe him to be divine, be considered a Christian? Why or why not?

4. Should someone who believes that Jesus is the Son of God but does not belong to or participate in a Christian church be considered a Christian? Why or why not?

5. Interpreters disagree on whether Jesus should be considered the "founder" of Christianity. Does this question have significance for contemporary Christians?

6. What seem to be the most significant differences among the historic movements within Christianity: Roman Catholicism, Eastern Orthodoxy, and Protestantism? Would Christianity be stronger if there were not such divisions? If so, what will cause the divisions to be overcome?

7. How might Christianity change in the next century, as the center of Christianity shifts from the developed countries of the northern hemisphere (Europe and the United States) to the developing countries of the south

(especially Latin America and Africa)? Will the changes strengthen or weaken Christianity?

8. Do you agree that the division between "traditionalists/conservatives" and "modernists/liberals" in Christianity is more important than the differences among the historic movements and denominations? Would Christianity be stronger in the twenty-first century if there were not such divisions? Why are conservative Christian churches growing in number, while more liberal churches are declining?

SOURCES AND SUGGESTIONS FOR FURTHER STUDY

BORG, MARCUS J., 1994. *Meeting Jesus Again for the First Time: The Historical Jesus and the Heart of Contemporary Faith.* San Francisco: HarperSanFrancisco.

DILLENBERGER, JOHN and CLAUDE WELCH, 1987. *Protestant Christianity Interpreted through its Development.* 2nd ed. New York: MacMillan.

CARMODY, DENISE LARDNER and JOHN TULLY CARMODY, 1996. *Roman Catholicism: An Introduction.* Upper Saddle River, NJ: Prentice Hall.

HAUER, CHRISTIAN E. and WILLIAM A. YOUNG, 2001. *An Introduction to the Bible: A Journey into Three Worlds.* 5th ed. Upper Saddle River, NJ: Prentice Hall.

HICK, JOHN H. and BRIAN HEBBLETHWAITE, eds., 1980. *Christianity and Other Religions.* Philadelphia: Fortress.

JENKINS, PHILIP, 2002. *The Next Christendom: The Coming of Global Christianity.* New York: Oxford University.

MCFAGUE, SALLIE, 1987. *Models of God: Theology for an Ecological, Nuclear Age.* Philadelphia: Fortress.

MCGRATH, ALLISTER E., 2002. *The Future of Christianity.* London: Blackwell.

MARTIN, DAVID, 2001. *Pentecostalism: The World Their Parish.* London: Blackwell.

POPE-LEVINSON, PRISCILLA and JOHN R. LEVINSON, 1992. *Jesus in Global Contexts.* Louisville: Westminster/John Knox.

WALKER, WILLISTON, et al., 1985. *A History of the Christian Church.* 4th ed. New York: Charles Scribner's Sons.

WARE, TIMOTHY, 1993. *The Orthodox Church.* New York: Penguin.

WIGGINS, JAMES B. and ROBERT S. ELLWOOD, 1988. *Christianity: A Cultural Perspective.* Englewood Cliffs, NJ: Prentice Hall.

WUTHNOW, ROBERT, 1995. *Christianity in the Twenty-first Century.* New York: Oxford University.

Web Sites

www.acs.ucalgary.ca/%7Elipton/christian1.html
> (a web guide for the study of Christianity, maintained by the University of Calgary library; extensive links to churches, movements, etc.)

americancatholic.org
> (on being a Roman Catholic today; sponsored by the Franciscan Order)

ocf.org
>   (links to a variety of sites on Eastern Orthodoxy)

www.clas.ufl.edu/users/gthursby/rel/xprotest.htm
>   (links to sites for Protestant denominations and movements)

TIME Refer to Pearson/Prentice Hall's **TIME Special Edition: World Religions** magazine for these and other current articles on topics related to many of the world's religions:

•◆ *The Religious Experience: The Legacy of Abraham*
•◆ *Christianity: Missionaries Under Cover; The Lord's Business*

Prentice Hall's **Research Navigator** helps students in their further study of the world's religions. Visit *http://www.researchnavigator.com* for help on the research process and access to databases full of relevant material, including the New York *Times*.

CHAPTER

12

Islam—The Way of Submission to Allah

INTRODUCTION

Islam is both the youngest and, along with Christianity, the fastest growing of the world's major religions. In the early twenty-first century about 1.3 billion people (or one in five people in the world) are Muslims. Muslims come from every nationality and culture, from the southern Philippines to Nigeria. The single largest Muslim community in the world is in the Pacific nation of Indonesia, where 80 percent of the population of 235 million are Muslims. Significant numbers of Muslims are also found in the nations of the former Soviet Union, North and South America, Africa, China, and Europe. About 18 percent of the world's Muslims live in the Arab countries of the Middle East. Islam is (or soon will be) the second largest religion in the United States.

Islam means both submission and peace. According to Muslim teaching, the fundamental purpose of human life is to submit to the will of God (*Allah* in Arabic). Submission leads to peace in this life and in the hereafter. The word *Muslim* means "one who submits."

According to Islam, Allah has spoken through a long line of prophets, but Allah's final and definitive revelation was to a man named Muhammad, who lived in Arabia in the seventh century C.E. Muslims believe that the words of God to Muhammad are recorded, as they were heard, in their holy book, the *Qur'an*. As with the other monotheistic religions, the revelation of God laid forth an ethical lifestyle for the faithful to follow.

Since September 11, 2001, interest in Islam outside the Muslim world has risen rapidly. Unfortunately, the exploitation of Islamic teachings by Osama bin Laden and those responsible for the deaths of thousands of innocent people on that day has created confusion about Islam. Our task in this chapter is to look beyond distortions and stereotypes to try to understand what Islam actually is. In this chapter we will trace the development of Islam from the time of the Prophet Muhammad to the present worldwide Islamic revival. Then we will describe the Muslim worldview and reflect on the situation of Islam in the twenty-first century.

STAGES OF DEVELOPMENT AND SACRED TEXTS

According to Muslim teaching, Islam did not begin with the revelation received by Muhammad in the seventh century C.E. The truth of Islam was revealed to all of Allah's prophets, beginning with Adam and Noah, and through them to every people and nation through history. However, because we have discussed some of the earlier revelations in the previous two chapters, it is appropriate to begin this chapter with the one Muslims believe to be the final prophet: Muhammad, who received a revelation that summed up and perfected all that had been made known by Allah through earlier prophets.

Arabia in the Seventh Century C.E.

 Tour *The Sacred World* CD!

The indigenous religion of pre-Muslim Arabia was animistic. The high god in the tribal polytheism was called *Allah* ("the God"); Allah was surrounded by a pantheon of other deities and spirits, including demonic spirits called *jinn*. In the Arabian city of *Mecca*, located on the major north-south caravan route, a large black meteor was venerated as a spirit in an enclosure called the *Kaaba* ("cube"). Each year time was set aside for pilgrimages to the Kaaba, and various tribes vied to control it.

The Prophet Muhammad

 Tour *The Sacred World* CD!

The Prophet Muhammad was born in 570 or 571 C.E. He was orphaned soon after his birth and adopted by his uncle, *Abu Talid*, a leader of the Quraish tribe of Mecca. Muhammad had no formal education and remained illiterate throughout his life. As he grew, he was known for his spirituality, truthfulness, generosity, sincerity, and ability to arbitrate in disputes. He was always a believer in the one God and rejected the idolatry so common in Arabia at the time.

At age twenty-five Muhammad married a forty-year-old widow named *Khadija*, whose wealth allowed Muhammad freedom for private spiritual discipline and reflection on the situation of people in the world around him. In the years after his marriage, Muhammad spent time meditating in the hills surrounding Mecca. He had become convinced of the coming judgment that Zoroastrianism, Judaism, and Christianity describe, and agonized over the fate of those who worshipped idols. He was also concerned about the oppression of the poor and weak in society.

While Muhammad was meditating during the month of Ramadan on Mt. Hira in his fortieth year, an angel, whom he later learned was Gabriel, appeared and spoke to him. Gabriel commanded him to "Read [or, Recite] in the name of thy Lord." This was the first of a number of such revelations Muhammad received during the next twenty-three years. He memorized what he heard, and it was written down by others. The content of these visions became the Muslim sacred text, the Qur'an.

Muhammad began to proclaim a message of the absolute unity of Allah. Because the people of Mecca benefitted from the pilgrimages to the shrines at the Kaaba, they did not respond enthusiastically to Muhammad's challenge to worship Allah alone.

Muhammad's first convert was his wife, Khadija. Then his cousin, 'Ali (who had married Muhammad's daughter, Fatima), and a slave that Muhammad had freed,

Zayd, accepted Muhammad's call to an exclusive faith in Allah. A friend, *Abu Bakr,* converted next. Then others slowly joined them, mostly from the lower classes of Meccan society. As opposition grew, Muhammad sent some of his followers to Abyssinia (the present Ethiopia) to avoid persecution, and perhaps to prepare the way for his joining them.

In 622 Muhammad did make a journey, but not to Ethiopia. Rival groups in the Arabian city of Yathrib (later called *Medina,* or "City of the Prophet") asked Muhammad to come to resolve property disputes. Opposition in Mecca had grown to the point that Muhammad's life was in danger, so he left Mecca and went to Medina. His migration (*Hijra*) from Mecca to Medina marks the beginning of the Muslim calendar. Dates are listed A.H. (for "year of the *Hijra*"). In Medina Muhammad gathered a faithful following. Here Muhammad established the first truly Islamic community, the model for all later Islamic societies.

Only a year after Muhammad's arrival in Medina, his Meccan opponents organized an attack on their rival. The conflicts were at first caravan raids, but gradually escalated into a full war. By 629 the new faith Muhammad proclaimed had become so strong that the Meccans could not resist when Muhammad brought some of his followers to Mecca for a pilgrimage. A year later Muhammad led a force that conquered Mecca. He forgave his former enemies, but destroyed the idols in the *Kaaba,* leaving only the black meteoric stone and its enclosure intact. According to Muslim belief, the *Kaaba* had been built by the Prophet Abraham and his son Ishmael. Muhammad reestablished the rite of pilgrimage to Mecca, which Muslims believe had been initiated by Abraham himself.

From this point on Islam grew steadily, and Muhammad was the undisputed political as well as religious leader of Arabia. Tribal leaders swore their loyalty to Muhammad, and he began to invite other nations to join the new "nation of Islam."

When Muhammad died in 632, at the age of sixty-three, he left no provision for succession. His friend Abu Bakr emerged as the first *caliph* ("successor"), but, as we shall see, the question of the rightful succession to Muhammad was to be the issue that led to the major division in Islam.

The Holy Qur'an

Tour *The Sacred World* CD!

The Holy Qur'an ("reciting, recitation") is, for Muslims, the direct Word of Allah. It is the final, definitive revelation to humanity. Muslims believe that the Qur'an is the unadulterated record of God directly speaking to all humanity. The collected revelations are for Muslims a guide to individual and collective life and thought.

Muslims believe that the Qur'an is eternal and irrevocable. It cannot be translated for it is God's own speech; to try to express it in another language distorts its meaning. Therefore, Muslims, regardless of their native tongue, strive to memorize the Qur'an in Arabic. Many commit all 114 *surahs* ("chapters") of the Qur'an (about the length of the Christian New Testament) to memory. Those who do are called "guardians of the Book in the heart." The first words that a baby born into a Muslim family hears are verses from the Qur'an, as are the last words a dying Muslim is told. The Qur'an is also used to teach children to read Arabic.

The *surahs* of the Qur'an (after the first) are organized in terms of length, approximately from the longest to the shortest, rather than in terms of topic or date of receipt of the revelation. Each *surah* has a name rather than a number, usually taken from a word unique to the surah. Some examples are "Night," "The Cow," and "Unity." Together they form a mosaic of repeated images and themes.

The content of the Qur'an ranges from hymns in praise of Allah and the myriad of "signs" of Allah in the world to warnings about the coming Day of Judgment. Many exhortations to pious living, reminders of God's involvement with people in the past through a series of prophets, and guidelines for personal as well as social morality are also found.

Muslims call the Qur'an simply "The Book." They recognize the legitimacy of the Scriptures of Jews, Christians, and Zoroastrians (although they feel they were corrupted during transmission), but the Qur'an is the final and definitive Word of God. It sums up and corrects the revelations given to the earlier prophets of the other traditions. When Muslims pray, they recite verses from the Qur'an. It is chanted, sung, and meditated upon. To touch "the Book" one must be ritually pure.

The Qur'an is the principal foundation for all aspects of Muslim life. Its language sets the standards for determining grammatical rules in Arabic. Its guidelines are used as the basic laws in Muslim societies. Artists paint its verses on buildings with an elaborate calligraphy. Ordinary people pattern their speech and their behavior after it.

The Spread of Islam and the Rise of Islamic Civilization

Despite the problems of succession, Islam quickly began to move beyond Arabia. Muhammad had united the desert tribes of the peninsula into an awesome fighting force, and the Byzantine and Persian Empires that controlled the Middle East were in decline.

Muhammad's friend Abu Bakr, the first caliph, died within a year of succeeding the Prophet. The second caliph, *'Umar,* remained in power from 634 until 644. Under his leadership, the ancient city of Damascus fell in 635 to Muslim forces, as did most of Syria. By 637 the Sassanid Empire centered in what is now Iran had fallen to the Muslim armies. In 638 Jerusalem was conquered, and all of Palestine was soon under Arab control. Unlike other conquerors, the Muslims did not destroy Jerusalem. The Jewish and Christian inhabitants greeted the Muslims as liberators, and, in turn, the Muslim army respected these "people of the Book" and their places of worship. By 611 Egypt fell, and Muslim armies began to move across North Africa.

As a result of these conquests, the treasuries of Medina filled with tribute. When 'Umar was assassinated by a Persian slave in 644, Muhammad's father-in-law, *'Uthman,* succeeded him. He ruled until 656. After a long campaign (640–49), Persia fell to the Muslims. Three years later, most of Asia Minor was in Muslim hands.

The next caliph was Muhammad's son-in-law and cousin 'Ali. 'Ali's two sons were Muhammad's only male descendants. He took power amidst controversy and soon was forced to flee into Iraq. In 661 'Ali was murdered.

After 'Ali's death, the *Ummayad* dynasty began. The Ummayads were members of Muhammad's tribe, who argued that succession should be kept within the tribe, but not limited to Muhammad's immediate family or associates. The Ummayads established their capital in Damascus, and ruled over a vast empire stretching ultimately from southern France to China. In 711 Muslim armies crossed the Mediterranean and entered Spain, initiating the Moorish culture that dominated Spain for nearly eight hundred years. The northward expansion of Muslim political power was not halted until the Battle of Tours in 732.

In 750 the *'Abbasid* dynasty replaced the Ummayad (except in Spain) and moved the center of Islamic rule to Baghdad, Iraq, where they ruled until 1258. Baghdad became a center of Islamic culture and religious cooperation, with Jews and Muslims working together. Their scholarship preserved the works of Greek philosophers and scientists. The 'Abbasid dynasty succeeded in spreading Islam to the East, into India and ultimately into China.

In the early ninth century the united Muslim Empire began to split into competing factions. Spain remained under Ummayad control, and Cordoba became a great cultural center. Egypt, Syria, and Palestine fell under the influence of dynasties more oriented toward the *Shi'ite* branch of Islam (see below). Then the *Seljuk* Turks gained power in the Middle East. They were the ruling power when the Christian Crusaders entered the region. One of the greatest of all Muslim leaders, *Salah-al-Din,* led the resistance to the Crusaders, recapturing Jerusalem in 1187. Jerusalem was rebuilt with the massive walls that still demarcate the old city.

The spread of Islam into sub-Saharan Africa had begun early in Islamic history, with communities established in East Africa (in what is now the Sudan and Somalia). North African traders carried Islam into West Africa. By the fourteenth century Indonesia had become a Muslim region, and the faith was carried into other Pacific islands. The growth of Islam in Africa and the Pacific region continued despite the European colonization of these areas.

Mongols from eastern Central Asia invaded the Middle East in the thirteenth century under the leadership of Genghis Khan, and held power in Iraq and Persia for a century. The power of the Muslim faith proved strong, as many of the Mongols converted. The erosion of Mongol control opened the way for the emergence of new Islamic empires, including the Moghul Empire of India and the Ottoman Empire centered in Asia Minor.

The Islamic civilizations of the Middle East brought about great advances in medicine, mathematics, physics, astronomy, geography, architecture, art, literature, and history that were to have a profound influence on Western culture. Mathematical systems and innovations such as the Arabic numerals, algebra, trigonometry, and the vital concept of *zero* (from the Arabic word *sifr*) entered Europe by way of Islam. The navigational instruments that were to make possible the voyages of discovery by European explorers also were developed by Muslim scientists. For eight hundred years Arabic was the major intellectual and scientific language of the world.

Muslim armies had reached India by the eighth century, but it was the largely peaceful migration of Muslims across the Indus River into India that led to Muslim control in parts of India by the early thirteenth century. Most of India came under Muslim control by 1526, and the Moghul Empire was created. Famous Moghul rulers such as Akbar ruled much of India until the British rose to power, finally abolishing the Moghul Empire in 1857.

The Ottomans, named after Othman, the first ruler of the Ottoman Empire, were nomadic Turkish tribes who migrated from Central Asia into Asia Minor, the modern Turkey. They seized Constantinople in 1453, and the Ottoman Empire became the most powerful in the world during the sixteenth and seventeenth centuries. The empire reached the height of its power under Suleiman the Magnificent, who ruled from 1520 until 1566. His armies conquered Hungary and northern Africa. Ottoman territorial expansion continued until Austrian and Polish troops turned back an assault on Vienna, Austria in 1683. Hereafter, the power of the empire began slowly to wane. The Ottoman was the last great classical Muslim empire to fall, lasting until World War I. With the creation of the Republic of Turkey in 1922, it officially came to an end.

By the eighteenth century many parts of the Muslim world had already begun to feel the impact of European expansionism. By the nineteenth century and continuing into the early twentieth century, European powers (especially Great Britain,

France, and Holland) had established colonies in formerly Muslim areas, from North Africa to Southeast Asia. Colonial rule replaced centuries-old Islamic institutions.

Many Muslims today believe that the decline of Islamic civilization occurred not only because of external European domination but also because of weakening faith among Muslims. Only through a revitalization and renewal of Islam would the situation change, they claimed. The stage was set for the revival of Islam that continues today, and to which we will return. First however, we will introduce the major branches of Islam.

The Branches of Islam

Islam has not splintered into as many factions as other religions. There is still a remarkable unity within Islam, a testament, Muslims believe, to its clarity of teaching and inclusiveness. However, the Muslim world *is* divided into two great movements—*Sunni* and *Shi'ite*—principally over the question of proper succession to the Prophet Muhammad.

Sunni: **The Way of Tradition**   The Sunni is the largest of the two main branches of the Islamic family; roughly 85 percent of the Muslims in the world identify themselves as Sunni Muslims. The name "Sunni" comes from *sunna* ("way, manner of acting").

The Sunni branch of Islam is committed to following the faith and practice established by Muhammad and the four "righteous caliphs," the first four successors of Muhammad. The primary authority, of course, is the Qur'an, the Word of Allah revealed to Muhammad and collected by the first caliphs. However, some circumstances require guidance that the Qur'an does not cover directly. In this case, appeal is made to the *hadith* ("speech, news"), short narrative reports of what the Prophet said, did, and allowed (or did not allow), as well as indications of his attitude while he ruled in Medina. As time passed, the validity of various *hadith*—or "traditions" as we might call them—was tested on the basis of the chain of transmission through which they passed from Muhammad's time onward. For Sunni Muslims the Qur'an and *hadith* serve as the primary source of guidance for all aspects of communal and personal life.

As time passed, circumstances arose for which neither the Qur'an nor *hadith* gave clear guidance. To fill the void Muslim scholars appealed to two other sources to determine the proper path. One was to seek the consensus (*ijma'*) of the Muslim community, at first in Medina at the time of Muhammad, but later of the local Muslim community where a decision was needed. Another was to draw an analogy (*qiyas*) from the teachings of the Qur'an or *hadith* and apply them to the new circumstance. For example, although the Qur'an does not specifically outlaw the use of drugs such as cocaine, its prohibition of other intoxicants may serve as an analogy for taking a stand against illicit drug use today. *Qiyas* also opened the way for the application of reason to the determination of the right decision. The role of Muslim legal scholars was enhanced by the need for scholars (*ulama*) to determine consensus and draw analogies.

The term that developed to cover the entire body of authoritative Muslim teaching on how to live was *Sharia* ("Way"). It is often translated simply as "law," but its range of meaning is wider, including personal and social morality, religion, and philosophical reflection, in addition to legal matters. Today Sunni Muslims believe that both individual and communal life should be guided by the Sharia, for it is the way of life ordained by Allah. Traditionally, Islam has recognized no distinction between sacred and secular, between matters of religion and civil concerns.

Four separate Sunni legal schools or traditions developed different emphases regarding the various sources of authority in the determination of Sharia. All four arose during the first two centuries of Islamic history.

The earliest was the *Hanifite* School, established in the eighth century in Iraq. It favors the use of analogy to determine the right path when the Qur'an is not clearly relevant. Hence, this school favors the use of rational judgment of what is best for the common good, even if (in some, very special cases) the ruling conflicts with the apparent meaning of the Qur'an. On this basis, scholars of this school argued that the Qur'an's directive that thieves should have their hands cut off does not apply in all times and places. The Hanifite School is most influential today in Iraq, Pakistan, India, and Central Asia.

The *Malikite* School, established in Medina in the eighth century, used both the Qur'an and *hadith* to determine the proper path, but turned, where necessary, first to the consensus of the community and, finally, to analogy. It is the major school in some areas of North Africa, Egypt, and eastern Asia.

The *Shafi'ite* School also emerged in the eighth century, and was the first to distinguish clearly the four sources of authority mentioned above. This school, like the Malikite, theoretically gives equal authority to the Qur'an and *hadith*, but tends toward the *hadith*'s authority in cases of dispute. This school deemphasizes the role of reason in determining Sharia, appealing more strongly to consensus. Its influence is strongest in Indonesia, but is also felt in Egypt (the Cairo area), eastern Africa, southern Arabia, and southern India.

The last school to develop, the *Hanbalite,* is the most conservative and today the most controversial. It arose in Baghdad, Iraq, in the ninth century and reacted against the reliance on "opinion" in other schools. This school maintains that the Qur'an holds supreme authority. The *hadith* is its only other recognized source of authority. It relies on individual responsibility to follow the dictates of the Sharia, refusing to use speculation to fill in the details. Saudi Arabia and Afghanistan (while under Taliban rule) are the only two modern countries in which the Hanbalite School has dominated—though, as we shall see, its influence has recently spread.

All the Sunni schools are bound together by their allegiance to the Prophet and the Qur'an and basic Muslim theology and ethics, but they differ significantly in their understanding of how Muslims should live in the modern world. We will see more of this diversity when we discuss the status of Islam in the twenty-first century.

Shi'ite: **The Party of 'Ali**   The smaller of the two major movements within Islam (comprising about 15 percent of the Muslim world) is known as the "Party (*Shia*) of 'Ali." As noted, 'Ali was the fourth caliph. He was the cousin of Muhammad, as well as his son-in-law, husband of Muhammad's daughter, Fatima. According to Shi'ites he was the *first* legitimate successor to Muhammad; the first three were "usurpers." 'Ali's youngest son, *Husain,* attempted to succeed his father when 'Ali was murdered, but Husain was captured at Karbala (in modern Iraq) and executed by the Ummayads in 680. The martyrdom of Husain became one of the central dates in the Shi'ite calendar, commemorated with an annual festival in which men whip themselves to identify with the martyr's suffering. The sites of the murders of 'Ali and Husain in Iraq are places of pilgrimage for Shi'ites. Because of the pattern established by Husain, and an ongoing history of persecution, Shi'ites place a particular importance on martyrdom for the true faith.

The Shi'ites call the proper successors of Muhammad *imams* ("he who stands before") rather than caliphs. Imam has various meanings in Islam, because it is also used to refer to those who lead the community in prayer. However, for Shi'ites *the*

Imam is the one endowed with supernatural authority to interpret Sharia during the period in which he rules. 'Ali was the first Imam. Because their decisions on Muslim life carry the authority of Allah, the teachings of Imams in Shi'ite communities are regarded as infallible. Although not a "prophet," the Imam stands as Muhammad did to the people of his age, manifesting perfectly the will of Allah to the community. There is a central Imam in every age, according to Shi'a, but sometimes he is hidden. Love and devotion for 'Ali, and subsequent Imams, is at the center of Shi'ite teaching and worship.

Different Shi'ite sects recognize various numbers of Imams after Husain, before the line was broken and the principle of the "Hidden Imam" began. One sect is known as the "Seveners," for they acknowledge seven Imams after Husain. Another is called the "Twelvers."

Another important Shi'ite belief, which distinguishes the movement, is the notion that one of the hidden Imams will return as the *Mahdi* ("the guided one"). In the *hadith,* the term *mahdi* is sometimes used to refer to a descendant of Muhammad who will restore the purity of the faith. In the Shi'ite movement it is restricted to one of the hidden Imams. The Twelvers, for example, believe that the Twelfth Imam will return as the Mahdi. The time of the Mahdi's appearance is not known, so Shi'ites believe they must live in a constant state of preparation and expectancy. When the Mahdi comes he will lead the entire world into a new age of justice. Many Shi'ites believe the present world is corrupt and awaits the purification of the Mahdi. There are great temptations in the present age, they believe, to turn away from the true faith.

Shi'ites also have a somewhat different view of the Qur'an than Sunnis. Since it does not mention 'Ali, they claim that the revelations received by Muhammad must have been tampered with by the "usurpers" before they were written down. The Qur'an must be carefully interpreted in order for its true, and sometimes hidden, meanings to be understood.

At any time, a small number of interpreters of the Sharia who are particularly learned are accorded in Shi'ite communities the title *Ayatollah* ("Sign or Reflection of Allah"). An Ayatollah is considered to be so righteous and so steeped in the true faith, that he can make independent judgments that carry the authority of the Imam. The most famous of the modern Ayatollahs has been Ayatollah Khomeini of Iran.

The Shi'ite branch is in the majority in modern Iran and Iraq, and is an influential minority in other Muslim countries, including Syria, Lebanon, Saudi Arabia, Yemen, and Pakistan. Smaller numbers of Shi'ites live in India.

Sufi: **The Mystical Movement**

Tour *The Sacred World* CD!

Sufi ("wool clad") is the name given to the mystical movement in Islam. Sufi refers to the woolen garments worn by early members of the school to demonstrate their disdain for worldly things. Like the mystical branches of other religions, Sufism defies easy classification. As one Sufi teacher has observed, "Trying to describe Sufism in conventional language is like trying to send a kiss by a messenger." For Sufis the conventional teachings of Islam are like a shell, and the Sufi wisdom is the hidden kernel inside.

Sufis trace the origin of their movement to Muhammad and the Qur'an, pointing to stories such as the account of Muhammad's ascension to heaven, the so-called "Night Journey," as indications of a hidden, mystical teaching. The Sufis rejected the turn toward worldly ambition that marked the caliphate, and maintained that Muhammad himself taught a simple, spiritual lifestyle.

Mansur al-Hallaj (858–922) was the most prominent and controversial of the early Sufis. He is most famous for declaring in a state of mystical union with Allah, "I am Truth!" Since "Truth" is one of the names for Allah, al-Hallaj was dismembered by other Muslims for blasphemy.

Martyrdoms such as Mansur's forced the Sufis underground. By the twelfth century, secretive Sufi brotherhoods, focusing on saints (*wali*) who had profound mystical experiences, had formed to initiate new members into the mystical teaching. Those initiated were called by the name *fakir* (Arabic for "poor") or *darwish* (Persian for "poor," taken over into English as "dervish"), because of the ascetic lifestyle they practiced. Sometimes fakirs demonstrated their denial of the flesh by walking on hot coals or performing similar feats. Members of an order called the *Mawlawis* practiced a form of ecstatic dancing in which they revolved majestically in circles, like planets around the sun.

Sufi saints became the object of veneration, with intercessory prayers said to them and pilgrimages made to their tombs. To some other Muslims this was a form of idolatry.

However, during the Middle Ages, Sufis also tried to demonstrate that they were just as loyal to the teachings of Islam as other Muslims. Al-Ghazzali (1058–1111), a Baghdad professor, succeeded in synthesizing Sunni teaching with Sufi mysticism in works such as *The Revival of the Religious Sciences.*

The Sufi contention that true religion consists of inward experience of holiness rather than external forms has served as a balance to the more legalistic and ritualistic aspects of Muslim life. Sufi poetry and parables are among the true gems of religious literature. Here is one example from the famous thirteenth-century Sufi poet Rumi (Rumi 1994):

When the rose is gone and the garden faded
you will no longer hear the nightingale's song.
The Beloved is all; the lover just a veil.
The Beloved is living; the lover a dead thing.
If love withholds its strengthening care,
the lover is left like a bird without wings.
How will I be awake and aware
if the light of the Beloved is absent?
Love wills that this Word be brought forth.

The Revival of Islam

Tour *The Sacred World* CD!

Since the decline of European colonialism, beginning after World War I and accelerating after World War II, Islam has undergone an exciting period of reform and revitalization. In general, Muslims have sought ways to express the uniqueness of their heritage in response to the incursions of European (Western) ideas and values. Three different types of responses may be identified (Esposito 1998). Conservative movements have sought to purify Muslim life from what are perceived to be the corrosive influences of secular, Western culture, and to return to the values of the past that caused Islam to flourish. Secular movements are committed to revitalizing Muslim life through critical incorporation of the modern Western ideal of separation of the religious and secular spheres. Modernist movements have attempted to reform Muslim societies through reaffirming basic Muslim values and applying them to the challenges of a changing world, letting go of what are viewed as unnecessary social customs. In this section we will survey a range of conservative, secular, and modernist reform and revitalization movements.

Conservative Movements

THE *WAHHABI* MOVEMENT   The first modern movement to try to purify Islam was the Sunni *Wahhabi* movement of Arabia, which adopted the *Hanbalite* view that the true way is found in rigid adherence to the Qur'an and ways of Muhammad as expressed in the *hadith*. Its founder, Ibn al-Wahhabi (1703–1791), taught that all forms of *shirk* ("idolatry") must be rooted out and crushed, including the Sufi veneration of saints. The Wahhabis (or *muwahhidun*, "unitarians") destroyed shrines and suppressed all activities associated with them. A strict, simple lifestyle was seen as the proper way to live.

When the *Sa'ud* family, which had been in alliance with the Wahhabi movement since its creation, consolidated their control of much of the Arabian peninsula by the mid-twentieth century, the teachings of the Wahhabi were used to guide the practice of Islam in the modern nation of Saudi Arabia. In Saudi Arabia religious police still seek out those who are in violation of the Sharia, and courts impose the penalties called for in the Qur'an and *hadith* (including beheading for adultery) on violators. Men and women are kept strictly separate in public places, even though women are allowed to hold professional and other high positions (in keeping with the principles of the Qur'an that women should have equal opportunity).

With the support of the Saudi government and wealthy individuals, the Wahhabi movement has spread internationally through the building and support of schools (*madrasas*), mosques, and other institutions. As a result, Wahhabism has taken root in Afghanistan, Pakistan, various Central Asia republics, China, Africa, Southeast Asia, and in selected cities in the United States and Europe.

THE MUSLIM BROTHERHOOD   Another manifestation of the commitment to purify Islam from perceived corruption is the Muslim Brotherhood, which was founded in Egypt in 1928 by Hasan al-Banna (1906–1949) and today is active in a number of countries. It is an educational and political movement with the goal of raising awareness in the Muslim world of the need to purge negative, secular influences from Islamic societies. It also seeks to replace powerful elites in Muslim countries, viewed to be under the direct or indirect control of Western powers, with truly Islamic leaders. Hasan taught that Muslims are caught in a struggle (*jihad*) between the forces of Allah and Satan, good and evil, ignorance (*jahiliyyah*) and truth. He viewed the Brotherhood as a nucleus that would serve as the impetus for a truly reformed Muslim society guided by Sharia. He was assassinated by the Egyptian secret police in 1949.

Radicalized by the repression of the Muslim Brotherhood in Egypt, another Brotherhood leader, Sayyib Qutb (1906–1966), rejected the nonviolent strategies of Hasan and issued a call to arms. He is regarded as "godfather to Muslim extremist movements around the globe" (Esposito 2002: 56). Although imprisoned, Qutb published more than forty books spelling out his revolutionary ideology. These writings have had a powerful impact on Osama bin Laden and other Muslim extremists. Just as the Prophet Muhammad and his followers had to take up arms to withstand the pagan forces of evil and ignorance, modern Muslims, Qutb asserted, must engage today in an armed struggle against the secular, materialistic West and corrupt Muslim leaders who are influenced by the West.

Inspired by Qutb's fiery rhetoric, a number of small groups sprang up in Egypt intent on crushing the secular regime of Gamal Abdel Nassar. Qutb was executed in 1966, but his influence lived on. After negotiating a peace treaty with Israel and forging a relationship with the United States, Nassar's successor, Anwar Sadat, was assassinated in 1982 by military officers associated with a faction of the Muslim Brotherhood. Although still officially outlawed in Egypt, the Muslim Brotherhood has been allowed an increasing role in Egyptian political life.

HAMAS   During the first Palestinian *intifada* ("uprising") in the late 1980s, members of the Muslim Brotherhood in the territories occupied by Israel also rejected the group's nonviolent strategy and formed *Hamas,* a movement committed to the armed liberation of Palestine. Hamas is the acronym for *Harakat Al-Muqawama Al-Islamiya fi Filistin* ("the Islamic Resistance Movement in Palestine"). Hamas is also the Arabic word for "zeal, courage, or bravery." The organization seeks to create a Palestinian Islamic state to replace the Jewish State of Israel. It is committed to military action as a legitimate means to free Palestine. Attacks on the "Zionist occupiers" began in 1989 with the kidnapping and killing of Israeli soldiers, civilians, and tourists. In 1992 Hamas initiated car bombings; in 1994 suicide bombings (or as Hamas calls them, martyrdom actions) became the preferred strategy, as they continue to be. Hamas is the largest among several Muslim groups committed to using such tactics to liberate Palestine. The Israeli government has responded with retaliatory strikes on Hamas strongholds after suicide bombings, and targeted assassinations of Hamas and other militant leaders.

THE *TALIBAN*   In 1996, amidst the chaos that followed the expulsion of the Soviet army, the *Taliban* movement seized power in Afghanistan and created the rigidly conservative Islamic Republic of Afghanistan. The movement was led by students who learned the Wahhabi version of Islam in *madrasas* ("seminaries") in neighboring Pakistan. While greeted initially as liberators who restored order to wartorn Afghanistan, the Taliban soon imposed their revolutionary, puritanical version of Islam. Women were prohibited from leaving their homes to go to work, and girls were not allowed to attend schools. In public women had to wear *chadors,* entirely covering their bodies. Men were forced to wear beards, and music and television were banned. Muslims around the world condemned the Taliban as distorters of Islam, and only three nations (Saudi Arabia, Pakistan, and the United Arab Emirates) recognized the Taliban government.

OSAMA BIN LADEN AND *AL-QAEDA*   The Taliban gave refuge to Osama bin Laden, a Saudi who had become the best-known proponent of a worldwide Islamic revolution against the West. He was the son of a wealthy Saudi family who had been radicalized when he joined the movement to liberate Afghanistan from occupation by the Soviet Union in the 1980s. Schooled in the Wahhabi version of Islam—which views anyone (including other Muslims) who engages in "un-Islamic" behavior as a *kufr* ("unbeliever")—bin Laden became convinced that a global struggle (*jihad*) against the West was necessary to defend Islam. Although bin Laden had received American support during the war in Afghanistan, he came to view the United States as the principal source of the evil threatening Islam. In Afghanistan he established *al-Qaeda* ("the base"), a network for those who embraced his militant, revolutionary ideology.

When United States troops entered Saudi Arabia during the first Persian Gulf War in 1991, bin Laden claimed that infidels had invaded the most holy Muslim land. Al-Qaeda was linked to the 1993 bombing of the World Trade Center in New

York, the bombing of a U.S. military compound in Saudi Arabia in 1996, and other terrorist attacks. By 1994 the Saudi Arabian government had renounced bin Laden for his extremism and revoked his citizenship. He took refuge in the Sudan, but was expelled in 1996 and returned to Afghanistan. With the support of the Taliban leader, Mullah Omar, bin Laden established camps to train young Muslims from around the world in his extremist ideology and in guerilla tactics. In August, 1996, bin Laden issued a Declaration of Jihad to drive out U.S. forces from Saudi Arabia, overthrow the Saudi government (which bin Laden claimed was a den of unbelievers), and support revolutionary, Islamic groups around the world, especially in Palestine.

Bin Laden and his followers skillfully used the international media and the internet to promote his cause. In a 1998 interview, bin Laden justified his call for terrorist attacks (Esposito 2002: 24–25):

> There is no doubt that every state and every civilization has to resort to terrorism under certain circumstances for the purpose of abolishing tyranny and corruption. . . . The terrorism we practice is of the commendable kind for it is directed at tyrants, the traitors who commit acts of treason against their own countries and their own faith and their own prophet and their own nation. Terrorizing those and punishing them are necessary measures to . . . make things right.

As a self-appointed religious leader, in 2000 bin Laden issued a *fatwa* ("religious edict") calling for Muslims to kill U.S. citizens. On September 11, 2001, the call was heeded by a group of nineteen hijackers who flew commercial airliners into the twin towers of the World Trade Center and the Pentagon, killing thousands of innocent people from ninety countries, including many Muslims. The United States and a coalition of other nations responded by initiating a campaign against al-Qaeda and other international terrorist groups. By 2002 bin Laden's camps in Afghanistan had been destroyed, the Taliban regime had been removed from power, and terrorist targets were being struck in other countries. Although at this writing the fate of Osama bin Laden is unknown, many of his key lieutenants have been killed or captured, and the ability of al-Qaeda to mount massive attacks such as those of September 11th seems to have been reduced. However, bombings linked to al-Qaeda–related cells in Saudi Arabia and Morocco in May, 2003, and continued indications of the likelihood of new terrorist attacks in the United States and other western countries, suggest that bin Laden's brand of extremist Islam continues to draw support and inspire suicide missions against civilian targets. The invasion of Iraq in 2003, led by the United States, has been cited by al-Qaeda as one more example of the continuing assault by the West on the Islamic world.

THE ISLAMIC REPUBLIC OF IRAN   The leading example of Shi'ite efforts to purify Islam from Western influences is the Islamic Republic of Iran. After several decades of secular reform in Iran under Shah Mohammad Reza, a revolution brought Ruhallah Musavi Khomeini (who was accorded the honorific title Ayatollah), whom the Shah had exiled, and other Shi'ite leaders to power. Devoted Shi'ites saw in the Shah's persecution of the Ayatollah Khomeini and other leaders a modern reenactment of the Ummayad attack on Husain. The dramatic success of the revolution inspired not only Shi'ites but many in Sunni communities as well. Khomeini returned from exile in 1979, the Shah was driven from the country, and an Islamic Republic was formed. The intent of this radical revolution was to create a purified Muslim nation.

Although he was not President or Prime Minister, Khomeini took the position of Guiding Legal Expert, which gave him power to intervene in any area in which he perceived a threat to the will of Allah. The militant Revolutionary Guards were an effective force in thwarting any opposition. They also confronted the "Great Satan" (the United States) through taking American hostages in the late 1970s. During the 1980s, war with Iraq tested the resolve of the Iranians.

Conservative Shi'ite groups in other Muslim countries, such as the *Hezballah* ("Army of Allah") in Lebanon, swore loyalty to the Ayatollah Khomeini and acted as his proxies in guerilla warfare against American, European, and especially Israeli interests. After the death of Khomeini in 1989, moderates were elected to the Iranian parliament. However, their efforts at reform have been thwarted by the conservative clerics of Iran who remain in control.

OTHER MOVEMENTS   Militant Sunni Islam has enjoyed a resurgence in Pakistan and other nations that had at one time turned away from traditionalism. In Pakistan the *Jamaiyyat-i-Ulama-i-Islam* (JUI), a religious party dedicated to creating a puritanical Muslim government, has garnered popular support, but also the opposition of the current Pakistani government. A victory in the early 1990s by strongly conservative Islamic candidates in Algerian national elections was voided by a military coup, which has sparked violent demonstrations in the years since.

In summary, as the twenty-first century begins, the conservative response to the modern world continues to gain strength in Islam. Traditionalist movements have had the most success among the poor and disadvantaged, who respond enthusiastically to calls for a return to the social justice found in the Qur'an and *hadith*. It is important to note that only a very small minority of conservative Muslims support the violence called for by leaders like Osama bin Laden, but the belief in the critical importance of the "Islamicizing" of Muslim societies is widespread in the modern Muslim world. Whether conservatives committed to nonviolent change (in order to create societies more firmly based on Sharia) can successfully distance themselves from the terrorism of extremists like bin Laden remains to be seen.

Secular Movements   Although conservative "Islamicists" garner the most attention among the Muslim responses to the modern world, there are other movements. The secular response to Western influences has sought to separate religion from civil affairs. In Turkey the "Young Turks," who overthrew the Ottoman Empire after World War I, abolished the religious courts and prohibited various public expressions of Islam such as the wearing of *hijab* ("veils") by women. An effort was made to orient Turkey toward the West instead of the rest of the Muslim world. However, the trend toward secularization has been reversed in Turkey, with the electoral success of conservative religious parties, and the reintroduction of the teaching of Islam in schools and other measures.

Secularization (although not to the same extent as in Turkey) was introduced by the Baath party in Syria and Iraq, and has also been influential in Algeria, Albania, Libya, and Egypt. However, in all these countries conservative movements are on the rise, with intense opposition to secularization because of the threat the conservatives feel it poses to the ideal of a true Islamic society.

Modernist Movements   Modernist movements, which arose in nineteenth-century Egypt and India, have tried to steer a middle course between extreme conservatism and secularism. The leaders of modernist movements have argued for a return to the basic values of Islam in order to bring democracy and justice to society, while turning away from customs (such as the segregation of women and men) that have developed in Muslim societies over the centuries. Modernists view such customs as cultural and not part of the essential teachings of Islam.

One influential modernist leader was Jamal al-Din Afghani (1839–1897), who helped spark resistance to British rule in Egypt and who campaigned for a pan-Islamic movement to unite the Muslim world across national boundaries. Another was his student Muhammad Abdul (1849–1905).

Modernists say that Muslims need not turn to the West to learn of democracy and freedom, for Islam manifests these ideals. For example, the assertion of rights for women in Muslim societies, they argue, is not an imposition of Western values but a reaffirmation of the egalitarian principles of the Qur'an. Modernists have also emphasized the teaching that reason cannot contradict revelation, and called for the wider use of Western science, technology, and education to modernize Muslim societies. Like conservatives, modernists argue that all of life should be in conformity with Islamic teaching, but they disagree as to what are essential values that should guide society.

Since September 11, 2001, modernist (and many conservative) Muslim leaders have spoken out vigorously against what they claim is the "hijacking" of Islam by extremists like Osama bin Laden (see, for example, El Fadl 2002 and Wolfe 2002). Modernist Islam is particularly strong today in Muslim communities in Western countries, and in Muslim nations that have dealt directly with the social and economic problems in which extremism is bred.

THE ISLAMIC WORLDVIEW

Despite the diversity we have noted in Islamic history, there is a common core of teaching that virtually all Muslims affirm.

Humanity: From a Single Soul

Tour *The Sacred World* CD!

According to the Qur'an, humans are created from the earth, with Allah breathing His spirit into humanity (*Surah* 32:6–9 [Ali 2002: 272]; cf. 15:28–29, 22:5):

> Such is He, the Knower of all things, hidden and open, the Exalted (in power), the Merciful;—
>
> He who has made everything which He has created Most Good: He began the creation of man with (nothing more) than clay.
>
> And made his progeny from a quintessence of the nature of a fluid despised;
>
> But He fashioned him in due proportion, and breathed into him something of His Spirit. And He gave you (the faculties of) hearing and sight and feeling (and understanding); little thanks do you give!

Gender equality is suggested in the creation of male and female from a single soul (4:1). According to Islam, humans have been created for the purpose of submission to the divine will. Humans have the ability to reason and can determine for themselves that submitting to Allah is the purpose of life. As in Judaism and Christianity, Islam teaches that humans have been given power by Allah over the earth and its creatures (7:10).

Problem: Rejecting Allah's Guidance

Unlike Christianity, Islam has no doctrine of "original sin." Indeed, each child is born with an inner disposition toward virtue, knowledge, and beauty. Allah is gracious in offering humans guidance in the fulfillment of His will, especially in the gift of the Qur'an.

In His mercy Allah desires humans to submit willingly. Because God is omniscient, He knows who will respond to His will and who will not. He appoints the term of each person's life (40:67). Some passages in the Qur'an imply that Allah not only knows the fate of humans, He controls what happens to them day to day. This attitude is expressed in the common expression in Muslim countries, "If Allah wills. . ." (*im' shallah*). Other passages in the Qur'an, however, imply that humans have freedom to decide whether to submit to the will of Allah or to try to resist it. The tension between free will and predestination is one with which Muslim theologians have wrestled over the centuries.

Muslims view life as a testing ground, in which humans are being given the chance to submit willingly to Allah. Muslims agree that humans who try to reject Allah's guidance will find themselves under Allah's power, one way or another. Those who reject Allah's guidance worship other powers, whether another god or something secular. Therefore, another way of stating the basic problem to be overcome is idolatry, the human tendency to worship the creation rather than the creator—for all other powers in the universe, spiritual or secular, are dependent on Allah.

Cause: Distraction

Even though Allah has sent prophets throughout history to point humans toward the righteous way to live, humans stray from this path. For Islam the cause is "distraction." Humans are distracted from the path Allah has revealed by *jinn*, the evil spirits, who appeal to the earthly nature of humans, causing them to forget what their higher, spiritual soul (which is aware of Allah) is telling them to do. Humans are also distracted by the idolatrous tendency discussed above.

Like traditional Judaism and Christianity, Islam also teaches that an evil angel (Satan, or, here, *Iblis*) tries to lure people into turning away from the one true God (7.16–18).

Humans are not by nature corrupt, for as creatures in Allah's image that would imply some imperfection on the part of the Creator. Nevertheless, only the prophets such as Muhammad and Jesus (and in Shi'ite Islam, the Imams) are free from distraction. They can therefore be models for others to follow to overcome this flaw.

End: Paradise and the "House of Islam"

Just as Zoroastrianism, Judaism, and Christianity, Islam is eschatological. Muslims believe that Allah revealed to Muhammad the truth of the "end time," although not when it would be.

The Qur'an points to a Day of Judgment, when people will be judged on the basis of their deeds recorded in a heavenly book, and be led either to heaven or hell (*Surah* 39.68–73 [Ali 2002: 309]):

> The Trumpet will (just) be sounded, when all that we are in the heavens and on earth will swoon, except such as it will please Allah (to exempt). Then will a second one be sounded, when, behold, they will be standing and looking on!
>
> And the Earth will shine with the glory of its Lord: the Record (of deeds) will be placed (open); the prophets and the witnesses will be brought forward; and a just decision pronounced between them; and they will not be wronged (in the least).
>
> And to every soul will be paid in full (the fruit) of its deeds; and (Allah) knows best all that they do.

The Unbelievers will be led to Hell in crowds: until, when they arrive there, its gates will be opened[. . . .]

And those who feared the Lord will be led to the Garden in crowds: until behold, they arrive there; its gates will be opened; and its Keepers will say: "Peace be upon you! You have done well! You enter here, to dwell therein."

Islam also paints a picture of the goal toward which societies are oriented. It is expressed in the oft-repeated phrase *dar al-islam* ("house of Islam or peace"). The ideal society is one that has willingly made the revelation of Allah the basis of its life. Such a society is a truly just and compassionate community. This is a goal that can be achieved before the end time. Just as Medina, then all Arabia, and other nations, submitted themselves to the will of Allah, so can all societies. The conservative interpretation of *dar al-islam* is that the Sharia should be the only law in a society, for all areas of life must be submitted to the will of Allah revealed in the Qur'an and the other recognized sources of determining the right path.

Another important and related Muslim principle is *umma* ("people"). It is the ideal of a single, worldwide Muslim community. Rooted in the Qur'an, *umma* has been used as the basis for various pan-Islamic movements, which have sought to overcome the national and ethnic divisions within Islam. Extremists like Osama bin Laden have attempted to appeal to the concept of the *umma* to enlist the global Muslim community in their terrorist campaigns.

Islam also looks toward the arrival of the figure known as the *Mahdi,* who will bring about a final age of peace and harmony.

Means: A Life of Submission

Tour *The Sacred World* CD!

Islam has no priesthood, no intermediaries between humans and Allah. Each individual and each society is responsible for making the decision to submit willingly to Allah. Islam teaches that all those who examine life rationally will come to faith in Allah and the desire to live a life of submission.

According to the Qur'an, true joy is found in "remembering" Allah. The concept does not mean merely calling Allah to mind, but acting on the basis of a relationship of submission established with Allah. Islam teaches that the right way to live is to submit to Allah and to abide by His teaching revealed through prophets like Moses and Jesus, and finally Muhammad. The Qur'an speaks of the righteous life on almost every page, with its commitment to personal piety and social justice, as the following excerpt suggests (*Surah* 2.177 [Ali 2002: 16]):

It is not righteousness that you turn your faces toward East or West: but it is righteousness—to believe in Allah and the Last Day and the Angels, and the Book, and the Messengers, to spend of your substance, out of love for Him, for your kin, for orphans, for the needy, for the wayfarer, for those who ask, and for the ransom of slaves, to be steadfast in prayer, and practice regular charity [. . .] Such are the people of truth, those who fear Allah.

For the individual the "*five pillars*" constitute the foundation of living. These are the obligations all Muslims recognize. Muslims call them the *'ibadat* ("acts of service").

The Five Pillars   The first of the pillars is repetition of the creed: *La ilaha illa Allah; wa-Muhammadan rasulu Allah* ("There is no God, but Allah; and Muhammad is His messenger [or prophet]"). Called the *shahadah* ("bearing witness"), it is recited daily in Arabic by all Muslims, regardless of their native tongue.

For Islam, Muhammad is the "seal" of the prophets, the last messenger of Allah to humanity. Allah has sent a messenger in every era, beginning with Adam, the first man, and including Noah, Abraham, Ishmael, Isaac, Jacob, Joseph, Job, Moses, Arran, David, Solomon, Elijah, Jonah, John the Baptist, and Jesus. Those who accept these revelations as they have been written down are "People of the Book" or "People of the Covenant" and are deserving of special status and protection, according to the Sharia. However, as we have already noted, Muslims believe these writings have been distorted in transmission and introduce ideas (such as the divinity of Christ) that are not authentic revelations.

Only the revelation that Muhammad recited (the Qur'an) is undefiled, the pure and unadulterated Word of Allah. Muslims do not believe that Muhammad was or is *divine,* any more than any other human being. While they venerate him and seek to follow his example, they do not worship him. You will find no shrines to Muhammad, no statues or pictures to which people bow down.

The way one becomes a Muslim is simply by reciting the *shahadah* with faith. The faithful Muslim recites the creed every day, and it is ideally the last words on a dying Muslim's lips. Once a person has recited the creed in faith, the rest of the pillars are then his or her duty.

The second pillar is daily prayer (*salat*), which Muslims are required to perform five times a day (dawn, noon, mid-afternoon, sunset, and evening). One can always recognize a Muslim community by the sound of the *muezzin* ("crier") calling the faithful to prayer at the five appointed times. He climbs the tall *minaret* ("tower") of the *masjid* (also called the *mosque*) and delivers the *adhan* ("call to prayer"). Four times he calls *Allahu akbar* ("God is most Great!"), then twice the *shahadah.* Then twice each he cries "Come to prayer! Come to salvation!" The vocal call to prayer was chosen by Muhammad to distinguish Muslim practice from Christian and Jewish, which use a bell or wooden clapper and a ram's horn, respectively, to summon worshippers. Today, accommodation has been made to modern technology in some Muslim communities, as timed tape recordings of the *muezzin* replace the human crier.

When responding to the call to prayer, Muslims first purify themselves. At mosques water is usually available for a cleansing of the hands, face, mouth, nose, teeth, and feet. If no water is available, sand is permissible for some of the purificatory acts. If the prayer is in the mosque, worshippers remove their shoes. The worshippers then position themselves facing in the direction of Mecca. The prescribed prayers are said with accompanying bending, bowing, and ultimately prostration on the knees, with head and hands on the ground. This posture symbolizes complete and total submission to Allah. While prostrate the worshipper cries three times in Arabic, "Glory be to my Lord, the Most High!" Most of the prayer is in praise of Allah, but it ends with an expression of concern for others.

Friday is the day of congregational prayer in the Muslim house of worship, the *masjid* (mosque). The mosque is the center of the Muslim community. If possible, Muslims should come to the mosque for daily prayer. However, on Friday it is an obligation for males to come for the noon prayer. On Friday, after the prayer, led by any pious Muslim male functioning as *imam,* the assembled congregation listens to a sermon delivered by a Muslim man learned in the faith. Mosques have tended in Muslim societies to serve as community centers. Since there is no recognized distinction between religion and politics in traditional Islam, the sermons can be calls

The Muslim place of communal prayer and other gatherings is called the masjid (Arabic for "place of worship or bowing down") or mosque. The magnificent Jama Masjid ("Mosque of Friday") in Delhi, India, was built by the Mughal Emperor, Shahjahan, between 1644 and 1658. From the masjid's towers (minarets) worshippers are called to daily prayer.

to political action in the strongest and most unambiguous terms. In many Muslim communities only men come to the mosque for prayer, and women pray at home; where women are allowed to pray in the mosque they do so separately from men, usually in an enclosed area behind the men, so as to avoid the distraction associated with the intermingling of men and women.

The third pillar is almsgiving (*zakat*, which means "purity, integrity"). This is, in effect, a tax on certain kinds of property, including both money and goods, which is paid at the end of each year. Its purpose is to provide for the needs of the poor of the community and for the upkeep of the mosque and other religious institutions. The *zakat* may constitute from 2½ to 10 percent of a person's disposable wealth, depending on the type of property.

The fourth pillar is fasting (*sawm*) during the entire month of *Ramadan*. All Muslims who are sane and in good health are expected to abstain from eating, drinking, smoking, and sexual intercourse during daylight hours each day of this holy month. Mothers nursing infants and travelers are exempted from the rules concerning nourishment. Muslims observing the Ramadan fast usually eat a meal before dawn and another large meal when the Sun sets. Ramadan is the ninth month of the Islamic lunar calendar, thus its dates shift on the solar calendar. Muslims believe that this was the month when Muhammad received his first revelation.

The last pillar is the pilgrimage to Mecca (*hajj*). The Qur'an requires every Muslim man and woman to make the journey to the holiest city of Islam, Mecca, at least once in a lifetime. It is modelled on Muhammad's pilgrimage to Mecca a short time before his death in 632. The *hajj* always takes place in the twelfth month of the lunar calendar. As pilgrims approach Mecca they remove their national dress, and don the simple white garments of pilgrims. This symbolizes their unity with one another as brothers and sisters, regardless of their race, nation, or economic status.

Upon arrival in Mecca, the pilgrim circumambulates the Kaaba seven times. Then the pilgrim goes to a spot where the footprint of Abraham, who built the Kaaba, is preserved. Next the pilgrim visits the well of Zamzam, a site important in the story of Hagar and Ishmael. Hagar, who was a servant of Sarah, the wife of the prophet Abraham, gave birth to Abraham's first son, Ishmael. Muslims believe that the promises Allah gave to Abraham to make of his descendants a great nation passed to Ishmael's family (rather than Isaac's, as Jews believe). According to both Muslim and Jewish tradition, Hagar and Ishmael had to flee because of Sarah's jealousy. On the *hajj,* Muslims run between two "hills" to reenact the flight of Hagar and Ishmael, at the point where she ran back and forth seeking help.

With these acts complete, the *hajj* proper begins. The pilgrims travel for several days to Mina and then Arafat, twelve miles from Mecca. At Arafat they stand from noon to sunset asking for Allah's forgiveness, in apparent anticipation of standing before Allah at the final judgment. The next day the pilgrims return to Mina to cast stones at a pillar representing the forces of evil, commemorating Abraham's rejection of the devil's temptation to disobey God's command that he sacrifice his son Ishmael. They then sacrifice an animal, reenacting Allah's sparing of Ishmael because of Abraham's faithfulness. The final acts of the *hajj* are the shearing of a male pilgrim's hair (and the trimming of a woman's), followed by a three-day festival and a farewell circumambulation of the Kaaba.

Each Muslim is also expected to observe a series of dietary guidelines such as avoiding the eating of pork, the drinking of wine and other intoxicants (extended today by analogy to illicit drugs), and gambling.

It is difficult for persons raised in societies that assume a distinction between religious and secular institutions to understand that no such demarcation has been traditionally recognized in Islam. It was not until Muslim nations came under European influence that the pattern of separating religious and nonreligious life occurred. Traditionally, all of a society's institutions and all societies must submit themselves to the will of Allah revealed through the Prophet. This has meant organizing all of life according to the dictates of the Sharia.

Jihad   One of the most interesting and misunderstood aspects of the Muslim conception of submitting all of life to Allah is *jihad.* Jihad is usually assumed in the non-Muslim world to mean only "holy war," and to refer to a presumedly Islamic idea that Muslims must use aggressive violence to annihilate all the enemies of Allah. (Indeed, this has been the claim of extremists like Osama bin Laden.) In fact, *jihad* means "striving" or "exertion" in Arabic, and refers in general to the Muslim's duty of strenuous exertion in the cause of Allah. According to the *hadith,* the "great *jihad*" is the individual Muslim's struggle against all forms of inner evil; the "lesser *jihad*" is the armed conflict in defense of the faith or its propagation. If a believer is killed in a "lesser *jihad,*" that person goes directly to paradise, without having to wait for the judgment at the end of time.

If the Muslim world is the *dar al-Islam* ("the house of submission"), the rest of the world is *dar al-Harb* ("the house of warfare"). The requirement of jihad is to work vigorously to extend the *dar al-Islam,* by persuasion wherever possible, and through force if necessary. However, force is to be used only to defend against attack by infidels. In fact, the Qur'an forbids the use of force in conversion; people must be allowed to choose freely (2:256).

Reality: The Signs of Allah

The Qur'an includes numerous verses that assert that Allah is the Creator of the heavens and the earth, acting alone (*Surah* 32.4 [Ali 2002: 271]):

> It is Allah Who has created the heavens and the earth, and all between them, in six Days, and is firmly established on the Throne (of authority): you have none, besides Him, on a Day, to protect or intercede (for you): will you not then receive admonition?

Although Allah is separate from the creation, its order and beauty are "signs of Allah" that human reason can discern. Islam has traditionally supported science, the application of human reason to the understanding of the natural world, in the belief that scientific discoveries will inevitably confirm the truth revealed by Allah.

The world is a place of goodness, to be enjoyed. Islam in general has never been ascetic in its attitude toward life in the world.

Like the other major religions that arose in the regions, Islam has a linear view of time. As noted above, Islam dates its calendar from the migration (*hijra*) of Muhammad from Mecca to Medina in 622 C.E.

Sacred: There Is No God but Allah

Islam is strictly monotheistic. Throughout the Qur'an Allah is heralded as the only God (*Surah* 2.255 [Ali 2002: 25]):

> Allah! There is no God but He,—the Living, the Self-subsisting, Eternal.

The Muslim creed—"There is no God but Allah"—and the phrase used by the *muezzin* in calling a Muslim community to prayer—*Allahu akbar* ("God is most great!")—summarize well the basic Muslim attitude toward the sacred. Allah is personal; He alone is supreme. According to the Qur'an Allah has ninety-nine names, but transcends them all. As the first *surah* of the Qur'an makes unmistakably clear: Allah is the transcendent, omnipotent creator, who rules and judges over all. Allah cannot be represented by any image, so you will find no statues or pictures of Allah in mosques or any Muslim home. It is even considered blasphemous to create pictures of humans, for they reflect the image of Allah.

Since Allah is beyond direct human knowing, human knowledge of Allah depends on two sources. If humans observe the creation with minds unclouded by idolatry, they will inevitably come to an awareness of the Creator. Where science seems to contradict what Allah has revealed, then our understanding is inadequate or incomplete. Further study will yield results that are in harmony with what Allah has made known. Allah's ultimate revelation, of course, is the Qur'an, His direct word to all humanity. Its words are Allah's words; therefore to hear them and to recite them is the holiest of actions.

Muslims believe that Allah is the same God who spoke to Zoroastrians, Jews, and Christians. Unfortunately, although the prophets Allah chose to speak to these peoples fulfilled their roles, those who wrote down and transmitted the words have distorted Allah's truth. For example, the Christian idea of the Trinity is blasphemous, for it creates three gods instead of the one true God. Despite what Christianity says, Allah had no son (*Surah* 23.91 [Ali 2002]):

> No son did Allah beget, nor is there any god along with Him, behold, each god would have taken away what He had created, and some would have lorded it over others! Glory to Allah! (He is free) from the (sort of) things they attribute to Him!

Allah is the Supreme Lord, but there are other divine beings in the Muslim spiritual hierarchy. Angels exist as Allah's spiritual messengers; the most famous is Gabriel who was Allah's envoy in delivering the Qur'an to Muhammad. Angels such as Gabriel and Michael are sent by Allah to lead people to the right path. The Qur'an also speaks of an angel who opposes Allah, *Iblis,* the Muslim Satan or Devil. In the Qur'an, Iblis is also identified as one of the *jinn,* spirits, some of whom are good and others evil (although the term usually connotes evil spirits). As the chief of the evil *jinn,* Iblis is a creature of fire who opposes the angels, who are creatures of light. Iblis rules over hell until the final judgment. The existence of Iblis helps to mitigate the more troublesome implications of strict monotheism, giving a place for a force of evil. However, the Qur'an makes clear that Iblis has no power independent of Allah. He is Allah's servant, who may even in the end be redeemed by Allah.

Most Muslims seem to accept fatalism as a natural corollary to belief in Allah's power. Muslims theologians, however, have tried to maintain a balance between Allah's omnipotence and the need to maintain some sense of spontaneity and freedom in the natural world. For the vast majority of Muslims the belief that everything happens as Allah wills, and only as Allah wills, is comforting rather than puzzling.

ISLAM IN THE TWENTY-FIRST CENTURY

Tour *The Sacred World* CD!

Much as are Judaism and Christianity, as the twenty-first century begins, Islam is at a crossroads. Will the influence of traditionalists who intend to restore a "pure" Islam prevail? Or will modernists committed to the reform of Islam, inspired by the basic principles of the tradition rather than detailed laws or customs, win the support of the Muslim world? Or perhaps a secularist backlash to the harshness of the conservative revival, especially in its extreme form, will emerge, and those who wish to follow the Western model of separation of the secular and the spiritual will regain the influence they once had. For the foreseeable future, all three of these trends will continue, and, as some Muslim leaders have described it, a "battle for the heart of Islam" will continue well into the twenty-first century.

Unfortunately, an ongoing backlash in the non-Muslim world after September 11, 2001, will also affect the status of Islam and Muslims in the years ahead. Christian leaders, who influence the views of millions, speak of Islam as a "religion of violence and hate" and perpetuate stereotypes of Islam as old as the Christian Crusades. Expressions of hate are directed against Muslims, ranging from insults shouted at Muslim women wearing head scarves to random killings of Muslims.

Surely, understanding of what Islam actually is, as this chapter has attempted, will continue to be critically important as the century unfolds.

CHAPTER SUMMARY

Islam is the second largest and one of the two fastest growing religions in the world. Early in the twenty-first century, the Muslim population had swelled to 1.3 billion.

Our survey of the stages of development and sacred texts of Islam included discussion of the life Muhammad, in the context of his times; Muhammad's hearing and recitation of the Word of Allah and its commitment to writing as the Qur'an; the spread of Islam beyond Arabia; the emergence of divisions within Islam—into the Sunni and Shi'ite branches, as well as the mystical movement (Sufi); and the various responses of Islam—ranging from very conservative to secularist—to the modern world. We focused special attention on the extremist version of Islam advocated by Osama bin Laden and others.

In our analysis of the worldview of Islam we examined the broad consensus in the Muslim community on issues such as the nature of humanity, the basic human problem (the rejection of Allah's guidance), the cause (distraction by lesser powers and the worship of them), the goal (paradise for the individual after death and the creation of the "house of Islam" on earth), the means to the goal (a life of submission for individuals through observing the "five pillars," and of submission of society through allegiance to the Sharia), and a strict monotheistic understanding of the sacred ("there is no God but Allah!").

We concluded with discussion of challenges facing Islam and those seeking to understand Islam in the twenty-first century.

IMPORTANT TERMS AND PHRASES

Abu Bakr, 'Ali, Allah, *allahu akbar,* al-Qaeda, *ayatollah,* caliph, *dar al-Harb, dar al-Islam,* dervish, *fatwa,* five pillars, *hadith, hajj, hijra,* Hamas, Husain, Iblis, *ijma', imam, im' shallah, jihad* (greater and lesser), *jinn,* Kaaba, Khadija, Mahdi, Mecca, Medina, *musjid,* mosque, *muezzin,* Muhammad, Muslim Brotherhood, Osama bin Laden, People of the Book, *qiyas,* Qur'an, Ramadan, Salah-al-Din, seal of the prophets, *shahadah,* Sharia, Shi'ite, *shirk,* Sufi, Sunni, *surah,* Taliban, *ulama, umma,* Wahhabi

QUESTIONS FOR DISCUSSION AND REFLECTION

1. Compare and contrast the Muslim narrative of the life of Muhammad with the stories of the lives of Jesus (see Chapter Eleven), Siddartha Gautama (see Chapter Four), and Mahavira (see Chapter Five).

2. Compare and contrast Muslim beliefs about Muhammad with Christian beliefs about Jesus, Buddhist beliefs about Siddartha Gautama, and Jain beliefs about Mahavira.

3. Compare and contrast Muslims beliefs about the Qur'an with Jewish beliefs about the Torah and Christian beliefs about the Old and New Testaments.

4. What accounts for the rapid spread of Islam in the early centuries after its founding, its later decline, and its revival in the mid-to-late twentieth and early twenty-first centuries?

5. Compare and contrast the responses to the modern world in Islam with those found in Christianity and Judaism.

6. What is Osama bin Laden's understanding of Islam and the Qur'an? The vast majority of Muslims believe Osama bin Laden and extremists like him have "hijacked" Islam. What do they mean?

7. How have the events of September 11th, 2001, affected your understanding of and attitude about Islam? Did you encounter any discriminatory and hateful comments or actions against Islam or Muslims after September 11th? If so, what were they and how did you respond?

8. Some Christian leaders have described Islam as "a religion of hate and violence." Based on your initial study of Islam, do you agree with that assessment?

9. The Qur'an speaks of the "bliss" that awaits believers. From a Muslim perspective, how is bliss found? Compare this approach to "bliss" with the Buddhist understanding (see Chapters Four and Eight).

10. Why is Islam growing rapidly in the developing countries of Africa and Asia?

11. What needs to happen for greater understanding and cooperation to occur among the religions that all recognize Abraham as an ancestor: Judaism, Christianity, and Islam?

SOURCES AND SUGGESTIONS FOR FURTHER STUDY

ALI, ABDULLAH YUSUF, TRANS., 2002. *The Qur'an: Translation.* 9th ed. Elmhurst, NY: Tahrike Tarsile Qur'an.

ARMSTRONG, KAREN, 2002. *Islam: A Short History.* New York: Modern Library.

CRAGG, KENNETH AND R. MARSTON SPEIGHT, 1998. *The House of Islam.* 3rd ed. Belmont, CA: Wadsworth.

EL FADL, KHALED ABOU, 2002. *The Place of Tolerance in Islam.* Boston: Beacon.

EL FADL, KHALED ABOU, 1996. *Islam and Democracy.* New York: Oxford University.

EL FADL, KHALED ABOU, 1998. *Islam: The Straight Path,* 3rd ed. New York: Oxford University.

EL FADL, KHALED ABOU, 2002. *Unholy War: Terror in the Name of Islam.* New York: Oxford University.

ESPOSITO, JOHN L., 2002. *What Everyone Needs to Know about Islam.* New York: Oxford University.

HUNTINGTON, SAMUEL, 1998. *The Clash of Civilizations and the Remaking of the World Order.* New York: Touchstone.

LEWIS, BERNARD, 2003. *What Went Wrong: The Clash Between Islam and Modernity in the Middle East.* New York: HarperPerrenial.

NASR, SEYYED HOSSEIN, 2002. *Islam: Religion, History, and Civilization.* San Francisco: Harper-SanFrancisco.

NASR, SEYYED HOSSEIN, 2002. *The Heart of Islam: Enduring Values for Humanity.* San Francisco: HarperSanFrancisco.

NASR, SEYYED HOSSEIN, ET AL., 1988. *Shi'ism: Doctrines, Thought, and Spirituality.* Albany: State University of New York.

PICKTHALL, MARMADUKE, TRANS., 1953. *The Meaning of the Glorious Koran: An Explanatory Translation.* New York: New American Library.

RUMI, JALALUDIN, 1994. *Teachings of Rumi,* trans. E. H. Whinfield. London: Octagon Press.

TAMIMI, AZZAM AND JOHN L. ESPOSITO, ED., 2000. *Islam and Secularism in the Middle East.* New York: New York University.

VIORST, MILTON, 2001. *In the Shadow of the Prophet: The Struggle for the Soul of Islam.* Boulder, CO: Westview.

WOLFE, MICHAEL, ED., 2002. *Taking Back Islam: American Muslims Reclaim Their Faith.* Emmaus, PA: Rodale.

Web Sites

islam101.com
>   (an introductory site on Islam)

www.uga.edu/islam/
>   (site maintained by Prof. Alan Godlas at the University of Georgia, with excellent links for the study of Islam)

al-islam.org
>   (a general site on Islam, with a Shi'ite orientation)

ias.org
>   (the site of the International Association of Sufism)

islamdenouncesterrorism.com
>   (a site explaining why Islam is opposed to terrorism)

TIME   Refer to Pearson/Prentice Hall's **TIME Special Edition: World Religions** magazine for these and other current articles on topics related to many of the world's religions:

- ➜ *The Religious Experience: The Legacy of Abraham*
- ➜ *Islam: The Women of Islam; A Jihadi's Tale; As American As . . .; Voices of Islam*
- ➜ *The Impact of Religion: In the Heart of Hate*

    Prentice Hall's **Research Navigator** helps students in their further study of the world's religions. Visit *http://www.researchnavigator.com* for help on the research process and access to databases full of relevant material, including the New York *Times.*

CHAPTER

13

Sikhism—The Way of the Guru

INTRODUCTION

The placement of Sikhism in a survey of the world's religions poses a problem. Since Sikhism emerged in India, it would be appropriate to discuss Sikhism along with the other religions of South Asia (Hinduism, Buddhism, and Jainism). However, Sikhism arose against the background of Hinduism and Islam, so we have delayed our discussion of Sikhism until readers have had the opportunity to encounter the basic history and teachings of Islam.

As we examine Sikhism we will point out Hindu and Muslim elements. However, its "syncretistic" context (combining and synthesizing beliefs) should not be allowed to obscure the uniqueness of Sikhism. It stands alone as a distinct and important religion. It is today a global religion.

We will first discuss the stages of development and sacred texts of Sikhism, from its founder Nanak through the modern period. Then we will introduce the Sikh worldview, before concluding the chapter with a discussion of Sikhism in the twenty-first century.

STAGES OF DEVELOPMENT AND SACRED TEXTS

Founder: Nanak

Tour *The Sacred World* CD!

Once Islam had come to dominate much of India, a series of Hindu reformers came under the influence of the strict monotheism and anticeremonialism of the Muslim faith. They applied these ideals to the *bhakti* movements within Hinduism (see Chapter Three), and proclaimed a message of liberation from the cycle of rebirth through heartfelt devotion to the one true God for anyone, regardless of caste.

One such reformer was a weaver named *Kabir* (1440–1518). Although born a Muslim, he accepted the Hindu analysis of the human predicament, while rejecting the authority of the Vedas in resolving it. Kabir combined Hindu *bhakti* devotionalism with Muslim Sufi mysticism (see Chapter Twelve), and taught a path of love of God, which leads to absorption into the divine. He carried his message across the north Indian plain, winning devotees to this synthesis of the two religions. He also emphasized the need for the guidance of a spiritual teacher, a *guru*. In his poems, Kabir challenged the narrowness of Hindus and Muslims. One can still find in India small sects that claim to follow Kabir.

One of those who came under the influence of Kabir was *Nanak*. He was born in 1469 to Hindu parents in the Punjab region, in an area which is now part of Pakistan, about thirty-five miles from the city of Lahore. It was a time of turmoil, with recurrent hostility between Hindus and Muslims.

According to his religious biography, from an early age Nanak was a poet who tended toward religious musing. His father was intent on having him follow the family tradition and become a businessman. Nanak entered business, married and had two sons. But he showed no proclivity for commerce. Like other founders of religions, Nanak left his family in order to devote himself to his spiritual quest. He spent increasing time singing hymns to God. One of his friends, a Muslim minstrel named Mardana, joined with him in a small band dedicated to discovering the truth.

The turning point for Nanak came when he was thirty. According to one tradition, he was bathing when he disappeared in the water. Those present assumed he had drowned, but he had actually been taken into the presence of God. God commissioned Nanak to go and repeat the Divine Name and tell others to do likewise. God also challenged him to remain unpolluted by the world, to practice charity, ritual bathing, service, and meditation. When Nanak reappeared, he uttered the words that were to become the theme of his message: "There is no Hindu; there is no Muslim."

Like other religious founders, Nanak wandered through the region, teaching his message to any who would listen. He travelled with Mardana and together they sang praises to God, who had revealed himself to Nanak as the *True Name*. Nanak wore a combination of Hindu and Muslim garments. According to some traditions they travelled to Arabia, where they visited the holy cities of Islam, Mecca and Medina. In all his travels, Nanak's greatest success came in the Punjab region of his birth.

Among Nanak's poems is the following evocation of the human relationship with God (Cole and Sambhi 1978: 39):

> Oh, my mind, love God as a fish loves water:
> The more the water, the happier the fish,
>   the more peaceful his mind and body.
> He cannot live without water even for a moment.
> God knows the inner pain of that being without water.

When Nanak neared death in 1538, his Hindu and Muslim followers debated over the fate of his body. Following their heritage, the Hindus wanted to place his body on a pyre and cremate him. In accord with their tradition, the Muslims wanted to bury him. One night, the dying Guru Nanak told his Hindu devotees to place flowers on his left side and his Muslim disciples to lay flowers to his right. Those whose flowers remained fresh in the morning, he said, would have the right to his body. He drew a sheet over his body. In the morning, when his followers withdrew the sheet, his body was gone and the flowers on both sides were fresh.

The Gurus after Nanak

For the first two hundred years after the death of Nanak, the community of his followers had a series of human leaders. The community became known as *Sikhs* (from the Sanskrit word for "disciple"). The first Guru (as the Sikh leaders were called) after Nanak was Angad (1504–1552). He compiled a collection of Nanak's and his own hymns, and established the custom of a communal feast for disciples known as the *langar.*

The fifth Guru, Arjan (1503–1606), compiled the *Guru Granth Sahib* (also called the *Adi Granth*), the Sikh scripture (see below). He also built a Temple in the middle of a pool, at a site in Punjab that became known as *Amritsar* ("the pool of immortality"). Arjan helped establish a unique Sikh identity and functioned as a political and economic leader. As a result of his political activity, Arjan was arrested, tortured, and killed by Muslim leaders.

Arjan's son succeeded him as Guru Har Gobind (1606–1645). As the sixth Guru he followed his father's political direction and created the first Sikh army, leading them into battle against the Muslim Moghuls. The pacifism taught by Guru Nanak had fallen victim to the growing hostility between Sikhs and Muslims.

The tenth and last human Guru, Gobind Singh (1675–1708), created a military fraternity that still plays a prominent role in Sikh life. The account of its formation, the "Five Beloved Ones," is one of the most powerful Sikh narratives. It tells of Gobind Singh calling for volunteers who would surrender themselves completely in order to protect Sikhism. Five of his disciples responded. One by one Gobind Singh called them into his tent. Each time the Guru emerged with a bloody sword, indicating that the volunteers had given their lives for their Guru. Only after all five had willingly gone into the tent, did the Guru present them alive to the gathered congregation as the *Panj Pyares* (Five Beloved Ones).

Called the *khalsa* (the "pure"), the members of the fraternity Gobind Singh created become through initiation *singhs* ("lions"). The ceremony includes *amrit* (holy nectar) and water stirred by a sword (indicating strength), into which sweets have been placed (suggesting compassion). As their distinguishing marks they wear the same "five k's" that were first bestowed on the Five Beloved Ones: *kesh,* uncut hair; *kangha,* comb; *kachh,* short pants; *kara,* steel bracelet; and *kirpan,* sword. Male members of the *khalsa* wear turbans to cover their long hair. From the beginning, men of all castes have been eligible for membership; in more recent times, girls have been included as initiates, taking the name *kaur* ("princess"). The Singhs were a fearsome fighting force, starting the tradition that the finest soldiers in India would be Sikhs. Today, although Sikhs constitute only about 1.5 percent of the Indian population, roughly 30 percent of the Indian army is Sikh.

Guru Adi Granth (The Granth Sahib)

After Guru Gobind Singh's assassination, he was succeeded not by a human leader, but (at his direction) by the Sikh Scripture, the *Adi* ("first") *Granth,* as Guru. (The text is also known as the *Guru Granth Sahib.*) Since 1708, Sikhs have venerated the Granth as their spiritual leader, considering the collection the embodiment of the ten human gurus. Each morning a copy of the Granth is symbolically enthroned and worshipped at the Golden Temple in Amritsar; at night it is put to rest. Sikh children are typically given a name whose first letter is taken from the first letter of a verse of the Adi Granth chosen at random.

The Granth Sahib ("Book of the Lord") includes about six thousand hymns: those of Nanak and the next four Gurus as well as compositions by Kabir, and other Hindu and Muslim poets. Over two thousand hymns are attributed to the fifth Guru, Arjan, who compiled the collection.

The Resurgence of Sikhism in Modern India

After the demise of the Mughal Empire in India, a Sikh empire (1801–1849) under Maharaja Ranjit Singh was formed. Despite the Muslim persecution of Sikhs, the Sikh empire practiced toleration of Muslims. When the British government took control of India in 1848, Sikhs put up the noblest resistance. They were subdued, and their empire ended. However, their fierce fighting and pledge of loyalty after defeat won the respect of British authorities.

The British gave the Sikhs considerable autonomy under their rule, although this only caused many Sikhs to long for full independence. Sikhs were active participants in the movement for Indian self-determination. One of the major turning points in the struggle was the massacre by British forces of 379 unarmed persons, mostly Sikhs, rallying in the holy Sikh city of Amritsar in 1919.

When Britain withdrew from India in 1947, creating the nations of India and Pakistan, the results were tragic for the Sikhs. Their Punjabi homeland was split between the two countries. More than two million Sikhs had to flee Pakistan, even as Muslims flocked from India into the new Muslim state. Holy sites, including the birthplace of Nanak, were left behind in Pakistan, as were many profitable Sikh farms. Sikhs were not adequately compensated for their economic losses, and Sikh political autonomy was thwarted by increasing centralization in the new India. One Sikh leader bitterly summarized the situation by saying, "After independence the Hindus got India, the Muslims got Pakistan; we got nothing."

Punjab is the richest agricultural area of India. Under Sikh leadership, about 80 percent of the food produced in India comes from the Punjabi region. However, in a democratically elected central government, the Sikhs can wield little political power. They were unable, for example, to stop the diversion of water from the Ganges River into Hindu areas.

Most Sikhs are political moderates; one of them (Zail Singh) took the symbolic office of President of India in 1982. However, frustration over their impotent political situation has led some Sikhs to call for the creation of an independent Sikh nation, to be known as *Khalistan* ("land of the pure"). Drawing on their militant heritage and fired by a new spirit of Sikh traditionalism, some Sikh extremists formed a paramilitary force, which mounted assaults on Hindu civilians. In June, 1984, the Indian army responded to these attacks by moving against Amritsar, where the extremists had their headquarters and arsenal. In the assault, twelve hundred Sikhs and two hundred soldiers were killed. Four months later, two of Indian Prime Minister Indira Gandhi's elite Sikh bodyguards assassinated her. Thousands of Sikhs were slaughtered by Hindus in a wave of retaliatory violence. Indira Gandhi's son and successor, Rajiv Gandhi, sought reconciliation with the Sikhs, and an accord was reached in 1985. However, violence has continued, with additional assaults on Amritsar and assassinations by Sikhs of government officials.

In addition to the emergence of Sikh traditionalism in India, more moderate forms of Sikhism have enjoyed a resurgence, some outside India. After 1947 many Sikhs migrated to England, and to the Western United States and Canada. They formed communities, which in some areas have attracted converts to the healthy lifestyle of the religion.

THE SIKH WORLDVIEW

Although Sikhism is an amalgamation of Hindu and Muslim teachings, it may be more accurate to say that it is a manifestation of the basic Indian worldview, expressing the Hindu *bhakti* viewpoint with certain Muslim (largely Sufi) adaptations.

Humanity: A Pearl in an Oyster

For Nanak all humans are inherently good. Like a pearl in an oyster, we only await the shell to be opened so that the pearl may emerge. In other words, humans have a spiritual nature, which is pure and good and eternal.

Human souls reflect the image of the True Name, as this passage from the Adi Granth testifies (Singh 1962: 825):

> Wondrous and peerless is the Gospel of the Lord:
>   Our Soul is the image of the Transcendent God.

Like Islam, Sikhism stresses the equality of all humans, for God's light dwells equally in all, regardless of gender, caste, or religion. At Sikh holy sites, members of untouchable castes are invited to bathe in the purificatory water alongside Brahmins.

Problem: Living Apart from God

Unfortunately, humans choose to live in a way that distorts their spiritual nature. In short, we live apart from God and are stuck in the unending cycle of rebirth. Sikhs accept the idea of *karma* (see Chapter 3) as an impersonal law that explains the entrapment of the soul. Because of *maya* (illusion), we are unaware that our true nature is hidden.

Cause: Egoism

The cause of our entrapment is egoism, leading lives that revolve around the fulfillment of earthly desires, as another passage from the Adi Granth teaches (Singh 1962: 644–45):

> The elephant is lured by lust to his enslavement and he goeth as he's led by
>   another.
> And the deer is lured to death by the sweet melodies of music.
> Seeing his family the man is enticed away by the sense of possessiveness and
>   the love of Maya (the illusory material world).
> And then one becometh a part of it and owneth it he,
>   but it for sure leaveth him in the end.
> Without God all other lives are painful.

This again shows the influence of both Hinduism, with an emphasis on attachment to the self caused by desire, and Islam, with an emphasis on idolatry (worshipping earthly things, rather than God). Egoism involves lust, anger, greed, attachment, and pride.

End: Absorption in God

Like other religions originating in South Asia, Sikhism envisions release from the cycle of rebirth as ultimate transformation. For Sikhs the image of liberation is absorption into God, blending our light with the eternal light. The Adi Granth describes this state of union poetically (Singh 1962: 87):

> I wandered and wandered and there arrived at my Home;
> And I found what I had longer for.
> O Saints, he, the Guru, Satiates all, and Awakens our Intuition to see our
>   Lord[. . .]
> I have described Him as I Saw Him;
> But he alone hath his Taste who Knoweth His Mystery;
> And one's Light Mergeth in the All-light, for, Nanak, the One alone
>   Pervadeth all.

This reflects the influence of Hindu devotionalism as well as the mystical teaching of Muslim Sufism that God saturates all reality. The bliss of absorption into God can be reached in this life, by those who follow the right path.

Means: Praise and Compassion

Tour *The Sacred World* CD!

Like many Hindu *bhakti* schools, Sikhism teaches that the way to reach liberation is through devotion to the one true God, and that in the current evil age the best way to show devotion is through repetition of the name of God. However, praising God's name must not be mindless repetition. It must be a kind of meditation, which focuses and stills the mind and which takes root at the depths of one's being. The prayer of the repetition of God's name is far better than pilgrimages to shrines, worshipping images, or practicing asceticism. Devout Sikhs rise before dawn, bathe, and recite the *japji*, which begins with the *Mul* (root) *Mantra* (Macauliffe 1963: 195–96):

> There is but one God whose name is true, the Creator, devoid of fear and
>   enmity, immortal, unborn, self-existent; by the favour of the Guru.
>   REPEAT HIS NAME
> The True One was in the beginning;
>   The True One was in the primal age.
> The True One is now also, O Nanak;
>   The True One also shall be.
> By thinking I cannot obtain a conception of Him, even though I think
>   hundreds of thousands of times.
> Even though it be silent and I keep my attention firmly fixed on Him, I cannot
>   preserve silence.
> The hunger of the hungry for God subsideth not though they obtain the load
>   of the worlds.
> If man should have thousands of devices, even one would not assist him in
>   obtaining God.
> How shall man become true before God?
> How shall the veil of falsehood rent?
> By walking, O Nanak, according to the will of the commands
>   preordained[. . . .]

Faithful Sikhs also offer evening prayers, devoting up to two hours a day to this individual worship.

In houses of worship known as *gurdwaras* ("house or gateway of the Guru"), Sikhs gather intermixed by caste and gender for *kirtan* (congregational worship). The Guru Granth Sahib is displayed regally at the front of the sanctuary and honored by respected men in the *sangat* (congregation), who wave symbolic whisks over it, as servants would a king. When they enter, Sikhs bow before the Guru Granth Sahib. Songs of praise are sung and the Adi Granth is read aloud. At night the book is lovingly returned to a place of rest.

Each individual must learn to discipline himself or herself; there is no one formula for all to follow. The guidance of the Guru Granth Sahib is essential, however. Without a guide we will only wander aimlessly, unable to reign in our egos.

In addition to the repetition of God's name, Sikhism stresses lives of compassion. Sikhism does not subscribe to the social barriers of the caste system, and men and women are treated equally. The symbol of Sikh compassion is the *langar,* the feast of the Sikh community. When a *langar* is held, it must be opened to everyone, especially those who are hungry because of poverty. Sikh *gurdwaras* also serve as way stations for travelers in need of a place to rest.

Unlike other religions originating in India, the eating of meat is not seen as wrong by Sikhs. Sharing the Muslim view that God gave lesser animals to humans for food, Sikhs believe it is permissible to consume the flesh of clean animals.

Reality: Penetrating the "Wall of Falsehood"

According to Sikh teaching, God created the material world by drawing the veil of *maya* around himself. Thus the world has reality, but it is a snare, a "wall of falsehood" for those seeking spiritual liberation. It must be penetrated by those who would see true Reality. The true Reality is One, like the Advaitan teaching of philosophical Hinduism (see Chapter Three), but true Reality is the personal God, as Islam and devotional Hinduism hold.

Sacred: The True Name

According to Sikhism God is One, supreme, the uncreated creator of all things, the all-knowing and all-compassionate. God's love is inexhaustible. God is the True, the ultimately Real. God is beyond our ability to describe or name. In Sikh writings God is addressed as Father, Lover, Master, and the True Creator (the Hindu name *Hari* ("Kindly") is also common). However, when speaking of God, Sikhs prefer True Name (*Nam*), because all other specific names are limiting.

Sikhism is monotheistic, for the True Name is the transcendent creator of all. However, the True Name also pervades all reality. As one of the Gurus said (Cole and Sambhi 1978: 74): "God abides in everything. See him, therefore, in your heart."

SIKHISM IN THE TWENTY-FIRST CENTURY

At the beginning of the twenty-first century, the number of Sikhs worldwide stood at about 23 million, making Sikhism the fifth largest of the world's religions (after Christianity, Islam, Hinduism, and Buddhism). The vast majority of Sikhs still live in northwest India, in the Punjab region and in Delhi. However, there is a sizeable Sikh diaspora. At last estimate, several hundred thousand Sikhs lived in the United

Preparations for the traditional langar (feast) at a Sikh place of worship (gurdwara) in Delhi, India. The communal meal prepared by Sikhs is open to all, regardless of gender, ethnicity, religion, or social status. It symbolizes the Sikh commitment to the equality of all people.

Kingdom, the same number in Canada, and up to two hundred thousand in the United States.

The violence spawned by the movement to create an independent Sikh homeland has subsided, though the fervor for Khalistan has not. One of the hundreds of web sites dedicated to the movement (www.panthkhalsa.org) includes the following appeal:

> No nation can survive without political power. We must rededicate ourselves to the freedom of the Sikh Nation and to accomplishing our dream of Raj Kare Ga Khalsa, a free Khalistan[. . . .] Sikhs who do not support Khalsa Raj are hypocrites who are lying to the Guru. Political power is the sine qua non for the survival of any nation.

However, not all Sikhs are comfortable with such militancy. They point to the tolerance and respect taught by Nanak and the emphasis on personal spirituality in Sikh tradition. They advocate a Sikhism that recognizes the truth of all religions and promotes unity rather than division among peoples.

CHAPTER SUMMARY

Sikhism began in India in the fifteenth century C.E., founded by a poet and religious teacher named Nanak, who sought to reconcile Hindus and Muslims by synthesizing the two religions. Guru Nanak drew particularly on Hindu devotionalism (*bhakti*) and Islamic mysticism (Sufi).

Nanak's pacifism was replaced by Sikh militancy when Muslims began persecuting Sikhs and killing the successors of Nanak as Guru. After ten human Gurus, the Sikh scripture (the Adi Granth) was installed as Guru. A militant fraternity was created to protect Sikhs from persecution, and Sikh warriors gained a reputation for their military prowess. After the British left India, the Sikh homeland was divided between India and Pakistan, causing millions of Sikhs to flee into India. A movement to create an independent Sikh homeland (Khalistan) gained strength, leading to a violent confrontation between Sikh militants and the Indian government. Though the violence has subsided, the campaign for Khalistan still has wide Sikh support. However, other Sikhs reject this militancy as antagonistic to the Sikh tradition of respect for all peoples and religions.

Influenced by Islam, Sikhism is monotheistic, worshipping the one God known to Sikhs as True Name. As with Hindu teaching, humans are understood to be trapped in a cycle of rebirth by attachment to the material world. Following the *bhakti* tradition, Sikhs sing praises to God. Sikhism has also been influenced by the Muslim commitment to social justice and equality of all people before God. It reflects the mystical trends in both Hinduism and Islam, speaking of "absorption into the True Name" as the ultimate transformation.

As we begin the twenty-first century, some Sikhs continue to struggle for greater autonomy or an independent homeland in India, while others are more focused on their individual spiritual journeys.

IMPORTANT TERMS AND PHRASES

Amritsar, Guru, Guru Adi Granth (Guru Granth Sahib), Guru Gobind Singh, *japji*, Kabir, *kaur*, *khalsa*, *kirtan*, *langar*, *maya*, Nanak, Punjab, Sikh, Singh, True Name, five k's

QUESTIONS FOR DISCUSSION AND REFLECTION

1. Compare and contrast the Sikh account of the life of Nanak with the narratives of the founders of other religions you have studied.
2. Was it inevitable that Sikhism would turn away from peaceful practices and toward the use of violence?
3. What are the adavantages and disadvantages of a sacred text, rather than a human leader, serving as the Sikh Guru?
4. Should Sikhs have their own independent homeland? If so, on what territory (India and/or Pakistan) should Khalistan be created? Are Sikhs justified in using violence to attain independence from India? Why is it unlikely that the central governments of India and Pakistan would allow an independent Sikh nation?

SOURCES AND SUGGESTIONS FOR FURTHER STUDY

COLE, W. OWEN AND PIARA SINGH SAMBHI, 1978. *The Sikhs: Their Religious Beliefs and Practices.* London: Routledge and Kegan Paul.

MACAULIFFE, M. A., 1963. *The Sikh Religion: Its Gurus, Sacred Writings and Authors.* Vol. 1. Delhi: S. Chand.

MCLEOD, W. H., 1989. *The Sikhs.* New York: Columbia University.

OBEROI, HARJOT, 1994. *The Construction of Religious Boundaries: Culture, Identity, and Diversity in the Sikh Tradition.* Chicago: University of Chicago.

SINGH, DARAM, 1997. *Sikhism: Norm and Form.* New Delhi: Vison and Venture.

SINGH, GOPAL, TRANS., 1962. *Sri Guru Granth Sahib.* Vol. III. New York: Taplinger.

SINGH, GOPAL, TRANS., 1979. *A History of the Sikh People 1469–1978* New Delhi: World Sikh University.

SINGH, HARBANS, 1964. *The Heritage of the Sikhs.* New York: Asia Publishing House.

Web Sites

sikhs.org
> (a "Sikhism home page")

allaboutsikhs.com
> (a "gateway to Sikhism")

 Prentice Hall's **Research Navigator** helps students in their further study of the world's religions. Visit ***http://www.researchnavigator.com*** for help on the research process and access to databases full of relevant material, including the New York *Times*.

CHAPTER

14

The New Religious Movements—Renewal and Innovation

INTRODUCTION

A survey of the world's religions would not be complete without attention to religions that have sprung up in the modern era. Almost all of the religions discussed in this chapter originated in the nineteenth or twentieth centuries. Some emerged from the major religions discussed in the previous chapters. Others are religions with a spiritual ultimacy, but which do not claim to be associated with any of the major religions. Still others are secular religions with material patterns of ultimacy.

After accounting for the rapid growth of these religions and discussing the problems associated with studying them, we will examine a representative sampling of new religious movements. In selecting from among the thousands of new religions estimated to be practiced by nearly two hundred million people today, we have chosen religions that are well-established in North America.

The Rapid Growth of New Religious Movements

Why are there so many new religions and why are they growing in popularity? The reasons are debated by interpreters; here are but a few possible explanations.

One cause is the growing individualism in the modern world. Even in cultures with a strong tradition of group solidarity, such as Japan, people are increasingly willing to step out on their own, and turn from the traditional religious commitments of their families. A characteristic of new religions is that they often provide an alternative communal atmosphere.

A related reason is growing alienation from traditional religions, creating an environment in which people are more willing to associate with religions that offer alternative approaches to basic human questions and responses to contemporary ethical issues.

On the other hand, some new religions claim to return to the "true teachings" of a religious tradition, and appeal to some people's desire to retreat from the chaos and confusion they perceive in the modern world.

Other new religions appeal to many people's fears and fascination about the future, offering myths that guarantee that those who embrace them will have their futures secured when the "end" comes.

The rapid development of the Internet and other innovative forms of communication must also be considered a factor in the rapid growth of new religions. New religions now have access to fairly inexpensive means to communicate their messages, and to research that shows them how to "package" their messages effectively so that people today will respond. Many new religions are making more effective use of modern communications technology than the more traditional religions.

Another factor is the bureaucratization of some of the major religions, which has made it more difficult for people to see them as communities responsive to their spiritual needs. New religions effectively address the needs of persons in a way that often seems less organizationally structured than major religions.

Finally, many people today yearn for clear and straightforward messages expressed by forceful leaders. A common denominator of most new religions is the presence of a charismatic leader, who has a vivid and appealing message that is delivered in an engaging style of communication.

Problems in Studying New Religious Movements

The "Cults" Controversy Many of the religions discussed in this chapter have been called "cults" or "sects." Speaking descriptively, a *cult* may be considered a religious movement that focuses on one aspect of a religion or a single figure (such as a particular saint in Christianity); a *sect* is a religious group that has split from another movement or is a particular group within a larger religion. However, in common usage the terms "cult" and "sect" have become negative labels to refer to religious groups in which, it is argued, fanatical loyalty to a central leader clouds the members' judgment and causes them to sacrifice their individual will and identity for the sake of the group. From this perspective, cults and sects subject people to psychologically coercive recruitment and indoctrination practices ("brainwashing") and practice rejection or hatred of the rest of society. Portrayed negatively, cults and sects are "parasitic," receiving funding through deception for the personal gain of the leadership elite, but performing no service for society.

After such horrific events as the mass suicide of nine hundred people at the People's Temple in Guyana in 1978, and the tragic deaths of more than ninety people at the Branch Davidian compound in Waco, Texas in 1993, concern has grown and questions have been raised (but not resolved) about how such "dangerous groups" can be effectively monitored and controlled.

In the highly charged religious atmosphere of the early twenty-first century, the debate rages over which new religious movements are "dangerous" and which are merely unique but legitimate expressions of the human quest for ultimate transformation. Some observers might consider the movements discussed in this chapter offensive "cults or sects" that should be exposed as such. Others would remind those critics that some of the major religions of today (for example, Christianity) were condemned as dangerous cults or sects when they originated.

Many experts on the new religions to be discussed in this chapter now contend that the term "cult" (and, to a lesser extent, "sect") has become so loaded and devalued that it should not be used at all in serious discussion. We will honor that recommendation.

We choose the more neutral designation "new religious movements" to name the religions discussed in this chapter, in order to maintain the descriptive approach to the study of religions outlined in Chapter One. Our intention in this text is to describe, not evaluate, these movements. However, where serious charges have been made by responsible critics about activities of the religion being discussed, these allegations will also be noted.

Classifying the New Religious Movements   In this work, we will organize our study of new religious movements on the basis of types, related to the basic theme evident in the religion. We have chosen to highlight the following orientations, because they seem to be the most common among the new religious movements. We have selected only a few of the myriad new religious movements to illustrate each type.

- Preparing for the End: Apocalyptic New Religious Movements
- Faith and Spirit: New Religious Movements of Healing and Awareness
- Reviving the Church: Christian New Religious Movements of Renewal
- Nature and Spirit: Earth-based and Ecological New Religious Movements
- Liberation and Enlightenment: New Religious Movements with Asian Roots
- African-American and Afro-Caribbean New Religious Movements
- Native American New Religious Movements
- Focusing on the Human and the Natural: Secular New Religious Movements
- The Quest for Unity: Universalist New Religious Movements

PREPARING FOR THE END: APOCALYPTIC NEW RELIGIOUS MOVEMENTS

Among the most well-known new religious movements in the early twenty-first century are those with apocalyptic orientations. They claim to reveal the secrets of an end time, which are essential to receive in order to be prepared when the end comes (typically with a violent conflict) and a new age begins. Because the apocalyptic theme is central to Christian tradition, many new religious movements in this group have Christian roots. We will discuss two Christian apocalyptic new religious movements (Seventh-Day Adventism and the Branch Davidians). Other new religious movements focused on preparing for the end may draw on Christian imagery, but in association with other traditions. In this section we will examine one such religion (Aum Shinryko).

Seventh-Day Adventism: Living in the Final Days

The fourth of the Ten Commandments in the Bible says, "Remember the sabbath day, to keep it holy." For Seventh-Day Adventism, the commandment means that keeping holy the Jewish sabbath (from sundown Friday to sundown Saturday) is incumbent on Christians as well as Jews. Keeping the "seventh day" (rather than Sunday, the first day of the week) as the weekly holy day, and a firm belief that

Jesus Christ will return soon (*advent* here refers to the Second Coming of Christ) to begin the promised Kingdom of God on earth, distinguishes Seventh-Day Adventism.

Seventh-Day Adventism is an example of a *millenarian movement.* In general, millenarian movements expect that supernatural powers are about to bring a new age to earth. As a result, restoration and salvation will come to the community of true believers. "Millenarian" specifically indicates a period (typically 1,000 years) in which a divine figure (Jesus in Christianity) will reign on earth, either before or after another final age begins, or as the only end time.

Although now a global movement, Seventh-Day Adventism traces its roots to the biblical interpretation of William Miller (1782–1849), who calculated the date for Second Coming (advent) of Christ and the end of the world. Miller predicted the end would begin sometime between March 21, 1843, and March 21, 1844. When the end time did not dawn, one of Miller's followers recalculated the date to October 22, 1844. Thereafter, some of the smaller groups that had formed in response to Miller's predictions joined to form Seventh-Day Adventism. One of the principal figures was a woman named Ellen White (1827–1915), believed by Adventists to be a prophet of God.

The major beliefs of the movement are that in 1844 Christ began the process of judging the sins of both the living and the dead; that we are now living in the final days before the end time; that when Christ comes he will take the faithful with him to begin the thousand-year rule; and that after this "millennium" a final battle between God and Satan will lead to the creation of a new earth, which will be the eternal home of the righteous.

There were estimated to be between ten and eleven million Seventh-Day Adventists worldwide early in the twenty-first century.

Branch Davidians: Unlocking the Seven Seals

Until the spring of 1993 few people had heard of small religious movement known as the Branch Davidians. That quickly changed on February 18, 1993, when agents from the Federal Bureau of Alcohol, Tobacco, and Firearms (ATF) failed in an attempt to enter a hundred-member Branch Davidian community called Mt. Carmel outside Waco, Texas, to execute a search warrant for illegal weapons. Four ATF agents and a number of Branch Davidians were killed in an exchange of gunfire. A siege of Mt. Carmel then began, headed by the Federal Bureau of Investigation. Branch Davidian leader David Koresh and his followers inside Mt. Carmel refused to surrender, and a standoff ensued. Attempts to negotiate a peaceful resolution continued for fifty-one days, until Mt. Carmel burned to the ground on April 19th after tanks sprayed a powerful chemical into the building. Eighty-six members of the community (including seventeen children) died.

The Davidian movement, as it was first known, was founded in 1934 by Victor Houteff, a Seventh-Day Adventist, who taught that the Second Coming of Jesus was imminent. Houteff taught that the eternal Kingdom of David, promised in the Old Testament, would then begin. A year later he opened a commune called Mt. Carmel, located near Waco, Texas.

After Houteff's death in 1955, his wife Florence assumed leadership of the Davidians and announced that on April 22, 1959, during the Jewish Passover, the eternal Kingdom of David would begin on earth. When it did not come, a new movement, called the Branch Davidians, split from the main group and took control of Mt. Carmel.

In 1987 a young convert named Vernon Howell became the Branch Davidian leader. He changed his name to David Koresh, taking the names of the ancient Israelite King David and the Hebrew name of the Persian king Cyrus, whom the prophet Isaiah named as a messiah (anointed one) of God. Koresh announced that he was a messiah sent by God as a divinely inspired teacher during the last days before the return of Christ. He fathered a number of children by different Davidian women (some only teenagers), claiming that in so doing he was planting the seeds of the new age. Despite later reports, Koresh never claimed to *be* Jesus Christ; rather, he believed himself to have been anointed by God to open the Seven Seals described in the New Testament Book of Revelation. Davidians believe that the opening of the seals will lead to the final judgment, in which the forces of evil will be vanquished and God's elect will inherit the eternal kingdom.

Unfortunately, when the ATF attempted a forced entry into Mt. Carmel, David Koresh and his followers believed that the final battle prophesied in the Book of Revelation had begun. Surrender to the forces of "Babylon" was not in the "script" the Davidians believed they must follow. They lived in their own symbolic world, defined by their understanding of the apocalyptic signs in the Bible. Only David Koresh was authorized by God to unlock the code.

The FBI negotiators could make little sense of the biblical language Koresh used when they talked with him, calling it "Bible babel." During the standoff, several scholars of new religious movements who understood the apocalyptic worldview of the Davidians worked out a method that would enable the Davidians to surrender without compromising their understanding of the Seven Seals. However, the scholars were unable to convince the FBI to allow Koresh time to finish a commentary on the Seven Seals, and the federal authorities decided they would have to take action to end the standoff. Computer disks taken from Mt. Carmel by Davidians who escaped in the final conflagration showed that Koresh was indeed working on the commentary and it was nearly finished.

Fortunately, lessons were learned as a result of the tragedy at Waco. In its aftermath, the FBI formed a group of scholars of new religious movements who serve as consultants if and when federal agencies find themselves dealing with groups like the Branch Davidians. In addition, the news media, whose sensationalized stories about Koresh and the Davidians helped create the atmosphere that led to misunderstanding, has become more (if not fully) responsible in its coverage of new religious movements. Perhaps most importantly, as a result of the loss of life at Waco, the public is becoming cautious in accepting uncritically prejudicial portrayals of new religious movements.

Aum Shinryko: Teaching the Supreme Truth

In 1986 a blind Japanese yoga teacher named Chizuo Matsumoto (b. 1955) claimed to have been enlightened while meditating alone in the Himalaya Mountains. He returned to Japan, changed his name to Asahara Shoko, and founded a new religious movement called Aum Shinryko ("Teaching of the Supreme Truth"). Asahara claimed that he had received divine instruction to establish a spiritual kingdom on earth called the Shambhala Kingdom.

In 1989 Aum Shinryko was granted legal recognition by the Japanese government and established a political party, *Shinrito* (Supreme Truth Party), with the claim that political action aimed at spreading the truths of the movement was necessary to save the world.

When Aum Shinryko was sued by disgruntled members, Asahara announced that the movement would be unable to save the world and members should prepare themselves for an inevitable final battle. He instructed them to build nuclear fallout shelters and separate themselves from the world. In order to prepare for the coming end, they were told to practice a rigid asceticism and recognize Asahara as absolute ruler.

In 1991 Asahara announced that he was Christ returned to earth. He warned of the coming apocalypse, saying it would involve chemical weapons. Aum Shinryko membership gradually grew to about eleven hundred. Most were idealistic, educated young professionals who had become disillusioned with the materialism of modern Japanese society.

The Aum Shinryko worldview accepts the Buddhist teachings on suffering, reincarnation, karma, and enlightenment through meditation. It also draws on Tantric Buddhism (see Chapter Eight), claiming that certain supernatural powers such as levitation may be attained through the release of the *kundalini* power within. From Hinduism, Aum Shinryko draws devotion to Shiva, the god of destruction and regeneration, and the guru tradition. In addition to claiming to be Christ returned to initiate the new age, Asahara said he was an incarnation of Lord Shiva. Through a process of blood initiation, he taught that his followers would attain buddhahood. Members also wore special headgear that they believed attuned their brain waves with Asahara's.

When Aum Shinryko withdrew from society, Asahara incorporated apocalyptic teachings from the New Testament Book of Revelation and the popular Prophecies of Nostradamus. He instituted the "Lotus Village Plan," teaching that if Aum Shinryko members formed small communes devoted to him they would survive the nuclear holocaust. After the final conflict, these communes would become the basis for a new, ideal world society. Influenced by the Lotus Sutra's teaching of an age of the Destruction of Dharma (see Chapter Eight), Asahara taught that the current age was corrupted by materialism.

In 1993 Asahara ordered Aum Shinryko scientists to produce sarin nerve gas, saying that it was needed to defend against an imminent gas attack by the American military in Japan. In 1994, at Asahara's command, Aum Shinryko members released sarin gas, killing seven and injuring hundreds. That same year he proclaimed himself emperor.

The sarin attack was not linked to Aum Shinryko until the next year. After a government raid on the group's headquarters in Osaka, Japan, members released sarin gas into the Tokyo subway system on March 20, 1995, killing ten and injuring thousands. Asahara and two hundred of his followers were arrested. Asahara was charged with murder for the sarin deaths and for the killing of Aum Shinryko opponents. A seven-year trial of Asahara did not end until 2003; as of this writing, a final verdict has not been rendered. Several other Aum Shinryko leaders have received death sentences for their parts in the sarin attacks and other murders. Aum Shinryko subsequently survived a government attempt to disband it, but its reorganized membership fell to several hundred.

FAITH AND SPIRIT: NEW RELIGIOUS MOVEMENTS OF HEALING AND AWARENESS

Some new religious movements place special focus on spiritual awareness and healing. These movements are typically started by teachers who have discovered a path to awareness of the true spiritual nature of humanity. We will examine two such movements in this section: Christian Science and International Raelian Religion.

Christian Science: Recovering Lost Healing

In 1866 Mary Baker Eddy (1821–1910), who had been studying various forms of spiritualism, experienced a miraculous healing after a serious injury. Mrs. Eddy devoted the rest of her life to the promotion of Christian healing. Her book, *Science and Health with a Key to the Scriptures,* the primary supplement to the Bible in Christian Science, appeared in 1875. Four years later the Church of Christ (Scientist) was organized, with headquarters in Boston, Massachusetts (home of the Mother Church). The goal of the movement was to recover original Christianity, with its emphasis on healing, which had been lost as Christianity evolved. Each congregation is expected to make available a reading room in which the public has access to Christian Scientist publications, including the highly respected newspaper *The Christian Science Monitor.*

In accord with Mrs. Eddy's teachings, the Bible and her book are the pastor in Christian Science, so there is no professional clergy. At services, portions of Scripture and *Science and Health* are read, and members witness to their faith experiences. Instead of ministers or priests, some lay members (male or female) function as "practitioners." They specialize in the healing ministry of the church, which takes place outside the context of the services, usually in the members' homes.

Christian Science teaches that God is the Divine Mind, the only principle that really exists. In *Science and Health,* Eddy defined God in the following terms (Eddy 1906: 465, 587, 256):

> God is incorporeal, divine, supreme, Infinite Mind, Spirit, Soul, Principle, Life, Truth, Love.

> GOD. The great I AM; the all-knowing, all-seeing, all-acting, all-wise, all-loving, and eternal; Principle; Mind; Soul; Spirit; Life; Truth; Love; all substance; intelligence.

> Love, the divine Principle, is the Father and Mother of the universe, including man.

Only Mind and Spirit are real; matter is an illusion. Since sickness strikes the material body, it cannot be real. The error is in thinking it is. The same is true of sin and death. Error is overcome through prayer. As a believer develops spiritually, the error is transformed, apparent sicknesses disappear, and the believer becomes healthy, happy, and holy.

According to the teaching of Christian Science, humans are Spirit, and therefore perfect. Anything that detracts from this perfection is a product of false thinking that can be corrected through purifying thought and gaining a deeper understanding of God and humanity in God's image and likeness. Mrs. Eddy answers the question "What is man?" in these words (Eddy 1906: 475):

> Man is not matter [. . .] The Scriptures inform us that man is made in the image and likeness of God. Matter is not that likeness. The likeness of Spirit cannot be so unlike Spirit. Man is spiritual and perfect; and because he is spiritual and perfect, he must be so understood in Christian Science. [. . .]
> Man is incapable of sin, sickness, and death. The real man cannot depart from holiness [. . .]

Christian Scientists typically refuse medical treatment. Critics charge that this has resulted in a great deal of unnecessary pain and suffering. Civil courts have held Christian Scientist parents accountable for withholding treatment from their children.

Membership statistics for Christian Science are not released. Outside observers estimated the membership in 2000 to be about 150,000. The Church does report 2,200 separate congregations in 70 countries.

International Raelian Religion: Preparing for the Elohim

On December 13, 1973 extraterrestrial beings called Elohim (a Hebrew word meaning "those who came from the sky") appeared in a flying saucer to Claude Vorilhon, a French journalist. They gave him the name Rael, and told him that he had been chosen to tell humans the truth about humans and the Elohim.

In six hourlong meetings the Elohim told Rael that humans had been created not on earth but on another planet, by Elohim who had mastered genetics and cell biology. They also instructed him to build an embassy in Jerusalem to prepare for the coming of the Elohim to earth. According to Rael, the Elohim told him that once world peace had been achieved, they would come to teach humans their extraordinary technology. International Raelian Religion was created to achieve these two objectives. Raelians believe that Buddha, Moses, Jesus, Mohammed, Joseph Smith, and other prophets were messengers from the Elohim. Rael is the last in this long line of prophets.

The core of Raelian teaching is a creation narrative, which reinterprets the Genesis account in accord with the message Rael received. The laboratories where humans were created are the Garden of Eden in the Genesis story. When humans became aggressive, the Elohim expelled them from the laboratories. All the prophets, Rael among them, are the product of the interbreeding of Elohim and humans to which Genesis alludes (4:6, 6:2). The prophets carry messages adapted to the cultures in which they live.

According to the Raelian worldview, we are now living in the Age of Apocalypse, which began when the first atomic bomb was dropped on Hiroshima, Japan in 1945. The dawning of the apocalyptic age was also marked by the creation of the Jewish state of Israel and breakthroughs in medicine and technology. In particular, innovations in human genetics and understanding of DNA have humanity at the threshold of creating life.

According to Rael, life has infinite levels. The Earth is one tiny atom in a gigantic structure, which itself is one atom of an even bigger being. God is infinite. A unique teaching is that it is not the soul, but the recreation of an individual from his/her DNA that guarantees eternal life. On the basis of this belief, Raelians have taken a special interest in the science of cloning. In 2002 unsubstantiated claims of successful human cloning by Raelian scientists working in a company called Clonaid brought global attention to the Raelian movement.

Raelians also believe that a system of world government called "humanitarianism" should be created, governed by those who are most intelligent. A meditative technique for "awakening the mind" called "sensual meditation" is taught at Raelian seminars.

The Raelian Movement claims about 40,000 members, with the majority in France, Canada, and Japan. By 1997, the Movement had raised approximately seven million dollars for the construction of the embassy for the Elohim, but had been unsuccessful in convincing the government of Israel to allow it to be built in Jerusalem.

REVIVING THE CHURCH: CHRISTIAN NEW RELIGIOUS MOVEMENTS OF RENEWAL

Many new religious movements have emerged with a leader who is inspired to renew an existing religion, believing that the religion needs to be restored to the original vision of its founder—with modifications that have been supernaturally revealed to the new leader. The Christian new religious movements we have already encountered could be considered from this perspective, and other movements associated with other religions have similar qualities. However, the two new religious movements introduced in this section (The Church of Jesus Christ of Latter-day Saints, or Mormons; and the Holy Spirit Association for the Unification of World Christianity, or Unification Church) focus especially on the restoration of true Christianity.

The Church of Jesus Christ of Latter-Day Saints (the Mormons): Christ's Kingdom in America

The founder of the Church of Jesus Christ of Latter-day Saints was Joseph Smith (1805–1844). Like other religious founders, Smith was seeking for the truth amidst a variety of spiritual paths when he experienced a revelation. For Smith revelation came in 1822, when an angel named Moroni told him about golden plates containing the word of God in a language called reformed Egyptian hieroglyphics. Moroni told Smith he had been chosen to dig up these buried plates. Smith found them a year later near Manchester, New York. He was equipped with two special stones, the Urim and Thummim, to enable him to read the plates. He eventually translated them as the Book of Mormon in 1830.

The movement begun by Smith proclaimed that Christ's kingdom would come in America. Within a year, he and his wife Emma had attracted a thousand followers. He led them first to Ohio, then to Missouri. (Smith believed the New Jerusalem would arrive in Independence, Missouri.) Called now Mormons, Smith and his followers sparked opposition because of their attacks on the validity of other Christian groups. Driven out of Missouri, Smith established an autonomous Mormon enclave in Nauvoo, Illinois. From there missionaries spread out to carry the Mormon faith. Thousands of converts came to join the Nauvoo community. Hostility grew, and Smith was killed by an angry mob in 1844.

After Smith's death, the movement split. Members of Smith's family joined a remnant of other followers who had stayed in Missouri and formed the Reorganized Church of Jesus Christ of Latter-day Saints (RLDS). Today the world headquarters of this 250,000-member movement (now known as the Community of Christ) is in Independence, Missouri. They reject the name "Mormon."

The "Mormons" are those who associate with those followers of Smith who accepted the leadership of Brigham Young (1801–77). They retained the name Church of Jesus Christ of Latter-day Saints (LDS). Brigham Young led the famous migration to Utah, beginning in 1847. Near the Great Salt Lake, Young and his followers transformed a desolate area into a thriving region that they called Deseret, from the Reformed Egyptian word for "honey bee." When they arrived, Utah was part of Mexican territory. When the United States took control, opposition to Young led ultimately to the dissolution of the church corporation in 1887. In 1890 the Church officially abandoned polygamy after it had been outlawed. After Utah achieved statehood, Mormons settled into their roles as citizens and focused on the development of the Church.

LDS doctrine is rooted in basic Christian teachings, but with some unique interpretations based on the revelation Smith received. For Mormons matter is eternal, and God is a self-created being with a material body. There are other gods of other worlds; Mormons worship the god of this world. Humans now living may one day become gods in their own worlds because of the coming of Christ. The godhead consists of three separate gods: Heavenly Father, Jesus Christ, and Holy Ghost. Jesus Christ is the eldest "spirit child" who came to earth as Jehovah (as described in the Old Testament).

Christ's kingdom will be established on earth, in America. Everyone is eligible to enter Christ's kingdom, but only through LDS baptism in an immersion ceremony conducted by a member of the priesthood. Those who are dead may be vicariously baptized (the basis for the elaborate genealogical records kept by the Church). Before the kingdom comes, those who have died but are baptized wait in heaven. There they live with material forms just like their earthly bodies.

According to Mormon belief, eternal life after death in heaven has three levels. In descending order they are the Celestial Kingdom, the Terrestial Kingdom, and the Telestial Kingdom. The Celestial Kingdom itself has three levels. The highest is reserved for persons who have been obedient to Mormon teachings and married in an LDS temple. Males at this level become gods of their own worlds. This level is the only one in which the Heavenly Father lives and rules. The other two levels are also reserved for LDS members. The second kingdom, the Terrestial, is for those who have not yet heard the Restored Gospel as taught by the LDS church. Jesus will visit this kingdom, but not the Heavenly Father. The Telestial is for those who have heard but rejected the Restored Gospel. Beneath all these is the Second Death or Outer Darkness, reserved for the especially wicked.

Mormons consider marriages eternal; families will be rejoined in heaven. The central unit in Mormon life is the family, and a great deal of emphasis is placed on preserving and strengthening it. There is no professional Mormon clergy. Every male may become a priest (of the order of Aaron or Melchizedek). The religious status of a woman is dependent on her husband.

The organization of the church is hierarchical. All leaders are male. At the head are the Council of Twelve Apostles and a President, considered the successor to Joseph Smith. Like Smith the President can receive revelations that define basic church doctrine. For example, a revelation given in 1978 allowed African-American males to be admitted to the priesthood for the first time. At the local level individual congregations form wards, headed by an appointed bishop. The world headquarters of the Mormon Church are located in Salt Lake City, Utah.

The Book of Mormon includes not only teachings on how Mormons are to live, but also a detailed account of the early history of America. According to the narrative, a group known as the Lamanites (the ancestors of the American Indians) and the Nephites (their foes) both descended from the "lost tribe of Israel" that came to America about 587 B.C.E. Christ appeared to the Lamanites after his resurrection, promising to return to America to establish his kingdom on earth. The Lamanites rebelled against the truth and attacked the Nephites. The only Nephites to survive were Mormon, who wrote the story we have just summarized on the golden plates that Joseph Smith translated, and his son Moroni. As stated above it was Moroni who, as an angel, led Smith to the plates.

Besides the Book of Mormon, two other works written by Smith, *Doctrine and Covenants* and *Pearl of Great Price,* are considered by Mormons necessary supplements to the Bible. The Bible alone does not contain the whole truth needed for salvation.

The Church of Jesus Christ of Latter-day Saints has grown to about 5.4 million members in the United States, with rapid expansion around the world through their international missionary efforts. In the early twenty-first century there were about 11.7 million Mormons in the world, with over 26,000 congregations.

The Holy Spirit Association for the Unification of World Christianity (the Unification Church): Restoration of Original Harmony

The Unification Church (officially called the Holy Spirit Association for the Unification of World Christianity) was established in 1954 in Korea. According to the church, Jesus appeared to its founder, the Reverend Sun Myung Moon (b. 1920), in 1936, instructing him to establish the Kingdom of God on earth. As a result Moon began a movement that became known as the Holy Spirit Association. It reached the United States by 1959. Eventually the offices of the world headquarters were established in and near New York City.

The church recognizes Rev. Moon's *Divine Principle* as a sacred text, which interprets the true meaning of the Christian Bible. The work presents a history of humanity that focuses on God's efforts to establish the divine Kingdom on earth. It teaches that the original harmony will be restored when a second Adam and a second Eve come to pay the price for human sin. Jesus was the second Adam, but he failed to marry, so only a spiritual restoration occurred, with the Holy Spirit as the bride of Jesus. Jesus died unnecessarily, because of the failure of John the Baptist to prepare the way for him properly, Rev. Moon contended. The material world remained under the power of Satan. The time is near, Rev. Moon wrote, when a new messiah will appear, the Lord of the Second Coming. He will come to Korea, where he will marry so the full price of the sin of humanity can be paid and the model for the new, spiritual family can be created. The new messiah, a Third Adam, will bring God's kingdom to earth. Rev. Moon does not overtly claim to be this messiah, but he and his wife are enacting the prophecies associated with his coming.

As spiritual parents to all members of the church, Moon and his wife arrange and preside over the marriages of their "children" in mass ceremonies called Blessings. Members must themselves pay "indemnity" for human sinfulness through sacrificial good deeds. The raising of money for the church is the primary means of paying this indemnity. The church teaches that Satan is still alive and at work in the world, trying to deflect Moon and his followers from the mission given to him by Jesus himself.

The movement vigorously supports the role of the United States as leader of the free world. It opposes abortion, defends "family values," and supports private religious education. The church publishes *The Washington Times*, a daily newspaper. The church maintains that it recognizes and supports other religions, and only asks that this openness be reciprocated. Members of the church have been given the derogatory name "Moonies," and have been the target of "deprogrammers" hired by concerned parents whose sons or daughters have joined. The church responds that overzealous recruiting by some misguided members has been curbed, and that the church seeks only recognition and the opportunity to function as a legitimate Christian denomination.

NATURE AND SPIRIT: EARTH-BASED AND ECOLOGICAL NEW RELIGIOUS MOVEMENTS

Two types of new religious movements are particularly concerned with the relationship between the spiritual and the natural. Some, like Wicca, are inspired by the indigenous religions we have encountered in Chapter Two. Others, like Deep Ecology, have emerged out of the modern environmental movement.

Wicca: Renewing European Witchcraft

The word "witch" conjures up an image of an old woman dressed in black with a pointed hat, stirring a cauldron, casting evil spells. However, another, more positive understanding of witches and witchcraft has been developed by a modern movement called *Wicca*.

Wicca (the Old English word for "wise") is the name given to a very loosely connected movement committed to restoring the witchcraft traditions of pre-Christian Europe. Wicca is the root of the English word "witch." Modern Wicca began in England, as a result of the work of Gerald Gardner (1884–1964), and spread to the United States by the mid-1960s. The movement is based on what can be recovered from the ancient tradition (now mostly lost or distorted, Wiccans admit, after centuries of Christian suppression), combined with newly devised rituals that reflect the basic principles of the indigenous worldview.

In the Wiccan religion all members are considered witches, meaning "seekers of the ancient wisdom." There is no hierarchy, but in practice one witch assumes leadership, and is sometimes called the priestess. Members form their own groups known as "covens," some of which are for women only (called Dianic), with others open to both men and women. The covens are small, usually limited to thirteen members, and there is no central organization among them. Other larger groups have developed beyond the coven level to provide coordination and opportunities for networking. The only connection among covens and larger groups is a loose network of internet bulletin boards, newsletters, other publications, and conferences that draw various covens and other groups together.

The goal of Wicca is to enable members to reestablish the harmony with the earth lost in modern civilizations. Wicca teaches the indigenous idea of the interconnectedness of all of life, and stresses that humans are part of nature not her masters. The worldview is biocentric.

The Wiccan view of the sacred is that all nature is spiritually alive. However, as in other indigenous religions, there are gods. One deity is the male Lord of animals, death, and the beyond, called the *Horned God*, symbolized by the sun. Increasingly, the more important deity for the practice of Wicca is the *Goddess*, who appears in three aspects reflective of the cycle of life, and, in particular, the phases of the moon: the maiden, the mother, and the crone (old woman). There is no strict distinction drawn between the gods and nature; the gods are present in nature, in everyone, and in all of life. Their energy is the energy of nature, not a power infused into nature from outside.

Wiccan rituals involve the creation of sacred space, through purification involving the four elements (fire, water, earth, and air) and the demarcation of the four cardinal directions. The creation of the space is called "casting the circle." Ritual objects such as swords, knives, wands, and chalices are used. Worshippers stand and dance in circles. In some covens, at some times, they are skyclad (naked), to manifest their sense of oneness with nature and the beauty of the natural body. The ceremonies involve the use of chanting and dancing to raise the spiritual energy within the circle, then the focusing of the energy into a "cone." When the witch in charge senses intuitively that the energy is at its peak, it is directed at a particular goal decided upon by the group. The goal usually involves the well-being of a particular person or group, or the healing and harmony of the environment. Many Wiccans today seek to apply the power politically, to effect changes in policies deemed detrimental to the well-being of Mother Earth.

Wiccan magic is "white magic," not the so-called "black magic" associated with the use of magical powers for destructive ends. The identification of witchcraft with evil is, they believe, the result of prejudice. Wiccans point out that the image of the "witch" (boiling toads in a cauldron to cast evil spells, and riding on a broomstick) is due more to the hysterical response to witchcraft by church authorities in Christian Europe in the eleventh and twelfth centuries than to historical reality.

One distinctive Wiccan ritual is the "drawing down of the moon." The moon, representing the three phases of the Goddess, is magically "drawn down" into an individual who then exhibits to the coven the force of the Goddess. The individual takes the role of the shaman in other indigenous religions, becoming "possessed" by the spirit world and manifesting the power of that world to others. The Goddess uses the person to instruct the group in the ways of wisdom.

As in indigenous religions, Wiccans have no written Scriptures. They do find meaning in ancient myths, such as the story of the Greek gods Demeter and Persephone. The chief source of revelation is nature. There is no founder, or single central leader.

The Wiccan calendar reflects the cycle of nature, with special rituals held at the summer and winter solstices, and fall and spring equinoxes. At the winter solstice the Horned God is born anew each year. In Spring he becomes the Goddess's lover. At Halloween he dies, and the Goddess becomes the crone of winter.

Deep Ecology: Ecological Egalitarianism

Ecology is the scientific study of the interconnectedness of all living things in the environment. The "environmental movement" is composed of individuals and organizations who are trying to raise peoples' awareness of the current ecological crisis (see Chapter Fifteen) and influence public policy to address it. The phrase "Deep Ecology" first appeared in the 1970s to refer to the spiritual dimension of this modern environmental movement, and as an attempt to address the concern that the traditional spirituality of Western religions is antithetical to the preservation of the balance of nature.

Deep Ecology goes beyond "shallow ecology" to a deeper and fuller, more comprehensive worldview. Deep Ecologists seek to replace the Western understanding of nature with a biocentric, ecological egalitarianism. Every living being has a "right to be" that must be respected. Humans have failed to recognize the right to "self-realization" of other beings, as they are expressed in natural patterns. Humans must reawaken to their place in the natural community. For Deep Ecologists, nature as a whole is ultimate and environmental activism the means of transformation in response to this ultimacy. All forms of anthropocentrism must be overcome.

According to some Deep Ecologists, the material standard of living in industrialized societies must be "drastically reduced" and the human population should be lowered significantly. From this perspective, the time is past for gradual reformation of our approach to restoring the balance of life. Radical steps are necessary and they must be taken now. This attitude has inspired some in groups such as

Greenpeace and Earth Now to take direct action to challenge practices they deem environmentally irresponsible.

Deep Ecology calls not so much for sacrifice on the part of the individual, as for an expanded awareness of "self-interest." Influenced by Buddhism, Deep Ecologists speak of an "eco-self," an understanding of human identity that does not separate the "self" and "nature."

It is important to note that Deep Ecology is not a unified movement; it is a spiritual perspective that is emerging simultaneously in a variety of contexts. People who are active in traditional religions, as well as others who are not religious at all in a traditional sense, are becoming increasingly aware that the ecological crisis requires spiritual transformation. Some are motivated by the spiritual values of indigenous religions. Others find a basis for their beliefs in the traditional religions of the Middle East, which speak of the human responsibility to be God's stewards of the earth and recognize the divine presence in nature. Some Christian theologians are speaking of the "cosmic Christ," meaning that God's incarnation in Christ includes a recognition that the earth itself is the "body of Christ." Still others see in Eastern religions like Daoism or Zen Buddhism a spiritual awareness of the inherent harmony of all life.

Some persons base their understanding of Deep Ecology on the *Gaia* hypothesis of scientist James Lovelock, who asserted that the earth, the life on the earth, and the atmosphere surrounding the earth constitute one living, self-regulating being whom he called Gaia (from the Greek name for the Earth as a goddess). Still other Deep Ecologists believe in the emergence of a new "planetary consciousness" that is replacing the anthropocentric thinking of earlier generations. Supporters of this "New Age" spirituality often gather in small communities that emphasize planetary harmony, and practice a lifestyle of cooperation with nature. In 1987 New Age spiritualists gathered at especially sacred locations around the world to celebrate a "harmonic convergence" in which they sought to raise energy to transform the anthropocentric worldview.

Ecofeminism has emerged in recent years as a movement that shares some concerns with Deep Ecology, but goes beyond it in the analysis of the roots of the environmental crisis. Ecofeminism focuses on women's potential to take the lead in bringing on an ecological revolution. They join Deep Ecologists in saying that more than gradual reform of our attitude toward the environment is necessary. But they criticize Deep Ecologists for not being radical enough in their critique of the role played by male domination in creating the cultural values that led to the ecological crisis.

It remains to be seen whether these various and quite distinct proponents of Deep Ecology will join together to express in a more unified way their common understanding of the spiritual relationship that humans must foster with the earth and all of life. Some observers think that Deep Ecology has the potential to spark a universal spiritual renewal and reformation as profound as any in history. Many Deep Ecologists maintain that human survival depends on this spiritual transformation—otherwise, extinction of the human species will inevitably occur to restore the ecological balance that humans have callously disrupted.

LIBERATION AND ENLIGHTENMENT: NEW RELIGIOUS MOVEMENTS WITH ASIAN ROOTS

Many new religious movements have roots in the religions of South and East Asia. In this section we will examine one religion with a South Asian background—The International Society for Krishna Consciousness (the Hare Krishnas), and two with roots in East Asia—Falun Dafa (also known as Falun Gong) and Soka Gakkai.

The International Society for Krishna Consciousness: The Hare Krishnas

In 1966 Abhay Charan De, a seventy-year-old owner of a small Indian pharmaceutical firm, arrived penniless in New York City. Seven years earlier he had taken the vow of a *sannyasin* (see Chapter Three). He came to the United States to fulfill a promise he had made to his spiritual teacher in 1936 to bring the teaching of "Krishna Consciousness" to the West. He became the leader of a movement, the International Society for Krishna Consciousness (ISKCON), which has been the principal point of contact with the Hindu tradition for millions of Americans and others.

A.C. Bhakitvedanta Swami Prabhupada, as his followers came to know him, taught a message he believed had been passed from guru to guru for literally thousands of years. According to this tradition, in the present materialistic age (the last before the current cosmic cycle ends in destruction) people should chant the holy names of God as the simplest and surest way to find spiritual fulfillment.

Upon his arrival in New York, Swami Prabhupada began chanting the names of God in Tompkins Square Park on the Lower East Side. Gradually he began to attract followers who had dropped out of mainstream American culture. Eight years later, nearly seventy centers of the International Society for Krishna Consciousness had opened around the world, with twenty-eight in the United States.

Devotees became known as "Hare Krishnas," because of their simple chant:

Hare Krishna, Hare Krishna, Krishna, Krishna, Hare, Hare
Hare Rama, Hare Rama, Rama, Rama, Hare, Hare

Krishna and Rama are divine names in Sanskrit. Krishna is an epithet meaning "beloved" or "all-attractive." According to the movement, the translation of the chant is:

O all-attractive, all pleasing-Lord, O energy of the Lord,
please engage me in your devotional service

By chanting the names of the Lord in faith, devotees believe that they are being drawn into the presence of the Supreme Lord of the Universe. Krishna Consciousness is a Vaishnavite *bhakti* movement that historians trace to a sixteenth-century teacher named Chaitanya. The principal text for the movement is the *Bhagavad Gita*, which members believe to be the literal word of Krishna.

Devotees have attracted a great deal of attention by asking for donations for copies of the Swami's translation of the Gita and other movement literature at airports and other public places. Some members devote themselves entirely to the movement and maintain a rigorous lifestyle, living in the centers. Other devotees live outside the centers, and participate to varying extents in the center's cycle of group chanting (*kirtan*) before images of Krishna. All members individually maintain their spiritual focus through chanting the names of God on *japa* beads throughout the day.

After Swami Prabhupada's death in 1977, the leadership of the movement passed to a council. The movement has experienced some bitter divisions and much negative publicity, yet continues to function as the most successful example of the *bhakti* branch of the Indian religious tradition outside South Asia. By the early twenty-first century, the International Society for Krishna Consciousness had developed into a worldwide confederation of approximately 10,000 temple members and 250,000 congregational devotees. The movement includes more than 350 centers around the world, as well as 60 rural communities, 50 schools, and 60 restaurants (where a vegetarian cuisine is featured).

Falun Dafa (Falun Gong): Cultivating the Universal Life Energy

The movement known as Falun Gong or Falun Dafa was founded in 1992 by Master Li Hongzhi in China. Less than a decade later it claimed about one hundred million followers in more than thirty countries. It describes itself as "an advanced system of cultivation and practice (*qigong*)," for improving one's physical and psychological health, moral development, and spiritual enlightenment. *Qi* (also written as *ch'i;* see Chapter Six) is the universal life energy, and *gong* refers to the cultivation of that energy.

Dafa refers to the "great law of the universe." The *falun* is the "law wheel" located in each person's lower abdomen. It is a spinning body of energy, a microcosm of the universe. Through a series of five sets of exercises known as *falun gong*, practitioners synchronize the *falun* with the universe's rotations and absorb the cosmic energy. The influence of the Buddhist *dharma chakra* (wheel of dharma), Tantric Buddhist *kundalini* meditation, and the Daoist set of exercises known as *tai ch'i* are evident in the movement's teachings. The exercises can be done individually, but when done in a group an energy field radiating peace is created by the practitioners.

Falun Gong focuses on cultivation of *xin xing* (mind nature) and its assimilation to *zhen-shan-ren* (truthfulness-compassion-forbearance), which is the ultimate nature of the universe. The entire system is described in Master Li Hongzhi's book *Zhuan Falun,* which has been translated into dozens of languages. Followers claim that, as a result of the practice, they have improved their health, reduced stress, and become more moral. They also testify to the developing spiritual enlightenment they experience.

When it was founded, Falun Dafa was officially registered by the Chinese government as a form of *qigong* rather than a religion. However, in 1996 Master Li Hongzhi withdrew Falun Dafa from the goverment's list, because the other *qigong* schools were only concerned with health and fitness.

In 1999, when Falun Dafa members began gathering in public to protest distortions of its teachings appearing in magazines and newspapers, the Chinese government banned the movement, declaring it to be a "dangerous cult" that promoted "pseudo-science." Government authorities are apparently concerned that Falun Dafa might undermine the state's communist ideology and be a focus for a popular opposition movement. They point to other similar movements in Chinese history that became instigators of chaotic rebellions. The government has also claimed that thousands have died as a result of the Falun Dafa exercises and in "cultic" mass suicides. There is no independent evidence in support of these allegations.

In response, Master Li Honghzi has said that Falun Dafa has no political aspirations and is nothing more than a movement to help persons improve themselves physically and morally. Falun Dafa members have been imprisoned in China for illegal public gatherings and for refusing to stop the practice of *falun gong*. In 1999 a warrant for the arrest of Master Li Hongzhi was issued. However, several years earlier he had left China and settled in New York State.

Falun Dafa claims that it is not a religion, because it has no organized structure and no rituals. However, from the perspective of the definition of religion adopted in this work, Falun Dafa is a spiritual religion with its own means of transformation in response to perceived ultimacy.

Soka Gakkai: The Society for Value Creation

Soka Gakkai ("The Society for Value Creation") is a lay movement within the Nichiren school of Buddhism (see Chapter Eight). It was started by a high school principal named Tsunesaburo Makiguchi (1871–1944) before World War II. Makiguchi and some of his followers were imprisoned during the War because they rejected the call to exclusive loyalty required by State Shinto. The founder died in prison.

After the War, Soka Gakkai's commitment to individualism and this-worldly results, as well as its separation from State Shinto, made it popular. It experienced rapid growth during the 1950s under the leadership of Josei Toda, who had been imprisoned with Makiguchi. In 1975, Soka Gakkai International (SGI), an international umbrella organization encompassing groups in various nations, was created. The current SGI Chairman is Ikeda Daisaku. In 1991 the lay movement split from the major monastic Nichiren Buddhist school in Japan, Nichiren Shoshu. By the early twenty-first century SGI claimed twelve million members in 186 countries.

Adapting the teachings of Nichiren and the Lotus Sutra to the contemporary world, Soka Gakkai stresses self-improvement for individuals leading to beauty, truth, and especially benefit. Happiness is the ultimate value in Soka Gakkai.

Each person can become a Buddha through chanting "Hail to the Lotus Sutra!" (*nam-myo-ho-renge-kyo*) and meditating on a *gohonzon* ("personal worship object"), a mandala with the names of principal figures of the Lotus Sutra at the center. The chant brings members into harmony with the energy radiating from all the Buddhas mentioned in the Lotus Sutra, and the central Buddha Reality at the core of all being. Members gather in *zadankai* (discussion) groups to help one another see that which is impeding the achievement of happiness. Converts are encouraged to destroy all signs of other religions in their homes, such as Bibles and Shinto *kami* shelves (see Chapter Nine).

According to Nichiren Buddhism, *now* is the time for world salvation through turning to the truth of the Lotus Sutra. Soka Gakkai recognizes the legitimacy of *shakubuku* ("break and subdue"), in which devotees try to win converts by showing them the error of their present beliefs and the truth of the Lotus Sutra.

In addition to drawing individuals into the movement, Soka Gakkai seeks to influence the course of national as well as international events. In Japan Soka Gakkai organized the *Komeito* ("Clean Government") Party, which continues to hold seats in the Japanese parliament. On the world stage, Soka Gakkai is active in movements to achieve world peace and ultimately a "Third Civilization" in which Buddhism and society will be yoked.

AFRICAN-AMERICAN AND AFRO-CARIBBEAN NEW RELIGIOUS MOVEMENTS

Slaves captured in Africa and transported to North and South America brought with them their native African religions. We have already briefly discussed two new religious movements with roots in the Yoruba tradition: Santeria and Vodun, or Voodoo (see Chapter Two). In this section we will examine a new religious movement that emerged in the United States (the Nation of Islam) and another with roots in the Caribbean (Ras Tafari).

The Nation of Islam: The "Black Muslims"

The Nation of Islam was established in Detroit, Michigan in 1930. Members of the movement are popularly known as the "Black Muslims," although this is not a name used or preferred within the Nation of Islam. Its founder, Wallace Fard, proclaimed that he had come from the Muslim holy city of Mecca to reveal to Black Americans that their salvation would come through self-knowledge, in which they recovered a sense of their own glorious history and accepted the essentially deceptive character of whites. The charismatic Fard organized a Temple, a University of Islam, and a paramilitary force called the Fruit of Islam. He published *The Secret Ritual of the Nation of Islam* and *Teaching for the Lost Found Nation of Islam in a Mathematical Way.*

When Fard disappeared in 1934, his chief disciple, Elijah Muhammad, became the movement's leader. Elijah Muhammad taught that Fard was an incarnation of Allah, and that he was Fard's messenger. He urged his fellow Blacks to withdraw from white society and create their own institutions. Under Elijah Muhammad's leadership, Nation of Islam mosques were established in urban areas across the United States. The Nation created its own schools, stores, houses, and farms.

The traditional teachings of the Nation of Islam were that whites are the personification of evil in the world. Humanity was originally black; the white race was created by a black scientist named Yakub who rebelled against Allah. If Blacks are to realize their destiny, they must purge themselves from all white influences. As the religion of the whites, Christianity is dangerous and must be avoided. Followers are to maintain a strict lifestyle, with prayer five times a day, no intoxicants or tobacco, a pure diet, and no illicit sex.

In the 1950s Malcolm X emerged as a key figure in the movement. (Members of the nation of Islam typically dropped their last name, considering it a "slave" name assigned to them by whites, and used "X" instead.) Malcolm X had been converted to the Nation of Islam in prison, and attributed his salvation to Elijah Muhammad. Malcolm became a charismatic exponent of the movement and helped win many converts. However, after a pilgrimage to Mecca, he began to question whether the Nation of Islam was in harmony with traditional Islamic teaching about universal brotherhood. Malcolm was killed by supporters of Elijah Muhammad in 1965.

After Elijah Muhammad's death in 1975, his son Wallace D. Muhammad assumed leadership. Influenced by Malcolm X's proposals to bring the Nation more into line with the racially inclusive teachings of traditional Islam, he opened the movement to people of all races and changed its name to The World Community of al-Islam in the West, and then later to the American Muslim Mission.

Some Black Muslims rejected this shift and sought to maintain the ideology of racial separatism. Louis Farrakhan became the primary spokesman for this wing of the movement, which retains the original name. In 1995 Minister Farrakhan organized the Million Man March in Washington, D.C., to challenge African-American men to assume their responsibility morally and spiritually. In recent years leaders of the factions have met to work toward healing the division between them.

The Ras Tafari Movement: The Black Messiah

The Ras Tafari Movement (also known as Rastafarianism) began in 1930 when Crown Prince *Ras Tafari* became Emperor Haile Selassie of Ethiopia. The coronation seemed to be in fulfillment of a prophecy made by Marcus Garvey, a Black nationalist leader from Jamaica. When Garvey was preparing to go to the United States from Jamaica in 1916, he told the Blacks of Jamaica to look to Africa where a Black King, who would be their redeemer, would be crowned. The Ethiopian king was addressed with titles associated with Christ in the Bible (King of Kings and Conquering Lion of the Tribe of Judah), adding weight to the view that Haile Selassie was the long-awaited Black Messiah. The Ras Tafari movement emerged out of the enthusiasm. Its principal leader was Leonard Howell, who organized the movement near Kingston, Jamaica.

The movement split into an old school that emphasizes a return to Africa, and a new school that focuses on improving the quality of life for Blacks in Jamaica and elsewhere. Reggae music and artists such as Bob Marley have been associated with the new school.

Ras Tafari teachings include the belief that Haile Selassie is the living God; the black man is superior to the white man; Jamaica is hell and Ethiopia is heaven; Haile Selassie has provided for the return of Blacks to Africa; and Blacks will one day rule the world. Rastafarianism rejects modern industrial life as an evil system introduced by whites to enslave blacks, and idealizes a return to simpler, more natural ways of life in Africa. Ras Tafari men are distinguished by a unique hairstyle called dreadlocks, in which the hair is allowed to grow to look like the mane of a lion—as a symbol of the natural life. Rastafarian ritual is famous because of the smoking by some members of what Rastafarians call *ganja* (marijuana). There is an ongoing movement in the United States to defend Ras Tafari ritual use of *ganja,* claiming that it is protected under the First Amendment guarantee of freedom of religion.

The Ras Tafari movement spread from Jamaica throughout the Caribbean and to the United States and Canada. Emperor Haile Selassie, who died in 1974, repudiated the claims made about him by Rastafarians, but his refusal to cooperate with the ideology did not discourage members of the movement.

As the twenty-first century began, estimates of the number of followers of the Ras Tafari movement range as high as seven hundred thousand.

NATIVE AMERICAN NEW RELIGIOUS MOVEMENTS

In Chapter Two we encountered the traditional religions of Native American nations, focusing on the Oglala Lakota as an example. In addition to tribal religions, Native Americans have created pan-national new religious movements, including the Native American Church.

The Native American Church: Peyote Religion

Peyote is a small, spineless, blue-green cactus that grows in the deserts of Mexico and certain areas in the Southwestern United States. The "buttons" that grow atop the clusters of the cactus are dried, and either chewed or consumed in a tea. The peyote consumer typically experiences a euphoric state in which time stands still; during this state visions often come.

Reports from sixteenth-century Spanish missionaries speak of the importance of peyote among indigenous peoples of Mexico. The ritual consumption of peyote continued through the centuries, and spread into the tribes of the American southwest, such as the Kiowa. The visions received while under the influence of peyote were considered to be a form of communication with the spirit world, which helped the worshipper maintain harmony with the spirits. Soon after European contact, peyote users began associating consumption with Christianity, calling peyote the "flesh of God," a symbol of Christ.

When the United States government began to outlaw native religious practices, including the use of peyote, in the late nineteenth century, a group of Native Americans responded by incorporating peyote into a new religious movement, which eventually became known as the Native American Church of Christ. The first efforts at organization were in Oklahoma, Indian Territory.

From Oklahoma the Native American Church (NAC) spread through the western and midwestern states. When it reached Canada it became known as the Native American Church of Christ in North America. As the twenty-first century began, the Church claimed more than a quarter million members. It has served to bring a sense of spiritual unity to native Americans across tribal boundaries. Typically, members of the NAC participate in both their own tribal rituals *and* the rites of the Church.

Whether the NAC is Christianity adapted to indigenous ways or indigenous religion adapted to Christianity is a matter of dispute within and outside the Church. The two basic divisions within the NAC, the Cross Fire and Half Moon Fireplaces, reflect this tension. Both claim to be Christian. However, the Cross Fire Fireplace maintains a stronger Christian orientation, using the Bible in services and taking an evangelical approach to Christianity. The Half Moon Fireplace uses the name of Jesus in songs, but is not so overtly Christian.

The peyote ritual is quite formalized, with variations depending on the leadership of the ceremony. A peyote ritual in the Southwest typically begins on Saturday evening and lasts through the night until noon on Sunday. The officiant is called the Peyote Chief, and he is assisted by a Fire Chief, Drum Chief, Road Man, and Cedar Man. After purification, participants consume a few buttons through chewing them or drinking a peyote tea. Through the night songs are sung, and more buttons and/or tea are consumed, until visions are attained. It is clear that the intent of the ritual is to communicate with the spirit world for the purpose of receiving spiritual power, guidance, and healing. Spirit intermediaries, such as Thunderbird, carry the people's petitions. The ritual objects typically used in the all-night ritual include a gourd rattle; an iron kettle partially filled with water, the water drum; an eagle feather; cedar incense; and sage.

Even though the Bureau of Indian Affairs reversed a half-century of trying to eliminate peyote use in 1940 and recognized its legitimacy, the dispute over peyote continued. In 1961 the NAC was finally recognized as an official religious organization by the federal government. A few years later, however, in reaction to the abuses of the drug culture of the 1960s, Congress listed peyote among "dangerous drugs" (despite a lack of scientific evidence to support this claim, supporters of the NAC point out). In 1990 the United States Supreme Court upheld the right of states to ban the use of peyote without violating the constitutional guarantee of freedom of religion. Deeply concerned by the implications of this decision for the religious feedom of all Americans, a coalition of religious organizations joined with the NAC in mounting a campaign for federal legislation to guarantee the rights of NAC members to use peyote ritually. The campaign succeeded in convincing Congress in 1994 to pass amendments to the American Indian Religious Freedom Act of 1978, which legalized the ceremonial use of peyote by Indians in all fifty states. However, subsequent court rulings have again raised concern.

FOCUSING ON THE HUMAN AND THE NATURAL: SECULAR NEW RELIGIOUS MOVEMENTS

The new religious movements discussed so far in this chapter have all focused on spiritual patterns of ultimacy. However, as we noted in Chapter One, our definition of religion allows for secular movements to be considered religions, with nonspiritual ultimacies. Three new religious movements in this category are Secular Humanism, Marxism, and one of the most controversial new religious movements, Satanism.

Secular Humanism: Humanity as Ultimate

One result of the secular challenge to spiritual ultimacy in the modern age has been the emergence of groups that consider humanity itself to be ultimate. The idea of treating humanity as a substitute for God as the basis for a new religion can be traced to the French philosopher and founder of modern sociology, Auguste Comte (1798–1857). Comte organized a *Church of Humanity* in Paris, substituting a calendar celebrating the achievements of scientists for the Catholic calendar commemorating the miracles of saints.

Comte's Church of Humanity faded away, but the notion of a humanistic substitute for traditional religion continued. In 1876 Felix Adler, who had studied to be a rabbi but turned away from traditional Judaism, organized the *Ethical Culture Society* in order to inculcate moral values without religious dogma, ritual, and legalism. Today, centers of the Society (linked together as the American Ethical Union) support charitable causes and offer members worship that focuses on inspirational readings, music, and lectures in place of theistic ritual. Members may, if they choose, retain belief in God, since there are no doctrinal requirements, but the activities of the group are nontheistic.

The *American Humanist Association* (AHA) is probably the most active secular humanist organization today. Its origins can be traced to the 1920s when a group of Unitarian ministers and others turned away from theism and embraced a secular philosophy based on humanism. In 1933 eleven prominent humanists (among them the educational leader John Dewey) issued "A Humanist Manifesto," which rejected supernatural explanations, calling the universe "self-existing" and regarding humanity as part of nature. The AHA formally organized in 1941. In 1973 the "Humanist Manifesto II" appeared as a "consensus statement on social policy." It provides a set of principles for the Association's program.

"Humanist Manifesto III: Humanism and Its Aspirations" was subsequently published, with signatures by 19 Nobel Laureates. It begins with the following definition of humanism (www.americanhumanist.org/3/HumandItsAspirations.htm):

> Humanism is a progressive philosophy of life that, without supernaturalism, affirms our ability and responsibility to lead ethical lives of personal fulfillment that aspire to the greater good of humanity.

It expresses the following as principles guiding the humanist philosophy:

- Knowledge of the world is derived by observation, experimentation, and rational analysis.
- Humans are an integral part of nature, the result of unguided evolutionary change.

- Eth cal values are derived from human need and interest as tested by experience.
- Life's fulfillment emerges from individual participation in the service of humane ideals.
- Humans are social by nature and find meaning in relationships.
- Working to benefit society maximizes individual happiness.

In place of ministers, the American Humanist Association licenses counselors to perform weddings and funerals for people who prefer a "secular clergy." Approximately twenty per cent of the AHA membership is composed of college students organized as the Humanist Student Union of North America. The AHA has affiliates in thirty two states.

Marxism: Toward a Classless Society

Karl Marx (1818–1883) would not be pleased if he knew that the system named after him appeared in a survey of the world's religions *as* a religion! Marx was a German philosopher who became convinced that traditional religion was an "opiate of the masses" that rendered people powerless to confront the real forces of economic oppression from which they needed liberation. Marxists are typically "scientific atheists" who seek to understand history from a strictly materialistic standpoint.

How then can we call Marxism a religion? The argument that Marxism is a "secular religion" with its own distinctive means of transformation in response to perceived ultimacy has already been introduced in Chapter One. We will provide a fuller analysis of the religious characteristics of Marxism here.

According to Marxism, humans are material beings, with no souls or spiritual natures. There is no God outside humanity guiding or sustaining humanity. Humans create what they are by their own labor. They use their intelligence and creative abilities to produce from the natural world the goods necessary for life. What humans deserve and desire is control over their own productive capacities and material well-being in this world. However, production is not an individual enterprise; it requires division of labor. This division leads to some people controlling the means of production, with the rest (workers) having only their labor to sell in order to attain goods. According to Marx, history is an inevitable struggle between the ruling and working classes. At the heart of this struggle is private ownership of the means of production. Until the community as a whole controls production, social and economic inequalities will result in alienation for the workers. The ruling classes will use religion and other social institutions to control workers.

According to Marx, in the modern world the oppressive ideology is Capitalism, which emphasizes the concentration of wealth in the hands of a few. Capitalists control the means of production, and use their power to exploit workers. Workers must organize and seize control of the means of production. The ultimate result will be a classless, communist society, a utopia in which all peoples' material needs will be met through an equitable distribution of the wealth produced by labor.

Although Marxism denies any spiritual ultimacy, it replaces it with a secular ultimacy. For Marx, his scientific theory was ultimate. For followers of Marx, the Communist Party became ultimate. Practically, the leaders of Communist Revolutions such as Lenin, Stalin, Mao, and Fidel Castro in Cuba became substitute deities, with rituals focusing on them (such as the obligatory pilgrimage to Lenin's Tomb in Red Square in Moscow). The means of ultimate transformation are political and economic, the work of the people organized by the Party in bringing about the classless society. Therefore, it is essential for the Party to remain in power for the transformation to occur.

Our contention is not that Marxism *must* be a religion. Some Marxists utilize Marxism as a political and economic theory, but do not accord it the status of ultimacy. For example, some Christians who advocate "liberation theology" (see Chapter Eleven) draw on Marxism to diagnose the ills of their societies, but retain their allegiance to a spiritual power as the ultimate source of the needed transformation.

Satanism: Indulging Self

In the contemporary popular media, Satanism has become virtually synonymous with ritualized murders conducted by people described simply as "Satanists." Various groups have mobilized to challenge the influences of Satanism in popular culture, as for example in heavy metal rock music.

Few people are aware that in addition to such (quite rare) examples of what might be called "spontaneous" Satanism, there are organized Satanic movements, some of which have U.S. government recognition as legitimate religions, and which claim absolutely no connection to the lurid "Satanic" activities just cited.

"Formal" Satanism is divided into three distinct orientations. Some Satanists accept the Christian understanding of Satan as the evil opponent of God, the Prince of Darkness, whom they worship as the true power of the universe. They look forward to a life after death in Satan's realm. A second attitude accepts the idea of a personal Satan, but regards him as the heroic rebel against the Christian God who attempts to thwart natural human desires. His presumed evilness is a Christian distortion, designed to make people feel guilty, they say. These might be called forms of spiritual Satanism.

Our focus in this section is on the third type of formal Satanism, which holds that the personification of Satan in general is a projection of Christian guilt and insecurity. The true "Satan" is the life force itself, these movements claim, and all the natural impulses associated with life in the flesh. Worship of Satan is seen as a celebration of this natural life force, freed from the repressions of hypocritical Christian morality. Adherents of this understanding reject as childish and silly the view of Satan as a personal god, and as wishful thinking any hope of an afterlife. Thus, this type of Satanism is properly considered a secular religion.

There is no single, centralized Satanic movement of this type. Instead there are a number of groups that have developed around charismatic leaders. They are part of a tradition that arose in the late nineteenth and early twentieth centuries in Europe. One of the key figures in the tradition of hedonistic rejection of Christian morality was Aleister Crowley (1875–1947), a magician and author who advocated that "Do what you will shall be the whole of the Law."

The two most widely known modern secular Satanic movements in the United States endorse the view that Satan is nothing more than a symbol for humanity's carnal desires. In 1966 Anton LaVey organized the *Church of Satan* in San Francisco. LaVey was put off by the hypocrisy of "good Christians," whom he would see engaging in immoral behavior on Saturday night and then proclaiming their piety in church on Sunday morning. He challenged people to be honest with the fact that what they truly worship is their own natural desires. LaVey taught his followers to indulge themselves, so long as they did not hurt anyone who did not want to be hurt. The highly dramatic rituals of the Church of Satan included the traditional "black mass," in which the elements of the Catholic mass are parodied. (For example, the altar would be a nude woman; and instead of praying for others, curses would be hurled, with members ventilating their anger). With the publication and notoriety of his *Satanic Bible* in 1969, LaVey's movement grew. Satanic churches were opened in major cities throughout the United States and Europe. However, the membership was never very large, probably numbering in the hundreds.

Tension soon developed within the movement. Some members believed that LaVey was concerned only with the money and fame the Church of Satan was bringing to him, not with the religion itself. In 1975, Dr. Michael Acquino, who had been attracted to the Church of Satan because of its materialistic ideology, withdrew to form the *Temple of Set* (named after the Egyptian deity Seth, the source, Acquino argues, of the name Satan). In recent years the Temple of Set has largely replaced the Church of Satan as the major organized "Satanic" movement in the United States. According to its literature, the Temple of Set does not try to recruit members. In fact, those who desire to join are carefully screened to ensure that they are not mentally or emotionally unstable.

The basic principle of all forms of organized Satanism is that humans should pursue and enjoy natural pleasure and power and not feel guilty about their physical desires. Humans are animals and should simply be free to live out rather than repress their natural instincts (so long as they do not interfere with others' rights to do the same). Satanists believe that there is nothing wrong with individualistic egoism. Some observers say that this message seems frightfully similar to the consumerist ideal, which seems to resonate in modern, Western culture, that everyone should "grab as much as you can get" and "look out for number one." Dr. Acquino has contended that in consumerist societies such as the United States most people are latent Satanists and just don't realize it!

THE QUEST FOR UNITY: UNIVERSALIST NEW RELIGIOUS MOVEMENTS

Our final group of new religious movements are those that seek to draw on the truths of all religions and promote a new age of global unity, in which there will be equality and justice in all areas of life. Two such religions are the Baha'i Faith, a universalist new religious movement with its roots in Islam, and the Unitarian Universalist Association, a movement that emerged from Christianity.

The Baha'i Faith: Toward World Unity

In 1844 a young Iranian Shi'ite Muslim (who was also influenced by Sufi mysticism) named Mirza Ali Muhammad (1819–50) proclaimed that he was the *Bab-ub-Din* ("Gate of the Faith"). According to the beliefs of the Shi'ite sect to which he belonged, the Bab was claiming to be the twelfth Imam who had disappeared and would return as the Mahdi, the messiah who would restore a purified Islam (see Chapter Twelve). His followers became known as *Babis* and in 1848 withdrew from Islam. For most of his ministry the Bab was imprisoned; in 1850 he was executed. Before he died he announced that another would follow him, who would be the prophet of a new, universal religion.

While in prison in 1852, one of the Bab's followers, Mirza Husayn Ali (1817–92), experienced a call to be the prophet of God for the modern age, whom the Bab had foretold. In 1863 he publicly proclaimed himself as a prophet in the succession of Moses, Jesus, and Muhammad. His followers called him *Baha'u'llah* ("The Glory of God") and the religion he established became known as the *Baha'i* ("Glory") Faith.

Baha'u'llah spent the rest of his life persecuted and under arrest, transported from one location to another, finally spending his last years under fairly liberal house arrest in Acre, Palestine. Even though imprisoned, he nurtured the Baha'i Faith and wrote a number of works used today by Baha'is for worship and study. He also communicated with world leaders, urging that they dedicate themselves to world peace and understanding. Baha'u'llah prophesied the coming together of all humanity and the regeneration of the entire universe in these words (Baha'u'llah 1952: 243):

> I testify that Thou art the Lord of all creation, and the Educator of all beings, visible and invisible. I bear witness that Thy power hath encompassed the entire universe, and that the hosts of the earth can never dismay Thee, nor can the dominion of all peoples and nations deter Thee from executing Thy purpose. I confess that Thou hast no desire except the regeneration of the whole world, and the establishment of the unity of its peoples, and the salvation of all them that dwell therein.

Upon Baha'ullah's death, his son, known as Abdul Baha ("Servant of Glory"), succeeded him. Abdul Baha (1844–1921) established branches of the movement in the United States and developed the teachings of his father as they are understood in the West. Abdul Baha's son, Shoghi Effendi ("Guardian of the Cause;" 1898–1957), succeeded him and continued his father's missionary and organizational work. After Shoghi Effendi's death, leadership passed to a Universal House of Justice.

The Baha'i Faith teaches that all religions are true, for they all come from the same source. In virtually every age God reveals the truth through a designated prophet. Baha'u'llah, however, as the prophet of the modern age, is the last and greatest of these messengers. God is one, and so is humanity. All prejudice must be overcome, for all humans are members of the same family. The Baha'i Faith teaches that in the modern age science and religion must cooperate, for their teachings balance one another. Any religion that makes a claim contrary to science is distorting the truth. The freedom of each individual to pursue the truth must be protected. Equality between men and women is also stressed. The Baha'i Faith also strongly advocates world peace and calls for universal education and a universal language to help attain this goal.

The extremes of wealth and poverty must also be eliminated, the Baha'i Faith teaches, if world peace is to be realized. A universal court must be given the power to judge international disputes, so war can be avoided. The Baha'i Faith advocates a theory of work that considers it service to God. In keeping with its pragmatic orientation, the Baha'i Faith rejects a literal interpretation of heaven and hell. The souls of humans are eternal, but heaven and hell are not "places" where they go, but rather states of existence measured by the degree of harmony with God that the soul exhibits. The Baha'i worldview is essentially positive. No separate force of evil (like Satan) is recognized; evil is merely the lack of goodness.

The Muslim background of the Baha'i Faith is evident in the movement's attitude toward worship. Daily prayer is mandated, and fasting during one of the nineteen months in the Baha'i calendar is recommended. There is no special clergy to conduct services, which are usually held in a member's home. Worship is uncomplicated, with prayer and readings from the writings of Baha'u'llah and often from the sacred texts of other religions. Individual Baha'i congregations are administered by nine-member Local Spiritual Assemblies. Each country has a National Spiritual Assembly, also with nine members. The number nine, the largest whole number, symbolizes the world unity Baha'i seeks to promote. Local communities typically do not have separate buildings in which they worship. However, magnificent Houses of Worship have been constructed on all five continents. The North American House of Worship is located on the shore of Lake Michigan in Wilmette, Illinois.

In the early twenty-first century the Baha'i Faith reported about five million members in 230 countries and territories, coming from more than two thousand ethnic groupings. It is one of the world's largest religions in terms of the number of countries in which its adherents are found. The largest concentration of members is in the United States, but the movement is growing in the developing world because of its commitment to universal justice and acceptance of diverse cultures.

Unitarian Universalist Association: The Unity of God

The Unitarian Universalist Association was created in 1961 as the result of a merger between the American Unitarian Association and the Universalist Church of America. In that sense it is a new religion. However, the two movements that merged have long histories.

Unitarianism was a movement that rejected the orthodox Christian teaching of the Trinity in favor of an affirmation of the unity of God. The roots of Unitarianism are found in the early Christian trinitarian disputes, some leaders of the Protestant Reformation who questioned the trinity, and the Enlightenment criticism of revealed religion. The movement spread from England to the United States, where it gained a strong foothold in New England. Among its principal teachings were a commitment to interpret the Bible rationally, a dedication to follow the example of Jesus but not assert that he is God, and a strong devotion to serve humanity and right the wrongs of society. Many of the strongest opponents of slavery in the United States were Unitarians. The idea of human perfectibility through education was also a strong tenet. Respect for the integrity of individual conscience meant that Unitarianism had no creeds to which members pledged allegiance. Transcendentalist authors like Ralph Waldo Emerson gave literary expression to many Unitarian principles.

Unitarianism had always been a middle- and upper-class movement. The movement with which it merged in 1961 had its roots in a lower-class movement in England that emphasized the love of God, which will eventually restore all humanity to harmony with God and one another. Universalism was more evangelical and accepting of orthodox Christian teachings than Unitarianism, but it did emphasize the unity of God.

Since the merger, Unitarian Universalism (UU) has been principally (but not exclusively) a movement among highly educated, middle- to upper-class Americans. However, its openness to other religions and other cultures has won interfaith admiration among people of various cultural and ethnic backgrounds. In recent decades some groups within Wicca (see above) have found a home in UU churches, creating the Covenant of Unitarian Universalist Pagans. The basis of UU teaching is the free and open search for truth, with the recognition that truth can be found among all religious traditions. However, it finds in the Judeo-Christian expression of love of God and love of neighbor the core truth needed today. Its goal is the creation of a world community of justice and peace.

There is no set liturgy for worship in Unitarian Universalism, so Protestant-style services of prayer, praise, readings, and sermons often alternate with experimental services and programs on current social issues.

In the early years of the twenty-first century there were about one thousand UU congregations in North America, with approximately a million members, linked together through the Unitarian Universalist Association headquartered in Boston, Massachusetts.

CHAPTER SUMMARY

Hundreds, perhaps thousands, of "new religions" have sprung up in recent decades. We began this discussion of a representative sampling of "new religions" by raising the issue of how they should be approached. A significant number of people consider them all to be "sects" and "cults," which are a danger to individuals and society. However, to judge them negatively simply because they have arisen only recently is unfair. In this chapter we sought to objectively describe the selected religions, observing the principle stated in Chapter One that we should seek to understand religions before we evaluate them. We adopted the designation "new religious movements" for this group of religions.

We organized the new religious movements studied around a group of basic orientations:

- Preparing for the End: Apocalyptic Movements (Seventh Day Adventism, Branch Davidians, and Aum Shinryko)
- Faith and Spirit: Movements of Healing and Awareness (Christian Science and International Raelian Religion)
- Reviving the Church: Christian Movements of Renewal (The Church of Jesus Christ of Latter-day Saints and The Holy Spirit Association for the Unification of World Christianity)
- Nature and Spirit: Earth-based and Ecological Movements (Deep Ecology and Wicca)
- Liberation and Enlightenment: Movements with Asian Roots (The International Society for Krishna Consciousness, Falun Gong, and Soka Gakkai)
- African-American and Afro-Caribbean Movements (The Nation of Islam Ras Tafari)
- Native American Movements (The Native American Church)
- Focusing on the Human and the Natural: Secular Movements (Humanism, Marxism, and Satanism)
- The Quest for Unity: Universalist Movements (The Baha'i Faith and the Unitarian Universalist Association)

IMPORTANT TERMS AND PHRASES

(The following are in addition to the names of the new religious movements and their leaders.)

advent, casting the circle, Celestial Kingdom, Church of Humanity, Clonaid, coven, cult, *dafa,* decreeing, Divine Mind, drawing down the moon, ecological egalitarianism, Elohim, *falun,* Gaia, Goddess, *ganja, gohonzon,* Horned God, Lotus Sutra, Lotus Village Plan, magic, mantra, millenarian, Mormon, Moroni, Mount Carmel, peyote, sect, Seven Seals, Third Adam, *qigong,* witch, *zadankai*

QUESTIONS FOR DISCUSSION AND REFLECTION

1. Do you agree that the designations "cult" and "sect" should be avoided in a descriptive study of new religious movements?
2. Why are new religious movements in general springing up and growing rapidly in the contemporary world?
3. Does the rapid growth of new religious movements threaten the major religions discussed in earlier chapters, or do they enhance them by adding variety and competition?

SOURCES AND SUGGESTIONS FOR FURTHER STUDY

BAH'A'ULLAH, 1952. *Gleanings from the Writings of Bah'a'ullah,* trans. Shoghi Effendi. Wilmette, IL: Baha'i Publishing Trust.

EDDY, MARY BAKER, 1906. *Science and Health with a Key to the Scriptures.* Boston: Trustees under the Will of Mary Baker Eddy.

Web Sites

Several web sites provide introductions to the above new religious movements and sources for further study, including books and articles as well as links to appropriate web sites.

religiousmovements.org
    (a University of Virginia site, maintained by faculty and students)

religioustolerance.org/var_rel.htm
    (maintained by the Ontario Consultants on Religious Tolerance)

www.cesnur.org
    (the Center for Studies on New Religions)

Prentice Hall's **Research Navigator** helps students in their further study of the world's religions. Visit *http://www.researchnavigator.com* for help on the research process and access to databases full of relevant material, including the New York *Times*.

III

The World's Religions and Contemporary Ethical Issues

W hat are the most important ethical issues that the world faces in the twenty-first century? Among the most significant are the following, which we will address in the next four chapters:

- the ecological crisis that threatens to destroy the balance of life on the planet;
- the widening gap between rich and poor, and a perceived crisis of economic justice;
- the proliferation of ever more violent wars, and the rise of international terrorism, threatening global peace and stability;
- the ongoing debate over capital punishment: if and when society has the moral right to take the life of an individual who has violated society's laws;
- the deep divisions over the morality of abortion: whether there is a "right to life" for unborn babies, and who has the right to make reproductive choices for women;
- the question of euthanasia: whether and when there is a "right to die" (an issue becoming ever more acute because of modern medicine's ability to prolong life);
- the changing attitudes toward gender roles in society and the rights and status of women; and
- the question of sexual orientation, and in particular whether the view that homosexuality is a violation of the "natural order" is justified.

Religion is at the center of the discussions and debates swirling around each of these issues. Our goal in these chapters will be to examine a representative sampling of the responses of the world's religions to these dilemmas. Our purpose is to provide a context in which readers can reflect on and discuss these critically important questions, drawing on and responding themselves to the various religious perspectives.

CHAPTER

15

The Ecological and Economic Crises—Humans and Resources

THE ECOLOGICAL CRISIS: IS THE BALANCE OF LIFE ON PLANET EARTH IN JEOPARDY?

The Nature of the Issue and the Role of Religion

As the twenty-first century begins, there is wide agreement among scientists that the balance of life on planet earth is in danger. The issues are familiar:

- ozone depletion, releasing ultraviolet radiation that threatens to severely damage humans, other animals, and plants;
- emissions resulting in the "greenhouse effect" and the dangerous elevation of the earth's temperature, with a host of negative consequences;
- deforestation, including, but not limited to, the important tropical rain forests;
- pollution of the air, earth, and water;
- desertification, caused by depletion of the earth's soils through current agricultural practices;
- population growth that threatens to exceed the carrying capacity of the earth, unless we learn to distribute resources more equitably;
- extinction of species, which threatens the planet's biodiversity;
- consumption of natural resources faster than they can be replenished; and
- the proliferation of nuclear, biological, and chemical weapons of mass destruction.

For several decades, many interpreters (e.g., White 1967) have argued that the very roots of the modern environmental crisis are found *in* the teaching of *Western* religions that humans are distinct from nature and have a divinely sanctioned right to exploit nature. Many today are saying that since the roots of the present environmental crisis *are* spiritual, the solutions must come from religious sources as well. At the least, it is clear that any analysis of the ecological crisis must include attention to the possible role religions have played in creating it, and their potential for resolving it.

Religious Responses

Indigenous Religions   In Chapter Two we described the indigenous worldview as *biocentric* and *animistic,* meaning that all living beings are seen as members of one interdependent, spiritual community. From this perspective, it is critically important that humans live in harmony with the rest of the natural world. We can summarize these responses by identifying five themes, using Native American examples to illustrate them (Young 2002: 339–48):

INTERCONNECTEDNESS: WE ARE ALL RELATED   The traditional worldviews of the indigenous cultures we have studied all affirm that other beings are alive and conscious just as humans, and, with humans, form a single ecological community. A sense of kinship with all beings has caused Native Americans to approach other beings as brothers and sisters. Other animals are considered fellow "people" whose rights must be honored and who have a great deal to teach those who are attentive. Stones, trees, mountains, lakes, and all other "natural objects" also are alive, and can educate those willing to listen to them.

In such an interconnected world, humans must understand their place. In the words of a Taos Pueblo saying, "We are in one nest" (Hughes 1983: 15).

REVERENCE: ALL OF LIFE IS SPIRITUAL   In Native American teachings, the world in which all things are living and all are interrelated is spiritual. Therefore, the proper response is reverence.

The Diné (Navajo) goal of life, expressed in the word *hozho* (balance, harmony, beauty), expresses this attitude of reverence. In the words of the famous Diné prayer (Hughes 1983: 13):

> In beauty I walk,
> With beauty before me, I walk.
> With beauty behind me, I walk.
> With beauty below me, I walk.
> With beauty above me, I walk.
> With beauty all around me, I walk.
> It is finished in beauty.

MOTHER EARTH: THE WOMB OF LIFE   Another commonly held belief among Native American nations is that the Earth as a whole is alive and must be treated with respect. Although "sometimes male, or often sexless, the earth is indeed widely linked to femininity and motherhood" (Bierhorst 1994: 9).

This attitude toward the earth as mother caused Hopi farmers to resist the use of steel plows, because a plow "unnecessarily and cruelly tears the skin of the earth mother" (Loftin 1991: 9). It is also common to see references to plants as the dress of Mother Earth or as parts of her body. Like a mother, the earth gives birth to life.

EMBEDDEDNESS: WE ARE THE LAND AND THE LAND IS US   Another common ecological theme in indigenous religions might be called "embeddedness." From this perspective, we are part of the land and the land is part of us. As Jimmie Durham, a Cherokee artist, has written: "In *Ani Yonwiyah,* the language of my people, there is a word for land: *Eloheh.* This same word also means, history, culture and religion. This is because we Cherokees cannot separate our place on earth from our lives in it, nor from our vision and our meaning as a people" (Hughes 1983: 60).

A common phrase for this sense of embeddedness is "sense of place," an awareness that the world in which we live is a "sacred geography," in which the sacred history of a people is entwined with particular places.

RECIPROCITY: LIVING IN HARMONY   In the indigenous worldview, the world exists in a delicate balance, so humans must always act reciprocally, taking only that which is truly needed and replacing whatever is used. Everything done is seen as part of a sacred interaction between humans and the rest of nature.

Reciprocity means that if humans show proper respect, the spirit beings will respond favorably and assist humans as they seek to live harmoniously. This attitude is especially evident in the traditional farming practices of Native American communities. The Hopi, for example, were taught by the god of this world, Massaw, to reverence the earth as a relative and to treat the earth as they would expect to be treated.

Reciprocity is also evident in traditional Native American hunting and gathering techniques. The pueblo people who hunt antelope believe that "[w]aste of meat or even the thoughtless handling of bones cooked bare will offend the antelope spirits. Next year the hunters will vainly search the dry plains for antelope" (Silko 1996: 27). The Menominee people of Wisconsin who gather wild rice always make sure some of the rice falls into the water so that there will be a crop the following year.

The Tewa people of the American Southwest have a phrase that sums up well the indigenous ecological ethic. Tewa elders say, "Look to the mountain, to remind people that in their dealings with the earth, they must always take a long term perspective and think not merely of the immediate results of their actions, but of the impact on the land over thousands of years and on future generations" (Cajete 2002: 149).

Religions of South and Southeast Asia   South and Southeast Asia are not immune from the environmental destruction that plagues the world. For example, the rain forests of Southeast Asia are being exploited as ruthlessly as the rain and old growth forests of the Americas. The world's worst nonnuclear industrial accident occurred in Bhopal, India. Many of India's sacred rivers, including the Ganges, are polluted by municipal and industrial wastes.

The tragedy of these developments is at least twofold. First, they threaten the physical and social well-being of the peoples of South and Southeast Asia, as environmental degradation does elsewhere. Second, the environmental abuse stands in marked opposition to the understanding of nature present among most of the religions of Asia. As we shall see, Hinduism, Buddhism, and Jainism have ecological perspectives that run counter to the values supporting the abusive actions such as those listed above.

HINDUISM   The hymns of the Rig Veda reflect an awareness of the presence of the sacred in nature. For example, in a hymn to Aranyani, the goddess of the forest, the spiritual nature of the forest is celebrated in these words: "The forest creaks like a cart at eventide. Who tarries in the forest-glade, thinks to himself, 'I heard a cry'. Sweet-scented, redolent of balm, replete with food, yet tilting not, mother of beasts, the Forest Deity, her have I magnified with praise" (*Rig Veda* X.146. Cited by Chaitanya 1983: 129.)

Several ethical values that crystallized during the classical period of Hinduism reflect ecological sensitivity. According to Hindu teaching, even that which appears to be physical is in truth manifestation of the the spiritual (whether the impersonal Brahman or the Supreme Lord). This perspective might be described as *ecocentric,* for at the center is life itself imaged as an interconnected, spiritual whole.

The Hindu preference for vegetarianism, veneration of cows, and the general teaching of noninjury (*ahimsa*) flow from this understanding of spirituality. Anthropocentrism and its attendant attitude of the human right to exploit nature is not part of the basic Hindu worldview.

Another ecologically oriented Hindu value is restraint. It is an aspect of the Hindu ideal of the renunciation of attachment to one's actions in order to break free from the effects of the law of karma, expressed so vividly in the Bhagavad Gita.

Finally, the concept of karma (shared with other religions that emerged in India) has environmental implications. According to the law of karma, we are in a very real way the product of our past actions. It "binds [humanity] into the strongest community with natural processes and makes [humans] co-implicate, as it were, with them" (Deutsch 1989: 265).

Many Hindu leaders today are trying to balance a concern for the well-being of all life in their own tradition with the need to develop the material resources of the land to provide adequately for people. It is a delicate balancing act!

THERAVADA BUDDHISM   According to the stories of the life of Buddha preserved in Theravada tradition, he himself was in harmony with nature. He was born under a tree, and experienced enlightenment in a forest, on the banks of a river. Snails crawled on his head to protect him from the sun. In his preaching he used tales of animals, from his own past lives, implying that animals' lives were every bit as important as humans'.

One of the principal values the Buddha taught was *metta,* loving kindness for all beings. Theravada Buddhism holds that compassion should be displayed not selectively, but to all living beings. One Theravada text expresses this value (*Metta Sutta, Khuddakapatha.* Badiner 1990: 12) in this way: "As a mother with her own life guards the life of her own child, let all-embracing thoughts for all that lives be thine."

Vietnamese monk Thich Nhat Hanh expresses the basic Buddhist attitude concerning nature in these words (Harvey 2000: 151):

> We should deal with nature the way we should deal with ourselves! We should not harm ourselves; we should not harm nature [. . .] Human beings and nature are inseparable.

The fact that all beings share in the reality of impermanence (*anicca*) creates a sense of mutuality among humans and nonhuman life. Just as nonhuman living beings have "no eternal self," neither do humans. In addition, like other South Asian religions, Buddhism endorses the value of *ahimsa* (noninjury), with its important environmental implications.

JAINISM   Jainism offers perhaps the most radical environmental ethic of all the world's religions. It could be argued that given the depth of the crisis, the Jain approach to ecological responsibility offers the best hope for resolution. Jainism introduced the ideal of *ahimsa* into Indian culture and has always exemplified it most vividly. The ideal Jain lifestyle is one of respect for all life forms, even those that most people would find offensive. As one scholar has observed, the Jain view of nonviolence refers not only to human-human relationships but also to "species-species relationships and human-earth relationships" (Chapple 2001: 214).

Religions of East Asia   China, Japan, South Korea, and Taiwan certainly face serious environmental problems as the twenty-first century begins. The rapid economic growth in these countries has come at a significant environmental cost. However, as in South Asia, the religions of East Asia have a strongly ecological orientation that can serve as a resource in confronting these problems and developing the will to overcome them in East Asia and beyond.

DAOISM   The basic concepts of philosophical Daoism have clear implications for the present ecological crisis. Among them are "reversion, the constancy of cyclical change, *wu wei* ('actionless activity'), and the procurement of power by abandoning the attempt to 'take' it" (Goodman 1980: 73).

As we noted in Chapter Six, the Dao is the eternal process whereby everything comes into existence and passes out of existence. This is sometimes called the principle of reversion (*Daodejing*, Poem 40). It can be observed in such natural phenomena as the changing of the seasons and the birth, life, and death of all living beings. It can be argued that "much of our ecological crisis is caused by our failure to understand the simple truth of reversion." We pretend that we can simply throw things away and they will be gone forever, hiding from the simple truth that "things are only moved around; sooner or later they will be back" (Goodman 1980: 75).

The Daoist ideal is to utilize the natural cycles with a minimum of human involvement. Industrialized societies have moved to the opposite extreme, trying to improve life by maximizing human manipulation of nature. For example, on a mechanized farm, the farmer seeks to increase productivity by using chemical fertilizers. However, fertilizers sometimes increase short-term productivity but interfere with natural processes, with negative long-term results. Daoist agriculture is suspicious of such intervention and seeks to control pests through organic means, accepting poor crops as a result of weeds or insects as a part of the natural process, secure in the knowledge that nature will take care of the situation in a balanced way.

Paradoxically, Daoists believe that *wu wei* ("actionless activity"), or nonintervention with the ways of nature, is a means of control. *Wu-wei* is not passivity in the face of the forces of nature, but learning to respond to, rather than trying to coerce, them. For example, by closely observing the natural flow of water in a given area, the irrigation ditches that a farmer builds will work by harmonizing with the way of nature.

In its approach to energy production, Daoism would seek the path of generating power naturally. Ideally, there should be no waste, no residue. Daoism is suspicious of too much organization and centralization. The point is not to do without technology, but to let nature guide the technology needed.

Daoism does not treat nature in general, but in the concrete. From a Daoist perspective, we will never resolve the environmental crisis merely "by appeal to universal principles." Instead, we "must apply ourselves to the aesthetic task of cultivating an environmental *ethos* in our own place and time, and recommending this project to others by our participation in their environments" (Ames 1986: 348).

The Daoist attitude of the interrelatedness of all things challenges the anthropocentrism that can cause environmental insensitivity. As the modern science of ecology is recognizing, and Daoism has always asserted, we are all a part of an interdependent whole. Humanity does not stand outside this reality, but is simply one part of the organic process of the totality of nature (Ip 1986: 102–05). This is yet another expression of the *ecocentric* perspective.

CONFUCIANISM   On the surface, Confucianism would not appear to be concerned about the environment. Confucian teaching focuses on humans and their relations with one another. However, by extension Confucianism makes an important contribution to the quest for ecological responsibility. Confucian teaching views humans in the context of their social relations, never atomistically as Westerners tend to do. "Confucius posits a social model of human individuality which is an analogue of ecology's model of species adapting to niches in the economy of nature and thus acquiring their specific characteristics" (Callicott 1987: 129). From this perspective, humans are members of a biological community, in which they must practice the Confucian virtues of propriety, reciprocity, and concern for others (see Chapter Seven).

Confucianism (like Daoism) reflects the East Asian worldview that holds that "all of the parts of the entire cosmos belong to one organic whole and that they all interact as participants in one spontaneously self-generating life process" (Wei-Ming 1989: 67). This notion of organic continuity and dynamism, echoed by modern ecologists, is, many argue, one of the principal starting points for developing a responsible environmental ethic today. In her study of the ecological teachings in Confucianism, Mary Evelyn Tucker concludes that the "holistic and dynamic understanding of the world and the role of humans which we find in Confucianism could bring us far in the revisioning so necessary for dealing with our current ecological crisis" (Tucker 2001: 344).

MAHAYANA BUDDHISM   Among the Mahayana schools, Zen has the most important environmental implications. It too has an *ecocentric* perspective. If all reality is, in truth, the Buddha-nature, as Zen teaches, then the attitude of egoism that contributes to abuse of the environment is undermined. Zen teaching (as expressed, for example, in the art that it inspires), emphasizes the harmony of nature and the place of humans within the processes of nature. The mystical experience of *satori* is of a harmony beyond description, which leads to a calm and peaceful lifestyle of balance, with all of the "grasping" that has created the environmental crisis overcome. Zen students seek to awaken to an identity with all beings, thus emptying themselves of awareness of a separate self. A Korean Zen master, Samu Sunim, has said, "Everything depends on others for survival and nothing really exists apart from everything else. Therefore, there is no permanent self or entity independent of others. Not only are we interdependent, but we are an interrelated whole. As trees, rocks, clouds, insects, humans and animals, we are all equals and parts of our universe" (cited by Donegan 1990: 197).

The Mahayana Hua-yen Sutra uses the image of the Net of Indra to illustrate the interdependence of all reality (Cook 1977). According to this text, in the abode of the god Indra there is a net that stretches infinitely in all directions, with a jewel on each point or "eye" of the net. Each jewel in the net reflects and contains all the other jewels. And in each jewel is another net. The image symbolizes a cosmos in which all members are interrelated and infinite. What affects one member affects all. There is no hierarchy, no center (for all are at the center). In this universe everything is needed, everything valuable. "It is not just that 'we are all in it' together. We all *are* it, rising or falling as one living body" (Callicott and Ames 1989: 229).

The leader of Tibetan Buddhism, the Dalai Lama, captured the Buddhist attitude of compassion for all living things in these words: "Our mother planet is telling us, 'My dear children, behave in a more harmonious way. Please take more care of me!'" (Vittachi 1989).

SHINTO   The ecological perspective in Shinto is also *ecocentric* and reflects the Shinto principle of *cultivation*.

One symbol of the ecocentric principle is the *torii,* the gateway outside a Shinto shrine. The freestanding, open gateway indicates the lack of separation—as well as the necessary balance—between the manmade and the natural.

The paper walls of Japanese houses, which are sensitive to changes in light, wind, and temperature, also reflect a sense of the participation of nature in that which humans create (Shaner 1989: 166).

The theme of cultivation (*shugyo*) refers to the importance of the development of character in Japanese culture. Cultivation "depends upon an emotional engagement with nature and others" (175). From this perspective, as we seek to develop ourselves we must always realize that we are part of a larger social and natural whole. There is a long tradition in Japanese culture of seeking "a keen emotional sensitivity to and empathy with the natural environment" (177).

The harmony of nature is a basic Shinto principle. Here family imagery is used in a Shinto text to speak of the harmony that needs to be maintained (*Oracle of the God of Atsuta.* Aston 1905: 370):

> All ye men who dwell under Heaven. Receive the just commands of the Gods. Regard Heaven as your father, Earth as your mother, and all things as your brothers and sisters. You will then enjoy this divine country which excels all others, free from hate and sorrow.

Religions Originating in the Middle East   Many contemporary environmentalists charge that the monotheistic religions that developed in the Middle East (Judaism, Christianity, and Islam) are to a significant degree responsible for the current ecological crisis. Their reasoning is that these religions have distanced the sacred from nature, and created the attitude that humans may exploit nature at will, since this prerogative has been given to humans by the Creator. In their view, the result has been unchecked abuse of the environment in the West (and elsewhere, as Western influence spreads). Since this discussion has arisen largely in the context of Christianity, we will examine it in more detail below. In response to this criticism, Jewish, Christian, and Muslim leaders have sought to both answer it and search within their own traditions for a responsible environmental ethic.

JUDAISM   In developing a contemporary Jewish ethic for the environment, four themes are being highlighted: divine ownership of nature, respect for the natural order, maintenance of the harmony of the earth, and reverence for the sacred quality of the natural world (Helfand 1986: 40–50).

Divine Ownership of Nature The theme of divine ownership of nature derives from the affirmation that "the earth is the Lord's and the fullness thereof" (Psalm 24:1). Although humans have a special place in creation as God's partners, the earth does not belong to humans to do with as we please. The Tanak in general makes clear that, as the Lord asserts, "The land is mine" (Leviticus 25:23).

Respect for the Natural Order Therefore, humans must follow the divine plan in their treatment of nature, according to Jewish law. In a commentary on the Book of Ecclesiastes, the rabbis wrote (*Midrash Kohelt Rabbah* 7:20; cited in Dorff 2001: 105–06):

> At the time time that the Holy One, blessed be He, created the first man, he took him and showed him all the trees of the Garden of Eden and said to him: "Look at how beautiful and praiseworthy are my creations. Everything that I created, I created for you. Pay attention not to spoil or destroy my world, for if you spoil it, there is none to fix it after you."

In this regard, attention has been drawn by Jewish interpreters to the Biblical precept that "in case you lay siege to a city many days by fighting against it so as to capture it from them, you must not ruin its trees by wielding an axe against them; for you should eat from them, and you must not cut them down" (Deuteronomy 20:19). According to Rabbinic interpretation of this precept, unnecessary destruction of nature is not permissible. This law "has been expanded to form a protective legal umbrella encompassing almost the entire realm of ecological concerns." This attitude extends to a concern for the protection of endangered species in Jewish tradition (Helfand 1986: 44–45).

Maintenance of the Harmony of the Earth In the Talmud and among commentators, the principle of *yishuv ha-aretz* ("settlement of the land") has been applied to create an ethic of maintaining the harmony of the earth. For example, the Mishnah forbade the raising of goats and sheep in the land of Israel because of their propensity to defoliate the land. The fourteenth century code of Jacob ben Asher, the *Tur,* extends the principle to *yishuv ha-olam* ("settlement of the world"). Thus, the Jewish community outside the borders of Israel was implored to act with environmental responsibility (Helfand 1986: 46–47). This principle can form a basis for Jewish endorsement of the modern argument that nature has rights that must be respected.

Reverence for the Sacred Quality of the Natural World The awareness of the sacred quality of all creation should give humans a sense of humility. Although we treat the land "as if" we were its masters, we must never forget that we are but a part of God's larger whole. That awareness instills in us a feeling of harmony with all creation. As the Talmud says, "He who goes out in the spring and views the trees in bloom must recite, 'Blessed is He who left nothing lacking in His world and created beautiful creatures and beautiful trees for mankind to glory in'" (*Berakhot,* 43a. Cited in Helfand 1986: 49).

The twentieth-century Jewish philosopher Martin Buber contrasts two ways that humans relate to others, whether they be humans or other beings. When we relate in an "I-it" manner, we treat the "other" as an object or thing; the relationship is exploitative. When we enter into an "I-Thou" relationship, we affirm the worth and dignity of the other; the relationship is reciprocal. For Buber, God is the "Eternal Thou" (Buber 1970). The ecological challenge is to relate to all of nature not as "it" but as "Thou." Many Jews are recognizing that within their tradition there are the resources for responding to that challenge.

CHRISTIANITY   In 1966 Lynn White, an interpreter of the history of science and technology, dropped the first bombshell in the modern debate over the role of both Judaism and Christianity in the ecological crisis. White argued that Western civilization had exploited nature to the extent that the quality, if not the very survival, of its life was threatened. The reason, White said, was a dualistic ethical system that sharply discriminates between humans and nature. That ethic is based on the biblical tradition that informs Judaism and Christianity. Because of biblical texts, like the first chapter of Genesis, these religions have assumed that humans are separate from, rather than part of, the natural community. Moreover, humans are told by God, according to Genesis, that nature exists solely for their benefit. White concluded that "Christianity is the most anthropocentric religion the world has seen" (White 1967: 1205). He argued that meaningful change in the treatment of nature would not occur in the West "until we reject the Christian axiom that nature has no reason for existence save to serve man" (1207). White also pointed to the Christian hostility toward animism as another basis for the attitude that nature is mere matter for humans to use as they choose, rather than living reality to be reverenced. He concluded that "since the roots of our [ecological] trouble are so largely religious, the remedy must also be essentially religious, whether we call it that or not. We must rethink and refeel our nature and destiny" (1207).

Interpreters have highlighted other aspects of traditional Christianity's hostility toward nature. One is the attitude that the wilderness is a cursed land, which must be subdued and "humanized." Some assert that Christianity has also emphasized other-worldly concerns, which leaves the earth as merely a place of testing and preparation for heavenly existence (Nash 1989: 91).

By the 1970s a consensus had emerged among many interpreters, which pointed to the following aspects of the view of nature associated with Christianity (Callicott and Ames 1989: 3–4):

- God—the locus of the holy or sacred—transcends nature.
- Nature is a profane artifact of a divine craftsman-like creator. The essence of the natural world is unformed matter.
- Humanity exclusively is created in the image of God and is, thus, segregated, essentially, from the rest of nature.
- Humanity is given dominion by God over nature.
- God commands humans to subdue nature and multiply themselves.
- The world is hierarchically organized: God over humanity, humanity over nature.
- The image-of-God in man is the ground of man's intrinsic value. Since nonhuman natural entities lack the divine image, they are morally disenfranchised. They have, at best, instrumental value.
- The rest of nature exists as a means to support human ends.

In modern times, a number of Christians have sought to respond to these assertions by developing a Christian ecological ethic that inspires environmental responsibility. Some Christian interpreters have pointed out that in addition to the "domination of nature" theme of Genesis, there are other Scriptural injunctions and images that support Christian environmental responsibility. Protestant theologian Richard Cartwright Austin summarizes positive Biblical teachings on the environment in these words (Austin 1988: 18):

> The Bible's ecological perspective is remarkable, for it brings nature within the community of covenant love and moral responsibility. The Lord tends a landscape which, though often injured by human oppression, yearns to flourish under just treatment and, beyond that, to respond compassionately to humans needs.

When we turn to the New Testament, we find a number of ecologically related themes. The first is an important aspect of the message of Jesus, according to the first three gospels—the Kingdom of God. The Kingdom is God's new beginning, a time of the renewal of the covenant that extends to all of creation (Austin 1988: 115–26).

Another source of Christian ecology is the New Testament concept that Christ is present in the entire cosmos, with the implication that if Christ is divine, then all reality is sacred (e.g., Colossians 1: 15–17).

The Apostle Paul envisioned all creation participating in God's redemption (Romans 8: 21): "the creation itself will be set free from its bondage to decay and will obtain the freedom of the glory of the children of God."

During the Middle Ages, St. Francis of Assisi (1182–1226) addressed nonhuman beings as "brother" and "sister" and the earth as "mother." St. Francis "implicitly accorded to all creatures and natural processes a value entirely separate from human interest. Everything had a direct relationship with God" (Nash 1989: 93).

Early in the twentieth century, Albert Schweitzer not only espoused a philosophy of life rooted in Christianity (which he called "reverence for life"), he modeled it in his work in Africa and his theological writings. According to Schweitzer, "the great fault of all ethics hitherto has been that they believed themselves to have to deal only with relations of man to man" (cited in Spring 1974: 1).

Catholic scientist and theologian Pierre Teilhard de Chardin developed a vision of a process of cosmic redemption that has inspired a great deal of ecological reflection. The process philosophy of Alfred North Whitehead has also influenced many theologians (beginning with Charles Hartshorne) to take seriously the reality of God as a dynamic presence amidst, rather than separate from, nature. One "process theologian," Daniel Day Williams, wrote, "Our modern experience of nature leads many theologians to affirm more emphatically the divine immanence in the world. God [. . .] is the creative spirit and the ultimate order that makes process possible and order intelligible." (Williams in Barbour 1972: 58).

The first papal statement specifically on the environment came in 1971 when, in an apostolic letter (*Octogesima Adveniens*), Pope Paul VI warned that industrial society was causing "dramatic and unexpected changes in the natural order" (Jakowska 1986: 134). On the fifth World Environment Day in 1977, Paul VI said that the fulfillment of the Kingdom of God on earth includes an ecological dimension: "nature will regain the lost balance and will participate in the liberation of all God's children" (135).

Pope John Paul II continued the strong environmental statements of his predecessor. For example, on the eight hundredth anniversary of the birth of Saint Francis of Assisi in 1982, he warned that "we cannot continue as predators, destroying what was provided through God's wisdom; we must respect nature in order to preserve a suitable environment for future generations" (Jakowska: 136).

By the 1980s many other church leaders had signed on as Christian environmentalists. For example, in 1988 Archbishop Robert Runcie of the Anglican Church made a statement that increasing numbers of Christians could endorse (Cited in Vittachi 1989: 93):

> At the present time, when we are beginning to appreciate the wholeness and interrelatedness of all that is in the cosmos, preoccupation with humanity can seem distinctly parochial. We need now to extend the area of the sacred and not to reduce it[. . . .] The nonhuman parts of creation would then be seen as having an intrinsic value of their own rather than being dependent for value on their relation to human beings.

Well-known evangelist Billy Graham, known principally for his concern for the salvation of individuals, also expressed the view that "we Christians have a responsibility to take a lead in trying to take care of the Earth" (Stone 1989: 79).

However, a reaction against what has become known as "ecotheology" has sprung up among both Catholic and Protestant leaders who see it as an undermining of Christianity's central teachings. For example, Archbishop Robert Dwyer of Los Angeles warned that such views were "anti-human" and could lead to human self-extinction. And Protestant writer Richard Neuhaus claimed that those who advocated the rights of nature were deflecting Christianity from its proper concern for the plights of humans. Nevertheless, by the 1990s most Christians were at least giving lip service to, and many were becoming much more involved in, the movement to preserve the environment and restore the balance of life.

Other Christians who support the goals of the environmental theologians question whether simply teaching people about the spiritual nature of creation and appealing to human goodness is sufficient. For example, "Christian realist" Reinhold Niebuhr (1892–1971), made the following observation (Ayers 1986: 166):

> our present environmental crisis is due not only to the wrongheaded thinking and mistaken feelings present in individuals [. .] but also to the perceived vested interests, the collective egoism, of groups, social, economic, political, and religious. For example, in his better moments an individual executive of an industry might be persuaded of the need to be concerned about the environment, and yet, because of his own ego interests and the vested interest of the firm, he might be unable to restrain this industry from polluting the environment.

From this point of view, a combination of moral persuasion and coercive action are necessary to meet environmental challenges.

ISLAM   Islam shares with traditional Judaism and Christianity both the view that humans have a divinely given authority over other creatures and the theme of stewardship of the earth. Islam's environmental ethic balances the need to provide for human well-being from the resources of nature with respect for the balance of nature. From a Muslim perspective, "such an approach would maintain man's position on the earth as ecologically dominant, but at the same time regulate his behavior by clearly defined measures of reward and punishment; both in this world as well as in the other world" (Zaidi 1986: 112).

Like Judaism and Christianity, Islam teaches that God has created the natural world for the benefit of humans and has given humankind the responsibility for the care of the nonhuman world, as this hadith illustrates (*Hadith of Bukhari.* Dermenghem 1958: 117):

> According to Abu Hurairah, the Messenger of God [Muhammad] said "A man travelling along a road felt extremely thirsty and went down a well and drank. When he came up he saw a dog panting with thirst and licking the (moist) earth. 'This animal,' the man said, 'is suffering from thirst just as much as I was.' So he went down the well again, filled his shoe with water, and taking it in his teeth climbed out of the well and gave the water to the dog. God was pleased with his act and granted him (pardon for his sins)."

Traditional Islam has a deep sense of reverence for nature as Allah's creation. The creation is ordered harmoniously. The Qur'an makes abundantly clear that the earth belongs to Allah, and that humans are His stewards (or viceroys). Humans are held accountable for how they function in this capacity. According to the Qur'an, they are not to take actions that disrupt the environment (*Surah* 15: 19–20. Ali 2002: 162):

> And We have spread out the earth (like a carpet); set thereon mountains firm and immovable, and produced therein all kinds of things in due balance.
> And we have provided therein means of subsistence,—for you and for those whose sustenance you are not responsible.

Creation is full of the signs of Allah, which cause reflective humans to have reverence for and respect the divine order inherent in nature. The major ecological problem is not "human dominance," from a Muslim perspective, but the materialism and greed characteristic of Western culture, which has turned from its spiritual roots. A society based on Islam accepts human control of nature, but within the limits set forth by Allah. Muslim leaders have a responsibility to insure that the programs of development necessary to better the conditions for humans do so in a way in that preserves the environment (Zaidi 1986: 120–22).

SIKHISM   Like the other religions in this group, Sikhism asserts that humans have a divinely ordained responsibility as caretakers of the earth, who are to use the resources of the earth wisely and well.

New Religious Movements   Among the thousands of new religious movements there is no uniformity on any of the ethical issues discussed in this volume. For each issue we will be able to sample only a few from the variety of these responses. We have already discussed the environmental teachings of Deep Ecology and Wicca in Chapter Fourteen.

THE INTERNATIONAL SOCIETY FOR KRISHNA CONSCIOUSNESS   In response to a request for ISKCON positions on current social issues, Drutakarma Dasa, a member of the movement for over thirty years and an editor of ISKCON publications (including *Back to Godhead* and *ISKCON World Review*), made the following statement on the ecological crisis (Dasa 1992):

> The root of the environmental crisis is a spiritual one. The world has for several centuries been dominated by a mechanistic, materialistic, and essentially godless view of the universe. And from this has grown an industrial-consumer civilization

bent on exploiting and dominating matter to the maximum extent possible. The environment has suffered from this. Responding to the environmental crisis, the International Society for Krishna Consciousness offers a new way of looking at the universe, as the energy and property of God, who offers humans an opportunity to develop their dormant God consciousness and return to their original spiritual home. Meanwhile, humans can use the resources of nature in a balanced, harmonious way, consistent with the primary goal of developing God consciousness. In order to demonstrate this, the International Society for Krishna Consciousness has established over 50 spiritually-centered rural communities, striving for self-sufficiency by cow protection and agriculture. Their motto is simple living and high thinking.

SECULAR HUMANISM   The *Humanist Manifesto II,* published by the American Humanist Association, includes as one of its seventeen basic principles the following statement on the environment (AHA 1973):

> The world community must engage in cooperative planning concerning the use of rapidly depleting resources. The planet earth must be considered a single ecoystem. Ecological damage, resource depletion, and excessive population growth must be checked by international concord. The cultivation and conservation of nature is a moral value; we should perceive ourselves as integral to the sources of our being in nature. We must free our world from needless pollution and waste, responsibly guarding and creating wealth, both natural and human. Exploitation of natural resources, uncurbed by social conscience, must end.

THE ECONOMIC CRISIS: WHY HUNGER AND ABJECT POVERTY IN A WORLD OF PLENTY?

The Nature of the Issue and the Role of Religion

In 2000 a group of 191 nations developed the Millennium Development Goals. The goals included halving the number of those living in extreme poverty by 2015. Two years later, world leaders gathered in Johannesburg, South Africa, for a summit to develop strategies to realize this goal. It will not be easy, for the gap between the rich and the poor in the world continues to widen, especially in the United States. In 2003 the Worldwatch Institute reported that "while the global economy has grown sevenfold since 1950, the disparity in per capita income between the 20 richest and 20 poorest nations more than doubled between 1960 and 1995[....] Of all high-income nations, the United States has the most unequal distribution of income, with over 30 percent of income in the hands of the richest 10 percent and only 1.8 percent going to the poorest 10 percent" (Worldwatch 2003: 88).

The World Bank defines "absolute poverty" as a condition affecting roughly 20 percent of the world's population, characterized by "malnutrition, illiteracy, disease, short life expectancy and high rates of infant mortality." In the early twenty-first century this means that over one billion people are the "absolutely poor." Roughly another billion live a subsistence lifestyle—which, although not life-threatening, condemns people to having little more than the very minimal necessities.

The thesis that religion plays a central role in shaping economic life has widespread acceptance today. If we are to understand such economic issues as the distribution of wealth and the growing disparity between rich and poor, and how to respond to them, we must examine religious teachings.

Religious Responses

Indigenous Religions

AFRICAN   The Yoruba have a number of proverbs that teach the dignity of hard work: "Weeping will not save anyone from penury," "The pretended illness of the indolent is incurable," "Labor is the cure of poverty" (Abogunrin 1989: 282–83). These would seem to challenge the stereotype that indigenous people lack initiative. However, Yoruba tradition also teaches that those who by their labor acquire wealth are expected to share their resources with others. Riches pass away ("money comes and goes like the showers of rain"), so what a person should strive for is a good name. A reputation is gained not by the accumulation of wealth but by generosity. Giving freely to the poor is rewarded in life beyond death.

Unfortunately, both Western economic-growth models and indigenized socialist models have proven ineffective in helping the economic plight of many indigenous peoples. The poor have become poorer and the rich richer. According to the World Bank, 38.1 percent of Sub-Saharan Africans (180 million people) lived on less than one dollar a day in 1987. Statistics compiled in 1999 showed that the percentage had grown to 39.1 percent (219 million people). Some African leaders maintain that a return to the values of traditional cultures will lead to the development of indigenous models of economic development.

NATIVE AMERICAN   Ohiyesa (Charles Eastman), a Dakota Elder, characterized his peoples' approach to material possessions in these moving words (Eastman 1971: 99–100, 101):

> It was our belief that the love of possessions is a weakness to be overcome. Its appeal is to the material part, and if allowed its way will in time disturb the spiritual balance of the man[. . . .] The Indian in his simplicity literally gives away all that he has, to relatives, to guests of another tribe or cleen, but above all to the poor and aged, from whom he can hope for no return.

Native Americans seem to have had a sense of the necessity of considering "sustainability" in their economic decisions. "Indian technology was certainly capable of doing more damage to the environment than was actually done. Such skilled hunters could have depleted the birds and animals. Fishing weirs could have been left closed, instead of being opened to let many of the migrating fish through. . . . It was not lack of technology, but the basically ecological attitudes of the Indians, that prevented exploitation" (Hughes 1983: 98).

Religions of South and Southeast Asia

HINDUISM   According to Hindu tradition, wealth or poverty is a result of a person's own karma [action]. A starving untouchable is enduring the unfortunate consequences of behavior in a past life. By contrast, a wealthy merchant is benefitting from the karmic influences of a previous existence or prior actions in this life. Since the caste system and the law of karma are believed by Hindus to be rooted in the very nature of the cosmos itself, the concept of social inequities being "unjust" is a difficult one for traditional Hinduism to accept. To the degree that traditional Hinduism still dominates life in India, what outsiders would view as oppression and injustice is seen by rich and poor alike as inevitable and unchangeable.

On the other hand, reformers like Mahatma Gandhi have drawn on other traditional teachings, such as *ahimsa* (noninjury), to press for programs designed to alleviate poverty, hunger, and homelessness in India. Adapting the tradition of renunciation to modern problems, the Ramakrishna Order has opened clinics and other social service agencies across India to respond to human suffering. In addition, a relatively strong Communist movement in India, as well as other types of socialist groups, have influenced social developments in some regions of India. Regardless of the sources, the contemporary leaders of India are committed to what they realize will be a long struggle to transform Indian society on the basis of the principles of equal rights and equal justice. Tremendous strides (in the face of almost overwhelming odds) are being made in the areas of distribution of food, housing, and health care, and a lower percentage of Indians lives in abject poverty today than before the modern state originated.

THERAVADA BUDDHISM   The fundamental Buddhist teaching that craving must be overcome has profound economic implications. Economic systems in the West are based on the idea of insatiable consumption. What might be called "Buddhist economics" is based on "simplicity, frugality, and an emphasis on what is essential—in short, a basic ethic of restraint" (De Silva 1990: 15). From a Western perspective, development occurs as more desires are fulfilled; from a Buddhist perspective, true development is in the reduction of desires. In the words of E. F. Schumacher, writing in his now classic work *Small Is Beautiful: Economics as if People Mattered,* "the Buddhist sees the essence of civilization not in a multiplication of wants but in the purification of human character" (Schumacher 1973: 52).

The basic Buddhist teaching of the "Middle Way" between self-indulgence and self denial means that it is not wealth itself that is the problem or the enjoyment of material things. Wealth itself is not evil; it how it is made and used, and, most importantly, the attitude one has toward it that are most important. According to the *Dhammapada,* "contentment is the greatest wealth" (Harvey 2000: 187). "The keynote of Buddhist economics, therefore, is simplicity and non-violence. From an economist's point of view, the marvel of the Buddhist way of life is the utter rationality of its pattern—amazingly small means leading to extraordinarily satisfactory results" (Schumacher 1973: 54).

In terms of the issue of wealth and poverty, the Buddhist perspective minimizes the intense competition for limited resources characteristic of societies that focus on consumption as the accepted goal. Extremes of wealth and poverty develop where the quality of life is measured by the amount of material goods one possesses. Since basic Buddhism teaches people not to strive for material well-being, but to measure the quality of life on the basis of the overcoming of craving, people in traditional Theravada Buddhist societies instinctively use resources modestly. And "people satisfying their needs by means of a modest use of resources are obviously less likely to be at each other's throats than people depending on a high rate of use" (Schumacher 1973: 55).

Beggars in a market in South India. As the twenty-first century began, over one billion of the world's people lived in extreme poverty.

Since Buddhism teaches reverence for all life, it instinctively counts the cost of using up nonrenewable resources. From a Buddhist perspective (Schumacher 1973: 57),

> non-renewable goods must be used only if they are indispensable, and then only with the greatest care and the most meticulous concern for conservation[. . . .] a population basing its economic life on non-renewable fuels is living parasitically, on capital instead of income.

The Buddhist approach to economic life favors self-sufficiency, with local communities supporting themselves using the resources at hand. In the developing world this model makes people themselves accountable for producing what they need to live, without becoming dependent on the uncertainties of large-scale trade and commerce. In this way communities need not be trapped by the boom-and-bust cycles of such economic activity. However, it must also be acknowledged that the Buddha's emphasis on diligence and hard work is compatible with the entrepreneurial spirit found in capitalism (Harvey 2000: 209).

Buddhism may indeed offer a middle way between unabashed materialism and traditionalist stagnation. The former has led to disastrous results—"a collapse of the rural economy, a rising tide of unemployment in town and country, and the growth of a city proletariat without nourishment for either body or soul" (Schumacher 1973: 58). The latter has proven incapable of adapting to changing circumstances of life, and has left people in backward conditions that have condemned them to absolute poverty. Buddhism offers an economic "middle way" (Payutto 1994).

As the twenty-first century begins, various attempts are underway in Theravadan countries to draw on Buddhism in economic policy. In Sri Lanka, for example, the *Sarvodaya Sramadadana* movement ("Sharing Energy for the Awakening of All") fosters the economic and cultural development of impoverished villages by implementing the middle path taught by the Buddha. The movement "criticizes both capitalism and socialism for focusing only on economic activity" and ignoring traditional spiritual values It is perhaps the most influential movement in "engaged Buddhism," which seeks to solve social problems with techniques drawn from Buddhist tradition (Harvey 2000: 227–34).

JAINISM   The Jain virtue of *aparigraha* (nonattachment) is particularly relevant to a discussion of economics and social justice. According to this virtue, "one should set a limit to one's own needs and whatever surplus one may accumulate beyond these needs should be disposed of through charities" (Jain 1989: 80). It thus provides for the equitable distribution of wealth without the necessity of government intervention or revolutionary struggle on the part of the dispossessed. Jains view it as the only peaceful way the growing gulf between the rich and the poor can be bridged.

Religions of East Asia

DAOISM   The poems of the Daodejing suggest a Daoist approach to economics. If modern consumer society is based on the principle of striving for success and prosperity, Daoist philosophy proposes that such ambition is a recipe for poverty. If you pursue success, it will elude you (9). To be truly rich, be content with what you have (33). If your sense of fulfillment depends on the accumulation of material things, you will never be filled (44). The more you give to others, the wealthier you will be (81).

When societies are in harmony with the Dao, their factories build that which people need to live. When they are not, they produce weapons of war (53). Daoist philosophy does not, however, support government intervention in peoples' lives in order to take care of them. Such welfare undermines their self-reliance. Trust the people, the Daodejing says, then leave them alone (57, 75). Philosophical Daoism supports small-scale, local enterprises in which people support themselves rather than elaborate trade, communication, and transportation networks that complicate life (80).

CONFUCIANISM   As with Buddhism, for Confucianism the goal of economic activity is not material prosperity but moral development. From a traditional Confucian perspective, individuals and societies must place morality ahead of material gain. As Master Meng (Mencius) said, "If righteousness be put last, and profit be put first, they [i.e., government and common people alike] will not be satisfied without snatching all" (cited by Tse 1989: 112). Societies should be structured on moral, rather than business, relationships.

Confucianism also recognizes that in order to have the personal security necessary to develop morally, a person must be free from poverty and be able to own the goods necessary to provide for basic needs. Therefore, it is not opposed to the market economy and free trade.

The role of the government in the economy, in the Confucian model, is neither direct ownership of business nor a completely laissez faire approach. Rather, government should supervise the conduct of business to insure against monopolies and exploitation (Tse 1989: 112–13).

The success of the economies of East Asian countries that have a Confucian heritage may be taken as evidence that this approach is practical. When the pursuit of wealth is not the primary end, prosperity seems naturally to follow (see Tai 1989 and Zhang 1999).

MAHAYANA BUDDHISM   One interpreter has argued that Mahayana Buddhism can provide the religious basis for the emergence of a new, global economic order, just as Protestantism was once the motivating force for the development of modern capitalism, claiming that "[j]ust as once before Reformation Protestantism was the transformation of Christianity in the shift from medievalism to modernism, so now is Reformation Buddhism part of the transformation from European to planetary culture" (Thompson 1989: 25).

The post–World War II Japanese "economic miracle" is rooted in a mix of Confucian and Buddhist values. The Buddhist contribution has particularly been in the commitment of companies to the welfare of their employees (Harvey 2000: 235–37).

Religions Originating in the Middle East   As we shall see, the religions that originated in the Middle East (Judaism, Christianity, and Islam) are conducive to the development of free enterprise economies that rely on individual initiative. However, they all express deep concern for the poor who cannot provide for themselves, regardless of the economic system in place, and link care for the impoverished to God's will and plan for the earth.

JUDAISM   The Tanak contains no specific economic principles for the distribution of wealth. However, the practices suggested in the legal sections, many of the utterances of the prophets, comments in the historical sections, and observations in the Psalms and wisdom writings show an unmistakable bias in favor of those on the economic margins of society.

The laws of the Torah again and again admonish the Israelites to provide for the widow, orphan, and sojourner in their midst (e.g., Exodus 22:21–24). The system of sabbatical years provided for the needs of the poor, that they might have access to food (Exodus 23:11, Leviticus 19:9–10) and have their debts cancelled (Deuteronomy 23:24–25).

Calls for rulers and people to bring justice to the poor, because of their oppression, can be found in virtually all of the prophetic books (e.g., Ezekiel 22:29, 31). For example, the Prophet Amos indicts the northern Kingdom of Israel for the treatment of the poor, identifying the needy as the righteous (2:6–7):

> Thus says the LORD:
> For three transgressions of Israel,
>   and for four, I will not revoke the punishment;
> because they sell the righteous for silver,
>   and the needy for a pair of sandals—
> they who trample the head of the poor into the dust of the earth,
>   and push the afflicted out of the way

Other indictments of the rich for their treatment of the poor are found throughout the collected sayings of the other eighth-century B.C.E. Israelite prophets (e.g., Isaiah 1:23, 2:7, 5:8 and Micah 2:2).

The Psalms portray God as having a special concern for the poor. For example, Psalm 10 appeals to God's caring for the poor to motivate the Lord to act, and calls those who are "greedy for gain" the wicked (10: 2–4).

The Book of Proverbs chastises individuals who are poor because of their laziness (e.g., 6:11, 13:8), but makes clear that many are poor because of the social system in which they must live (13:23). Another proverb says simply, "Those who oppress the poor insult their Maker, but those who are kind to the needy honor him" (14:31).

The Talmud calls for employers to treat their workers justly, saying that "whoever withholds an employee's wages, it is as though he has taken the person's life from him" (*Bava Metzia* 112a, cited in Shapiro 1989: 172).

Because capitalism favors "individual autonomy and dignity, the free exercise of reason and intellectual curiosity, the adaptation of scientific knowledge to the practical world via technological innovation, freedom from and of religion, and human creativity," it has been favored by many Jews, especially those in the Reform movement of Western Europe and the United States. In countries that adopted capitalism, Jews were allowed to participate in the economic system and achieve emancipation (Shapiro 1989: 174).

Many Jews have flourished in the open competition of capitalist economies. However, success has made Judaism and Jews easy and convenient targets at times of economic disruption. Antisemitism continues to be a serious problem in countries with capitalist economies, although (as evidenced in the former Soviet Union) command economies can also foster prejudice against Jews. In addition, Jewish teachers are well aware of the potential for abuse in a capitalist economy, and many Jewish groups and individuals have been active in efforts to assist and empower those left out in the competition.

CHRISTIANITY   Christianity has been attacked by a host of critics who challenge the hypocrisy of Christians on the issues of wealth and poverty. The French existentialist Jean-Paul Sartre, for example, said, "The poor are hungry, and they are offered a crucifix" (cited in Ferré and Mataragnon 1985: 111). Many critics today view Christianity as at least partially responsible for the tremendous gap between rich and poor. They point to Christianity's perceived other-worldly emphasis that has been used to try to convince poverty-stricken people to accept their fate in this world, because of the hope of reward after death. Critics also interpret the role of Protestant Christianity in the rise of modern capitalism as a sign that Christianity supports the inequitable distribution of wealth.

However, to suggest that Christianity unequivocally supports laissez faire capitalism would be inaccurate. In fact, some modern Christians indict the capitalist system as a manifestation of sinful selfishness, and call for an economic transformation based on biblical teachings. For example, evangelical Protestant ethicist Ronald Sider has written, "From the perspective of biblical revelation, property owners are not free to seek their own profit without regard for the needs of the neighbor. Such an outlook derives from the secular laissez-faire economics of the deist Adam Smith, not from Scripture" (Sider 1977: 114).

Protestant Christian interpreters such as Sider have based their contention—that Christians should seek economic relationships ordered to ensure that the needs of the poor are addressed—on an analysis of Biblical passages. In addition to the Old Testament passages cited in the section of Judaism, references to the poor are found on almost every page of the New Testament. Here is a representative selection of passages cited to argue that Christians must place a high priority on responding to the material needs of the poor: Matthew 25:31–46; Mark 10:21 and parallels in Matthew and Luke; Luke 1:46–53, 4:16–21, 6:20, 6:24, 10:29–37, 12:13–21, 14:12–24, 19:1–10; John 12:6, 13:29; Acts 2:44–45, 4:32; 1st Corinthians 11:17–22; 2nd Corinthians 8:9, 8:13–15; 2nd Thessalonians 3:10; James 1:27, 2:2–4, 5:3–5.

Despite the seemingly unequivocal and extensive New Testament evidence that (in its origins) Christianity was especially concerned with the poor and suspicious of unwarranted and excessive wealth, many interpreters over the years have tried to suggest that several key passages show that Christians should not try actively to challenge the underlying causes of poverty.

The most famous such passage is a statement of Jesus in the gospels of Mark (14:7), Matthew (26:11), and John (12:8). Quoting Deuteronomy (15:11), in response to the disciples' complaint that the expensive oil a woman was using to anoint him could be sold and the money given to the poor, Jesus says, "you always have the poor with you, and you can show kindness to them whenever you wish; but you will not always have me." For countless Christians this has been understood as endorsement of a permanent social stratification in which some are rich and others poor. However, biblical scholars have pointed out that the statement is speaking to the particular circumstance of the moment, not to the inevitable situation for all times. "The statement," comments New Testament scholar Vincent Taylor, "is not intended to assert that poverty is a permanent social factor" (cited by Miranda 1982: 59).

In the period after the writing of the New Testament, other Christian teachers dealt with the distribution of wealth. For example, St. Ambrose wrote, "What you give to the poor you do not take from your own property; rather you give back to him what is already his." (cited in Ferré and Mataragnon 1985: 114).

During the Protestant Reformation, the Reformers took an active interest in the needs of the poor. For example, the British reformer and "founder" of Methodism, John Wesley, said that any Christian who takes for himself anything more than the "plain necessaries of life, lives in an open, habitual denial of the Lord." He has "gained riches and hell-fire!" (Sider 1977: 172–73).

As we have already mentioned, Max Weber developed the theory, accepted by many today, that Protestantism (especially in its Calvinist form) provided the motivation for the development of capitalism through emphasizing work as a way of life, worldly asceticism, and rationalism.

Over the years the Roman Catholic Church has not shied from wrestling with this dilemma. In a series of encyclicals, beginning one hundred years ago, all modern popes have responded. For example, two papal encyclicals, *Laborem exercens* (1981) and *Sollicitudo rei socialis* (1988) maintain that there must be an "effective search for appropriate transformation of the structure of economic life" in a Christian spirit. They further claim that the abolition of poverty has taken on a world dimension requiring the transformation of unjust structures to which the masses have no access (Levi 1989: 45).

In addition to the official teaching of the Catholic church, as exemplified in the encyclicals, a movement has emerged in Catholicism in recent decades that takes a more activist approach to the problem of poverty. Called *liberation theology,* this movement has had a profound effect not only on Roman Catholicism but on other Christian churches. According to liberation theology, the God of Christian revelation is the God of the oppressed. This means both that God shares in the suffering of the poor and that God is involved in their struggle to be liberated. The liberation is not merely spiritual, but that of human lives from economic inequality and political repression.

By 1980 church teaching and most liberation theologians had agreed that at the root of the problem of excessive wealth amidst grinding poverty was a global capitalism in which "internal colonialists" cooperated with external capitalists (multinationals and developed-world organizations like the International Monetary Fund) to repress the poor.

Christian critics of liberation theology counter by charging that "while poverty and underemployment are still with us and probably always will be, it is nevertheless true that capitalism has produced the greatest and most widely distributed material well-being of any economic system" (Williamson 1979: 11).

Increasingly, as the twenty-first century begins, the phenomenon known as "globalization" is at the center of discussion of the relationship between Christianity (and other religions) and economic justice. Globalization is the rapid expansion, beginning after World War II, of laissez faire capitalism around the world. Supporters claim that only through a world network of free trade, in which people all over the world are able to participate freely in the global market, will poverty be alleviated. Critics argue that, instead of helping the poor, globalization is further concentrating the wealth of the world in a handful of multinational corporations and billionaire capitalists. Instead of aiding the poor, globalization chains them to market forces that only exacerbate their misery and drown them in the symbols and rituals of the consumerist religion promoted in the international market place. Local cultures and religions are steamrolled, they say, by the juggernaut of global capitalism.

Pope John Paul II has spoken vigorously against the more insidious effects of globalization. In May 2003, he said that globalization has not delivered on the promises of its enthusiasts—higher standards of living and social and political progress. "It is disturbing," the Pope said, "to witness a globalization that exacerbates the conditions of the needy, that does not sufficiently contribute to resolving the situations of hunger, poverty and social inequality, that fails to safeguard the natural environment" (Rifkin 2003).

Many modern Christian analysts of economics are calling for a truly new economic order, neither capitalist nor socialist, that emphasizes sustainability and equitable distribution on a regional basis (Cobb 1986: 173):

> Whereas we have pursued universal affluence chiefly by increasing the total quantity of goods and services available, and we have concerned ourselves only secondarily about their distribution, the goal of living within renewable resources forces a reversal. Since global growth will be limited, and since in many areas there must be substantial reduction of production, appropriate distribution of goods to all becomes the primary concern.

For many Christians, the most important issue is what can be done practically, at a local level, to alleviate the economic injustice in the world. For Ronald Sider the mandate is clear for Christians living in the affluent world (1977: 175):

> We Christians [. . .] are caught in an absurd, materialistic spiral. The more we make, the more we think we need in order to live decently and respectably. Somehow we have to break this cycle because it makes us sin against our needy brothers and sisters and, therefore, against our Lord.

ISLAM   As part of its modern revival, Islam is now engaged in a thorough soul-searching concerning its economic teachings. Islamic theorists are looking to their own tradition—especially the Qur'an, and the economic practices of Muhammad during the creation of the first Muslim community in Medina—to chart a different course than either of the two dominant Western economic models: capitalism and socialism. In so doing, the issue of distribution of wealth is of critical concern. As with Christianity, there is no single point of view in Islam on economic issues. We will give here only a sense of the modern discussion.

According to one expert, there are some key characteristics in the Islamic approach to economics (Bannerman 1988: 97–98):

> the right to private ownership of property, positive encouragement of the exploitation of resources, approval of material progress and prosperity, co-operation and mutual responsibility, acceptance of the rights of others, social justice, equitable distribution of wealth, prohibition of interest, and abstention from certain malpractices such as fraud, gambling, extortion, monopoly practices, hoarding, and the like.

Since Allah is the real owner of all creation (Qur'an 24:33), human ownership is as a trustee and is subject to two moral imperatives (Bannerman 1988: 98):

> good management on behalf of the real owner and the requirement to apply surplus wealth productively in pursuit of social justice and the general good. [. . .] Although equitable distribution of wealth is deemed necessary, it is not absolute: disparities in wealth distribution are acceptable, since men are not endowed with equal intelligence, ability, and skills, and the more fortunate are not expected to hide their greater wealth.

The Qur'an states that those able to work who do not, deserve their poverty (4.95). However, those unable to work have a right to share in the wealth of the community (51.19, 70.24–25). Wealth itself is not unethical, but how it is acquired and distributed can be. Wealth may not be gained through cheating, robbery, or deception. As noted in Chapter Twelve, the *zakat,* the purifying or alms tax, requires that

2½ percent of all acquired and held wealth must be spent on the needy each year (9:60). A series of regulations requires just treatment of debtors, widows, the poor, and orphans (90:13–16) and slaves (24:33). Additional charity beyond the tax (*sadaqa*) is highly commended. People should not keep more wealth than they need for their family's present needs. Usury is strongly condemned (2.279).

The main difference between Islamic economics and capitalism is the absence of interest as a source of income. The principal distinction from socialism is the recognition of private property rights. Islamic economics differs from both in the structuring of moral values into the system itself. The materialistic systems think that "livelihood" is the fundamental human problem and economic progress the ultimate end of human life. Islam recognizes these as subordinate goals (Shafi 1975: 2).

The objects of the distribution of wealth in Islam are as follows (Shafi 1975: 7–10):

- the establishment of a natural and practical system of economy, thus the natural force of supply and demand is recognized (Qur'an 43:32);
- enabling everyone to get what is rightfully due to him (including those who have not participated in the production of wealth, if Allah directs that they be cared for); and
- eradication of concentrations of wealth (Qur'an 59:7).

According to capitalism, wealth is distributed only among those who have taken part in producing it through capital, labor, land, and entrepreneurship or organization. Thus it is distributed through interest, wages, rent, or profit. Islam allows for all but the first, and adds those who Allah directs as "secondary" recipients of wealth (Shafi 1975: 10–11).

However, according to this interpretation of Islamic teaching, socialism is not the answer. "If the Socialist system is adopted and all capital and all land are totally surrendered to the state, the ultimate result can only be this—we would be liquidating a large number of smaller Capitalists, and putting the huge resources of national wealth at the disposal of a single big Capitalist—the State—which can deal with this reservoir of wealth quite arbitrarily. Socialism, thus, leads to the worst form of concentration of wealth." By allowing for property and rent as sources of income (in addition to wages), Islam overcomes the problems inherent in socialism. By outlawing interest and structuring in a long list of people who have a "secondary right to wealth," Islam avoids the concentration of wealth that is the great evil of capitalism (Shafi 1975: 13).

Allowing the loaning of money only without interest forces the lender to share in the profit *or* loss of the borrower. "Thus, under the Islamic system of economy, Capital and Entrepreneur become one and the same, and their share in the distribution of wealth is 'Profit' not 'Interest.'" (Shafi 1975: 18).

Some Muslim scholars have been critical of the gap between the Muslim ideal of social justice and the reality in many Muslim societies. As in other religious traditions, self-criticism is an important safeguard against smugness and arrogance. One Muslim teacher, Riffat Hassan, observed (1982: 54) that

> for hundreds of years now, Muslim masses have patiently endured the grinding poverty and oppression imposed on them by those in authority. Not to be enslaved by foreign invaders whose every attempt to subjugate them was met with resistance, Muslim masses were enslaved by Muslims in the name of God and the Prophet, made to believe that they had no rights, only responsibilities; that God was the God of Retribution, not of Love; that Islam was an ethic of suffering, not of joyous living; that they were determined by "Qismat" [fate], not masters of their own fate.

The popularity of Islamicist groups like the Muslim Brotherhood and Hamas (see Chapter Twelve) can be attributed in large measure to their work to alleviate the suffering of those who have not benefitted from the globalized economy and who are victims of the inept management of national economies by corrupt regimes.

SIKHISM   According to the Adi Granth, "He alone has found the right way who eats what he earns through toil and shares his earnings with the needy" (1245; cited in Nesbitt 1996: 111). Evidence of the Sikh commitment to hard work and self-reliance is seen in the prosperity created by the hundreds of thousands of Sikhs who had to flee Pakistan after the partition of India in 1947. Many created successful farms in the Punjab, and have shared their wealth in keeping with the Sikh principle that a tenth of earnings should be given to those in need (Nesbitt 1996: 113).

New Religious Movements

THE HOLY SPIRIT ASSOCIATION FOR THE UNIFICATION OF WORLD CHRISTIANITY: THE UNIFICATION CHURCH   The following statement expresses the teaching of the Unification Church on economic justice (Anderson 1985: 120):

> In the Unification Church, God is viewed as the parent of the world with all people as God's children. When we talk about rich and poor nations in relationship to theology, this concept becomes a central factor. Any discussion of the relationship between rich and poor nations necessarily involves the belief that people of all nations are siblings. The sibling metaphor denotes a relationship that goes beyond economic or military considerations.

THE BAHA'I FAITH   Although the Baha'i Faith recognizes that wealth earned by hard work in an honorable profession is ethical, Baha'i teachers have had a great deal of concern about the disparity between rich and poor. According to Baha'i principles, the rich (who, on a world scale, include the American middle class) are obligated to give of their wealth for the poor. Baha'u'llah echoed other great religious leaders when he said, "O Ye that Pride Yourselves on Mortal Riches! Know ye in truth that wealth is a mighty barrier between the seeker and his desire, the lover and his beloved. The rich, but for a few, shall in no wise attain the court of His presence nor enter the city of content and resignation" (cited in Thomas 1984: 95). He also said, "Nobody should die of hunger; everybody should have sufficient clothing; one man should not live in excess while another has no possible means of existence" (cited in Thomas 1984: 97). From a Baha'i perspective, both societies and individuals have an obligation to respond to the needs of the poor.

CHAPTER SUMMARY

Two of the most important issues facing humanity in the twenty-first century are the ecological crisis and the problem of world poverty. They raise fundamental questions of how we as humans relate to the environment, and how we use and share the resources of the earth. In this chapter we first introduced each of these issues and how religions in general have related to them. Then we explored the responses to each issue of many of the religions of the world.

IMPORTANT TERMS AND PHRASES

absolute poverty, *ahimsa,* anthropocentric, biocentric, Buddhist development, Christian realists, Confucian development, cultivation (*shugyo*), deforestation, desertification, Earth Summit, ecocentric, ecotheology, Gaia, *hozho,* I-Thou, embeddedness, interconnectedness, Islamic economics, karma, Kingdom of God, laissez faire, liberation theology, *metta,* Mother Earth, Net of Indra, nonattachment, ozone depletion, patriarchy, reciprocity, reverence for life, reversion, settlement of the land (*yishuv ha-aretz*), signs of Allah, sustainability, *wu wei, zakat.*

QUESTIONS FOR DISCUSSION AND REFLECTION

For each of the contemporary ethical issues discussed in Chapters 15–18, scenarios will be suggested as a basis for discussion and reflection. The following scenario combines the issues discussed in this chapter.

Imagine that you are attending a United Nations Summit on the Environment and Sustainability. Representatives of the world's religions have been invited to the summit to discuss the teachings of their religions on how to address the ecological crisis and the problem of global economic injustice. They are urged to find common ground, to help guide the efforts of the U.N. and member countries to address these critical issues. In a group setting, individual students should represent the various religions and engage in dialogue about their responses to the issues. Individually or in a group, attempt to draft a statement drawing on and attempting to synthesize the best of the teachings of the world's religions in response to each of these issues.

SOURCES AND SUGGESTIONS FOR FURTHER STUDY

GENERAL SOURCES FOR THE STUDY OF WORLD RELIGIONS AND ETHICAL ISSUES (FOR CHAPTERS 15–18)

Note: Listings for selections from these sources in Chapters 15–18 will refer to individual essays and the titles of the books in which they appear.

CARMODY, DENISE LARDNER AND JOHN TULLY CARMODY, 1988. *How to Live Well: Ethics in the World Religions.* Belmont, CA: Wadsworth.

CRAWFORD, S. CROMWELL, ED., 1989. *World Religions and Global Ethics.* New York: Paragon.

CROTTY, ROBERT B., MARIE T. CROTTY, AND ARNOLD D. HUNT, EDS., 1991. *Ethics of the World Religions.* San Diego: Greenhaven.

FASCHING, DARRELL J. AND DELL DeCHANT, 2001. *Comparative Religious Ethics: A Narrative Approach.* Oxford: Blackwell.

JUDD, DANIEL K., ED., 2003. *Taking Sides: Clashing Views on Controversial Issues in Religion.* Guilford, CT: McGraw-Hill/Dushkin.

LAWTON, CLIVE, AND MORGAN, PEGGY, EDS., 1996. *Ethical Issues in Six Religious Traditions.* Edinburgh: Edinburgh University.

MAY, LARRY, SHARI COLLINS-CHOBANIAN, AND KAI WONG, 2002. *Applied Ethics: A Multicultural Approach.* 3rd ed. Upper Saddle River, N.J.: Prentice Hall.

RUNZO, JOSEPH AND NANCY M. MARTIN, ED., 2001. *Ethics in the World Religions.* New York: Oneworld.

TWISS, SUMNER B. AND BRUCE GRELLE, ED., 1998. *Explorations in Global Ethics: Comparative Religious Ethics and Interreligious Dialogue.* Boulder, CO: Westview.

WOLFE, REGINA WENTZEL AND CHRISTINE E. GUDORF, ED., 1999. *Ethics and World Religions: Cross-Cultural Case Studies.* Maryknoll, NY: Orbis.

THE ECOLOGICAL CRISIS

General

FLAVIN, CHRISTOPHER, 2002. "Preface," *State of the World 2002: A Worldwatch Institute Report on Progress Toward a Sustainable Society,* ed. Linda Starke. New York: Norton, xix–xxii.

CALLICOTT, J. BAIRD, 1994. *Earth's Insights: A Survey of Ecological Ethics from the Mediterranean Basin to the Australian Outback.* Berkeley: University of California.

FOLTZ, RICHARD C., ED., 2003. *Worldviews, Religion, and the Environment: A Global Anthology.* Belmont, CA: Wadsworth.

GOTTLIEB, ROGER S., ED., 1996. *This Sacred Earth: Religion, Nature, Environment.* New York: Routledge.

HARGROVE, EUGENE, ED., 1986. *Religion and Environmental Crisis.* Athens: University of Georgia.

KINSLEY, DAVID, 1995. *Ecology and Religion: Ecological Spirituality in Cross-Cultural Perspective.* Englewood Cliffs, NJ: Prentice Hall.

LOVELOCK, JAMES E., 1982. *Gaia: A New Look at Life on Earth.* New York: Oxford University.

LOW, ALAINE AND SORAYA TREMAYNE, 2001. *Sacred Custodians of the Earth? Women, Spirituality and the Environment.* New York: Berghahn.

MAGUIRE, DANIEL C., 2000. *Sacred Energies: When the World's Religions Sit Down to Talk about the Future of Human Life and the Plight of this Planet.* Minneapolis: Fortress.

NASH, RODERICK, 1989. *The Rights of Nature: A History of Environmental Ethics.* Madison: The University of Wisconsin Press, 1989. (See especially "The Greening of Religion," 87–120.)

ROCKEFELLER, STEVEN C. AND JOHN C. ELDER, 1992. *Spirit and Nature: Why the Environment Is a Religious Issue: An Interfaith Dialogue.* Boston: Beacon.

SPRING, DAVID AND EILEEN, ED., 1974. *Ecology and Religion in History.* New York: Harper & Row.

TUCKER, M. E. AND J. A. GRIM, EDS., 1994. *Worldviews and Ecology: Religion, Philosophy, and the Environment.* Maryknoll, NY: Orbis.

VITTACHI, ANURADHA, 1989. *Earth Conference One: Sharing a Vision for Our Planet.* Boston: New Science Library.

WHITE, LYNN, JR., 1967. "The Historical Roots of Our Ecological Crisis." *Science* 155 (1967), 1203–07. (Included in Spring 1974: 15–31).

Indigenous (Native American)

BIERHORST, JOHN, 1994. *The Way of the Earth: Native America and the Environment.* New York: Morrow.

CAJETE, GREGORY, 2002. "Look to the Mountain: Reflections on Indigenous Ecology." In May, Collins-Chobanian, and Wong, *Applied Ethics,* 148–57.

GRIM, JOHN A., ED., 2001. *Indigenous Traditions and Ecology: The Interbeing of Cosmology and Community.* Cambridge, MA : Harvard University.

HUGHES, J. DONALD, 1983. *American Indian Ecology.* El Paso: Texas Western.

LOFTIN, JOHN D., 1991. *Religion and Hopi Life in the Twentieth Century.* Bloomington: Indiana University.

REED, GERARD, 1986. "A Native American Environmental Ethic: A Homily on Black Elk." In Hargrove, *Religion and Environmental Crisis,* 25–52.

SILKO, LESLIE MARMON, 1996. *Yellow Woman and a Beauty of the Spirit.* New York: Simon and Schuster.

VECSEY, CHRISTOPHER AND ROBERT W. VENABLES, ED., 1980. *American Indian Environments: Ecological Issues in Native American History.* Syracuse, NY: Syracuse University.

WEAVER, JACE, ED., 1996. *Defending Mother Earth: Native American Perspectives on Environmental Justice.* Maryknoll, NY: Orbis.

YOUNG, WILLIAM A., 2002. "The Ecocrisis and Native American Spiritual Traditions." *Quest for Harmony: Native American Spiritual Traditions.* New York: Seven Bridges, 329–62.

South and Southeast Asian Religions

Hinduism

CALLICOTT, J. BAIRD AND ROGER T. AMES, ED., 1989. *Nature in Asian Traditions of Thought: Essays in Philosophy.* Albany: State University of New York.

CHAITANYA, KRISHNA, 1983. "A Profounder Ecology: The Hindu View of Man and Nature." *The Ecologist* 13: 127–35.

CHAPPLE, CHRISTOPHER KEY, ED., 2000. *Hinduism and Ecology: The Intersection of Earth, Sky, and Water.* Cambridge, MA: Harvard University.

DEUTSCH, ELIOT, 1989. "A Metaphysical Grounding for Natural Reverence: East-West." In Callicott and Ames, *Nature in Asian Traditions of Thought,* 259–65.

Theravada Buddhism

BADINER, ALLAN HUNT, ED., 1990. *Dharma Gaia: A Harvest of Essays in Buddhism and Ecology.* Berkeley, CA: Parallax.

DE SILVA, PADMASIRI, 1990. "Buddhist Environmental Ethics." In Badiner, *Dharma Gaia,* 14–19.

HARVEY, PETER, 2000. "Attitude to and Treatment of the Natural World." *An Introduction to Buddhist Ethics.* Cambridge: Cambridge University, 150–86.

TUCKER, MARY EVELYN AND DUNCAN RYUKEN WILLIAMS, 1997. *Buddhism and Ecology: The Interconnection of Dharma and Deeds.* Cambridge, MA: Harvard University.

Jainism

CHAPPLE, CHRISTOPHER KEY, 2002. *Jainism and Ecology: Nonviolence in the Web of Life.* Cambridge, MA: Harvard University.

CHAPPLE, CHRISTOPHER KEY, 2001. "Pushing the Boundaries of Personal Ethics: The Practice of Jaina Vows." In Runzo and Martin, *Ethics in the World Religions,* 197–215.

East Asian Religions

Daoism

AMES, ROGER T., 1986. "Taoism and the Nature of Nature." *Environmental Ethics* 8: 317–49.

CALLICOTT, J. BAIRD, 1987. "Conceptual Resources for Asian Traditions of Thought: A Propaedeutic," *Philosophy East and West* 37: 115–30.

CHENG, CHUNG-YING, 2002. "On the Environmental Ethics of the *Tao* and the *Ch'i.*" In May, Collins-Chobanian, and Wong, *Applied Ethics,* 158–66.

GIRADOT, N. J., JAMES MILLER, AND LIU XIAOGAN, 2001. *Daoism and Ecology: Ways within a Cosmic Landscape.* Cambridge, MA: Harvard University.

GOODMAN, RUSSELL, 1980. "Daoism and Ecology." *Environmental Ethics* 2: 73–80.

IP, PO-KEUNG, 1986. "Taoism and the Foundations of Environmental Ethics." In Hargrove, *Religion and Environmental Crisis,* 94–106.

Confucianism

TUCKER, MARY EVELYN, 2001. "Confucian Cosmology and Ecological Ethics: *qi, li,* and The Role of the Human." In Runzo and Martin, *Ethics in the World Religions,* 331–45.

TUCKER, MARY EVELYN AND JOHN BERTHRONG, ED. 1998. *Confucianism and Ecology: The Interrelation of Heaven, Earth, and Humans.* Cambridge, MA: Harvard University.

WEI-MING, TU, 1989. "The Continuity of Being: Chinese Visions of Nature." In Callicott and Ames, *Nature in Asian Traditions of Thought,* 67–78.

Mahayana Buddhism

COOK, FRANCIS, 1977. *Hua-yen Buddhism.* University Park: Pennsylvania State University.

DONEGAN, PATRICIA, 1990. "Haiku & the Ecotastrophe." In Badiner, *Dharma Gaia,* 197–207.

Shinto

ASTON, W. G., 1905. *Shinto: The Way of the Gods.* London: Green & Co.

PICKEN, STUART D. B., 2002. *Shinto Meditations for Revering the Earth.* Berkeley, CA: Stone Bridge.

SHANER, DAVID EDWARD, 1989. "The Japanese Experience of Nature." In Callicott and Ames, *Nature in Asian Traditions of Thought,* 163–82.

Religions Originating in the Middle East

Judaism

BERNSTEIN, E., ED. 1998. *Ecology and the Jewish Spirit: Where Nature and the Sacred Meet.* Woodstock, NY: Jewish Lights.

BUBER, MARTIN, 1970. *I and Thou,* trans. Walter Kaufmann. New York: Simon and Schuster.

DORFF, ELLIOT N., 2001. "Doing the Right and the Good: Fundamental Convictions and Methods of Jewish Ethics." In Runzo and Martin, *Ethics in the World Religions,* 89–113.

HELFAND, JONATHAN, 1986. "The Earth is the Lord's: Judaism and Environmental Ethics." In Hargrove, *Religion and Environmental Crisis,* 38–52.

TIROSH-SAMUELSON, HAVA, ED. 2002. *Judaism and Ecology: Created World and Revealed Word.* Cambridge, MA: Harvard University.

Christianity

AUSTIN, RICHARD CARTWRIGHT (four volumes in a series entitled *Environmental Theology*):

   1987a. *Baptized into Wilderness.* Atlanta: John Knox.

   1987b. *Hope for the Land: Nature in the Bible.* Atlanta: John Knox.

   1988. *Beauty of the Lord: Awakening the Senses.* Atlanta: John Knox.

   1990. *Reclaiming America: Restoring Nature to Culture.* Abingdon, VA: Creekside.

AYERS, ROBERT H., 1986. "Christian Realism and Environmental Ethics." In Hargrove, *Religion and Environmental Crisis,* 154–71.

BARBOUR, IAN, 1972. Earth Might Be Fair: Reflections on Ethics, Religion, and Ecology. Englewood Cliffs, NJ: Prentice Hall.

HESSEL, DIETER T. AND ROSEMARY RADFORD RUETHER, EDS., 2000. *Christianity and Ecology: Seeking the Well-being of Earth and Humans.* Cambridge, MA: Harvard University Center for the Study of World Religions.

JAKOWSKA, SOPHIE, 1986. "Roman Catholic Teaching and Environmental Ethics in Latin America." In Hargrove, *Religion and Environmental Crisis,* 127–53.

MCDANIEL, JAY, 2000. *Living from the Center: Spirituality in an Age of Consumerism.* St. Louis: Chalice.

MCFAGUE, SALLIE, 1993. *The Body of God: An Ecological Theology.* Minneapolis: Fortress.

STONE, PAT, 1989. "Christian ecology: A growing force in the environmental movement." *Utne Reader* 36 (Nov./Dec.), 78–79.

Islam

ALI, ABDULLAH YUSUF, TRANS., 2002. *The Qur'an: Translation.* 9th ed. Elmhurst, NY: Tahrike Tarsile.

DERMENGHEM, EMILE, 1958. *Muhammad and the Islamic Tradition,* trans. J. M. Watt. New York: Harper and Brothers.

KHALID, FAZLUN M. AND JOANNE O'BRIEN, ED., 1992. *Islam and Ecology.* New York: Cassell.

ZAIDI, IQTIDAR H., 1986. "On the Ethics of Man's Interaction with the Environment: An Islamic Approach." In Hargrove, *Religion and Environmental Crisis,* 107–26.

New Religions

International Society for Krishna Consciousness

DRUTAKARMA DASA, 1992. Personal correspondence.

Secular Humanism

AMERICAN HUMANIST ASSOCIATION (AHA), 1973. *Humanist Manifestos I and II.* New York: Prometheus.

ECONOMIC JUSTICE

General

BROWN, LESTER, 2001. *Eco-Economy: Building an Economy for the Earth.* New York: Norton.

COWARD, HAROLD, ED., 1995. *Population, Consumption, and the Environment: Religious and Secular Responses.* Albany: State University of New York.

COWARD, HAROLD AND DANIEL C. MAGUIRE, ED., 2000. *Visions of a New Earth: Religious Perspectives on Population, Consumption, and Ecology.* Albany: State University of New York.

FERRÉ, FREDERICK AND RITA H. MATARAGNON, EDS., 1985. *God and Global Justice: Religion and Poverty in an Unequal World.* New York: Paragon.

KNITTER, PAUL F. AND CHANDRA MUZAFFAR, EDS., 2002. *Subverting Greed: Religious Perspectives on the Global Economy.* Maryknoll, NY: Orbis.

RIFKIN, IRA, 2003. *Spiritual Perspectives on Globalization: Making Sense of Economic and Cultural Upheaval.* Woodstock, VT: SkyLight Paths.

TAWNEY, R. H., 1962. *Religion and the Rise of Capitalism.* Gloucester, MA: P. Smith.

WEBER, MAX, 1930. *The Protestant Ethic and the Spirit of Capitalism,* trans. Talcott Parsons. London: Allen and Unwin.

WORLDWATCH INSTITUTE, ED., 2003. *Vital Signs 2003: Trends That Are Shaping Our Future.* New York: Norton.

Indigenous

African

ABOGUNRIN, SAMUEL O., 1989. "Ethics in Yoruba Religious Tradition." In Crawford, *World Religions and Global Ethics,* 266–96.

ANSAH, JOHN K., 1989. "The Ethics of Traditional African Religions." In Crawford, *World Religions and Global Ethics,* 241–65.

Indigenous (Native American)

EASTMAN, CHARLES, 1971. *The Soul of the Indian.* New York: Johnson Reprint Co. (Original edition, Boston: Houghton Mifflin, 1911.)

Religions of South and Southeast Asia

Theravada Buddhism

HARVEY, PETER, 2000. "Economic Ethics." *An Introduction to Buddhist Ethics,* 187–238.

PAYUTTO, P. A., 1994. *Buddhist Economics: A Middle Way for the Market Place.* Bangkok: Buddhadhamma Foundation.

SCHUMACHER, E. F., 1973. *Small Is Beautiful: Economics As If People Mattered.* New York: Harper & Row.

Jainism

JAIN, PREM SUMAN, 1989. "The Ethics of Jainism." In Crawford, *World Religions and Global Ethics,* 65–88.

Religions of East Asia

REDDING, S. GORDON, 1990. *The Spirit of Chinese Capitalism.* New York: W. deGruyter.

Confucianism

TAI, HUNG-CHAO, 1989. *Confucianism and Economic Development: An Oriental Alternative?* Washington, DC: Washington Institute.

TSE, CHUNG, 1989. "Confucianism and Contemporary Ethical Issues." In Crawford, *World Religions and Global Ethics,* 91–125.

ZHANG, WEI-BIN, 1999. *Confucianism and Modernization: Industrialization and Democratization of the Confucian Regions.* New York: St. Martin's.

ZHANG, WEI-BIN, 2000. *On Adam Smith and Confucius: The Theory of Moral Sentiments and The Analects.* Commack, NY: Nova Science.

Mahayana Buddhism

QUEEN, CHRISTOPHER S. AND SALLIE B. KING, EDS., 1996. *Engaged Buddhism: Buddhist Liberation Movements in Asia.* Albany: State University of New York.

THOMPSON, WILLIAM IRWIN, 1989. "Pacific Shift." In Callicott and Ames, *Nature in Asian Traditions of Thought,* 25–36.

Religions Originating in the Middle East

BARBER, BENJAMIN R., 1995. *Jihad vs. McWorld.* New York: Times.

WILSON, RODNEY, 1997. *Economics, Ethics, and Religion: Jewish, Christian, and Muslim Economic Thought.* New York: New York University.

Judaism

LEVINE, AARON, 1993. *Economic Public Policy and Jewish Law.* New York: Yeshiva University.

NEUSNER, JACOB, 1998. *The Economics of the Mishnah.* Atlanta, GA: Scholars.

SHAPIRO, RAMI M., 1989. "Blessing and Curse: Toward a Liberal Jewish Ethic." In Crawford, *World Religions and Global Ethics,* 155–87.

Christianity

COBB, JOHN B., JR., 1986. "Christian Existence in a World of Limits." In Hargrove, *Religion and Environmental Crisis,* 172–87.

LEVI, WERNER, 1989. *From Alms to Liberation: The Catholic Church, the Theologians, Poverty, and Politics.* New York: Praeger.

MCDANIEL, JAY, 1985. "The God of the Oppressed and the God Who is Empty." In Ferré and Mataragnon, *God and Global Justice,* 185–204.

MIRANDA, JOSÉ, 1982. *Communism in the Bible,* trans. Robert R. Barr. Maryknoll, NY: Orbis.

SIDER, RONALD J., 1977. *Rich Christians in an Age of Hunger: A Biblical Study.* New York: Paulist.

WILLIAMSON, RENÉ DE VISME, 1979. *The Integrity of the Gospel: A Critique of Liberation Theology.* Media, PA: The Presbyterian Lay Committee.

Islam

ALI, ABDULLAH YUSUF, TRANS., 2002. *The Qur'an: Translation.* 9th ed. Elmhurst, NY: Tahrike Tarsile.

BANNERMAN, PATRICK, 1988. *Islam in Perspective: A Guide to Islamic Society, Politics, and Law.* New York: Routledge.

CHOUDHURY, MASUDUL ALAM, 1997. *Money in Islam: A Study in Islamic Political Economy.* New York: Routledge.

CHAPRA, M. UMER, 1992. *Islam and the Economic Challenge.* Herndon, VA: International Institute of Islamic Thought.

HASSAN, RIFFAT, 1982. "On Human Rights and the Qur'anic Perspective." In *Human Rights in Religious Traditions,* ed. Arelene Swidler. New York: Pilgrim, 51–65.

MANNAN, MUHAMMAD ABDUL, 1987. *Islamic Economics: Theory and Practice.* Boulder, CO: Westview.

SHAFI, MUFTI MUHAMMAD, 1975. *Distribution of Wealth in Islam.* Karachi, Pakistan: Begum Aisha Bawany Wakf.

TURNER, BRIAN S., 1974. *Weber and Islam: A Critical Study.* London: Routledge & Kegan Paul.

Sikhism

NESBITT, ELEANOR, 1996. "Sikhism." In Lawton and Morgan, *Ethical Issues in Six Religious Traditions,* 99–134.

New Religious Movements

The Holy Spirit Association for the Unification of World Christianity: The Unification Church

ANDERSON, GORDON L., 1985. "God is Parent: Rich and Poor Nations are Siblings." In Ferré and Mataragnon, *God and Global Justice,* 120–35.

The Baha'i Faith

THOMAS, JUNE MANING, 1984. "Poverty and Wealth in America: A Baha'i Perspective." In *Circle of Unity: Baha'i Approaches to Social Issues,* ed. Anthony A. Lee. Los Angeles: Kalimar, 91–116.

Web Sites

ECOLOGICAL CRISIS

www.hds.harvard.edu/cswr/ecology
environment.harvard.edu/religion
> (the Harvard University series on "Religions of the World and Ecology")

www.earthcharter.org
> (the Earth Charter Initiative)

nrpe.org
> (the National Religious Partnership for the Environment)

ECONOMIC JUSTICE

www.religion-online.org/cgi-bin/relsearchd.dll/listcatitems?cat_id=70
> (links to articles on religion and economic justice)

Prentice Hall's **Research Navigator** helps students in their further study of the world's religions. Visit *http://www.researchnavigator.com* for help on the research process and access to databases full of relevant material, including the New York *Times*.

CHAPTER

16

War and Capital Punishment—Society and Violence

WAR: WHEN, IF EVER, IS WAR JUSTIFIED?

The Nature of the Issue and the Role of Religion

Today wars are raging around the world. Since September 11th, 2001, the ongoing "war on terrorism" has dominated world attention. In addition, the 2003 war in Iraq, the intractable Palestinian-Israeli conflict, and smoldering hostilities in more than two dozen other countries demonstrate that war is a sad but seemingly inevitable fact of human relations.

What is the cost of war? In the twentieth century approximately one hundred million people lost their lives as a result of wars. The cost of war is also economic. The United States, between the end of World War II in 1945 and 1990, spent more than ten trillion dollars on the military. What could you buy with that much money? "The answer is everything—everything in the United States except the land; every skyscraper, house, ship, train, airplane, automobile, baby diaper, pencil. Everything could be purchased for ten trillion dollars" (Vittachi 1989: 30). As the twenty-first century began, the countries of the world were spending over eight hundred billion U.S. dollars a year on military expenditures.

Given the immensity of the cost of war, is war ever justified? What is the relationship between the world's religions and wars? Religion has been and continues to be used to justify some of the most terrible conflicts in human history. Yet religions have also inspired great sacrifice by those who have fought in wars now widely accepted as just wars against oppressors who had to be stopped. As we shall see, religions have also encouraged many to work tirelessly to find nonviolent solutions to the conflicts that cause wars.

Religious Responses

Religions of South and Southeast Asia

HINDUISM   As in other religions, there is an inherent ambiguity in Hinduism on the subject of war. On the one hand, the Aryan culture in which the Vedic literature was written was dominated by conflict. According to the Rig-Veda, one of the four social classes present since creation was the *kshatriya* or warrior class. From this point of view, wars are an inevitable reality, especially in this final age of the present cosmic cycle, *Kali Yuga,* when hostility and tension are high among peoples.

On the other hand, the Hindu virtue of *ahimsa* (noninjury), shared with other religions of South and Southeast Asia, has contributed to a pacifist streak in India. Mohandas Gandhi turned ahimsa into a political strategy known as *satyagraha,* using nonviolent resistance rather than armed conflict to end British rule in India (Gandhi 2002). Unfortunately, after independence Gandhi's charisma could not thwart the internecine struggle between Hindus and Muslims, which led to many deaths. India today has become a nuclear power, and has flexed its military muscles in border clashes with its nuclear neighbor Pakistan, and in support for the emergence of the nation of Bangladesh in what was once East Pakistan. Most recently, the ongoing conflict in Kashmir has threatened to erupt into a wider, perhaps even nuclear, war between India and Pakistan. Sporadic violence between Hindus and Muslims within India, as well as between Sikhs and Hindus, seems intractable.

THERAVADA BUDDHISM   Although Theravada Buddhist texts recognize that violence sometimes results from unjust social situations, they acknowledge no circumstances under which violence can be justified in order to redress grievances.

The dominant Theravada position requires "a sound causal analysis of situations and circumstances in which violence and social conflicts arise and attempts to enlighten men on ways to prevent violence from ever taking place" (Premasiri 1989: 62). Violence begets violence, according to Theravada teaching, and the only way to bring peace is through nonviolence. In the *Jataka* tales there is a story of a king who opens the gates to an attacking army. He is imprisoned, but the invading king comes to recognize his own error, releases the leader, and leaves the kingdom in peace. A saying in the *Dhammapada* makes the point succinctly (223; Harvey 2000: 242):

> Conquer anger by love, conquer evil by good, conquer the stingy by giving, conquer the liar by truth.

According to general Buddhist teaching, at the root of all injurious actions, including war, are greed and delusion. In addition to attachment to material things, attachment to dogmatic opinions leads to the distorted views that result in conflict among people and nations. With this sensitivity to the basic causes of war, Buddhism offers means to resolve conflicts nonviolently. Buddhist monks and nuns have served as mediators in disputes, drawing on the basic Buddhist values of lovingkindness, compassion, empathetic joy, and equanimity to defuse volatile situations. For example, in the ongoing conflict in Sri Lanka, while some Buddhist monastics have advocated violence against the Hindu Tamils as justifiable self-defense, others have joined with Buddhist lay leaders in seeking to end the bloodshed through peaceful negotiation (Harvey 2000: 275–77). Winner of the Nobel Peace Prize, Aung San Suu Kyi of Burma, draws on Buddhist ideals in her struggle against the military junta that rules Burma (Myanmar).

JAINISM Jainism stands opposed to war. The *Uttradhyayana* says, "If you want to fight, fight against your passions." However, as Jain scholar Sagarmal Jain points out, "perfect nonviolence is possible only on a spiritual plane.[...] The problem of war and violence is mainly concerned with worldly beings.[...] Jainism permits only a householder and not a monk to protect his rights through violent means in exceptional cases. But the fact remains that violence for Jainas is an evil and it cannot be justified as a virtue" (www.fas.harvard.edu/~pluralsm/affiliates/jainism/article/worldproblems.htm).

Religions of East Asia

DAOISM The Daodejing expresses the view that wars do more harm than good, as is the case with all unnatural exertions of force (72). Those seeking to live in harmony with the Dao detest the weapons of war, for they inspire fear. The more weapons, the less security there is (57). Yet there are times in this world when war is necessary. When those times come, weapons should be employed with utmost restraint and war entered into with sorrow (31). As in personal defense, the Daoist strategy in war is to draw on the power exerted by the enemy rather than trying to overwhelm the foe with your own force (69). Nations not in harmony with the Dao have great storehouses of weapons (46) and meddle unnecessarily in the affairs of other nations (61).

CONFUCIANISM War was a fact of life in ancient China, as it has been in all civilizations. Confucius does not seem to have been a pacifist, but he did urge that if people are asked to go to war, they must have an understanding of the reasons for it and the potential cost. For example, in the *Analects* (13:30), Confucius is purported to have said: "Leading an uninstructed people to war is to throw them away" (Ware 1955: 88).

MAHAYANA BUDDHISM As in the Theravada branch, the dominant Mahayana position is that violent responses to threats only beget more violence. The leader of Tibetan Buddhism, the Dalai Lama, who won the Nobel Prize for Peace, has steadfastly spoken out against the use of violence to resolve disputes in the world. For example, after the September 11, 2001, terrorist attacks, the Dalai Lama questioned whether a "war on terrorism" was the best response. He warned against "a cycle of violence and counter-violence that did little to solve the original problem" (www.news.com.au). Another Mahayana leader, Thich Nhat Hanh of Vietnam, has advocated an "engaged Buddhism" that works nonviolently for peace and justice (Nhat Hanh 1987).

However, Mahayana Buddhist schools have not always followed the course of nonviolence in their teachings on war. Some Mahayana texts "contain passages which allow killing in constrained circumstances provided it is motivated by compassion and carried out with 'skillful means' [...] Over the centuries, Chinese and Japanese military forces have used Buddhist symbols [...] to empower their actions and intimidate opponents" (Harvey 2000: 263).

Zen Buddhism contributed to the famed warrior (*samurai*) culture in Japan. It was one of the influences on the *bushido* ("way of the warrior") code (see Chapter Nine). The Zen ideal of "spontaneous reaction free from discriminating thought was influential on martial arts [in Japan], such as swordsmanship and archery. The idea that even life and death are empty, essenceless phenomena also helped develop a lack of hesitation, and lack of fear of death, in battle" (Harvey 2000: 266).

Recent research has documented a close association between Zen Buddhism and Japanese militarism before World War II. Zen masters provided a spiritual basis for the suicidal loyalty that the Japanese military exploited, arguing that war and killing are sometimes necessary to promote the universal harmony the Buddha taught (Victoria 2000).

SHINTO   Shinto is certainly not a pacifist religion. Among the *kami* is *Hachiman,* god of war. War heroes have often been elevated to the status of *kami,* with shrines created to honor them. As we have seen in Chapter Nine, Shinto was also closely associated with the rise of militarism in twentieth-century Japan. Proponents of militaristic patriotism in contemporary Japan often draw on Shinto to promote their cause. However, the focus of Shinto is the promotion of harmony and purity, and there is no necessary connection between the basic teachings of the religion and the promotion of war.

Religions Originating in the Middle East

JUDAISM   War is a recurrent theme in the Tanak. God is described as a warrior (e.g., Exodus 15:3, Psalm 24:8, and Isaiah 42:13). Israel's enemies are God's enemies (Judges 5:31, First Samuel 30:26), and God leads Israel into battle (Exodus 14:13–14; Joshua 10:11, 24:12; First Samuel 17:45). This is the root of the Judeo-Christian notion of "holy war," in which conflicts against enemies who oppose the divine will are seen as sanctioned by God (see also Joshua 8:1, Judges 4:14–15, First Samuel 23:4, Second Kings 3:18). The guidelines for "holy war" are most clearly expressed in the Tanak in Deuteronomy 20. Some in the Jewish and Christian communities are willing to apply this biblical perspective to contemporary conflicts, such as the Israeli-Palestinian conflict or the U.S.-led war on terrorism.

By contrast, according to the biblical narrative, God could withdraw divine protection from the Israelite nation, and "use" a foe to punish Israel for its sins (Isaiah 5:26–28; Jeremiah 5:15–17; Ezekiel 21:1–32). This perspective has also been applied by contemporary interpreters. Some of the prophets looked beyond divine judgment and envisioned a time of peace, when wars would be obsolete (e.g., Isaiah 2:1–4), inspiring some Jews today to take pacifist positions in the face of the horrors of modern warfare.

Two events during the Jewish war against Rome (66–70 C.E.) point to different Jewish strategies in the face of overwhelming force. The first occurred at Masada, a desert refuge near the Dead Sea. There the Zealot defenders committed suicide rather than surrender to the Roman Army. The second took place when the famous Yohanan ben Zakkai had his disciples spirit him from Jerusalem in a coffin, so that he could negotiate with the Roman general Vespasian to be allowed to set up an academy of Jewish learning at Yavneh in Galilee. Of these situations, one counsels defiance and the other accommodation. In the latter case, the "surrender" of Yohanan ben Zakkai secured the future for Judaism by preserving the traditions of the past and passing them to the future (Shapiro 1989: 179).

The slaughter of six million Jews during the Holocaust (1933–1945) has imprinted the lesson that Jews must be prepared to defend themselves and not depend on others. Therefore, the fanatic resistance of Masada is a symbol of uncompromising defiance against enemies, characteristic of the policies of the modern State of Israel.

These policies have caused tension in the Jewish community, with some uneasy about the State of Israel's retaliatory policy, which extracts quick and harsh vengeance against Palestinians, including the striking of civilian targets when Israeli civilians are attacked. Some Jews in Israel are committed to renouncing such violent tactics and working toward reconciliation with the Palestinians. For example, a group known as the Coalition of Women for Peace has issued the following statement (www.coalitionofwomen4peace.org):

> The militarism, which permeates Israeli society, must [. . .] end. As long as the governments of Israel continue to be dominated by generals and a belief in violence as a political strategy, we will never get to peace. To end the conflict we must resolve problems through wisdom, not force.

CHRISTIANITY   Within Christianity we find positions on the morality of war ranging from the pacifism of the "Peace Churches" (like the Mennonites and Church of the Brethren) to the ideology of "holy war," which equates a particular war with the will of God.

There is no single, inclusive teaching on war in the New Testament. Some texts seem to support pacifism. In the Sermon on the Mount, Jesus teaches his disciples to practice nonresistance in the face of violence. "Do not resist an evildoer. But if anyone strikes you on the right check, turn the other also" (Matthew 5:39). Some Christians extend this teaching to wars, arguing that Christians are not allowed to participate in acts of violence against any evildoers. However, others point out that Jesus seemed to accept the inevitability of war (Matthew 5:44). Yet Jesus apparently *did* rebuke those who tried to advance his cause through violence (John 18:36, Matthew 26:52–54).

The Apostle Paul, however, instructed Christians to accept the authority of the state (Romans 13:1–7). Many Christians have argued that this passage means Christians must participate in wars authorized by the legal authority in the nation in which they live.

Building on this biblical teaching, the fifth century theologian Augustine developed the theory of "just war," which has dominated Christian teaching on war ever since (see Lackey 2002). Augustine said that to be just a war must be authorized by legitimate rulers, be fought to restore peace and to obtain justice, and be motivated by Christian love. For Augustine, no one should participate in war who has not overcome hate in his own heart. Wars should be conducted without unnecessary violence, indiscriminate killing, endangering innocents, or looting.

In the eleventh century, in response to an appeal from the Eastern Emperor at Constantinople, Pope Urban II urged Christians to undertake a crusade to liberate the Holy Land from "pagan" control. This began a process in the Church that made war sacred, and viewed the enemy as a demonic force. The enemies (in this case Muslims) were portrayed in the imagery of the Book of Revelation as the forces of the Antichrist. In other cases the "infidels" have been Native Americans in the nineteenth century, the North Vietnamese and Viet Cong in the 1960s and '70s, Saddam Hussein and the Iraqis during the wars of 1990–91 and 2003, and Osama bin Laden and al-Qaeda during the war against terrorism.

When the technology of war became more deadly with the introduction of gunpowder, some Christian intellectuals—like the humanist Erasmus (1466–1536)—condemned war. Erasmus argued that once wars become just, they then become glorious, and Christians must oppose them. The main leaders of the Protestant Reformation, however, accepted the "just war" teaching. However, many leaders of the Anabaptist wing of the Reformation did reject violence, and taught that restoration of New Testament community included pacifism.

Christians took positions of leadership in revolutionary wars such as the American War of Independence, but the pacifist movement has gained strength as warfare has become ever more bloody, and the ideology of "total war" has become the accepted military doctrine. After the slaughters of World War I, the "war to end all wars," a mood of pacifism swept through Christian churches in Europe and the United States.

Unfortunately, the world again erupted in violence, and the next cycle did not end until atomic bombs had been dropped by the United States on Japanese civilians, thousands of noncombatants had been killed in the devastating firebombing of British and German cities, and millions of Jews and others had been slaughtered in German death camps.

Ironically, nuclear weapons accomplished what politics could not, a situation in which all-out conflict was too terrible to be allowed to happen. Many Christians became active in the Nuclear Disarmament movement and worked in opposition to other conflicts, such as the Vietnam War of the 1960s and '70s. However, the majority of Christians continued to affirm the teaching of "just war."

In general, then, Christians today typically take one of four positions on war (Clouse 1981):

- *nonresistance,* with a willingness to serve in noncombatant roles such as the medical corps;
- *pacifism,* in which Christians refuse to cooperate in any way with the state's prosecution of wars, including for some the paying of taxes used to support the military;
- *just war,* following the historical criteria established by Augustine and affirmed by many Christian teachers since; or
- *crusade* or *preventive war,* in which the utter depravity of the enemy is thought to justify the prosecution of war by Christians in the most violent way possible.

The Christian attitude toward war is complicated by the teaching found in the Bible (especially the apocalyptic Books of Daniel and Revelation) about a great conflict between God and Satan at the end of history. Christians who believe the apocalyptic passages in the Bible should be interpreted literally claim that Armageddon is inevitable, and associate particular modern nations with the forces of goodness and evil. For some Christians nuclear war is part of the plan of God, and they oppose any efforts to negotiate nuclear disarmament. Other Christians, who reject a literalist view of Scripture, contend that the Bible's apocalyptic imagery is symbolic and should not be used to try to predict the future. They say that Christians should be motivated by the apocalyptic books to work cooperatively to achieve the divine plan of bringing to earth the peaceful and just kingdom of God portrayed in Revelation.

ISLAM   After the attacks of September 11, 2001, interest in the Muslim teaching about war has taken on a sense of urgency. Were the actions of the nineteen Muslim men who hijacked commercial airliners that day, killing thousands of innocent people, sanctioned by the teachings of Islam? Or was theirs a distorted understanding of the Muslim teaching about when acts of war are justified?

As in other areas of Muslim life, the Qur'an is the primary source for an understanding of Islamic teaching on war. The Qur'an clearly says that Allah approves of Muslims engaging in war. The disagreement among interpreters rests on the issue of whether only defensive wars are permissible. The ambiguity seems to be in the text itself. For example, *Surah* 2.190 speaks of fighting those who fight you, but not starting the hostilities. That would seem to rule out Muslim participation in offensive military actions. However, the very next verse admonishes Muslims to kill enemies wherever you find them, for persecution is worse than slaughter. This has been taken to support Muslim armies moving preemptively against enemies.

The consensus of interpreters today is that Muslims may only engage in defensive wars. As in Judaism and Christianity, there are strict limitations governing how the wars may be conducted. For example, women, children, and the elderly may not be made targets of warfare, nor may farm animals or crops. Every effort must be taken to protect the environment during warfare, including the air, water, and even trees.

War falls under the dictates of *jihad* ("struggle"), which, as we have seen, refers to the Muslim's obligations to resist or struggle against evil. The principal or greater *jihad* is the individual Muslim's struggle against evil. The lesser *jihad* is war to defend Islam and Muslims under attack.

One Muslim scholar, Sobhi Mahmassani, has characterized the contemporary Islamic teaching on war in this way (cited by Mayer 1991: 203):

> Islamic law[. . . .] is essentially a law of peace, built on human equality, religious tolerance and universal brotherhood.
>
> War, in theory, is just and permissible only as a defensive measure, on grounds of extreme necessity, namely to protect the freedom of religion, to repel aggression, to prevent injustice and to protect social order[. . . .]
>
> This defensive war, when permissible, is moreover subjected by Islamic jurisprudence to strict regulations and rules[. . . .]
>
> Thus, a declaration of war has to be preceded by notification sent to the enemy. Detailed provisions are laid down for the use of humane methods of warfare and fair treatment of enemy persons and property. Acts of cruelty and unnecessary destruction and suffering are expressly proscribed. Provision is also made for the termination of war and the settlement of its consequences.

However, a minority of Muslims in various countries believe that, as victims of a violent campaign of colonialism and imperialism, they have a right to strike out preemptively against all Western targets in the defense of Islam. Excerpts from a July 20, 1988, speech by Ayatollah Khomeini, the Shi'ite leader of the Islamic revolution in Iran, reflect this attitude (cited by Mayer 1991: 207):

> O Muslims of all the world [. . .] think of attacking the enemies of Islam, because glory in life can be achieved through struggle[. . . .] it is necessary to break the sovereignty of global infidelity, particularly of the United States[. . . .]
>
> We must smash the hands and the teeth of the superpowers, particularly the United States. And we must choose one of two alternatives—either martyrdom or victory, which we both regard as victory[. . . .]

Rhetoric such as this has inspired groups like Hezbullah in Lebanon, Islamic Jihad and Hamas in Palestine, and al-Qaeda to engage in terrorist acts against civilians, such as the attacks on September 11, 2001. In 2000 the leader of al-Qaeda, Osama bin Laden, issued a *fatwa* (religious edict) claiming that Islam was under siege by its historic enemies, Christianity and Judaism, and calling all Muslims to a global *jihad* in which civilians were legitimate targets.

Groups such as al-Qaeda number in the thousands in their membership. The vast majority of the world's 1.3 billion Muslims strongly reject these groups' interpretation of Muslim teaching on war. To condemn Islam as a violent religion because of the actions of men like Osama bin Laden and his supporters would be comparable to condemning Christianity because of the Christian hate groups that label Jews and Muslims as enemies of God, and that have killed innocent people on the basis of their twisted interpretations of the Bible.

There are many alternatives to the extremist and violent interpretations of Islam dominating the news in the early twenty-first century. Unfortunately, they are not nearly as widely known. For example, Uztaz Mahmoud Mohamed Taha, known as the "African Gandhi," created an Islamic movement in Sudan to resist colonialism with the same strategy Gandhi used in India (cf. Taha 1986). He also stood in opposition to extremist forces intent on imposing their repressive version of Sharia throughout the Sudan and was martyred for his beliefs in 1985. His was a "humane and liberating understanding of Islam as an alternative to the cruel and oppressive interpretation underlying recent events in Iran, Pakistan, and Sudan, and the equally negative traditionalist view prevailing in Saudi Arabia and other parts of the Muslim world" (Smith-Christopher 2001: 256). His message has been heard and is being promoted by other courageous Muslim scholars and leaders today.

SIKHISM   As discussed in Chapter Thirteen, Sikhism originated with a commitment to end the religious violence that plagued India in the seventeenth century. However, circumstances forced Sikh Gurus to advocate the taking up of arms for self-defense. As Guru Gobind Singh said, "When all efforts to restore peace prove useless and no words avail, Lawful is the flash of steel, it is right to draw the sword" (Nesbitt 1996: 123-4).

New Religious Movements

INTERNATIONAL SOCIETY FOR KRISHNA CONSCIOUSNESS   The founder of the International Society for Krishna Consciousness, A. C. Bhaktivedanta Swami Prabhupada, has advocated the position that conflicts will not end until nationalism is overcome. Nationalism is, from this perspective, merely one manifestation of the ignorance that comes from attachment to the material world. Nationalism creates a sense of "enemy" and "friend" that can be transcended only through perception of the true, spiritual self. According to Srila Prabhupada, "Because people are identifying with this material world, they are thinking 'I am an Englishman,' 'I am this,' 'I am that.' But if one chants the *Hare Krishna mantra,* he will realize that he is not this material body." (Drutakarma 1992: 54). Only through such spiritual realization will people develop the sense of identify necessary to overcome nationalism and the wars that nationalism breeds.

THE BAHA'I FAITH   'Abdu'l-Baha' wrote in 1912 that "when perfect equality shall be established between men and women, peace may be realized for the simple reason that womankind in general will never favor warfare. Women will not be willing to allow those whom they have so tenderly cared for to go to the battlefield. When they shall have a vote, they will oppose any cause of warfare" (Pokorny 1984: 7).

The Baha'i ideal is a unified world in which national loyalties have been transcended and people share a commitment to the well-being of all. The task of the

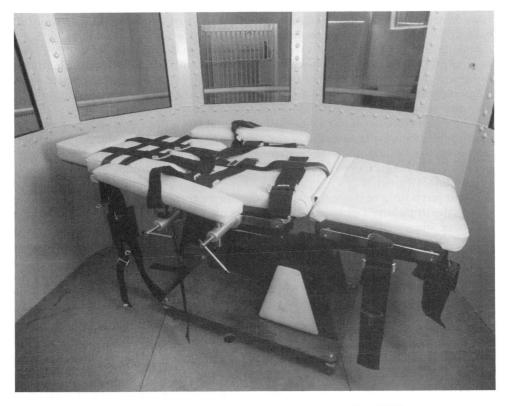

Lethal injection chamber at a U.S. prison. Early in the twenty-first century, about 3,500 men and women were awaiting execution on death row in American prisons.

Baha'i community is to model the "new world order," and, by the spreading of the teachings of Baha'u'llah and other Baha'i leaders, to show others the way to find world unity.

CAPITAL PUNISHMENT: WHEN MAY THE STATE TAKE A CRIMINAL'S LIFE?

The Nature of the Issue and the Role of Religion

On the day I am writing these words, the State of Oklahoma is putting to death Robert Wesley Knighton for the January 8, 1990, murder of Richard and Virginia Denney in rural Oklahoma. Knighton took sixty-one dollars, a pocketknife, some cigarettes, and a run-down truck from his victims. Nine months later he was sentenced to death for the murders. Watching Knighton as he receives a cocktail of lethal chemicals this evening will be Sue Norton, one of the victims' daughters. She and her husband will be present at Knighton's request.

At a clemency hearing about a week before the execution, Norton spoke about how God had moved her to forgive Robert Knighton. She befriended him in prison and pleaded for his life before the Oklahoma Board of Pardons and Paroles. At the same hearing, another of the Denney children spoke of her desire to see Knighton executed, that "justice may be done." This situation reflects the deep division among religious people, even in the same families, on the question of whether society should take the lives of persons convicted of brutal crimes such as the one that Knighton committed. Motivated by their faith, some strongly oppose capital punishment, while others believe it to be a moral and just punishment, sanctioned by the same faith.

The United States is one of the last democracies in the world that imposes the death penalty. In the last decade of the twentieth century, about one hundred men and women in total have been executed each year in the states in which the death penalty is legal. As the twenty-first century begins, a debate is raging over whether it should be abolished.

Our purpose here is not to review all the arguments in the general moral debate on the death penalty, but to examine the specific teachings of the world's religions that have addressed this issue.

Religious Responses

Indigenous Religions   On the one hand, putting to death those who have seriously violated the social order, or captives taken in battle, has long been practiced by indigenous cultures. The punishment is usually carried out in a ritual manner, and is deemed essential to restoring harmony with the spirit world. On the other hand, the tradition of restorative justice in many indigenous cultures supports other, nonlethal forms of punishment, in which the one who has violated the culture's norms repairs the damage done.

Like other people of color, indigenous people in the United States have been disproportionately sentenced to death when tried in courts outside their own traditional cultures. Principally for that reason, opposition to capital punishment is presently the prevailing perspective among indigenous peoples living under laws that come from outside their traditional cultures.

South and Southeast Asian Religions   There is no single position on capital punishment in the religions of South and Southeast Asia (Hinduism, Theravada Buddhism, Jainism). The position is taken by some that the death penalty is necessary to discourage acts of violence and murder. However, the commitment to *ahimsa* (noninjury toward all forms of life) mitigates against support for the death penalty in these religions. In addition, the law of karma dictates that a person will suffer the consequences of a crime in this life and the next without the State taking his or her life. The Buddhist Peace Fellowship is a group actively working against the death penalty on the basis of Buddhist values. Despite these religious objections, India retains the death penalty for some crimes.

East Asian Religions

CONFUCIANISM   Confucian teaching endorses capital punishment. A passage from the writings of the early Confucian scholar Mencius provide the basis for Confucian teaching (cited in Tse 1989: 116):

> When men kill others, and roll over their bodies to take their property, being reckless and fearless of death, among all the people there are none but detest them:—thus, such characters are to be put to death, without waiting to give them warning.

The justification for capital punishment implied in this passage is that some people choose to deny their own human nature (characterized by *jen* or "humaneness") when they commit acts such as murder and robbery. Such people have separated themselves from humanity and therefore "ought to be removed from the human world" (Tse 1989: 116).

MAHAYANA BUDDHISM   In a statement supporting an international moratorium on capital punishment, Tenzin Gyatso, the fourteenth Dalai Lama, stated (www.againstdp. org/dalai.html):

> The death penalty fulfills a preventive function, but it is also very clearly a form of revenge. It is an especially severe form of punishment because it is so final. The human life is ended and the executed person is deprived of the opportunity to change, to restore the harm done or compensate for it. Before advocating execution we should consider whether criminals are intrinsically negative and harmful people or whether they will remain perpetually in the same state of mind in which they committed their crime or not. The answer, I believe, is definitely not. However horrible the act they have committed, I believe that everyone has the potential to improve and correct themselves. Therefore, I am optimistic that it remains possible to deter criminal activity, and prevent such harmful consequences of such acts in society, without having to resort to the death penalty.

Religions Originating in the Middle East   Among the world's religions, the most vigorous debate about capital punishment is found in the religions originating in the Middle East (Judaism, Christianity, and Islam).

JUDAISM   The legislation found in the Tanak provides for capital punishment in a number of circumstances, based on the principle of *lex talionis*—"life for life, eye for eye, tooth for tooth" (Deuteronomy 19:21). After the great flood, capital punishment seems to have been established as a basic law for all humanity; "whoever sheds the blood of man, by man shall his blood be shed" (Genesis 9:6). Jewish (and Christian) supporters of capital punishment point to these seemingly clear calls for the death penalty to defend their position. However, opponents argue that the law of retribution was actually a step toward the limitation of unwarranted revenge rather than a sanction for it. They also point out that provisions for the death penalty in the Tanak are balanced by calls for mercy, such as this passage from the Book of the Prophet Ezekiel: "As I live, says the Lord God, I have no pleasure in the death of the wicked, but that the wicked turn from their ways and live" (33:11).

The Talmud significantly limited the conditions under which capital punishment could be imposed. In general, the Talmud substitutes financial payment for literal application of the principle of "an eye for an eye." Jewish opponents of the death penalty claim that this general principle and specific restrictions effectively abolished capital punishment in the Jewish community. Testimony in capital cases had to be presented by two eyewitnesses of the crime, who were required to acknowledge that they knew the one they were testifying against could be put to death.

Jewish opponents of the death penalty also argue that the death penalty has a brutalizing effect, and that since Judaism is committed to reverence for life, it cannot support capital punishment. The Union of American Hebrew Congregations, an association of Reform Jewish Rabbis, has issued the following statement: "We appeal to our congregants and to our co-religionists and to all who cherish God's mercy and love to join in efforts to eliminate this practice [of capital punishment] which lies as a stain upon civilization and our religious conscience."

The State of Israel eliminated the death penalty, except in the cases of treason and genocide. It has been applied only once, in the case of Adolf Eichmann, who was convicted of coordinating much of the implementation of the Nazi plan for the extermination of the Jews during the Holocaust. However, the policy of assassination of leaders of Palestinian militias may be considered a form of extrajudicial capital punishment.

The Orthodox, Reform, and Conservative branches of American Judaism have joined in opposing capital punishment both on the grounds that it is incompatible with the standards of American democracy and because of Jewish tradition.

CHRISTIANITY   Surveys indicate that most Christians in the United States support capital punishment. When asked to draw upon their religious tradition to defend their viewpoint, most name the Old Testament principle of "an eye for an eye" and the New Testament teaching that Christians should support the efforts of the legitimate civil authority to maintain order.

Christian opponents of the death penalty most often cite the teaching of Jesus concerning forgiveness and his rejection of the law of retribution. In the Sermon on the Mount, for example, Jesus said, "You have heard that it was said, 'An eye for an eye and a tooth for a tooth.' But I say to you, Do not resist an evildoer. But if anyone strikes you on the right cheek, turn the other also" (Matthew 5:38–39). Supporters counter by pointing out that this applies to the Kingdom of God, which has not yet fully arrived. In the meantime, the laws of the state must remain in force. Christian critics of the death penalty also draw on the Apostle Paul's statement on the need to leave vengeance to the Lord (Romans 12:17–21). Supporters point out that this verse is followed by Paul's admonition for Christians to accept the authority of the state.

Opponents also cite Jesus's opposition to capital punishment in a specific case, when he told those who were about to stone a woman caught in adultery, "Let anyone among you who is without sin be the first to throw a stone at her" (John 8:7). Finally, they claim that the sacrifice of Jesus on the cross removes its necessity. "Christ died that others may live. By trading places with the guilty and the enemy, by dying in the place of the murderer Barabbas, Christ closed off the Old Testament reason for the death penalty" (Zehr: 21).

Since the reinstitution of the death penalty in the United States in 1976, a number of Protestant Christian churches have expressed qualified support or outright opposition. A statement of the Christian Reformed Church in North America, adopted in 1981, is typical (National Coalition 1988):

> Given that human life is sacred, that the magistrate is fallible, that time for repentance is desirable, and that imprisonment will normally satisfy the demand for justice, we conclude that, though judicial executions may sometimes be divinely sanctioned and be in society's best interests, it is not desirable that capital punishment be routinely inflicted upon persons guilty of murder in the first degree. Only under exceptional circumstances should the state resort to capital punishment.

In 1980 the U.S. Roman Catholic Bishops issued a statement on capital punishment. It expresses opposition on the same grounds used to oppose abortion: that all life, from conception onward, is sacred and must be protected (National

Coalition 1988):

> abolition of capital punishment is [. . .] a manifestation of our belief in the unique worth and dignity of each person from the moment of conception, a creature made in the image and likeness of God.[. . .] We do not wish to equate the situation of criminals convicted of capital crimes with the condition of the innocent unborn or of the defenseless aged or infirm, but we do believe that the defense of life is strengthened by eliminating exercise of a judicial authorization to take human life.

Attention has been drawn to Catholic opposition to the death penalty by Sister Helen Prejean, CSJ, who told the story of her work with death-row inmates and the families of their victims in the book *Dead Man Walking*, the basis of the widely acclaimed movie of the same title.

ISLAM   Capital punishment is allowed in Islamic law. However, because Allah is the giver and taker of life, the application of the death penalty must be carefully guided by the principles Allah has established. Under Muslim law, when a family has been aggrieved by a crime, their wishes must be considered in deciding on the punishment to be meted out. Capital punishment is one of three permissible options the family of a victim may request for those responsible for their grief: life for life, a fine, or forgiveness. One is not necessarily favored over the others—although, as in the other monotheistic religions, forgiveness is a central value in Islam.

As in Judaism, indiscriminate retaliation is not allowed in Islam. *Surah* 6.151 says "take not life which Allah hath made sacred, except by way of justice and law" (Ali 2002: 89; cf. 17.33). Given this emphasis, concern over racial bias in the application of the death penalty in the United States has caused some American Muslims to oppose it.

In practice, although capital punishment is recognized as legitimate, Muslim societies differ in its application, depending on the scholarly interpretation deemed most authoritative in particular situations.

SIKHISM   Sikhs share the South Asian perspective that individuals suffer in accord with the law of karma, in this life or in another birth. However, according to Sikh teaching, there are circumstances in which the death penalty is the necessary punishment. A Sikh who is put to death defending the faith is revered as a martyr (*shahid*) (Nesbitt 1996: 118).

New Religious Movements

THE INTERNATIONAL SOCIETY FOR KRISHNA CONSCIOUSNESS   Drutakarma Dasa explains the Hare Krishna position on capital punishment as follows (1992):

> The Vedas and books of social codes such as the *Manu-samhita* sanction capital punishment. According to the laws of karma, a killer must suffer in the next life by being killed violently. But if the killer receives capital punishment in this life, the killer is freed from any further violent karmic reaction in the next life. Capital punishment is thus a legitimate resource for the state in its dealings with criminals, and in the context of the law of reincarnation, is in fact merciful.

UNITARIAN UNIVERSALIST ASSOCIATION   The General Assembly of the Unitarian Universalist Association has adopted resolutions opposing the death penalty on a number of occasions. These resolutions have urged the complete abolition of capital punishment as "inconsistent with respect for human life; for its retributive, discriminatory, and non-deterrent character" (National Coalition 1988: 44).

CHAPTER SUMMARY

 In this chapter we explored the relationship between religion and socially sanctioned violence. According to the world's religions, are wars ever justified as a means to resolve disputes among nations or groups? How do religions respond when societies use the death penalty as a punishment for those who violate the laws of the society? We learned that on each issue there are a range of views, both among and within religions.

IMPORTANT TERMS AND PHRASES

ahimsa, al-Qaeda, Armageddon, costs of war, Hachiman, Holocaust, holy war, *jihad,* just war, *kshatriya, lex talionis,* Masada, nonresistance, nonviolent resistance, pacifism, preventative war, total war

QUESTIONS FOR DISCUSSION AND REFLECTION

1. Suppose that, in the days following September 11, 2001, representatives of the world's religions have gathered. In a group setting, have members represent various religions. First discuss the roles that religions may have played among those who planned and carried out the attacks. Next consider what guidance the world's religions have to offer to political leaders, who must decide how to respond to the attacks. Can you reach consensus on these questions? If so, what might the consensus be? If not, why not?

2. Suppose that the United States Senate and House Justice Committees have called a joint hearing on a bill to abolish the death penalty in federal law. Representatives of the world's religions have been invited to testify. In a group setting, have members represent different religions, and groups within religions, in which there is disagreement on capital punishment. Convene the hearing and have the representatives testify. Others in the group are members of the congressional panel, who should raise questions after listening to the testimony, and discuss whether and how the views of these religions should influence them as they decide whether the Committee should recommend that the Senate and House adopt the legislation.

SOURCES AND SUGGESTIONS FOR FURTHER STUDY

WAR

General

APPLEBY, SCOTT, 2000. *The Ambivalence of the Sacred: Religion, Violence, and Reconciliation.* Lanham, MD: Rowman & Littlefield.

BROWN, ROBERT McAFEE, 1987. *Religion and Violence.* Philadelphia: Westminster.

ELLIS, MARC H., 1997. *Unholy Alliance: Religion and Atrocity in Our Time.* Minneapolis, MN: Fortress.

FERGUSON, JOHN, 1978. *War and Peace in the World's Religions.* New York: Oxford University.

GOPIN, MARC, 2000. *Between Eden and Armageddon: The Future of World Religions, Violence, and Peacemaking.* New York: Oxford University.

JUERGENSMEYER, MARK, 2000. *Terror in the Mind of God: The Global Rise of Religious Violence.* Berkeley: University of California.

LACKEY, DOUGLAS, 1989. *The Ethics of War and Peace.* Englewood Cliffs, NJ: Prentice Hall.

LEFEBURE, LEO D., 2000. *Revelation, the Religions, and Violence.* Maryknoll, NY: Orbis.

VITTACHI, ANURADHA, 1989. *Earth Conference One: Sharing a Vision for Our Planet.* Boston: New Science Library.

Religions of South Asia

Hinduism

GANDHI, MOHANDAS K., 2002. "The Practice of Satyagraha." In May, Collins-Chobanian, and Wong, *Applied Ethics,* 285–90.

ROSEN, STEPHEN J., ED., 2002. *Holy War: Violence and the Bhagavad Gita.* Hampton, VA: Deepak Heritage.

Theravada Buddhism

HARVEY, PETER, 2000. "War and Peace." In *An Introduction to Buddhist Ethics: Foundations, Values, and Issues.* New York: Cambridge University, 239–85.

PREMASIRI, P. D., 1989. "Ethics of Theravada Buddhism." In Crawford, *World Religions and Global Ethics,* 36–64.

BARTHOLOMEUSZ, TESSA J., 2002. *In Defense of Dharma: Just War Ideology in Buddhist Sri Lanka.* New York: Routledge.

Religions of East Asia

Confucianism

WARE, JAMES R., 1955. *The Sayings of Confucius.* New York: New American Library.

Mahayana Buddhism

NHAT HANH, THICH, 1987. *Being Peace.* New York: New York University.

VICTORIA, BRIAN, 2000. *Zen at War.* New York: Weatherhill.

Religions Originating in the Middle East

Judaism

SHAPIRO, RAMI M., 1989. "Blessing and Curse: Toward a Liberal Jewish Ethic." In Crawford, *World Religions and Global Ethics,* 155–87.

Christianity

BAINTON, ROLAND, 1960. *Christian Attitudes Toward War and Peace.* Nashville: Abingdon.

CLOUSE, ROBERT G., ED., 1981. *War: Four Christian Views.* Downers Grove, IL: InterVarsity.

DOMBROWSKI, DANIEL A., 1991. *Christian Pacifism.* Philadelphia: Temple University.

LACKEY, DOUGLAS P., 2002. "Just War Theory." In Mays, Collins-Chobanian, and Wong, *Applied Ethics,* 275–84.

RAMSAY, PAUL, 1961. *War and the Christian Conscience.* Durham, NC: Duke University.

SCHLABACH, THERON F. and RICHARD T. HUGHES, ED., 1997. *Proclaim Peace: Christian Pacifism from Unexpected Quarters.* Urbana: University of Illinois.

WOOD, JOHN, 1998. *Perspectives on War in the Bible.* Macon, GA: Mercer University.

Judaism, Christianity, and Islam

NELSON-PALLMEYER, JACK, 2003. *Is Religion Killing Us? Violence in the Bible and the Quran.* Harrisburg, PA: Trinity.

SMITH-CHRISTOPHER, DANIEL L., 2001. "'That Was Then. . .': Debating Nonviolence within the Textual Traditions of Judaism, Christianity, and Islam." In Runzo and Martin, *Ethics in the World Religions,* 251–69.

Islam

ALI, ABDULLAH YUSUF, TRANS., 2002. *The Qur'an: Translation.* 9th ed. Elmhurst, NY: Tahrike Tarsile.

DONNER, FRED M., 1991. "The Sources of Islamic Conceptions of War." In Kelsay and Johnson, *Just War and Jihad,* 31–69.

ESPOSITO, JOHN L., 2002. *Unholy War: Terror in the Name of Islam.* New York: Oxford University.

HAFEZ, MOHAMMED M., 2003. *Why Muslims Rebel: Repression and Resistance in the Islamic World.* Boulder, CO: Lynne Rienner.

KELSAY, JOHN, AND JAMES TURNER JOHNSON, EDS., 1991. *Just War and Jihad: Historical Perspectives on War and Peace in Western and Islamic Traditions.* New York: Greenwood.

LAWRENCE, BRUCE B., 2000. *Shattering the Myth: Islam Beyond Violence.* Princeton, NJ: Princeton University.

MARSDEN, PETER, 2002. *The Taliban: War and Religion in Afghanistan.* New York: Zed.

MAYER, ANN ELIZABETH, 1991. "International Law and the Islamic Tradition of War and Peace." In Kelsay and Johnson, *Just War and Jihad,* 195–226.

TAHA, MAHMOUD MOHAMED, 1986. *The Second Message of Islam,* trans. Abdullah Ahmed An-Na'im. Syracuse, NY: Syracuse University.

Sikhism

NESBITT, ELEANOR, 1996. "Sikhism." In Lawton and Morgan, *Ethical Issues in Six Religious Traditions,* 99–134.

New Religious Movements

WESSINGER, CATHERINE, 2000. *How the Millennium Comes Violently: From Jonestown to Heaven's Gate.* New York: Seven Bridges.

International Society for Krishna Consciousness

DRUTAKARMA DASA, 1992. "Peace and the New Nationalism," *Back to Godhead,* 25–26, 52–54.

The Baha'i Faith

POKORNY, BARD, 1984. "A Worldwide Movement for Peace." *Circle of Unity,* 135–53.

CAPITAL PUNISHMENT

ALI, ABDULLAH YUSUF, TRANS., 2002. *The Qur'an: Translation.* 9th ed. Elmhurst, NY: Tahrike Tarsile.

BAILEY, LLOYD R., 1987. *Capital Punishment: What the Bible Says.* Nashville: Abingdon.

BEDAU, HUGO A., ED., 1982. *The Death Penalty in America.* New York: Oxford University.

DRUTAKARMA DASA, 1992. Personal correspondence.

GROSSMAN, MARK, 1998. *Encyclopedia of Capital Punishment.* Santa Barbara, CA: ABC-CLIO.

HOOK, DAVID AND LOTHAR KALIN, 1989. *Death in the Balance: the Debate over Capital Punishment.* Lexington, MS: Lexington.

HOUSE, H. WAYNE and JOHN HOWARD YODER, 1991. *The Death Penalty Debate*. Dallas: Word.

KASHER, AVA, 1989. "Jewish Ethics: An Orthodox View." In Crawford, *World Religions and Global Ethics*, 129–54.

MEGIVERN, JAMES J., 1997. *The Death Penalty: An Historical and Theological Survey*. New York: Paulist.

National Coalition to Abolish the Death Penalty, 1988. *The Death Penalty: The Religious Community Calls for Abolition*. Washington, DC: National Interreligious Task Force on Criminal Justice.

OTTERBEIN, KEITH, 1986. *The Ultimate Coercive Sanction: A Cross-Cultural Study of Capital Punishment*. New Haven, CT: HRAF.

PREJEAN, HELEN, 1994. *Dead Man Walking: An Eyewitness Account of the Death Penalty in the United States*. New York: Vintage.

STASSEN, GLEN H., 1998. *Capital Punishment: A Reader*. Cleveland: Pilgrim.

TSE, CHUNG M., 1989. "Confucianism and Contemporary Ethical Issues." In Crawford, *World Religions and Global Ethics*, 91–125.

ZEHR, HOWARD, n.d. *Death as a Penalty: A Moral, Practical and Theological Discussion*. Elkhart, IN: Mennonite Central Committee.

Web Sites

WAR

www.ppu.org.uk/learn/infodocs/st_religions.html
>(short essays on the positions of various religions on war, as well as on pacifism and just war theory)

www.ipacademy.org
>(site of the International Peace Academy)

CAPITAL PUNISHMENT

religioustolerance.org/execut7.htm
>(positions of various religious groups on the death penalty)

web.amnesty.org/pages/deathpenalty_index_eng
>(Amnesty International's campaign to end the death penalty)

prodeathpenalty.com
>(a site with pro–death penalty links)

 Prentice Hall's **Research Navigator** helps students in their further study of the world's religions. Visit *http://www.researchnavigator.com* for help on the research process and access to databases full of relevant material, including the New York *Times*.

CHAPTER

17

Abortion and Euthanasia— Life and Death

ABORTION: RIGHT TO LIFE OR RIGHT TO CHOOSE?

The Nature of the Issue and the Role of Religion

In communities across the United States, "pro-life" and "pro-choice" forces gather for yet another round in one of the most intractable ethical disputes of modern times. Both sides claim that their positions have religious validity. The Congress of the United States debates a "partial abortion" bill, as its proponents call it. They claim it protects babies who would be viable if delivered normally from being brutally killed. Its opponents say it is a part of a carefully calculated campaign to undo the gains made in protecting a woman's reproductive freedom.

On January 22, 1973, in a decision known as Roe v. Wade, the United States Supreme Court effectively legalized abortions. Most of the more than one million abortions performed in the United States each year are elective. Some opponents of abortion have become increasingly aggressive in their attempts to end what they call a "slaughter of innocents." Several physicians who performed abortions have been killed by abortion opponents, and abortion clinics have been bombed, with deaths resulting. Advocates of abortion rights have used the courts to restrict the tactics of pro-life groups.

Does a woman have a right to choose to terminate a pregnancy through abortion? If so, in what circumstances? Does an unborn child have a "right to life"? If not, why not? When does life begin? Is abortion a symbol of the deterioration of modern society's values, or of the growing recognition of the autonomy and dignity of women? We will step back here from the immediacy of the abortion debate as it rages today and seek to understand the full range of teachings in the world's religions concerning this controversial issue.

Many who engage in abortion protests are motivated by religion to support the "right-to-life," but others who support reproductive "freedom of choice" for women also claim to be guided by their religious views.

Religious Responses

Indigenous Religions

AFRICAN   For indigenous religions in general, all life is sacred, for all life is the realm of the spiritual. The Akan and Ewe people of Ghana reflect an awareness of the sanctity of life in the frequency of the term "life" in personal names and common greetings. Since abortion results in the taking of life, it is viewed as a "bad act." During pregnancy, a variety of rituals surround the expectant mother to protect both her and the unborn child (Ansah 1989: 261–62).

The indigenous attitude toward marriage and family life also support a negative attitude toward abortion. Prosperity is measured by the number of children in the family, and a large family is necessary to provide for the welfare of elders. Therefore, abortion is thought to be a maladaptive behavior, and is discouraged on those grounds.

NATIVE AMERICAN   Because of their reverence for life, most Native Americans oppose abortion. However, concern for protecting the harmony of the earth has caused others to support abortion as a means to protect the land against overpopulation. In addition, polls show that increasing numbers of Native American women are defending their right to make their own reproductive choices, even when that means having an abortion.

Religions of South and Southeast Asia

HINDUISM   Abortion has been legal in India since 1971, when the Medical Termination of Pregnancy Act was passed as part of the government's strategy to slow population growth. About four million medically induced abortions are reported annually in India. A similar number of illegal abortions not medically performed may occur.

Traditional Hinduism opposes abortion. The classical texts consider it a violation of dharma. Up to 80 percent of Hindu women consider abortion wrong (Menski 1996: 33). In the Vedic tradition, the fetus is inviolable and abortion is not an option, for it would be a violation of the moral principle of *ahimsa* (noninjury) to all living beings.

Ahimsa, however, is not absolute when the rights of humans conflict. When a woman risks "grave injury," abortion is permissible. Some Hindu scholars argue that the rights of an adult human being with familial obligations outweigh those of a human being whose karmic state in the current life has not yet developed. Under these circumstances a woman's right to have an abortion must be recognized, they maintain.

In cases of fetal deformity, Hindu leaders oppose abortion because it interferes with the child's karmic development (Crawford 1989: 27). They also consider the use of abortion for sex selection to be infanticide, and thus immoral. Although illegal in India, abortions of female fetuses simply because they are female are still widespread. More generally, many Hindus are concerned at the use of elective abortion for birth control.

In the final analysis, however, Hinduism is a religion that recognizes that each person must make his or her own ethical decisions, because each person alone suffers or enjoys the karmic consequences of them.

THERAVADA BUDDHISM   According to the Theravada Buddhist interpretation of the Buddha's teachings, each person is on his or her own on the journey toward nirvana. Each of us must make and take responsibility for ethical decisions, guided by the Buddha's teaching (dharma) and following the example of the Buddha. According to the rules stipulated for Buddhist monks, abortion would seem to be unacceptable, because it involves the taking of a human life already existent (Harvey 2000: 313):

> When a monk is ordained he should not intentionally deprive a living being of life, even if it is only an ant. Whenever a monk deprives a human being of life, even down to destroying an embryo, he becomes not a true renouncer.

Most Theravada commentators adopted the view that the migration of consciousness occurs at conception, and therefore that all abortion incurs the karmic burden of killing a living being. The Jataka tales describe the destiny of those who conduct abortions as the same as those who commit matricide, and adulterers (Harvey 2000: 315).

However, in sorting through the myriad of circumstances that surround specific situations, individuals must decide for themselves what course to take in the case of abortion (as with other ethical issues). What counts, from a Theravada perspective, is the "goodness of the intention," for that determines the karmic effect (Premasiri 1989: 56–57; cf. Morgan 1996: 77). Hence, there are circumstances in which an abortion may be necessary, as when there is a threat to the life of the mother.

JAINISM   Because of its central emphasis on the principle of *ahimsa,* Jainism is generally opposed to abortion. However, some Jains accept that there are circumstances in which abortion is necessary to prevent a greater harm. For example, if a woman's life is in jeopardy and can only be saved through a therapeutic abortion, the procedure, they would argue, is warranted.

Religions of East Asia

DAOISM   Abortion is not directly addressed in the Daodejing or other ancient Daoist texts. Since abortion interferes with the natural process of pregnancy and birth and Daoism teaches that the way of nature should not be resisted, opposition to abortion can be inferred. However, Daoism also holds that governments should not unnecessarily intrude into the lives of citizens. Therefore, from a Daoist perspective laws against abortion would seem also to be unnecessarily intrusive.

CONFUCIANISM   Confucianism does not address abortion directly. Guidance comes from drawing implications from basic Confucian virtues. It seems clear that Confucian ethics are neither "pro-life" nor "pro-choice," for both positions focus on the rights of an individual. From a Confucian perspective, neither the fetus nor the mother has rights independent of the network of social relationships in which they exist. Because Confucian values are social values, based on the five basic human relationships (see Chapter Seven), decisions about abortions must be made in the context of these relationships. Because a woman is in a subordinate position to her husband, she is not acting in her proper role if she claims the right to make an autonomous moral decision about abortion or anything else. However, she is also in a relationship with her unborn child, so she has the responsibility to express her moral sense of what that relationship obliges (Jones 1999: 182–83).

Application of the Confucian values of *jen* (humaneness) and *shu* (reciprocity) would seem to mitigate against abortion. Moreover, social harmony depends on respect for life, which abortions would seem to undermine.

In countries influenced by Confucianism, the preference for sons has led to the use of abortion for sex selection. For example, it is estimated that thirty thousand female fetuses are aborted each year in South Korea simply because of their sex. In response, the South Korean government has instituted strict laws against abortion for sex selection. Vietnam has also banned the practice.

In China today the traditional preference for male children is combined with the government policy of limiting family size to one child because of the concern with overpopulation. Defenders of the policy argue that even late-term abortions are morally justifiable given the need to control population (Qiu 2002). Abortions for sex selection are common in Chinese families in which the parents (especially the father) wants to be sure the one child is a son.

MAHAYANA BUDDHISM   Because oral contraceptives have been banned in Japan, in recent decades up to half of pregnancies have ended in abortion. One commentator has concluded that in modern Japan "there is a consensus that abortion constitutes a painful social necessity and as such must remain legal and available" (LaFleur 2002: 548). Fear of overpopulation has also been cited as a reason for the acceptance of abortion in Japan. Consequently, the fundamental morality of abortion has not been the subject of the same public controversy in Japan as in Western countries.

Many women who have had abortions in Japan are turning to the *bodhisattva* Kannon, making offerings so that the aborted fetuses (*mizuko*) will be blessed and reborn once again as humans and eventually as buddhas (Smith 1992: 418–19). Discussion of abortion in Japan has focused on "criticism of those temples [. . .] which employ the notion of 'fetal retribution' to coerce the 'parents' of an aborted fetus into performing rituals that memorialize the fetus [. . .]" (LaFleur 2002: 548).

Religions Originating in the Middle East

JUDAISM   There is broad consensus among branches of Judaism on two aspects of the abortion question. First, human life *is* sacred; therefore, abortion is a serious moral issue, not just a matter of convenience. Second, when a mother's life is at stake or even threatened, the life of the mother must have priority and the fetus must be aborted (Goldman 1978: 35).

Beyond these two points, however, there is considerable disagreement. The only explicit statement in the Tanak on abortion can be interpreted to support either side of the debate. The Covenant Code in the Book of Exodus (Exodus 21:22–25) states:

> When people who are fighting injure a pregnant woman so that there is a miscar-
> riage, and yet no further harm follows, the one responsible shall be fined what the
> woman's husband demands, paying as much as the judges determine. If any harm
> follows, then you shall give life for life, eye for eye, tooth for tooth, hand for hand,
> foot for foot, burn for burn, wound for wound, stripe for stripe.

The "pro-life" interpretation of this passage is that it cannot be used to justify abortion, because the loss of the unborn baby is accidental, not intentional. The abortion is spontaneous, not induced. Opponents of allowing induced abortions also point out that even though the abortion was accidentally induced, it was still punished. Just because the punishment was a fine does not mean that the fetus is not human. Only premeditated murder is outside the provision that a ransom be paid in similar circumstances.

The "pro-choice" interpretation is that the passage does not view the fetus as a person with rights. The concern is the life and well-being of the mother. Even though the passage deals with a spontaneous abortion, the basic principle applies to induced abortions: the mother *is* a person, and an injury to her must be taken seriously, whereas the fetus is *not* a person.

Pro-life advocates point to a number of other texts in the Tanak that they think show God's concern for the unborn (e.g., Numbers 35:33, Psalm 51:5, Psalm 139:13, and Jeremiah 1:5), while pro-choice supporters quote a passage from Ecclesiastes which suggests that there is a radical distinction between life before and after birth (Ecclesiastes 6:3).

Perhaps the passage from the Hebrew Bible most quoted by opponents of abortion is the fifth commandment, "Thou shalt not kill" (Exodus 20:13). Since they consider an unborn child to be a human being, they believe the commandment applies to the killing of the child through abortion. Supporters of the right to abortion claim that since the fetus is not a person, the commandment is irrelevant to abortion. Further, they point out that the Bible does not rule out all killing, only the unjustified taking of life. Therefore, according to this argument, in cases where the abortion is justified, abortion is not a violation of the commandment even if the fetus is considered a person. In response, "pro-life" advocates claim that the commandment applies to the taking of innocent life, and no life is more innocent than an unborn child's.

Another debated text comes from the Book of Genesis: "Whoever sheds the blood of a human, by a human shall that person's blood be shed; for in his own image God made humankind" (Genesis 9:6).

There is obviously no *single* Jewish position on abortion. Individual Jewish communities must struggle with the conflicting interpretations of their legal tradition and come to their own understanding of what Torah teaches them on this controversial issue. In general, the three major modern movements within Judaism take the following positions (Goldman 1978: 49–59):

- *Orthodox.* The unborn child has a right to life. Even if a pregnancy is the result of rape or incest, or if tests reveal abnormalities, that right may not be abridged unless the life of the mother is threatened.
- *Conservative.* The mother has power over the fetus, but she must have valid and sufficient reasons for depriving it of potential life. Therapeutic abortions are permissible when the basic health of the mother, psychological as well as physical, is threatened. Rape or incest is a sufficient cause for an abortion to be sought. Where deformity is a certainty, abortion is allowed, but not if it is only a possibility. Abortions for convenience, however, are not acceptable.
- *Reform.* Most Reform Rabbis affirm the Conservative position, and add that social and economic factors may be taken into account in determining whether an abortion is moral.

In summary, the Jewish position is that abortion is moral only when the life of the mother is threatened, on the basis of the duty of self-preservation (*pikuah nefesh*). However, within Judaism there is wide disagreement about what constitutes a legitimate threat to the life of the mother (Biale 1984: 219–238). The strictest interpretation is that abortion is acceptable only if the mother's physical life is in danger. More lenient interpreters include in the principle of self-protection other threats, such as physical pain, mental anguish, or even social disgrace.

CHRISTIANITY (ROMAN CATHOLICISM)   The position of the Roman Catholic Church on abortion is quite clear. Abortion is murder, even if it is carried out with the best of intentions.

The teaching of the Church is that life begins at conception, and no artificial means may be used to interrupt the natural development of life. As Catholic theologian John Noonan puts it, "once the humanity of the fetus is perceived, abortion is never right except in self-defense" (2002: 504). According to Church teaching, to take the life of an unborn child, unless the life of the mother is actually at stake, would be for humans to substitute their judgment for God's will.

Historians point out that the teaching of the Church has not always been so clear-cut on abortion. Until 1588 Catholic theologians and Popes condoned abortion at up to eighty days for the female fetus and up to forty days for the male. In 1588 Pope Sixtus V outlawed all abortions; in 1591, however, Pope Gregory XIV overruled his predecessor's decree and allowed abortions at up to forty days for both the male and female fetus. "That is how the matter stood till 1869 when Pius IX forbade all abortions at any time" (Gregory 1983: 36).

Catholic opposition to abortion was reaffirmed by the Second Vatican Council, and a series of subsequent papal pronouncements and other Church statements, including the 1974 Declaration on Procured Abortion. In the Church's view, abortion is an attack on the principle of the "sanctity of life," which is essential to the Christian faith.

In the opinion of defenders of the Church's teachings, the Roman Catholic church is today—just as in ancient times—surrounded by a society that accepts and unduly practices abortion.

Mother Teresa, famous for her care of the dying in Calcutta, India, and her strong stand for the sanctity of life in all circumstances, was probably the most effective Catholic spokesperson for the unborn. In 1989 she told a forum of global spiritual leaders, "Every second so many little ones are being aborted [. . .] We in our mission are fighting abortion by adoption. We see now those little ones have brought so much joy into homes where the family cannot have a child." (Cited in Vittachi 1989: 64–65).

Although the Church hierarchy strongly opposes abortion, polls indicate that most Catholics in the United States support a woman's right to choose. They find support among Catholic leaders who think that the Church's teaching does not accurately reflect Catholic tradition. These "pro-choice" Catholics point out that the theologian whose views most shaped Catholic doctrine, Thomas Aquinas, believed that "the embryo is certainly not a human being during the early stages of pregnancy, and that, consequently it is not immoral to terminate pregnancy during this time, provided there are serious reasons for such an intervention" (Father Joseph F. Doncell, cited by Gregory 1983: 33).

Another Catholic "pro-choice" leader, Father Joseph O'Rourke, has written, "If the Church was to stand sincerely against abortion, it would re-orient its social and relief services to stop the 100 spontaneous abortions (miscarriages) for every 200 live births in the Third World, attacking the malnutrition, poverty and medical ignorance that is the cause of this hidden plague, rather than lobbying against the rights of American women" (Gregory 1983: 34).

Despite such strong American voices questioning the Church's teaching on abortion, Pope John Paul II has reaffirmed the Church's ban and shows no signs of reconsidering it. There is considerably more support for the official teaching among Catholics in other parts of the world.

CHRISTIANITY (PROTESTANTISM) Protestant Christians have *no* consensus on the question of abortion! All positions, ranging from the most extreme "pro-life" to the most radical "pro-choice," can be found in Protestant circles. We will first summarize some of the arguments made by Protestant opponents of abortion, then look at the points made by supporters of abortion rights.

Protestants claim that the principal, if not sole, source of authority on matters of faith and practice is the Bible. Therefore, the debate among Protestants about what the Bible has to say about abortion is particularly important.

The passages from the Tanak cited above all figure in the Protestant discussion. "Pro-life" Protestants add a feature in the interpretation of Exodus 21:22–25. The Greek translation says that a death penalty is to be imposed on the perpetrator if the fetus is "perfectly formed." This translation suggests that when fully formed the fetus is a human being, and the forced miscarriage is murder.

There is no explicit reference to abortion in the New Testament, but that has not stopped Christians on both sides of the abortion argument from appealing to the New Testament for support. Abortion opponents, for example, cite Luke 1:44, in which Elizabeth (the mother of John the Baptist) says, "the child in my womb leaped for joy." "Pro-life" advocates make the point that in the New Testament there is no distinction between a child in the womb and a child after birth (Brown 1977: 120). The account of the birth of Jesus (e.g., Matthew 1:20–21) shows, according to this perspective, that conception rather than birth marks the beginning of a person's life and that God has a plan for persons before they are born. Protestant opponents of abortion often argue that the special concern Jesus showed for the weak and powerless naturally extends to the unborn, and is made even stronger by the love Jesus showed for children.

Protestant opponents of abortion also cite the leaders of the Protestant Reformation in support of their position. John Calvin, for example, wrote that "the fetus, though enclosed in the womb of its mother is already a human being, and it is almost a monstrous crime to rob it of the life which it has not yet begun to enjoy" (Calvin 1950. 3.41,42).

Major twentieth-century Protestant theologians have also spoken strongly against abortion, the "pro-life" community asserts. For example, Dietrich Bonhoeffer, a German Lutheran pastor martyred during World War II because of his opposition to the policies of Adolf Hitler, wrote that "the simple fact is that God intended to create a human being and that this human being has been deliberately deprived of his life. And that is nothing but murder" (cited in Brown 1977: 127, 128).

The basis for the Protestant support for abortion rights can be summarized in this statement: "[Women] are recognized as creative, loved and loving human beings who have achieved full personhood. In the sight of most Protestant denominations, to equate personhood with an unborn fetus is to dehumanize a woman, to consider her a mere 'thing' through which the fetus is passing. To deny this essential tenet of our beliefs—the concept of personhood—would constitute a gross violation of our Christian faith" (Theresa Hoover, United Methodist Church; cited in Gregory 1983: 40–41).

In response to the "pro-life" argument that the Bible regards the fetus as a person, "pro-choice" interpreters of the Bible point to several Biblical texts that support the view that personhood does not begin before birth, especially Genesis 2:7. Also cited is Genesis 1:26–28, with the view taken that "image of God" is a spiritual rather than physical understanding of human nature. "The Biblical portrait of person, therefore," one pro-choice Protestant has argued, "is that of a complex many-sided creature with god-like abilities and the moral responsibility to make choices. The fetus hardly meets those characteristics[. . . .] The one who unquestionably fits this portrayal is the woman [. . .] The abortion decision focuses on the personhood of the woman, who in turn considers the potential personhood of the fetus in terms of the multiple dimensions of her own history and the future." (Simmons: 7, 8).

Statements in support of a woman's right to choose an abortion have been made since the 1970s by the American Baptist Churches, U.S.A.; the United Methodist Church; the Lutheran Church in America; the United Church of Christ; the United Presbyterian Church (U.S.A.); the Christian Church (Disciples of Christ); the Church of the Brethren; the Moravian Church in America; the Protestant Episcopal Church; and the Reformed Church in America.

For abortion-rights advocates the issue is at its heart one of religious liberty. Just when "personhood" begins is a religious issue, they argue, and any law that imposes one understanding of this complex issue on all people is a violation of the freedom of religion of those who do not agree.

Some Christians have sought to move beyond the rhetoric of the "pro-life" and "pro-choice" camps, to search for common ground. For example, these advocates of a "middle way" focus on providing access to prenatal care for women who choose to bring a child to term. They also work to provide care for children to increase their opportunities to grow into healthy adults. More and better information on birth control and adoption must be made available, they agree. If steps like these were taken, perhaps the "abortion epidemic" would be curbed (as abortion opponents desire), as would the restrictions on women's access to legal, safe abortions (as supporters of abortion rights want to ensure).

ISLAM   According to the Qur'an (*Surah* 16.5), Allah ordains how long the fetus remains in the womb and when a baby is born. This would seem to imply that Muslims should not condone forced abortions, because they would challenge the will of Allah. However, *Surah* 32.9 suggests that the fetus is not alive until "ensoulment" or "quickening" (cf. 40.68), the point at which Allah breathes the spirit into the fetus. This has opened the door for the ruling that guides other Muslim teaching on the topic: that before such time as Allah breathes the spirit into a child (six weeks is the accepted threshold), abortions are not in violation of the Sharia. However, the reason for the abortion must be compelling.

SIKHISM   Abortion is not in keeping with fundamental Sikh principles. As one modern Sikh commentator has said, "Abortion is taboo as it is an interference in the creative work of God. If the conception has taken place it would be a sin to destroy life" (Nesbitt 1996: 116). However, Sikh women are under the same cultural pressure to produce sons as other Indian women, and some resort to abortion for the purpose of sex selection.

New Religious Movements

THE CHURCH OF JESUS CHRIST OF LATTER-DAY SAINTS (THE MORMONS)   The position of the Latter-day Saints on abortion was expressed by President Gordon Hinckley (1998):

> What has happened to our regard for human life? How can women, and men, deny the great and precious gift of life, which is divine in its origin and nature? How wonderful a thing is a child. How beautiful is a newborn babe. There is no greater miracle than the creation of human life.

> Abortion is an ugly thing, a debasing thing, a thing which inevitably brings remorse and sorrow and regret.

THE INTERNATIONAL SOCIETY FOR KRISHNA CONSCIOUSNESS   According to Drutakarma Dasa, the Hare Krishna position is that abortions are not to be condoned (Dasa, 1992):

> According to Vedic books of knowledge, the persons involved in abortion must themselves be aborted in future lives. The Vedas say that the soul is present in the embryo from the moment of conception[. . . .] Although the movement does not become directly involved in partisan political affairs, I think it is fair to say that we would regard the outlawing of abortion as a step in the right direction.

EUTHANASIA: A "GOOD DEATH" OR "PLAYING GOD"?

The Nature of the Issue and the Role of Religion

"Euthanasia" comes from the Greek words that mean "good death." The term was coined by Sir Thomas More (1478–1535) to describe "the painless and merciful killing of incurables" (Goldman 1978: 171). In general usage, euthanasia refers to the ending of a life because of the belief that death would be preferable to life. Suicide can be considered self-imposed euthanasia, but the term usually is limited to cases in which the action (or inaction) of a second party results in the death of a person. "Mercy killing" is frequently used as a synonym for euthanasia.

Euthanasia may be either voluntary or involuntary. Voluntary euthanasia occurs when a person asks someone else to enable his or her death. For example, a person unable to move, but still alert, asks a friend to help him take an overdose of sleeping pills. Involuntary euthanasia means that the person whose life is taken is not active in the decision making process. This usually occurs when a person is incapacitated and unable to make his or her wishes known. For example, a husband takes a gun and shoots his wife who is suffering from Alzheimer's disease, her brain function having atrophied to the point that she is unable to make her will known.

Euthanasia is also either passive or active. "Passive euthanasia" (sometimes called anti-dysthanasia) refers to a situation in which action is withdrawn or withheld and a person is allowed to die. In a case that received national attention, the parents of Nancy Cruzan, a Missouri woman diagnosed to be in a "persistent vegetative state," received court approval (after a long legal battle) to have the feeding tubes that were keeping her alive removed. It can be argued that the act was "passive euthanasia," for Ms. Cruzan was "allowed to die" rather than killed, or that it was "active euthanasia" because she was actively denied food.

"Active euthanasia" means that an action causes the person to die. The case of a husband shooting his wife is a clear example of active euthanasia. Another is a medical practitioner administering a drug that results in the early death of a terminally ill person, in an attempt to alleviate the suffering of the patient and/or the patient's family. The line between active and passive euthanasia can easily blur, however. When a plug is pulled from a respirator and the patient, who was being kept alive by the machine, dies, is that passive or active? It is active in the sense that a concrete action (pulling the plug) occurred. It is passive because the "action" simply allowed the natural process of dying to continue; the person was not actively killed.

This is an important distinction, because "passive euthanasia" is widely viewed as ethical, whereas "active euthanasia" is still considered homicide. Those who engage in active "mercy killing" are often tried and sometimes (but rarely) convicted of a serious crime. Some today argue, however, that the distinction between "active" and "passive" euthanasia is morally irrelevant, since the end (a "good death") is the same, and may be much more humane when active steps are taken to accomplish it. What is critical is the intention behind the action (Rachels 2002).

The world's religions, as we shall see, have been deeply involved in the attempt to respond to the issues raised by euthanasia.

Religious Responses

Indigenous Religions   The Akan and Ewe people of Ghana are opposed to euthanasia because of a firm belief that life itself is the highest of human values. Since the end of euthanasia is the destruction of life, it cannot be permitted. One proverb puts it this way: "no form of life should be considered unworthy of living" (Ansah 1989: 262).

However, euthanasia is practiced in other indigenous cultures. Allowing an elderly person to go off alone and die is sanctioned by some groups as an acceptable way of putting the well-being of the group before the individual's "right to life."

Religions of South and Southeast Asia

HINDUISM   In Hinduism, death is merely the gateway into another existence. However, active euthanasia runs counter to the basic Hindu worldview and the principles of dharma and karma. "Actively [cutting] short a life through medical intervention would be viewed as destructive of one's dharma by interrupting the working out of karma in the patient's life. Active euthanasia would produce negative karma for both the patient and the physician" (Hamel 1991: 97).

However, voluntary euthanasia, which does not require active intervention, is another matter. Some Hindu *sadhus* (holy men) have chosen voluntary starvation as an extreme expression of their renunciation of attachment to the material self, but the practice is not common. One of the disciples of Mahatma Gandhi, Vinobha Bhave, chose to end his life by stopping the intake of food. In keeping with the Hindu tradition of respect for the right and obligation of individuals to chart their own destinies, no effort was made to stop Bhave from his act of voluntary euthanasia.

THERAVADA BUDDHISM   Buddhism has traditionally emphasized the importance of meeting death mindfully, since the last moment of one life can be particularly influential in determining the quality of the next rebirth. "Buddhism has long recognized persons' rights to determine when they should move on from this existence to the next. The important consideration here is not whether the body lives or dies, but whether the mind can remain at peace and in harmony with itself" (Becker 2002: 614). Active euthanasia impedes the individual's ability to meet death mindfully. The Buddha strongly condemned a monk or nun who aided another's suicide, for "[t]o kill a person deliberately, even if he or she requests this, is dealt with in the same way as murder" (Harvey 2000: 294).

By contrast, the Buddhist teachings of impermanence and compassion suggest an awareness that passive euthanasia may be the most appropriate response to terminal illness. Buddhists are supportive of the hospice movement, which focuses on allowing the individual to meet death openly and directly, while providing compassionate support during the dying process. "The ideal is to die without anxiety regarding those one leaves behind and in a conscious state which is also calm and uplifted" (Harvey 2000: 292).

JAINISM   On the one hand, Jainism would seem to advocate euthanasia, since Mahavira and other heroes of the faith took a path of voluntary euthanasia as a way of overcoming their karmic build up. However, when euthanasia is understood to mean the compassionate relieving of the suffering of another, Jainism opposes it. Since suffering is caused by one's own karma, no one else can relieve the cause of suffering. Moreover, *ahimsa* forbids the taking of another life, even when that being is near death. Therefore, Jainism is opposed to the practice of euthanasia, but not to the practice of self-starvation if chosen by an enlightened being who is ready to rise to the top of universe.

Religions of East Asia

DAOISM   To extend a person's life artificially is to resist the natural processes of the Dao. Therefore, passive euthanasia, in which the process of death is allowed to take its natural course, is not in conflict with Daoist ethics. The poems of the Daodejing speak of "embracing death," which means accepting the natural flow of life and death. However, to take action to interrupt the natural process creates an imbalance of the *yin* and *yang* forces. Consequently, active euthanasia would typically be avoided by those surrendering to the harmony of the Dao. However, there are no absolutes from a Daoist perspective, so there may be situations in which the unfolding process of the Dao includes actions leading to death.

CONFUCIANISM   The Confucian virtue of filial piety mitigates against support for euthanasia involving the elderly. Respect for elders implies that no action be taken to hasten the death of an older person. In addition, the virtues of humaneness (*jen*) and reciprocity (*shu*) imply a reluctance to engage in behavior in which life is put in jeopardy. However, while its emphasis is on harmonious life in this world, Confucianism does not place an absolute value on bodily life. The pursuit of righteousness is more important than the mere perpetuation of physical existence. There may be circumstances in which a "good death" is preferable to a purposeless life. In those cases euthanasia, even of the active type, may be the moral choice from a Confucian perspective.

MAHAYANA BUDDHISM   In Japanese Buddhism there is ambiguity on the issue of euthanasia. On the one hand, the Japanese term for euthanasia is *anrakukoku,* which in Buddhist terminology is another name for the Pure Land, to which devotees of Amida Buddha expect to go after death. When a person is facing imminent death, "it is morally acceptable to assist his suicide, particularly if the motive is mercy" (Becker 2002: 615).

Among the samurai in Japan, the practice of an attendant assisting in the warrior's suicide (*seppuku*) is well known. Few warriors had the strength to cut their own necks or spines, and it was considered acceptable for an attendant to deliver the lethal blow. Thus, "the *samurai's* code of suicide included a provision for euthanasia" (Becker 2002: 616).

On the other hand, Zen Buddhist masters instruct their disciples to live naturally. This presumably means that life should be allowed to take its course, without undue interference. One master expressed the Buddhist position by saying, "Buddha said, 'Don't kill all life.' Many machines and drugs are not necessary. Let all beings live in a natural way. When you die, where do you go?" (cited in Larue 1985: 135). When one dying Buddhist teacher was offered drugs to alleviate his pain, "he told them not to worry about that. He sat with one of the attendants supporting his head. A doctor began to give him oxygen, but with a wave of his hand he motioned him away" (Larue 1985: 136). However, if the mind is unable to focus due to pain, the use of drugs may be permissible, even if they hasten death, "because clarity of consciousness at the moment of death is so important in Buddhism" (Becker 2002: 618).

The Dalai Lama has spoken against euthanasia, saying that "it is best to face suffering, which is karmically caused, in the present, human life, where one is better placed to bear it than in, say, an animal rebirth." However, he recognizes that there comes a time when keeping a person alive longer has no point (Harvey 2000: 303–04).

Religions Originating in the Middle East

JUDAISM   The Tanak establishes precedents for Jewish (and Christian) acceptance of euthanasia, but not without raising questions about it. According to the Book of Judges, Abimelech initiated voluntary euthanasia, asking his armor-bearer to kill him after he had been fatally wounded by a millstone dropped by a woman during a siege (Judges 9:54).

However, the death of King Saul, who also requested a servant to kill him after he had been wounded in battle, is problematic (Second Samuel 1:6–10). The man who killed Saul was put to death by King David, indicating that this case of euthanasia was deemed a capital crime (although political considerations are also implied as the basis for King David's action).

Most Jewish authorities today reject "active euthanasia" on the grounds that no human has the right to take another's life, even in cases of extreme suffering. The Biblical legislation that most Jewish interpreters understand as ruling out active euthanasia includes Genesis 9:6, Exodus 21:14, Leviticus 24:17, Numbers 25:30, and, especially, the commandment: "Thou shalt not kill."

However, there is disagreement on the validity of "passive euthanasia." The Talmud recognizes a state called *gosses,* in which death is imminent (when a person can no longer swallow his or her saliva). Even in this state a person must be considered a human being, and it is immoral to hasten death. The medieval *Mishneh Torah,* compiled by Moses Maimonides, sums up the Talmudic teaching in this way (*Judges, Laws of Mourning* 4:5; cited by Hamel 1991: 55):

> One who is in a dying condition is regarded as a living person in all respects. It is not permitted to grind his jaws, to stop up the organs of the lower extremities, or to place metallic or cooling vessels upon his navel in order to prevent swelling. He is not to be rubbed or washed, nor is sand or salt to be put upon him until he expires. He who touches him is guilty of shedding blood. To what may he be compared? To a flickering flame, which is extinguished as soon as he touches it. Whoever closes the eyes of the dying while the soul is about to depart is shedding blood.

However, other sources acknowledge that actions which prolong dying should be avoided (*Sefer Hasidim,* 234, 723; cited in Larue 1985: 22–23).

The current positions of the three major branches of Judaism on euthanasia may be summarized as follows (Goldman 1978: 177–81):

- *Orthodox.* Active euthanasia is condemned as murder by all Orthodox authorities. However, there is disagreement on the circumstances under which the withdrawal of treatment, or the use of drugs that may hasten death while relieving suffering, are appropriate.

- *Conservative.* There is no consensus, but Conservative Rabbis tend to be more liberal than Orthodox scholars in assessing when the artificial prolongation of life may be terminated in order to allow a patient to die naturally.
- *Reform.* Leading Reform Rabbi Solomon B. Freehof took the position that the act of killing a patient, no matter what the motivation, is absolutely forbidden. However, there are circumstances, he said, when death may be allowed to come. The Reform community is more willing to recognize a "right to die" that must be respected.

CHRISTIANITY (ROMAN CATHOLICISM)   The teaching of the Roman Catholic Church on this issue is most clearly expressed in the Vatican's 1980 Declaration on Euthanasia, approved by Pope John Paul II (cited in full in Larue 1985: 35–43). The Declaration begins by recalling the Second Vatican Council's affirmation of the "right to life" and its condemnation of crimes against life "such as any type of murder, genocide, abortion, euthanasia, or willful suicide." Its central assertion (Larue 1985: 38) is that:

No one can in any way permit the killing of an innocent human being, whether a foetus or an embryo, an infant or an adult, an old person, or one suffering from an incurable disease, or a person who is dying. Furthermore, no one is permitted to ask for this act of killing, either for himself or herself or for another person.

However, the Declaration does allow for passive euthanasia when "death is imminent." Then "it is permitted in conscience to take the decision to refuse forms of treatment that would only secure a precarious and burdensome prolongation of life, so long as the normal care due to the sick person in similar cases is not interrupted" (Larue 1985: 42).

CHRISTIANITY (PROTESTANTISM)   In its deliberations on euthanasia, the Lutheran Church (Missouri Synod) has raised the issue of the appropriateness of such distinctions as "passive" and "active," suggesting that they only serve to confuse. A 1979 document of this denomination stipulates that euthanasia should be understood to mean "direct intervention, the killing of a human being, with our without his knowledge or consent" (Larue 1985: 66). Therefore, according to this Protestant denomination, it is "contrary to God's Word and will and cannot be condoned or justified" (64).

Other Protestant Churches may or may not use the phrase "passive euthanasia," but the ethical stance is virtually the same: active euthanasia is not acceptable, but the withholding or withdrawing of treatment may be permissible. A United Methodist statement, adopted in 1980, is typical (Larue 1985: 87):

we recognize the agonizing personal and moral decisions faced by the dying, their physicians, their families, and their friends. Therefore, we assert the right of every person to die in dignity, with loving personal care and without efforts to prolong terminal illnesses merely because the technology is available to do so.

Some Protestant Christian ethicists have pointed out the ambiguity in the position that extraordinary means of treatment may be withheld from a dying patient. What is ordinary treatment in one circumstance (for example, antibiotics to treat bronchitis in a healthy person) may be extraordinary in another (antibiotics used to treat pneumonia in a dying person). This has led some Christians to advocate what they call "situational" or "contextual" ethics, in which the basic Christian principle (love God and your neighbor as yourself) is applied, taking into account the unique dynamics of the particular situation. This opens the door for deciding that in some cases "active euthanasia" may be the moral decision for a Christian.

ISLAM   The Qur'an teaches that Allah preordains the time of a person's birth and death. For example, *Surah* 6.2 reads, "He it is Who created you from clay, and then decreed a stated term (for you), And there is in His Presence another determined term; yet you doubt within yourselves!" (Ali 2002: 76). Although there is no direct Muslim position on euthanasia, the clear implication is that to actively kill a dying person would be an interference with the divine plan. Suffering is also a part of Allah's punishment for sin, and any unnatural termination of suffering would affect a person's paying the price for sin and thus finding redemption.

SIKHISM   Although no particular pronouncements on euthanasia have been made by Sikhs, emphasis is placed on care of sufferers. As one commentator has observed, "There is no place in Sikh thought for deliberately ending the life of the incurably ill or irreversibly senile. All Sikhs are to accept what God gives as an expression of the divine will" (Nesbitt 1996: 116).

New Religious Movements

SOKA GAKKAI   A leader of the Nichiren School of Buddhism in the United States has expressed the Soka Gakkai view of euthanasia in these words (Larue 1985: 137):

> I agree that it is unbearable to see a loved one in extreme pain. In such a condition, that person feels he has no reason to live, so he wants to be allowed to die. The people close to him will think that they should allow his wish to be granted out of their own sense of compassion. But isn't this too materialistic a view of life? Moreover, the truth of life reveals that death is not the final solution to the problem of suffering. The people who cannot bear to see their loved one suffer from pain will be able to stop their own suffering by allowing the person to die, but the karma of suffering still exists within that person's life. The only possible solution is to infuse that person with the life-force to change his own karma for the better. This is why we need Nichiren Daishonin's Buddhism.[. . .] the hope of being freed from suffering can only be realized when we have strong faith in the Gohonzon.

SECULAR HUMANISM   Leaders of Humanist movements such as the Ethical Union and the Ethical Culture Society have not only endorsed passive euthanasia, like most other religions surveyed here, they have spoken in defense of active euthanasia. One Ethical Union leader has written, for example, "When a relative or friend or professional person is party to an act of euthanasia, every effort should be made to remove this act from the category of criminal action subject to criminal punishment—*provided* the suffering is unbearable and the illness terminal and hopeless, *and* the sufferer has fervently requested such action in the presence of witnesses, *and* written and sworn affidavits are furnished" (cited in Larue 1985: 130).

The American Humanist Association included euthanasia, suicide, and the right to die with dignity among the freedoms claimed in its 1973 *Humanist Manifesto II.*

CHAPTER SUMMARY

Is there a right to life? Is there a right to die? Who has the right to make these life-and-death decisions? What do the world's religions have to say about these fundamental ethical questions as they relate to the contentious issues of abortion and euthanasia? These are issues many readers of this book will have encountered themselves, or with family members or friends. In this chapter we first discussed the nature and scope of abortion and euthanasia as they relate to religion, and then surveyed the responses of many of the world's religions to these issues of life and death.

IMPORTANT TERMS AND PHRASES

active euthanasia, *ahimsa,* elective abortion, *gosses,* karmic effect, filial piety, "good death," involuntary euthanasia, Medical Termination of Pregnancy Act (India), mercy killing, *mizuko,* passive euthanasia, persistent vegetative state, right to die, right to life, Roe v. Wade, viable, voluntary euthanasia

QUESTIONS FOR DISCUSSION AND REFLECTION

1. Imagine that a friend has come to you saying that she is considering having an abortion. She tells you that she became pregnant after a "one-night stand" with a man she had just met at a party. She does not want to tell him that she is pregnant, because she is afraid he will try to talk her into having the baby. She says it is her right to decide whether to have the abortion or not. She says the religion of her family is strongly against abortion, but that she has heard not all religions are anti-abortion. She knows that you are aware of what various religions teach about abortion, and asks you to explain to her which of the religious teachings about abortion you find most persuasive and why. What do you tell her?

2. You are the parent of a twenty-year-old college student who is in a persistent vegetative state after a car accident: since the accident, your son has not regained full consciousness. You think that he may have squeezed your hand at times in response to something you've said, but you are not sure. The doctors tell you that these are involuntary reactions and that his condition will almost certainly never improve. They suggest that you authorize stopping the feedings through a tube in his stomach that are keeping him alive, so that "nature can run its course." You are accustomed to seeking guidance from a variety of religious traditions in making ethical decisions. You have friends who practice a number of the world's religions. What questions would you ask them as you consider whether to stop feeding your son through a tube, and what might they tell you from their different perspectives? What would you decide to do, and what role would the religious teachings play in your decision?

SOURCES AND SUGGESTIONS FOR FURTHER STUDY

LIFE AND DEATH

DRUTCHAS, GEOFFREY G., 1998. *Is Life Sacred?* Cleveland: Pilgrim.

MCCANCE, DAWNE C., ED., 1998. *Life Ethics in World Religions.* Atlanta, GA: Scholars.

ABORTION

General

BRODY, BARUCH, 1975. *Abortion and the Sanctity of Life*. Cambridge, MA: MIT.

GREGORY, HAROLD, ED., 1983. *The Religious Case for Abortion*. Ashville, NC: Madison and Polk.

MAGUIRE, DANIEL, 2002. *Sacred Choices: The Right to Contraception and Abortion in Ten World Religions*. Minneapolis: Fortress.

SCHWARTZ, STEPHEN, 1990. *The Moral Question of Abortion*. Chicago: Loyola University.

STEFFEN, LLOYD, ED., 1996. *Abortion: A Reader*. Cleveland: Pilgrim.

WENZ, PETER S., 1992. *Abortion Rights as Religious Freedom*. Philadelphia: Temple University.

Indigenous Religions

African
ANSAH, JOHN K., 1989. "The Ethics of Traditional African Religions." In Crawford, *World Religions and Global Ethics,* 241–65.

Religions of South and Southeast Asia

Hinduism
CRAWFORD, S. CROMWELL, 1989. "Hindu Ethics for Modern Life." In Crawford, *World Religions and Global Ethics,* 5–35.

LIPNER, JULIUS J., 1989. "The Classical Hindu View on Abortion and the Moral Status of the Unborn." In *Hindu Ethics: Purity, Abortion, and Euthanasia,* ed. Harold G. Coward. Albany: State University of New York, 41–70.

MENSKI, WERNER, 1996. "Hinduism." In Lawton and Morgan, *Ethical Issues in Six Religious Traditions,* 1–54.

Theravada Buddhism
HARVEY, PETER, 2000. "Abortion and Contraception." *An Introduction to Buddhist Ethics,* Cambridge: Cambridge University, 311–52.

FLORIDA, R., 1991. "Buddhist Approaches to Abortion." *Asian Philosophy* 1: 39–50.

KEOWN, DAMIEN, ED., 1998. *Buddhism and Abortion*. New York: Macmillan.

LECSO, P. A., 1987. "A Buddhist View of Abortion." *Journal of Religion and Health* 26: 214–18.

MORGAN, PEGGY, 1996. "Buddhism." In Lawton and Morgan, *Ethical Issues in Six Religious Traditions,* 55–98.

PREMASIRI, P. D., 1989. "Ethics of Theravada Buddhism." In Crawford, *World Religions and Global Ethics,* 36–64.

Religions of East Asia

China
QIU, REN-ZONG, CHUN-ZHI WANG, and YUAN GU, 2002. "Can Late Abortion Be Ethically Justified?" In May, Collins-Chobanian, and Wong, *Applied Ethics,* 539–44.

Confucianism
JONES, CHARLES B., 1999. "A Bundle of Joy: A Confucian Response." In Wolfe and Gudorf, *Ethics and World Religions,* 177–84.

Mahayana Buddhism

LaFleur, W. A., 1992. *Liquid Life: Abortion and Buddhism in Japan*. Princeton: Princeton University.

LaFleur, W. A., 2002. "Contestation and Consensus: The Morality of Abortion in Japan." In May, Collins-Chobanian, and Wong, *Applied Ethics*, 545–55.

Smith, Bardwell, 1992. "Buddhism and Abortion in Contemporary Japan: Mizuko Kuyo and the Confrontation with Death." In *Buddhism, Sexuality and Gender,* ed. Jose Ignacio Cabezon. Albany: State University of New York.

Religions Originating in the Middle East

Judaism

Biale, Rachel, 1984. *Women and Jewish Law: An Exploration of Women's Issues in Halakhic Sources*. New York: Schocken, 219–38.

Bleich, J. David, 1981. "Abortion and Jewish Law." *New Perspectives on Human Abortion,* ed. Thomas W. Hilgers, Dennis Horan, and David Mall. Frederick, MD: University Publications of America, 405–19.

Cohen, Armond, 1967. "A Jewish View Toward Abortion." *Abortion in America: Medical, Legal, Anthropological and Religious Considerations,* ed. Harold Rosen. Boston: Beacon, 166–74.

Goldman, Alex J., 1978. "Abortion." *Judaism Confronts Contemporary Issues.* New York: Shengold, 35–62.

Christianity

Brown, Harold O. J., 1977. *Death Before Birth.* Nashville: Thomas Nelson.

Calvin, John, 1950. *Commentaries on the Last Four Books of Moses.* Grand Rapids, MI: Eerdmans.

Connery, John S., 1977. *Abortion: The Development of the Roman Catholic Perspective.* Chicago: Loyola University.

Melton, J. Gordon, ed., 1989. *The Churches Speak on Abortion: Official Statements From Religious Bodies and Ecumenical Organizations.* Detroit: Gale Research.

Noonan, John T., Jr., 2002. "An Almost Absolute Value in History." In May, Collins-Chobanian, and Wong, *Applied Ethics*, 504.

Simmons, Paul D., n.d. *Personhood, the Bible, and the Abortion Debate.* Washington, DC: Religious Coalition for Abortion Rights.

Vittachi, Anuradha, 1989. *Earth Conference One: Sharing a Vision for Our Planet.* Boston: New Science Library.

Islam

Ali, Abdullah Yusuf, trans., 2002. *The Qur'an: Translation.* 9th ed. Elmhurst, NY: Tahrike Tarsile.

Sikhism

Nesbitt, Eleanor, 1996. "Sikhism." In Lawton and Morgan, *Ethical Issues in Six Religious Traditions,* 99–134.

New Religious Movements

Drutakarma Dasa, 1992. Personal correspondence.

Hinckley, Gordon B., 1998. The Teachings of Gordon B. Hinckley, Salt Lake: Deseret.

EUTHANASIA

General

HAMEL, RON P., ED., 1991. *Choosing Death: Active Euthanasia, Religion, and the Public Debate.* Valley Forge, PA: Trinity.

HORAN, DENNIS J. AND DAVID MALL, 1977. *Death, Dying, and Euthanasia.* Washington, DC: University Publications of America.

HUMPHRY, DEREK, 1988. *The Right to Die: Understanding Euthanasia.* New York: Harper & Row.

LARUE, GERALD A., 1985. *Euthanasia and Religion: A Survey of the Attitudes of World Religions to the Right-to-Die.* Los Angeles: Hemlock Society.

LARUE, GERALD A., 1996. *Playing God: Fifty Religions' Views on Your Right to Die.* Wakefield, RI: Moyer Bell.

MANNING, MICHAEL, 1998. *Euthanasia and Physician-Assisted Suicide: Killing or Caring?* New York: Paulist.

RACHELS, JAMES, 2002. "Active and Passive Euthanasia." In May, Collins-Chobanian, and Wong, *Applied Ethics,* 561–65.

Buddhism

BECKER, CARL B., 2002. "Buddhist Views of Suicide and Euthanasia." In May, Collins-Chobanian, and Wong, *Applied Ethics,* 609–19.

HARVEY, PETER, 2000. "Suicide and Euthanasia." *An Introduction to Buddhist Ethics,* 286–310.

KEOWN, DAMIEN, 1995. *Buddhism and Bioethics.* New York: St. Martin's.

Judaism

GOLDMAN, ALEX J., 1978. "Euthanasia." *Judaism Confronts Contemporary Issues,* New York: Shengold, 171–91.

KAPLAN, KALMAN J. AND MATTHEW B. SCHWARTZ, 1998. *Jewish Approaches to Suicide, Martyrdom, and Euthanasia.* Northvale, NJ: Jason Aronson.

Christianity

GEIS, SALLY B. AND DONALD E. MESSER, 1997. *How Shall We Die? Helping Christians Debate Assisted Suicide.* Nashville: Abingdon.

GILL, ROBIN, ED., 1998. *Euthanasia and the Churches.* New York: Cassell.

LARSON, EDWARD J. AND DARREL W. AMUNDSEN, 1998. *A Different Death: Euthanasia and the Christian Tradition.* Downers Grove, IL: InterVarsity.

Islam

ALI, ABDULLAH YUSUF, TRANS., 2002. *The Qur'an: Translation.* 9th ed. Elmhurst, NY: Tahrike Tarsile.

Web Sites

ABORTION

re-xs.ucsm.ac.uk/ethics/abortion/religionandabortion.html
> (links to sites on the teachings of various religions on abortion)

nrlc.org
> (National Right to Life Committee)

rcrc.org
> (Religious Coalition for Reproductive Choice)

EUTHANASIA

euthanasia.com
> (a site committed to the fundamental belief that the intentional killing of another person is wrong)

www.endoflifechoices.org
> (advocate for options in dying for the terminally ill)

CHAPTER

18

Gender and Sexual Orientation—Roles and Identity

THE CHANGING ROLES OF WOMEN: LIBERATION OR CONFUSION?

The Nature of the Issue and the Role of Religion

Gender is an issue that all religions and contemporary students of religion must face. As one scholar put it, "It is no longer possible to study religious practice or religious symbols without taking gender—that is, the cultural experience of being male or female—into account" (Bynum, Harrell, and Richman 1986: 1–2). Gender is an inevitable ingredient in the human attempt to portray the sacred and the human experience of ultimacy.

We need first to distinguish between "sex" and "gender" as the terms are used in academic discussions today. "Sex" refers to the differences attributable to biology, while "gender" refers to the distinctions between male and female humans beings "that are created through psychological and social development within a familial, social, and cultural setting" (Bynum, Harrell, and Richman 1986: 7). To a significant degree, therefore, gender is "culturally constructed" and may have considerably different meanings in different settings.

The tendency toward male domination in the world's religions (called *patriarchy*) has inspired movements that have touched virtually all religions in an effort to liberate women from what are considered oppressive religious structures. These movements have also sparked resistance among traditionalists, who view attempts to elevate the status of women as an assault on an ordering of life and gender relations that has sacred sanction.

A full appreciation of the world's religions requires that we look at what they teach about gender, and how they respond to the current controversies surrounding gender issues.

Religious Responses

Indigenous Religions

AFRICAN   Among the Akan and Ewe peoples of modern Ghana, traditional roles for women persist (Ansah 1989: 256–57). A growing number of women have pursued educations and achieved considerable social equality in the cities; however, traditional society is clearly patriarchal, and women who do not entirely break away from these patterns of male dominance rarely challenge them from within.

In Yoruba culture, women as well as men are expected to have a vocation, often tending their own farms or engaging in other money-raising activities. However, the husband is considered the head of the home and the principal breadwinner. Women are priests in many religious groups, with men worshipping under their leadership. However, some groups that focus on ancestral spirits bar women's participation. Despite these leadership roles, women are still stereotyped in Yoruba society as being too emotional and unable to keep secrets (Abogunrin 1989: 280).

In African as well as other indigenous religions, special rites of passage for women relating to fertility play an important role. Specific rituals for women at puberty, marriage, childbirth, menopause, and death are found in virtually all indigenous cultures. The seclusion rites associated with menstruation also symbolize the power associated with the feminine in indigenous religions. All of these enable women in indigenous cultures to feel a sacral importance tied to gender, and a special empowerment separate from men. Women's societies typically oversee all these gender-specific rituals for women, creating an independent source and arena of sacral influence for women, as well as a special sense of community among women.

The disfiguring practice of clitoridectomy common in a number of cultures in Africa and Asia is an ongoing concern. It is often called female genital mutilation (FGM) by those seeking to end the practice. The practice is found in communities in which indigenous traditions dominate (where it is often carried out by a female shaman), but it is also found in Muslim and some Christian communities in Africa (see subsequent sections regarding those religions). In this procedure, the external genitalia of girls (as young as infants, but usually older) are removed or mutilated and their vulvas sewn shut, leaving an opening only large enough for urination and menstruation. It is estimated that about two million girls in Africa are made to endure clitoridectomies each year. The purpose is to insure virginity and to eliminate sexual sensation. It may also be that the clitoridectomy is thought to remove any signs of maleness in the girl (the clitoris being perceived as a type of penis) and the belief is also widely held that a woman's clitoris will grow disgustingly large if the procedure is not done.

An international movement has emerged in the developed world, championed by Pulitzer-prize-winning African-American novelist Alice Walker, to try to force an end to the practice (Walker and Parmar 1996). Supporters of this position argue that FGM should be "on the list of unacceptable practices that violate women's human rights, and we should be ashamed of ourselves if we do not use whatever privilege and power has come our way to make it disappear forever" (Nussbaum 2002: 34). Many educated African women also want to end FGM as a violation of women's human rights, but others join traditionalists in viewing the efforts of Walker and others as examples of "cultural condescension." One Kenyan women's rights leader made the point this way: "Let indigenous people fight it according to their own traditions. It will die faster than if others tell us what to do." In response, Walker has said, "Torture is not culture." (Kaplan 1993: 124).

NATIVE AMERICAN   As noted in Chapter Two, the Oglala Lakota traditionally address the sacred using both masculine and feminine imagery, as Father or Grandfather and Mother or Grandmother. As in other indigenous religions, the sky was associated with the masculine and the earth with the feminine. This balancing of the masculine and the feminine in approaching the holy is seen also in the openness in the principal role of shaman to both men and women.

Women play a crucial role in Lakota mythology (e.g., White Buffalo Calf Woman). Moreover, in the myth of origins it is a woman who coaxes the Buffalo People to come from their subterranean world to the earth, and who (with the trickster figure) instructs them in the ways of culture (see Powers 1986: 35–52).

In her study of Oglala women, Marla Powers has demonstrated that despite a superficial male dominance—much overemphasized by outside observers—Lakota women were and are in key positions of leadership (1986). If anything, the subordination of traditional male roles on the reservations has elevated the status of women.

In short, American Indian women have not been as meek, docile, and subordinate to men as the dominant culture has asserted. Women "have always formed the backbone of indigenous nations on this continent" (Jaimes and Halsey 2002: 401).

Religions of South and Southeast Asia

HINDUISM   On the one hand, women are idealized in traditional Hindu culture. As one text says, "Women must be honoured by their fathers, brothers, husbands and brothers-in-law, if they desire their own welfare. Where women are honoured, there the gods are pleased" (cited in Menski 1996: 42).

However, the actual treatment of women is different. She is to be subordinate first to her father, then to her husband, and finally to her sons. A married woman has traditionally been taught to view her husband as her god. Several traditions illustrate the Hindu heritage of male dominance. One is the ancient (but still very influential) preference for male offspring. According to the Code of Manu, sons alone are able to rescue the souls of ancestors from hell so that they may continue their spiritual progress toward liberation. The Code also states that the first-born son is the only child born for the sake of dharma; others are the fruit of passion (Crawford 1989: 21–22). According to Hindu teaching, the principal dharma of the woman is to give birth to sons.

A second tragic tradition that demonstrates the oppression of women in traditional Hindu society, is the practice of female infanticide. Because a father must supply dowries for his daughters, they can become a financial drain. According to tradition, only a son can light the fires on a parent's funeral pyre; many couples, therefore, continue having children until a son is born. As one father of three daughters, whose wife had just given birth to a first son, said (in front of his daughters) in a 1993 interview, "Now I finally feel fulfilled." Tragically, this attitude can result in the killing of female newborns (although Indian law strictly forbids infanticide); with a reassertion of Hindu traditionalism, this practice seems to be on the rise. In lower-caste families, some "parents reluctantly poison the newborn girl, justifying it as a shortening of her suffering from one life to one hour"

(Crawford 1989: 22). It is so common that prosecution of parents who kill their female infants is rare.

In Hindu families who can afford it, female infanticide has been replaced by abortion. Amniocentesis or sonograms are used to determine the gender of the fetus; if it is a girl, the woman has an abortion. Some clinics offer "package deals," gender determination and abortion (if the fetus is female) for one low price. According to the 2001 census, there were 933 females per 1,000 males in India. Without abortion for sex selection, the numbers of male and female births would be equal.

The tradition of arranged marriage at a very young age also serves to restrict opportunities for women. Traditionally, Hindu women are betrothed well before puberty, married shortly thereafter, and become mothers of several children while still in their early teens. Married women are expected to be docile, even worshipping their husband's big toe. The Code of Manu says that women are to be loyal and faithful even if their husbands are unfaithful, drunk, abusive, or deformed.

The fourth tradition is *sati,* in which a widow immolates herself on her husband's funeral pyre, because her life symbolically ends with his death (Hawley 1994). (*Sati*—literally, "good woman"—was the name of a goddess, who committed suicide after her husband, the god Shiva, was insulted.) The practice was ostensibly voluntary (it is not directly enjoined in any Hindu code of law), but sometimes apparently resulted from the pressure of greedy relatives who wanted the wife's inheritance. It was outlawed in 1829, under pressure from British authorities and Hindu reformers. The practice continues today in only a handful of highly publicized cases, but the symbolism of a woman's identity being tied to the males in her life continues.

Another indication of the oppression of women is the "dowry death," in which a woman is killed (often in a cooking "accident") by her in-laws who are upset because the woman's family has not paid the agreed-upon bride price or dowry (or it is judged to be insufficient). Although outlawed, dowry deaths still occur in twenty-first-century India. At least sixteen women a day are victims of dowry-related murders, according to estimates by the Indian government; many of these crimes go unpunished.

Women have traditionally been restricted from serving as priests, the role being reserved for male members of the *brahmin* class. Women were for centuries forbidden from studying Sanskrit, the language in which the Hindu sacred texts are written.

In traditional Hinduism there are also hints of another perspective, in which women are seen as the spiritual equals of men. In some branches of Hinduism, especially some of the *bhakti* (devotional) movements, women have been accorded equal spiritual status. The influential Bhagavad-Gita teaches that women may become devotees of the Supreme Lord and enjoy the spiritual benefits of divine service in the same way as men. Tantric movements have also allowed women an alternative to the subordination in more traditional Hindu circles (Young 1987: 88–89).

In its conception of the sacred, traditional Hinduism also supports gender equality, even female superiority. The feminine power, *shakti,* is "the energy of both creation and destruction. It is the principle of passion and change" (Carmody 1989: 42). In divinity, the dark, mysterious, feminine shakti is balanced by the passionless, constant, intellectual male side of deity.

The primal mother in Hindu mythology is *Adi Shakti.* According to the myths associated with her, she alone existed in the beginning. Desiring a partner, she created the male gods Brahma, Vishnu, and Shiva. Only *Shiva* accepted her proposal of

Ardhanarishvara, a half-male and half-female representation of the god Shiva, represents the balance between masculine and feminine energy in the Hindu understanding of the sacred.

marriage, and he becomes prominent, replacing her. Adi Shakti is still worshipped as goddess of the harvest in rural India (Carmody 1989: 42–43).

"[Adi Shakti] [. . .] enjoyed a reputation as a supreme deity who creates, preserves, and destroys as well as defends dharma by battling the demons to preserve the order of society and cosmos" (Young 1987: 90). There have not been many attempts to utilize the myth of Adi Shakti to claim a more central role for women in Hindu society.

On the other hand, a myth associated with the popular goddess Kali illustrates how tales of the gods served to give a sacred basis for suspicion of female passion and female subordination in traditional Hindu society. After killing an evil giant and his army, Kali broke into a highly charged dance that threatened to shake apart the whole world. She stopped only when Shiva lay down at her feet, for as a devout wife she would not step on her husband. What was the moral of the story, according to traditional Hindu interpretation? "Unless husbands control their wives, the world will surely collapse" (Carmody 1989: 46).

Mahatma Gandhi stressed equality for women in the independence movement (although he attempted to exert control over his own wife!). Civil legislation in the secular state of India now guarantees political rights for women. The 1947 Constitution banned discrimination against women in social, political, and economic settings. In India women have entered into virtually all professions. While many Western countries still have a "glass ceiling" for women in fields like politics, women in India have moved to the top in a variety of areas. The most famous example is Indira Gandhi, who served as Prime Minister of India from 1966 (in several nonconsecutive terms) until she was assassinated in 1984.

At present, tension runs high in India between groups and leaders who wish to preserve a modern, secular state, and others who want to create a Hindu state, which would include a return to the more traditional gender relations described above. If the turn toward Hindu traditionalism continues, "the advances of the last century for women may be endangered" (Young 1994: 133). There has even been renewed public support for the practice of *sati*, with Hindu leaders arguing that if suicide and even active euthanasia are increasingly accepted in the West, Hindu women should have the right of voluntary *sati* (Young 1994: 119–23).

THERAVADA BUDDHISM   Siddartha Gautama apparently regarded women and men as spiritual equals. According to Theravada tradition, the Buddha, speaking about the pursuit of enlightenment, said, "whoever has such a vehicle, whether a woman or a man, shall indeed, by means of that vehicle come to *nirvana*" (*Suttanipatta* I.33. Cited by Young 1987: 106). In contrast to Hindu orthodoxy, the Buddha allowed women to lead a monastic life. The first *sangha* of nuns was instituted five years after the Buddha's enlightenment. The number of nuns in Theravada countries has increased in recent decades, to the current total of over thirty thousand (Harvey 2000: 383–91, 396).

Throughout history, however, monks have far outnumbered nuns in Theravada Buddhism (e.g., in modern Thailand, by about twenty-five to one.), giving the religion a distinctly male orientation. Monks are, in fact, regarded as superior to nuns. The teaching of dharma has been a function of men, with monks teaching nuns but typically not the other way around. Nuns were taught to take on a male way of thinking in order to pursue enlightenment. Buddha is reputed to have said that the admission of women would diminish the life of the sangha. In short, "in all Buddhist sects throughout the Buddhist world, men have always dominated and still dominate" (Barnes 1987: 131).

The popular belief that birth as a woman indicated bad karma from a previous life found its way into Buddhism from Hinduism, despite the Buddha's teaching about gender equality. According to a famous story, when one of Buddha's disciples asked how the monks were to conduct themselves with women, Buddha answered, "As not seeing them." If a woman should see the monk he should not talk to her, and if she speaks first, then the monk should "keep awake" (Carmody 1989: 69). The Theravada commentator Buddhaghosa wrote graphic descriptions of women as made of "flesh that would soon decay, bodies that would rot in the grave and be foul smelling" in order to discourage monks from being seduced by women (Carmody 1989: 71). However, it may be that such texts should be interpreted as more reflective of the general early Buddhist rejection of "worldliness" than as purposefully antifeminine (Barnes 1987: 110–14; Harvey 2000: 379–80).

The ambiguity of the Theravada attitude toward women is shown in another story of two monks travelling through the forest. They came to a river swollen by spring rains and found a woman standing on the edge, debating how to cross. One of the monks offered her a ride on his back, and she accepted. On the other side of the river, the woman and the monks parted ways. Some miles later the monk who had not carried the woman criticized his companion for his intimacy with a woman. In response, he said, "I put the woman down hours ago. Why are you still carrying her?" (Carmody 1989: 85).

In traditional Theravada areas, lay women tend shrines and, most importantly, earn merit by providing food for monks as they make their morning rounds. In contrast to Hindu practice, Buddhist women were given the choice whether to marry or pursue enlightenment as nuns. Married women were still expected to be docile and serve their husbands, but they were given more responsibility to manage the financial affairs of the household.

In some Theravada countries in recent years, orders of nuns have begun to play a more prominent role (Barnes 1994: 138–45, 152–59), in some cases taking the lead in addressing social problems. In addition, Theravada laywomen have been instrumental in leading the Buddhist revival in Sri Lanka and other countries, even taking on the role of meditation teachers (Barnes 1994: 145–46, 148–49, 150–51). An International Buddhist Women's Association holds periodic "Daughters of the Buddha" conferences to address women's issues.

JAINISM   The equal status of men and women has been implemented more fully in Jainism than in Theravada Buddhism. In the early religious order of the founder (Mahavira), women outnumbered men, and in the legends of Jainism women play central and important roles. Throughout Jain history, women have been recognized for their learning and their contributions in all fields.

Religions of East Asia

DAOISM   In the earliest religion of China women functioned alongside men as shamans, making the power of the sacred accessible to their communities. In fact, the Chinese word for shaman—*wu*—referred originally to a woman (Reed 1987: 170).

Chinese society was and is patriarchal, but there is a strong feminine presence in the Chinese understanding of reality. According to Chinese teaching, "male" and "female" are functional expressions rather than biological classifications. In all reality both the male (*yang*) and female (*yin*) are present; they are complementary, with no distinction of superiority and inferiority. For the well-being of the whole, both are necessary (Reed 1987: 165–66).

In the Daodejing feminine imagery is prominent in the poems that point to the fundamental cosmic reality—the Dao. For example, the sixth poem speaks of the Dao as the Great Mother. The womb is another symbol for the Dao, as is a nurturing breast. The Dao is seemingly docile, like the woman's role in society, yet through the quiet and hidden "it all gets done." The successful way is not the aggressive style associated with the male role, but the responding and apparently submissive mode of the female. This is true power, the way of the Dao. For Daoist thinkers, the subordination of women was one of the social pretensions that must be discarded in order to allow life to occur naturally and spontaneously.

In the other branch of Daoism, the "religious," women have functioned as masters and alchemists, and were ordained as priests. They participated in the esoteric *chiao* ritual tradition. A primary deity in Daoist mythology is the Jade Mother. Communities of Daoist women were formed, in which women pursued the Daoist paths to "immortality." In a Daoist temple in modern Taiwan, lay women perform faith-healing rituals, laying their hands on the sick or on their clothing (Reed 1987: 180).

CONFUCIANISM   According to the early Confucian texts, "the female was inferior by nature, she was dark as the moon and changeable as water, jealous, narrow-minded, and insinuating. She was indiscreet, unintelligent, and dominated by emotion" (Giusso 1981: 59). The subordination of earth to heaven was applied to the dominant status of men over women.

The basic relationships of Confucian ethics place the man in the position of superiority over the woman—in the family and in society. As girls, women were to obey their fathers, as mature women their husbands, and as old women their elder sons (Kelleher 1987: 140).

In traditional Confucian society there was simply no place for women in government and commerce. Women's education, under the guidance of the Confucian ethic, was limited to practical skills such as sewing and caring for men. They were to be the keepers of the morals of the home, treating all (including the husband's concubines) with respect (Carmody 1989: 96–98). The Chinese symbol of "wife" includes a broom, indicating the priority of her domestic status.

With the development of Neo-Confucianism came increased emphasis on the importance of chastity and asceticism for women. Models for women included a woman who resists being raped by throwing herself off a high cliff, and another who mutilates her body rather than remarry and dishonor her dead husband (Kelleher 1987: 156).

By the nineteenth century this had led to severe oppression of women, which inspired a reform movement within Chinese society. Women played key roles in these attempts to modernize China. One traditional practice that was a symbol of the subordination of women, the footbinding of baby girls, was a particular target of reformers (the practice had left many women hobbled and unable to walk naturally). Feminist reformers also opposed arranged marriages, and supported increased educational opportunities for women.

In the 1940s the Communist revolution highlighted the Confucian subordination of women as an example of the inequities of traditional Chinese society that needed to be overturned. The Communists included women in the unions organized to further workers' rights. When Mao Zedong came to power, arranged marriages were outlawed and steps were taken to curb female infanticide. However, the traditions of treating women as inferiors did not disappear, and the Communist system has been dominated by patriarchal attitudes (Levering 1994: 176–91).

It has been in the resurgent Chinese religions that women have been most active as leaders in recent decades (Levering 1994: 191–221). Chinese women are increasingly active politically as well. The democratic movement that climaxed in the occupation of Tienanmen Square in 1989 involved many women student leaders, who argued that the Communist Party has not lived up to its promise to liberate women in Chinese society.

In Taiwan, traditional Confucian values still dominate, but there are signs of change. These changes are being brought by educated, economically independent women who are challenging their traditional subordination (on the basis of a reassertion of the egalitarian nature of basic Confucian virtues), and by the upsurge of interest in new religious movements (Reed 1994).

MAHAYANA BUDDHISM   In Mahayana Buddhist tradition women may take the bodhisattva vow and become objects of devotion; there are also feminine Buddhas (Young 1987: 121–23). The most famous bodhisattva is Kannon, the popular goddess of mercy in Japan (known as Kuan Yin in China). The background for Kannon is the Indian Buddha Avalokiteshvara; his characteristics were transferred to Kannon. Women often turn to Kannon for assistance in becoming pregnant and giving birth to healthy children. Kannon and other feminine Mahayana "deities" embody the compassion at the heart of Buddhist teaching (Harvey 2000: 365–66).

One famous Mahayana text focuses on a nun named Lion's-Yawn (enlightenment is sometimes called "the Lion's Roar" in Mahayana schools), who offers sophisticated instruction to seekers after enlightenment (Paul 1979: 94–105).

Another key feminine figure in Mahayana teaching is Queen Srimala, who is portrayed in *The Sutra of Queen Srimala Who Had the Lion's Roar* as "the ideal layperson whose teaching about the Tathagatagarbha [the womb of suchness, or reality] greatly helps those desiring Buddhist salvation" (Paul 1979: 289–302). Queen Srimala teaches her hearers to give birth to the buddha nature within them.

The Lotus Sutra has a prominent role for *nagas,* female beings with lovely human faces and the bodies of snakes. The nagas continually shed their skin, constantly renewing themselves. The princesses among the nagas were the models of wit and beauty and had reached the state of *prajna-paramita.*

The very important concept of *prajna-paramita* ("the wisdom that goes beyond") is also known as the Mother of All Buddhas, representing the enlightenment that enables reality to be seen as it truly is (Harvey 2000: 361). The association of the wisdom that gives meaning to all reality with feminine symbolism is a characteristic of other religions as well; the Chinese Dao and Christian Holy Spirit, for example, have feminine overtones (Carmody 1989: 77).

In the tantric *Vajrayana* ("Diamond Vehicle") school of Mahayana Buddhism popular in Tibet, women played a prominent role (Barnes 1987: 127–28; 1994: 159–60). Among the teachers (*siddhas*) who were thought to have reached perfect enlightenment were women. They taught their followers to stop thinking of themselves as concrete enough to be bound by social conventions. Thus, adherents engaged in various forms of "crazy wisdom," in which ordinary dietary and sexual taboos were purposefully broken. In this school *taras* (goddesses) were portrayed as consorts of the buddhas and played an important role in popular piety (Carmody 1989: 83). Among twenty-four forms, Green and White *taras* are among the best loved deities in Tibet. "They are seen as graceful, attractive, and approachable, and as ever ready to care tenderly for those in distress" (Harvey 2000: 361).

An a order of nuns established in China in the fourth century C.E. has continued in an unbroken tradition to the present time, providing an opportunity for women to live active, respected lives outside the typical family structure. They are particularly noted as teachers of the Buddhist scriptures (Young 1987: 123–27).

Buddhist teaching has also supported women's claims for political authority and independence. For example, in the nineteenth century, women silk workers in Guangdong refused to marry and lived together, the lay equivalent of an order of nuns (Young 1987: 132).

In the United States, Buddhist women have played a prominent role in the spread of Mahayana teaching (Young 1994: 161–62). For example, the founder of the famous Shasta Abbey in California, a Soto Zen institution, was Jiyu Kennett Roshi, an Englishwoman who became a Zen master in Japan and founded the Abbey in 1970.

With a shared concern in the overcoming of the dualistic thought patterns linked to patriarchy and Western religions, there are signs at present of Buddhist and feminist thinkers joining together (Young 1994: 168–69).

SHINTO   In early Japanese history, female spiritual functionaries called *miko* occupied an important role, as noted in Chapter Nine. At the center of Japanese mythology is Amaterasu, the sun-goddess and ancestress of the Japanese imperial family. A female priesthood continues today at Shinto shrines, including Amaterasu's Grand Shrine at Ise, and in popular Shinto practice many women are spiritual mediums and ascetics. Therefore, in traditional Japanese culture and religion women have had a central role. Shinto tries to harmonize life with the natural, and thus the beauty, fertility, and spontaneity associated with the feminine has highlighted women. However, the hard, uncompromising, disciplined aspects of nature (considered "masculine") have caused Shinto also to support the subordination of women (Carmody 1989: 125).

With the introduction of Chinese cultural influence and Confucian values, the subordination of women took firm hold in Japan and continued until modern times. During the long feudal period, when militarism was dominant, women married to samurai warriors were expected to carry a dagger and commit suicide in a variety of circumstances. For example, if passion for a wife was keeping a samurai warrior from complete devotion to his lord, the wife's duty was to take her own life (Carmody 1989: 118).

Leadership by women in many of the Japanese "new religions," which manifest both Shinto and Buddhist influences, has increased the status of women, restoring the shamanic role of early times (Young 1994: 146–50). In most of these religions a woman who suffered emotional or physical trauma had a vision that healed her. She then became a source of healing for others, and a religious movement formed around her (see, for example, Nakamura 1989).

The phenomenon of the Japanese *geisha* is also important to understand (Dalby 1983). Geishas are women who provide entertainment and companionship for men, while the wife cares for the home and family. While geishas seem to most outsiders to be merely a symptom of a male-dominated society that reserves some women as "playthings" for men and restricts the wife to the home, this has not been the view traditionally taken by most women in Japan. In fact, geishas are more economically independent than other Japanese women. The teahouses run by geishas are women's worlds. Men are customers, but women are in charge. Geisha families provide a warm and supportive atmosphere for the young women who are accepted as apprentices. At the same time, wives are freed from the necessity of playing a romantic role with their husbands and can dedicate themselves to the management of the household and nurturing of children. However, this division does support male domination in Japanese society. Both geishas and wives are expected to have the well-being of men as their principal concern, meeting men's needs so that they may be freed to perform in the world of business and industry.

An emergent women's movement in Japan is beginning to challenge male dominance and discrimination. For example, the "glass ceiling" phenomenon is still a major problem for Japanese women seeking careers. The traditional attitude that women must be subordinate to men and concern themselves with the well-being of their families rather than any individual career aspirations still dominates in Japan. Whether this *should* change, and what the effects on Japanese society will be if it does, is a fascinating topic to discuss.

Religions Originating in the Middle East

JUDAISM   The Torah portrays God's intention as equality among men and women. In the first creation account in Genesis, both male and female are created in the image of God (1:26), with no hierarchical ordering. In the second creation narrative, woman is created from the flesh of man, not as a subordinate but in order to fulfill him. In the Garden, Eve is portrayed as intelligent and practical. However, when Adam and Eve together violate God's command, the relationship of equality and mutuality is broken.

The legislation in the Torah assumes male dominance. A girl was the property of her father; when she married she became her husband's chattel. Her most important role was to produce sons to perpetuate her husband's name. Adultery was treated as a violation of the property rights of a woman's father or husband (Leviticus 20:10–11). A woman was expected to come to marriage as a virgin, and if her husband could prove that she was not, he could have her stoned (Deuteronomy 22:13–21). A woman had no rights to initiate divorce, but she was not to be divorced without a substantial basis (Deuteronomy 21:1–4).

The legislation in the Tanak may support women's subordination, but the narratives are replete with stories of women who are wise and powerful. In the Book of Ruth, for example, two women (Ruth and Naomi) take charge in a situation stacked against them, and defend their own rights and interests. Although the dominant imagery for God in the Tanak is masculine, texts such as Jeremiah 31:20 show that feminine metaphors could be used by Biblical authors to speak of God.

According to the traditional point of view, the Talmud treats the male as normal, with the female capable of being only a marginal Jew. Since her time was given over to husband and family, she was not expected to recite the morning prayer or attend the synagogue service on Sabbath. Her purpose was to support her husband's and sons' efforts to study and keep the Torah in the community, and to ensure that the dietary laws and Sabbath restrictions in the home were observed. Her greatest fear was infertility, for to be childless was in effect to be "dead." The Talmudic attitude toward women is summed up in the famous phrase, "Happy is he whose children are sons and woe to him whose children are daughters."

Since the emergence of the Reform movement in the nineteenth century, however, male dominance in Jewish tradition has been challenged. In 1846 a conference of Reform Jews called for full equality for women in all areas of religious life. The Reform movement introduced a rite of passage for Jewish girls (*bat mitzvah*), so that they could symbolically become members of the Jewish community, just like boys. Since 1972 Reform Judaism has ordained women as rabbis, and Conservatives have followed suit. Only Orthodox Judaism does not allow women to serve as rabbis.

Among the feminist critics of patriarchy in religion are Jewish women such as Naomi Goldenberg, Rita Gross, Judith Plaskow, and Ellen Umansky, who have written movingly of the need for the empowerment of women in Jewish life and thought. They have found in traditional Jewish sources glimpses of a spirituality to which Jewish women can relate (e.g., Wegner 1988), and through their own creative imaginations have begun to explore and renew that spirituality. As Judith Plaskow has written, in defense of her work in attempting to recover a "primordial Torah" that is not distorted by patriarchy (1989: 41, 49):

> To accept androcentric texts and contemporary androcentric histories as the whole of Jewish history is to enter into a secret collusion with those who would exclude us from full membership into the Jewish community[. . . .] Beginning with the conviction of our presence both at Sinai and now, we rediscover and invent ourselves in the Jewish communal past and present, continuing the age-old process of reshaping Jewish memory as we reshape the community today.

CHRISTIANITY   From the origins of Christianity until the present, there has been tension between two perspectives, "one affirming the equivalence of man and woman as human persons and the other defining woman as subordinate to man" (Ruether 1987: 208). In this section we will trace this tension through the history of Christianity.

In the New Testament, the Apostle Paul acknowledged spiritual equality when he wrote, "in Christ there is neither male nor female" (Galatians 3:28). However, Paul also seemed to endorse the subordination of women in the home and Christian community. Women were, for example, not to speak in worship, according to the Apostle (First Corinthians 14:34–36).

In the Gospels women are not among the formal inner circle of Jesus, but play important roles among the disciples, including being the first to witness the resurrection of Jesus, the defining moment in Christian history. One scholar summarizes the attitude of Jesus toward women in this way (Witherington 1984: 127):

> Jesus broke with both biblical and rabbinic traditions that restricted women's roles in religious practices, and [. . .] rejected attempts to devalue the worth of a woman, or her word of witness. Thus, the community of Jesus, both before and after Easter, granted women together with men (not segregated from men as in some pagan cults) an equal right to participate fully in the family of faith.

In the rest of the New Testament women are described in a number of leadership roles (e.g., Acts 18:14–26; Romans 16:6, 12; Philippians 4:2–3), even as stipulations are given about their subordinate status (e.g., Colossians 3:18–4:1, First Timothy 2:11–15). There is considerable evidence to support the view, advanced by feminist scholar Elisabeth Schüssler-Fiorenza, that the earliest Christian community was "radically egalitarian" in its treatment of men and women (1983).

However, with the growing influence of Hellenistic ideas on Christianity, the situation changed. Most influential was the incorporation of the dualistic conception of body and soul borrowed from Greek culture. Women were thought to be more "carnal" and thus, like other manifestations of the body, should be kept subordinate.

Over time the ideal spiritual woman came to be the virgin, who resisted bodily desires. That idealization of virginity had a profound effect, many believe, on the development of the relations between men and women in Western culture in general. The ideal Virgin, of course, was Mary, who became venerated as the Mother of God, and who could intercede for sinners with her Son.

The growth of monastic movements for women in the Middle Ages did provide a refuge for women from dominance by men, since many convents were led by women and provided women creative outlets denied to them in secular society. In the larger society, however, women were likely to be blamed as the source of all ills because of their seductive powers. The leading medieval theologian, Thomas Aquinas, followed his mentor Aristotle, calling female nature essentially defective, a "misbegotten manhood" (cited in Carmody 1989: 174). If a medieval woman displayed any spiritual power herself, she could be branded a witch and burned alive at the stake.

The Protestant Reformation ostensibly restored the spiritual equality of the genders found in the New Testament. Each believer stood before God, saved by the grace of God received in faith. Women and men had equal access to the throne of grace, according to Reformation leaders. However, the subordination of women in society continued. According to Martin Luther, a woman's role was determined by her procreative function (Carmody 1989: 174–75). Luther also held that women bore a greater portion of the curse of original sin than men, thus justifying their subordination. John Calvin said that election by God was irrespective of gender (or social status), but at the same time affirmed the Augustinian view of the subordination of women as part of the original order of creation (Ruether 1987: 222).

Despite their leadership roles in the New Testament communities, women were denied early official status as ordained church leaders. That practice continues in the Roman Catholic Church, Eastern Orthodoxy, and a number of Protestant churches. Among the Reformers only the "radicals" of the Anabaptist wing allowed women to have leadership roles. However, beginning in recent decades many other Protestant denominations have opened ordination to women. Women's movements—pressing for full access for women to all roles of leadership, and equal treatment in all areas of church life—have developed in most Christian churches in the West.

A feminist critique and reformulation of Christianity from within has emerged in recent decades. One of the first feminist Christian theologians was Rosemary Radford Ruether. She has emphasized the need to face up to the oppression of women within Christian history, alongside the subjection of racial and ethnic minorities, as a starting point in a fundamental rethinking of Christian faith. Her radical reformulation includes speaking of divinity as God/ess, who liberates us from the distortions and alienations of patriarchal-hierarchical society (1983).

Another of the many feminist reformulations of Christian imagery is Sallie McFague's *Models of God* (1987). McFague, a Protestant theologian, calls her approach a "metaphorical theology," in which she is "trying out" new ways of speaking of the mysteries of Christian thought. She uses the image of God as Mother to speak of the creative activity of God. Elizabeth Johnson's *She Who Is* is a new understanding of the mystery of God by a contemporary Catholic feminist theologian.

Some Christian feminists, frustrated with the slow pace of change (or resistance) in traditional churches, have created their own worshipping communities called "women-church." They provide an opportunity for women to express feminist experience in worship, study, and reflection (Ruether 1994: 284).

"Womanist" theology has emerged as a distinct movement within Christianity: In this movement African-American women reflect on the meaning of God in terms of their own experiences (Williams 1989).

Opposing the feminists who look beyond Christianity for a meaningful spirituality are Christian traditionalists who defend the spritual equality of women, but point out that the New Testament, which they consider to be God's inspired word, subordinates women to men in leadership roles in the church and in the family.

ISLAM   Before the Prophet Muhammad received his revelation from Allah and the religion of Islam originated on the Arabian peninsula, the status of women was desperate. Unwanted female children were buried alive, and women were treated as objects to be bought, sold, and inherited. Islam is credited with giving to women in the Arab world a status and dignity unrivalled in other regions until modern times.

Muslims point out that Islam has largely been spared the upheaval that has occurred in Judaism and Christianity as a result of a feminist critique of male dominance. Most Muslims take this as evidence that women in Islam have an ideal status, which should be the norm for other religions. Outside critics, and some Muslim reformers, suggest that the suppression of women in Islam is so significant that attempts to challenge traditional understandings of gender are very difficult to initiate and sustain.

The place to begin a study of the status of women in Islam is with passages from the Qur'an that deal with gender. Two are particularly important. *Surah* 4 in the Qur'an begins with these verses (*Surah* 4:1, 3–4; Ali 2002: 46):

> O mankind! reverence your Guardian-Lord, Who created you from a single Person, created, of like nature, his mate, and from them twain scattered (like seeds) countless men and women;—reverence Allah, through Whom you demand your mutual (rights), and (reverence) the wombs (that bore you): for Allah ever watches over you[. . . .]
>
> If you fear that you shall not be able to deal justly with the orphans, marry women of your choice, two, or three, or four, but if you fear that you shall not be able to deal justly (with them), then only one, or (a captive) that your right hand possesses that will be more suitable, to prevent you from doing injustice.
>
> And give the women (on marriage) their dowery as a free gift; but if they, of their own good pleasure, remit any part of it to you, take it and enjoy it with good cheer.

Like the Genesis account of the creation of man and woman, this text implies a complementary relationship between the two sexes, with woman created from man as "mate." One revolutionary feature is that the text assumes that women have rights that must be protected. A woman's property cannot merely be taken over when she marries. This breaks from the tradition of male "ownership" of women. The text authorizes polygamy (or, more accurately, polygyny—a plurality of wives, because it was necessary for the protection of women in a society in which so many men died in battle). However, it places strict limits on the practice, making the welfare of the woman the primary concern. In contemporary Islam, polygyny is rare, because of changed circumstances.

A later passage in the same *Surah* (34–35) says clearly that men have authority over women. Therefore, "good women are the obedient." Rebellious wives are to be confined to other beds and scourged, but are to be treated well if they again become obedient. The effect of this passage is to sanction patriarchy within Islam.

Surah 24:30–31 includes the text that is the basis in the Qur'an for the modest dress and veiling of women practiced in traditional Islamic societies. The verses say (Ali 2002: 228):

> Say to the believing men that they should lower their gaze and guard their modesty: that will make for greater purity, for them: and Allah is well acquainted with all that they do.

> And say to the believing women that they should lower their gaze and guard their modesty; that they should not display their beauty and ornaments except what (must ordinarily) appear thereof; that they should draw their veils over their bosoms and not display their beauty except to their husbands, their fathers [. . .] and that they should not strike their feet in order to draw attention to their hidden ornaments.

The passage implores *both* male and female believers to be modest, but only women are admonished to cover themselves until they are past childbearing age.

In traditional Muslim societies two practices developed to enable women to fulfill their responsibility to be modest. One is seclusion (*purdah*), under which women do not participate in the public worship in the mosque (or, if they do, are separated from men) and do not engage in activities outside the home unless chaperoned by male relatives or kept separate from men. The result was the creation of a woman's "life apart." The rationale for *purdah* is that it allows women to be freed from social pressures so that they can devote themselves to home and family. However, it has also had the effect of creating a two-tiered, gender-determined society in traditional Islamic cultures.

The other practice is veiling or covering (*hijab* or *sitr*). No specific type of veil is mentioned in the Qur'an. There are in fact various cultural traditions of covering in different Muslim societies, ranging from a head scarf to covering the face (*nigab*)— both with loose fitting clothes for modesty, to covering the whole body (except for hands and feet) with the head entirely enclosed and the woman's face entirely hidden (*chador*). Veiling was apparently first adopted by upper-class, urban women so that they could practice "seclusion" and still go out in public. In the contemporary world, "veiling" allows "lower-class women, unable to afford expensive 'Western' attire, [to] recover an affordable means to gaining respect and status in society" (Davary 1999: 154–55).

In the strictest Muslim societies, a religious police looks for women in violation of these restrictions and forcibly returns them to their homes and their husbands. For example, although women in Saudi Arabia have access to education and may take on professional roles, they are not allowed to drive automobiles or appear in public without proper covering.

With the revival of traditional Islam sweeping the Muslim world, women who had given up the *hijab* are returning to it. For some women it is a sign of disenchantment with secular, consumerist values that treat women as sex objects, and a symbolic way of expressing a desire to return to the traditional values of Islam. For others it is a way to move freely and safely about in public.

Reform movements within Islam have argued that the traditions of "seclusion" and "veiling" should not be considered basic Muslim teachings, but customs that developed after the time of Muhammad. They argue that these customs thwart the basic Muslim value of equality of men and women, and are rooted in men's desire to control and dominate women.

However, Islamic movements such as the Taliban in Afghanistan instituted the repression of women in the guise of restoring Islamic values. These expressions of Islamic extremism have been denounced across the Muslim world, by both modernists and traditionalists, who agree that they have no place in an authentically Muslim society.

Although not mentioned in the Qur'an, female circumcision as a rite of passage for girls is found in some Muslim societies (Hermansen 1999: 26–33 and Kassam 2001: 10–22). Although not found in the land where Islam originated, its practice is widespread in Muslim communities in Africa, where it is also associated with indigenous traditions (as previously noted). There is controversy among Muslims about whether the practice is sanctioned by Muslim law. Muslim proponents of female circumcision point out it is found in several sayings reported by tradition (*hadith*) of the Prophet Muhammad. One says, "Circumcision is a *Sunna* (tradition) for men and a mark of respect for women." They also argue that it protects women from promiscuous behavior by lowering their sexual desire, and that there is no definitive medical evidence proving it is any more harmful to women than circumcision is for males.

Muslims who oppose female circumcision (preferring to call it female genital mutilation) assert that because the Qur'an says nothing about the practice, and because the *hadith* that mention it are considered weak in their connection to the Prophet by most Muslim scholars, it should not be considered required. It is, they say, a cultural practice for which its defenders have sought religious sanction. Opponents also say that in the absence of a clear mandate in Sharia for the procedure, the medical evidence showing that harm is done to young women physically and psychologically should be given the strongest weight. There is a principle in Muslim law that, where possible, unnecessary harm should be prevented, and female circumcision, they say, is one such case.

In cultures where female circumcision is common, some Muslim parents of girls have found a compromise by having a minor, symbolic small cut performed in a sanitary setting, instead of the harsher, often unsanitary removal of the clitoris and labia, and vaginal narrowing. The alternative preserves the ritual and cultural significance but avoids the harmful effects.

Another problem women face in some Muslim societies is a practice known as "honor killings" (Kassam 2001: 122–26). It is difficult to estimate the severity of the practice, but each year a number of cases are reported. Honor killings take place in the Middle East and in South Asia. A woman may be killed by her in-laws simply because they suspect her of an extramarital affair that has brought shame to the family. Fathers or brothers may also kill an unmarried daughter or sister who they believe has had an illicit relationship with a man. A woman who attempts to divorce her husband may also be made the target of an honor killing by her own family. There is nothing in the Qur'an or *hadith* to support such violence against women, but the tradition in Islam of families having the right to settle disputes within the family has been used to minimize the consequences for those who carry out honor killings. Muslims seeking to end the practice claim that it is part of a pattern of domination of and violence against women that contradicts the most basic Islamic values.

SIKHISM   According to Sikh teaching, men and women are equal in the eyes of the Creator. Women are as eligible as men for initiation into the Sikh Khalsa. However, although the early Guru condemned customs like female infanticide, Sikh women have suffered under the same forms of oppression as Hindu women (Nesbitt 1996: 121–22).

New Religious Movements

WICCA   In Wicca teaching all nature is spiritually alive. However, as in other indigenous religions, there are gods. One deity is the male Lord of animals, death and the beyond, called the Horned God, symbolized in the sun. Increasingly, the more important deity for the practice of Wicca is the Goddess, who appears in three aspects reflective of the cycle of life (and, in particular, the phases of the moon): the maiden, the mother, and the crone (old woman). According to the Wiccan writer Starhawk, "the image of the Goddess inspires women to see ourselves as divine, our bodies as sacred, the changing phases of our lives as holy, our aggression as healthy, our anger as purifying, and our power to nurture and create, but also to limit and destroy when necessary, as the very force that sustains all life" (1979: 9).

THE BAHA'I FAITH   One of the twelve principles of the Baha'i Faith, first enunciated in 1912, is that there is equality between men and women. The prophet for the modern age, Baha'u'llah, had said that "the capacity of woman has become so awakened and manifest in this age that equality of man and woman is an established fact" (cited in Schoonmaker 1984: 142). Baha'is believe that with "the emergence of womankind as a full and coequal partner with mankind [. . .] human civilization will take the next vital step forward" (143). It is education, according to Baha'i teaching, that will enable women to realize this equality.

HOMOSEXUALITY: ORIENTATION, PREFERENCE, OR PERVERSION?

The Nature of the Issue and the Role of Religion

"Sexual orientation" is one of the most hotly debated topics in the world today, at least in the developed world. In particular, debate focuses on same-sex relations— "homosexuality"—and so will our discussion. Homosexuality has been "officially" defined as "a predominant, persistent, and exclusive psychosexual attraction toward members of the same sex" (Kanoti and Kosnik 1978: 671). Before we proceed, we must acknowledge that "homosexuality" was "constructed" as a concept in nineteenth-century Europe, and its helpfulness in understanding same-sex relations in other cultures is limited.

Same-sex relations are found in all cultures and have been a part of human experience since the beginning of recorded history. Four types of homosexual relations have been found in all major culture areas (Greenberg 1988: 25–26). They are *transgenerational homosexuality,* which is found primarily among males, and between an older, more assertive male and a younger partner; *transgenderal homosexuality,* in which one of the partners assumes a gender role that does not correspond with his or her biological sex; *egalitarian homosexual relations* between two members of the same sex, sometimes in association with a particular life phase; and *class-distinguished homosexuality,* involving same-sex relations between members of different social classes.

As we will see, in a number of religions various expressions of homosexuality are accepted as normal. However, in Western societies homosexuality has been judged negatively since about the eleventh century, to a significant degree because of the way homosexuality is viewed in the Western religions.

The debate about homosexuality has become particularly heated in recent decades in the West, as more scientists and physicians have expressed the view that homosexuality is much more a matter of genetic determination than psychosocial conditioning or free choice, and is therefore not abnormal and need not be "treated" (see Burr 1993). This has put increasing pressure on religions to renounce traditions that say that homosexuality departs from the sacred ordering of human life. Many "modernists" among Western religious traditions (especially in Judaism and Christianity) have accepted this challenge and have taken the position that homosexuality is as valid an expression of human sexuality as heterosexuality. In response, "traditionalists" have vigorously defended classical teachings that portray homosexual behavior as wicked.

Our purpose will not be to try to resolve this complicated issue, but to provide readers with various points of view represented in the world's religions so that they may be better informed as they confront the controversy themselves.

Religious Responses

Indigenous Religions

AFRICAN   With regard to homosexuality among peoples who practice indigenous African religions, the evidence is ambiguous. There seems to be both condemnation and acceptance, depending on the culture and the observer reporting.

Among many traditional African peoples, like the Akan and Ewe of Ghana, homosexuality today is simply outside the normal frame of reference. To them it is simply inconceivable "that a person can have sexual desire toward another person of his own sex. Even animals, they contend, distinguish between male and female in their sex life" (Ansah 1989: 257).

Among the Yoruba, "homosexuality, lesbianism, and having sex with animals are not only taboos, but are regarded as mental illnesses that require as much treatment as those who eat sand or potsherd" (Abogunrin 1989: 280).

These negative attitudes may very well reflect the influence of Western cultural incursions. Awareness that most Europeans and Americans did not approve of

A demonstration for the rights of gays and lesbians. As the twenty-first century begins, sexual orientation and the status and rights of gay, lesbian, bi-sexual, and transgendered people continue to spark impassioned debates among as well as within religious communities.

homosexuality probably led to the concealment of more positive perspectives. One study (Baum 1993) found that various forms of homosexuality are accepted in many traditional African cultures. For example, transgenderal homosexuality is found among the peoples of south and central Africa. It is often associated with religious roles, as the person in the transgenderal role is seen to combine both male and female spiritual power. In the religion of the Ila of Zambia, the male *mwaami* (prophet) might dress as and live among women (although there is no indication that this meant engaging in sexual relations with men). The transgenderal role is taken typically as the result of a dream or vision.

NATIVE AMERICAN   A survey of studies of Native American groups identified 113 in which homosexual relations have existed, including thirty-three in which female homosexuality is found (Williams 1986: 3–4). Examples of egalitarian and transgenerational homosexuality are found. However, most are transgenderal, occurring with the framework of the man-woman role known to observers as *berdache*.

The term *berdache* apparently comes from the Arabic word *bardaj*, meaning a boy slave kept for erotic purposes (Herdt 1987: 450). It was apparently first applied to transgendered men by French missionaries and explorers (Baum 1993: 7). It has been adopted for general usage in the modern study of gender roles to describe men who dress and live as women and women who dress and live as men (the former is most common). *Berdaches* are found in a number of indigenous societies, including most Native American groups (Roscoe 1987). *Berdaches* are found, for example, in both Hopi and Lakota societies. They were noted not only for their cross-dressing and sexual relations with persons of the same biological sex, but for spiritual power. They often mediated between the human and supernatural realms (fulfilling the role of shaman), or between the sexes.

Berdaches are considered especially spiritual persons, whose sacred power can be drawn on by other members of the group. Among the Lakota, for example, male *berdaches* join with postmenopausal women in the preparations for the sun dance. They also give special names and medicine bags to boys "in order to protect them against illness and to enhance their sacred power (*wakan*)" (Baum 1993: 16).

By the late nineteenth century, Euroamerican suppression led to the near disappearance of the *berdache* role among Native Americans. Indian agents, for example, often forced male berdaches to wear male clothes in an effort to "break them" of their "perverse" ways. Missionaries condemned them because of the rejection of homosexuality in traditional Christianity. One Lakota healer described the effect such hostility had on *winktes* (the Lakota name for *berdaches*): "The missionaries and government agents said *winktes* were no good, and tried to get them to change their ways. Some did, and put on men's clothing. But others, rather than change, went out and hanged themselves" (Williams 1986: 183). However, the institution has continued into the present in some Native American communities. *Berdaches* have been stereotyped by some modern interpreters as "ridiculed outcasts," but in most indigenous societies they are still considered holy persons.

Religions of South and Southeast Asia

HINDUISM   Traditional Western scholarship on India has taken the position that there is less emphasis on homosexuality in India than in other cultures. This position reflects, in part, the biases of interpreters who, like A. L. Basham, state that the slight attention to homosexuality in early literature shows that "ancient India was far healthier than most other ancient cultures" (Basham 1954: 172; cited by Sharma 1993: 48). While not as judgmental, modern Indian political leaders have also taken the view that homosexuality is not very evident in Indian culture. J. L. Nehru, for example, said that "homosexuality was evidently neither approved nor at all common in India" (cited by Sharma 1993: 69). Leaders like Nehru have tended to associate homosexuality with the "vices" of minorities who had occupied India, the Muslims and the British.

It is true that references to homosexuality are rare in classical Hindu texts, and where they occur the setting suggests that homosexual practice was not viewed positively. Homosexuality was seen as fundamentally incompatible with the fulfillment of the goals of dharma (duty) and *artha* (material well-being). Not to marry and bear children may be seen as a violation of dharma within the *varna* (class) system. However, in pursuit of the goal of *kama* (pleasure), homosexuality was seen as acceptable. According to the *Kamasutra,* "the experience of physical love between two people of either the same or opposite sex is to be engaged in and enjoyed for its own sake as one of [the] arts [of love]" (Sharma 1993: 59).

Like the *berdache* in Native American cultures, the *hijra* in India is an institutionalized "third gender" role (Nanda 1985). *Hijras* are devotees of the Mother Goddess, *Bahuchara Mata.* Typically, *hijras* are men who live and dress as women. Although they dress as women, they do not attempt to "pass" as women. *Hijras* have an important ritual role and are often employed to perform at birth ceremonies and weddings. They burlesque behavior ordinarily associated with women in Hindu society, and use "coarse and abusive" speech (Nanda 1985: 38). Some interpreters point out that like the "contraries" in other cultures, Hindu *hijras* provide an acceptable outlet for the tensions that build up as a result of the limitations of normal social interaction. For the most part, they are not only tolerated but valued in Indian society. There are an estimated half million *hijras* in modern India, most living in communities under the leadership of a guru.

In general, the fact that all the major Hindu deities (such as Shiva) have both feminine and masculine aspects has contributed to a more tolerant attitude in India toward homosexual and bisexual orientation. According to Hindu mythology, Samba, the divine son of the god Krishna, "not only engaged in homosexuality but also dressed as a woman to seduce the wives of other gods" (Herdt 1987: 450). In addition, the Hindu capacity to allow seeming contradictions to confront one another without resolution has supported a more accepting attitude toward homosexuality than has been traditionally found in Western religions.

THERAVADA BUDDHISM   In general, Buddhism recognizes only two types of sexuality: "that of celibate monks and nuns and that of married householders engaged in heterosexual family life. Homosexual activity would seem to most Buddhists to break the third precept [regarding refraining from misuse of the senses]" (Morgan 1996: 63). However, not all commentators agree that homosexual acts are implied in the third precept (Harvey 2000: 421–22).

Although not discussed often, homosexual acts are proscribed in Theravadan texts. Buddhaghosa wrote that "desire and attachment in men for men, in women for women" are "wrong practices" (Harvey 2000: 421). However, in the important Jataka Tales, which portray the previous lives of the Buddha, there is no warning against homosexual relationships. Indeed, some commentators find in the stories an "implicit affirmation" of homosexuality. The Buddha's affection for his disciples (and theirs for him, and one another) at times seems, according to this view, homoerotic (Cabezon 1993: 88–89).

It should be noted that in Buddhist ethical teaching there are no moral absolutes that are uniformly applicable, so right action must be determined in the contexts in which people find themselves.

Religions of East Asia

DAOISM AND CONFUCIANISM   Christian missionaries and other early Western visitors were shocked to find widespread acceptance, even promotion, of same-sex relations in Chinese society. When these Westerners expressed moral outrage to their Chinese acquaintances at this tolerance of homoerotic behavior, they were met with surprise and were told that no one had ever said such behavior was wrong. Because of gender segregation, both male and female homosexuality was quite common in Chinese history before modern times. It may have reached its peak during the Northern and Southern Sung Dynasties (960–1279).

This cultural toleration of homosexuality is not, however, the whole story. Both Confucian and Daoist teachers developed arguments against same-sex relations (Wawrytko 1993: 204–10). Many Confucian teachers have argued that homosexuality poses a threat to social solidarity by undermining the propagation of the family line. Daoist rejection of homosexuality has been rooted in the assumption that it leads to an imbalance in *yin* and *yang* energies. In male-female sexual relations there is a balance of *yin* and *yang;* in same-sex relations there is an imbalance. The double *yang* energy in male-male relations is most dangerous, because the two assertive forces are more likely to conflict.

Under Communism, active oppression of homosexuals has been the official policy. At its most extreme, homophobia led to the execution of homosexuals in "reeducation" camps at the height of the Cultural Revolution. "In present-day China, homosexuals still pursue their proclivities at the risk of their lives, although discretion is more likely to be rewarded by official blindness" (Wawrytko 1993: 206).

MAHAYANA BUDDHISM   Japanese society may very well be the most permissive in terms of prevalent attitudes toward homosexuality. The general cultural attitude toward sexuality in Japan is summed up well by Edwin Reischauer, one of the most respected experts on Japan in the West (cited by Wawrytko 1993: 211):

> The Japanese do not share Western views about the sinfulness of sexual relations. To them they have always seemed a natural phenomenon, like eating, which is to be enjoyed in the proper place. Promiscuity is in itself no more of a problem than homosexuality. Their attitudes have thus in a sense been permissive.

It was not uncommon for Buddhist monks to take younger male lovers during the period before Westerners arrived (Cabézon 1993: 91). A famous seventeenth-century work, *The Great Mirror of Male Love* by Ihara Saikaku, extolled male homosexuality.

On the other hand, while an accepting attitude dominates, condemnations of homosexuality are found in Japanese Buddhism. For example, a tenth-century Tendai monk claimed that "homosexuals go straight to hell, because of their moral transgressions and worldly attachment." Some Zen masters warn that monks who have sex "with novices and young boys [. . .] experience bad karmic results" (Harvey 2000: 428).

The current Dalai Lama has expressed the view that "homosexual conduct is not a fault as long as both partners agree to it, neither is under vows of celibacy, and the activity does not harm others." However, he has also written that a sexual act is only proper "when the couples use the organs created for sexual intercourse and nothing else." He has also spoken out vigorously against discrimination based on sexual orientation (Harvey 2000: 432–33).

SHINTO Shinto has traditionally had a rather permissive attitude toward sexuality as a natural expression of humanity. Homosexual relationships are tolerated as long as the partners have a commitment to one another. Shinto concern for "pollution" has contributed to the acceptance and promotion of male homosexuality in Japan. Two of the three main sources of ritual pollution (childbirth, menstruation, and death) are linked exclusively to women (Wawrytko 1993: 212–19).

The most famous expression of male homosexuality in Japan was the pederasty common in the samurai class during the Kamakura Period (1192–1336). Indeed, transgenerational homosexuality was valued in the feudal order of Japanese society, which did not end until the beginning of the Meiji era in 1868. Shoguns and samurai often kept young male lovers for emotional support as well as sexual expression. The attitude was that women were for producing heirs, whereas boys were for pleasure and companionship (Herdt 1987: 448).

Likewise, lesbianism has been a feature of Japanese culture, though it is not openly expressed. According to one interpreter, women in Japan have been drawn together "by the alienating social climate as well as by prevailing misogyny" (Wawrytko 1993: 213).

Religions Originating in the Middle East

JUDAISM In a long list of forbidden sexual relations, the Holiness Code in the Book of Leviticus includes the following: "You shall not lie with a male as with a woman; it is an abomination" (18:22). In the penalty section for violating the rules of the community, the Code stipulates, "If a man lies with a male as with a woman, both of them have committed an abomination; they shall be put to death; their blood is upon them" (Leviticus 20:13). Some interpreters note that in ancient Israel cultic prostitution involving male homosexual activity was an issue of great concern, and claim that these strident statements must be understood in that context. Others say the laws are clear and speak for themselves, condemning homosexuality as an abomination in the eyes of God.

In the story of the destruction of Sodom and Gomorrah in the Book of Genesis (Genesis 19:1–38), the desire of the men of Sodom to have sexual relations with the young men visiting Lot's home (19: 5) is apparently one of the sins for which the city is destroyed. The modern term "sodomy," which refers in part to homosexual acts, derives from this story. Interestingly, Talmudic interpretation focuses not on homosexuality in the passage, but on the "Sodomites as mean, inhospitable, uncharitable, and unjust" (Eron 1993: 109).

The implicit prohibition of male homosexual behavior in the Tanak is reinforced and stated explicitly in the Talmud. In the medieval code of Maimonides, female homosexuality is also condemned, but is not regarded as seriously as male homosexuality. The clearest explanations for the prohibition of homosexual behavior are that it thwarts procreation, which is the purpose of human sexuality, and destroys family life.

Unambiguous condemnation of homosexuality has continued to the present in Orthodox Judaism. David Feldman, an authority on Jewish law and sexuality, has expressed the view that "the elements of the Jewish legal-moral-social view of homosexuality are simple. The practice is condemned as sinful, an 'abomination'" (Feldman 1983: 426). Feldman points out that for Jewish law the modern debate over the causes of homosexuality is irrelevant. What is condemned are homosexual acts, regardless of the reasons behind them. Jewish law, he says, condemns homosexual behavior not only because it thwarts procreation and undermines family life, but because it runs counter to the very structures of creation as described in the Book of Genesis (428). In defending the traditional perspective, many interpreters have distinguished condemnation of homosexual behavior from rejection of persons who experience homosexual preferences (e.g., Kahn 1989: 53).

Scholars of the Conservative Movement have appealed to the concept of "constraint" to respond to the issue of homosexuality (Kahn 1989: 56). The *halakhah* recognizes that "constraint" may be "an excusing factor in circumstances beyond one's control." This is the *halakhic* basis for judging a person not guilty of a violation of the law because of the threat of punishment, or temporary mental illness. If modern research is correct in the view that homosexuality is not a matter of choice, but of basic sexual orientation, then homosexuals are "constrained" by this orientation and their violation of the commandments must be excused. As once Conservative scholar said, "The most truly Jewish stance would be one that takes with equal seriousness both the authority of traditional standards and the significance of modern knowledge" (cited by Kahn 1989: 56).

The Reconstructionist and Reform Jewish communities have tended to take a more liberal attitude toward homosexuality. Some scholars in these communities repudiate the traditional condemnation, invoking the authority of fundamental moral principles such as respect for the dignity of persons and the value of commitment in human relationships (Umansky 1985: 9–15). Others argue that *halakhah* has always been interpreted in the particular social context of the affected Jewish community (Kirschner 1988: 452). In the modern context, in which the traditional assumption that homosexuality is a "perversion" of normal sexuality has been undermined in the scientific community, should not the Jewish community take a more tolerant and open attitude? Homosexuality, they argue, would seem to be "an expression of diversity rather than perversity" (456).

For many in the Jewish community, especially in Reform congregations, the approach to be taken toward homosexual persons is clear: "to rescind the ancient denunciation of homosexuals and to recognize that all persons, in their unique sexual being, are the work of God's hands and the bearers of God's image" (Kirschner 458; see also Soloff 1983: 417–24).

Taking advantage of this new attitude of openness, the first gay synagogues opened in 1973 in the United States, west coast. The Reform movement's Union of American Hebrew Congregations accepted four homosexual congregations into membership; soon the movement spread to other parts of the country. One participant in Congregation Beth Simchat Torah, a synagogue for gays in New York City, writes, "My involvement in Congregation Beth Simchat Torah over the years has helped me form my own theology; I have only one identity, one self. The feeling of two conflicting identities, one gay and one Jewish, was a false consciousness. I need to be part of a Jewish community. For me, CBST is that community" (Rabinowitz 1983: 435).

The emergence of these gay synagogues caused a "backlash" in the Reform community, as many lay people and some Rabbis stepped forward to challenge acceptance of the open practice of homosexuality. For example, respected Reform Rabbi Solomon Freehof stated that homosexual marriages are "a contravention of all that is respected in Jewish life" (Lehrman 1983: 393). One Reform interpreter attempted to counter the use of modern research to justify acceptance of homosexuality by pointing out that the traditional rejection "is based on the empirical lesson of history: that permanent, joyous, sexually faithful bonding between men and women produces stable families and societies and is, thus, fundamentally important for human survival and growth" (394).

To defend an attitude of tolerance toward homosexual persons, some Jewish scholars have noted the parallel between treatment of Jews and gays in European history. In his study of the history of the treatment of homosexuals in Europe, one scholar noted that "the fate of Jews and gay people has been almost identical throughout European history, from early Christian hostility to extermination in concentration camps. The same laws which oppressed Jews oppressed gay people; the same groups bent on eliminating Jews tried to wipe out homosexuals" (Boswell 1980: 15). In response, some defenders of the traditional Jewish rejection of homosexuality point out that Jews can and should vigorously defend the human and civil rights of gay, lesbian, bisexual, and transgendered people without condoning their sexual behavior.

CHRISTIANITY   The teaching of Christian churches in the United States on homosexuality ranges from full acceptance of homosexual orientation and practice within committed relationships by the Society of Friends (the Quakers) and the Moravian Church, to vigorous denunciation of homosexuality (no matter how it is approached) among such conservative Protestant denominations as the Southern Baptist Convention, to a variety of positions in between.

A Christian denomination that is dominated by persons of homosexual orientation, the Metropolitan Community Church, has provided a place of acceptance for persons who were forced out of or did not feel comfortable in "straight" churches.

We will here summarize the contemporary teaching of the Roman Catholic church, conservative and so-called "mainline" Protestant churches, and the dispute over the New Testament texts which deal with homosexuality.

The Roman Catholic Church has maintained an unchanging rejection of homosexual practice, while being less clear on the issue of "homosexual orientation." In 1986 the Roman Catholic Congregation for the Doctrine of the Faith sent to the Bishops of the Church a statement entitled "On the Pastoral Care of Homosexual Persons." Although not a statement of the Pope and not regarded as "infallible" teaching, it establishes the current view of the Catholic hierarchy. On the basis of the teachings of Scripture, the statement concluded that the Church's rejection of homosexual behavior is based on "the solid foundation of a constant Biblical testimony" (Williams 1987: 260). It went on to make the controversial claim that homosexuality must be considered an "objective disorder" while at the same time strongly affirming the intrinsic dignity of gay persons. "Therefore special concern and pastoral attention should be directed toward those who have this condition, lest they be led to believe that the living out of this orientation in homosexual activity is a morally acceptable option. It is not" (Williams 1987: 264). Defenders of the 1986 statement have tried to make clear that it is not a condemnation of homosexual persons, any more than saying that a person has a tendency toward the moral evil of irascibility is a rejection of the person. "One's personality cannot be reduced to sexual orientation" (Williams 1987: 268).

Catholic critics of the 1986 statement have pointed out that it fails to acknowledge sufficiently the modern advances in understanding homosexuality. The Bible's assumptions that heterosexuality is the norm, and homosexuality is a voluntary choice that thwarts what is normal, have both been undermined, critics say, by contemporary research.

The Roman Catholic Church in the United States has tended toward a more open attitude on the question of homosexuality than the Church at large. For example, in 1983 the senate of priests of the Archdiocese of San Francisco published a pastoral plan that said that homosexuality must be addressed not only by church teaching but also in terms of the results of modern research and the real experiences of homosexual persons. It said that the feelings of many homosexual persons that their sexuality is right and good must be considered (Nugent and Gramick 1989: 27).

Conservative Protestant churches have based their positions on homosexuality almost exclusively on the Bible. For most, the New Testament's clear rejection of homosexual behavior makes obvious that there is no basis for Christians to condone it today. The passage cited most frequently is from the Apostle Paul's letter to the Romans. In speaking of the human tendency not to honor God, although God is clearly revealed in the ordering of creation, Paul uses homosexual behavior by women and men as an example (1:26–27). In his list of "wrongdoers" in First Corinthians 6:9, Paul mentions both male prostitutes and "sodomites." First Timothy 1:10 includes sodomites among examples of "the godless and sinful." These texts, combined with the Old Testament passages cited above, clearly leave no room, many conservative Protestants argue, for tolerance of homosexual activity.

In 1988 the Southern Baptist Convention adopted a resolution condemning homosexuality as "an abomination in the eyes of God, a perversion of divine standards, and a violation of nature" (Nugent and Gramick 1989: 25). In 1992 two Southern Bapitist congregations that had ordained an openly homosexual person into the ministry and blessed a homosexual union were expelled from the Convention. Programs designed to help homosexual persons repent and be delivered from their presumed sinfulness have been developed by some conservative Protestant churches as a form of pastoral ministry to gays and lesbians.

While considering homosexual behavior sinful, some conservative Protestants have cautioned against singling out homosexuality for condemnation. They point out that homosexual behavior is not given special prominence in lists of sins in the Bible. They warn that too much emphasis on homosexuality by Christians has helped create a climate in which homosexual persons are themselves sinned against and subjected to unwarranted restrictions in society. They maintain that the moral rejection of homosexual behavior should not be the basis for laws that discriminate against homosexual persons (Smith 1969).

More liberal, "mainline" Protestant Christian churches have attempted to balance the traditional understanding of the biblical teaching on homosexuality with the emergent modern understanding that homosexuality is not necessarily "abnormal." As in the Reform community in Judaism, various responses have emerged. The discussion has tended to focus on the issue of whether openly gay persons should be allowed to be ordained as ministers. In 1972 the United Church of Christ became the first Christian denomination to ordain a self-proclaimed gay. In 2003 an American Episcopal priest who acknowledged being in a homosexual relationship was ordained as a bishop. Other "mainline" churches such as the United Methodists and Presbyterians have attempted to draw on modern research in developing a more tolerant and accepting attitude toward homosexuals, while still refusing to ordain openly gay and lesbian persons as ministers or church officers, because of the seemingly clear Biblical denunciation of homosexual behavior.

In recent decades some Christian scholars have begun to question the traditional understanding of the Bible's teaching on homosexuality. In his study of the New Testament and homosexuality, Robin Scroggs (1983) concluded that the social contexts in which the New Testament was written must be taken into account in evaluating particular texts. Scroggs pointed out that committed homosexual relationships between adults were unknown in New Testament times. Therefore, the Biblical denunciation of particular types of homosexual acts, such as male prostitution and man-boy relationships, should not be turned into an absolute standard used to condemn all forms of homosexual behavior today. This becomes a basis for a position that holds that in the context of loving and committed relationships, homosexuality meets the New Testament criteria for what is moral sexual behavior just as much as heterosexuality.

In summary, the attitudes toward homosexuality found among Christian churches and individuals can be categorized as follows (Nugent and Gramick 1989: 31–42):

- *Rejecting-Punitive.* According to this view both homosexual behavior and the homosexual condition/orientation are sinful. The basis is the clear Biblical teaching—which, at its extreme, treats homosexual behavior as a capital crime. Some who take this position go so far as to argue that the "plague of AIDS" is God's punishment on homosexuals for their sinfulness. Within this framework it is also believed that all homosexuals who are truly repentant are able to go through a process of spiritual conversion, leaving their sinful condition and behavior behind.

- *Rejecting-Nonpunitive.* This perspective rejects homosexual acts but not homosexual persons. The behavior is regarded as "intrinsically evil," often because it seems to those who take this view to be an affront to the biological differences between the two sexes. Many supporters of this position are willing to acknowledge that some persons have a constitutional homosexual orientation that cannot be changed. Those persons unable to change their orientation must, however, remain celibate or else they violate God's law, they argue.

- *Qualified Acceptance.* This position states that while homosexual activity may, in some instances, be acceptable for Christians, it is always inferior to heterosexual expression. It is based on endorsing the research that homosexual orientation is not a matter of choice, while maintaining the authority of the Christian teaching that the norm for human beings is heterosexuality. Homosexual "marriages" are, from this viewpoint, necessary accommodations to the reality of homosexuality, but are not of the same moral quality as heterosexual unions.

- *Full Acceptance.* According to this position, homosexuality is as much a part of the divine plan for creation as heterosexuality. Indeed, homosexuality is an expression, it is held, of the rich diversity of creation. The standard for sexuality should not be procreation or the male/female union, it is argued, but the quality of the relationship of the two persons regardless of gender. For advocates of this position, Christian churches should recognize homosexual marriages as just as valid as heterosexual unions, and sanction rituals for both.

ISLAM   Two verses from the Qur'an are cited to show that male homosexuality in Islam is considered a violation of Allah's will for men (7: 80–81, 26:165–66; Ali 2002: 96, 243).

> We also sent Lut (Lot): he said to his people: "Do you permit lewdness such as no people in creation (ever) committed before you?
> For you practice your lusts on men in preference to women: you are indeed a people transgressing beyond bounds.
> Of all the creatures in the world, will you approach males,
> And leave those whom Allah has created for you? Nay, but you are a people transgressing (all limits)!

There are no references to lesbian acts in the Qur'an. All Islamic legal schools consider homosexual acts to be unlawful, though they differ on the question of what type of punishment is appropriate.

Despite the legal view, Islam has generally been more tolerant in practice toward homosexuality than traditional Judaism or Christianity. One reason may be the existence in pre-Muslim Arabia of age-structured homosexuality. The most tolerant attitude in Islam toward homosexuality is found in the mystical branch (Sufism). Many Sufis have regarded homosexual relations "as an expression of the spiritual link between man and God" (Herdt 1987: 447–48).

A number of groups have formed to support gay and lesbian Muslims. For example, *Al-Fatiha* is an "international organization for lesbian, gay, bisexual, and transgender Muslims, including those questioning their sexual orientation and/or gender identity, as well as their friends, families, partners, and allies." The group's mission is to "work in order to enlighten the world that Islam is a religion of tolerance and not hate, and that Allah (God) loves His creation, no matter what their sexual orientation might be."

SIKHISM   As in traditional Judaism, Christianity, and Islam, the norm for Sikhs is marriage of men and women and the bearing of children. Although homosexuality was not directly addressed by the Sikh Gurus, one modern commentator speculates that "any surrender to instincts incompatible with conjugal fidelity or to the proper role of men and women as marriage partners would be condemned" (Nesbitt 1996: 107). However, a tradition of tolerance has led to acceptance of gays and lesbians within some Sikh communities.

New Religious Movements

THE INTERNATIONAL SOCIETY FOR KRISHNA CONSCIOUSNESS   Drutakarma Dasa (1992) reports that the position of the Hare Krishna movement on homosexuality is that it would not be allowed for initiated members, for they commit themselves to having no illicit sex. Illicit sex involves sex outside marriage and sex within marriage not for procreation. Thus, practicing homosexuals may not be initiated, and are banned from positions of leadership in the movement. Previous homosexual practice does not disqualify someone from initiation, and practicing homosexuals who are not initiated are not excluded from attending temple functions and practicing Krishna consciousness as much as they can.

CHAPTER SUMMARY

Want to have an impassioned discussion? Raise the two issues discussed in this chapter—gender roles and the status of women, and homosexuality. As we have seen in this chapter, the teachings of the world's religions on these two topics engender heated arguments, often within the same religion. We began discussion of each issue by clarifying the concepts and the role of religion in relation to them. Then we surveyed the responses of the world's religions to these issues, which will undoubtedly remain hotly debated well into the twenty-first century.

IMPORTANT TERMS AND PHRASES

abomination, Adi Shakti, Amaterasu, *bat mitzvah, berdache,* chattel, class-distinguished homosexuality, clitoridectomy, construction of homosexuality, Dao, dharma (woman's), egalitarian homosexuality, female genital mutilation, female infanticide, feminist theology, footbinding, gay synagogues, geisha, gender hierarchy, gender versus sex, God/ess, *hijab, hijra,* Kali, Kamasutra, Kannon, Metropolitan Community

Church, *nagas,* objective disorder, patriarchy, *prajna-paramita, purdah, sati, shakti,* sodomy, tantric, *taras,* third gender, transgenerational homosexuality, transgenderal homosexuality, virginity (idealized), White Buffalo Calf Woman, women-church, womanist theology, *winktes, yin/yang*

QUESTIONS FOR DISCUSSION AND REFLECTION

1. Suppose that at a family meal you are asked to deliver the blessing. You decide to begin your prayer with "Mother God. . ." You can hardly get out an "Amen" when your father says, "In *this* house God is our father, *not* our mother! I don't want to hear you start a prayer like that again!" Imagine that you respond by trying to educate your father on the various feminine images of the sacred you have encountered in your study of the world's religions. What would you say? Do you think that it is appropriate to address the Holy in feminine imagery?

2. Imagine that you are in a discussion among friends about the rights of women, and one says, "Religions oppress women. They teach that women are inferior to men and don't allow them to be religious leaders. No self-respecting woman should be religious!" Based on what you have learned in this chapter, how would you respond?

3. A friend confides to you that she is a lesbian. She says that she is feeling overwhelmed by guilt because she learned growing up in her church that homosexuality is an "abomination" against God and nature. She is afraid to talk with her parents because this is their belief. Knowing that you have taken several religious studies classes, she asks you, "Do all religions condemn homosexuality? Is homosexuality a sin?" How would you respond?

SOURCES AND SUGGESTIONS FOR FURTHER STUDY

GENDER ROLES AND THE STATUS OF WOMEN

General

BYNUM, CAROLINE WALKER, STEVAN HARRELL, AND PAULA RICHMAN, 1986. *Gender and Religion: On the Complexity of Symbols.* Boston: Beacon.

CASTELLI, ELIZABETH A., ED., 2001. *Women, Gender, Religion: A Reader.* New York: Palgrave.

CARMODY, DENISE LARDNER, 1989. *Women and World Religions.* Englewood Cliffs, NJ: Prentice Hall.

CHRIST, CAROL AND JUDITH PLASKOW, EDS., 1979. *Womenspirit Rising: A Feminist Reader in Religion.* San Francisco: Harper & Row.

FALK, NINA AUER AND RITA M. GROSS, 1989. *Unspoken Worlds: Women's Religious Lives.* Belmont, CA: Wadsworth.

GREEN, M. CHRISTIAN AND PAUL D. NUMRICH, 2001. *Religious Perspectives on Sexuality: A Resource Guide.* Chicago, IL: Park Ridge Center.

KING, URSULA, ED., 1995. *Religion and Gender.* Cambridge, MA: Blackwell.

PLASKOW, JUDITH AND CAROL CHRIST, 1989. *Weaving the Visions: New Patterns in Feminist Spirituality.* San Francisco: HarperSanFrancisco.

RUNZO, JOSEPH AND NANCY M. MARTIN, EDS., 2000. *Love, Sex and Gender In the World Religions.* Boston: Oneworld.

SHARMA, ARVIND, ED., 1987. *Women in World Religions.* Albany: State University of New York.

SHARMA, ARVIND, ED., 1994. *Today's Woman in World Religions.* Albany: State University of New York.

SHARMA, ARVIND AND KATHERINE YOUNG, 2002. *Her Voice, Her Faith: Women Speak on World Religions.* Boulder, CO: Westview.

Indigenous (Religions)

African

ABOGUNRIN, SAMUEL O., 1989. "Ethics in Yoruba Religious Tradition." In Crawford, *World Religions and Global Ethics,* 266–96.

DORKENOO, EFUA, 1995. *Cutting the Rose: Female Genital Mutilation—The Practice and Its Prevention.* London: Minority Rights Group.

KAPLAN, DAVID A., 1993. "Is it Torture or Tradition? The genital mutilation of young African girls sparks an angry intellectual debate in the West." *Newsweek,* December 20: 124.

NUSSBAUM, MARTHA, 2002. "Judging Other Cultures: The Case of Genital Mutilation." In May, Collins-Chobanian, and Wong, *Applied Ethics,* 23–36.

TOUBIA, NAHID, 1988. *Female Genital Mutilation: An Overview.* Geneva: World Health Organization.

WALKER, ALICE AND PRATIBHA PARMAR, 1996. *Warrior Marks: Female Genital Mutilation and the Sexual Blinding of Women.* San Diego: Harcourt Brace.

Native American

JAIMES, M. ANNETTE WITH THERESA HALSEY, 2002. "American Indian Women at the Center of Indigenous Resistance in Contemporary North America." In May, Collins-Chobanian, and Wong, *Applied Ethics,* 401–11.

POWERS, MARLA, 1986. *Oglala Women: Myth, Ritual, and Reality.* Chicago: University of Chicago.

Religions of South and Southeast Asia

Hinduism

GROSS, RITA, 1979. "The Second Coming of the Goddess: Hindu Female Deities as Resource for the Contemporary Rediscovery of the Goddess." *Anima* 6: 48–59.

HAWLEY, JOHN S., ED., 1994. *Sati, the Blessing and the Curse: The Burning of Wives in India.* New York: Oxford University.

MENSKI, WERNER, 1996. "Hinduism." In Morgan and Lawton, *Ethical Issues in Six Religious Traditions,* 1–54.

YOUNG, KATHERINE K., 1987. "Hinduism." In Sharma, *Women in World Religions,* 59–103.

YOUNG, KATHERINE K., 1994. "Women in Hinduism." In Sharma, *Today's Woman in World Religions,* 77–135.

Theravada Buddhism

BARNES, NANCY SCHUSTER, 1987. "Buddhism." In Sharma, *Women in World Religions,* 105–33.

BARNES, NANCY SCHUSTER, 1994. "Women in Buddhism." In Sharma, *Today's Woman in World Religions,* 137–69.

GROSS, RITA M., 1993. *Buddhism after Patriarchy: A Feminist History, Analysis and Reconstruction of Buddhism.* Albany: State University of New York.

HARVEY, PETER, 2000. "Sexual Equality." *An Introduction to Buddhist Ethics.* Cambridge: Cambridge University, 353–410.

PAUL, DIANA Y., 1979. *Women in Buddhism.* Berkeley, CA: Asian Humanities.

Religions of East Asia

Daoism

GIUSSO, RICHARD, ED., 1981. *Women in China.* New York: Philo.

LEVERING, MIRIAM, 1994. "Women, the State, and Religion Today in the People's Republic of China." In Sharma, *Today's Woman in World Religions,* 171–224.

REED, BARBARA, 1987. "Taoism." In Sharma, *Women in World Religions,* 161–81.

REED, BARBARA, 1994. "Women and Chinese Religion in Contemporary Taiwan." In Sharma, *Today's Woman in World Religions,* 225–43.

Confucianism

KELLEHER, THERESA, 1987. "Confucianism." In Sharma, *Women in World Religions,* 135–59.

LI, C., ED., 2000. *The Sage and the Second Sex: Confucianism, Ethics, and Gender.* Chicago: Open Court.

Mahayana Buddhism and Shinto

DALBY, LIZA CRIHFIELD, 1983. *Geisha.* Berkeley: University of California.

NAKAMURA, KYOKO MOTOMOCHI, 1989. "No Women's Liberation: The Heritage of a Woman Prophet in Modern Japan." In Falk and Gross, *Unspoken Worlds,* 134–44.

Religions Originating in the Middle East

Judaism

GREENBERG, BLU, 1988. *On Women and Judaism: A View from Tradition.* Philadelphia: Jewish Publication Society.

PIRANI, ALIX, ED., 1991. *The Absent Mother: Restoring the Goddess to Judaism and Christianity.* London: Mandala (HarperCollins).

PLASKOW, JUDITH, 1979. "The Coming of Lilith: Toward a Feminist Theology." In Christ and Plaskow, *Womenspirit Rising,* 198–209.

PLASKOW, JUDITH, 1989. "Jewish Memory from a Feminist Perspective." In Plaskow and Christ, *Weaving the Visions,* 39–50.

PLASKOW, JUDITH, 1990. *Standing Again at Sinai: Judaism from a Feminist Perspective.* San Francisco: Harper & Row.

UMANSKY, ELLEN M., 1989. "Creating a Jewish Feminist Theology." In Plaskow and Christ, *Weaving the Visions,* 87–198.

WEGNER, JUDITH ROMNEY, 1988. *Chattel or Person: The Status of Women in the Mishnah.* New York: Oxford University.

Christianity

JOHNSON, ELIZABETH A., 1993. *She Who Is: The Mystery of God in Feminist Theological Discourse.* New York: Crossroads.

McFAGUE, SALLIE, 1987. *Models of God: Theology for an Ecological, Nuclear Age.* Philadelphia: Fortress.

MOLLENKOTT, VIRGINIA, 1983. *The Divine Feminine: The Biblical Imagery of God as Female.* New York: Crossroad.

RUDY, KATHY, 1997. *Sex and the Church: Gender, Homosexuality, and the Transformation of Christian Ethics.* Boston: Beacon.

RUETHER, ROSEMARY RADFORD, 1983. *Sexism and God-Talk: Toward a Feminist Theology.* Boston: Beacon.

RUETHER, ROSEMARY RADFORD, 1987. "Christianity." In Sharma, *Women in World Religions,* 207–33.

RUETHER, ROSEMARY RADFORD, 1989. "Sexism and God-Language." In Plaskow and Christ, *Weaving the Visions,* 151–62.

RUETHER, ROSEMARY RADFORD, 1995. *New Woman, New Earth: Sexist Ideologies and Human Liberation.* Boston: Beacon.

SCHÜSSLER-FIORENZA, ELISABETH, 1983. *In Memory of Her.* New York: Crossroad.

STUART, ELIZABETH AND ADRIAN THATCHER, 1996. *Christian Perspectives on Sexuality and Gender.* Grand Rapids, MI: Eerdmans.

UNITED STATES CATHOLIC CONFERENCE, 1998. *From Words to Deeds: Continuing Reflections on the Role of Women in the Church.* Washington, DC: USCC.

WILLIAMS, DELORES S. 1989. "Womanist Theology: Black Women's Voices." In Plaskow and Christ, *Weaving the Visions,* 179–86.

WITHERINGTON, BEN, 1984. *Women in the Ministry of Jesus.* Cambridge: Cambridge University.

Islam

AHMED, LEILA, 1992. *Women and Gender in Islam: Historical Roots of a Modern Debate.* New Haven, CT: Yale University.

ASK, KARIN AND MARIT TJOMSLAND, EDS., 1998. *Women and Islamization: Contemporary Dimensions of Discourse on Gender Relations.* New York: Oxford University.

DAVARY, BAHAR, 1999. "A Matter of Veils: An Islamic Response." In Wolfe and Gudorf, *Ethics and World Religions,* 153–59.

EL-SOLH, CAMILLIA FAWZI AND JUDY MABRO, EDS., 1995. *Muslim Women's Choices: Religious Belief and Social Reality.* Providence, RI: Berg.

HADDAD, YVONNE YAZBECK AND JOHN L. ESPOSITO, EDS., 1998. *Islam, Gender, and Social Change.* New York: Oxford University.

HERMANSEN, MARCIA K., 1999. "A Question of Compromise: A Muslim Response." In Wolfe and Gudorf, *Ethics and World Religions,* 26–33.

KASSAM, ZAYN, 2001. "Islamic Ethics and Gender Issues." In Runzo and Martin, *Ethics in the World Religions,* 115–34.

AL-SABBAGH, MUHAMMAD LUBFTI, 1996. *Islamic Ruling on Male and Female Circumcision.* Alexandria, Egypt: World Health Organization.

SMITH, JANE I., 1987. "Islam." In Sharma, *Women in World's Religions,* 235–50.

SMITH, JANE I., 1994. "Women in Islam." In Sharma, *Today's Woman in World Religions,* 303–25.

Sikhism

NESBITT, ELEANOR, 1996. "Sikhism." In Lawton and Morgan, *Ethical Issues in Six Religious Traditions,* 99–134.

New Religious Movements

Wicca

STARHAWK, 1979. *The Spiral Dance: A Rebirth of the Great Goddess.* New York: Harper & Row.

The Baha'i Faith

SCHOONMAKER, ANN, 1984. "Revisioning the Women's Movement." *Circle of Unity: Baha'i Approaches to Current Social Issues,* ed. Anthony A. Lee. Los Angeles: Kalimat 135–63.

HOMOSEXUALITY

General

BAIRD, ROBERT M. AND M. KATHERINE BAIRD, 1995. *Homosexuality: Debating the Issues*. Amherst, NY: Prometheus.

BULLOGH, VERN, 1976. *Sexual Variance in Society and History*. Chicago: University of Chicago.

BURR, CHANDLER, 1993. "Homosexuality and Biology." *Atlantic*, 271: 47–65.

COMSTOCK, GARY DAVID, 1996. *Unrepentant, Self-Affirming, Practicing: Lesbian/Bisexual/Gay People Within Organized Religion*. New York: Continuum.

COMSTOCK, GARY DAVID AND SUSAN E. HENKING, 1997. *Que(e)rying Religion: A Critical Anthology*. New York: Continuum.

GREENBERG, DAVID F., 1988. *The Construction of Homosexuality*. Chicago: University of Chicago.

HASBANY, RICHARD, ED., 1989. *Homosexuality and Religion*. New York: Harrington Park.

HERDT, GILBERT, 1987. "Homosexuality." *Encyclopedia of Religion*, Vol. 6, ed. Mircea Eliade. New York: Macmillan, 445–53.

KANOTI, GEORGE A. AND ANTHONY R. KOSNIK, 1978. "Homosexuality: Ethical Aspects." *Encyclopedia of Bioethics*, ed. Warren T. Reich, Vol. 2. New York: Free Press, 671.

OLYAN, SAUL M. AND MARTHA C. NUSSBAUM, EDS., 1998. *Sexual Orientation and Human Rights in American Religious Discourse*. New York: Oxford University.

SHALLENBERGER, DAVID, 1998. *Reclaiming The Spirit: Gay Men and Lesbians Come to Terms with Religion*. New Brunswick, NJ: Rutgers University.

SULLIVAN, ANDREW, ED. 1997. *Same-Sex Marriage: Pro And Con—A Reader*. New York: Vintage.

SWIDLER, ARLENE, ED., 1993. *Homosexuality and World Religions*. Valley Forge, PA: Trinity.

Indigenous Religions

African

ABOGUNRIN, SAMUEL Ò., 1989. "Ethics in Yoruba Religious Tradition." In Crawford, *World Religions and Global Ethics*, 266–96.

ANSAH, JOHN K., 1989. "The Ethics of Traditional African Religions." In Crawford, *World Religions and Global Ethics*, 241–65.

BAUM, ROBERT, 1993. "Homosexuality and the Traditional Religions of the Americas and Africa." In Swidler, *Homosexuality and World Religions*, 1–46.

Native American

ROSCOE, WILL, 1987. "Bibliography of Berdache and Alternative Gender Roles among Native American Indians." *Journal of Homosexuality* 14: 81–171.

WILLIAMS, WALTER L., 1986. *The Spirit and the Flesh: Sexual Diversity in American Indian Culture*. Boston: Beacon.

Religions of South and Southeast Asia

Hinduism

BASHAM, A. L. 1954. *The Wonder That Was India*. New York: Grove.

NANDA, SERENA 1985. "The Hijras of India: Cultural and Individual Dimensions of an Institutionalized Third Gender Role." *Journal of Homosexuality* 11: 35–54.

SHARMA, ARVIND, 1993. "Homosexuality in Hinduism," In Swidler, *Homosexuality and World Religions*, 47–80.

Theravada Buddhism

CABEZON, JOSÉ IGNACIO, 1992. *Buddhism, Sexuality, and Gender.* Albany: State University of New York.

CABEZON, JOSÉ IGNACIO, 1993. "Homosexuality and Buddhism." In Swidler, *Homosexuality and World Religions,* 81–101.

DE SILVA, A. L., "Homosexuality and Theravada Buddhism." www.buddhanet.net/homosexu. htm. May 15, 2003.

HARVEY, PETER, 2000. "Homosexuality and Other Forms of 'Queerness'." *An Introduction to Buddhist Ethics,* 411–34.

MORGAN, PEGGY, 1996. "Buddhism." In Lawton and Morgan, *Ethical Issues in Six Religious Traditions,* 55–98.

Religions of East Asia

Daoism and Confucianism

WAWRYTKO, SANDRA A., 1993. "Homosexuality and Chinese and Japanese Religions." In Swidler, *Homosexuality and World Religions,* 199–230.

Mahayana Buddhism and Shinto

WATANABE, TUNEO AND IWATA JUN'ICHI, 1989. *The Love of the Samurai: A Thousand Years of Japanese Homosexuality in Japan.* London: GMP.

Religions Originating in the Middle East

Judaism

BALKA, CHRISTIE AND ANDY ROSE, EDS., 1989. *Twice Blessed: On Being Lesbian, Gay and Jewish.* Boston: Beacon.

BOSWELL, JOHN, 1980. *Christianity, Social Tolerance and Homosexuality: Gay People in Western Europe from the Beginning of the Christian Era to the Fourteenth Century.* Chicago: The University of Chicago.

ERON, DAVID, 1993. "Homosexuality and Judaism." In Swidler, *Homosexuality and World Religions,* 103–34.

FELDMAN, DAVID, 1983. "Homosexuality and Jewish Law." *Judaism* 32: 426–29.

KAHN, YOEL H., 1989. "Judaism and Homosexuality: The Traditionalist/Progressive Debate." *Journal of Homosexuality* 18: 47–82.

KIRSCHNER, ROBERT, 1988. "Halakhah and Homosexuality: A Reappraisal." *Judaism* 37: 450–58.

LEHRMAN, NATHANIEL S., 1983. "Homosexuality and Judaism: Are They Compatible?" *Judaism* 32: 392–404.

RABINOWITZ, HENRY, 1983. "Talmud Class in a Gay Synagogue." *Judaism* 32: 433–43.

SHNEER, DAVID AND CARYN AVIV, EDS., 2002. *Queer Jews.* New York: Routledge.

SOLOFF, RAV A., 1983. "Is there a Reform Response to Homosexuality?" *Judaism* 32: 417–24.

STONE, KEN, ED., 2001. *Queer Commentary and the Hebrew Bible.* Cleveland: Pilgrim.

UMANSKY, ELLEN M., 1985. "Jewish Attitudes Towards Homosexuality: A Review of Contemporary Sources." *Reconstructionist* 51: 9–15.

Christianity

CARMODY, DENISE AND JOHN CARMODY, 1993. "Homosexuality and Roman Catholicism." In Swidler, *Homosexuality and World Religions,* 135–48.

CLARK, J. MICHAEL, 1997. *Defying the Darkness: Gay Theology in the Shadows.* Cleveland: Pilgrim.

COLEMAN, GERALD, 1987. "The Vatican Statement on Homosexuality." *Theological Studies* 48: 727–34.

ELLISON, MARVIN M., 1993. "Homosexuality and Protestantism." In Swidler, *Homosexuality and World Religions,* 149–80.

GAGNON, ROBERT A. J., 2001. *The Bible and Homosexual Practice: Texts and Hermeneutics.* Nashville: Abingdon.

GLASIER, CHRIS, 1988. *Uncommon Calling: A Gay Man's Struggle to Serve the Church.* San Francisco: Harper & Row.

GRAMICK, JEANNINE AND PAT FURVEY, EDS., 1988. *The Vatican and Homosexuality.* New York: Crossroad.

MCNEILL, JOHN J., 1993. *The Church and the Homosexual.* Boston: Beacon.

MELTON, J. GORDON, ED., 1991. *The Churches Speak on Homosexuality: Official Statements from Religious Bodies and Ecumenical Organizations.* Detroit: Gale Research.

NUGENT, ROBERT AND JEANNINE GRAMICK, 1989. "Homosexuality: Protestant, Catholic, and Jewish Issues." *Journal of Homosexuality* 18: 7–46.

SCROGGS, ROBIN, 1983. *The New Testament and Homosexuality.* Philadelphia: Fortress.

SIKER, JEFREY, ED., 1994. *Homosexuality and the Church: Both Sides of the Debate.* Louisville: Westminster John Knox.

SMITH, B. L., 1969. "Homosexuality in the Bible and the Law." *Christianity Today* 13: 935–38.

WILLIAMS, BRUCE, 1987. "Homosexuality: The New Vatican Statement." *Theological Studies* 48: 259–77.

WINK, WALTER, 1999. *Homosexuality and Christian Faith.* Minneapolis: Fortress.

Islam
DURAN, KHALID, 1993. "Homosexuality and Islam," *Homosexuality and World Religions,* 181–97.

New Religious Movements
DRUTAKARMA DASA, 1992. Personal correspondence

Web Sites

THE ROLE OF WOMEN
directory.google.com/Top/Society/People/Women/Religion_and_Spirituality/
   (links to sites dealing with women and religion)

HOMOSEXUALITY
www.religion-online.org/cgi-bin/relsearchd.dll/listcatitems?cat_id=58
   (links to articles on religion and homosexuality)

www.religioustolerance.org/hom_isla.htm
   (a site on views of homosexuality in Islam)

IV
Conclusion

❧

*A*s we complete our descriptive survey of the world's religions, emphasizing their worldviews and responses to contemporary ethical issues, several questions remain for us to consider. What does the future hold for the world's religions? How will they relate with one another? What are the prospects of cooperation in addressing critical issues? What impact will September 11, 2001, and its aftermath have on relations among the world's religions? While none of us has a crystal ball, we can examine indications in the present of what may transpire as the twenty-first century unfolds.

CHAPTER

19

The Future of the World's Religions

HOW THE WORLD'S RELIGIONS WILL RELATE TO ONE ANOTHER: THREE POSSIBLE FUTURES

There would seem to be at least three possible paths religions may take in their relationships with one another: *exclusivism, inclusivism,* and *pluralism.* At the present, signs of each are apparent.

Exclusivism

When proponents of a particular religion assert that their religion alone is true, they are maintaining a position of *exclusivism.* Advocates of exclusivism usually take the position that their religion will ultimately win worldwide allegiance, either through divine intervention, successful evangelism, or both. This attitude is most common in religions such as Christianity and Islam, which share a strong sense of being commissioned by the one true God to carry the religion to the ends of the earth so that all may have an opportunity to be saved by or surrender to God. However, there are movements within other, less evangelistic religions, that also have exclusivist orientations. For example, the Nichiren school of Buddhism has a worldview in which its message is seen as essential for individual well-being and world peace. In addition, some of the new religious movements we have studied firmly believe that their teachings are true to the exclusion of the claims of other religions. Some would argue that religion is by nature exclusivist, since particular perceptions of ultimacy make other claims necessarily subordinate. How, they ask, can more than one perception of ultimacy be true, if that which is perceived is truly ultimate?

As the twenty-first century begins, religions and movements within religions that advocate exclusivism are on the rise. The term "fundamentalism" has been adopted to describe this growing exclusivist orientation (see Marty and Appleby

1991–95; Armstrong 2000; and Almond 2003). Although the term was coined to describe a movement within modern Protestant Christianity (see Chapter Eleven), it is now used to describe trends within all major religious traditions. For example, observers speak of the rise of Islamic fundamentalism throughout the Muslim world; Jewish fundamentalism, especially in Israel; and the resurgence of Hindu and Sikh fundamentalism in India. A recent work suggests that conflict between fundamentalist movements, focused in the developing world, will dominate the religious situation in the twenty-first century (Jenkins 2002).

Anthropologist Richard Antoun has identified the following recurrent themes in his own cross-cultural study of fundamentalism (Antoun 2001):

- the quest for purity in an impure world
- a struggle of good against evil
- protest, outrage, certainty, and fear
- strict adherence to traditions
- literal belief in the absolute truth of a sacred scripture
- a stand against the rapid change of the contemporary, globalized world
- opposition to the ideology of modernism
- opposition to the secularization of society
- the infusion of daily and leisure activities with religious meaning

Why is exclusivism on the rise? While there is no single reason, observers usually point to the rapid globalization and secularization of the modern world, which has put pressure on traditional religious worldviews. In response, some within the religions reacts vigorously by reasserting traditional beliefs and values. Within this movement there may be those willing to use extreme measures, including violence, to turn back the forces they see as enemies of the truth.

Inclusivism

The *inclusive* attitude is that all religions will be subsumed within one universal religion, for all religions point toward the same spiritual ultimacy (e.g., Hick 1982). That religion could be a universalistic religion already in existence, such as the Baha'i Faith (see Chapter Fourteen), or it might be some religion that has not yet developed. According to this view, as people become more aware of the need for global unity they will seek one all-embracing religion that manifests the one Truth toward which all other religions point. Movements often described as "new age" speak of an emerging "planetary consciousness" as evidence that the inclusive vision is beginning to be realized. Individual religions will not so much be repudiated as transcended, they say, shed as does a butterfly slipping free from the cocoon in which she has matured.

The Universe Story (Berry and Swimme 1992) is one attempt to formulate a new, inclusive myth appropriate for the scientific worldview of the twenty-first century. It is a new sacred narrative based on the insights of modern science. The story begins with "the primordial flaring forth of the vast energies," fifteen to twenty billion years ago, and continues "through the galactic formations, the shaping of the solar system, of the Earth, of living beings, and of the human species, along with the historical development of humans through the ages." It envisions the new biological era into which we are now entering as the Ecozoic Era, "a period we humans would be present to the earth in a mutually-enhancing manner" with the realization that all beings form with humans "a single community with a common destiny."

Some interpreters have suggested that inclusivism may be viewed as a form of exclusivism, for its proponents believe that eventually humanity will come together in the affirmation of a single shared perception of ultimacy, transcending others.

Pluralism

The third possibility for future relationships among the world's religions is *pluralism,* in which the religions of the world will continue as distinct perceptions of ultimacy, but grow ever more respectful of one another. According to the pluralist perspective, religions will continue to affirm their own perceptions of ultimacy in the future, but without the need to deny the truths apprehended in other traditions. Groups within a number of religions have moved in this direction, and there is now a quite long history of dialogue among faiths at local, national, and world levels.

In an affirmation of pluralism, representatives of the world's religions gathered in 1993 in Chicago for a Parliament of the World's Religions, to commemorate the one-hundredth anniversary of the first Chicago Parliament of Religion. The Parliament included both traditional, spiritual religions and representatives from various secular traditions. Among the stated goals of the 1993 Parliament was to hold a celebration, with openness and respect, of the rich diversity of religions. A subsequent Parliament of the World's Religions was convened in Cape Town, South Africa, in 1999. The 2004 Parliament in Barcelona, Spain focused on the theme "Pathways to Peace: The Wisdom of Listening, the Power of Commitment." The sponsoring group of the parliaments plans to hold similar gatherings of world religious leaders every five years.

One of the concrete results of the 1993 Parliament was a proposal called "A Global Ethic" (Küng 1993). This declaration addresses many of the contemporary ethical concerns that we have discussed in this book. Its principal author was Hans Küng, a Roman Catholic Christian and ecumenical theologian, and it was accepted by the two hundred religious leaders gathered for the Parliament. After describing a "world in agony" as a result of abuses of the Earth's ecosystems, poverty, hunger, and wars, the Global Ethic proposes a set of core values found in the world's religions. These include:

- interdependence and respect for the community of living beings
- individual responsibility
- a commitment to treat each person humanely
- an ability to forgive
- service of others, especially the poor, disabled, and marginalized
- equal partnership of women and men
- rejection of violence as an acceptable means for resolving disputes
- justice, truthfulness, compassion, and fairness
- prayer and meditation as a means to transform individual consciousness in order to transform the Earth
- a readiness to sacrifice

The Global Ethic makes clear that it is not claiming that religious people have a corner on the truth, but that "as religious and spiritual persons we base our lives on an Ultimate Reality, and draw spiritual power and hope therefrom, in trust, in prayer, in meditation, in word, or silence. We have a special responsibility for the welfare of all humanity and care for the planet Earth." It rejects exclusivism and inclusivism and calls for pluralism, stating that "we do not mean a global ideology or a single unified religion beyond all existing religions, and certainly not the domination of one religion over all others" (Küng 1993).

The spreading influence of the United States around the world may assist in the acceptance of pluralism. As the Pluralism Project at Harvard University has demonstrated, the United States has become the world's most diverse religious nation, and an attitude of respect among religions dominates (Eck 2001).

The influence of a deeply-rooted tradition of pluralism in India may also inspire greater understanding among religions in the twenty-first century. Despite politically-motivated religious violence in India in recent decades (see Chapters Three and Thirteen), the heritage of openness and mutual acceptance remains strong. For example, in early 2000, after a Christian missionary and his two children had been burned alive by Hindu extremists, leaders of all the major religions of India—Hindus, Muslims, Sikhs, Christians, Jains, Parsis—came together at the spot of the killings to honor the missionary and renounce violence in the name of religion.

THE SEARCH FOR COMMON GROUND: THE ECOLOGICAL CRISIS

On May 6, 1992, Mikhail Gorbachev, former president of the Union of Soviet Socialist Republics, symbolically ended the Cold War era at Westminster College in Fulton, Missouri, from the same podium at which former British Prime Minister Winston Churchill began it by speaking in 1946 of the "Iron Curtain" descending across Europe. Gorbachev proclaimed that "humanity is at a turning point" and said that, for the first time, "the resources of the world can be focused on solving problems in non-military areas: demography, ecology, food production, energy sources, and the like." He warned that "despite all the efforts being made to prevent ecological catastrophe, the destruction of nature is intensifying." He claimed that the ecological crisis "compels governments to adopt a world perspective and seek generally acceptable solutions." Gorbachev called for the United Nations to be the forum for developing the cooperative structures for globally confronting the crisis (Gorbachev 1992).

A month later the United Nations sponsored a Conference on Environment and Development (commonly called the "Earth Summit") in Rio de Janeiro, Brazil, setting in motion a detailed set of steps for nations to take to restore the environment. At a parallel Global Forum, concerned citizens, including many religious leaders, met to try to launch a global "environmental revolution," which, if it succeeds, "will rank with the Agricultural and Industrial Revolutions as one of the great economic and social transformations in human history" (Brown 1992: 174).

A decade later, many of the steps called for in the Earth Summit had yet to be implemented, and the United Nations convened a World Summit on Sustainable Development in Johannesburg, South Africa, in a further attempt to develop international consensus to take action to address the crises of the environment and global poverty.

After the 1992 gathering in Rio, a group of religious leaders and others gathered in the belief that the needed environmental revolution requires a fundamental ethical and spiritual reorientation. They have drafted a document called the "Earth Charter" (www.earthcharter.org). It lays forth a vision and a set of principles that will enable humans to become "a family of cultures that allows the potential of all persons to unfold in harmony with the Earth Community. We must preserve a strong faith in the possibilities of the human spirit and a deep sense of belonging to the universe." In a series of regional events, the Earth Charter has been adopted by citizens, who pledge to devote themselves to its implementation.

If the vision of the Earth Charter is realized, it will probably not be due to global summits as much as to individuals reorienting their own lives. As the current Dalai Lama said at a gathering of world religious and political leaders, "When we talk about global crisis [. . .] we cannot blame a few politicians, a few fanatics, or a few troublemakers. The whole of humanity has a responsibility because this is our business" (Vittachi 1989). Or, in the oft-quoted words of René Dubos, "Think globally; act locally."

Indeed, as the twenty-first century begins, a new phenomenon known as "glocalization" is emerging to counter the forces of globalization—which, some believe, threaten to draw all peoples, cultures, and religions into a homogenized global consumerism. "Glocalization" seeks to blend the local religious values of a community with the tools of globalization. For example, in Bangalore, India, computer technicians place garlands on their computers and offer prayers as they begin their work days, so that the work they do on these instruments of the globalized world may be guided by their sense of spiritual duty and not merely by the desire for selfish gain (Rifkin 2003).

The logo for a multinational corporation placed on a boat for religious pilgrims seeking detachment from the material world on the Ganges River in India suggests the challenges of twenty-first century globalization to traditional religions.

A volume prepared for the 1999 Parliament of the World Religions described the two paths that we humans may take in the twenty-first century (Barney 2000: 73):

> Down one path is a tragic wasteland. The climate has become hotter than today; floods and droughts are more frequent and more violent. Massive amounts of soil have wasted into the sea. Most forests are gone. A large fraction of Earth's species are extinct, and the remaining ones are being lost rapidly. Oil and natural gas are gone.
>
> Nine-tenths of the human population lives in hopeless poverty. Education and health services are gone. Economic, environmental, and moral decay spread uncontrollably. Ever wider areas cease to have any semblance of social order. Ethnic and religious rivalries fuel hatred, corruption, atrocities, and warfare[. . . .]
>
> One-tenth of the human population ignores what is happening to the nine-tenths. The one-tenth attempts to maintain a rich, consumptive, industrialized economy by using military forces to obtain foreign resources (especially coal and uranium), to slow the migration of refugees, to slow drug trafficking and to counter terrorist attacks[. . . .]
>
> Down the other path is a different Earth. A just, sustainable development for the whole earth has become the principal goal of every nation and people. The peoples are united in planet-wide efforts to understand Earth and its peoples and to envision what Earth and its people can become. Protection of Earth has become a top priority for every person. Human ignorance, poverty, bigotry are recognized everywhere as primary threats to national security and the future of Earth.

Which path humans take will depend in significant measure on their perceptions of ultimacy, and how they shape their lives in response to those perceptions.

THE WORLD'S RELIGIONS AFTER SEPTEMBER 11, 2001

The horrific events of September 11, 2001, placed another choice clearly before the world community. On the one hand, that day marked a dramatic victory for religious exclusivism (see Lincoln 2002 and Kimball 2002). The hijackers who flew the planes into the World Trade Center towers and the Pentagon were motivated by a narrow and exclusivist understanding of Islam. In response, a number of Christian leaders, motivated by their own exclusivist visions, claimed that the terrorist attacks demonstrated that Islam is a religion of hatred and violence that must be confronted and overcome. Ironically, but not surprisingly, reports of acts of hatred and violence against Muslims increased dramatically in the aftermath of September 11th (Eck 2001: xiv–xv).

As the news of these statements and the reports of violence against Muslims spread across the Muslim world, the numbers of Muslims calling for a confrontation with the "Crusaders" and "Infidels" who were attacking Islam also rose. In the West, even before September 11th, scholars had warned of a twenty-first-century "clash of civilizations" that will pit the Muslim and Christian worlds against one another in a battle for world domination (Huntington 1998).

On the other hand, since September 11th many others in the Muslim and Christian communities have been motivated to work toward greater understanding and respect among followers of the world's two largest religions. Proponents of dialogue point out that Christians and Muslims, as well as Jews, are children of Abraham and share a spiritual and ethical heritage that must not be ignored. Angered by the "hijacking" of Islam by the September 11th terrorists, Muslims have begun confronting extremists who cloak their own twisted ideology of hatred in the language and symbols of Islam. Christians who knew virtually noting about Islam have taken it upon themselves to learn how Islam—as understood and practiced by the vast majority of 1.3 billion Muslims throughout the world—*is* a religion of peace that promotes the same basic values of justice, equality, and respect as do the other two Abrahamic religions. As one woman, interviewed at an open house sponsored by an Islamic center in Texas after 9/11, said, "The time of not getting to know each other is over" (Eck 2001: xvi).

These two trends have extended beyond Islam and Christianity since September 11th, and are now shaping interactions among religious communities around the world. As the twenty-first century begins, it is certainly an open question which will prove more powerful—fear and hatred, or openness and respect. Readers of this book will have their own roles to play as the future unfolds. Having become more informed about the diversity of the world's religions, and the basic commitment of those religions to the values that nurture strong and good persons and societies, you will make conscious decisions not only about how to be religious yourselves but how to view and interact with people of other religions.

IMPORTANT TERMS AND PHRASES

exclusivism, inclusivism, pluralism, fundamentalism, *The Universe Story*, Parliaments of the World's Religions, A Global Ethic, Earth Summit, Earth Charter, September 11, Abrahamic religions

SOURCES AND SUGGESTIONS FOR FURTHER STUDY

ALMOND, GABRIEL, ET AL., 2003. *Strong Religion: The Rise of Fundamentalisms around the World.* Chicago: University of Chicago.

ARMSTRONG, KAREN, 2000. *The Battle for God.* New York: Knopf.

ANTOUN, RICHARD T., 2001. *Understanding Fundamentalism: Christian, Islamic and Jewish Movements.* Walnut Creek, CA: AltaMira.

BARNEY, GERALD O., ED., 2000. *Threshold 2000: Critical Issues and Spiritual Values for a Global Age.* Ada, MI: CoNexus.

BERRY, THOMAS AND BRIAN SWIMME, 1992. *The Universe Story: From the Primordial Flaring Forth to the Ecozoic Era—A Celebration of the Unfolding of the Cosmos.* San Francisco: HarperCollins.

BROWN, LESTER, 1992. "Launching the Environmental Revolution," in *State of the World 1992.* ed. Linda Starke. New York: W. W. Norton, 174–90.

COWARD, HAROLD, 1985. *Pluralism: Challenge to World Religions.* Maryknoll, NY: Orbis.

ECK, DIANA L. 2001. *A New Religious America: How a "Christian Country" Has Become the World's Most Religiously Diverse Nation.* San Francisco: HarperCollins.

GORBACHEV, MIKHAIL, 1992. "Drawing Back the Curtain," speech delivered at Westminster College, Missouri on May 6.

GYATSO, TENZIN, THE FOURTEENTH DALAI LAMA, 1999. *Ethics for the New Millennium.* New York: Riverhead.

HICK, JOHN, 1982. *God Has Many Names.* Philadelphia: Westminster.

HUNTINGTON, SAMUEL, 1998. *The Clash of Civilizations and the Remaking of the World Order.* New York: Touchstone.

JENKINS, PHILIP, 2002. *The Next Christendom: The Coming of Global Christianity*. New York: Oxford University.

KIMBALL, CHARLES, 2002. *When Religion Becomes Evil*. San Francisco: HarperCollins.

KÜNG, HANS, ED., 1993. *Towards a Global Ethic: An Initial Declaration*. New York: Continuum.

KÜNG, HANS, ED., 1998. *A Global Ethic for Global Politics and Economics,* trans. John Bowden. New York: Oxford University.

LINCOLN, BRUCE, 2002. *Holy Terrors: Thinking about Religion after September 11*. Chicago: University of Chicago.

MARTY, MARTIN AND R. SCOTT APPLEBY, EDS., 1991–95. *Fundamentalisms Observed*. (Also subsequent volumes in the Fundamentalism Project series.) Chicago: University of Chicago.

RIFKIN, IRA, 2003. *Spiritual Perspectives on Globalization: Making Sense of Economic and Cultural Upheaval*. Woodstock, VT: SkyLight Paths.

SMITH, HUSTON, 2001. *Why Religion Matters: The Fate of the Human Spirit in an Age of Disbelief*. San Francisco: HarperSanFrancisco.

VITTACHI, ANURADHA, 1989. *Earth Conference One: Sharing a Vision for Our Planet*. Boston: New Science Library.

Web Sites

www.nain.org
(North American Interfaith Network)

astro.temple.edu/%7Edialogue/geth.htm
(Center for Global Ethics)

www.cpwr.org
(Council for a Parliament of the World's Religions)

fas.harvard.edu/~pluralsm/
(Pluralism Project at Harvard University)

www.earthcharter.org
(Earth Charter Project)

millenniuminstitute.net
(Millennium Institute, providing tools for achieving environmentally sustainable development)

TIME Refer to Pearson/Prentice Hall's **TIME Special Edition: World Religions** magazine for these and other current articles on topics related to many of the world's religions:

➤ *The Impact of Religion: Cult Shock; Relaxing in a Labyrinth; Will Politicians Matter?; Essay—God Is Not On My Side. Or Yours.*

 Prentice Hall's **Research Navigator** helps students in their further study of the world's religions. Visit *http://www.researchnavigator.com* for help on the research process and access to databases full of relevant material, including the New York *Times*.

GLOSSARY

Note: *Names of persons are not included in the glossary. Consult the index for the pages upon which they appear.*

Abrahamic religions—religions that claim descent from Abraham as an ancestor (Judaism, Christianity, Islam).

Advaita Vedanta—Sanskrit for "nondual [interpretation of] the Vedanta [Upanishads]"; Hindu philosophical school that stresses the oneness of all reality (monism).

advent—in Christianity, refers to the Second Coming of Christ. "Adventist" groups, such as the Seventh Day Adventists, calculate the time of and prepare for the return of Christ. Also, the season of preparation for the celebration of the birth of Christ (Christmas).

Agamas—Sanskrit for "tradition"; used for texts in both Hinduism and Jainism.

agnosticism—the view that it is impossible for humans to know whether spiritual reality exists.

ahimsa—noninjury to all life, a concept found in Jainism, Hinduism, and Buddhism.

Ahura Mazda—"Wise Lord," the Zoroastrian designation for the one God, creator and judge of the universe.

Allah—the Arabic term for "God."

Allahu akbar—"God is most great." A frequent expression in Islam.

al-Qaeda—Arabic for "the base." An Islamic terrorist network responsible for the September 11, 2001, attacks and others.

Amaterasu—in Shinto, the sun goddess.

Amitabha—in Pure Land Buddhism, the heavenly Buddha of the Western Paradise; called *Amida* in Japan.

Amritsar—Punjabi city sacred to Sikhs; location of the Golden Temple.

Analects, The—the reputed sayings and conversations of Confucius.

anatman—literally, "no *atman*"; Buddhist teaching that humans have "no permanent self or soul."

Angra Mainyu—the evil spirit in Zoroastrian cosmology.

anicca—Pali for "impermanence"; Buddhist concept that all reality is constantly changing and without any permanence.

animism—the belief, common in indigenous religions, that all reality is infused with spirits or a spiritual force and is therefore alive.

anthropocentric—the view that humans are at the center of creation; the traditional perspective in religions originating in the Middle East (Judaism, Christianity, Islam).

anti-Semitism—attitude and acts of hatred against Jewish people and Judaism.

apocalyptic—referring to the revelation of the secrets of the end time.

apostolic succession—the doctrine that authority in the Christian church is determined by a line of succession from the apostles of Jesus.

arhant—Theravada Buddhist term for someone who has followed the teachings of the Buddha and attained enlightenment.

Armageddon—literally, "Mount Megiddo." Designates the final battle associated with the coming of the end time.

asceticism—active self-denial for the purpose of spiritual fulfillment.

Ashkenazim—Jews who fled persecution in Western Europe and settled in Eastern Europe during the Middle Ages.

assimilation—giving up or modifying one's own religious beliefs and practices in order to adapt to a dominant religion and culture.

atheism—the denial of the existence of a personal god (see theism)—or, for some today, of any spiritual reality. Theoretical atheism is the position that no such deities or spiritual reality exists. Functional atheism holds that even if deities or spiritual reality exists, humans are on their own in reaching the ultimate goal.

atman—Sanskrit for "eternal soul."

Avalokitesvara (Avalokita)—the bodhisattva of compassion. As male in Tibet (*Chenrezig*), watches over people and is incarnate in the Dalai Lama. Female in China and Japan (see **Kuan Yin**).

avatar—Hindu concept of the incarnation of earthly manifestation of a deity.

Avesta—Persian for "instruction"; the primary collection of Zoroastrian sacred texts.

avidya—Sanskrit for "ignorance." In Hinduism, the concept of ignorance of true, spiritual reality.

Ayatollah—"sign or reflection of God." An title of honor in Shi'ite Islam.

Bar (Bat) Mitzvah—Hebrew for "son (daughter) of the commandment"; the Jewish rite of passage through which one becomes an adult member of the Jewish community.

Bardo Thodol—the Tibetan Book of the Dead, with instructions for the intermediate state (*bardo*).

berdache—in the modern study of gender roles, describes a man who dresses and lives as a woman and a woman who dresses and lives as a man.

Bhagavad-Gita—Sanskrit for "Song of the Lord"; a section of the *Mahabharata*. Regarded by many as the crowning achievement of Hindu literature, synthesizing the major strands within Hindu teaching.

bhakti—Hindu concept of devotional service to a personal God. The spiritual path of devotion is known as *bhakti-yoga*.

biocentric—the perspective that all living beings form one community; humans are not at the center.

bodhi—Sanskrit for "enlightenment." In Buddhism, the tree under which Siddartha Gautama experienced enlightenment is called the *bodhi tree*.

bodhisattva—Sanskrit for "a being intended for enlightenment"; in Mahayana Buddhism, one who has taken a vow to delay his or her own experience of **nirvana** in order to aid others.

Bon—the pre-Buddhist religion of Tibet.

Brahma—Hindu god of creation.

Brahman—In Hinduism, the spiritual oneness of all reality.

Brahmin—In the Hindu class system, the highest of the four traditional classes; the "priestly" class.

Buddha nature—the Mahayana Buddhist concept that all reality is infused with Buddhahood.

bushido—Japanese for "military warrior way"; the code of belief and conduct of the samurai warrior, synthesizing Confucian, Zen Buddhist, and Shinto teaching.

caliph—Arabic for "successor"; in Islam, political successors to the Prophet Muhammad.

canon—a collection of sacred writings deemed authoritative by and for a religious group.

caste—from the Portuguese *casta*, meaning "race"; used to designate the elaborate, stratified system found in traditional Hindu society.

casting the circle—in Wicca, a ritual used to create sacred space.

Celestial Kingdom—in the cosmology of the Church of Jesus Christ of Latter-day Saints, the highest of the three levels of heaven.

charismatics—in Christianity, refers to groups, individuals, churches that emphasize the role of the Holy Spirit manifest in ecstatic gifts like speaking in tongues.

cheng-ming—the Confucian virtue of "rectification of names."

ch'i (also written as *qi*)—in the Chinese worldview, the vital energy that animates all living beings.

consubstantiation—the belief that in the sacrament of Holy Communion the body and blood of Christ are actually present with or alongside (but not replacing) the physical elements of bread and wine.

consumerism—term used to designate a modern secular religion in which the acquisition of material things is ultimate.

conversion—the process of deliberate change from one religion to another.

cosmic Christ—in Christianity, the teaching that Christ is present in all reality. Sometimes called the "third nature" of Christ (alongside the human and divine).

cosmos—ordered reality as a whole. In religions, ultimacy is typically the source of cosmos.

cosmology—the study of (or a view of) how the universe (all reality) is ordered. A *cosmogony* is a theory or story of how the cosmos originated.

coven—the small groups into which Wiccans are informally organized, and in which rituals are performed.

covenant—an agreement characterized by mutual loyalty and trust. In Judaism and Christianity, refers to pacts between God and his chosen people.

cult—descriptively, a movement that focuses on one person or god. Often used negatively for a religious movement deemed dangerous.

dafa—in Falun Gong teaching, the "great law of the universe."

Dalai Lama—"Ocean of wisdom"; the title of the chief spiritual and temporal leader of the Tibetan people. The current (fourteenth) Dalai Lama is Tenzin Gyatso.

Dao—the mysterious, unnameable cosmic power that is the source and end of all reality according to philosophical Daoism.

Daodejing (Tao-te-ching)—a collection of eighty-one enigmatic poems traditionally ascribed to the legendary figure Lao Zi. The basic text of Daoist philosophy.

dar al-Islam—Arabic for "house of peace"; a symbol of the ideal of political unity established by submission to the will of Allah. Contrasted with *dar al-harb*, "house of war."

de (te)—Chinese for "power" or "virtue."

devi—Sanskrit for "goddess." In Hinduism, various *devi* are worshipped.

dhamma—Pali term (similar to **dharma**) that describes the Buddha's teaching, followed by all who seek to lead a Buddhist lifestyle.

dharma—Sanskrit for "duty" or "the way things are intended to be"; also translated as "law." In Hindu society, "social dharma" is determined by caste, whereas "eternal dharma" refers to the duty to pursue a path leading to liberation from the cycle of rebirth.

Diaspora—the dispersion (scattering) of the Jewish people from their homeland.

divination—methods of discovering the nature and significance of events, usually future ones.

Divine Mind—In Christian Science, the name for God.

doctrine—a religious teaching expressed in rational, discursive form. For example, the "doctrine of the trinity."

dualism—the view that reality is divided into two, and only two, basic principles or forces (one material and the other spiritual), which are mutually opposed and/or complementary.

dukkha—Pali for "suffering." According to Buddhist belief, suffering caused by craving is the condition from which humans need to be liberated.

ecocentric—the perspective that the entire earth is interconnected, with no single center.

ecumenical—from the Greek for "the whole inhabited world"; in Christianity, used to refer to the movement for increased cooperation and unity among Christian churches.

eightfold path—the Buddhist path to nirvana implementing the teaching of the "Middle Way" between self-indulgence and self-denial.

Elohim—Hebrew for "god" or "gods." In the International Raelian Religion, the *elohim* are "those who came from the sky" in a flying saucer to teach humanity.

eschatology—teaching about or study of the "end time," which will occur at the climax of history, according to the religions that originated in the Middle East.

ethics—principles of right conduct, and the study of them.

fakir—Arabic for "poor"; in Sufism, a seeker of the way to union with Allah.

falun—According to Falun Gong teaching, the "law wheel" located in each person's abdomen.

fatalism—the view that events are predetermined.

fatwa—in Islam, a formal opinion treating a moral, legal, or doctrinal question, issued by a recognized scholar.

female genital mutilation (FGM)—the disfiguring and/or removal of female sexual organs as part of a rite of passage for girls. Particularly common in Africa.

fetish—a sacred object thought to have special powers.

filial piety (xiao)—Chinese value of reverence for one's social superiors, coupled with respectful treatment of social inferiors by superiors; expressed in five basic relationships. Emphasized in Confucianism.

five pillars—the basic obligations that individual Muslims observe. They include (1) the profession of faith; (2) daily prayer; (3) the alms tax for the needy; (4) fasting during the month of Ramadan; and (5) taking the *hajj* (pilgrimage) to Mecca at least once.

Four Noble Truths—the basic teaching of Buddhism, expressed by Siddartha Gautama in his Deer Park Sermon: (1) life is painful; (2) the cause of this suffering is desire; (3) there is a way to overcome this suffering; (4) the way is the eightfold path.

fundamentalism—a movement within a religion that stresses the absolute, unchanging, and unequivocally true nature of the movement's core teachings. First used to refer to a movement in Christianity; now frequently applied to movements in other religions.

Gaia—the Greek name for the earth goddess. The Gaia Principle (developed by James Lovelock) holds that the earth is a single unified organism.

ganja—the Rastafarian word for marijuana; it is smoked ritually by some members of the movement.

Goddess—in Wicca, the principal deity, manifested as maiden, mother, and crone (old woman). Her power is called upon in Wiccan rituals.

gohonzon—a "personal worship object" used by members of Soka Gakkai to help them meditate on the truths of the Lotus Sutra.

gospel—the Christian proclamation of the "good news" of salvation through Jesus Christ. Also, a literary term for writings that narrate this proclamation as expressed in the life, death, and resurrection of Jesus.

grace—in Christianity, refers to the free gift of salvation through Jesus Christ.

guru—a spiritual teacher; in Sikhism, a leader of the religion.

Guru Adi Granth (Guru Granth Sahib)—the Sikh sacred text.

hadith—Arabic for "speech, news, event": refers to the narratives (or traditions) of what the Prophet Muhammad said, did, or was like when he established the first Muslim community in Medina. After the Qur'an, the major source for determining **Sharia.**

haggadah—a Hebrew term referring to an interpretation of the **Tanak** that is homiletical rather than legal in nature.

hajj—the pilgrimage to Mecca, which every Muslim must try to make at least once during his or her life.

halakah—Hebrew for "to walk, go, follow"; a terms used in Judaism to designate an authoritative instruction on the way a Jew seeking to be obedient to God should act.

Hasidism—a Jewish movement that began in eighteenth-century Europe, which emphasizes the joy of following the **Torah.**

hijab—in Islam, head coverings worn by women in keeping with the Qur'an's admonition of modest dress.

hijra—Arabic for "emigration"; the emigration of the Prophet Muhammad from Mecca to Medina in 622 C.E. Muslims date their calendar from this event.

Holocaust—the mass killing of approximately six million Jews in Europe by the German Nazis during World War II.

high god—in indigenous religions, a deity who is responsible for creating the world, but who then withdraws. Other gods are often more actively worshipped.

Horned God—in Wicca, the male god, associated with the sun.

Iblis—In Islam, a name for **Satan,** who is considered to be the personification of evil and chief of the **jinn.** He rules over hell until Judgment Day, after having been banished from heaven for his disobedience to God.

I Ching—Chinese "Book of Changes," the classic text on **divination.**

imam—Arabic for "one who stands before"; in Sunni Islam, the leader of worship in the **mosque.** In Shi'ite Islam, a spiritual successor to the Prophet Muhammad who is endowed with the power to interpret the truth in the age in which he lives.

im' shallah—Arabic for "if God wills"; a common expression in Islam.

indigenous—originating in or pertaining to a particular area or region. Indigenous religions are those native to a geographical area, such as Native American religions.

Indus Valley Civilization—a sophisticated urban culture that flourished along the banks of the Indus River in South Asia, from about 2500 to 1500 B.C.E.

jihad—Arabic for "struggle, exertion," referring to the obligation of all Muslims to struggle against error and idolatry. The "greater" jihad is the individual's personal struggle; the "lesser" jihad is the struggle of the Muslim community to defend itself against those who would destroy the faith.

jina—"conqueror"; the Jain term for someone who has attained liberation.

jinn—Arabic for "spirits," some (like **Iblis**) are evil, while others are good.

jiva—In Hinduism, the physical/psychological/social **karmic** self, which acts, but which is not eternal; in Jainism, the spiritual, eternal soul (contrasted with *ajiva*).

jnana yoga—In Hinduism, the path of knowledge.

justification by faith—the Christian teaching that humans receive redemption from sin through trust in what God has done in Jesus Christ, not by any merit of their own.

just war—the teaching found in the religions that originated in the Middle East that wars are just if they meet certain criteria (such as being declared by legitimate authorities, and minimizing civilian casualties).

Kaaba—Arabic for "cube": the central shrine of Islam, located in the Grand Mosque of Mecca. It symbolizes the center of the world and is visited by Muslims on the *hajj*.

Kabbala—Jewish mysticism.

Kali—Hindu goddess of death, destruction, and renewal.

kami—Japanese for "the sacred"; anything that inspires awe or reverence. *Kami-no-michi* ("Way of the Kami") is the Japanese phrase used to describe Japanese indigenous religion (Shinto).

karma—Sanskrit for "action"; the law that explains human behavior as the chain of causes and effects resulting from desire. According to the religions that originated in South Asia, karma binds us to the cycle of rebirth. In Pali, written as *kamma*.

karma-yoga—in Hinduism, the way of action.

khalsa—"pure"; the members of the Sikh military fraternity, distinguished by the wearing of the "five k's": *kesh*, uncut hair; *kangha*, comb; *kach*, short pants; *kara*, steel bracelet; and *kirpan*, sword.

Kingdom of God—the reign of God on earth, to be established at the end of the current age.

kirtan—a ritual featuring devotional songs, found especially in Hinduism and Sikhism.

koan—a puzzle used in Zen **meditation.**

Krishna—Hindu god prominent in the **Bhagavad Gita.** Devotees of Vishnu consider Krishna to be an **avatar** of Vishnu.

Kuan Yin (Kannon, Koan-Eum)—Chinese (Japanese, Korean) names for the bodhisattva of mercy, who has maternal compassion for all.

lama—in Tibetan Buddhism, a spiritual teacher.

li—the Confucian virtue of "propriety, right form," as expressed in the proper conduct of ritual and right behavior in relationships.

liberal—referring to a movement within a religion that stresses the importance of adapting the religion's teachings and practices as times change.

Lotus Sutra—a Mahayana Buddhist text stressing that the true Buddha is the cosmic Buddha who wants to show compassion for all beings.

magic—the manipulation of other beings through spells, incantations, or other means; in Wicca, the focusing of the five senses to effect change, always positively.

Mahayana—literally, "large raft"; used to refer to one of the two branches of Buddhism, dominant in East Asia and Vietnam. So named because of the belief that its teachings provide a "large raft" to carry people across the river of rebirth to liberation.

Mahdi—arabic for "the guided one"; in Islam in general, a descendant of the Prophet Muhammad who will restore justice on earth. In Shi'ite Islam, a messianic **imam** who will appear in order to end corruption.

Maitreya—the next Buddha to appear, who will lead many followers to liberation.

mandate of heaven—in China, the right to rule, withdrawn when a leader or regime fails to fulfill the responsibility to maintain harmony and rule justly.

mantra—a sacred syllable, word, or phrase, used in meditation.

maya—"illusion"; the concept in Hinduism that reality as experienced is not true reality and constitutes a veil that must be penetrated.

Mecca—the Arabian city at the center of the Muslim world. When Muslims pray, they prostrate themselves in the direction of Mecca.

Medina—the Arabian city to which the Prophet Muhammad emigrated in 622 C.E., and where he established the first Muslim community.

meditation—focused, disciplined concentration intended to lead to experience of the sacred.

messiah—Hebrew for "anointed one"; the hoped-for descendant of King David who will appear to restore Israel to glory.

Midrash—interpretation of the Tanak in a verse-by-verse commentary. May be **haggadic** or **halakhic.**

millenarian—referring to the belief that supernatural powers are about to bring a new age on earth, which will totally transform life and bring restoration and salvation to the community of believers who have faithfully received the message of the coming end time.

Mishnah—Hebrew for "teaching, tradition, study"; the **oral Torah** as it existed in written form in the late second or early third century C.E.

mitakuye oyasin—Lakota for "all my relations." Used in Lakota rituals to emphasize that they are "for everyone and everything."

Mitzvah (plural **mitzvoth**)—Hebrew for "commandment"; collectively, the laws traditional Jews believe to have been revealed to Moses by the Lord, which all Jews are to keep for all time.

moksha—Sanskrit for "liberation"; refers to the South Asian teaching of liberation from the cycle of rebirth.

monasticism—a way of life withdrawn from ordinary pursuits and dedicated to the sacred.

monism—the view that all reality is one, typically emphasizing spiritual unity.

monotheism—the belief in one all-powerful personal deity who created, sustains, and will judge the cosmos.

Mormon—the prophet recognized by the Church of Jesus Christ of Latter-day Saints as the author of the Book of Mormon. The name "Mormon" is used to refer to members of the LDS Church.

Moroni—the son of Mormon, who, as an angel, appeared to Joseph Smith and directed him to the golden tablets on which the Book of Mormon was inscribed.

mosque (or **masjid**)—a communal place of prayer and gathering for Muslims.

mysticism—directed, unmediated experience of the ultimate, and the path that leads to such experience.

myth—a story about the sacred, which is foundational, creating the basic patterns of life for people who accept the story as true for them. A **cosmogonic** myth tells the story of the ordering of reality, and an **eschatological** myth tells the story of the end of the current age and the beginning of a new one.

neo-paganism—the movement that seeks to restore suppressed indigenous beliefs and practices, especially of Europe.

nirvana—the state of bliss that comes when desire and attachment are overcome. Particularly associated with Buddhism.

Ogun—the most widely worshipped **orisa**; the Yoruba god of war and iron, with associated powers of both formation and destruction.

Olorun—"owner of the sky"; the Yoruba **high god,** Lord above all, who dwells in the heavens and is the source of all life.

oral Torah—legal teachings that supplement the written **Torah** (the Hebrew Bible), which appeared first orally among Torah teachers but were committed to writing by the late second or early third century C.E. as the **Mishnah,** and grew to encompass the whole **Talmud.**

original sin—the Christian teaching that all humans are sinful at birth, or are born with a tendency to sin.

orisa—the Yoruba name for spirits.

orthodox—referring to authoritative, right beliefs in a religious community.

Pali Canon—the Theravada Buddhist scripture, consisting of the *Tripitaka* ("three baskets"): the baskets of disciplinary regulations, discourses, and higher philosophy.

pantheism—the belief that all reality is infused with God.

Parsis—"Persians," the name for the Zoroastrian community in India.

patriarchy—male dominance over women.

Passover—the Jewish festival commemorating the deliverance of the Hebrew slaves from Egyptian bondage.

Pentecostal—in Christianity, a movement emphasizing restoration of the gifts of the Holy Spirit described in the New Testament.

People of the Book—in Islam, designates religions that have sacred texts, especially Judaism and Christianity.

peyote—a small cactus that contains a drug that causes visions or feelings of euphoria when consumed; used as a sacrament in the Native American Church.

Pharisees—a party within Judaism, active in the last centuries B.C.E. and first century C.E., composed of lay people dedicated to keeping the commandments of the written and oral Torahs;

opposed to the Sadducees. Contemporary Judaism descends from Judaism as understood by the Pharisees.

pietism—a Christian movement that emphasizes personal spiritual devotion over corporate worship and assent to doctrine.

polytheism—belief in a multiplicity of personal deities.

pope—title for the Bishop of Rome; leader of the Roman Catholic Church.

prajna—Buddhist term for "wisdom." *Prajna-paramita* is the wisdom that goes beyond ordinary knowledge to an intuitive experience of the ultimate truth.

profane—the opposite of sacred; ordinary reality, which is yet to be ordered by the sacred.

prophet—someone commissioned by God to carry a message to a particular people.

Punjab—the traditional homeland of the Sikhs, now divided between Pakistan and India.

Pure Land (Western Paradise)—the paradise that awaits those devoted to **Amitabha (Amida) Buddha.**

Qur'an—Arabic for "recitation"; the collections of revelations received by the Prophet Muhammad from God (Allah) through the angel Gabriel.

rabbi—Hebrew for "my master"; Jewish teachers who interpret the **Torah** for others and serve as leaders of Jewish communities.

Reconstructionism—in Judaism, the modern movement that views Judaism as an evolving civilization and interprets religious teaching in light of scientific understanding.

Reform—in Judaism, the modern movement that stresses loyalty to the essence of the Jewish tradition while adapting Jewish principles to changing times and different cultures.

revelation—the manifestation of ultimacy to humans.

ren (or **jen**)—the Confucian virtue of humaneness.

rites of passage—rituals that mark and facilitate the transition from one state of life to the next, typically at birth, puberty, marriage, and death.

ritual—symbolic action in response to perceived ultimacy, based on myth.

Rosh Hashanah—the Jewish new year, which occurs in the fall; along with **Yom Kippur,** the "high holy days" in the Jewish ritual calendar.

sabbath—the Jewish holy day, beginning at sundown on Friday and ending at sundown on Saturday, commemorating the "day of rest" after the six days of creation.

sacraments—in Christianity, the signs of God's grace; rituals, through which believers participate in the spiritual reality to which the rituals point.

sacred—that which is ultimate, either of a spiritual or secular nature, and which orders reality for believers.

sacred hoop—symbol of the Oglala Lakota nation; an unbroken circle.

sacred pipe—holy object, symbolizing the universe, smoked in Oglala Lakota rituals.

sacrifice—a ritual in which worshippers present offerings to deities or spirits in exchange for benefits they are seeking.

Sadducees—a movement within Judaism, active in the last centuries B.C.E. and first century C.E., composed of priests and their supporters; opposed by the Pharisees.

samsara—Sanskrit for the "cycle of rebirth."

sangha—the Buddhist order of monks and nuns.

Santeria—a new religious movements with roots in Yoruba religion, which combines **orisa** with Catholic saints. Developed in Cuba and spread throughout the Caribbean and into the United States.

Satan—Hebrew for "adversary," borrowed from Persian.

Second Coming—in Christianity, the expected return of Jesus Christ at the end of history to inaugurate the **Kingdom of God** on earth.

sect—a religious movement that split from another group; used negatively as a synonym for cult.

secular—having to do with this observable reality, as opposed to the spiritual. Secular religions have nonspiritual, this-worldly ultimacies.

Sephardim—Jews who fled persecution in Western Europe and settled in the Middle East during the Middle ages.

Septuagint—the Greek translation of the **Tanak.**

shakti—Sanskrit for "power, energy"; in Hinduism, the active energy of a deity, personified as a goddess. *Shaktism* is the practice of seeking to identify with this active power and draw upon it for material or spiritual pursuits.

shaman—in an indigenous religion, a holy person who, having been "possessed" or "taken over" by spiritual powers, becomes an intermediary between the spirit world and the people.

Shang Ti—Chinese for "Ruler on High"; central deity in ancient Chinese mythology, guarantor of the moral order and of rulers' authority.

Sharia—the path or way Muslims are to follow; hence, Muslim "law."

Shi'ite—the smaller of the two main divisions of Islam; split over the issue of rightful succession to the Prophet Muhammad.

Shinto Myth—the indigenous Japanese story of creation and of Japan as the land of the **kami.**

Shiva—Hindu god of destruction and rejuvenation.

Sikh—Sanskrit for "disciple"; the followers of Guru Nanak.

Spenta Mainyu—the good spirit in Zoroastrian cosmology.

spiritual—referring to a level of existence beyond the ordinary, material, temporal reality of this world. In contrast to "secular" reality.

Sufi—the mystical movement within Islam.

Sun dance—Oglala Lakota ritual of rejuvenation.

Sunni—the larger of the two main branches of Islam; where the Qur'an is not explicit this movement appeals to *sunna* (the manner of behavior associated with the Prophet Muhammad, known via **hadith**).

sunyata—an important Mahayana Buddhist teaching regarding the "emptiness" or "openness" of all things and our perceptions of things.

surah—one of the divisions (chapters) of the **Qur'an.**

sutras—collections of aphorisms, sayings.

symbol—any object, word, or action which points toward and allows experience of and/or participation in perceived ultimacy.

synagogue—Hebrew for "assembly"; in Judaism, a place of prayer and study.

sweat lodge—Oglala Lakota ritual of purification.

taboo—an object, action, or person that must be avoided because of its potentially injurious power and/or polluted status.

Talmud—Hebrew for "learning"; in Judaism the collection composed of the **Mishnah** and further interpretation (*Gemara*). Constitutes the fullest expression of the **oral Torah.**

Tanak—an acronym from the Hebrew names for the three sections of the Hebrew Bible—Torah, Prophets, Writings; used as a designation for the Hebrew Bible.

Tantra—Sanskrit for "that which extends, spreads." In a broad sense, tantrism is a religious practice outside the **Vedic** tradition, including rituals open to persons not of the **Brahmin** class. Practiced in Hinduism, Tibetan Buddhism, and Jainism, tantrism attempts to harness corporeal energy, ultimately for the highest spiritual purposes.

theism—belief in one or more personal deities.

Theravada Buddhism—literally, "Way of the Elders"; surviving school of one of two branches of Buddhism, found in Southeast Asia.

Third Adam—according to the teaching of the Unification Church, a messiah who will appear to pay the full price for the sin of humanity and establish the Kingdom of God on earth; Jesus was the second Adam.

T'ien—Chinese for "heaven"; in ancient China, the impersonal power with which the emperor was in harmony, as long as he ruled justly.

Torah—Hebrew for "instruction, law"; God's revelation of instructions to the Jewish people. Often used to refer to the first five books of the Hebrew Bible. See also **oral Torah.**

totem—an animal, plant, or object with which a group develops a special relationship.

tradition—the handing down of beliefs and practices considered as a dynamic collection.

transcendent—removed from or "above" the secular, profane world. In contrast to "immanent."

transubstantiation—in Christianity, the belief that through the proper consecration during the sacrament of Holy Communion the elements of bread and wine become the substance of the body and blood of Christ.

trinity—in Christianity, the doctrine of one God, three "persons" (father, son, holy spirit).

True Name—the Sikh name for the one God.

Tunkashila—Oglala Lakota word for "grandfather." In prayers, **Wakan Tanka** is often addressed as Tunkashila.

ulama—in Islam, scholars responsible for interpreting **Sharia.**

umma—Arabic for "community"; often used for the entire community of Muslims throughout the world.

untouchables—in traditional Hindu society, those "below" the caste system because of the impurity associated with their occupations, and thus not members of any of the four classes. Also known as the "scheduled castes." Mahatma Gandhi called the untouchables *harijan*, children of God. Increasingly, they are known as *dalits*, oppressed ones.

Upanishad—Sanskrit for "to sit nearby"; philosophical utterances, collected in a section of the **Vedas,** that are the basis of later philosophical reflection in Hinduism.

Vedas—Sanskrit for "knowledge"; the sacred writings of the Aryans, deemed canonical by later Hinduism. Basic collections include hymns to the gods (*Rig-Veda*), ritual materials and directions for the sacrifices and invocations for the gods (*Yajur-Veda*), verses from the *Rig-Veda* arranged musically (*Sama-Veda*), and hymns together with spells and incantations (*Atharva-Veda*).

Vishnu—Hindu god of preservation and love; appears on earth in various forms (**avatars**) in times of crisis.

vision quest—a Lakota ritual in which the participant spends time alone, often on a hill or mountain, fasting and waiting for a vision from the spirit beings that will give guidance for life.

wakan—Oglala Lakota for "holy" or "sacred." *Wakana* is "holiness." A *wicasa wakan* is a holy man; a *winyan wakan* is a holy woman (shaman). **Wakan Tanka** is the Great Mystery.

White Buffalo Calf Woman—Oglala Lakota mythic figure who brought the **sacred pipe** to the people and instructed them in how to live harmoniously.

Wicca—Old English for "wise." The word from which the term "witch" derives; taken as the name for a movement that seeks to restore pre-Christian European indigenous religion.

wu wei—Daoist concept of "actionless action."

Yiddish—a dialect of German that borrowed extensively from Hebrew, spoken in Jewish communities of Eastern Europe (the **Ashkenazim**).

yin and yang—the complementary, opposite forces present in all reality, according to the traditional Chinese worldview. The *yin* force is dark, mysterious, wet, female; the *yang* force is bright, clear, dry, and male.

yoga—Sanskrit for "to yoke or join"; refers to a variety of methods that seek to join the individual soul (**atman**) to the Ultimate, and thus achieve liberation from rebirth. See **bhakti yoga, karma yoga, jnana yoga.**

Yom Kippur—the Jewish "day of atonement." With **Rosh Hashanah,** the "high holy days" of the Jewish ritual calendar.

Zionism—the political movement dedicated to the creation of a Jewish homeland, where all Jews of the world may come and live without fear of persecution.

PHOTO CREDITS

INDEX